SHAMHART (1147)
AND THE MENG (1630)

SHAMHART (1147)
AND THE MENG (1630)

James L. Meng

Matchstick Literary
1-888-306-8885
www.matchliterary.com
orders@matchliterary.com

DEDICATION
TWO IMPORTANT MENG FAMILIES IN MY LIFE

This book is dedicated to the outstanding memories of my parents, my heroes in life, Edward J. Meng and Jessie F. Meng. No one could ever ask for a more dedicated and loving parents than Ed and Jessie. I am eternally grateful for their influential lifelong guidance and love.

This book is also dedicated to the love of my life, the beautiful Beverly Ann, my nourishing wife of almost 50 years, my best friend and mother of two totally outstanding children, Heather and Erik.

God has truly blessed my life with the love of great parents and family.

James L. Meng

TABLE OF CONTENTS

INTRODUCTION

The researching for this book has been both time-consuming and rewarding. One product of this effort is a renewed appreciation not only of what our ancestors accomplished in their lives but the dilemmas they faced leaving their homelands, friends, and possessions to go to a virtually unknown land called America. Furthermore, they did this by crossing the Atlantic in a small sailing ship or, at best, an early steamship, both with limited navigation skills.

The first section of this book reports the results of a Meng DNA test. In 2009, a DNA test was made on JAMES L. MENG. This test revealed his Y-DNA, which remains intact over the centuries and is passed down along his paternal lines from father to father . . . etc. Thus, the DNA testing of JAMES L. MENG provided the Y-DNA results for *all* male Mengs. The Meng DNA was further defined as part of the Haplogroup R1b. This identification connected *all* male Mengs to John Hanson, the American patriot who was the first president of the Continental Congress in 1781.

Family lore has said the name "Meng" must have been shortened when they arrived in America. In reality, the name was not shortened; in fact, there are Mengs with a very colorful and historic past that are all related in America, Germany, and New Zealand. However, there was a name change from Meng to Ming as reflected the HOYT B. MING's "John Christopher Meng and Many Descendants (The Ming Family)" section of this book. A noble branch of the Meng genealogical tree has been traced back to the 1500s with the BOYNEBURGS from Hessen, Germany. This line also resulted in the RUBENKAM family immigrating to America.

The first known American Meng has been traced back to the birth of NICHOLAS MENG in 1630 in Ladenburg, Rhein-Neckar-Kreis in Baden-Württemberg Although as epic as this event may have been to humankind, other less important events need to be at least mentioned: events like John Winthrop's delivery of his famous "City upon a Hill" sermon while en route to Colonial America, a sermon that my hero (President Ronald Reagan) cited in 1974; Judith Leyster painting her self-portrait; etc.

JOHAAN (JOHN) CHRISTOPH (CHRISTOPHER) MENG was the first Meng who landed in America in 1728 and settled in Philadelphia County, Pennsylvania. The Meng family subsequently prospered and became very involved in the American Revolutionary War. For example, JOHN MELCHIOR MENG, a loyalist, was tried for treason.

CHARLES MENG, born in Pennsylvania in 1769, was a captain under Gen. GEORGE WASHINGTON, and his son, JAMES M. MENG (got to love that name), became a major in the militia. Many of the Mengs were very active in our Revolutionary War. Some were officers, including a very interesting document in Gen. George Washington's own handwriting noting WOLLERY MENG, dated June 3, 1775. WOLLERY MENG was also a neighbor to fellow mason BENJAMIN FRANKLIN who participated either very directly or indirectly, I think, in the Boston Tea Party of 1773 along with another relation, mason and patriot, PAUL REVERE. It is also interesting to note that a Meng relative, SARAH SHELTON, married still another patriot Patrick Henry. The Mengs then drifted South, where historic Meng homes can be found today in Union and Winnsboro, South Carolina. Col. JAMES MENG (1770–1824) is buried in the Presbyterian Cemetery in Union, South Carolina. A fascinating history of the revolutionary Mengs by Hoyt B. Meng documenting all the above is included. In addition, a unique invitation via the World Wide Web to listen to the "Indian War Whoop" and his other music by HOYT MING and his PEP-STEPPERS is offered. Background information on this very interesting HOYT MING family and the historic involvement of his music in record recordings, movies, concerts, and stages are available for the reader.

The information contained within this book may apply to direct Meng descendants and the Shamhart descendants through the Trexler line, who desire to join the DAR or SAR.

Another group of related Mengs has been traced back to Hohen-Sülzen, Germany. This group or line started with JOHANN STEPHAN MENG born in 1725. In 1869, REICHARD MENG, a farmer, found two stone coffins from the fourth century with Roman skeletons inside in his backyard. In addition, one coffin contained third-century Roman glasses. One of these glasses is the famous *vas diatretum* currently displayed in the Mainz museum.

There are still many original Meng homes in existence today in Hohen-Sülzen. For example, the Meng family home at 25 Hauptstrasse is pictured.

Another branch of the Meng genealogy tree started with REICHARD MENG (1799–1871) and his son KARL PHILLIP MENG (1834–1885), who decided in 1863 to go to Australia but for some unknown reason ended up in Ashley/Christchurch area in New Zealand. This started a new Meng line formerly unknown to the family. Many of the New Zealand Mengs' difficulties in their new country are chronicled in the first section of this book, including pictures of headstones, events, and comments on their lives.

There are descendants of KARL PHILLIP MENG still living in New Zealand today.

A third group of Mengs then came to America from the small town of Monsheim, Germany. Monsheim is located very close to Hohen-Sülzen, so the families from these two towns intermingled. WILHELM MENG, who was born in 1755, is recognized as the start of the Monsheim Mengs.

CONRAD MENG, born in 1784 and immigrated to America in 1837, is recognized as the start of the Mengs of Freeburg, Illinois.

Copies of actual family documents from various Monsheim churches are contained within for review. This raw information is offered for those who wish to pursue the Meng genealogy further.

LOUIS MENG (1837–1882), my great-great-grandfather, came to America and owned and operated a "dry goods and groceries, hardware, etc.," in Lementon, Illinois, near Freeburg, Illinois. A copy of his business ledger contains many of the townspeople's names who were doing business with him in the 1870s. Also noted in this section of the book are newspaper articles on LOUIS MENG's children, some of which I knew when I was a child. The balance of the Freeburg Meng section addresses the children of

FRIEDERICH MENG, my grandfather. His children were my uncles, aunt, and, of course, my father, EDWARD JOHN MENG.

Since I obviously know more about my immediate family, I devoted considerable efforts toward my parents, EDWARD JOHN MENG and JESSIE FRANCES (née SHAMHART) MENG. To this end, I have included my father's interesting 40-year career in the US Postal Service, years of civic service and awards, Rotary International, and years of providing an excellent parenting role model to his two sons, EDWARD SHAMHART and JAMES LEROY MENG. Also included in the book is considerable information on my life, my marriage to BEVERLY (née LEWIS) MENG and our children, HEATHER ANDREA MENG and ERIK JAMES MENG. Additional connections to the MENG genealogical tree include the families of KOESTERER and VOGT.

The last section of the Meng family reflects the life of WILMER W. MENG (1903–1995) who had a unique life. In 2004, an 800-seat state-of-the-art concert hall at California State University in Fullerton, California, was named after Wilmer's wife, VAUGHNCILLE JOSEPH MENG!

The next major section of this book addresses my mother's side of the family, the Shamharts. Unlike the Meng side, whose name was not modified, the Shamhart name had several variations. To look at the name "Shamhart," many believe it may be English or Irish. Wrong! The Shamharts were 100% German just like the Mengs. For example, other modifications or variations of the name Shamhart include SCAPAHARDA, OBERSCHABBEHARD, NEIEDERSCHABBEHARD, SCHABBEHARAD, SCHABBEHAR, and SHAPPARD.

The 2009 DNA test referenced earlier also revealed the mtDNA of JAMES LEROY MENG. The female mtDNA, unlike the male Y-DNA, does not remain constant, thus will mutate over the centuries as it passes down along maternal lines from mother to mother. This test revealed a connection to Marie Antoinette, Alexandra Feodorovna, and Catherine Fisher (b. 1957), author, broadcaster, and adjudicator in Newport, Wales.

The Shamhart line is traced back to 1147. This was the year that the start of the Second Crusade was announced by Pope Eugene III and was the first of the Crusades led by European kings, namely Louis VII of France and Conrad III of Germany. Although the aforementioned 1147 events may have been regarded as important, they were all overshadowed by the birth of a baby SCAPAHADR in Steinhagen, Germany. The complete genealogical family tree of the Shamhart line from 1147 in Germany to 1939 in America is offered by a good friend and Shamhart relative, Herr Werner Schabbehard in Bielefeld, Germany. This amazing document represents years of work and is provided for your review.

SIMON HENRICH SCHAMHARDT was born in Varenholz, Germany, in 1792 and a picture of his 1793 home as it appears today in Varenholz, follows. His descendants subsequently immigrated to Guernsey County, Ohio, where his line eventually led to Newton, Jasper County, Illinois. HENRY (HENRICH) SHAMHART was a private in the Maryland militia during the War of 1812 serving under Captain Williams. His service pension records are also provided.

The Shamharts were also involved in the American Civil War (1861–1865). A very unique and interesting daily account of Union soldier, HENRY SHAPPARD, during the Civil War is a must read.

Henry's daily record, originally written in German, provides valuable insight into a soldier's life during the war.

Like the Meng section of the book, I have also included information on the Shamhart's families that I knew as a child. For example, these entries will read "Who were CHARLIE and MARY SHAMHART?" etc.

These accounts were added in an attempt to provide a personality of these people and get away from the straight genealogical statistical data.

Additional family connections to the Shamhart genealogical tree also includes the FOSTER, TREXLER, and CRAIL families with US congressman JOE CRAIL's connection to LADY CAMPBELL, DUKE of ARGYLL and the DUKE of MARLBOROUGH.

Like everyone else in this book, they all had real lives with successes and failures, a personality, thus were much more than born, married, child 1, 2, 3, and died. In addition, pictures of many Shamharts that my mother and grandmother knew and had saved in boxes have been added. Again, my objective is to record what I observed, real live people, when visiting the Shamharts in Newton, Illinois.

Finally, I, like many others, believe we are also a product of our environment. That is, what was going on in our parents' lives and affected them subsequently affected us as a child. With this thought in mind, I have included many references and documents of the time period from 1930 to 1950 in which my parents and I were involved.

For example, the effects of the Great Depression of the 1930s in which President Franklin D. Roosevelt made worse with and uncertainly, big spending and regulations that only prolonged the Depression. World War II subsequently resolved the Depression but created new problems for our parents. This was a traumatic time that our parents and relatives lived through and never got over.

A copy of FDR's proclamation to close all the American banks in 1933, a copy of a "war ration book," a copy of the first instrument of surrender by Germany dated May 5, 1945, Japan's surrender agreement signed September 2, 1945 ending World War II, etc., are all in the book.

During World War II, women began working in the factories for the first time, initiating a culture change to American society. Women working outside the home were a completely new concept in the 1940s. Bev's mother, VELMA V. LEWIS, was one of the Rosie the Riveters in California welding ships for the war effort. See the LEWIS section of this book. All of the above and more had a tremendous impact on the way our parents lived. Their experiences and lessons then influenced the children.

As the lives of our parents improved with the end of World War II, life in the 1950s was a great time to grow up. Having graduated in 1957 from Granite City High School, I had the fortunate experience to see the transition from a wartime economy and atmosphere to peacetime.

The 1983 movie titled *A Christmas Story*, directed by Bob Clark, is reflective of the 1940s and 1950s time during my youth. The nine-year-old character, Ralphie, in the movie could have easily been James Meng receiving his authentic "decoder ring" from some faraway place called Battle Creek. Youth organizations of the time and a new music style called rock and roll that we listened and danced to and a new invention called TV, etc., are mentioned.

NOTE OF APPRECIATION

The Germany research was accomplished by Herrn Werner Schabbehard in Bielefeld, Germany. Werner is a Shamhart relative who traced the Shamhart line back to 1147 and connected the Meng line back to 1630. He spent countless hours tracing our family with phone calls and e-mails to various German destinations, translating documents from old German and French to present-day German and then on to English. Werner has also spent countless hours on the phone with James L. Meng discussing his research.

The final product of all of Werner's work is an expansion of the family roots in Germany, information that would be very difficult if not impossible to know and pass on to future generations. A big *Danke Schoen* is due to Herrn Werner Schabbehard from all present and future Mengs for his tireless and informative work.

Werner Schabbehard behind the family tree of the Shamhart ancestors

CHAPTER 1
THE MENG Y-DNA

The Y-DNA in all males, unlike the female mtDNA, remains intact over the centuries and is passed down along paternal lines from father, to father, to father . . . etc. Thus, the DNA testing of one male Meng's DNA will provide the Y-DNA of all male Meng's.

In 2009, James L. Meng participated in the Genebase Company's Ancestry DNA project. The results of these test revealed in part that the Meng Y-DNA has a strong prediction paternal Haplogroup R for over the past 150,000 years. More specifically, the Meng DNA is part of the Haplogroup R1b. The Y-DNA Haplogroup R is perhaps the most prominent Y-DNA linage on earth today. The preeminent Haplography R is also the most prominent Haplogroup in Europe at 50% and in United States at 42%. The origin of Haplogroup R dates back to 30,000–35,000 years ago in the Paleolithic era and Pleistocene epoch.

Famous R people, other than the legendary Mengs of Freeburg, Illincis, include Patriot John Hanson, the president of the First Continental Congress (1781–1782) under the Articles of Confederation. Information regarding John Hanson's involvement in the founding of America will follow.

The Mengs and Shamharts Returning to their Roots

The first edition of this book is currently in 34 University and Public libraries in addition to many private libraries across America, Germany, Scotland and New Zealand. The book has also appeared in several newspapers as shown in the following presentation to Frau Petra Hollander of the Steinhagen, Germany Archives.

Zeitung für Steinhagen

Von Steinhagen in die USA

Ein Amerikaner erforscht mit Hilfe des heimischen Genealogen Werner Schabbehard seine Wurzeln

Von Annemarie
Bluhm-Weinhold

Steinhagen (WB). Was verbindet einen einflussreichen Gewerkschaftsmann aus dem US-Bundesstaat Illinois mit Steinhagens historischer Keimzelle Scapaharda? Der Stammbaum. Denn James L. Meng führt seine familiären Wurzeln nach Deutschland, nach Steinhagen – und letztlich auf den Stammsitz der Schabbehards zurück. Mit Hilfe aus der »alten Heimat«, nämlich von Werner Schabbehard, hat der Amerikaner seine Familienforschung in einem Buch veröffentlicht.

Es ist ein dicker Wälzer, mehr als 700 Seiten stark, der jetzt auch im Steinhagener Gemeindearchiv bei Petra Holländer liegt und dort für jedermann einsehbar ist. In jahrelanger genealogischer Kleinarbeit ist er entstanden. Denn die Mengs, James Leroy und Gattin Beverly, führen ihre Wurzeln nicht nur ins Westfälische, sondern auch in diverse Familienverbünde in Süddeutschland zurück. Gut, wenn man da einen Fachmann in der weitverzweigten Sippe weiß: Denn Werner Schabbehard, der in Bielefeld lebt, ist seit 13 Jahren, oftmals unterstützt vom befreundeten Genealogen Ulrich Siebrasse, dabei, Genaueres über die Ober- und Niederschabbehards, Schamharts und Shappards in Erfahrung zu bringen, die sich von Steinhagen aus nicht nur in westfälisch-lippischen Raum, sondern auch jenseits des Atlantik verbreiteten.

Am Anfang steht Scapaharda, 1147 in einer Urkunde König Konrads III. erwähnt. Aus dieser Bestrung gingen die Höfe Steinha-

Werner Schabbehard hat ein Exemplar der amerikanischen Familienchronik Petra Holländer und dem

gen Nr. 2 und 3, später Nieder- und Oberschabbehard, heute der Westfalenhof und der Hof Steinhagen, hervor. Doch der Bielefelder Genealoge hat quer durch die Jahrhunderte insgesamt 40 Schabbehards auf Steinhagener Höfen ausfindig gemacht. »Die Schabbehards haben an der Kolonialisierung Steinhagens mitgewirkt«, sagt er nicht ohne familiäres

Selbstbewusstsein. Seit dem Jahr 2000 erforscht er schon seine Familiengeschichte.

Und so war er gern bereit, dem ihm unbekannten James Leroy Meng, geboren am 25. April 1939 in Granite City, Madison County, Illinois, USA, behilflich zu sein, mehr über die Vorfahren seiner Mutter Jessie Francis Shamhart in Erfahrung zu bringen. »Sie ist eine Nachfahrin der Auswanderer, die im 17. Jahrhundert vom Hof Oberschabbehard, Steinhagen Nr. 3, zunächst nach Varenholz an der Weser übersiedelten, und 1802 nach Amerika auswanderten.«

Der Bielefelder hat gemeinsam mit Ulrich Siebrasse viel geforscht in Steinhagener Kirchenbüchern, im Landeskirchenamt in Bielefeld, in Varenholz und im Staatsarchiv Detmold. Und so ergibt sich ein sehr greifbares Bild: Hermann Schabbehaar, mit 57 Jahren am 21. Dezember 1700 in Varenholz gestorben, wurde um 1644 in Steinhagen geboren. Über die im westfälisch-lippischen Raum einflussreiche Familie von Wendt, deren sich das Steinhagener Oberschabbehards abgabepflichtig waren, kam er in den nahe Vlotho gelegenen Ort. Am 13.

Gemeindearchiv überlassen. Dafür hat er auch in Süddeutschland geforscht.   Foto: Bluhm-Weinhold

April 1760 wurde dort Simon Heinrich Schamhart geboren. 1791 heiratete er Amalie Christina Korf. Das Paar errichtete 1793 ein Haus in Varenholz und machte sich zehn Jahre später auf den Weg nach Amerika. Ins gelobte Land? Über die Beweggründe kann Werner Schabbehard in den von ihm geschriebenen Kapiteln in der amerikanischen Familienchronik nur spekulieren: Waren es die damals inflationsartigen Preise und Steuern, die Arbeitslosigkeit, die sie aus der Heimat vertrieben? Was er sicher weiß: Simon Heinrich Schamhart wollte heimlich sein Haus verkaufen. Doch ein Gespräch in der Kirche wurde bekannt, und Schamhart musste Hab und Gut unter staatlicher Aufsicht veräußern – und natürlich Zoll zahlen an die Obrigkeit, weiß Werner Schabbehard aus einer Zeitungsnotiz.

In Amerika siedelten sich die Nachkommen in Guernsey County Ohio an. Von dort aus führt die Linie offenbar weiter nach Newton, Jasper County, Illinois, dem Geburtsort von James Mengs Mutter.

@   www.schabbehard.de

James L. Meng

Das Haus, das Heinrich Simon Schabbehard 1793 baute und vor der Auswanderung verkaufte, steht heute noch in Varenholz.

2

John Hanson—An American Patriot and James L. Meng's DNA Relative

John Hanson

According to a Genetrack Biolab DNA test, the Y chromosome found in James L. Meng, thus all male Meng's, was also found in the American patriot John Hanson. The match was 17/20 markers, which is considered a very high probability.

John Hanson was born on April 3, 1715, in Charles County, Maryland. His career in public service began in 1750, when he was appointed sheriff of Charles County, Maryland. In 1757, he was elected to represent Charles County in the lower house of the Maryland General Assembly. He was a leading and vocal opponent of the 1765 Stamp Act and the Townshend Acts. After our War of Independence, John Hanson served in the Maryland House of Delegates in 1777, the first of five annual terms. In 1779, he was selected as a delegate to the Second Continental Congress.

Patriot John Hanson was the president of the Continental Congress from November 5, 1781 to November 3, 1782, under the Articles of Confederation which he signed in 1781. Consequently, he has been mistakenly identified as the first president of the United States. He died on November 15, 1783.

President of Congress John Hanson's bronze statue stands in the US Capitol

3

CHAPTER 2
THREE MENG GENEALOGICAL TREE BRANCHES

Meng family tree is firmly rooted in Hessen, Germany, with HEIMBROD VON BOYNEBURG in the 1500s. This noble branch of the Meng/Ming tree, which includes the RUBENKAM family, will follow in extensive detail.

From these roots grew three distinct branches of the family. The Meng immigration to America and New Zealand started in the German towns of Ladenburg, Hohen-Sülzen, and Monsheim. These branches can also be called the Pennsylvania branch, the New Zealand branch, and the Illinois branch of the Meng genealogical tree.

The first branch of the American family tree begins in Germany with NICHOLAS MENG, born in Ladenburg, Rhein-Neckar-Kreis in Baden-Württemberg, Germany, in 1630. JOHANN MARTIN MENG married ANNA SABINA BLACKLEIN. They had a son named JOHANN CHRISTOPH MENG born in 1697. JOHANN CHRISTOPH MENG sailed on the ship *Mortonhouse* to America on August 24, 1728. He and his wife DOROTHEA (née BAUMANN) with their son and daughter traveled to Philadelphia, Pennsylvania. Information on the Meng branch in Pennsylvania was researched by Hoyt B. Meng in his essay titled "John Christopher Meng and Many Descendants (The Ming Family)." Hoyt's heritage was subsequently connected to the Meng tree by Herrn Werner Schabbehard, a Shamhart relative in Bielefeld, Germany.

Incidentally, to put this event in a time reference, the JOHANN CHRISTOPH MENG family sailed to America 48 years before Gen. George Washington crossed the Delaware River on December 25, 1776, during the American Revolutionary War.

A second branch of the Meng genealogical tree starts with REICHARD MENG whose son, KARL PHILLIPP MENG, immigrated from Hohen-Sülzen (Germany) to Ashley (New Zealand) on the ship *Sebastopol* in 1863. KARL PHILLIPP MENG died on January 22, 1859, and is buried in the Flaxton Cemetery in Christchurch, New Zealand (see "The Karl Meng Family in New Zealand"). Interesting information on the NZ genealogical Meng branch and the history of the town of Hohen-Sülzen and life in New Zealand was compiled again by Werner Schabbehard and Belinda Lansley.

A third branch of the Meng genealogical tree started with CONRAD MENG, who was born on July 9, 1834, in Monsheim, Germany. He immigrated to the town of Freeburg in St. Clair County, Illinois, on August 1, 1837. He arrived in America on the ship *Manchester*. CONRAD MENG is viewed as having started the Illinois branch of the Meng genealogical tree (see the "Nachkommen von Wilhelm Meng"). The following Illinois information was once again developed by Werner Schabbehard in Germany and James L. Meng in America.

The First Known American Meng, Nachkommen von Nicholas Meng (1630)

In addition to the monumental and epic event of the first known Meng, Nicholas Meng being born in 1630, there were also six other events, some say of much less significance and influence to the history of the world.

These incidental events include (1) John Winthrop delivers "City upon a Hill" sermon aboard the *Arbella*, heading en route to Colonial America (referenced by my hero President Ronald Reagan in his January 25, 1974, speech to the first CPAC Conference); (2) Judith Leyster paints self-portrait; (3) Rembrandt paints *Jeremiah Mourns the Destruction of Jerusalem*; (4) the Winthrop Fleet departs from Yarmouth, Isle of Wight, for Colonial America; (5) the Winthrop Fleet arrives in Salem, Massachusetts; and (6) the Sack of Magdeburg.

The Sack of Magdeburg (Magdeburgs Opfergang or Magdeburger Hochzeit in German) refers to the siege and subsequent plundering of Magdeburg by the army of the Holy Roman Empire during the Thirty Years' War. The siege lasted from November 1630 until May 20, 1631.

THE MENGS FROM LADENBURG, DEUTSCHLAND

The next question is what and where is Ladenburg, Deutschland? Ladenburg is a town in the district of Rhein-Neckar-Kreis in Baden-Württemberg, Germany. It is situated on the right bank of the Neckar 10 km east of Mannheim and 10 km northwest of Heidelberg. It has an old town from the late Middle Ages. Its history dates back to Celtic and Roman ages. The first time this village was populated was between 3000 and 200 BC. It then consisted of a Celtic settlement Lopodunum (Seatower). In the year 40 the Romans populated the town as a farmer or military outpost and kept its Celtic name.

The local territory formed the civilian district of *Civitas Ulpia Sueborum Nicretum* (Neckarsuebi) of which Lopodunum was the chief town. In AD 74, the Romans founded the town Auxiliarkastelle, which was the center of the future town. The garrison included a cavalry of the Canaefaten. In addition to the world-renowned Nichlolas Meng being born in 1630, other notable people born in Ladenburg include the Bavarian war ministers Franz Xaver and Friedrich von Herling. The man who is regarded as the inventor of the automobile, Karl Benz, spent his last days of his life in Ladenburg between 1906 and his death in 1929.

Copies of the official church records connecting the Meng family to Ladenburg, Germany, and the Nachommen Meng will follow.*

Coat of arms of Ladenburg

The Meng-Shamhart book is in the Ladenburg City Archives

---

* Sack of Magdeburg" Wikipedia, The Free Encyclopedia. Also on this page, is the engraving of the Sack of Magdeburg by Mathäus Merian.

The next several pages are from the church book of Ladenburg, Germany. Johann Martin* and Hans Meng are shown on page 212, numbers 2110 and 2111. They are also provided in their totality for others who may want to research the Meng genealogy further. Although not a very exciting read, this information was difficult to obtain thus provided for others who may want to research the Meng genealogy further.

Ladenburger Kirchenbücher
Teil I

Reformierte und lutherische
Kirchenbücher
von 1649–1821

bearbeitet
von
Karl Diefenbacher
Oberstudiendirektor a/D.

MENG

2109   8 ...: Niclauß Meng, Wagner, +17.11.1668, und Anna Barbara ... siehe Ämterbuch
S: 138;
   5 Kdr: Kind +29.3.1670 alt 13 J. - Knabe +12.11.1667 alt
   2 J. - Anna Maria get.4.11.1668 - Anna Sara (siehe 132) - Catharina (siehe
   3631).

2110   8 ...: Johann Martin Meng, kof.1679 alt 15 J., (8 II siehe 2111) und Anna
Barbara ...,
   3 Kdr: Anna Margaretha *+ 23.11./9.12.1687 - Johann Martin *18.5.1689
   - Ludwig *21.4.1693.

2111   8 9.1.1697: Hans Martin Meng, Witwer, Beisitzer, (8 I siehe 2110), und Anna
Sabina Biacklein (To des Hans Jacob B., Bü in Heidelberg),
   Kind: Johann Christoph get. 22.9.1697.

2112   8 13.8.1698: Heinrich Meng, Witwer, Schuhmacher, und Maria Elisabeth
Trilch (aus 3250).

2113   8 ...: Johann Wilhelm Meng, Beständer auf dem Rosenhof, +24.9.1765 alt 48
J., und Maria Apollonia ... + 19.12.1774 alt 40 J. (8 II siehe 917),
   2 Kdr: Georg Wilhelm (siehe 2116) - Johann Christoph get.17.2.1766.

2114   8 20.5.1774: Johann Valentin Meng, Schmiedemeister in Neckarhausen, und
Margaretha Volckert *16.11.1751, +14.5.1806 (aus 3330),
   9 Kdr: Anna Maria (siehe 1053) - Alexander (siehe 2117 und 2121) - Sophia

---

* Johann Martin Meng's father, Neclaruss Meng, also on page 212, number 2109, is the Pennsylvania Meng genealogical branch.

(siehe 375) - Johann Jacob get.6.12.1780 - Maria Magdalena *11.12.1782, +1.9.1842 - Johann Martin (siehe 2118) - Sebastian *10.1.1787 - Johann Jacob Ü13.3.1790 - Michael *13.1.1794, +2.1.1795.

2115   8 15.7.1779: <u>Johann Georg Meng</u> von Neckarhausen, und <u>Anna Barbara Herauf</u> get.9.4.1759, +25.1.1809 (aus 1339),
        9 Kdr: Johann Georg get.24.6.1780 - Georg Wilhelm (siehe 2120 und 2122) - Johann Melchior *15.12.1783 - Anton *7.6. 1785 - Anna Margaretha *27.1.1787, +20.4.1794 - Valentin *24.12.189, +4.1.1790 - Johann Melchior (siehe 2124) - Johann Philipp * 15.5.1794 - Johann Valentin *27.10.1795, + 27.6.1815.

2116   8 10.8.1785: <u>Georg Wilhelm Meng</u>, Kutscher, Bauer von Edingen Bürger in Ladenburg, get.19.10.1763, +9.10.1843 (aus 2113), und <u>Susanna Louisa Sturm</u> *10.2.1765, +16.6.1819 (aus 3203),
        12 Kdr: Johann Christoph (siehe 2119) - Catharina *6.3.1785 - Susanna Maria (siehe 2238) - Catharina Margaretha *23.10.1787 - Georg Wilhelm *9.5.1789, +11.3.1790 - Michael (siehe 2123 und 2126) - Michael *+31.3./17.11.1791 - Michael Wilhelm *+16/23.12.1792 - Amalia *+2.3./4.11.1794 - Wilhelm *+ 6.5.1797 - Katharina *+ 6.5.1797 - Friedrich *21.3.1799, +23.6.1847.

2117   8 22.10.1797 in Neckarhausen: <u>Alexander Meng</u> von Neckarhausen get.19.9.1776, (8 II siehe 2121), (aus 2114), und <u>Catharina Margaretha Rausch</u> (To descendants Andreas R. von Wieblingen).

2118   8 12.8.1806 in Neckarhausen: <u>Martin Meng</u> in Neckarhausen, *24.11.1784 (aus 2114), und <u>Anna Margaretha Kleber</u> von Kleingemünd (To des Martin K., Ackersmann von Kleingemünd),
        Kind: Martin * 29.12.1806 in Neckarhausen.

2119   8 1.3.1808: <u>Christoph Meng</u>, Bürger und Schmieddmeister, *10.7.1783, +12.6.1814 (aus 2116), und <u>Eva Catharina Lösch</u> *... (8 II siehe 3523), (aus 1939),
        2 Kdr: Susanna Maria *21.1.1809 - Margaretha *20.3.1812, + 23.5.1876.

2120   8 3.5.1808" <u>Georg Wilhelm Meng</u> von Neckarhausen, *13.11.1782, + 12.9.1858 in Edingen (8 II siehe 2122), (aus 2115), und <u>Apollonia Ding</u> get.4.7.1770, +6.10.1811 (aus 543),
        Kind: Christoph *+ 6.8./11.9.1811 in Neckarhausen.

2121   8 ...: <u>Alexander Meng</u> (8 I siehe 2117), (aus 2114), und <u>Susanna Margaretha Gutmann</u> von Lindach bei Eberbach.

2122   8 9.3.1812 in Edingen: <u>Wilhelm Meng</u>, Witwer (8 I siehe 2120) (aus 2115), und <u>Anna Maria Hörauf</u> (aus 1342),
        Kind: Margaretha *3.9.1813 Neckarhausen.

2123   8 4.12.1816: <u>Michael Meng</u>, Schmied, +7.11.1849 alt 59 J., (8 II siehe 2126), (aus 2116), und <u>Anna Elisabeth Saam</u> von Schriesheim, +12.7.1819 alt 30 J. (To des Friedrich S., Müller in der Pflastermühle und der Elisabeth geb. Mack von Schriesheim),

     2 Kdr: Johann Ludwig *10.8.1816 - Georg Wilhelm *17.6.1818.

2124   8 13.4.1817: <u>Melchior Meng</u>, Leineweber in Neckarhausen *25.12.1790, +9.4.1855 (aus 2115), und <u>Barbara Schreckenberger</u>, kathol. (To des Sebastian Sch., Bauer in Neckarhausen und der Catharina geb. Lang),

     3 Kdr: Sebastian *3.7.1817, +27.7.1897 - Johann Georg *+29.10.1818 - Johann Georg *+ 28.5./20.9.1821.

2125   8 9.7.1818 in Neckarhausen: <u>Valentin Meng</u>, Witwer, Bauer zu Neckarhausen (So des Wilhelm M., Bü und Bauer zu Edingen und der Apollonia geb. Reimle von Neckarhausen), und <u>Anna Margaretha Reich</u> von Schönmattenwag (To des +Johann R., Papiermacher von Unterschönmattenwag und der Anna Maria geb.Flachs von Mudach).

2126   8 9.11.1819 in Neckarhausen: <u>Michael Meng</u>, Witwer, Hufschmied, Bauer, +7.11.1849 alt 59 J. (aus 2116), (8 I siehe 2123), und <u>Maria Elisabeth Quintel</u> aus Neckarhausen *22.7.1790, + 17.2.1847 (aus 2447),

     11 Kdr: Johann Caspar *21.9.1820 - Anna Barbara *22.11.1821, +28.3.1822 - Anna Barbara *+5.3./7.8.1823 - Christina *15.8.1824, +18.12.1904 - Anna Margaretha *21.12.1825 - Michael *21.10.1827, +4.6.1858 - Michael *+18.3/6.4.1829 - Magdalena *4.7.1830, +3.2.1831 - Helena *+3/25.8.1831 - Michael *20.6.1833 - Heinrich *26.10.1835.

MENK

2127   8 23.6.1739: <u>Jost Paul Menk</u>, Rotgerber von Niederingelheim, +17.3.1772 alt 60 J. (So des Jacob M., Ratsverwandter zu Oberingelheim) und <u>Dorothea Catharina Rautenbusch</u> get.3.2.1716, +29.7.1783 (aus 2472),

     14 Kdr: Anna Margaretha get. 16.3.1740 - Anna Maria get.16.3.1740 - Anna Barbara (siehe 1543) - Anna Christina (siehe 3054) - Catharina Elisabeth get.29.10.1743, +17.3.1773 ledig - Maria Margaretha get.18.7.1745 - Anna Christina Dorothea get.25.10.1746 - Elisabeth get.5.12.1747, +1.6.1776 - Johann Bernhard get.14.5.1749 - Joh.Philipp *10.11.1752 - Georg Adam get.15.8.1755 - Joh.Martin get.5.3.1757

BECKER

<u>132</u>   8 15.4.1673: <u>Johann Jacob Becker</u>, Hafner, +4.2.1715 luth., und <u>Anna Sara Meng</u> (aus 2109),

     5 Kdr: Johann Jacob get.15.12.1673, +1.6.1676 - Tochter *+19.8.1676

- Margaretha get.26.8.1677, +25.8.1680 - Margaretha get 10.11.1678,
+5.8.1680 - Hans Adam get.31.1.1681.
Karoline Elisabeth * 18.12.1893
Joseph * 22.7.1897 + 20.5.1900
Elisabeth Frieda * 21.9.1899 + 20.9.1928
8 Karl Probst
Joseph * 4.3.1898 + 3.9.1898

MENG

2447	8 29.1.1823 ev.: <u>Friedrich Jacob Meng</u>, Bauer, <aus I/2116> * 21.3.1799, und <u>Anna Barbara Scholl</u>, <aus I/2886> * 14.10.1800, + 30.1.1850.

10 Kinder:
Sophia Margaretha * 15.11.1823   <siehe 4149>
Anna Maria * 3.10.11826 + 7.2.1827
Johann Michael * 24.1.1858   <siehe 2451>
Johann Wilhelm * 12.6.1830 + 31.5.1832
Wilhelm * 29.11.1832   <siehe 2453>
Anna Maria * 6.1.1835 + 30.4.1835
Anna Maria * 26.8.1836   <siehe 1381>
Elisabetha * 20.1.1839
Ludwig * 10.12.1841 + 16.5.1841

2448   ... : <u>Michael Meng</u>, Ackersmann, <siehe I/2126>, und <u>Elisabeth Quintel</u>, von Neckarhausen.
        1 Kind:
        Helena * ... + 25.8.1836 alt: 21 Tage

2449   8 28.5.1846 ev.: <u>Georg Wilhelm Meng</u>, Ackersmann, <aus I/2123> * 17.6.1818, + 23.6.1882, und <u>Anna Maria Herre</u>, kath., (Tochter des Jakob Herre, Schuhmacher in Leutershausen und der + Eva Elisabeth geb. Pfisterer), + 9.3.1883, alt: 64 Jahre.
        7 Kinder:
        Katharina * 28.3.1847 + 13.1.1852
        Christine * 25.12.1848   <siehe 2075>
        Barbara * 6.7.1851   <siehe 3514>
        Catharina * 13.9.1853   <siehe 3970>
        Elisabeth * 19.9.1855   <siehe 3436>
        Heinrich * 1.5.1858
        Wilhelm * 25.10.1864 + 3.11.1864
        (Mädchen = kath., Knaben = ev.)

2450   * 15.8.1824 ev.: <u>Christine Meng</u>, <aus I/2126> + 18.12.1904.
        1 Kind:
        Ludwig * 3.7.1852 + 3.7.1859

2451   8 1.11.1855 ev.: <u>Johann Michael Meng</u>, Ackersmann, <aus 2447> * 24.1.1858,
        + 5.3.1892, und <u>Maria Elisabeth Nilson</u>, <aus 2710> * 4.1.1832, + 20.6.1891.
        8 Kinder:
        Carl * 5.8.1856   <siehe 2460>
        Franz * 30.1.1858   <siehe 2459>
        Christine Elisabeth * 12.11.1859 + 21.5.1860
        Carl Friedrich * 9.9.1861 + 22.10.1861
        Margaretha * 13.4.1864 + 25.7.1864
        Margaretha Elisabeth * 18.6.1865 + 14.10.1865
        Margaretha * 20.3.1870 + 20.6.1870
        Johann * 5.6.1872

2452   8 4.5.1856 ev.: <u>Johann Ludwig Meng</u>, Ackersmann, 1863 Fuhrmann, <aus
        I/2123> * 10.8.1816, + 16.3.1892, und <u>Maria Elisabetha Eisenhardt</u>, <aus
        I/0620> * 28.11.1831, + 13.3.1892.
        10 Kinder:
        Franz * 15.12.1855 + 24.10.1856
        Johann * 26.7.1857 + 19.5.1877 ledig
        Franz * 20.3.1859 + 4.5.1886 lediger Zigarrenarbeiter
        Theobald * 20.9.1861   <siehe 2463>
        Georg Wilhelm * 14.2.1863
        Louise * 22.9.1864 + 30.8.1876
        Christian Gottfried * 8.8.1866
        Elisabeth * 1.5.1869 + 1.8.1870
        Barbara * 1.5.1869 + 28.10.1869
        Ludwig * 8.11.1872

2453   8 27.11.1856 ev.: <u>Wilhelm Meng</u>, Bäckermeister, <aus 2447> * 29.11.1832, +
        13.1.1888, und <u>Anna Maria Wolf</u>, <aus 4142> * 16.12.1835, + 10.11.1908.
        10 Kinder:
        Anna Maria * 7.8.1857 + 21.12.1857
        Catharina Wilhelmina * 16.7.1858   <siehe 4167>
        Conrad Melchior * 16.8.1860
        Joseph Friedrich * 4.4.1862 + 24.10.1866
        Barbara Anna * 9.5.1864 + 10.9.1864
        Louise * 20.1.1867 + 2.7.1900 ledige Kellnerin
        Friedrich Adolf * 18.7.1868 + Heidelberg 7.4.1934
        Johann Emil * 13.2.1870 + 3.11.1875
        Kind +* 12.6.1873
        Karl Wilhelm * 14.9.1875

2454   8 25.1.1857 ev.: <u>Johann Kaspar Meng</u>, Ackersmann, 1867 Fuhrmann, <aus
        I/2126> * 21.9.1820, + 12.6.1878, und <u>Eva Vorgeitz</u>, <aus 3899> * 7.5.1832,
        + 6.3.1888.
        11 Kinder:

Maria Margaretha * 23.12.1857   \<siehe 2456\>
Elisabeth * 30.3.1859 + 10.6.1859
Adam Barbara * 27.10.1860   \<siehe 2457\>
Susanna * 5.7.1862 + 2.1.1863
Peter * 8.10.1863 + 14.10.1863
Elisabeth * 21.11.1864
Christine * 23.6.1866 + 24.8.1867
Wilhelm * 6.12.1867 + 27.4.1868
Johann Michael * 23.7.1869 + 31.7.1869
Johann Michael * 12.8.1871 + 16.9.1871
Carl Michael * 11.1.1875

2455   8 24.9.1868: <u>Heinrich Meng</u>, Taglöhner, \<aus I/2126\> * 26.10.1835, II. 8 mit Elisabeth Quintel, + 14.6.1909, und <u>Anna Margaretha Merkel</u>, (Tochter des Johann Peter Merkel, Leineweber und der Margaretha geb. Lauer), * Kleingemünd 9.11.1839, + 26.8.1900.
        4 Kinder:
        Johann Georg * 28.9.1868 + 20.10.1868
        Johanna * 29.10.1870 + 25.6.1871
        Johann * 10.11.1872 + 18.11.1932 8 Lina Fuchs
        Valentin * 28.4.1874 + 12.4.1893 ledig

2456   * 23.12.1857 ev.: <u>Margaretha Meng</u>, \<aus 2454\>.
        1 Kind:
        Eva Margaretha * 19.10.1880

2457   * 27.10.1860 ev.: <u>Barbara Meng</u>, \<aus 2454\>.
        1 Kind:
        Barbara Margaretha * 17.5.1883 + 7.7.1883

2458   8 31.3.1883 Weinheim: <u>Mathias Meng</u>, Ratschreiber in Neckarhausen, (Sohn des Johann Georg Meng, Landwirt, + 7.8.1888, alt: 65 Jahre 3 Monate 20 Tage und der + Margaretha geb. Dörrschuck, von Neckarhausen), und <u>Anna Rosina Eberle</u>, (Tochter des Christian Eberle, Gärtner und der Dorothea geb. Strauß, von Weinheim), * Weinheim ...
        4 Kinder:
        Friedrich Wilhelm * 24.1.1884
        Anna Dorothea   * 22.10.1884 + 23.10.1884
        Henriette Barbara * 22.10.1884 + 23.10.1884
        Philipp Ludwig * 4.9.1885

2459   8 5.5.1883: <u>Franz Meng</u>, Landwirt, \<aus 2451\> * 30.1.1858, + 20.10.1932, und <u>Margaretha Schmitt</u>, kath., \<aus 3272\> * 21.2.1860, + 4.12.1942.
        6 Kinder:
        Johann Michael * 8.2.1884

Barbara * 18.6.1885 + 10.8.1885
Johann * 14.7.1887 + 20.8.1887
Eva Katharina * 30.3.1991 + 8.1.1892
Barbara * 1.3.1893
Anna Maria * 19.2.1897 + 22.12.1904

2460   8 2.4.1887 Heidelberg : <u>Karl Meng</u>, Landwirt, <aus 2451> * 5.8.1856, +
7.9.1924, und <u>Katharina Lackert</u>, <aus 2147> * 14.1.1856, + 28.10.1930.
4 Kinder:
Hermann * 9.3.1888
Elisabeth * 3.11.1889
Friedrich * 29.1.1892 + 25.8.1892
Georg Friedrich * 18.7.1896

2461   8 31.1.1889: <u>Martin Meng</u>, Landwirt, (Sohn des + Martin Meng Landwirt
und der Katharina geb. Bühler, von Wieblingen), * Wieblingen 22.7.1858,
und <u>Margaretha Meng</u>, (Tochter des + Georg Meng, Bahnarbeiter und der
Margaretha geb.Derschuck, von Neckarhausen).

2463   8 10.6.1889 Hohensachsen: <u>Theobald Meng</u>, Fabrikarbeiter. <aus 2452> *
20.9.1861, + 1.1.1920, und <u>Katharina Meier</u>, (Tochter des + Johann Valentin
Meier und der Sophie Elise geb.Eichler, von Hohensachsen), * Hohensachsen
6.1.1857.
3 Kinder:
Anna Margaretha * 6.4.1890
Friedrich * 8.6.1892
Wilhelm * 20.5.1894

2464   + 20.12.1889: <u>Wilhelm Meng</u>, alt: 25 Jahre 6 Monate, lediger Fischer in
Neckarhausen, Sohn des Johann Georg Meng.

2465   8 ... ev.: <u>Wilhelm Meng</u>, Barbier, 1891 Taglöhner, und <u>Agnes Gütler</u>, kath., *
Steinseifersdorf in Schlesien 23.12.1865, + 2.11.1920.
8 Kinder:
Ludwig * 23.3.1890 + 9.4.1920 ledig
Eva * 30.10.1891 + 8.1.1892
Luise Elisabeth * 10.11.1892 + 11.8.1893
Christian * 4.12.1893 + 17.4.1894
Konrad * 16.2.1895 + 30.8.1895
Wilhelm Georg * 24.6.1896 + 31.7.1896
Franz * 23.7.1897
Friedrich * 27.2.1899
Mädchen = kath., Knaben ev.)

2466   + 22.2.1891 Mannheim: <u>Elisabeth Meng</u>, ledig von Ladenburg, wohnhaft in
Mannheim.

2467   8 ... : <u>Sebastian Meng</u>, Landwirt in Neckarhausen, <aus I/2124> + 28.7.1897, alt:
        84 Jahre 24 Tage. und <u>Elisabeth Merkel</u>, * 12.10.1834, + Heidelberg 25.2.1907.

ZEISEL

3631   8 17.1.1671: <u>Hans Wolf Zeisel</u> (Zahsel) aus Bayernland, und <u>Catharina Meng</u>
        (aus 2109); siehe Ämterbuch S: 181, 8 Kdr: Elisabeth get.20.12.1670 - Hans
        Jacob get.30.8.1672 - Simon get.23.3.1674 - Maria Magdalena get.16.6.1676 -
        Anna Maria get.9.3.1678, +17.4.1679 - Hans Nickel get.2 11.1679, +23.2.1680
        - Elisabeth get.29.12.1680 - Susanna get.18.10.1683.

3632   8 13.2.1672: <u>Simon Zeisel</u>, und <u>Maria Ursula Gieser</u> (aus 968), 5 Kinder:
        Maria Barbara get.6.12.1672 - Hans Heinrich get.16.6.1674 - Anna Bärbel
        get.23.1.1677 - Anna Margaretha get.14.2.1679 - Susanna get.20.4.1681.

THE MENG FAMILY TREE FROM LADENBURG, DEUTSCHLAND
NACHKOMMEN VON NICLAUß MENG

Erste Generation

1. Niclauß Meng[1] wurde 1630 geboren. Er starb am 17. November 1668 in Ladenburg, Rhein-Neckar-Kreis in Baden-Württemberg.

Niclauß war Wagner in Ladenburg, Rhein-Neckar-Kreis in Baden-Württemberg.

> Source: Churchbook Ladenburg, page 212, no. 2109; forwarded by Meng, Karl, farmer from 68526 Ladenburg, Rhein-Neckar-Kreis in Baden-Württemberg

Niclauß heiratete Anna Barbara NN[2] 1650 in Ladenburg.

> Source: Churchbook Ladenburg, page 212, no. 2109; forwarded by Meng, Karl, farmer from 68526 Ladenburg, Rhein-Neckar-Kreis in Baden-Württemberg

Niclauß und Anna hatten die folgenden Kinder:

+ 2 W   i.   Catharina Meng wurde 1651 geboren.

+ 3W   ii.   Anna Sarah Meng wurde 1653 geboren.

  4   iii.   NN Meng[3] wurde 1657 geboren. NN starb am 29. März 1670 in Ladenburg, Rhein-Neckar-Kreis in Baden-Württemberg.

He died 13 years old

> Source: Churchbook Ladenburg, page 212, no. 2109; forwarded by Meng, Karl, farmer from 68526 Ladenburg, Rhein-Neckar-Kreis in Baden-Württemberg

  5   iv.   NN Meng wurde 1659 in Ladenburg, Rhein-Neckar-Kreis in Baden-Württemberg geboren.

Estimated child, because a woman had very often every two years a child. So it seems understandable that in the years between 1657 and 1665 more children should have be born, but not to be find in the churchbook, because the churchbook started later.

One of these two children might have been the father of Johoem Otto Meng, a uncle to Johan Martin Meng * 1664/65

> Source: Schabbehard, Werner-ancestry research Bielefeld the first day of March 2011

6   v.   NN Meng wurde 1661 geboren.

Estimated child, because a woman had very often every two years a child. So it seems understandable that in the years between 1657 and 1665 more children should have be born, but not to be find in the churchbook, because the churchbook started later.

One of these two children might have been the father of Johoem Otto Meng, a uncle to Johan Martin Meng * 1664/65

Source: Schabbehard, Werner-ancestry research Bielefeld the first day of March 201

+   7 M   vi.   Johann Martin Meng wurde 1664/1665 gebcren. Er starb am 22. Oktober 1728.

8 M   vii.   NN Meng[4] wurde 1665 in Ladenburg, Rhein-Neckar-Kreis in Baden-Württemberg geboren. Er starb am 12. November 1667 in Ladenburg, Rhein-Neckar-Kreis in Baden-Württemberg.

Bei Tod 2 Jahre alt

Source: Churchbook Ladenburg, page 212 no. 2109

9 W   viii.   Anna Maria Meng[5] wurde 1668 in Ladenburg, Rhein-Neckar-Kreis in Baden-Württemberg geboren. Sie wurde am am 04. November 1668 in Ladenburg, Rhein-Neckar-Kreis in Baden-Württemberg getauft.

Source: Churchbook Ladenburg, page 212 no. 2109

10   ix.   NN Meng[6] wurde 1655 in Ladenburg, Rhein-Neckar-Kreis in Baden-Württemberg geboren.

Zweite Generation

2.   Catharina Meng (Niclauß) wurde 1651 in Ladenburg, Rhein-Neckar-Kreis in Baden-Württemberg geboren.

Catharina heiratete Hans Wolf Zeisel[7] am 17. Januar 1671 in Ladenburg, Rhein-Neckar-Kreis in Baden-Württemberg[8]. Hans wurde in Bayernland geboren.

Source: Churchbook Ladenburg, page 12 no. 132 [Churchbook registers, part I, reformed church registers of 1649-1821, worked on by Karl Diefenbacher, prical a/D.; copies forwarded by Mrs. Gudrun Best, Sekretariat Evangelische Kirchengemeinde Ladenburg, Kirchenstraße 28, 68526 Ladenburg8526 Ladenburg Rhein-Neckar-Kreis in Baden-Württemberg

The name of Zeisel could possible read Zahsel

17

Hans und Catharina hatten die folgenden Kinder:

11 W i.   Elisabeth Zeisel[9] wurde 1670 in Ladenburg, Rhein-Neckar-Kreis in Baden-Württemberg geboren. Sie wurde am am 20. Dezember 1670 in Ladenburg, Rhein-Neckar-Kreis in Baden-Württemberg getauft.

> Source: Churchbook Ladenburg, page 12 no, 132 [Churchbook registers, part I, reformed church registers of 1649-1821, worked on by Karl Diefenbacher, principal a/D.; copies forwarded by Mrs. Gudrun Best, Sekretariat Evangelische Kirchengemeinde Ladenburg, Kirchenstraße 28, 68526 Ladenburg8526 Ladenburg Rhein-Neckar-Kreis in Baden-Württemberg
>
> The name of Zeisel could possibly read Zahsel

12 M ii.   Hans Jacob Zeisel[10] wurde 1672 in Ladenburg, Rhein-Neckar-Kreis in Baden-Württemberg geboren. Er wurde am 30. August 1672 in Ladenburg, Rhein-Neckar-Kreis in Baden-Württemberg getauft.

> Source: Churchbook Ladenburg, page 12 no. 132 [Churchbook registers, part I, reformed church registers of 1649-1821, worked on by Karl Diefenbacher, principal a/D.; copies forwarded by Mrs. Gudrun Best, Sekretariat Evangelische Kirchengemeinde Ladenburg, Kirchenstraße 28, 68526 Ladenburg8526 Ladenburg Rhein-Neckar-Kreis in Baden-Württemberg
>
> The name of Zeisel could possibly read Zahsel.; copies forwarded by Mrs. Gudrun Best, Sekretariat Evangelische Kirchengemeinde Ladenburg, Kirchenstraße 28, 68526 Ladenburg8526 Ladenburg Rhein-Neckar-Kreis in Baden-Württemberg
>
> The name of Zeisel could possibly read Zahsel

13 M iii. Simon Zeisel[11] wurde 1674 in Ladenburg, Rhein-Neckar-Kreis in Baden-Württemberg geboren. Er wurde am 23. März 1674 in Ladenburg, Rhein-Neckar-Kreis in Baden-Württemberg getauft.

> Source: Churchbook Ladenburg, page 12 no. 132 [Churchbook registers, part I, reformed church registers of 1649-1821, worked on by Karl Diefenbacher, pricipal a/D.; copies forwarded by Mrs. Gudrun Best, Sekretariat Evangelische Kirchengemeinde Ladenburg, Kirchenstraße 28, 68526 Ladenburg8526 Ladenburg Rhein-Neckar-Kreis in Baden-Württemberg
>
> The name of Zeisel could possibly read Zahsel

14 W iv.   Maria Magdalena Zeisel[12] wurde 1676 in Ladenburg, Rhein-Neckar-Kreis in Baden-Württemberg geboren. Sie wurde am am 16. Juni 1676 in Ladenburg, Rhein-Neckar-Kreis in Baden-Württemberg getauft.

> Source: Churchbook Ladenburg, page 12 no. 132 [Churchbook registers, part I, reformed church registers of 1649–1821, worked on by Karl Diefenbacher, pricipal a/D.; copies forwarded by Mrs. Gudrun Best, Sekretariat

Evangelische Kirchengemeinde Ladenburg, Kirchenstraße 28, 68526
Ladenburg8526 Ladenburg Rhein-Neckar-Kreis in Baden-Württemberg

The name of Zeisel could possibly read Zahsel

15 W v.   Anna Maria Zeisel[13] wurde 1678 in Ladenburg, Rhein-Neckar-Kreis
in Baden-Württemberg geboren. Sie wurde am am 09. März 1678 in
Ladenburg, Rhein-Neckar-Kreis in Baden-Württemberg getauft.

> Source: Churchbook Ladenburg, page 12 no. 132 [Churchbook registers, part
> I, reformed church registers of 1649-1821, worked on by Karl Diefenbacher,
> principal a/D.; copies forwarded by Mrs. Gudrun Best, Sekretariat Evangelische
> Kirchengemeinde Ladenburg, Kirchenstraße 28, 68526 Ladenburg8526
> Ladenburg Rhein-Neckar-Kreis in Baden-Württemberg

> The name of Zeisel could possibly read Zahsel

16 M vi. Hans Nickel (Niclauß) Zeisel[14] wurde 1679 in Ladenburg, Rhein-
Neckar-Kreis in Baden-Württemberg geboren. Er wurde am 02.
November 1679 in Ladenburg, Rhein-Neckar-Kreis in Baden-
Württemberg getauft. Er starb am 23. Februar 1680 in Ladenburg,
Rhein-Neckar-Kreis in Baden-Württemberg.

> Source: Churchbook Ladenburg, page 12 no. 132 [Churchbook registers, part
> I, reformed church registers of 1649-1821, worked on by Karl Diefenbacher,
> principal a/D.; copies forwarded by Mrs. Gudrun Best, Sekretariat Evangelische
> Kirchengemeinde Ladenburg, Kirchenstraße 28, 68526 Ladenburg8526
> Ladenburg Rhein-Neckar-Kreis in Baden-Württemberg

> The name of Zeisel could possibly read Zahsel

17 W vii. Elisabeth Zeisel[15] wurde 1680 in Ladenburg, Rhein-Neckar-Kreis in
Baden-Württemberg geboren. Sie wurde am am 29. Dezember 1680 in
Ladenburg, Rhein-Neckar-Kreis in Baden-Württemberg getauft.

> Source: Churchbook Ladenburg, page 12 no. 132 [Churchbook registers, part
> I, reformed church registers of 1649-1821, worked on by Karl Diefenbacher,
> principal a/D.; copies forwarded by Mrs. Gudrun Best, Sekretariat Evangelische
> Kirchengemeinde Ladenburg, Kirchenstraße 28, 68526 Ladenburg8526
> Ladenburg Rhein-Neckar-Kreis in Baden-Württemberg

> The name of Zeisel could possibly read Zahsel

18 W viii. Susanna Zeisel[16] wurde 1683 in Ladenburg, Rhein-Neckar-Kreis in
Baden-Württemberg geboren. Sie wurde am am 18. Oktober 1683 in
Ladenburg, Rhein-Neckar-Kreis in Baden-Württemberg getauft.

> Source: Churchbook Ladenburg, page 12 no. 132 [Churchbook registers, part
> I, reformed church registers of 1649-1821, worked on by Karl Diefenbacher,
> principal a/D.; copies forwarded by Mrs. Gudrun Best, Sekretariat

Evangelische Kirchengemeinde Ladenburg, Kirchenstraße 28, 68526 Ladenburg8526 Ladenburg Rhein-Neckar-Kreis in Baden-Württemberg

The name of Zeisel could possibly read Zahsel

3. Anna Sarah Meng[17] (Niclauß) wurde 1653 in Ladenburg, Rhein-Neckar-Kreis in Baden-Württemberg geboren.

> Source: Churchbook Ladenburg, page 12 no. 132 [Churchbook registers, part I, reformed church registers of 1649–1821, worked on by Karl Diefenbacher, principal a/D.; copies forwarded by Mrs. Gudrun Best, Sekretariat Evangelische Kirchengemeinde Ladenburg, Kirchenstraße 28, 68526 Ladenburg8526 Ladenburg Rhein-Neckar-Kreis in Baden-Württemberg

Anna heiratete Johann Jacob Becker[18] am 15. April 1673 in Ladenburg, Rhein-Neckar-Kreis in Baden-Württemberg[19]. Johann starb am 04. Februar 1715 in Ladenburg, Rhein-Neckar-Kreis in Baden-Württemberg.

> Source: Churchbook Ladenburg, page 12 no. 132 [Churchbook registers, part I, reformed church registers of 1649-1821, worked on by Karl Diefenbacher, pricipal a/D.; copies forwarded by Mrs. Gudrun Best, Sekretariat Evangelische Kirchengemeinde Ladenburg, Kirchenstraße 28, 68526 Ladenburg8526 Ladenburg Rhein-Neckar-Kreis in Baden-Württemberg

Johann und Anna hatten die folgenden Kinder:

19 M i. Johann Jacob Becker[20] wurde 1673 in Ladenburg, Rhein-Neckar-Kreis in Baden-Württemberg geboren. Er wurde am 15. Dezember 1673 in Ladenburg, Rhein-Neckar-Kreis in Baden-Württemberg getauft. Er starb am 01. Juni 1676 in Ladenburg, Rhein-Neckar-Kreis in Baden-Württemberg.

> Source: Churchbook Ladenburg, page 12 no. 132 [[Churchbook registers, part I, reformed church registers of 1649-1821, worked on by Karl Diefenbacher, pricipal a/D.; copies forwarded by Mrs. Gudrun Best, Sekretariat Evangelische Kirchengemeinde Ladenburg, Kirchenstraße 28, 68526 Ladenburg8526 Ladenburg Rhein-Neckar-Kreis in Baden-Württemberg

20 W ii. NN Becker[21] wurde am 19. August 1676 in Ladenburg, Rhein-Neckar-Kreis in Baden-Württemberg geboren.

> Source: Churchbook Ladenburg, page 12 no. 132 [Churchbook registers, part I, reformed church registers of 1649–1821, worked on by Karl Diefenbacher, pricipal a/D.; copies forwarded by Mrs. Gudrun Best, Sekretariat Evangelische Kirchengemeinde Ladenburg, Kirchenstraße 28, 68526 Ladenburg8526 Ladenburg Rhein-Neckar-Kreis in Baden-Württemberg

21 W iii. Margaretha Becker[22] wurde 1677 in Ladenburg, Rhein-Neckar-Kreis in Baden-Württemberg geboren. Sie wurde am am 26. August 1677 in Ladenburg, Rhein-Neckar-Kreis in Baden-Württemberg getauft. Sie

starb am 25. August 1680 in Ladenburg, Rhein-Neckar-Kreis in Baden-Württemberg.

> Source: Churchbook Ladenburg, page 12 no. 132 [Churchbook registers, part I, reformed church registers of 1649–1821, worked on by Karl Diefenbacher, principal a/D.; copies forwarded by Mrs. Gudrun Best, Sekretariat Evangelische Kirchengemeinde Ladenburg, Kirchenstraße 28, 68526 Ladenburg8526 Ladenburg Rhein-Neckar-Kreis in Baden-Württemberg

22 W iv. Margaretha Becker[23] wurde 1678 in Ladenburg, Rhein-Neckar-Kreis in Baden-Württemberg geboren. Sie wurde am 10. November 1678 in Ladenburg, Rhein-Neckar-Kreis in Baden-Württemberg getauft. Sie starb am 05. August 1680 in Ladenburg, Rhein-Neckar-Kreis in Baden-Württemberg.

> Source: Churchbook Ladenburg, page 12 no. 132 [Churchbook registers, part I, reformed church registers of 1649–1821, worked on by Karl Diefenbacher, pricipal a/D.; copies forwarded by Mrs. Gudrun Best, Sekretariat Evangelische Kirchengemeinde Ladenburg, Kirchenstraße 28, 68526 Ladenburg8526 Ladenburg Rhein-Neckar-Kreis in Baden-Württemberg

23 M v. Hans Adam Becker[24] wurde 1681 in Ladenburg, Rhein-Neckar-Kreis in Baden-Württemberg geboren. Er wurde am 31. Januar 1681 in Ladenburg, Rhein-Neckar-Kreis in Baden-Württemberg getauft.

> Source: Churchbook Ladenburg, page 12 no. 132 [Churchbook registers, part I, reformed church registers of 1649-1821, worked on by Karl Diefenbacher, principal a/D.; copies forwarded by Mrs. Gudrun Best, Sekretariat Evangelische Kirchengemeinde Ladenburg, Kirchenstraße 28, 68526 Ladenburg8526 Ladenburg Rhein-Neckar-Kreis in Baden-Württemberg

7. Johann Martin Meng[25,26] (Niclauß) wurde 1664/1665 in Lambsborn, Landkreis Kaiserslautern in Rheinland-Pfalz geboren. Er starb am 22. Oktober 1728 in Speyer, Rheinland-Pfalz.

Johann war Beisitzer [official at the town office] in Ladenburg, Rhein-Neckar-Kreis in Baden-Württemberg.

Was confirmed 1679 in Ladenburg 15 years old. From this date he is born in 1674

> Source: Churchbook Ladenburg, page 212 no. 2110

He died 63 years old on a strong kolik, documentet in the churchbook of Speyer. From this date he is born in 1675

> Source: Mrs. Gisela Peschka from Evangelische Kirche der Pfalz

Johann heiratete Anna Sabina Biacklein[27,28] Tochter von Hans Jacob Braenklin am 09. Januar 1697 in Ladenburg, Germany[29] (1). Anna wurde im Februar 1668 in Speyer, Rheinland-Pfalz geboren. Sie starb am 25. August 1737 in Speyer,

Rheinland-Pfalz. Sie wurde am August 27, 1737 in Speyer, Rheinland-Pfalz bestattet.

She is the daughter of the Heidelberger citizen Hans Jacob Biacklein

She died as Anna Sabina Meng, Hans Martin Mengs left back widow 69 years 6 month

> Source: Mrs. Gisela Peschka from Evangelische Kirche der Pfalz
> Source: Churchbook Ladenburg, page 212 no. 2111

Johann und Anna hatten die folgenden Kinder:

+ 24 M i. Johann Christoph Meng wurde 1697 geboren. Er starb am. October 17, 1785.

Johann heiratete Anna Barbara NN[30] vor November 1687 (2).

> FamilySearch™
> Anna Barbara Compact Disc 141 - Pin2936496

Johann und Anna hatten die folgenden Kinder:

25 W ii. Anna Margaretha Meng[31] wurde am 23. November 1687 in Ladenburg, Rhein-Neckar-Kreis in Baden-Württemberg geboren. Sie starb am 09. Dezember 1687 in Ladenburg, Rhein-Neckar-Kreis in Baden-Württemberg.

> Source: Churchbook Ladenburg, page 212 no. 2110

26 M iii. Johann Martin Meng[32] wurde am May 18, 1689 in Ladenburg, Rhein-Neckar-Kreis in Baden-Württemberg geboren.

> Source: Churchbook Ladenburg, page 212 no. 2110

27 M iv. Ludwig Meng[33] wurde am 21. April 1693 in Ladenburg, Rhein-Neckar-Kreis in Baden-Württemberg geboren.

> Source: Churchbook Ladenburg, page 212 no. 2110

Dritte Generation

24. Johann Christoph Meng[34] (Johann Martin, Niclauß) wurde 1697 in Ladenburg, Rhein-Neckar-Kreis in Baden-Württemberg geboren. Er wurde am September 22, 1697 in Ladenburg, Rhein-Neckar-Kreis in Baden-Württemberg getauft. Er starb am Oktober 17, 1785 in Germantown, Pennsylvania, United States. Er wurde am Oktober 19, 1785 in Lower Burial Ground of Germantown, Germantown, Philadelphia Co., Pa. bestattet.

> Source: Churchbook Ladenburg, page 212 no. 2111

Johann heiratete Ursula Marquard[35] Tochter von Gabriel Marquard am Juli 08, 1722 in Mannheim, Baden-Württemberg[36] (1).

> Family Search Beta:
> Johann Christoph Meng
> Father: Johann Martin Meng
> Marriage: July 08, 1722 Mannheim (A. Mannheim), Baden, Germany
> Bride: Ursula Marquart
> Father: Gabriel Marquart
> Indexing Project (Batch) Number: M92143-8
> System Origin: Germany-EASy
> Source Film Number: 1192146

Johann heiratete Dorothe Baumann[37] am 29. Juni 1723 in Mannheim[38] (2). Dorothe wurde in Mannheim, Baden-Württemberg geboren. Sie starb 1759 in Germantown, Pennsylvania, United States.

> FamilySearth™
> DOROTHEA BAUMANN
> Spouse: CHRISTOPH MENG
> Marriage: 29 JUN 1723 Evangelisch, Frankenthal, Pfalz, Bayern

Johann und Dorothe hatten die folgenden Kinder:

28 W i. Anna Barbara Meng[39] wurde 1724 in Mannheim, Baden-Württemberg geboren. Sie wurde getauft am July 16, 1724.

> Family Search Beta:
> Anna Barbara Meng
> Christening: July 16, 1724 Mannheim, Baden, Germany
> Father: Johann Christoph Meng
> Mother: Dorathea [Baumann]
> Indexing Project (Batch) Number: C92143-2
> System Origin: Germany-EASy
> Source Film Number: 1192140

29 M ii. Melchior Meng[40] wurde am 10. April 1726 in Mannheim, Baden-Württemberg geboren. Er wurde am 12. April 1726 in Mannheim, Baden-Württemberg getauft. Er starb am 13. Oktober 1812 in Germantown, Pennsylvania, United States. Er wurde in Lower Burial Ground of Germantown, Philadelphia Co. PA bestattet.

> Family Search Beta:
> Johann Melchior Meng
> Christening: 12 Apr 1726 Mannheim, Baden, Germany
> Father: Johann Christoph Meng

Mother: Dorathea [Baumann]
Indexing Project (Batch) Number: C92143-2
System Origin: Germany-EASy
Source Film Number: 1192140

Melchior heiratete Elizabeth Vende[41] am April 15, 1788 in Philadelphia, Philadelphia, PA, United States; First German Reformed Church[42]. Elizabeth wurde ungefähr 1731 in Pennsylvania, US geboren. Sie starb am December 14, 1814 in Germantown, Pennsylvania, United States.

FamilySearch™
Elizabeth Vende Compact Disc 141-Pin 2936361
Birth: abt 1731 PA, USA
Death: December 14, 1814 Germantown, Philadelphia, PA, United States
Father: Frederick Vende Disc 141-Pin 2936362
Submitter: Charles Martin HANSEN
307 Russell Road Alexandria, Virginia 22301
Submission Search: 4530690-0413108215158

30 M iii. Jacob Meng[43] wurde 1729 geboren.

> Source: Hoyt B. Ming, 35 Magnolia Drive, Petal, MS 39465 and Wescott's History of Philadelphia, PA

+ 31 M iv. Ulrich (Wollery) Meng wurde am June 11, 1731 geboren. Er starb 1796.

32 M v. John Christopher Meng[44] wurde 1734 in Germantown, Pennsylvania, US geboren.

> Source: Hoyt B. Ming, 35 Magnolia Drive, Petal, MS 39465 and Wescott's History of Philadelphia, PA

33 W vi. Ann Dorthea Meng[45] wurde 1736 in Germantown, Pennsylvania, USA geboren.

> Source: Hoyt B. Ming, 35 Magnolia Drive, Petal, MS 39465 and Wescott's History of Philadelphia, PA

34 W vii. Susanne Meng[46] wurde 1740 in Germantown, Pennsylvania, US geboren.

> Source: Hoyt B. Ming, 35 Magnolia Drive, Petal, MS 39465 and Wescott's History of Philadelphia, PA

Johann heiratete Anna Catherein Gensel[47] am September 13, 1759 in Germantown Reformed Church, Philadelphia Co. PA[48] (3).

FamilySearchTM
Anna Catherine Gensel Compact Disc 141-Pin 2936461
Spouse: Johann Christopher Meng Disc 141-Pin 2936503
Marriage: September 13, 1759 Germantown Reformed Church, Philadelphia
Co. PA
Submitter: Charles Martin HANSEN
307 Russell Road Alexandria, Virginia 22301
Submission Search: 4530690-0413108215158

Vierte Generation

31. Ulrich (Wollery) Meng[49] (Johann Christoph, Johann Martin, Niclauß) wurde am
11.

Anhang A - Quellen

1. Ladenburger Kirchenbücher, page 212 no. 2109.
2. Ladenburger Kirchenbücher, page 212 no. 2109.
3. Ladenburger Kirchenbücher, page 212 no. 2109.
4. Ladenburger Kirchenbücher, page 212 no. 2109.
5. Ladenburger Kirchenbücher, page 212 no. 2109.
6. Ladenburger Kirchenbücher, page 12 no. 132, Ladenburger Kirchenbücher, Teil I,
   Reformierte Kirchenbücher von 1649-18.
7. Ladenburger Kirchenbücher, page 12 no. 132, Ladenburger Kirchenbücher, Teil I,
   Reformierte Kirchenbücher von 1649-18.
8. Ladenburger Kirchenbücher, page 12 no. 132.
9. Ladenburger Kirchenbücher, page 12 no. 132.
10. Ladenburger Kirchenbücher, page 12 no. 132.
11. Ladenburger Kirchenbücher, page 12 no. 132, Ladenburger Kirchenbücher, Teil I,
    Reformierte Kirchenbücher von 1649-18.
12. Ladenburger Kirchenbücher, page 12 no. 132.
13. Ladenburger Kirchenbücher, page 12 no. 132.
14. Ladenburger Kirchenbücher, page 12 no. 132.
15. Ladenburger Kirchenbücher, page 12 no. 132.
16. Ladenburger Kirchenbücher, page 12 no. 132.
17. Ladenburger Kirchenbücher, page 12 no. 132.
18. Ladenburger Kirchenbücher, page 12 no. 132.
19. Ladenburger Kirchenbücher, page 12 no. 132.
20. Ladenburger Kirchenbücher, page 12 no. 132.
21. Ladenburger Kirchenbücher, page 12 no. 132.
22. Ladenburger Kirchenbücher, page 12 no. 132.
23. Ladenburger Kirchenbücher, page 12 no. 132.
24. Ladenburger Kirchenbücher, page 12 no. 132.
25. Ladenburger Kirchenbücher, page 212 no. 2110.

26. Evangelische Kirche der Pfalz
27. Evangelische Kirche der Pfalz
28. Ladenburger Kirchenbücher, page 212 no. 2111.
29. Ladenburger Kirchenbücher, page 212 no. 2111.
30. Family Search, Compact Disc 141-Pin2936496.
31. Ladenburger Kirchenbücher, page 212 no. 2110.
32. Ladenburger Kirchenbücher, page 212 no. 2110.
33. Ladenburger Kirchenbücher, page 212 no. 2110.
34. Ladenburger Kirchenbücher, page 212 no. 2111.
35. Family Search Beta, Indexing Project (Batch) Number: M92143-8.
36. Family Search Beta, Indexing Project (Batch) Number: M92143-8.
37. Family Search, no reg. no.
38. Family Search, no reg. no.
39. Family Search Beta, Indexing Project (Batch) Number: C92143-2.
40. Family Search Beta, Indexing Project (Batch) Number: C92143-2.
41. Family Search, Submission Search: 4530690-0413108215158.
42. Family Search, Submission Search: 4530690-0413108215158.
43. Hoyt B. Ming, MS 39465 and Wescott's History of Philadelphia, PA.
44. Hoyt B. Ming, MS 39465 and Wescott's History of Philadelphia, PA.
45. Hoyt B. Ming, MS 39465 and Wescott's History of Philadelphia, PA.
46. Hoyt B. Ming, MS 39465 and Wescott's History of Philadelphia, PA.
47. Family Search, Submitter: Charles Martin HANSEN 307 Russell Road Alexandria, Virginia 22301.
48. Family Search, Anna Catherine Gensel Disc 141 Pin 2936491.
49. Hoyt B. Ming, MS 39465 and Wescott's History of Philadelphia, PA.
50. Hoyt B. Ming, MS 39465 and Wescott's History of Philadelphia, PA.
51. Hoyt B. Ming, MS 39465 and Wescott's History of Philadelphia, PA.
52. Hoyt B. Ming, MS 39465 and Wescott's History of Philadelphia, PA.
53. Hoyt B. Ming, MS 39465 and Wescott's History of Philadelphia, PA, Gen. of PA Families.
54. Hoyt B. Ming, MS 39465 and Wescott's History of Philadelphia, PA.
55. Hoyt B. Ming, MS 39465 and Wescott's History of Philadelphia, PA.
56. Hoyt B. Ming, MS 39465 and Wescott's History of Philadelphia, PA.

Nachkommen von Niclauß Meng

h. means marriage; g. means born; t. means death

1. **Niclauß Meng (g. 1630;t.1668)**
   oo: Anna Barbara NN (h. 1650)
   2. Catharina Meng (g. 1651)
      oo: Hans Wolf Zeisel (h. 1671)
      3. Elisabeth Zeisel (g.1670)
      3. Hans Jacob Zeisel (g.1672)
      3. Simon Zeisel (g.1674)

3. Maria Magdalena Zeisel (g.1676)
3. Anna Maria Zeisel (g.1678)
3. Hans Nickel (Niclauβ) Zeisel (g.1679;t.1680)
3. Elisabeth Zeisel (g.1680)
3. Susanna Zeisel (g.1683)
2. Anna Sarah Meng (g.1653)
oo: Johann Jacob Becker (h.1673;t.1715)
3. Johann Jacob Becker (g.1673;t.1676)
3. NN Becker (g.1676)
3. Margaretha Becker (g.1677;t.1680)
3. Margaretha Becker (g.1678;t.1680)
3. Hans Adam Becker (g.1681)
2. NN Meng (g.1657;t.1670)
2. NN Meng (g.1659)
2. NN Meng (g.1661)
2. Johann Martin Meng (g.1664;t.1728)
oo: Anna Sabina Biacklein (g.1668;h.1697;t.1737)
3. Johann Christoph Meng (g.1697;t.1785)
oo: Ursula Marquard (h.1722)
oo: Dorothe Baumann (h.1723;t.1759)
4. Anna Barbara Meng (g.1724)
4. Melchior Meng (g.1726;t.1812)
oo: Elizabeth Vende (g.1731;h.1788;t.1814)
4. Jacob Meng (g.1729)
4. Ulrich (Wollery) Meng (g.1731;t.1796)
oo: Margaret Jones (h.1757)
5. John Meng (g.1758)
oo: Sarah Colliday (g.1737;h.1760;t.1778)
5. Charles Meng (g.1769)
oo: Esther Morris (h.1794)
4. John Christopher Meng (g.1734)
4. Ann Dorthea Meng (g.1736)
4. Susanne Meng (g.1740)
oo: Anna Catherein Gensel (h.1759)
oo: Anna Barbara NN (h.1687)
3. Anna Margaretha Meng (g.1687;t.1687)
3. Johann Martin Meng (g.1689)
3. Ludwig Meng (g.1693)
2. NN Meng (g.1665;t.1667)
2. Anna Maria Meng (g.1668)
2. NN Meng (g.1655)

CHAPTER 3
HOYT BERTRAND MING AND THE JAMES L. MENG CONNECTION

In 1991, I received a phone call from Mr. Hoyt Bertrand Ming. He asked if we were related to the Mengs in Pennsylvania. I replied not that I knew of but some people ask with the name of *Meng*, if we are Chinese. We then had a very long and enjoyable conversation discussing the Meng families in Illinois, Pennsylvania, and in the Southern states. Hoyt subsequently sent me a copy of his first essay titled "Northern Roots and Southern Trails" on September 29, 1991. His transmittal letter for his information is included. It was decided at that time if a relationship between the Illinois and Pennsylvania families did exist; we agreed that the connection would be in Germany. Twenty years pass. Enter good friend and Shamhart relative, Herr Werner Schabberhard, who in 2010 documented a descendent of Nicholas Meng and Johann Christoph Meng settling in Philadelphia, Pennsylvania. Thus the connection of my known ancestors and Hoyt Ming's ancestors was made with the Ladenburg official church book records cited earlier.

The John Christopher Meng connection may also explain the Meng Y-DNA noted in chapter 1, being present in patriot John Hanson who was born in 1715 in Charles County, Maryland. Again, this relationship, which until now was unknown, also connected the Meng genealogical history back to 1630 and beyond.

In 2011, I was successful in re-contacting the Ming family. Hoyt's widow, Scottie Ming, informed me that her husband, Hoyt B. Ming, had died in 2009. She also stated that his previous essay had been updated in 2005 and retiled "John Christopher Meng and Many Descendants (The Ming Family)." Hoyt's revision includes Norma (née Ming) Graham's (his middle daughter) work tracing the Meng/Ming line back to the Boyneburgs of Germany (excerpts included). The numerous connections with our nation's founding fathers and a noble branch of the Meng genealogical tree have opened an impressive expansion of the Meng heritage.

You are also invited to go on the World Wide Web for Hoyt B. Ming and listen to some classic American old-time fiddling music performed by his father, Hoyt Lester Ming. Of particular interest is the "Indian War Whoop" and (my favorite) "The Monkey in the Dogcart" by Hoyt Ming and his Pep-Steppers. You cannot keep from whistling or tapping your foot when listening to their music: absolutely great folk music, authentic "Americana" at its best. A collection of newspaper clippings referencing the Pep Steppers' numerous performances are included.

Scottie Meng's very interesting essay "Some of My Personal Experiences with Hoyt Lester Ming and His Family" will close this chapter, providing valuable personal insight into this loving family. And, obviously, special thanks for Scottie Ming for graciously continuing the Hoyt Ming contributions to the Meng/Ming family history.

September 29, 1991

Dear Mr. Meng,

I appreciate your response to my letter. I enjoyed it very much. Apparently, we are not from the same family in America; but probably from the same family much earlier in Germany.

I am sending you two manuscripts that are roughly written, as I am no writer, that will let you know some about my German ancestors. Also, you will find a lineage chart and a copy from an earlier manuscript (author unknown) that mentions the spelling Menge. The manuscripts will probably bore you, but may be helpful should you research your past.

The early passenger list of immigrants arriving in America mentions John C. Meng 1728, Michael and Adam Meng in the 1750's and Peter Meng in 1802. I believe Peter went westward, but your ancestors probably came at a later date. Col. James Meng had two brothers that moved to the Lexington area of Missouri about 1840. They were Wollery and Samuel. Samuel had a son that was a doctor. There was a James Meng in 1850 Mississippi that was also a doctor. He was born ca. 1825 in Pennsylvania.

Col. James Meng was born in 1771 in Philadelphia, PA, and died in Union, SC. He did not participate in either war. The title Revolutionary Soldier was a label given to many of the militia men during the early years of America. His father, Wollery, was in the revolution, and a grandson, James, my great uncle, a brave Rebel, was killed in Antonia, GA, during the Civil War.

Please send me as much information about your ancestry as possible without too much inconvenience or expense on your part. I will enjoy the history and will keep it in our (my wife and I) personal library.

I almost forgot, the name Meng was changed to Ming by my grandfather, as my great-grandfather's signature is Charles Meng. But the name is spelled both ways in documents all the way back to the 1700's. Officials have often spelled the name phonetically.

Again, thank you for your letter.

Sincerely,
Hoyt B. Ming

P.S. My wife, (Scottie) facetious as she is, added the word brave before rebel.

Note: For more information on this very interesting Hoyt Ming (Meng) family, see Scottie Ming's great informative background history on page 112".

THE PENNSYLVANIA BRANCH OF
THE MENG GENEALOGICAL TREE
INTRODUCTION

The following Meng history begins with the first Meng (Ming) to arrive in America in 1728. The story then takes the reader to his sons: one who was tried for treason during the American Revolution, and another son who served honorably in the Continental army under Gen. George Washington. Intriguing also is his son's wife, who was descended from preachers educated in Calvinism and also linked, beyond a doubt, to the noble Boyneburg family of Germany. And then to a grandson who married a granddaughter of Samuel Shelton. She had a cousin, Sarah Shelton, who married Patrick Henry. This same grandson had a granddaughter that became the First Lady of Texas in 1903. And there are many more articles of interest.

This family history includes the maternal ancestors of three separate generations of Ming families. Some of the dates are as early as the fifteenth century, with some specific details in the sixteenth century.

There are many misspelled words and capital letters where there normally would be a small letter. The words were typed as they were recorded and documented (e.g., Manheim, Mannheim). The same applies to the punctuation.

Betty Drake best explains the different name spellings in "Meet Your Ancestors." "When communities were small and people were not mobile, a personal or first name was sufficient. The hereditary surname as we know it dates from 1,000 years.

"There are generally six sources of surnames: (1) geographic features; (2) occupation (mill—Miller, drives horse and cart—Carter); (3) bodily and personal features (Strong, Smart); (4) variations given on the father's given name (adding son, or deleting son, etc.); (5) animal and color names; and (6) Anglicized or Americanized names (name written as it sounded)."

"Anglicized or Americanized" words are the most common name changes in the early Ming family history. This frequently happened because the persons writing the legal records read and wrote English and the immigrants spoke and wrote German, and many names had to be spelled as they sounded.

To the Meng-Ming family: Be proud of your heritage.

Hoyt B. Ming

Scrapbook of Hoyt Bertrand Ming

Castle of Elberberg (ca. 1600).

Greentree Inn built (1748)

John C. Meng (1697–1785)
1750

James Meng House built (1832)

Culp House built (1857)

James Shelton Meng (b. 1824)
1875

Joseph Ming (1848–1920)
1890

Clough M Ming 1859–1934
1900

Sarah Burdine (b. 1846)
1915

Hoyt and his Pep Steppers (1928)

Sweet Potato Beds (1948)

Meng Creek, Union, SC (1992)

A few American Patriots involved with the Meng family

George Washington

Benjamin Franklin

John Hanson

Patrick Henry

See patriot Emanuel Trexler (1765–1830) in the Shamhart family line.

34

JOHN CHRISTOPHER MENG AND HIS DESCENDANTS ARRIVE IN PHILADELPHIA (1728)

Descendants of John Christopher Meng

Generation No. 1

1. JOHN CHRISTOPHER[2] MENG (*JOHANN MARTIN[1] MENGEN*) was born September 17, 1697 in Germany, and died October 17, 1785 in Germantown, PA. He married DOROTHE BAUMANN June 29, 1723 in Manheim, Germany[1], daughter of ANNA DORTHEA BAUMANIN. She was born in Germany, and died July 18, 1759 in Germantown, PA.

Notes for JOHN CHRISTOPHER MENG:
John C. Meng (pictured) came to America aboard the ship *Mortonhouse* in 1728. He was a mason and a builder and architect. According to the indenture of John (Johann) Christopher Meng, his surname in Germany was Mengen. In 1718, he finished his apprenticeship as a bricklayer in the city of Speyer and moved to Manheim to carry on his trade. In the records of the Reformation Church, Manheim, Germany, is the following: "John Christopher Meng born 22 Sept. 1697," and the same church has his marriage the 29th of June, 1723 to Anna Dorthea Baumann, daughter of John Wetzler and his wife Anna Barbara. "John Wetzler is mentioned upon church records as 'father-in-law.' Anna Barbara was known as Baroness von Ebstein, but from whom the dignity descended to her father research will show" ("John Christopher Meng and His Descendants," by Edwin C. Jellett, located in the library of the Genealogy Society of Pennsylvania). In later life, he had a shop in Germantown. A painting of John by his son, Christopher, is in the Genealogy Society and History of PA located in Philadelphia. The portrait was given to Charles S. Ogden by his uncle William Meng Alburger who in turn received it from his mother Susanna Alburger, née Meng (daughter of Melchoir Meng). Charles S. Ogden presented this portrait to the archives. Also, in the GSH of PA are copies from the family Bible (earlier notes written in German), two other paintings by his son, and another book of his son "Melchoir Meng and His Descendants," by William L. Hires.

Note: In the book *John Christopher Meng and His Descendants*, there is great detail of John's coming to America, his work in Germantown, and a printing of his will. According to his will, probated November 7, 1785, he married secondly, Catherine Schreiner. This marriage was sometime after 1759.

Catherine had the following children which became the stepchildren of John; Jacob, Nicholas, Charlotte (wife of Philip Will), and stepson John Gansel.

Also, in the book is a copy of his will and the mention of his son John Ulrich Meng (the author's fourth grandfather removed). In the same book is the mention of John Ulrich Meng's children which includes son James Meng (the author's third grandfather removed). Note: James Meng married in Virginia and by 1810 was in Union, South Carolina. James Meng's son, Charles Meng (the author's second grandfather removed) is proven by documents in court records in Union, South Carolina. The next generation is familiar history to the author.

John Christopher Meng's old resident number on Main Street in Germantown was 4912. ". . . and was torn down for the purpose of straightening the lines of Vernon Park . . . Meng's property extended back beyond Greene Street (see map, Vernon Park), and embraced a large portion of what is now Vernon Park. His meadow and spring house were still in existence up to the time when the meadow was filled in by the Department of City Property. Meng's garden was a very fine one, and through Kin, a neighbor, he acquired some of the rarest and finest specimens of trees and shrubs to be found in the country. Many of these are still in existence (1902), but many were destroyed in laying out the grounds for Vernon Park." Meng's property became the property of his son, John Melchoir the oldest son, after his death in 1785. Note: All of the sons of John Christopher Meng had the first name John. For this reason, they were usually referred to by their middle name. (There are many documents and writings, such as the above, about John Christopher Meng in the library in Germantown, PA.)

From the book *John Christopher Meng and His Descendants*: "The causes of the father's coming to America seem to have been a practical idea that he could accomplish more here than in Germany. He was thirty-one years old at this time and so his vision of life was a forward one. He certainly succeeded in his undertaking. We find that he was a 'master mason,' and builder in Germany, and that vocation was of prime importance in Germantown. He was just the man needed, for when he came prosperity was general and the fine colonial houses, for which Germantown is still famous, were then beginning to appear. To Christopher Meng, therefore, may be due much of the excellent stone construction of the ancient mansions . . . He helped establish the Germantown Academy, helped design it and helped build it. He does not appear to have bought up any established business; but started anew. That he had funds for fair proportions is readily seen, for every indication is that he was well born, educated, and of good commercial and technical experiences before he left Germany. He did not confine his business solely to builder operations, but early started, probably for the benefit of his sons, a small store or shop. Whether the merchandise therein was of implements pertaining to his trade or to agriculture, or general supplies, there is no specific evidence. In his later life, this shop occupied most of his attention.

> "Meng's first interest in land was his lease of some property. On December 15th, 1730, about two years after he arrived in Germantown, he purchased the land he leased, for £363-3s. In this deed he is mentioned as then being the keeper of a shop and also that two pieces of land had been in his occupancy by virtue of a lease for one year. These two pieces of land were on the Main Street (now Germantown Ave.). He built upon them early. Four years later, in 1734, he was taxed on fifteen acres and paid a quite-rent . . . These rents varied from one to six shillings per hundred acres yearly. Meng's

fifteen acres were valuable. In 1740, 22 July, he added ten acres more adjoining his other land, paying £14 to Peter Shoemaker, a turner, and Margaret his wife . . .

"The house Christopher Meng lived in is not still standing but it was converted into the tin shop No. 4912 Germantown Ave. . . . Christopher Meng and his son, John Melchoir, were trustees of the Old Academy at Germantown. The minutes of the meetings of the founders and trustees of this institution bear testimony to the high character and valued abilities of John C. Meng. He was on the first committee to raise funds to erect the building 1759 . . . 1760. Among managers of the building Mr. Meng was placed at the head of the committee . . .

"This worthy citizen brought from Mannheim a Bible in which were entered the vital statistics of the family. He died in the house of John Engle, Germantown, Oct. 17, 1785 . . ."

John is buried in the "Lower Burial Ground," or Hood Cemetery, on Germantown Road.

At his death of 88, his personal estate consisted of the following:

Cash
Two bonds of George Righter & John Fry due principle and interest
A note of hand of George Blife
A ten-plate stove
An old desk
A tea table
A Walnut ovel table
A small do
Seven rush bottom chairs
Nine silver tea spoons
Two small tables
A hye chest of drawers
A prefsing table
6 leather bottom chairs
A walnut stand
A walnut chest
A parcel of old books
A small chest and carpenter's tools and various other articles

"The tradition is that John Christopher Meng attended church until the preaching in English commenced, whereupon he never worshipped there again."

Note: Edwin C. Jellett, the author of *John Christopher Meng and His Descendants*, was a writer and resident of Germantown in the late 1800s, Pennsylvania.

Notes for DOROTHEA BAUMANN:
Dorothea was born Baroness von Epstein. In the church record, her marriage has her as being the daughter of John Wetsler and his wife Anna Barbara. The record further records John Wetsler as "father-in-law." Dorthea's mother Anna Barbara was known as Baroness von Epstein.

Children of JOHN MENG and DOROTHEA BAUMANN are:

i.   ANN BARBARA[3] MENG, b. 1724, Germany[2].

Notes for ANN BARBARA MENG:
Ann Barbara married John Van Lashet.

ii.   JOHN MELCHOIR MENG, b. April 10, 1726, Manheim, Land of Baden, Germany[2]; d. October 13, 1812, Germantown, PA.

JOHN MELCHOIR MENG FOUND GUILTY OF TREASON

Notes for JOHN MELCHOIR MENG:

John Melchoir Meng came to America with his family at the age of two. He married (first) Nov. 7, 1748, to Anne Marie Magdalena Colladay, a sister to Sarah that married Wollery Meng. He married (second) Elizabeth (Maulsby) Ax and (third) Elizabeth (Vende) Lehman. Melchoir was a carter and baker. In the journals of the Continental Congress are records of payments for carrying money by wagon to Cambridge, Virginia, New York, and Albany. In 1774, Melchoir was Tax Assessor for Germantown. Following the Battle of Germantown on Oct. 4, 1777 on May 21, 1778, Melchoir and his son Jacob were given word to render themselves to the authorities and stand trial for High Treason. Jacob was acquitted, but Melchoir was found guilty (home was used for a hospital by the British). In the *Pennsylvania Archives*, Series 6, can be found several pages listing the items of Melchoir's estate including four parcels of land in and around Germantown that were confiscated. He was released later, and it appears that most of his property was returned. The children of John Melchoir (all from his first wife Anna Marie Colladay) are: John Chistopher, born June 8, 1750; Anna Dorethea, born Feb. 8, 1754 and married Hugh Ogden; Juliana Catharine, died at the age of 17. Susannah, born April 7, 1758 and married Christian Alburger; Mary, born May 7, 1764 and married James Davis on April 9, 1791; Jacob, born April 1, 1756 married Massy Page of Philadelphia and they had a daughter, Massy, who married George Thomas; Daniel and Mary that died young. After Mary died young, their last child born in 1764 was also named Mary and she married James Davis. John Christopher was Lt. Colonel Assistant Deputy Quartermaster General of the Second Battalion Philadelphia Militia and was in the Battle of Germantown ("Melchoir Meng of Germantown and His Descendants," by William L. Hires). "Colonial Families of Philadelphia" reports that Melchoir had a principle at Germantown Academy, D. J. Dove that wrote the following poem:

> Melchoir Meng, the bell doth toll
> Melchoir Meng, the school is in.
>
> Be not surprised that Melchoir cries on Sunday
> He that cheats six, has cause to cry one day.
>
> Melchoir Meng and old Huck.
> We set down in our book as Continental Tories.
>
> Whenever Melchoir Meng mows his meadow it rains.

Melchoir Meng once owned most of the land that became Vernon Park in Germantown (*Guide to Historic Germantown*). "Vernon Park, on the west side of Main Street just above Chelton Avenue includes the old Wister Mansion and some adjoining properties. Most of the land formerly belonged to Melchoir Meng, whose house stood along the street, immediately adjoining what is now No. 5708 Main Street. Melchoir Meng shared with his neighbor Kurtz (1902, "Those planted on the Kurtz place have disappeared, but many of those given to Meng still exist in Vernon Park"), a great love for trees and plant life. John Wister, who bought the property and lived there for many years, preserved and added to the collection. Some of these rare specimens are still standing (1902), particularly noticeable being several great holly trees. Meng was one of the founders of the Germantown Academy, and at the Battle of Germantown his house was occupied by the wounded soldiers. His three daughters alone in the house ... They saw the stricken Colonel Bird brought in and laid upon the porch ... soon the house was filled with wounded men." Allowing the British to use his (Melchoir's) house for a hospital resulted in the charge and arrest of treason upon Melchoir. (Guidebook to Historic Germantown)

Note: John Wister, and owner of the Wister mansion, mentioned above was one of Philadelphia's most distinguished families. He was married to Anna Catharina Rubenkam (second marriage) and it was her sister, Catharina Juliana Rubenkam that married Jacob Colladay. Catharina and Jacob had a daughter, Sarah, that married John Wollery Meng and a daughter, Anna Maria, that married Melchoir Meng. (*The Pennsylvania Genealogical Magazine*, Volume XXII, No.2, 1961)

John Wister, son of John Wister Sr., was the the first cousin to the wives of John Wollery Meng and Melchoir Meng and became a congressman from that area.

Melchoir Meng's resident number was 5708 Main Street (see above). No. 5442 Main Street, the Morris House, opposite the square, was the residence of George Washington during a portion of 1793 and 1794. (*Guidebook to Historic Germantown*, 1902)

Vernon Park

"Most of the Meng property that lay north of the house, was purchased by John Wister (Melchoir Meng's wife Anna Maria's uncle) and merged in his estate of Vernon ... The old mansion now occupied by the Germantown Branch of the Philadelphia Free Library was built by James Matthews about 1803. John Wister Sr. purchased the property in 1812 (Melchoir died in 1812) and named it 'Vernon' in honor of the home of Washington, Mr. Wister being a great admired of the character and ability of that famous man ... As has already been stated Vernon embraced the greater part of the estate of John Christopher Meng ..." See Map, Vernon Park.

"The Academy Offered to Congress"

"The subject uppermost in the minds of the President and his cabinet, of the state and local authorities, and interested citizens, was, where shall Congress meet on the first Monday in December. The Academy building had all along been considered the only place available in Germantown, in case Congress should assemble here. On October 26th, 1793, the trustees had considered a proposal from the Governor of Pennsylvania that the buildings be occupied by the legislature of the State, but at the same meeting the information was received that Congress might need the school. A committee was appointed, consisting of Henry Hill, President of the Board; John Bringhurst, Samuel Mechlin, Melchoir Meng and Joseph Ferree, to provide other accommodations for the school, that the way might be clear for the public use of the property . . ."

A Fourth of July with the Meng family on Broadway

Mentioned earlier was Anna Dorethia, daughter of Melchoir and Anna Maria, that married Hugh Ogden. They had a granddaughter Hannah Zell. Hannah read in a speech in 1903 before the Site and Relic Society of Germantown the following: ". . . He (her great grandfather Melchoir) resided on Main Street in the house next to John Wister's which is now a tin store having been altered . . . At the time of the battle of Germantown, my grandmother, Dorthy Meng, was 23 years of age . . . and she told me these scenes herself . . . Her father, Melchoir Meng, was thought to be a Tory in those days, and he hastily left with his most valuable effects . . . These three young girls (his daughters) witnessed the fighting as the soldiers skirmished down the street. The house was taken for a hospital, on account of vessels of cider stowed in the cellar made into vinegar which was used to dress the wounds to bleeding. The officers (British) told them if they would stay up stairs they would protect them, which they did . . . I remember one Fourth of July when (as) a young girl, I ran to her and said, 'Come grandmother, look at the soldiers.' 'Oh!' she said shaking her head. I have seen one Fourth of July, the first one, and the others are nothing to me now." Note: Dorthy's father Melchoir was in jail on the first Fourth of July. Also, the author has a copy of a letter written to Hannah Zell in 1850 by a cousin Sarah Meng of Virginia. In her letter she mentions several events that happened earlier that have been collaborated by the authors research.

"1776" the Musical: On the website of James Troutman is a story behind the musical "1776." It is adapted from a screenplay about the hardships of the birth of our nation. The story takes place in Germantown, PA (In the town the Meng/Ming family first settled). The following is from the website:

"Mr. Melchior Meng"

"The play contains a reference to a Mr. Melchior Meng petitioning the Congress for payment for his dead mule, which had been employed in service to the Congress (This passage is not in the screenplay). There was a Melchior Meng living in Germantown at the time. He was a horticulturist whose house was used as an emergency hospital during the battle of Germantown."

Note: The part is used in the play, although it was not in the original screenplay. This author wrote the website for more information about Melchior being used in the play. He wrote back that he could not recall anything more.

iii. JACOB MENG, b. 1729, Germantown, PA[2].

2. iv. JOHN ULRICH (WOLLERY) MENG, b. June 11, 1731, Germantown, PA; d. September 1796, Culpeper, VA.

v. JOHN CHRISTOPHER MENG JR., b. February 6, 1734, Germantown, PA[2]; d. ca. 1754, West Indies.

Notes for JOHN CHRISTOPHER MENG JR.:
"One of our earliest Painters, who was cut off by death ere his undoubted talent had matured and secured to him fame and profit, was John Meng, born Germantown, son of John Christopher, he from early boyhood had evinced a decided vocation for the Painters Art. He was gifted by nature with artistic tastes, and soon acquired no little skill with the pencil and brush. But the practical old German did not approve of his son's choice of a profession. This opposition made things unpleasant for John; moreover, he felt that he must have a better tuition than he could get in Philadelphia." His full length self-portrait was exhibited in the art gallery in Westmoreland County Museum of Art in Greensburg, PA in 1959 (Source: Western PA Historical Mag). Three original paintings are in the Historical Society of Pennsylvania. He died in the West Indies.

vi. ANN DORTHEA MENG, b. 1736, Germantown, PA[2].

Notes for ANN DORTHEA MENG:
Dorothy married Jacob Scheriner. It is not known if she married Jacob before or after his mother married Dorothy's father.

More About ANN DORTHEA MENG:
Degree: 1793, Yellow fever in Germantown, Pa

vii. SUSANNE MENG, b. 1740, Germantown, Pa.

More About SUSANNE MENG:
Degree: 1741.

Generation No. 2

2. JOHN ULRICH (WOLLERY)[3] MENG (*JOHN CHRISTOPHER[2], JOHANN MARTIN[1] MENGEN*) was born June 11, 1731 in Germantown, PA[3], and died September 1796 in Culpeper, VA[4]. He married (1) MARGARET JONES 1757 in Philadelphia, PA, daughter of JOHN JONES SR. He married (2) SARAH COLLADAY January 10, 1760 in Germantown, PA[5], daughter of JACOB (GALATHE) and CATHARINA RUBENKAM. She was born May 17, 1737 in Philadelphia, Pa, and died 1778. He married (3) ESTHER MORRIS 1794 in Culpeper County, VA.

Notes for John Ulrich (Wollery) Meng:

"Wollery Meng, Sadler, begs leave to inform the public and his friends in particular, that he has just removed from Germantown to the corner of Fifth-street in (and) Market-street, Philadelphia, where he continues to carry on his trade in all its branches. Said Meng is well acquainted with the making and jacking of fire-buckets, and will paint and letter them agreeable to directions at a very reasonable price." (Penna. Journal. no.1530. April 2, 1772). Note from the author: The corner of Fifth and Market Street (the location of Wollery's shop) is on or next to Independence National Historic Park. "...A section of the park where Benjamin Franklin's home once stood ... Independence National Park located in downtown Philadelphia, is often referred to as the birthplace of our nation ..." (National Park Service US Dept. of the Interior)

In 1769 Wollery Meng paid taxes in Germantown, PA, and in 1774 he paid taxes in the city of Philadelphia, PA. Wollery was a captain in the Continental Service and also in the Philadelphia Brigade in 1777. He was a saddler by trade and is mentioned in a letter to the Board of War by General George Washington. The following is an excerpt from that letter: "Head Quarters, Valley Forge, January 24, 1778. Sir: I have received. your favor of the 8th. inst. and that of Mr. Nourse* of the 16th. Upon the receipt of yours some time ago, Upon the subject of the Leather in the Vatts at Germantown, I made inquiry and was told then as I am now, that except that which is fit to put into the Curriers hands is immediately worked up, and that which is not Sufficiently tanned is shifted into other Vatts, that it will be undoubtedly spoiled. As I had no person to superintend this Business I did not think it worth while to remove the leather, when there would have been almost an absolute certainty of its being ruined. I have seen nothing of Capt. Ming (John Wollory Meng), but if you will order him down, and he will prepare some Tanneries, at a convenient distance back from Germantown to receive the Leather, I will furnish a proper party and endeavor to bring it off. The less that is said of this matter, the better, as it must be executed with Secrecy and dispatch ..." He is also listed in "George Washington Papers" in Washington's Pocket-day Book & Cash-Memorandum in June 1775 in which is printed, "By Wollore Meng's acct. for cartooch boxes & c for Prince Wm Comp a Wch charge to them" (In Washington's hand writing).

THE GEORGE WASHINGTON CONNECTION

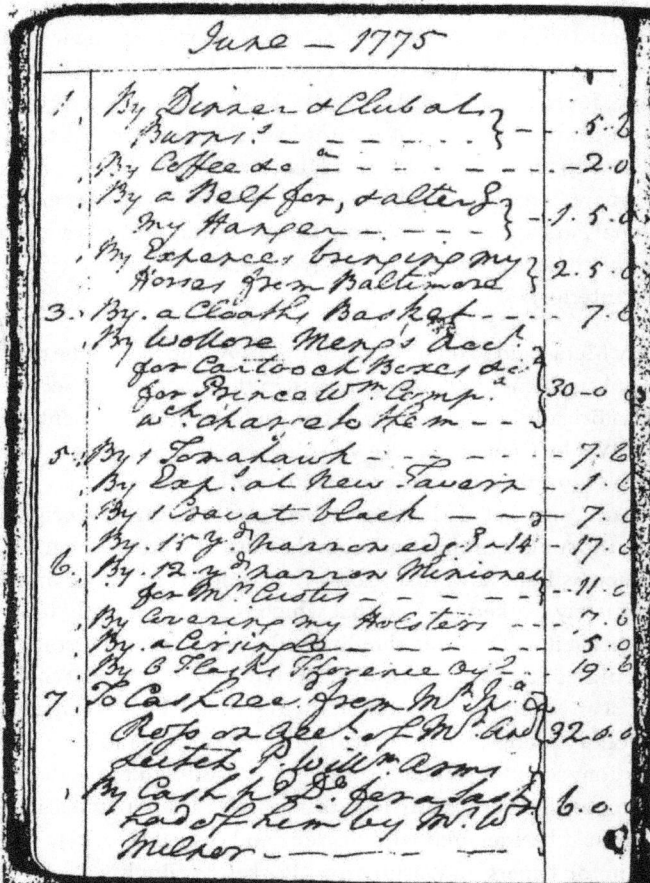

Above; George Washington's brown leather covered day-by-day notebook. The entry is June 3, 1775. It reads:

"BY WOLLORE MENG'S ACCT.
FOR CARTOOCH BOXES & c
FOR PRINCE WM COMP. a
Wch CHARGE TO THEM" } 30-00

NOTE: THE ENTRY IS GEORGE WASHINGTON'S HAND WRITING.

Wollery's Commission Paper 1778.

Wollery was secretary of the Germantown Library from 1759 to 1763 (PA Mag. Vol. 42) and received 300 acres of land in Westmoreland County in 1772. He was a Sadler in York County in 1780, and in 1782, he was a Sadler in Fredrick, Maryland. Wollery was first married to Margaret Jones in 1757 (PA Vital Records), and they had a son John Meng (DAR reg. 347692). Secondly, he married Sarah Colladay on January 7, 1760 (Pennsylvania Marriages), and after the death of Sarah Colliday (ca. 1778), Wollery married Esther Morris of Culpeper, Virginia, in 1794 (Genealogical and Historical Notes on Culpeper Co., VA). They had one son Wollery (DAR reg. ⌐08962) that married Dorthy North in Campbell County, Virginia. They later moved to Missouri.

THE BENJAMIN FRANKLIN CONNECTION

Wollery Meng became a mason in 1758, roster of the Freemen's Lodge. In the *Towne's Pennsylvania Evening Post* of May 22, 1777, he advertises the following: "Wanted immediately a few more workers, viz., saddlers, harness makers and shoemakers to be employed in the United States. Apply to Capt. Wollery Meng, Supt. of said factory." Also, in the *Pennsylvania Gazette* of May 31, 1775—"All sorts of military articles sold by Wolre (Wollery) Ming in Market Street about 10 doors down from the Goal."

In the provincial tax records for the city of Philadelphia in 1774 and in the order listed is the following: Robert Bass . . . 36.13, druggist; Benjamin Franklin, Esq'r . . . 3 acres . . . 331.15; Woolore Ming, sadler . . . 19.0; Eden Haydock . . . 79.18; Frederick Stonemetz, cooper (barrel maker) . . . 0. Ben Franklin was spending much of his time working with the Colonies and Great Britain in England at this time. He returned to Philadelphia two weeks before the Revolutionary War began in May 1775.

Ben Franklin was signer of both the Declaration of Independence and the US Constitution.

By 1794, Wollery and family were living in Culpeper, Virginia. Here he died in 1796. His last son Wollery Meng Jr. and son Samuel Meng would eventually move to Missouri. There the name was sometimes spelled Ming and many of their descendants live there today. One of the descendants of Wollery is said to have put in the first grocery store in Denver and later an opera house in Helena, Montana, named Ming Opera House. The author called the Chamber of Commerce in Helena in 1998 and verified the building was still there by that name. Refer to the notes of Wollery Ming Jr.

Notes for MARGARET JONES:
(See son John Ming)

Notes for SARAH COLLADAY:
Based upon the tax records recorded above, Wollery Meng, a saddler, lived next to Benjamin Franklin, Esq. Wollery Meng a Mason, and Benjamin Franklin who was a Grand Master of the Masonic lodge, were both Freemasons. Both along with Paul Revere, and other Masons, were deeply involved (as a Mason myself, I say very active) in the Boston Tea Party of December 16, 73.

Source Brother Edward Cair, Southern California Research Lodge.

Sarah Colladay, her last name has many different spellings in the early documents and writings. Among them are: Colliday, Kalledie, Galade, Galathe, Calleda. She was born in 1737 and married January 17, 1760 John Ulrich (Wollery) Meng. In the church papers her name is recorded as Sarah Galletin. The account written by Blasius Daniel Macknet of Sarah's ancestry is as follows: "Her father was a Burger's Son of Manheim in Platz (a place so called) and came to this Country with his Mother very young; his name was Jacob Colladay: his father died crossing the Ocean. Her Mother's name is Catharina Juliana, Father's Name Ribenkam (Rubenkam), was born 1703 in Wasinfried in Hessia where her father named Jn (Johann) Philip Ribenkam was a preacher, & preached the gospel 19 years and his father was a preacher at Eschwig (a place so called). Her Mother's name was Magretta (sic) Catharine, a minister's daughter of Saxone in Hessia, her father's name Sattorin, Her Mother's name Anna Julianna of Luninburg in Holstein. This may serve as a Memorandum, if perhaps sooner or later some of the Relations should come to visit this part of the world. Your grandmother, a Widow, came over with 6 grown children in 1726, Viz. Sons & 3 daughters the eldest Daughter she left in Germany in Berlinburg, where her Father died she is married to a Merchant of that place, named Holtzklaus who-with his Wife are, at this time dead. They left Issue, one daughter, who is married & lives in the house where her Mother died. Her Husband's name, is I believe, Reuschell. Here follows a list of your Mothers Children born in this Country Viz-

1 Margaret Catherina, born 1728 Sept 23 dead	
2 Anna Maria	1731 April 23
3 Jacob Colladay	1733 d 15
4 Catharine	1735 May 30
5 Sarah	1737 d 12
6 William	1738 Sept. 15
7 Susanna	1741 April 17

"And Whereas I was well acquainted with your Grand Mother, I can give her the Testimony that she was a pious good woman, led a virtuous life, & was an ornament to her Sex. The follies & pleasures of this world, she despised, & took upon her the Cross of Christ." Blasius Daniel Macknet. (Genealogy of Pennsylvania Families)

Blasius Daniel Macknet Jr. was the stepfather of Sarah Meng when he wrote her nativity. He was also the owner of the Green Tree Inn (pictured). The Green Tree Inn, built 1748 in Germantown, PA, is in existence as of this writing. It can also be researched on the Internet. Blasius Macknet Jr. purchased the Inn from Daniel Pastorius in which his father was the founder of Germantown.

For more information about Sarah's ancestors on her maternal side, refer to "Descendants of Heimbrod von Boyneburg," page 36 the noble blood ancestors; "Descendants of Freidrich Rubenkam," page 43 the early educated pastors; Also, "Descendants of Hans Gleim," page 47 that is interesting.

Child of JOHN MENG and MARGARET JONES is:

i.   JOHN[4] MENG, b. April 6, 1758, Germantown, PA.

Notes for JOHN MENG:

John Ming (Meng), his mother was Margaret Jones (first wife of Wollery), married Rebecca Shipley. The "Philadelphia Northern District Monthly Meeting Marriages 1772–1802," page 10 has the following: John Meng of Philadelphia, merchant, son of Wollery Meng of Frederick town, Maryland, married May 29, 1781, Rebecca Shipley, daughter of William Shipley of Philadelphia at Northern District Meeting House,

WITNESSES: Wollery, Dolly and Jacob Meng, William and Margaret Shipley, John and Catherine Jones (possibly father and mother of Margaret) and 59 others." John later moved to New Jersey. According to Philadelphia Will Abstracts, The Ming Message Board on the Internet has the following Children for John and Rebecca: William, Jon, Charles, Thomas Lockhart, Morris Shipley, and Joseph Ming. Morris Shipley Ming married Elizabeth Saxton, daughter of Gershom Saxton, and they had the following children: Mary Ann, Elizabeth born 1816 in NJ and married Joseph Baker, George, and William. Some of these Mings moved to Indiana. After the death of Rebecca Shipley, John married Rebecca Caskey 1797 (DAR, reg. 347692).

Note: Using written sources, John Ming and some members of the younger Wollery Ming family appear to be the first of the earlier Meng family to spell their name Ming rather than Meng.

Children of JOHN MENG and SARAH COLLADAY are:

ii. GEORGE[4] Meng, b. ca. 1766, Germantown, PA; d. Aft. 1804.

Notes for GEORGE MENG:

George's exact birth is not known but he appears to be one of the oldest sons of Wollery. He and his father, Wollery, are the only two Mengs listed on the tax records in Culpeper County, Virginia, in 1787. This information and the fact his mother was Sarah Colladay gives this writer reason to believe George was born about 1766. In 1801, George sold 499 acres of land near Frankfort, Kentucky. In 1802, George was back in Amherst County, Virginia, whereas he bought two acres for $1000. In Amherst, Virginia County deeds is the following: "page 29. Nov. 1803, George Meng, AC, to Dan'l Higginbotham, AC, Deed of Trust on debt to Rives Murphy & Co. 5 sh. Houses and lots in Warminster and where Meng lives—bought . . ." In 1804, George and Mary sold for 1420, two acres save a carriage house.

iii. ANNA MENG, b. Germantown, PA[6]; d. Germantown, PA.

Notes for ANNA MENG:

Ann may have died at a young age.

iv. WILLIAM MENG, b. May 24, 1761, Germantown, PA[7,8,9]; d. Aft. November 21, 1815, Fayetteville, NC[9,10].

Notes for WILLIAM MENG:

In some sources of the Meng family, it is mentioned that William died young, but this isn't true. His will in the archives in Raleigh, North Carolina, is proof that he was living in 1815. In his will, William mentions sister Sarah Meng, living in Martinsburg, Virginia. "Asked that he be buried on Harrington Hill in an enclosure of brick and a marble tombstone." Also he willed Sarah a gold locket and a clip of his mother's hair. As his father was married three times, this suggests that they had the same mother, Sarah Colladay Meng.

January 11, 1781, William was one of 23 men from Frederick, Maryland, that sent a message to Governor Lee: "May it please your excell'y in consequence of an Act of the General Assembly to encourage the raising of a Volunteer Troop of Light Horse in each County we the subscribers have enrolled for the purpose of forming ourselves into a Troop of Light Dragons on the Terms prescribed by law; and we take the Liberty to recommend Doctr. Philip Thomas to be commissioned as Captain, & John Ross Key esr. as Lieut to the troops by your excellency and the Honorable Council . . ." (The Maryland Militia in the Revolutionary War—Maryland Calendar of State Papers)

July 19, 1781, William wrote, from Frederick, Maryland, to Mr. Frank Willis Jur. the following: "In reply to enquiry as to the number of caps for Light Horse (Light Horse was the father of Robert E. Lee), he has on hand, says, those made for the Frederick town Troop are gone: but if he will wait about twelve days and will take them without 'Bearskin covers,' he can furnish a supply for good tobacco at two dollars hard money, pr: hundred: the price of the caps being three dolls: each. Can also furnish Saddles, bridles, holsters & c."

William Meng died at Fayetteville, North Carolina.

v.   SARAH MENG, b. ca. 1761, Germantown, PA[11]; d. September 5, 1856, Washington D.C..

Notes for SARAH MENG:

Sarah was a schoolteacher in Martinsburg, Virginia. According to one Meng family source, she died during a trip to Missouri to visit her brother Wollery. According to Catharine C. Davies, a descendant of Margaret Meng, Sarah Meng died at the home of Col. John James Abert in Washington DC on September 5, 1856. She is buried in Rock Creek Church Cemetery there in the original graveyard close to the old church. On the marker, an inscription gives her mother's name as Margaret, but her mother's name was Sarah Colladay Meng, the second wife of her father. As she was without close relatives and never married, it can be assumed that the person placing the marker was not real familiar with the family's early history. In 1850, Sarah wrote a letter to her niece Hanna Zell in Germantown, Pennsylvania. This writer has a copy of that letter. A quote from the letter: "My grandmother and her children (my mother being one) has been represented to me as an elegant accomplished woman. And her great grandmother and father both neatly allied to some of the most respectable in Hess and that the Prince and Princess of Hess castle stood as sponsor's for children. So you see this speck of noble blood running through the veins of the descendants is faithfully preserved on parchment…" Obviously she is referring to the noble blood in her mother's ancestors, the Boyneburgs. For more about the Boyneburgs, refer to "Descendants of Jost Boyneburg" near the back of this book.

vi. MARGARET MENG, b. 1765, Germantown, PA.

Notes for MARGARET MENG:
Margaret was christened at Market Square in Germantown in 1765. She married John Ebert a Frenchmen October 30, 1783 in Frederick County, Maryland. She was baptized on May 12, 1765. Very little has been found pertaining to their children, who were Sophea, married William Cookees; Marie, married a Major Swan and then a Mr. Brian; Louisa, married a Captain Nelson; Elizabeth, married a Mr. Barry; Matilda, married John Raser; John Ebert Jr., marriage unknown.

vii. CHARLES ULRIC MENG, b. ca. 1770, Germantown, P[12]; d. 1855, Prince William Co., Virginia.

Notes for CHARLES ULRIC MENG:
The 1850 census of Virginia has Charles Ulric born in Pennsylvania (ca. 1770) and died in 1855. He is listed as 80 years of age. A Kentucky history source has Charles (b. 1780) in Virginia and coming from Holland, but does not give a source to confirm this. As there are other sources that have Charles born in Pennsylvania, the author will use the census information. According to the book *John Christopher Meng and His Descendants*, by Edwin C. Jellett, Charles was the son of John Ulric (Wollery) Meng. Charles settled in Prince William County, Virginia, and married Victoria Tebbs, daughter of William H. Tebbs and wife Victoria (Haislip). Charles was a captain in the War of 1812 in Scott's Regiment of the Virginia Militia. He was also sheriff of Prince William County, Virginia. The known children of Charles Ulric and Victoria were Evelina Meng, Ellen Meng, Charles Henry Meng, James Madison Meng, Sarah Meng, Martha Meng, William, Edmond Meng, and Katherine (Catherine) Meng. All were born in Virginia. There may have been as many as 11 children.

James Madison Meng lived in Bourbon County, Kentucky. He was a Major in the CSA and born on February 22, 1812, and died on September 23, 1885, married Amanda Malvina Hall, daughter of Henry and Fannie (Talbot) Hall, and their children were Charles H. Meng, born April 25, 1843, in Kentucky, died July 11, 1925, married Sarah Katherine Calvert, born November 29, 1852, the daughter of Walter S. Calvert and Louisa M. Evans; James Augustus Meng born (ca. 1854). James Meng's wife was Julia. They were all of Bourbon County, Kentucky.

The children of Charles H. Meng, son of James Madison Meng and

Amanda Malvina Hall, were Calvert born ca. 1874, (?) Melvina (b. ca. 1876), Charles Mccleland (b. ca. 1881), James M. (b. ca. 1887), and Walter Stephenson Meng (b. ca. 1890). Walter married Sarah Amanda Jones on October 5, 1910. They had five children: Emily K., Walter S., Armanda, William J., and James. The ancestry of Katherine Calvert Meng, wife of Charles H. Meng above is directly linked to George Calvert, First Lord Baltimore. George Calvert, born 1679–80 in Yorkshire, England, was a man of distinction. The name Baltimore derives from February 18, 1621, when the king granted him 2,300 acres in county Longford, Ireland. Eventually, "These Longford estates were erected into the manor of Baltimore, from which he took his baronial title."

Walter S. Meng was married to Sarah J. (b. ca. 1890), and they had the following issue: Emily R. (b. ca 1912); Walter S. Jr. (b. ca. 1914); Sarah A. (b. ca. 1916); Billy J. (b. ca. 1918); James (b. ca. 1919); and Charles H. (b. 1922). Walter S. married Marjorie Jones.

3.   vii.   JAMES EDWARD MENG, b. 1771, Philadelphia, PA; d. September 14, 1824, Union, SC.

     ix.   SAMUEL MENG, b. December 17, 1777, Germantown, PA[13,14]; d. March 6, 1824, Calloway, MO.

Notes for Samuel Meng:

Samuel was born in 1777 (DAR) and was living in Buckingham County, Virginia, in 1810. He was married to Nancy Murray of Virginia on March 21, 1799. Their children were Sarah C. Ming (Meng) (b. Feb. 3, 1800), she married George Barber; William F. Meng (b. May 22, 1802), married Nancy Narvell; Mary A. Meng (b. Jan. 20, 1806–d. Mar. 11, 1808); Charles A. Meng (b. Jan. 31, 1809); Robert W. Meng (b. Jul. 4, 1811), married Lydia B. House; Samuel Thornton Meng (b. Mar. 13, 1813) in Virginia, married Elmira Harrison. Note: All the children of Samuel Meng Sr. were born in Virginia.

The children of Samuel Thorton Meng were (1) John William Meng, DDS born Calloway, Missouri (b. Oct 6, 1847), and married Rebecca Carter; (2) Elizabeth T. Meng, married William T. Fisher, sheriff of Nevada, Missouri; (3) Laura E. Meng, married Henry Reinhart; (4) Dr. Edwin Ruthven (b. Mar. 13, 1849) in New Bloomfield, Missouri, married Alice Johnson of St. Louis, Missouri, and was a physician at Barnes College; (5) Annie M. Meng married James F. Winn; (6) Virginia Lee Meng was unmarried; (7) Dr. James Samuel Meng, DDS of Dover, Missouri, was unmarried. John William Meng, DDS above served in the CSA as a member of Shelby's Brigade. Samuel died in 1824 in Missouri.

Child of JOHN MENG and ESTHER MORRIS is:

     x.   WOLLERY ULRICH[4] MENG, b. June 1795; d. December 12, 1850, Franklin Co., MO.

Notes for WOLLERY ULRICH MENG:

Wollery Ulrich Meng Jr. was the youngest son of Wollery and Esther (third wife). Wollery, like his father, was a tanner. He married Dorthea (Dorothy) North in 1819, daughter of William and Mary Franklin North. In 1837, Wollery and Dorothy sold their land in Campbell County, Virginia, and moved to Franklin County, Missouri. In Missouri, he took up farming. He is buried in the Meng Cemetery on the old Ming (many of these Meng's use the Ming spelling) farm in Missouri. In the Campbell County, Virginia, tax records of 1828, Wollery had one son over 12 and one over 16. He had five slaves and a two wheel carriage valued at $50.00.

The children of Wollery and Dorothy were William Owen Meng; Mary Ester (b. Aug. 13, 1822) and married David Pollard Wood (b. Feb. 2, 1818); James Morris Meng (b. May 16, 1824) married Jemima Osborn; Martha Meng married Chetham Lewis; John H. Meng (b. Feb. 6, 1831); Benjamin Franklin Meng (b. 1832); Charles Meng; Virginia Ester Meng married William Thomas North; Ann Marie Meng (b. 1841–d. 1843).

William Owen Meng above married Mary Ann Osborn daughter of William and Rebecca (Richardson) Osborn. William was a merchant and made trips to Montana with a brother to sell goods at the outposts. He ran a general store in New Haven, Missouri, from 1855 to 1861. He was postmaster there during the period 1855–61. He became a mason in 1858. About 1861, he and his family moved to Warrensburg, Missouri, where he ran a general store. It was ruined by raiders of the war from both sides, north and south. Afterward, he opened the Ming's Hotel. It burned, and he moved to Marshall, Missouri, and had a hotel there. It stayed in the family for many years. The children of William Owen and Mary: James W. Meng, Louise Meng, John Meng, Endora Virginia Meng (married James Albert Montgomery), Millard Meng, Charles Meng, Dr. Phil Meng, George Meng, and Fannie Meng.

Mary Ester Meng and David Pollard Wood had the following Children: James S. Wood, Leslie Wood, John William Wood, Dorothea Wood, Martha Agnes Wood, Charles B. Wood, and Mortimer Wood, who married Carrie Brown.

James Morris Meng, born in Campbell County, and Jemima had the following: William Meng married Celeste Jeffries; Robert P. Meng; Emmet Meng married Emma Wallace; Robert T. Meng; Clara W. Meng; Eugene Meng married Laura May; Fannie married Dr. James L. Wallace; and James M. Meng.

Martha Meng and Chetham Lewis had the following: Alice Lewis, Harry Lewis, Virginia Lewis, and Minnie(?).

John H. Meng (Ming) crossed the plains in 1851 to Colorado where he engaged in the mercantile business. He went back to Missouri and returned to Colorado in 1858, this time locating in Denver. Here he opened the first grocery store. In 1863, he went to Virginia City, Montana, and later opened a store. In Helena, Montana, he also opened an opera house and named it

Ming Opera House. The building was in existence in 1998 and used once a month for meetings by a local organization (the author called the city and verified this information). According to the story of "The Meng Family," "He became the owner of a large tract of land on the west side of the city of Helena where he built the first house on that side of the city." He continued business in Virginia City and Helena, keeping his interest in mining and stock raising (many thousand head). In 1868, he married Katharine L. Cole and had two sons, John H. Meng and James L. Meng. He was a member of the IOOF and of the Masonic Fraternity. He died on December 27, 1887.

Benjamin Franklin Meng was a merchant in Gray Summit, Missouri about 1854 to 1860.

Charles Meng; no information.

Virginia Ester Meng married William Thomas North and had the following issues: Alice North, Enlalie North, Arthur North, Mattie North, Adele North, Dorothea North, Louise Riggin, and Agnes Jones.

Ann Marie; no information.

Note: Information of the Wollery and Dorthy Meng descendants is taken from the story of "The Meng Family" sent to the author by Martha Meng of Bowling Green, Kentucky.

JAMES EDWARD MENG (1806)

Generation No. 3

3. JAMES EDWARD[4] MENG (*JOHN ULRICH (WOLLERY)*[3], *JOHN CHRISTOPHER*[2], *JOHANN MARTIN*[1] *MENGEN*) was born 1771 in Philadelphia, PA[15,16], and died September 14, 1824 in Union, SC[17]. He married SARAH (SALLY) LEWIS ca. 1800 in Virginia, daughter of JOHN LEWIS and ELIZABETH SHELTON. She was born ca. 1778[18], and died June 25, 1846 in Union, SC.

Notes for JAMES EDWARD MENG:
James Meng was an ensign in 1798 under Capt. Samuel Shelton in the Virginia Militia. In 1807, Prince Edward County, Virginia, James Meng was appointed and qualified as a justice. In 1806, he was appointed as one of two new captains in the Prince Edward County Militia. In 1807, he qualified for the office of magistrate (*The History of Prince Edward County*, by Herbert Clarence Bradshaw). James moved to Union, South Carolina, by 1810. The old home place was near the banks of what is now Meng's Creek. The old home, said to have been built in 1778, was torn down about 1970. According to Marion Johnson Bobo of Union, South Carolina, great-granddaughter of James Meng, "The family had a race track near the old home where the young men and their friends raced horses and showed off before their fair lady friends. They would throw javelins, or darts, through a ring from their horses, going breakneck speed." On James Meng's tombstone is "Col James Meng 53 years" and it is located in the Presbyterian Cemetery in Union, South Carolina. "Colonel James Meng was a long time resident of Union County. He was said to be very versatile, and considered to be the best tactician in South Carolina by Adjutant General Earle." (*Union County Heritage*, South Carolina). James was a charter member of the Union Library which was located in the courthouse. In 1821, James was one of the signers of the village of Union that petitioned the legislature to incorporate the town. Unfortunately the petition was rejected. The distilling of whiskey from corn became a local industry for the town by 1820. In that year, James was the leading distiller with 800 gallons (*Narrative History of Union County, SC*, by Allan D. Charles). The "Meng House" in Union was built in 1832 and is erect as of this article. It was purchased by Clough, James Meng's son about 1840. It has been the home of four generations of Meng descendants.

Note: The middle name "Edward" in the title of James Edward Meng comes from only one source, his great-granddaughter, Marion Bobo of Union, South Carolina. Marion Bobo is the author of "The James Edward Meng Family" in the book *Union County Heritage*.

James Meng's letter to the governor

A CLEAR VERSION OF JAMES MENG'S LETTER:

IN JUNE 1808, JAMES MENG WROTE TO GOVERNOR CABELL RESIGNING HIS COMMISSION AS CAPTAIN IN THE FIRST REGIMENT OF ARTILLERY OF THE VIRGINIA STATE MILITIA, STATING THAT HE HAD SOLD HIS LAND "WITH A VIEW OF REMOVING SOUTHWARD." THE RETURN ADDRESS ON THE LETTER WAS: "HERMITAGE, PR. EDW.", PROBABLY THE NAME OF HIS HOME.

THE LETTER FOLLOWS:

PRINCE EDWARD   JUNE 14TH:08

SIR,
    HAVING SOLD MY LAND IN THIS COUNTY, WITH A VIEW OF REMOVING TO THE SOUTHWARD, THE SETTLE-MENT OF MY AFFAIRS HAVE NECESSARILY ENGAGED SO MUCH OF MY TIME AS TO MAKE IT INCONVENIENT TO ATTEND TO ANY PUBLIC BUSINESS - THE 7TH SECTION OF THE MILITIA LAWS OF VA REQUIRES THE CONSENT OF A COURT MARTIAL OR THE EXECUTIVE OF THE COMMONWEALTH PREVIOUS TO AN OFFICERS RESIG-NATION. UNDER THE CIRCUMSTANCES STATED ABOVE I TAKE THE LIBERTY TO REQUEST, THAT YOU WILL PER-MIT ME TO RESIGN MY COMMISSION OF CAPT. IN THE FIRST REGIMENT OF ARTILLERY. SHOULD YOU THINK IT ADVISABLE, I WILL CALL A MEETING OF THE COMPANY, AND HOLD AN ELECTION FOR A SUITABLE CHARACTER TO FILL THE VACANCY.
    I AM SIR WITH THE HIGHEST RESPECT YR OBT SER.

HON H. CABELL ESQ.   JAMES MENG

Notes for SARAH (SALLY) LEWIS:

Sally is in the will of John Lewis Jr. dated July 16, 1780; Albermarle County, Virginia. "I bequeath to Sally Ming all property which came by first wife, her mother . . ." probated February 6, 1804. Sally had married James Ming (Meng) by this time. John Lewis Jr. was the son of John Lewis Sr. and grandson of Owen Lewis. Sarah's mother was Elizabeth Shelton. Sarah's grandfather, Samuel Shelton had a brother, Capt. John Shelton, that married Eleanor Parks, daughter of William Parks, first editor of "Virginia and Maryland." Their home was a country home named "Rural Plains." Capt. John Shelton and Eleanor had nine children and one of them, Sarah Shelton, married Patrick Henry in 1754 in the parlor at "Rural Plains" (*The Sheltons* by Mrs. A. E. Whitaker). Sally Ming had two brothers, Owen Lewis and Clough Lewis. Her grandmother was Judith Clough Shelton, daughter of Robert Anderson (1712–1792) and Elizabeth Clough (1722–1779) of Virginia. Elizabeth Clough was the daughter of Richard Clough. From this Richard Clough came the Clough name that would endure several generations in the Ming family. The author's grandfather was Clough Meng, grandson of Sally Lewis Meng.

Rural Plains

According to *The Sheltons* by Z. F. Shelton, John Shelton built the old Shelton home "Rural Plains" in 1670 in Hanover County, Virginia. "It is one of the few buildings standing in America that was built in that era and has not been remodeled. The home has always been in the hands of direct male descendants and is still the private home of the family although it is of great historic value and a large number of visitors are welcomed every year. Spacious lawns and large shade trees add to the welcome. In 1951, Mr. Z. F. Shelton and his family visited Rural Plains and were shown war relics including the sword worn by John Shelton when he was killed in the battle of Brandywire in 1777, also the place where Patrick Henry stood when he married. The home was under shell fire in three wars and the shell marks were in the walls to prove it." His children were Capt. John Shelton, Mary Shelton, Sarah Shelton, William Shelton, Elizabeth Shelton, and Thomas Shelton. His son William Shelton married Hannah Armistead and their son Samuel Shelton was the grandfather of Sally Lewis Meng. (*The Sheltons*)

For more on the maternal ancestors of Sally Meng, refer to the "Descendants of John Shelton (Chilton),"

NOTABLE MENG CONNECTIONS TO COLONIAL AMERICA

Children of JAMES MENG and SARAH LEWIS are:

i. JOHN L. WADDY[5] MENG b. ca. 1824.

Notes for JOHN L. WADDY MENG:
Very little has been found about John. After his father, Colonel James, died in 1824, he was living in the home of his brother Charles (Court of Equity, Union, SC).

ii. HENRY MENG, b. ca. 1800, Virginia[19]; d. ca. 1865.

Notes for HENRY Meng:
Henry Meng married Racheal R. Pearse in Wilkson County, Mississippi, on December 15, 1821. She died on April 1831. Henry was a mason and schoolteacher. He was admitted to the Holmesville, Mississippi, Lodge 69 in 1846 and in 1847 and 1848 was suspended. Henry sold his land in Union, South Carolina in 1829. Their son, James Shelton Meng (pictured), was born in 1824. In the 1860 census, Henry's household consisted of Elsebe (?) 60 years of age, and three other adults. James Shelton Meng, here forward, became a doctor. He was practicing medicine in Holmes County, Mississippi, in 1850 and in the Civil War as a surgeon. James married Caroline "Carrie" H. Gibson on December 11, 1854. Carrie was born on September 13, 1838, and died on May 28, 1919. Their children were Walter B. Meng, Maryland, born ca. 1856 and died February 25, 1886, married Annie M. Houch; Ida Shelton Meng, born July 21, 1857, and died October 2, 1858; Harry Herndon Meng, born December 24, 1859, and died May 30, 1945, married O'Delia Verna Engbarth, born August 1878 and died January 8, 1957; Alice Leslie Meng married Charles C. Campbell; Percy Meng; James Shelton Meng; Elizabeth "Bessie" Meng married Charles C. Cambell; Victor Meng; Lester Meng; Eustice Meng; and Grace Meng. James Shelton Meng died on January 14, 1891 in Vidalia, Louisiana.

The children of Harry Herndon Meng were Harry Herndon "Bootsie" Meng; Thelma "Haysis" Meng; John Raymond Meng, born August 15, 1898, and he married Carrie Elisabeth McCrary, born April 4, 1898; Lester Meng; and Delia Meng.

The children of John Raymond Meng and Carrie were John Raymond, Mary Elaine, Rae Elizabeth, and Louis Engbarth. Rae Elizabeth Meng was born on January 24, 1925, and married Charles Arthur Patout, born October 17, 1922. Issue: Charles Arthur Patout, David Joseph Patout, Raymond Paul Patout, Paul Dunkin Patout, Mary Elizabeth Patout, Patrick Oswell Patout, Barbara Rae Patout, and Jeanne Anne Patout.

In the Alexandra, Pineville Town Talk, on 2/31/1991: "Dr. James S. Meng became Vidalia's first mayor in 1875. This Meng dynasty only lasted a year." His photograph is hanging in the new city hall. In the La. Genal. Record, J. S. Meng is listed as being the Secretary of the School Board in Concordia Parish in 1877.

iii. JULIANNA MENG, b. ca. 1810, Va[20].

Notes for JULIANNA MENG:

Julianna (Julie Ann) Meng, the only available daughter of James, married a Hix in Union, South Carolina. This is based on an article in *Plantation Heritage* by Kenneth F., and Blanche Marsh, pub. 1962: "... built by Dr. James Edward Hix, a planter-doctor. His mother was a member of the aristocratic Meng family of Union." In *Will Book of Union* (B Transcripts) appear the following names, "James Meng, Charles Meng, and Julie Hix." Dr. Hix's home in Union on South Mountain Street was torn down in 1969 to make way for a supermarket. According to the census of 1860, it appears that Julianna may have remarried. Under the household of John Joiner is Julie Ann born in Virginia, age 50, and James Hix, physician, age 28, which is obviously her son. According to Union County Magistrates of 1865–1870 and published in the *Narrative of Union County*, South Carolina, Dr. James E. Hix owned 1,200 acres of land in 1865. His medical office was in the rear of the courthouse.

iv. CLOUGH S. MENG, b. 1802, Virginia[21]; d. 1870, Union, SC.

Notes for CLOUGH S. MENG:

Clough was born in Virginia. His first wife Martha and their only child died prior to 1827. Clough married secondly, Mary Giles (b. 1805). Clough was a Confederate soldier. He was in the Lt. Arty. Jeter's Co. (Macbeth Lt. Arty.). Clough and Mary had two daughters; Cornelia Meng that married Benjamin Dudley Culp on December 22, 1849, and Ann E. Meng that married Madison Wallace, and after his death, married John Thompson Hill in 1865. In her first marriage, she (Ann) had a son, Clough Wallace (b. 1851). Ann E. Meng and second husband John Thompson Hill moved to Union, where he operated a store and real estate firm known as J. T. Hill & Co. In 1965, he owned 2,496 acres. Clough owned a hotel in Union and the Meng House on Academy Street that is occupied as of this writing. The "Meng House" (pictured) was built in 1832. "The lumber for the Meng House was brought from Columbia and Charleston. Identical columned facades on two sides of the house were designed by W. W. James for Zachariah Herndon. However, four generations of the Clough Meng family have occupied the house" (Plantation Heritage). It has been mentioned that Zachariah sold the house to Clough Meng because of the nearby graveyard that was a depressing view.

The Culp House (pictured) is still standing today in Union, South Carolina, and was built by Clough Meng about 1857 as a wedding present to daughter

Cornelia, wife of Benjamin Dudley Culp. "This house served as a focal point for political activity during the mid-1800s" (Union County Heritage). "Mrs. Ann Hill (Ann Meng Hill) presented a flag (the flag is now in the Union Museum) to the Johnson Rifles, Union's first company of Confederate Volunteers from this porch . . . The campaign of 1876 for governor was a bitter one. During its course, Wade Hampton made what has been termed a fiery speech from the porch of this house in October of that year" (Plantation Heritage by Kenneth F. and Blanche Marsh). Wade Hampton was elected governor.

Benjamin Culp owned the Culp Rock Quarry and furnished the stone to build the Grace Methodist Church in Union. "Because of his gift Culp was given the privilege of naming the church. He said, 'It shall be called Grace and may it never fall from grace.'" (Names in South Carolina, Volumes XXV–XXX)

Pictures of three homes that Meng family members resided in during the 1800s at Union, South Carolina, are featured in *Plantation Heritage* by Kenneth F. and Blanche Marsh, printed in 1962; (1) Meng House, (2) Culp House, and the (3) James Hix house (son of Julianna Meng).

The Meng House

Four generations of Mengs occupied the Meng house during a period of about 120 years: (1) Clough and Mary Giles Meng, (2) Ann Meng Wallace, (3) Clough Wallace, and (4) Mrs. J Clough Wallace, granddaughter of Dr. James Hix until about 1970. The short street between the Meng house and the Culp House is named Wallace (understandable). According to the 1860 US census, living in the house was Clough Meng and wife Mary, daughter Ann Wallace and son Cluff (Clough), a neighborhood teacher, a teacher of the high school, five students, and eight other people.

4. v. CHARLES MENG, b. 1804, Prince Edward Co., VA; d. ca. 1860, Winston, Co., MS.

   vi. WILLIAM MENG, b. 1809, Prince Edward Co., VA; d. 1856, Union Co., SC.

Notes for William Meng:
William Meng married Sarah Jones, a daughter of Charles Jones, postmaster and schoolmaster at Jonesville, in Union County. Charles Jones built the "Wayside Inn" (in existence as of this writing) one mile north of Jonesville in 1811. William was a schoolteacher at Jonesville public school and a landowner. According to the 1850 census, he and Sarah had a daughter Frances born in 1830. In the UCH-SC is the following: "He (Charles Jones) had a small log school in the church yard of Gilead located a mile east of Jonesville. It was also used as a church (Union) until other churches were built . . . Charles Jones had a daughter who married a Meng and who owned the old Fowler place not far from the church in the rear. At her death she left the additional land for use of the church."

Wayside Inn

"The Brick House, just on the outskirts of Jonesville, was built by Charles Jones and was the Exchange Post for the Stage-Coach line between Charles Town (Charleston), South Carolina, and Asheville, North Carolina, where the horses were changed. Here the mails and passengers going either way were brought and the travelers refreshed." (UCH-SC)

vii. JAMES EDWARD MENG, b. January 16, 1810, Union, SC[22,22]; d. September 1, 1890, Union Co., SC.

Notes for JAMES EDWARD MENG:
Marion Johnson Bobo, granddaughter of James and Frances Meng, wrote the following in *Union County Heritage*: "My mother was born and reared in the home (believed built in 1778) that has been torn down to make room for the Jeter Long house near Meng's Creek on Highway 49 east of Union. It was a very spacious house with extensive grounds. Many noble people were entertained as guest there. It is said that Colonel William Washington's Cavalry camped near here before the Battle of Cowpens, when they were returning from a raid in Laurens County." James Edward Meng Sr. married Emily Jefferies on February 22, 1842. Their children were Amanda (b. ca. 1840), Chris (b. ca. 1842), Louis (b. ca. 1847), Bernice (b. ca. 1850), and William Owens (b. ca. 1850 and died young). Louis (Lewis) Meng was living in Gowdeysville, South Carolina, in 1880 when his family consisted of wife Addie (29) and son Willie (4) and Emma (2).

Emily Jeffries Meng died in 1855, and on November 25, 1856, James Edward Meng married Frances Amanda Hammond, born December 23, 1839, daughter of Philip T. Hammond of Union. Their children were Charles K., born December 27, 1857; Frances, born 1859; Mary Delilah, born November 11, 1861; James Edward, born October 11, 1864; Sallie Gillian, born April 19, 1867; Annie Thorn, born February 14, 1870; and Anna Elizabeth Hammond Meng, born May 21, 1880. (Family Bible records)

Charles K. Meng married Alcie Tolleson, and their children were Bernice, Ernest Clyde, and James Edward Meng; first child of Charles K. and Alcie Meng, Bernice (no information); second child of Charles K. and Alcie Meng, Ernest Clyde Meng, born April 2, 1880, and married Lily Delilah Olsen and had the following children: Bernice Evelyn, Willam Claude, Wesley K., Ernest C., Donald Lee, James Louis, Daniel Victor, and Eloise; Bernice Evelyn was born on March 6, 1920, and married Chris Panopulos; William Claude was born on February 13, 1922, and married Katherine Jo Buchanan on born 9, 1924, and they had the following children Claudia Jo Meng, born September 19, 1946, and married Nelden Halcolm Ward, born May 15, 1947; Ramonia Katherine Meng, born June 9, 1951, and married Daniel Burgdorf; Rafael Alexander Meng, born December 2, 1954, and married Coleen Ford; Wesley K. Meng (wife named Vona) was born on August 2, 1923, and had the following children: Jerry, Steven, and William Clyde;

Ernest C. Meng was born on January 16, 1925; Donald Lee Meng (wife named Kathy) was born on July 2, 1926 and had two children, Diana and Lisa; James Louis Meng was born on June 16,1930; Daniel Victor Meng was born on August 26, 1931, and married Ruth Ann; Eloise Alcie Meng was born on February 11, 1928, and married Jack Nelson and had two children, Gregg and Todd. Third child of Charles K. and Alcie Meng, James Edward Meng, had Ruth Lois and Betty.

Frances Meng, no information.

Mary Delilah Meng, born November 1861, married James Vernon Askew and their children were James L. (born 1882), Jackson R. (b. 1887), Lillie B. (b. 1892), Mildred (b. 1893), Willie F. (b. 1895), James V. (b. 1898), and Mary E. Askew (b. 1900).

James Edward Meng Jr. (b. 1864) and wife Elliot had the following children: C. Milton, Lillian, and Eddie.

Ann Thorn Meng married Willaim Chatman Johnson of Union, South Carolina, and they had the following children: William Douglas, born June 6, 1888; Richard Hughes, April 19, 1890; Mason Thorn, July 22, 1892; Clara Johnson, died young; Lois, died young; Lola Mae, March 20, 1899; Annie Willie, November 27, 1902; Marion Inez, January 15, 1905; Murray Fritz, May 15, 1907; Charles David, October 10, 1909; and Leroy Hammond, died in infancy.

Sallie Gillian and Anna Elizabeth Ming, no other information.

James Edward Meng Sr. was a large landowner. At one time, he owned land on the waters Browns Creek and sold it to his brother William. He moved to Fanning's Creek, and as of 1865 had 1,714 acres containing two mills near Jonesville.

viii. FRANCIS MENG, b. 1811, Union, SC; d. ca. 1827, Union, SC.

Notes for FRANCIS MENG:
Francis died when in teenage years.

ix. GARLAND MENG, b. 1817, Union, SC[22]; d. 1873, Union Co., SC.

Notes for GARLAND MENG:
Garland Thompson Meng married Susannah Ann Thomas (b. 1827). Susannah was the daughter of John P. and Jemima (Sims) Thomas of Union. Garland was a large landowner in Jonesville (1,068 acres in 1865, and 1,050 acres in 1870) that was spared by the Civil War. Garland was a Confederate soldier. He was a sergeant in the Fifth Troops Co. M. He also was a trustee for the New Hope Methodist Church near Jonesville. The children born to Garland and Susannah are Sarah Beona Meng that married Samuel W. T. Lanham that was the governor of Texas from 1903 to 1907 and a congressman from that state for 18 years; Frank Starr Meng that never married and died in 1893; J. Elma Meng that married Moses Wood; Emma T. Meng and son John Wallace T. Meng. John Wallace married Mary Leonard Johnson, and they had a son Bernard

Boyd Meng, born August 25, 1879, that married Minnie Lancaster, born September 10, 1879, in Union County. She was the daughter of Christopher C. and Ida Smith Lancaster. Their children are Ethel Wright Meng, born March 3, 1906, and married Donald W. Greer of Perris, California; Bernard Boyd Meng Jr., born June 13, 1908, in Union, South Carolina, and married Era Ann Collins of Metter, Georgia; Cammela Neil Meng, born August 6, 1910, and married Charles E. Tucker Sr. of Winnsboro, South Carolina; and Herbert Smith (Billy) Meng, born November 23, 1919, and married Margie Gayden Wylie of Winnsboro. Bernard Boyd Meng Sr. was superintendent of the Board of Public Works in Winnsboro until retirement in 1949.

Governor Lanham and First Lady Sarah B. Meng

Governor Lanham was born on July 4, 1846, in Spartanburg, South Carolina. At the age of 20, he married Sarah B. Meng (daughter of Garland Meng) in Union, South Carolina. They moved to Red River County, Texas, soon after. He was admitted to the bar in 1869 and became district attorney. In 1880, he was a presidential elector and served in the Eight District in Congress from 1883 to 1893 and 1895 to 1903. In 1903, he was elected governor. According to a resolution made by the CAMP state: At 16 he joined the army of Northern Virginia and surrendered at Appomattox. He did much to present and preserve the heroic deeds of the soldiers of the South. In the resolution, the CAMP went on to recognize Sarah Meng as being an asset on his behalf through her helpfulness and wisdom (Confederate Veteran, page 42). They last lived in Weatherford, Texas.

The Moseley Oak

Note: Near the home of Garland Meng in Union County was a large oak tree. According to an article in the *Union County Heritage-South Carolina*, "The Moseley Oak, named for Thomas 'Hi-Key' Moseley, celebrates a near fatal adventure of this intrepid scout for the Revolutionary General Daniel Morgan. Moseley was forced by a pack of wolves to spend the night in this tree. He escaped the next morning by shooting the leader of the pack, thus dispersing the menacing band of attackers. The tree became known to all in the surrounding county as Moseley's Oak."

Generation No. 4

4. CHARLES[5] MENG (*JAMES EDWARD*[4], *JOHN ULRICH (WOLLERY)*[3], *JOHN CHRISTOPHER*[2], *JOHANN MARTIN*[1] *MENGEN*) was born 1804 in Prince Edward Co., VA[23], and died ca. 1860 in Winston, Co., MS[24]. He married (1) NANCY in SC. She was born ca. 1815 in South Carolina, and died January 1850 in Winston Co., MS. He married (2) MARTHA HUDSPETH July 1, 1855 in Winston Co., MS[25]. She died ca. 1860.

Notes for CHARLES MENG:
Charles Meng lived in South Carolina from about 1810 to 1844. On September 12, 1831, Charles purchased 214 acres of land from his brother William Meng. On October 31, 1831, he sold the land to Z. Hooker and wife Mary A. Hooker. After the death of his

father, Charles became guardian to his younger brothers, James Edward and John Lewis Waddy. Charles was married first to Nancy (?) of Union, South Carolina, and they had the following children: Elizabeth (b. ca. 1837, SC); James F. (b. ca. 1838, SC) (died in the Civil War at Allatoona, GA); Julia (b. ca. 1840, SC); John (b. ca. 1844, MS); Joseph (b. ca. 1848, MS); and Charley (b. Dec. 1849, MS). Nancy died in January 1850 from childbed fever. The bond for Charles's marriage to Martha Hudspeth in 1855 is recorded in the courthouse in Louisville, Mississippi. His signature is written as Charles Meng. This is mentioned here as from then forward his sons spelled their name Ming (possibly excluding James that was killed in the Civil War).

According to Allan D. Charles in the book *Narrative History of Union Co., SC* on July 1, 1833, there was a "showdown" on the street in Union, South Carolina, in which Charles Meng was involved. "The town held its breath, for the whole community was watching. What happened next was variously reported, but it seemed that as Bobo and Rice drew within eight or ten paces of each other, both Rice and Gist pulled pistols on Bobo, who was ordered by Rice to halt. Bobo did so, and Rice cocked his gun as Gist stepped back whereupon William Rice Jr. came up and produced his pistol. At that moment, Charles Meng and John Rogers wrestled young Rice's weapon away from him, but Rice drew another pistol. Then Col. Robert Martin, Bobo's brother-in-law, seized Rice to prevent the lad from using his second weapon, and while Rice was scuffling with Martin, Bobo took the opportunity of coming up and delivering a couple of blows of his cane to Rice's head so that blood flowed." Sadly, Bobo died from a gunshot wound that day.

In courthouse records in Union, South Carolina, 1841,

> "Union District—An inquisition indented taken at the plantation of Wm. K. Clowney in said district 1 Sept. 1841 before Issac Gregory, coroner, upon review of the body of George, the property of said Wm. Clowney, then and there being dead, by the oaths of Wm. Long, Jos. Greer, Marshal Carroll, Wm. Gibson, Jas. Jackson, Jas Orr, A. Pearce, John Liles, Evans Williams, John Mays and Job Hammons, a lawful jury of inquest, do say that on Monday, 30 Aug. last the slave was shot with a shotgun on the plantation of Wm. Clowney by Charles Meng, the overseer of the Plantation, and died about dusk the following Tuesday evening . . . Joseph G. Clowney being sworn says that Charles Meng met him on the morning of the murder and said that there was a dead Negro in the field. Said Joseph asked how it happened, and he said it would not have happened if George had not run from him, he said he ordered him to stop and told him if he did not stop, he would shoot, and he did not stop . . . Summons for jurers issued same day . . . at Wm. K. Clowney's plantation." (Note: no other records pertaining to the trial are found by the author in the court records.)

Charles moved to Mississippi about 1844. In the 1850 census, his occupation is "overseer."

Notes for Martha Hudspeth:

In the marriage bond document, Martha is listed as Marthey T. Hudspeth. Little is known about Martha other than she was born in South Carolina (1860 census). Ayres (Aires) Hudspeth of Winston County had an aunt and a daughter named Martha Hudspeth, but little is known about them. It has been mentioned that Aires settled among the Indians in the early years in Mississippi. Tradition in the families of Clough Monk Ming, a son of Charles and Martha, is that they are part Indian. Charles was not Indian. Could Martha have been Indian, or part Indian? Clough was an orphan by the age of 10, or earlier, and living in the home of James Hemphill. Would he have known much about his mother? The writer concedes that there is no proof of Indian blood in this family, but as much of the belief has descended from Clough's oldest daughter, Leoda Ming Grant, the legend does warrant more study.

Children of Charles Meng and Nancy are:

i.   Elizabeth[6] Meng, b. ca. 1837.

ii. James F. Meng, b. ca. 1838; d. ca. October 1864, Altoona, GA..

Notes for James F. Meng:

James was in the Sixth Company of the Thirty-Fifth Mississippi Regiment of the Confederacy. He was killed in Altona (Allatoona), Georgia. The only record this writer found pertaining to this Company being in Allatoona was the night of October 8, 1864, and the next day in which the battle took place. As the battle lasted over into the afternoon and then the troops moved on leaving the dead behind, it may be reasonable to assume that James F. Ming (Meng) died that day, October 9, 1864. James married Melvina Knowles of Neshoba County, Mississippi, on February 22, 1859, in Winston County, Mississippi. She was the daughter of Lemuel and Dorothy Knowles. They had one son, James Lemuel Ming (b. ca. 1859). He being the grandson of Charles Meng, a member of the aristocratic family of Union, South Carolina, did not have life as easy as his earlier ancestors. The post-Civil War days in rural Mississippi for a young widow and her young son could have been cruel times. Luckily, for them her father Knowles, out of love for his daughter and grandson, brought them into his home in Neshoba County and cared for them until James was 21. James Lemuel in 1882 married Tex Anna Alla Pope. She was born in 1862. Their children were Nicey A., Ella U., Wilburn Jackson, Charles L., James Burl, and Nancy M. James Burl Ming first married Lillie and secondly married Clora Breazeale, born August 1893, daughter of John and Martha Breazeale. The children born to James B. Ming and Clora are James Freddie, Daniel, Maudeen, Jimmie Lou, Prentiss, and two children that died young, Lillie and Nesbert. Maudeen married Robert Shumaker of Scott County, Mississippi. They had two children, Robert (Bobby) L. Shumaker and Carolyn Shumaker. Bobby married Faith L. Foreman of Forest, Mississippi, and they have a son

Michael and a daughter, Alicia Hope Shumaker. Alicia Hope married Tony Sanford and had a daughter Brianna Sanford.

iii. JULIA MENG, b. ca. 1840.

iv. JOHN MENG, b. ca. 1844.

Notes for John Meng:
Very little is known about John. A rumor is he was killed in the Civil War, but no documentation has been found to substantiate this.

v. JOSEPH (MING) MENG, b. January 21, 1848, WINSTON Co., MS; d. June 11, 1920, Winston Co., MS.

Notes for Joseph (Ming) Meng:
Joseph Henry Ming (pictured) married Sarah Ann Bouchillon Taylor (her second marriage) July 18, 1868. She was born on June 26, 1841. Their children were Cassandra Josephine, born June 12, 1869 and died September 30, 1952; James Champion, born November 23, 1871 and died April 26, 1957; Finas Algernon Rianza, born August 3, 1874 and died February 13, 1958; Charles Bradshaw, born December 31, 1876 and died May 30, 1934; John C., born July 14, 1879 and died April 15, 1909; and Lucy L., born May 17, 1888 and died October 5, 1978. Joseph and Sarah are buried at Murphy Creek Cemetery near Louisville, Mississippi. More on these siblings below.

Children born to Sarah Ann Bouchillon Taylor and first husband James Arden Taylor were James Arden Taylor, born October 1, 1859; Nannie S. Taylor, born December 8, 1861; and P. Elizabeth Taylor, born July 5, 1864.

Children of Joseph Ming and Sarah Ann Bouchillon Taylor are as follows:

1. Cassandra Josephine Ming married Coley Ryanza Fulcher and their children were Lois Belle, born May 10, 1891; Henry Clarence, born November 15, 1892; Preston Parks, born February 25, 1895; Alberta Allene, born 1898; Willye Era, born October 16, 1901; and Olyn Dee, born October 26, 1906.
2. James Champion Ming and wife Georgia Ella, daughter of Henry Fulcher Jr. had the following issue: Ollie Inez Ming, born February 21, 1902; Gladys Waldene Ming, born May 21, 1904; Aubrey Watson Ming, born September 2, 1906; Claudia Edward Ming, born October 27, 1909; and Essie Ming, born January 12, 1912; Essie married Albert L. Parks and they had a daughter, Cubye Faye Parks.
3. Finas Algeron Rianza Ming married Letha Ann McCool, December 3, 1897, and their children were Hilery P. Ming, born January 18, 1902; Vernon Vane Ming, born June 9, 1904; Napoleon H. Ming, born November 8, 1905; Alvie Garland Ming, born February 21,

1910; Willie Mae Ming, born February 2, 1913; and Ccla P. Ming, born March 20, 1915.

4. Charles Bradshaw Ming married Clara Viola Warner on December 26, 1897. They had a son, Dewey Carl Ming, born October 4, 1898. Dewey Carl married Myrtly Era Easley, born May 2, 1900, and they had the following issues Carl Easley (Buff), bcrn September 8, 1920 and married Naomi Ming, born July 14, 1924, Sarah Ethel, Clara Susan, Charles Buster, Millye Edith, Kay Francis, and Michael Keith. Other children of Charles Bradshaw and Clara are Oscar Clyde Ming, born November 5, 1898; Lilly Nell Ming, born December 28, 1904; and Harold Spiva Ming, born June 30, 1909.

5. Lucy A. Ming married Robert A. Hill on September 17, 1978, and their children were Embree Gerald Hill, born November 21, 1909; Robert Guy Hill, born June 26, 1911; Grady Sanford Hill, born August 10, 1913; Sally Gertrude Hill, born October 16, 1915; Herbert Gilbert Hill, born December 15, 1918; James Graham Hill, born December 6, 1920; and Garvin Montgomery Hill, born February 16, 1925.

Bouchillon

Sarah Ann Bouchillon, wife of Joseph Ming, was the daughter of James Segang Bouchillon (b. 1806) and Lucinda Palmer Bouchillon (b. 1831). James Segang was the son of James Bouchillon (b. 1777) and Susannah Guillebeau. James was the son of Jean Bouchillon, born 1751 in France.

Note: For more information on the Joseph Ming family of Winston County, Mississippi, refer to "Charles Ming and Descendants" by Carl (Buff) and Naomi Ming, February 12, 1992, in the Winston County Library, or the Historical Library in Jackson, Mississippi.

vi. CHARLES (MING) MENG, b. December 13, 1849; d. April 27, 1901, Choctaw County, MS.

NAME CHANGE FROM MENG TO MING

Notes for CHARLES (MING) MENG:

Charles (Charley) Ming was born in December 1849, and in January the following year, his mother Nancy died of a fever. In Charles's generation, the spelling changed from Meng to Ming. Charley settled on 80 acres near the old Natchez Trace in Choctaw County, Mississippi. His wife was Mary A Smith, born January 30, 1859 and died November 24, 1937. They are buried at Pisgah Methodist Church in Choctaw County. Their children were Joseph H., born December 25, 1873; Thurman S., born December 23, 1875; Maggie, born November 30, 1877; Tennie, born April 30, 1880; Nannie; Homer, born May 30, 1890; Charles William, born May 21, 1887; and Jenny Lee, born December 11, 1884.

Joseph H. Ming married Liddie Franks, and they had the following four children: (1) Otho who married Courtney Jones had two children, Ella Jo and Travis Ming. Ella Jo married L. C. Gossett, and they had four children, Sandra, Vickie, Darlene, and Toni. Travis and wife Frances had Keith and Todd. (2) Vernon married Winnie Mills, and they had the following: a son Glennice and daughter Iva Jean. Glennice and wife Peggy had four children, Billy, Amanda, Melissa, and Jeremy Ming. Iva Jean married Homer Power, and they had Nicky and Lori. (3) Carrie; (4) Velma married Harry Dircks.

Maggie Ming married Sam Keen, and their children were (1) Mae Keen married Gordon Gray and had three children, Frances, Betty, and Alice; (2) Charlie whose first wife was named Patsy and his second wife was Ophie; (3) Mildred; (4) Stella; and (5) Sidney. Sidney Keen and wife Alice had four children, Sam, Martha, John, and Patricia.

Tennie Ming never married.

Thurman Ming married Mildren Raburn, and the children born to them are (1) Nolen; (2) Vada Ming Hale; (3) Ora Ming Strickland; and (4) Flora, twin sister of Ora. Nolen and wife Letha Ming had four children, Nolen Ming Jr., Jim Ming, Peggy Ming, and Charles. Nolen Jr. married Inez, and their children are Kathy, Ray, and Steve. Children to Jim are Tiger, John, and Tricia. Vada married a Hale, and their children are Hazel (first), whose children are Cookie, Debbie, Ricky, Jerry, Bryan, and Tommy. Wanda Hale (second) that married Bobby Hudspeth. Ora (third) married Ellis Strickland and had a son James. James Strickland and wife Glenda had Jim and Jamie. Flora, twin sister of Ora, died in 1914.

Nannie Ming married Charlie Franks, and their children are (1) Bertha Franks and (2) Mary Franks. Bertha married Tilden Parkes, and their children are Charles, Lamar, and Johnny. Children of Charles and wife Jean are Lynn and Jennifer. Lamar married Martha Dawn, and their children are Renee, Luke, and Dan. Children of Johnny and wife Ann are Jason and Allison. Mary Franks married Billy Power, and their children are Billye Gwynn and Bob. Billye Gwynn married Peck Reid, and their children are Beth, Edd, and Angelia. Children of Bob and wife Johnnie are Bill, Anissa, and Tom.

The children born to Homer Ming and Jewell Buck are (1) Sammie Lou, (2) Annie Noyce, and (3) Vonda Ming. Annie Noyce married Willie McMinn, and their children are Brenda, Ronnie, Bill, and Chuck. Vonda Ming married Morris Scrivner. Their children are Sandra, Gail, and Wick.

Children of CHARLES MENG and MARTHA HUDSPETH are:

vii.   FRED[6] MING, b. 1856, Winston, Co., MS[26].

Notes for Fred Ming:

At the age of 13, Fred was living in the household of William and Mary Norton in Winston County, Mississippi. Fred never married. According to his niece, Corrie Ming Blanton, when he was a young man, he fell from the side of a house trying to swat a wasp in the window and injured his head. The doctor placed a silver dollar inside his forehead. Little more is known about Fred.

5.   viii.   CLOUGH MONK MING (MENG), b. March 17, 1859, Winston, Co., MS; d. July 7, 1934.

Generation No. 5

5. CLOUGH MONK MING[6] (MENG) (*CHARLES[5] MENG, JAMES EDWARD[4], JOHN ULRICH (WOLLERY)[3], JOHN CHRISTOPHER[2], JOHANN MARTIN[1] MENGEN*) was born March 17, 1859 in Winston, Co., MS[27], and died July 7, 1934[28,29]. He married DORA L. EVANS December 26, 1888 in Home of William G. Burdine, daughter of EVANS and SARAH BURDINE. She was born March 18, 1872 in Choctaw Co., MS, and died September 6, 1951 in Choctaw Co., MS.

Notes for CLOUGH MONK MING (MENG):

Clough (pictured), Cluff, or Clough Ming was a farmworker and worked on numerous farms throughout Choctaw County, Mississippi. He was an orphan by age 10, and in 1870, he was living in the home of James C. and Mary Hemphill in Winston County. Clough was born just before the Civil War erupted and did not enjoy the financial life style as his earlier ancestors. Clough married Dora Evans (spelled Evins in the family Bible) on December 26, 1888, in the home of her uncle, William George Burdine, in Choctaw County. Clough worked most of his life as a farmer, but never owned his own home. In the final years of his life, Clough and Dora lived in a home next to his son, Hoyt Ming, on Baily Hill about five miles east of Ackerman. He is buried at Bethlehem in Choctaw County, Mississippi. Clough had an uncle Clough S. Meng, and great-great-grandmother Judith Clough. This is mention to establish the origin of the name.

The Clough Ming family Bible was presented to the library in Philadelphia, Mississippi, in 1991, by Leslie Flint for copying and depositing the handwritten information in the genealogy files of the library. Leslie Flint retained possession of the Bible. Leslie was the spouse of Christie Ming.

Notes for DORA L. EVANS:

After the death of Clough, Dora Evans Ming resided mainly in the home of her daughter Corrie Ming Blanton. She is buried next to her husband at Bethlehem Cemetery in Choctaw County. Dora was the daughter of Thomas (?) Evans and Sarah Ann Burdine. The author has no further information on Mr. Evans (spelled Evins in the family Bible) other than he resided in Choctaw County near Bankston in the 1870s. Dora's mother, Sarah Ann Burdine, was the daughter of Hamilton Burdine and Frances Caroline Sitton. Hamilton, born June 11, 1816, was from Easley, South Carolina, and the son of Richard Burdine of Easley, Pickens County, South Carolina. Richard Burdine, born August 6, 1773, and married to Martha "Patsy" Wilson, was the son of Samuel and Mary Eddins Burdine. Samuel was the son of Richard Burdine, a member of the Hebron Church in Madison, Virginia, in 1733.

Dora had the following siblings: John H. Streety (stepbrother), Thomas, Laura Nell, and Cora, and Ora, that died young. Laura Nell married Andrew Campbell on August 25, 1898.

In the Descendants of "Samuel Bourdine (Burdine)" and the "Burdine" family history by Arvalean L. Burdine Petrics, Dora's aunt "Dixie" Burdine relates the migration to Mississippi of the Burdine, Sitton, and Dacus families. This trip was by ox-drawn wagons in the late 1830s, and took about a month from Easley, South Carolina.

As a child, the author remembers visiting Henry Burdine, son of Billy George Burdine (brother to Sara Ann Burdine) in the 1940s. Two things stand out in the authors mind. (1) There was a long metal water pipe that extended from a pump (not electrified) from a lake down the hill to several twists under a black wash pot, and then into the house. When a fire was burning under the wash pot, they would have hot running water in the house. (2) An old flat bed truck (probably in the 1920s model) that had no roof over the cab, and no doors.

Pearl Burdine, brother to Henry, had a film developing studio in Chester. The author has some old photos that has his logo, "PEARL BURDINE PHOTO and KODAK finishing," Chester Miss.

For more on the maternal ancestors of Dora Ming, refer to "Descendants of Samuel Burdine," page 54.

Children of CLOUGH (MENG) and DORA EVANS are:

i.   LEODA[7] MING, b. August 15, 1889, Choctaw Co., MS; d. December 12, 1965, Dallas, TX.

Notes for LEODA MING:
Leoda married Wrenzo Grant. They had the following children: James, Tony, Junior, and Opal. Leoda and Wrenzo are buried in Dallas, Texas. Opal married Delbert Brogden. They had three children: Thomas and Joyce are the names of two.

ii.   HUBERT MING, b. May 18, 1893, Choctaw Co., MS; d. August 5, 1983, ITAWAMBA Co., MS.

Notes for HUBERT MING:
Hubert, farmer and mason, was a longtime resident of Itawamba County, and his last years were lived in Nettleton, Mississippi. He was first married to Ida Mae Baker. Their children were Carl, Catherine and Winnie. His second wife was Fleeta May Bethay, and their children were Charlotte, Norene, and Christine. On December 15, 1950, Charlotte married James Brietigan Waltz, born April 17, 1925. They have two daughters, Sandra Jean and Charlotte D'ann Waltz. Charlotte D'ann, born January 14, 1963, married Michael Terry Holloway, born May 1, 1960. Charlotte and Michael have one child, Jesse Colton Hanson Holloway, born June 29, 1994. Sandra Jean was born on December 8, 1951. She married first, David E. Anderson. Second, Sandra married Marshal Leigh Marymor, born April 21, 1953. Sandra and Marshall have a daughter, Nora Ann Marymor, born May 9, 1983.

iii.   JOHN CLINTON MING, b. December 19, 1895, Choctaw Co., MS; d. August 20, 1950, Choctaw Co., MS.

Notes for JOHN CLINTON MING:
John Clinton never married. He was a mason and was in the military during the World War I.

iv.   Ethel PLEMON MING, b. September 8, 1897, Choctaw, Co., MS; d. April 3, 1972, Choctaw, Co., MS.

Notes for ETHEL PLEMON MING:
Ethel was a farmer near Weir, Mississippi. He married Minnie Beatrice Dawkins, November 22, 1933. As this book covers the Ming family in depth, these notes will involve the family and ancestors of his wife. Minnie B. Dawkins Ming was the great-granddaughter of Reuben Dawkins. Reuben Dawkins was born on July 29, 1811, in South Carolina. He was living in Newberry County before moving to Mississippi about 1852. In Mississippi, he settled in Winston County. His wife was Louisa Miller (?), born September 22, 1822, and died in 1867. According to the "Annals of Newberry," Reuben was a private among 58 soldiers from Newberry that volunteered in the war with the Seminole in 1836. Reuben remarried about 1860. He died on January 19, 1887, in Winston County, Mississippi. His children by Louisa were Francis, born 1840, SC; RE, born 1842, SC; Nancy L., born 1844; Susan, born 1844, SC; Texanna, born 1848, SC; Ellen (Ella) L., born 1850, SC; James F., born 1852, MS; John, born 1855, MS; Jane, born 1857, MS; and Robert H., born 1861, MS. He married Maude Barron.

Listed on a Dawkins genealogy site on Ancestry.com is the following: Francis H., RE, Nancy L., Texanna, Ellen, John, Robert Henry, Frank (probably James Frank), and Catherine and JC (not listed above) moved to Winston County by wagon train. They arrived on November 9, 1852. "These people moved their church from Newberry SC to Winston County, MS. One couple remained with the church in SC. All other members of the congregation moved to Winston County, MS. Mr. Metts was the wagon master. Reuben Dawkins was a mason . . . Reuben Dawkins' daughter, Texanna, married Jim Dawkins. No relation. Jim and Texanna met in Alabama on the wagon train that brought the folks to MS . . . children of Jim and Texanna: Nola married Bud Leonard."

By 1871, Reuben was remarried. He and his new wife, Lisa (Elizabeth), had the following Children Hugh, born 1871, MS; Walter H. Dawkins, born 1872, MS; Rufus, born ca. 1876, MS. Elizabeth Dawkins (Reuben's wife) was born in South Carolina, February 16, 1834, and died July 22, 1915, in Winston County, Mississippi.

Walter H. Dawkins, son of Reuben and Elizabeth (Lisa), was born on September 29, 1872, in Winston County, Mississippi, and died on August 26, 1921. He married Callie Baker, born in Mississippi, January 22, 1875. After his death, she married a Smith and died on October 3, 1952. The children of Walter H. and Elizabeth Dawkins were Newman Clide, born May 15, 1892 in Winston County; Lula B., born 1894; Margia B., born 1898; and Nannie Sue. In 1900, Walter's mother, Elizabeth, Lula Baker, and sister-in-law (teacher) were living in the household (1900 census).

Newman Clide, son of Walter H. Dawkins, married Elizabeth Wylie, born November 17, 1888. Newman died on March 12, 1958, in Choctaw County. Elizabeth died on February 7, 1967, and their children were Albert, born March 14, 1913 and died December 12, 1977; Richard; Pansey, born July 27, 1915; Minnie Beatrice, born January 13, 1919; Mildred; Howard, born November 29, 1928 and died December 20, 1973; Myrtle, died young; and Robert was born on October 5.

Minnie Beatrice Dawkins, daughter of Newman Clide Dawkins, was born on January 13, 1919, and married Ethel Plemon Ming of Choctaw County, Mississippi. They resided for a while on Baily Hill in east Choctaw County and later moved a few miles NE of Weir, Mississippi. The children of Ethel and Minnie B. are Clovis Faye, born October 6, 1934; Doris Sherline, born January 2, 1937; and Plemon Olen, born March 19, 1940.

Clovis Ming, daughter of Ethel Ming, married Cecil Oakes. Presently they reside near West, Mississippi, and have two daughters, Janet Robinson and Jeanette Herod; two sons, Timothy and Brian.

Sherline married Willis Bonner and have a daughter Pam that married Harry Medders. Pam and Harry have a daughter, Brandy. Plemon Olen married Shirley Gladney and have a son, Steve. He and Joy Rigdon Ming have the following children, Ashlie Joy and Joshua Steve.

Minnie Beatrice Dawkins Ming went to her final resting place on November 25, 2004, at the age of 85. Her life exemplified a good Christian way of living. Some of her final words were "I love my children, I am ready to die, I'm going to Heaven."

v. TROY AMZY MING, b. March 1, 1900, Choctaw Co., MS; d. April 25, 1968, Clay Co., MS.

Notes for TROY AMZY MING:

Troy married Eva Cutts, and their children were, Mattie Rene, JT, Jeanette (married Kelly Unger), Bobby, and Charles (Sonny). Troy was in the cattle business at West Point, Mississippi. It has been told that he was the first cattle buyer for the Bryans Brothers meat packing plant in West Point.

6. vi. HOYT LESTER MING, b. October 6, 1902, Choctaw Co., MS; d. April 28, 1985, Choctaw Co., MS.

vii. ALVA MING, b. May 19, 1905, Choctaw Co., MS; d. NOVEMBER 22, 1954, Meridian, MS.

Notes for ALVA MING:

Alva never married. He died of an illness he had since he was a child. He is buried at Bethlehem Cemetery near Ackerman, Mississippi, along with his father Clough, Ethel Plemon, and John Clinton.

viii. BERLIN MING, b. June 24, 1908, Choctaw Co., MS; d. May 7, 1986, Memphis, TN.

Notes for BERLIN MING:

Berlin married Olene Wagner. They had the following children: Nadine, Dorthy, and Margaret. Berlin worked as a nightwatchman for the city of Memphis.

ix. CORRIE MING, b. April 23, 1911, Choctaw, Co., MS.

Notes for CORRIE MING:

Corrie married Izene Blanton, September 1, 1934, and their children are Nonaree and Carliss Robert Blanton. In the early years, the family lived on a farm near Weir, Mississippi, and Izene drove a school bus for the Weir school. Later, Izene and Corrie moved to Weir. Note: Bertrand and Hugh Tabor Blanton, brothers of Izene, lived their childhood in the home of Izene and Corrie. After the death of her husband, Corrie lived in Jackson, Mississippi. Nonaree married Glenn Calloway of Ackerman, Mississippi. Carliss R. Blanton and wife Nancy Smith (?) Blanton have one son, Robert Mitchell Blanton.

x. CHRISTIE CAMMIE MING, b. December 26, 1913, Choctaw Co., MS.

Notes for CHRISTIE CAMMIE MING:

Christie married Leslie Flint, July 7, 1941, in Neshoba County, Mississippi, and their children are Kathy Lee and Danny. Kathy married Michael F. Lahr.

They have one child, Chelsa. Kathy is a member of the DAR, national number 745324. Christie and Leslie are buried near Philadelphia, Mississippi.

Generation No. 6

6. HOYT LESTER[7] MING (CLOUGH MONK MING[6] (MENG), CHARLES[5] MENG, JAMES EDWARD[4], JOHN ULRICH (WOLLERY)[3], JOHN CHRISTOPHER[2], JOHANN MARTIN[1] MENGEN) was born October 6, 1902 in Choctaw Co., MS[30], and died April 28, 1985 in Choctaw Co., MS. He married ROZELLE INDIA YOUNG 1924 in Nettleton, MS, daughter of WILLIAM YOUNG and IDA MORGAN. She was born April 25, 1907 in Nettleton, MS, and died September 29, 1983 in Ackerman, MS.

HOYT LESTER MING'S PEP STEPPERS

Notes for HOYT LESTER MING:

Hoyt's business was growing sweet potatoes (pictured). For many years, he was a steward in the Mt. Airy Methodist Church in Choctaw County, Mississippi. His hobby was making music. He recorded "Indian War Whoop" in 1928 on Victor label (see picture "New Victor Record Hit"). The recording is in the Smithsonian Institute (Folkways section). From the obituary in the Clarion-Ledger April 29, 1985: "Ming begin teaching himself to play the fiddle at 15, and along with his wife (Rozelle) and their group, the 'Pep Steppers' (pictured-document), recorded his first record at Ellis Auditorium in Memphis in 1928 (February 13)." The Victor Records recording included four songs: "Indian War Whoop," "Old Red," "White Mule," and "Tupelo Blues." Except for his own entertainment and occasionally in church, or at a fiddlers contest, Hoyt retired from the fiddle until 1973. From an article published in the New York Press by Mike McGonigal: "In 1952, a compilation record, including Hoyt Ming's Indian War Whoop, unlike any before, or since, was released on Moses Asch's Folkways label. The eighty-four songs on the Anthology of American Folk Music not only pointed to the myriad bizarre and transcendent possibilities of American vernacular sound, they led the way to deep changes in our society, and in the habits of obsessive record collectors . . . # 34 Floyd (Hoyt) Ming and His Pep Steppers: 'Indian War Whoop' isn't that the coolest band name, like, ever? A high pitched violin plays a lovely, simple, plaintive melody . . ." The record is now in the Folkways section in the Smithsonian in Washington DC. In 1973, he and his newly organized band performed in the National Folk Festival at Wolf Trap, Washington DC. In 1984, Hoyt and son Bert performed in the World's Fair in New Orleans, Louisiana, in the folk music hall. "For Mississippi, he was probably one of the finest old-time fiddlers of his time," said Tom Rankin, folk life program director for the Mississippi Arts Commission (Clarion-Ledger, April 29, 1985). In 1975, Hoyt and the Pep Steppers recorded the tune "Rattlesnake Daddy" for the sound track of the movie *Ode to Billy Joe*. In 2001, "Indian War Whoop" was used in the movie *O Brother Where Art Thou?* The album by the same name containing the sound track won a Grammy in 2002. The tune is also included in the "Down from the Mountain" documentary. As of this writing, the original is included on the following albums, or CDs, "I'm a Man of Constant Sorrow, Bona Fide Bluegrass and Mountain Music, and Roots of American Fiddle Music." Hoyt's "Indian War Whoop" keeps on whoopin'. In 2004, the tune was made available for installing in cell phones for a ringtone.

Mr. Tom Rankin of the Mississippi Arts Commission once said of Hoyt, "He was a great ambassador of traditional music."

More About HOYT LESTER MING:

Occupation: Raised sweet potatoes and cotton.

Notes for ROZELLE INDIA YOUNG:

Rozelle Young Ming, usually referred to as Rose, had a great talent for music. She played the mandolin with the Pep Steppers and was know by many for her footwork when she played the musical instrument. Her parents were Will and Ida Morgan Young of Nettleton, Mississippi. Will Young was the son of James Young, and James Young was the great-grandson of John and Mary Young that came to America and settled in South Carolina about 1768 from Larne, Ireland. Her grandfather, Elias Morgan, was the son of Rueben Morgan Jr. of Newberry, South Carolina. Rueben was the son of Rueben Morgan Sr. and grandson of Thomas Morgan of Newberry. The earlier Morgans were patriots during the American Revolutionary War. Thomas owned 200 acres of land near Newberry, South Carolina.

Note: Rozelle was married in Nettleton, Mississippi, but in Monroe County.

Children of HOYT MING and ROZELLE YOUNG are:

i. GENEVA[8] MING, b. September 12, 1925, Choctaw Co., MS.

Notes for GENEVA MING:

After graduating From the University of Alabama, Geneva married John Lawrance Hunt. They have one daughter, Jennifer Hunt McCormick, and a son, Rex Hunt. Geneva and John have two grandchildren, Catherine Hunt (mother is Amanda L. Storment) and Ben McCormick. Geneva and John live in Frankfort, Kentucky.

ii. NORMA CHRISTIE MING, b. September 15, 1928, Choctaw Co., MS.

Notes for NORMA CHRISTIE MING:

Graduated from University of Alabama in the School of Education and married Sidney Graham. Their children are Sidney, Joyce, and Lisa. Their son Sidney married Tina (Stepfather was a Graham), and their children are Cole and Kaleb. Joyce married Larry Kuhn and have a daughter Jessica Ming Kuhn. Lisa married Brent Hoffort (a musician). As of 2005, Norma resided in Fort Walton Beach, Florida.

iii. HOYT BERTRAND MING, b. February 24, 1934, Choctaw Co., MS[31,32]; m. (1) PATRICIA JANE BASS; b. November 5, 1941, Memphis, TN; m. (2) SCOTTIE DIANN FOREMAN, January 2, 1970, Forest, MS; b. August 3, 1948, Jackson. MS.

WHO ARE THE HOYT MINGS?

Notes for HOYT BERTRAND MING:

Hoyt's first wife was Patricia Bass of Memphis, Tennessee. They had one daughter, Donna Carol, born December 27, 1963. Hoyt graduated from Mississippi State University in 1967 with a BS degree in general business. Hoyt married Scottie Diann Foreman in 1970, and they have one daughter Celia Diann. Hoyt and wife Scottie moved to Northport, Alabama, in 1997 so Scottie could pursue her career in psychology. Hoyt performed with father Hoyt L. Ming and the Pep Steppers at Wolf Trap Farms in Virginia at the National Folk Festival in 1973 and at the World's Fair in New Orleans folk music section in 1984. Before joining Fred's in 1967, Hoyt worked in the Union Planters Bank in Memphis, Tennessee, for seven years. He started as a "cotton runner" in 1956 and was assistant manager of the Transit Department before leaving at the end of 1964. Hoyt retired from Fred's in 1996. In 1992, Hoyt researched and wrote the "Ming/Meng Heritage Northern Roots and Southern Trails" that is in the archives in Salt Lake City, Utah.

Notes for PATRICIA JANE BASS:

Patricia was the daughter of Bryan Kelsey Bass and Jane Hardy Prowse, both from Memphis, Tennessee. Patricia Bass and Hoyt B. Ming have one daughter, Donna Carol Ming Renfrow. Donna married Tim Renfrow, and they have a daughter Savannah and a son Dylan. Tim has a daughter Jennifer by first wife Tracy Shawns Hammons.

Notes for SCOTTIE DIANN FOREMAN:

Scottie Diann Foreman Ming is the daughter of James Edward Foreman and Bobbye Jean Wardell Foreman of Forest, Mississippi. Scottie graduated with a BA degree in psychology at the University of Southern Mississippi in 1997. At the present, she is finance director at Tuscaloosa County Mental Retardation Authority in Northport, Alabama. Hoyt and Scottie have one daughter, Cecelia (Celia) Diann Ming Hill, born November 29, 1970. Celia served 12 years in the US Air Force and graduated with a BS degree in management of human resources at Faulkner University, Montgomery, Alabama, in 2004. She married Jimmy Hill of Gwinn, Michigan. They have two sons, Jarod Parker Hill and Caden Preston Hill.

Endnotes

1. *DAR # 506202, Ancestor, Wollery Meng.*
2. Edwin C. Jellett, *John Christopher Meng and His Descendants*, (Non-published; Located in the Genealogy Society of PA).
3. *SAR National # 141975.*
4. Applicate; Kathy Flint Lahr, *DAR National Number 745324, ancestor, Wollery Ulrich Meng.*

5. *SAR National # 141975.*

6. Edwin C. Jellett, *John Christopher Meng and His Descendants,* (Non-published; Located in the Genealogy Society of PA).

7. *TITLE.*

8. *Will of William Meng.*

9. Hoyt B. Ming, *Ming/Meng Heritage,* (Non-published, in the LDS Family Library, and Mississippi Library of History, Jackson, MS.)

10. *Will of William Meng.*

11. Edwin C. Jellett, *John Christopher Meng and His Descendants,* (Non-published; Located in the Genealogy Society of PA).

12. *TITLE.*

13. *DAR Register #438461 Samuel Meng.*

14. *TITLE.*

15. *Grave marker, Presbyterian Cemetery, Union, SC.*

16. Edwin C. Jellett, *John Christopher Meng and His Descendants,* (Non-published; Located in the Genealogy Society of PA).

17. *SAR National # 141975.*

18. Application by Kathy Lee Flint Lahr, *Dar Nat'l Number 745324, ancestor: Wollery 'Ulrich" Meng.*

19. *Census 1850, Pike Co., MS.*

20. *Census 1850, Union Co., SC; Household 552.*

21. Hoyt B. Ming, *Ming/Meng Heritage,* (Non-published, in the LDS Family Library, and Mississippi Library of History, Jackson, MS.).

22. Hoyt Ming, *Ming/Meng Heritage,* (Non-Published: In LDS Family Library, Salt Lake City, Utah).

23. Tony Russell, *Old Time Music,* (Simon A. Napier and Tony Russell, Proprietors; Printed in England).

24. *Census 1860.*

25. Members of the Winston Co. GHS, *Marriage Records of Winston Co., MS; V-1.*

26. *Census 1860, Winston, MS.*

27. *Grave marker; Bethlehem Cemetery, Ackerman, MS.*

28. *Birth Certficate; Dept. of Health, Jackson. MS.*

29. *Grave marker; Bethlehem Cemetery, Ackerman, MS.*

30. *Grave marker, Enon Cemetery, Ackerman, MS.*

31. *Birth Certificate; Dept. of Health, Jackson. MS.*

32. *TITLE.*

CHAPTER 4
THE NOBLE BRANCH ON THE MENG/MING GENEALOGICAL TREE

LINEAGE CHART

A Noble Branch of the Ming Tree

HEIMBROD IV VON BOYNEBURG-m. MARGARETHE VON ELBEN
    ISSUE:
        JOST

JOST VON BOYNEBURG-d. 1589, m. (1) CATHARINA VON BUTTLAR-d. 1554
    ISSUE:
        JOST (LT. COL.)
(2) ? VON FALKEN ROHRDA-d. 1556
    ISSUE:
        PHILIPP
        ASMUS (CAVALRY CAPT.)
(3) VERONIKA VON SCHETZEL-d. 1588
    NO ISSUE

JOST VON BOYNEBURG (LT. COL.)-b. 1554, d. APRIL 16, 1619 m. 1598 (1) ANNA
CATHARINA-d. 1600
    NO ISSUE

(2) ANNA VON HUNSTEIN-BORNHAGEN
ISSUE:
    ADAM-d. 1659
    <u>CURT LEOPOLD</u>
(3) AGNES VON KEUDEL
NO KNOWN ISSUE

<u>CURT LEOPOLD VON BOYNEBURG</u>-b. AUG. 18, 1609, d. 1673, m. SABINE SIBYLLE VON BOYNEBURG-m. ca. 1629 (COUSIN) b. 1611 d. 1674
ISSUE:
    ANNA SIDONIA
    JOST (m. AT ELBERBURG)
    AGRIPPINA
    <u>ANNA JULIANA</u>

<u>ANNA JULIANA VON BOYNEBURG</u>-b. ca. 1646, m. 1680 MATTHIAS SARTORIUS (Latinized version of SCHNEIDER). MATTHIAS MATRICULATED AT THE U. OF MARBURG MARCH 24, 1664.
ISSUE:
    MARGARETHA ELIZABETH-LIVED 6 YEARS
    <u>MARGARETHA CATHARINA</u>

<u>MARGARETHA CATHARINA SARTORIUS</u>-b. ca 1634 m. 1699 JOHANN PHILLIP RUBENKAM b. 1670, d. 1725
ISSUE:
    FRIEDRICH W.
    <u>CATHERINA JULIANA</u>
    JUSTICE W.
    MARGARETHA CATHERINA
    KARL W.
    ANNA CATHERINA
    JOHANNNA CATHERINA

<u>CATHERINA JULIANA RUBENKAM</u>-b. 1703, m. 1727 JACOB COLLIDAY (German spelling GALLADE) b. ca. 1706, d. BEFORE 1750
ISSUE:
    MARGRET CATHARINA
    ANNA MARIA-m. JOHN MELCHIOR MENG
    JACOB
    CATHARINE
    <u>SARAH</u>
    WILLIAM
    SUSANNA

SARAH COLLIDAY-b. MAY 12, 1737, d. 1778, m. ULRICH (Wollery) MENG (BROTHER TO MELCHIOR) IN PHILADELPHIA, PA JAN 10, 1760.
ISSUE:
WILLIAM
GEORGE
CHARLES
MARGARET
SARAH
JAMES E.
ANNA
SAMUEL

JAMES E. MENG-b. ca. 1771 PHILADELPHIA CO., PA, d. 1824 UNION CO, SC, m. SALLY LEWIS.-d. 1846 UNION, SC.
ISSUE:
CLOUGH
CHARLES
WILLIAM
JAMES E.
HENRY
GARLAND
FRANCIS
JOHN W.
JULIANA

CHARLES MENG (MING)-b. 1804 PRINCE EDWARD CO, VA, d. ca. 1860-1870 WINSTON CO, MS, m. (1) NANCY ? -b. ca. 1814, d. 1850 WINSTON CO, MS
ISSUE:
ELIZABETH
JAMES
JULIA
JOHN
JOSEPH
CHARLEY
(2) MARTHA HUDSPETH-d. 1868 WINSTON CO, MS
ISSUE:
FREDRICK
CLOUGH

The old country
Hessen (Hess)

"The country, known in early medieval times as Hessen centered around the Fulda, Werra, Eder and Lahn Rivers, forming part of the Frankish Kingdom under the Merovingian monarchs and the Carolingian sovereigns. At the time of the Rubenkam emigration to America, six principalities, distinguished from each other by additional and hyphenated names, comprised Hessen-Philippsthal, Hessen-Rheinfels-Rotenburg, Hessen-Rheinfels-Wanfried, Hessen-Darmstadt, and Hessen-Homburg. All of these were ruled by branches of the ancient House of Brabant; their ruling princes were called landgraves and their territories were known as landgraviates. The political division called Hessen-Rheinfels-Wanfried, the ancestral home of the Rubenkams, was a dependency of the more powerful landgraviate of Hessen-Kassel . . . Today (printed in 1961 in the PGM, Volume XXII, No. 2) Hessen lies directly west of the Eastern Zone of Germany. Wanfried, just inside the Western Zone, lies on the east bank of the Werra River. In 1693 it became the capital of the small landgraviate of Hessen-Rheinfels-Wanfried." Marburg is on the Lahn River and about 65 air miles southwest of Wanfried. Abertode is a village in Kreis Eschwege and is about six miles northwest of Eschwege. Eschwege is on the west bank of the Werra River and about 26 miles southeast of Kassel, and five miles west of Wanfried. The Sontra (see Boyneburg family) is a tributary of the Werra River and the rivers join north of Eschwege. ("The Rubenkam Family of Hessen," by Milton Rubencam, FASG)

Boyneburg is about 12 miles southwest of Eschwege and about two miles east of Wichmannshausen, which is on the Sontra River. In the Bild Atlas, the Boyneburg is marked as a tourist *aussichtspunkt* (vantage point). The area is now under study with archaeology digs.

Explanation: Hessen is the area and the dash separates the town such as Hessen-Kassel.

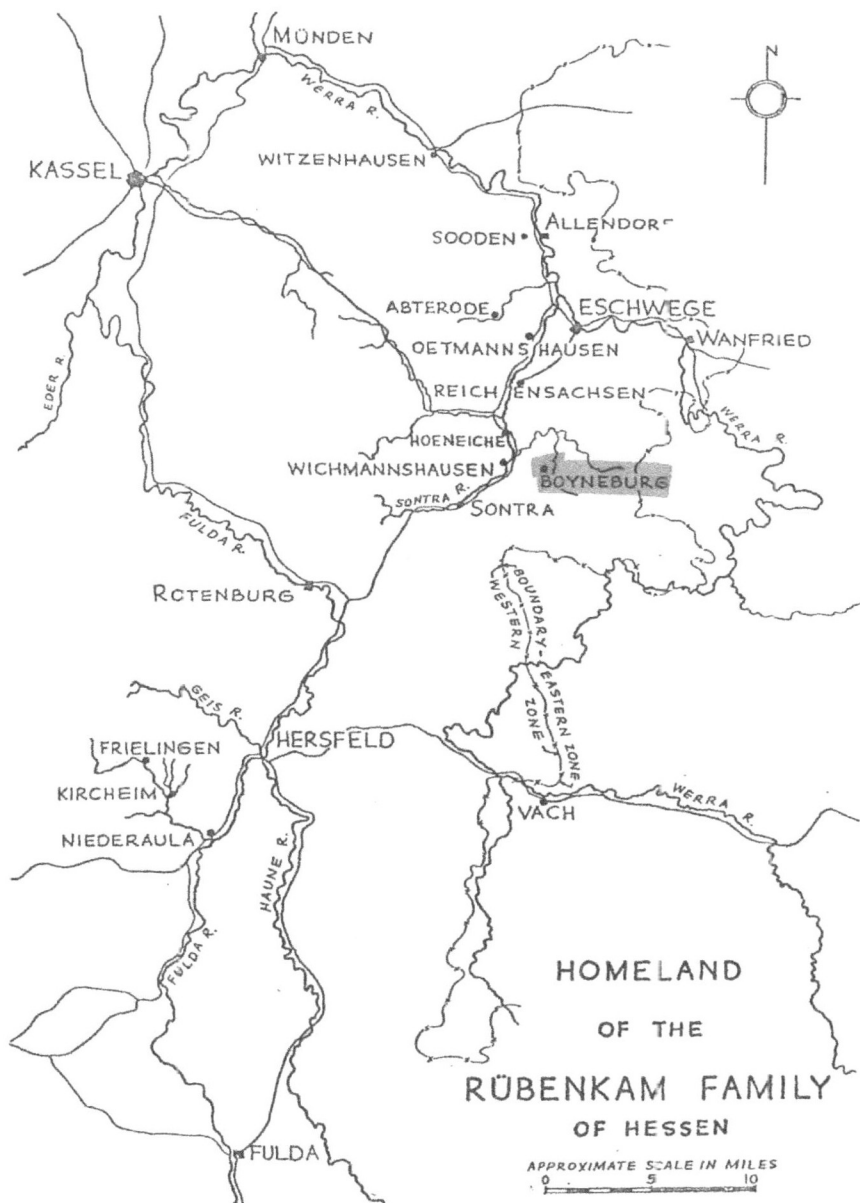

MÜNDEN

WERRA R.

WITZENHAUSEN

KASSEL

ALLENDORF

SOODEN

ABTERODE

ESCHWEGE

OETMANNSHAUSEN

WANFRIED

REICHENSACHSEN

EDER R.

WERRA R.

HOENEICHE

WICHMANNSHAUSEN

BOYNEBURG

SONTRA R.

SONTRA

FULDA R.

ROTENBURG

BOUNDARY—WESTERN ZONE

EASTERN ZONE

GEIS R.

FRIELINGEN

HERSFELD

KIRCHEIM

WERRA R.

NIEDERAULA

VACH

HAUNE R.

FULDA R.

HOMELAND

OF THE

RÜBENKAM FAMILY

OF HESSEN

APPROXIMATE SCALE IN MILES

0   5   10

FULDA

THE BOYNEBURG DESCENDANTS

Descendants of Heimbrod von Boyneburg

Generation No. 1

1. HEIMBROD[1] VON BOYNEBURG He married MARGARET VON ELBEN.

Notes for HEIMBROD VON BOYNEBURG:
"The Boyneburg family derives its name from the fortress (burg) of Boyneburg, which was a favorite residence of Emperor Frederick (I) Barbarossa in the twelfth century. It has been in the continuous possession of the House of Boyneburg for close to eight centuries, although it was abandoned as a residence in the fifthteen century when branches began to establish themselves in other castles and manor-houses." (*The Noble Ancestry of the Revercomb Family* by Milton Rubincam) *Note*: The Rivercomb (spelling change) family is of descent from the Rubenkam family.

Heimbrod IV von Boyneburg was a nobleman and a member of the early powerful Boyneburg family. The following is from a newspaper article in Germany, "Die Boyneburg am Ringgau," by Eduard Brauns; Translated into English by Hans Schneider, a friend of the writer's sister, Norma Ming Graham.

"Die Boyneburg am Ringgau"
(The Boyneburg in the Ringgau Area)

The old empire-fortress has rich historical past. Out of the valley of the rivers Sontra, Ulfe, and Netra on the western projection of the Ringgau, on a solid mountain 513 meters (about 1500 feet) high, in the older time a very powerful and proud castle stood, the empire fortress Boyneburg. Only a high tower, a chapel, and a few wall parts remain of the very rich historical past and significant construction close to the Hessen-Thuringischen border. Presumably the builders of Boyneburg were the powerful Earls of Northeim who needed a castle to guard their land in that area. Owners of the castle have been Earl Siegfried III who died in 1108. His son Siegfried IV, the last of the Earls of Northeim, was named "Comes de Boumeneburg." After he died in 1144, the castle was returned to the kingdom and became an empire-fortress in 1156. In this year King Fredrick Barbarossa signed a letter giving privileges to the monastery, Hildewarlshausen. The new owners of the Northeim-Fortress were the three lines of the lords of Boyneburg. Several times Emperor Barbarossa lived and ruled his land from his beloved castle, the Boyneburg. After coming back from his coronation in Italy, in the summer of 1166, and in 1188 when he was on his way to an empire meeting in Goslar and Mainz.

That was his last. He also built a chapel there honoring the Holy Virgin and St. Peter. After a fight for inheritance, the Earl Heinrich 1st from Brabard, took Hessen and eight fortresses along the river Werra, and also from Emperor Adolf von Nassu, the empire-castle Boyneburg. The lords of Boyneburg rebelled against their new ruler, Earl Heinrich I. In 1460, they compromised and received the deed for their castle and the surrounding villages. At the end of the 15th century, the lords of Boyneburg left their castle on the mountain and settled in the valley. Only an architect and a few soldiers were left behind. A hundred years later, only a caretaker lived there, checking the forest daily. He fed the priest after Sunday mass and guarded the prisoners. During the Thirty Years War (1618–1648), the proud empire-castle became plundered by General Tilly-Soldiers and finally in 1637 it was burned down by the Croation Soldiers. In 1672 the lords of Boyneburg divided the castle-forest in three equal parts to the three lines and let the castle rot down. The part that is left was founded in the 15th century and is on an outer part of the high plateau, which has been a hiding place at all times. A double trench with a pointed wall between divides the ruin from the other part of the plateau. The former castle yard is a narrow strip with the former five pointed tower on the south side, which was also the prison. In three stories you see loop-holes from where they could watch the three gates on the way to the castle yard. Over one gate the chapel was built by Barbarossa. In the year 1953, a variety of friends with the help of the Baron of Boyneburg and the Werra-Association restored the former chapel and the high tower.

By Eduard Brauns

This information was made possible by the writings of Milton Rubencam (see note below), also related to the Boyneburg family, and by Norma Ming Graham, who made a trip to Germany in 1994. While in Germany, she visited the Elberberg Castle that continues in the Butlar Family, and the village of Gut Boyneburg where the old castle ruins stand nearby, and continues in a branch of the Boyneburg family.

In 1998, the *Archäologische Denkmäler in Hessen*, a German published magazine, printed a story of archaeological digs around the castle (Boyneburg) ruin and grounds. The pictures tell an interesting story. A map shows the location of the digs, *schnitt* 1, 2, 3, and 4 near the ruin. Some of the items date back before the birth of Christ.

Note: "Mr. Rubincam is past president of the National Genealogical Society and of the Pennsylvania Historical Junto, vice president of the American Society of Genealogists, editor of the *National Genealogical Society Quarterly*, and editor of the recent publication of the American Society of Genealogists, 'Genealogical Research: Methods and Sources' (Washington, 1960)." ("The Noble Ancestry of the Rivercomb Family" by Milton Rubincam; footnote)

Child of HEIMBROD VON BOYNEBURG and MARGARET VON ELBEN is:

2.   i.   JOST[2] VON BOYNEBURG, d. 1589.

Generation No. 2

2. JOST² VON BOYNEBURG (*HEIMBROD¹*) died 1589. He married (1) CATHARINA VON BUTTLAR. She died 1554. He married (2) VON FALKEN ROHRDA. She died 1556. He married (3) VERONIKA VON SCHETZEL. She died 1588.

Notes for JOST VON BOYNEBURG:
Jost von Boyneburg was the son of Heimbrod IV Boyneburg and Margarethe von Elben. In the sixteenth century, he was co-owner of Elberburg Castle (pictured) in present-day Fritzlar, Germany. This was probably an inheritance as his father had obtained part ownership of the castle through his marriage to Margarethe, who is said to have descended from Emperor Charlemagne (*The Noble Ancestry of the Rivercomb Family*, by Milton Rubencam). According to Frau Butlar, the wife of a present-day descendant who lives in the village Elbenberg near the castle, the Boyneburgs had returned to their old homeland. The last 400 years, the Butlars have owned the Elberburg Castle.

Child of JOST VON BOYNEBURG and CATHARINA VON BUTTLAR is:

3.   i.   JOST³ VON BOYNEBURG, b. 1554; d. April 16, 1619.

Children of JOST VON BOYNEBURG and VON ROHRDA are:

     ii. PHILLIP³ VON BOYNEBURg.

     iii. Asmus von Boyneburg.

Generation No. 3

3. JOST³ VON BOYNEBURG (*JOST², HEIMBROD¹*) was born 1554, and died April 16, 1619. He married ANNA VON HANSTEIN-BORNHAGEN.

Notes for JOST VON BOYNEBURG:
Jost Boyneburg became a lieutenant colonel in the Hessian army. He died approximately six miles from the Boyneburg Castle. First, he married Anna Catharina, and she died in 1600 with no children. Second, he married Anna von Hunstein-Bornhagen, and they had two children, Adam Boyneburg and Curt Leopold Boyneburg. Third, he married Agnes Von Keudel with no issue.

Children of JOST VON BOYNEBURG and ANNA VON HANSTEIN-BORNHAGEN are:

4.   i.   CURT LEOPOLD⁴ von Boyneburg, b. August 18, 1609; d. 1673.

     ii. ADAM VON BOYNEBURG, d. 1659.

Generation No. 4

4. CURT LEOPOLD[4] VON BOYNEBURG (*JOST[3], JOST[2], HEIMBROD[1]*) was born August 18, 1609, and died 1673. He married SABINE SIBYLLE VON BOYNEBURG ca. 1629, daughter of SABINE SIBYLLE VON SCHOLLEY. She was born ca. 1611, and died 1674.

Notes for CURT LEOPOLD VON BOYNEBURG:
Sabine Sibylle von was Curt's first cousin.

Notes for SABINE SIBYLLE von BOYNEBURG:
Sabine Sibylle was the daughter of Jost Christoph Boyneburg, the grandson of the elder Jost von Boyneburg. (They were first cousins.)

Children of CURT VON BOYNEBURG and SABINE VON BOYNEBURG are:

5. i.   ANNA JULIANA[5] VON BOYNEBURG, b. ca. 1646.

    ii.   ANNA SIDONIA VON BOYNEBURG.

    iii. JOST VON BOYNEBURG.

    ### Notes for JOST VON BOYNEBURG:
    Married at Elberburg.

    iv.   AGRIPPINA VON BOYNEBURG.

Generation No. 5

5. ANNA JULIANA[5] VON BOYNEBURG (*CURT LEOPOLD[4], JOST[3], JOST[2], HEIMBROD[1]*) was born ca. 1646. She married MATTHIAS SARTORIUS 1680.

Notes for MATTHIAS SARTORIUS:
Matthias Satorius was pastor of Wichmannshausen, a village about three kilometers from Boyneburg castle. He was educated at the University of Marburg and graduated in 1664. He held the degree of magister, which is similar to MA degree.

Children of ANNA VON BOYNEBURG and MATTHIAS SARTORIUS are:

6. i.   MARGARETHA CATHARINA[6] SATORIUS, b. ca. 1684, Germany; d. 1727, Philadelphia Co., PA.

    ii.   Margaret Elizabeth Satorius.

Generation No. 6

6. MARGARETHA CATHARINA[6] SATORIUS (*ANNA JULIANA[5] VON BOYNEBURG, CURT LEOPOLD[4], JOST[3], JOST[2], HEIMBROD[1]*) was born ca. 1684 in Germany[1], and died 1727 in Philadelphia Co., PA[1]. She married JOHANN PHILLIP RUBENKAM July 19, 1699 in

Reichensachsen, Hessen Germany[1], son of ANDREAS RUBENKAM genannt
GLEIM. He was born April 20, 1670 in Wanfried, Germany, and died February 25,
1725 in Berleburg, Germany[1].

Notes for MARGARETHA CATHARINA SATORIUS:
Margaretha was baptized on February 26, 1684, at Reichensachsen, Germany. She was
nobly born to Anna Von Boyneburg genannt Hohenstein.

Notes for JOHANN PHILLIP RUBENKAM:
Johann Phillip Rubenkam (Rubencam) was the son of Andreas Rubenkam and the
grandson of Freidrich Rubenkam. He matriculated at the University of Marburg on
April 25, 1687, in theology. His professors were Dr. Samuel Andrea, second professor in
ordinary; Dr. Heinrich Duysing; Thomas Gautier, founder of the French community at
Marburg; Johannes May, professor of Greek and Posey; Maximilian Parcelli, professor
of eloquence and history; and Dr. Phillip Johann Tileman.

In 1692, he was granted "the expectancy (succession) to the parish at Wanfried
that had been held by his uncle Johannes Gleim, and in 1698, he became pastor there."
He married the daughter of Matthias Satorius, Margaretha. Margaretha's mother was
of the Boyneburg family and of noble blood. "In those days, when a man attained the
ministry, he was elevated to a social position 'nearly equal to nobility' and therefore was
eligible for the hand of a nobleman's daughter." Johann Philip was pastor at Wanfried for
nearly 19 years. Near the close of this time, it was said that his health had become bad.
"It appears, however, that an awkward situation had developed and that Rubenkam's
illness may have been a diplomat ailment, proposed as a smooth way to ease him out of
his office. "According to a letter written in 1716 by an Elder, Landgrave Wilheim, Johann
Phillip was refusing to conform to the Reformed religion as introduced into Hessen.
Soon after, he and his family moved westward taking up their exile at Berleburg, on the
Eder River . . ." There he died and was buried February 25, 1725. Margaretha died in
1727 and among 52 items listed in the estate was a "little still." (*The Rubenkam Family
of Hessen*, by Milton Rubenkam)

Johann's daughter Catharina Juliana married Jacob Colladay in 1727. They had
the following: Margaret Catherina (b. 1728), Anna Maria (b. 1731), Jacob Colladay (b.
1733), Catharine (b. 1735), Sarah (b. 1737) married Wollery Meng; William (b. 1738);
and Susanna (b. 1741).

Children of MARGARETHA SATORIUS and JOHANN RUBENKAM are:

i.   FRIEDRICH WILHEM[7] RUBENKAM, b. ca. 1702, Bristol Township, Philadelphia
     Co., PA[1].

     ### Notes for FRIEDRICH WILHEM RUBENKAM:
     Apparently, Friedrich never married.

ii. CATHARINA JULIANA RUBENKAM, b. ca. 1703, Bristol Township, Philadelphia
     Co., PA; d. February 16, 1774, Germantown, PA[1]; m. (1) BLASIUS DANIEL

MACKINET; m. (2) JACOB COLLADAY (GALATHE), November 24, 1727, Philadelphia, Pa[2]; b. 1707, Mannheim, Germany; d. ca. 1750, Germantown, Pa.

Notes for CATHARINA JULIANA RUBENKAM:
Godmother to Catharina was Catharina Agenta Crollius, daughter of the deceased Metropolitan of Sontra, Johannes Crollius II. Catharina Juliana Rubenkam is buried in the Upper Germantown Cemetery.

More About CATHARINA JULIANA RUBENKAM:
Baptism: October 4, 1703, Wanfried

Notes for BLASIUS DANIEL MACKINET:
Blasius Daniel Mackinet (Macknet) was the owner of the Greentree Inn (pictured) and was buried in Germantown Friends' ground on June 6, 1775. They had no children.

Notes for JACOB COLLADAY (GALATHE):
Jacob, his formal name was Johann Jacob Galathe (the name Colladay replaced Galathe when he came to America at an early age). He was baptized on February 3, 1707. Jacob and his family lived in or near Germantown, Pennsylvania. In the ledger of Benjamin Franklin in 1737 is the following: "Nov. 12, 1737 paid 2L & 4d to Jacob Koliday and charged to account of Wm. Deweese Jr." In 1737, Jacob purchased 94 acres in Philadelphia County (now Montgomery). After the purchase, Jacob built a paper mill on it. The mill was still in use to grind grain until 1939. The mill was on the banks of Sandy Run, a tributary of Wissahickon Creek. In 1740, he purchased 200 acres next to the 94 acres, but lying in the Upper Dublin Township. During his life, Jacob had been a busy man as he had been a miner, manufacturer of lime, manufacturer of paper, and a farmer at the same time. Jacob's daughter Sarah married John Ulrich (Wollery) Meng, son of John Christopher Meng. For more on Sarah and John Ulrich Meng, refer to the second generation in the "Descendants of John Christopher Meng."

iii.   JUSTUS WILHELM RUBENKAM, b. August 6, 1705.

Notes for JUSTUS WILHELM RUBENKAM:
Justus Rubenkam first married Katherine Conreds at First Presbyterian Church, Philadelphia, Pennsylvania. No known issue. Second, he married at the same church on April 2, 1742, Susanna Rittenhouse, daughter of Peter Rittenhouse. Their issue: Ann Rubenkam, Catherine Rubenkam, Margaret Rubenkam, Juliana Rubenkam, Sarah Rubenkam, Susanna Rubenkam, and Daniel Rubenkam.

iv.   KARL (CHARLES) WILHELM RUBENKAM.

Notes for KARL (CHARLES) WILHELM RUBENKAM:
Karl married Barbara Rittenhouse, daughter of Peter Rittenhouse.

More about KARL (CHARLES) WILHELM RUBENKAM:
Baptism: May 5, 1707

v.   ANNA CATHERINA RUBENKAM, b. February 25, 1709.

Notes for ANNA CATHERINA RUBENKAM:
Anna Catherina Rubenkam married John Wister in Philadelphia on November 10, 1737. They had the following issue: John Wister, Daniel Wister, William Wister, Catherine Wister, and William Wister. John Wister Sr. died in 1789

vi. JOHANNA CATHERINA RUBENKAM, B. MAY 31, 1711.

VII. MARGARETHA CATHERINA RUBENKAM, b. July 5, 1713.

DESCENDANTS OF FREIDRICH RUBENKAM

Descendants of Freidrich Rubenkam

Generation No. 1

1. FREIDRICH[2] RUBENKAM *(HANS CASPER[1])* was born ca. 1598, and died April 3, 1647. He married ANNA GERTRUDE UNDERBERG in Frielingen (?), Germany, daughter of NICHOLAS UNDERBURG and ANNA RICKGANS. She died February 11, 1681 in Oetmannshausen, Hessen.

Notes for FREIDRICH RUBENKAM:
A native of the city of Cassel, Freidrich was about 19 when he matriculated from the University of Marburg in 1617. This is the oldest Protestant University that was founded in 1527 by Landgrave Phillip the Magnanimous of Hessen. Here is where Luther and Zwingli had their dispute in 1529. "Freidrich majored in theology under such distinguished Reformed (Calvinist) savants as Johann Crocius, Raphael Egli, and Gregorius Schonfeld the Elder." He graduated in 1619 with a degree of magister which is "equivalent to the English master of arts." "He then served successively as a tutor in the noble families of Spede and von Hanstein at Frielingen, as pastor at Niederaula, near Hersfeld from 1623 to 1626 . . . Pastor Rubenkam and his family was caught in the whirlpool of the Thirty Years War . . . Rubenkam and his family took up exile at Abterode, a few miles northwest of Eschwege. There the pastor spent two years in exile, and then a reversal of fortune carried him back to his parish church at Frielingen. (On December 2, 1631 . . . the most illustrious and powerful Prince Wilhem, Landgrave of Hessen, took force and with the sword, and commanded that we preachers who had been previously driven away should be graciously restored to our former places . . . On the first day of Christmas Day 1631, we all began to sing Lobwasser's Psalms of David, and began with Psalm 130: Out of the depths.)" ("The Rubenkam Family of Hessen," by Friedrich Rubenkam)

> "Later that year the Rubenkams removed from Frielinger to Herolz, in the bishopric of Fulda, where they remained until 1635 when a sudden invasion of Croatians drove them out with great loss. Once again, they fled to Abterode. The year 1635 was a tragic one for Paster Rubenkam: in addition to the Croation invasion, the plague swept the land and four members of his family succumbed to its ravages: Freidrich's little daughters Elisabeth and Anna Sibylla were buried on October 5, 1635; a certain Hans Casper Rubenkam, Perhaps Freidrich's brother, was buried on October 30; and his mother-in-law, who had accompanied them on their flight, perished.
> "Freidrich remained at Abterode for about another year, and

then accepted a call to the ruined town of Wichmannshausen, where he was installed on October 22, 1636, as pastor by Inspector Casper Josephi of Alendorf. Wichmannshausen, on the Sontra River with a present population of 731 inhabitants, in the seventeenth century was an estate of the Boyneburg family, with which Pastor Rubenkam's grandson, Johann Phillip, was to ally himself matrimonially." ("The Rubenkam Family of Hessen")

Freidrich died in 1647.

Notes for ANNA GERTRUDE UNDERBERG:
Anna Gertrud Underburg was the daughter of Nicholas Underburg and his wife Anna Rickgans of Abterode, Germany. After the death of her husband, she lived at Oetmannshausen. In 1667, her son, Andreas Rubenkam, entered the University of Marburg.

Children of FREIDRICH RUBENKAM and ANNA UNDERBERG are:

2.   i.   ANDREAS[3] RUBENKAM, b. ca. 1642, Oetmannshausen, Germany; d. March 3, 1698, Eschwege, Germany.

    ii.   JOHANN GEORG RUBENKAM, b. ca. 1626.

Notes for JOHANN GEORG RUBENKAM:
Johann Georg Rubenkam married Juliana Margaretha Stuckrath. In 1667, he was tax collector (Rentmeister) of Eschwege. He married secondly, Elisabeth Rexrodt baptized on June 30, 1633.

    In the record is the following: "... he listed his house, farm, garden and barns, as well as his fields and meadows, specifically listing the following pieces of property owned by him: one acre of land behind the Freiheit; one acre of the old farms (ein acker adten Hoofe); One acre along the Kupferbach—literally Cooper Brook, apparently the name of a brook at or near Abterode; one acre ... and three quarters of an acre on the Middleburg, a hill near Abterode ..." ("The Rubenkam Family of Hessen")

    iii.   ELISABETH RUBENKAM, B. CA. 1631.

    IV.   ANNA SIBYLLA RUBENKAM, B. CA. 1632.

    V.   CHRISTOPH RUBENKAM.

    VI.   (UNNAMED) RUBENKAM.

    VII.   LAURENTIUS RUBENKAM.

Notes for LAURENTIUS RUBENKAM.
Laurentius had a son, Johann Heinrich, "while a student in the University of Hebron, he wrote a scholarly theological dissertation on the letters to the seven communities in Asia Minor (1693)."

viii. ANNA GERTRUDE RUBENKAM, b. ca. 1644.

Notes for Anna Gertrude Rubenkam:
Anna first married Otto Beck, and their issues were Christoph Beck, Johann Georg Beck, and Laurentius Beck. She second married Johannes Widitz and had a daughter, Catharine Julianna Widitz.

Generation No. 2

2. ANDREAS[3] RUBENKAM (*FREIDRICH*[2], *HANS CASPER*[1]) was born ca. 1642 in Oetmannshausen, Germany, and died March 3, 1698 in Eschwege, Germany. He married CATHARINA JULIANA GLEIM June 7, 1669, daughter of BALTHASAR GLEIM and ANNA CROLLIUS. She was born ca. 1647 in Rotenburg, Germany, and died November 22, 1722 in Eschwedge, Germany.

Notes for ANDREAS RUBENKAM:
Born in Oetmannshausen, Andreas moved to Eschwege where "on May 5, 1660, he was matriculated at the University of Marburg as a theological student under the name of Andreas Rubenkam Eschwegensis . . . Nine years later on June 7, 1669, Andreas Rubenkam married Catharina Juliana Gleim, who was born at Rotenburg about 1647, daughter of Pastor Balthasar Gleim and his wife Anna Margaretha Crollius. The Gleim ancestry of Andreas Rubenkam's wife has been traced with certainty to one Jacob Gleim who was born at Eschwege about 1530. He was a . . . master tanner, and was recorded as a householder at Eschwege in 1553 . . . The Crollius family first appears in the documents at Marburg in 1447 . . ." He, Andreas, became assistant pastor at Eschwege-Neustadt and pastor in 1672. Andreas' home on the marketplace was still standing about 1961. ("The Rubenkam Family of Hessen," by Milton Rubincam)

Notes for CATHARINA JULIANA GLEIM:
The ancestry of Catharina has been traced to Jacob Glime (Gleim), born at Eschwege about 1530. He was a Lobermeister (master tanner) and a householder at Eschwege in 1553. Jacob had two sons, Curt Gleim and Hans Gleim. Curt Gleim was born about 1565 and was a master tanner and had a son Hans Gleim. Catharina was the daughter of Pastor Balthasar Gleim and his wife Anna Margaretha Crollius. Pastor Balthasar Gleim, one of seven children, was the grandson of Curt Gleim and son of Hans and Anna Gleim. Balthasar was born about September 24, 1616. Catharina married Andreas Rubenkam.

For more on the descendants of this family refer to the "Descendants of Heimbrod von Boyneburg," generation no. 6, Margaretha Catharina Satorius and Johann Phillip Rubenkam.

Children of ANDREAS RUBENKAM and CATHARINA GLEIM are:

i.   JOHANN PHILLIP[4] RUBENKAM, b. April 20, 1670, Wanfried, Germany[1]; d.
     February 25, 1725, Berleburg, Germany[1]; m. MARGARETHA CATHARINA
     SATORIUS, July 19, 1699, Reichensachsen, Hessen Germany[1]; b. ca. 1684,
     Germany[1]; d. 1727, Philadelhia Co., PA[1].

Notes for JOHANN PHILLIP RUBENKAM:

Johann Phillip Rubenkam (Rubencam) was the son of Andreas Rubenkam
and the grandson of Freidrich Rubenkam. He matriculated at the University
of Marburg on April 25, 1687, in theology. His professors were Dr. Samuel
Andrea, second professor in ordinary; Dr. Heinrich Duysing; Thomas Gautier,
founder of the French community at Marburg; Johannes May, professor of
Greek and Posey; Maximilian Parcelli, professor of eloquence and history;
and Dr. Phillip Johann Tileman.

In 1692, he was granted "the expectancy (succession) to the parish at
Wanfried that had been held by his uncle Johannes Gleim, and in 1698, he
became pastor there." He married the daughter of Matthias Satorius, Margaretha.
Margaretha's mother was of the Boyneburg family and of noble blood. "In those
days, when a man attained the ministry, he was elevated to a social position
'nearly equal to nobility' and therefore was eligible for the hand of a nobleman's
daughter." Johann Philip was pastor at Wanfried for nearly 19 years. Near
the close of this time, it was said that his health had become bad. "It appears,
however, that an awkward situation had developed and that Rubenkam's illness
may have been a diplomat ailment, proposed as a smooth way to ease him out of
his office." According to a letter written in 1716 by an elder, Landgrave Wilheim,
Johann Phillip was refusing to conform to the Reformed religion as introduced
into Hessen. Soon after, he and his family moved westward taking up their exile
at Berleburg, on the Eder River . . ." There he died and was buried on February
25, 1725. Margaretha died in 1727, and among 52 items listed in the estate was
a "little still." ("The Rubenkam Family of Hessen," by Milton Rubenkam)

Johann's daughter Catharina Juliana married Jacob Colladay in 1727.
They had the following issues: Margaret Catherina (b. 1728), Anna Maria (b.
1731), Jacob Colladay (b. 1733), Catharine (b. 1735), Sarah (b. 1737) married
Wollery Meng; William (b. 1738); and Susanna (b. 1741).

Notes for MARGARETHA CATHARINA SATORIUS:

Margaretha was baptized on February 26, 1684, at Reichensachsen, Germany.
She was nobly born to Anna Von Boyneburg genannt Hohenstein.

ii. JOHANN FRIEDRIC RUBENKAM, b. January 25, 1672.

Notes for JOHANN FRIEDRIC RUBENKAM:

Matriculated at the University of Marburg on November 13, 1688, and was
rector of the Eschwege School.

iii. Anna Margaretha Rubenkam, b. November 4, 1673.

Notes for Anna Margaretha Rubenkam:
Anna Margaretha was born at Eschwege. She married Hieronymus Wigard Dircks (Dirksen), son of Friedrick Dirksen and wife Catharina Elizabeth Behran on June 1, 1769. Her husband matriculated at the University of Marburg in 1683 and became a teacher at Eschwege School in 1691 and in 1697 was chosen Konrector (rector). He was the editor of two theological works. Issues: Ernst Andreas Dircks and Catherina Margaretha Dircks. Catherina Dircks was born in 1702 and died in Berlin, Prussia, July 11, 1770. She married Johann Phillip Heinius (Hein) in 1725. Johann Phillip studied at Schmalkalden Gymnasium and the University of Bremen. He had many great accomplishments. One, he was elected to the Royal Accademy of Sciences at Berlin on April 19, 1732. In 1763, he was honored by a long audience with Frederick the Grear, king of Prussia, which touched on many topics. ("The Rubenkam Family of Hessen" by Milton Rubencam)

iv. Catharina Elizabeth Rubenkam, b. March 10, 1676.

Notes for Catharina Elizabeth Rubenkam:
Johann Andreas married Catharina Elisabeth Lober. He matriculated from the University of Marburg in 1696.

v. Johann Andreas Rubenkam, b. May 10, 1677.

vi. Michael Wilheim Rubenkam, b. August 19, 1680.

Notes for Michael Wilheim Rubenkam:
Michael matriculated at the University of Marburg in September 1696.

vii. Maria Juliana Rubenkam, b. June 25, 1684.

viii. Johann Karl Rubenkam, b. July 11, 1686.

ix. Johann Georg Peter Rubenkam, b. July 29, 1689.

Endnotes

1. Milton Rubencam, *The Pennsylvania Genealogy Magazine, The Rubenkam Family of Hessen.*

DESCENDANTS OF HANS GLEIM

Descendants of Hans Gleim

Generation No. 1

1. HANS[1] GLEIM was born ca. 1595 in Eschwege, Germany. He married ANNA SOILNER ca. 1615.

Child of HANS GLEIM and ANNA SOILNER is:

2.   i.   BALTHASAR[2] GLEIM, b. ca. September 24, 1616, Eschwege, Germany; d. December 23, 1675, Wanfried.

Generation No. 2

2. BALTHASAR[2] GLEIM *(HANS[1])* was born ca. September 24, 1616 in Eschwege, Germany, and died December 23, 1675 in Wanfried. He married ANNA MARGARETHA CROLLIUS July 17, 1644 in Eschwege, Germany, daughter of JOHANNES CROLLIUS and CATHARINA GEITER.

Notes for BALTHASAR GLEIM:
On April 9, 1635, Balthasar "matriculated a theological student at the University of Kassel which had temporarily replaced the University of Marburg during the Thirty Years' War." The ancestry of Balthasar Gleim (Glime) has been traced to Jacob Gleim who was born about 1530 in Eschwege. Jacob was a master tanner and had two sons, Curt and Jacob Gleim. Curt Gleim was a tanner also and lived in a section of Eschwege called Bruhl. He was born about 1565. In 1606, his property was valued at 175 gulden. Curt had a son Hans Gleim who followed his dad's business. Hans was born ca. 1595 and married Anna Soilner. Balthasar was one of their seven children. Balthasar Gleim became the pastor at Wanfried on the Werra River. ("The Rubenkam Family of Hessen," by Milton Rubencam)

Notes for ANNA MARGARETHA CROLLIUS:
The Crollius family first appears in the records at Marburg in 1447, with the name Contz Krol (Krul, Kroll). By 1656, the name Kroll was Latinized to Crollius. Contz Krol died about 1456. A son, Henne Kroll, was a woolenweaver at Marburg and was living as late as 1499. Henne Kroll's wife was Cathrein Krein and they had a son Michel (Michael) Kroll. Michel had a son Ebert that was a woolenweaver at Marburg in 1537. He had five sons and one, Matthaeus Kroll, was a woolenweaver in 1586 and was still living in 1632. He and wife Elisabeth had six children of which one, Jacob Kroll, was the landlord of the inn Zum Adler (At the Sign of the Eagle) at Marburg in 1618. He married Margarethe Ruppersburg. They had seven children. Of these seven, three are

known; Heinrich Kroll, a pastor of Breitenbach; Burkhard Kroll, a cavalryman and saddler in the army of the Duke of Saxe-Weimar; and Johannes Kroll that was born on September 1599 at Marburg.

Johannes Kroll (Crollius) was educated and received his master's degree at Marburg in 1617. In 1619, he married Catharina Geiter, daughter of Benedictus Geiter of Breithard in the Taunus Mountains. He became a rector (head) of the Eschwege School in 1629 and then assistant pastor at Eschwege-Neustadt in 1632. From 1634 to 1653, he was dean and court preacher at Rotenburg and, in the latter years, was the metropolitan (chief) of Hersfeld. He also became rector of the Hersfeld Gymnasium (classical school). He died at Hersfeld on October 19, 1669.

Catherine Geiter Crollius, wife of Johannes Crollius above, died on January 28, 1681, and is buried at Wanfried. Johannes and Catherine Crollus had the following children: Phillip Thomas, an attorney at Rottenburg; Anna Margaretha that married Balthasar Gleim and mother of Catharina Julina (Gleim) Rubenkam; Wilhelm Jost was a capitan in the militia and five times mayor of Hersfeld; Johannes Crollius II, metropolitan of Sontra; Anna Catharina; Johannes Laurentius, a doctor of theology and rector of the University of Heidelberg and of the University of Marburg in 1699; and one son that died young. ("The Rubenkam Family of Hessen," by Milton Rubencam)

Children of BALTHASAR GLEIM and ANNA CROLLIUS are:

i.   CATHARINA JULIANA[3] GLEIM, b. ca. 1647, Rotenburg, Germany; d. November 22, 1722, Eschwedge, Germany; m. ANDREAS RUBENKAM, June 7, 1669; b. ca. 1642, Oetmannshausen, Germany; d. March 3, 1698, Eschwege, Germany.

Notes for CATHARINA JULIANA GLEIM:

The ancestry of Catharina has been traced to Jacob Glime (Gleim), born at Eschwege about 1530. He was a Lobermeister (master tanner) and a householder at Eschwege in 1553. Jacob had two sons, Curt Gleim and Hans Gleim. Curt Gleim was born about 1565 and was a master tanner and had a son Hans Gleim. Catharina was the daughter of Pastor Balthasar Gleim and his wife Anna Margaretha Crollius. Pastor Balthasar Gleim, one of seven children, was the grandson of Curt Gleim and son of Hans and Anna Gleim. Balthasar was born about September 24, 1616. Catharina married Andreas Rubenkam.

For more on the descendants of this family refer to the "Descendants of Heimbrod von Boyneburg," generation no. 6, Margaretha Catharina Satorius and Johann Phillip Rubenkam.

Notes for ANDREAS RUBENKAM:

Born in Oetmannshausen, Andreas moved to Eschwege where "on May 5, 1660, he was matriculated at the University of Marburg as a theological student under the name of Andreas Rubenkamm Eschwegensis . . . Nine years later, on June 7, 1669, Andreas Rubenkam married Catharina Juliana Gleim who was born at Rotenburg about 1647, daughter of Pastor Balthasar

Gleim and his wife Anna Margaretha Crollius. The Gleim ancestry of Andreas Rubenkam's wife has been traced with certainty to one Jacob Gleim who was born at Eschwege about 1530. He was a . . . master tanner, and was recorded as a householder at Eschwege in 1553 . . . The Crollius family first appears in the documents at Marburg in 1447 . . ." He, Andreas, became assistant pastor at Eschwege-Neustadt and pastor in 1672. Andreas' home on the marketplace was still standing about 1961. ("The Rubenkam Family of Hessen," by Milton Rubincam)

ii.   PHILLIP GLEIM, b. 1649.

Notes for PHILLIP GLEIM:
Philip Gleim grauted from the Universities of Marburg, Bremen, Hanau, Helmstadt and Erfurt, judge and councillor at the Rotenburg Chancery.

iii.   JOHANNES GLEIM, b. 1653.

Notes for JOHANNES GLEIM:
Johannes Gleim graduated from the University of Marburg and was pastor at Wanfried and replaced his father as successor.

DESCENDANTS OF JOHN SHELTON (CHILTON)— THE PATRICK HENRY CONNECTION

Descendants of John Shelton (Chilton)

Generation No. 1

1. JOHN SHELTON[2] (CHILTON) (*JAMES[1] SHELTON*) was born Bef. 1649[1,2], and died 1706. He married JANE.

Notes for JOHN SHELTON (CHILTON):

John owned "Currioman" in Westmoreland County, Virginia. He bought "Carotoman" in Lancaster County. He was Vestryman in St. Paul Church in 1705. Built "Rural Plains" Shelton home in Hanover County in 1670. As of 1962, it was still owned by male descendants. This home was under shell fire in three wars. Record at "Rural Plains" in Richmond says John is son of James Shelton. "Rural Plains" is also the place that Sarah Shelton married Patrich Henry.

Early Sheltons

"It has always been conceded that the John Shelton of 'Rural Plains' was descended from Sir John Shelton, of Shelton Hall, Norfolk, England, and his wife Anne Boleyn. As Lady Anne Shelton was a great aunt of Queen Elizabeth's, the English records are very complete, and are part of the history of England in her Doomsday Book.

"After Elizabeth was crowned she sent for the family at Shelton Hall, who had given her shelter many times when she was so bitterly persecuted, and they lived at the Court for fifty years until the death of Elizabeth in 1603." ("The Shelton Family," by Mrs. A. E. Whitaker)

Children of JOHN (CHILTON) and JANE are:

i.   MARY[3] SHELTON.

Notes for MARY SHELTON:

Married John Sharp, Lancaster, Pennsylvania.

ii.   SARAH SHELTON.

Notes for Sarah Shelton:

First married Richard Grissage and second married Joseph Bickley.

iii. ELIZABETH SHELTON.

Notes for Elizabeth Shelton:
Married Byran Graves.

The Shelton House near Totopotomy Creek, Virginia, where Sarah Shelton married the Col. Patriot Patrick Henry.

iv. Thomas SHELTON, d. 1738.

Notes for THOMAS SHELTON:

v. CAPT. JOHN SHELTON, b. 1666[3,4]; d. 1726, VA[4].

Notes for Capt. John Shelton:
Signed name as Chilton Jr., first married Lattice Ball, second Mary Watts. Inherited d. "Currioman."

3. vi. WILLIAM SHELTON, b. 1676, Hanover Co., VA; d. 1734, Hanover, Co., VA.

Generation No. 2

2. WILLIAM[3] SHELTON (*JOHN SHELTON[2] (CHILTON), JAMES[1] SHELTON*) was born 1676 in Hanover Co., VA[4], and died 1734 in Hanover, Co., VA[4]. He married (1) HANNAH ARMISTEAD. He married (2) HANNAH ARMISTEAD December 10, 1698 in Elizabeth City Co., VA.

Notes for HANNAH ARMISTEAD:
Hannah was the daughter of Anthony Armistead.

Children of WILLIAM SHELTON and HANNAH ARMISTEAD are:

i. JAMES[4] SHELTON, d. 1753[4].

Notes for JAMES SHELTON:
James had land grants in Henrico County, Virginia (1723–1726), of 7,000 acres on record in Essex and Goochland Counties. He was appointed to supervise rebuilding the old capital at Williamsburg. He married Mary Bathurst. His son Bathurst Shelton (b. 1744) and Thomas Jefferson (third president) were rivals for the hand of "Patty" at William and Mary's College. (The Sheltons)

ii. JOHN SHELTON, d. September 11, 1777, Brandywine[4].

Notes for JOHN SHELTON:
John was a captain in the American Revolution. He enlisted on January 1, 1777, and was killed at Brandywine. He inherited "Rural Plains" and was in possession of "Currioman" when he was killed. He married Elanor Parks

about 1727, daughter of William Parks, first editor of Virginia and Maryland. Sarah, the daughter of John and Eleanor, born 1738, married Patrick Henry on October 1754, the early famous patriot.

iii. MARY SHELTON.

iv. DAVID SHELTON.

v. JOSEPH SHELTON.

Notes for JOSEPH SHELTON:
Will filled 1784.

vi. WILLIAM SHELTON.

vii. RALPH SHELTON, D. 1776.

viii. RICHARD SHELTON, D. BEF. 1780[4].

3. ix. SAMUEL SHELTON, b. 1703, Albermarle Co., VA; d. 1793, Albermarle Co., VA.

Generation No. 3

3. SAMUEL[4] SHELTON (WILLIAM[3], JOHN SHELTON[2] (CHILTON), JAMES[1] SHELTON) was born 1703 in Albermarle Co., VA[4], and died 1793 in Albermarle Co., VA[4]. He married JUDITH CLOUGH ANDERSON, daughter of ROBERT ANDERSON and ELIZABETH CLOUGH.

Notes for SAMUEL SHELTON:
According to the "History of Albermarle," by Edgar Woods, "Samuel Shelton was settled in Albermarle Co. from the beginning. In 1745 he purchased five hundred fifty acres of the twelve hundred acre tract on James River, granted to Thomas Gooles by 1732; the endorsement on the conveyance of this land made in 1788 expressly mentions the destruction of the records by the British in 1781. Samuel died in 1793. His wife's name was Judith and his children were Clough, Joseph, Samuel, David, Elizabeth, the wife of John Tindall, and the wife of John Lewis, who lived near Scot's Landing . . . Samuel (Junior) in the early part of the century was engaged in business in Warren, Virginia. In partnership with William Walker and John Staples, under the style of Samuel & Co., he conducted a large mill and distillery at that place. In 1810 he purchased from Governor W. C. Nicholas the Boiling Spring Plantation, which his son after sold to John Patterson the Governor's son-in-law. He died in 1826." ("History of Albermarle")

Samuel Shelton's granddaughter, Sally (Sarah) Lewis Meng married James Meng. For more on this family, refer to "John Christopher Meng and Many Descendants," generation 3.

Notes for JUDITH CLOUGH ANDERSON:
Judith Clough was the daughter of Robert and Elizabeth Clough Anderson.

Children of SAMUEL SHELTON and JUDITH ANDERSON are:

i.   ELIZABETH[5] SHELTON, d. Bef. 1792, Albermarle Co., VA[4]; m. JOHN LEWIS JR., Bef. 1780, Albermarle Co., VA[4]; b. 1749, VA[5]; d. 1804, Albermarle, Co., VA[6].

Notes for ELIZABETH SHELTON:
Elizabeth was married first to John Tindall. They had one daughter, Elizabeth Shelton Tindall. According to the book *Sheltons*, she married second John Lewis Jr. Her father was Samuel Shelton. In the will of Samuel Shelton, his grandchildren are mentioned, including Sarah (married James E. Meng), daughter of John Lewis Jr. Elizabeth Shelton's mother, Judith Clough, was the daughter of Robert Anderson and Elizabeth Clough. Elizabeth Clough was a daughter of Richard Clough and Ann Poindexter. Elizabeth Shelton's cousin, Sarah Shelton, married Patrick Henry. Although Elizabeth is not blood kin to Patrick, she is directly related to his offspring. Note: Sarah Lewis Meng was second cousin to Sarah, wife of Patrick Henry. Also, the relationship of Sarah Meng to the Clough family explains how the name "Clough" became a given name to some in the Ming family. For more on the descendants of Elizabeth, refer to "James and Sarah (Sally) Meng."

Notes for JOHN LEWIS JR.:
John Lewis first married Elizabeth Shelton, daughter of Samuel Shelton of Albermarle County, Virginia. Second he married Sarah Thomson, daughter of Waddy Thomson Sr.

ii.   JOSEPH SHELTON.

Notes for JOSEPH SHELTON:
Joseph was a colonel in Revolutionary War in Nelson County, Virginia Legislature (1813–1824); married Mary Harris on August 1, 1785, in Amherst.

iii. CLOUGH SHELTON, d. Nelson, Co., VA[7].

Notes for CLOUGH SHELTON:
Captain Clough was one of the signers of the Albermarle Declaration of Independence, served on the Virginia Line and was captured at Charleston, South Carolina. His wife was Mildred Fleming.

iv.   SAMUEL SHELTON, b. Albermarle VA; d. October 24, 1822, Union, SC.

Notes for SAMUEL SHELTON:

Moved from Albermarle to Union, South Carolina (ca 1801). (Note: There is a discrepancy here with the data of Samuel and the data in the book *The Sheltons*.)

v. DAVID SHELTON, b. 1750, Albermarle, Co., VA[8]; d. 1820, Fairfield, Co., SC.

Notes for DAVID SHELTON:

David was a captain in the Amherst County militia in Virginia in 1779.

Endnotes

1. Z.T. Shelton, *The Sheltons*, (Published 1962).
2. *Will dated Nov. 15, 1706, Westmoreland Co., VA.*
3. *The Shelton Family.*
4. Z.T. Shelton, *The Sheltons*, (Published 1962).
5. Sarah Travers Lewis (Scott) Anderson, *Lewises, Meriwethers and Their Kin.*
6. Rev. Edgar Woods, *Albermarle County in Virginia*, (The Green Bookman, Bridgewater, VA).
7. Z.T. Shelton, *The Sheltons*, (Published 1962).
8. *The Shelton Family.*

DESCENDANTS OF SAMUEL (BURDINE)

Descendants of Samuel Bourdin (Burdine)

Generation No. 1

1. SAMUEL BOURDIN[2] (BURDINE) *(MARC[1] BOURDIN)* was born ca. 1658 in Bordeaux, France. He married MARTHA CHARNEAU May 2, 1682 in Bordeau, France, daughter of PIERRE CHARNEAU and RACHEL ROY.

Notes for SAMUEL BOURDIN (BURDINE):
Samuel was apprenticed by his father to a master smith and jeweler in 1673.

Children of SAMUEL (BURDINE) and MARTHA CHARNEAU are:

2.   i.   RICHARD[3] BURDINE, b. ca. 1787, France; d. 1761, Culpepper, VA.

    ii.   PIERRE BURDINE BURDINE.

Generation No. 2

2. RICHARD[3] BURDINE *(SAMUEL BOURDIN[2] (BURDINE), MARC[1] BOURDIN)* was born ca. 1787 in France, and died 1761 in Culpepper, VA. He married CATHERINE TANNER, daughter of ROBERT TANNER.

Notes for RICHARD BURDINE:
Richard Burdine "was apparently the first of this family in America. According to the Treasurer's Report of 1733, Richard Burdine was listed as a member of the Hebron Lutheran Church, or 'Old Dutch Church' in Madison County, Virginia, in the same year that Rev. Casper Stoever became its pastor." According to the "Burdine Family," by Arvalean L. (Burdine) Petrics, often repeated legends is that Richard was a Huguenot who came from France to the Albermarle Sound in North Carolina. However, he was in Madison County, Virginia in 1733. Also, according to Rev. Stoever, his pastor in 1733, and printed reports in Weimer, 1738, the Burdines came from Alsace the Palatinate and neighboring districts of Germany and Switzerland. (Burdine Family)

Children of RICHARD BURDINE and CATHERINE TANNER are:

  i.   REGINALD[4] BURDINE.

  ii.   HANNAH BURDINE.

    Notes for HANNAH BURDINE:
    Married Robert V. Shotwell

iii.   BARBARA BURDINE.

Notes for BARBARA BURDINE:
Moved to Abbeville, South Carolina with brother Regina.d. Their descendant was governor of Georgia, Joe E. Brown, during Civil War.

iv.   NATHANIEL BURDINE.

Notes for NATHANIEL BURDINE:
Moved to Wilkes County, North Carolina; thence to Newberry, South Carolina, with his brother Samuel.

3.   v.   SAMUEL BURDINE, b. May 29, 1745, Madison Co., VA; d. Aft. October 12, 1818, SC.

Generation No. 3

3. SAMUEL[4] BURDINE (*RICHARD[3], SAMUEL BOURDIN[2] (BURDINE), MARC[1] BOURDIN*) was born May 29, 1745 in Madison Co., VA[1], and died Aft. October 12, 1818 in SC. He married MARY EDDINS 1771 in Virginia. She was born July 1, 1754[1].

Notes for SAMUEL BURDINE:
In 1784, Samuel patented 100 acres in Wilkes County, North Caro.ina. By 1790, he was in Newberry County, South Carolina, and there in 1792, he bought 200 acres on Kings Creek at old Saluda Road. On May 12, 1796, he purchased 996 acres on George Creek near Anderson, South Carolina (Burdine Family). An earlier source has Samuel married to Mary Fletcher. A more recent document clearly states that Samuel was married to Mary Eddins and Nathaniel to Anne Eddins (source: Carol Ann Burdine).

Children of SAMUEL BURDINE and MARY EDDINS are:

i.   JOHN[5] FLETCHER SR. BURDINE, b. January 21, 1772, Madison Co., VA[1]; d. May 7, 1845, Smithville, Ms.

Notes for JOHN FLETCHER SR. BURDINE:
John's grandson, William Murrah Burdine, in October 1898 moved to Miami, Florida, and founded the merchandising firm of Willia.m Burdine and Son. It was located on Miami Avenue, and shortly before his death, it was moved around the corner on Flagler Street, and which firm subsequently expanded into the large department store, Burdines, Inc.

4.   ii.   RICHARD BURDINE, b. August 6, 1773, Virginia; d. Septembe: 1, 1860, PICKENS Co., SC.

iii.   HENry BURDINE, B. 1774, MADISON, CO., VA1.
iv.   ABRAHAM BURDINE, b. 1776, Madison Co., VA[1]; d. Aft. 1821.

Generation No. 4

4. RICHARD[5] BURDINE (*SAMUEL[4], RICHARD[3], SAMUEL BOURDIN[2] (BURDINE), MARC[1] BOURDIN*) was born August 6, 1773 in Virginia, and died September 1, 1860 in Pickens Co., SC. He married MARTHA "PATSY" WILSON, daughter of JOHN WILSON. She was born 1777 in Wilkes Co., NC[1], and died November 10, 1861 in Pickens, SC.

Notes for RICHARD BURDINE:

Richard joined the Methodist Episcopal Church at six years old and spent his life being respected as a loved Christian man. The home of Richard and Patsy was about five miles southeast of the cemetery where they were buried in Pickens County. Their two-story log house had a date 1823 indicating when it was built. In 1832, Richard was a trustee in Greenville's New Buncombe Street Methodist Church. (Burdine Family)

Notes for MARTHA "PATSY" WILSON:

The house that Richard and Patsy lived in was a two-story made of logs in 1823. It was on the road leading into Greenville.

Children of RICHARD BURDINE and MARTHA WILSON are:

i. MARY "POLLY"[6] BURDINE.

    ### Notes for MARY "POLLY" BURDINE:
    Married John Latham.

ii. SAMUEL BURDINE.

    ### Notes for SAMUEL BURDINE:
    Resided in Cobb County, Georgia.

iii. JOHN BURDINE, b. December 25, 1801[1]; d. February 3, 1880, Pickens, SC[1].

    ### Notes for JOHN BURDINE:
    John was said to have founded Fairview Methodist Church near Pickens, South Carolina.

iv. ABRAHAM BURDINE, b. March 25, 1808[1]; d. September 12, 1849.

    ### Notes for ABRAHAM BURDINE:
    Married Mary Ann Spann.

5. v. HAMILTON BURDINE, b. June 11, 1816, Pickens Co., SC; d. June 12, 1864, SC.

Generation No. 5

5. HAMILTON[6] BURDINE (*RICHARD[5], SAMUEL[4], RICHARD[3], SAMUEL BOURDIN[2] (BURDINE), MARC[1] BOURDIN*) was born June 11, 1816 in Pickens Co., SC, and died June 12, 1864 in SC. He married (1) FRANCES CAROLINE SITTON February 27, 1834

in SC, daughter of JOHN SITTON. She was born August 27, 1820, and died September 16, 1848 in MS. He married (2) LOUISA HUGHES September 2, 1849 in Pickens Co., SC[1]. She was born 1818.

Notes for HAMILTON BURDINE:

Hamilton Burdine came to Mississippi by wagon train in 1830. This was about the time that the Choctaw and Chickasaw Indians were starting to move to Oklahoma. He came with the families of L. W. Dacus and John L. Sitton. It took about a month to travel from their homes in Pickens, South Carolina, to a place south of what is now Louisville, Mississippi. The name of the settlement was Lick Skillet. Before his death, he went back (leaving his estate in MS) to Pickens County, South Carolina, and there he died. Before his death, William (Billy) Burdine was born in Pickens County, South Carolina. At least two of his children, Sarah and Billy, lived out the remainder of their lives in Mississippi (Burdine Family). Sarah first married William Streety in 1865, in Alabama, and second married Thomas (?) Evans. They were married less than 10 years when he died. Little is known about Mr. Evans. They had a daughter Dora that married Clough Monk Ming.

Notes for LOUISA HUGHES:

Second wife of Hamilton Burdine, she was the daughter of Rev. James W. and Mary Jane Smith Hughes of the Upcountry Country area of South Carolina.

Children of HAMILTON BURDINE and FRANCES SITTON are:

i.   JOSEPH A.[7] BURDINE, b. October 4, 1835, Pickens, SC[1]; d. July 25, 1861.

ii. JOHN WESLEY BURDINE, b. January 29, 1837, Pickens Co., SC[1]; d. July 27, 1888.

iii. RICHARD PERSVILLE BURDINE, b. December 12, 1838, MS[1].

iv. HENRIETTA BURDINE, b. August 10, 1840, MS[1].

v.   JAMES HAMILTON, b. September 15, 1842, MS[1].

vi. ABRAM NEWTON BURDINE, b. August 10, 1844, MS[1].

vii. SARAH ANN BURDINE, b. October 26, 1846, Mississippi[2,3]; m. (1) WILLIAM J. STREETY, April 4, 1865, Shelby County, AL; m. (2) EVANS, ca. 1869.

Notes for SARAH ANN BURDINE:

Sarah (pictured) was first married to William J. Streety in Shelby County, Alabama. The rights of matrimony was observed by T. G. Evans; J. P. Sarah and William had a child, John H. Streety (b. 1866, MS). She then married an Evans. Sarah Ann Burdine and Sarah "Dixie" Burdine are sometimes confused as the same. Sarah Ann Burdine's father, Hamilton Burdine, and Sarah "Dixie" Dacus Burdine's father, L. W. Dacus, came to Mississippi (from Easley, SC) in the same wagon train in the 1830s. Sarah "Dixie" married Sarah Ann's brother

William George Burdine. It appears that after the death of Sarah Ann's second husband, Evans, she and the children lived in the home of William George Burdine.

Sarah Ann Burdine's parents were Hamilton Burdine and Frances Caroline (Sitton) Burdine. After the death of Frances Caroline, Hamilton married Louisa Hughes, and from this marriage William George "Billie" Burdine was born on May 29, 1854. "Billie" Burdine married Sarah "Dixie" Dacus, born October 24, 1862. It was their home which was at the time located on what is now the Leonard King place in Choctaw County near the Natchez Trace Parkway that Sarah's daughter Dora married Clough Ming.

Billie George is the ancestor of the Burdines now living in Choctaw County. He and half brother John Wesley Burdine have Masonic emblems carved on their tombstones (Choctaw Cemeteries).

Sarah Burdine's great-grandfather Samuel Burdine had a great-grandson William Murrah Burdine that built the huge retail store in Miami, Florida. The business became known as Burdines, Inc., and only recently became part of the giant federated stores retail chain.

viii. FRANCIS LEWIS, b. August 5, 1848, MS[4].

Children of HAMILTON BURDINE and LOUISA HUGHES are:

ix. THOMAS JOSHUS[7] BURDINE, b. July 17, 1850, Pickens Co., SC.

x. MARY ELIZABETH BURDINE, B. FEBRUARY 15, 1852, PICKENS CO., SC.

xi. WILLIAM (GEORGE) MULLINNAX BURDINE, B. MAY 29, 1854, PICKENS CO., SC; d. August 20, 1912, Choctaw Co., MS.

Notes for WILLIAM (GEORGE) MULLINNAX BURDINE:

William George (Mullinnex) Burdine a.k.a. "Billie" Burdine was married to Sarah Desdemonia "Dixie" Dacus. As William George had a sister Sarah Ann (the writer's great-grandmother) that married William Streety, the two Sarahs are sometimes confused. In the book *Burdine Family*, Ruth Grant entered the following written by Sarah "Dixie" Burdine for one of her sons:

> "November 27, 1933; Dear children, will tell you a little of the family history. My father, L.W. Dacus, and your grandfather, Hamilton Burdine, and great grandfather, John L. Sitton, and families left Pickens County, SC, in 1830 in covered wagons with ox teams for Mississippi to enter land for homes. They were one month on the road. They camped in a fort one night in Alabama, but did not sleep as so many men came in to spend the night. They had big pistols and dirk knives, and they found out they were robbers that had come to rob people.
>
> "The next night they camped at a creek. They had to ford all streams of water then. That was a place where people camped, and

there was a log where the Indians had cut off the heads of a man and his two daughters. Some of the people got away, but the Indians burned their wagons, and killed their oxen. There was grass about waist high everywhere, and they were afraid for all of them to go to sleep at once . . . they could hear a rattlesnake close by.

"They would camp about sun-up and travel until about the middle of the evenings and camp, again let the oxen graze and rest. The men would go a piece from the camp and kill a deer or turkey.

"They came to a little settlement in below Louisville, now called Grab All Town, and once called Lick Skillet in Winston County not far from Pearl River. Grandpa Sitton entered 160 acres of land and bought a lot of government land for 60 cents per acre. My father and Hamilton Burdine, your grandfather, came to Choctaw County the next year and entered land."

Another excerpt from the book: "Dec. 3, 1940—A few more lines. I have nine children living, 64 grandchildren, 38 great grandchildren, one hundred and 2 in all, 87 living. Been living on this place 46 years."

William George Burdine and "Dixie" had the following children: Talulah I. (Irene), Laura (Lollie), Adar Bell, French H. (Hughes), Willie Earl, George Pearl (know as Pearl G.), Charlie Marvin, Melvin Grover, Lanie Velmer, Sadie Gustavie, Gussie Hester, Cyril Fossie, and Henry Young. All of Henry's children were born at the old Burdine family home near Chester, Mississippi.

Endnotes

1. Arvalean L. Burdine Petrics, *History of Burdine Family, 1733 Madison Co., VA*, (Compiled by Toms River, NY 1875).
2. Arvalean L. Burdine Petrics, *History of Burdine Family*.
3. *TITLE*
4. Arvalean L. Burdine Petrics, *History of Burdine Family, 1733 Madison Co., VA*, (Compiled by Toms River, NY 1875).

DESCENDANTS OF HEIMBROD VON BOYNEBURG

1 Heimbrod von Boyneburg
....+ Margaret von Elben
....2 Jost von Boyneburg—1589
........+ Catharina von Buttlar—1554
........3 Jost von Boyneburg 1554–1619
.... + Anna von Hanstein-Bornhagen
............4 Curt Leopold von Boyneburg 1609–1673
.... + Sabine Sibylle von Boyneburg 1611–1674
.... 5 Anna Juliana von Boyneburg 1646–
....................+ Matthias Sartorius
...................6 Margaretha Catharina Satorius 1684–1727
...................+ Johann Phillip Rubenkam 1670–1725
.....................7 Friedrich Wilhem Rubenkam 1702–
.....................7 Catharina Juliana Rubenkam 1703–1774
.....................+ Blasius Daniel Mackinet
.....................*2nd Husband of Catharina Juliana Rubenkam:
.....................+ Jacob Colladay (Galathe) 1707–1750
.....................8 Margaret Catharena Colladay 1728–
.....................8 Anna Maria Colladay 1731–
.....................8 Jacob Colladay 1733–
.....................8 Catharine Colladay 1735–
.....................8 Sarah Colladay 1737–1778
.... + John Ulrich (Wollery) Meng 1731–1796
.... 9 George Meng 1766–1804
.... 9 Anna Meng
.... 9 William Meng 1761–1815
.... 9 Sarah Meng 1761–1856
.... 9 Margaret Meng 1765–
.... 9 Charles Ulric Meng 1770–1855
.... 9 James Edward Meng 1771–1824
.... + Sarah (Sally) Lewis 1778–1846
.... 10 John L. Waddy Meng 1824–
.... 10 Henry Meng 1800–1865
.... 10 Julianna Meng 1810–
.... 10 Clough S. Meng 1802–1870
.... 10 Charles Meng 1804–1860
..................................+ Nancy 1815–1850
..................................11 Elizabeth Meng 1837–
..................................11 James F. Meng 1838–1864

....11 Julia Meng 1840–
....11 John Meng 1844–
....11 Joseph Meng 1848–1920
....11 Charley Meng 1849–1901
.... *2nd Wife of Charles Meng:
....+ Martha Hudspeth—1860
....11 Fred Ming 1856–
....11 Clough Monk Ming (Meng) 1859–1934
....+ Dora L. Evans 1872–1951
.....................................12 Leoda Ming 1889–1965
.....................................12 Hubert Ming 1893–1983
.....................................12 John Clinton Ming 1895–1950
.....................................12 Ethel Plemon Ming 1897–1972
.....................................12 Troy Amzy Ming 1900–1968
.....................................12 Hoyt Lester Ming 1902–1985
....+ Rozelle India Young 1907–1983
.....................................12 Alva Ming 1905–1954
.....................................12 Berlin Ming 1908–1986
.....................................12 Corrie Ming 1911–
.....................................12 Christie Cammie Ming 1913–
.... 10 William Meng 1809–1856
.... 10 James Edward Meng 1810–1890
.... 10 Francis Meng 1811–1827
.... 10 Garland Meng 1817–1873
.... 9 Samuel Meng 1777–1824
.... 8 William Colladay 1738–
.... 8 Susanna Colladay 1741–
.....................7 Justus Wilhelm Rubenkam 1705–
.....................7 Karl (Charles) Wilhelm Rubenkam
.....................7 Anna Catherina Rubenkam 1709–
.....................7 Johanna Catherina Rubenkam 1711–
.....................7 Margaretha Catherina Rubenkam 1713–
.................6 Margaret Elizabeth Satorius
.... 5 Anna Sidonia von Boyneburg
.... 5 Jost von Boyneburg
.... 5 Agrippina von Boyneburg
...........4 Adam von Boyneburg—1659
....*2nd Wife of Jost von Boyneburg:
........+ von Falken Rohrda—1556
........3 Phillip von Boyneburg
........3 Asmus von Boyneburg
....*3rd Wife of Jost von Boyneburg:
........+ Veronika von Schetzel—1588

A Personal View of the Hoyt Mings
Some of My Personal Experiences with Hoyt Lester Ming and His Family
By Scottie Ming

Most of the facts about Hoyt L. and Rozelle Ming can be found in some the articles I sent. I am going to concentrate on who the people were and what they were like.

When they met Rozelle was 16 and Hoyt L. was in his 20s. They fell in love but Rozelle's parents refused to let her see Hoyt L. because he would "never amount to anything". After the Civil War his family lost everything and became share croppers. Rozelle's parents seriously underestimated Hoyt L.'s determination. They exchanged secret love letters through Rozelle's cousin. Hoyt L. would send the letters to Rozelle's cousin and she would give them to Rozelle. In this way they made plans to be married in Lee county, which is the next county over. When the day came they met in town, walked across the street to Lee county, and were married.

After they were married they moved to Choctaw county and began working and playing music together. Hoyt L. bought some land, becoming a land owner for the first time in his life—exceeding his father's accomplishments in his lifetime. Now for a home to call their own, Hoyt L. found an old house for sale. He bought it for $5 and dismantled it by himself. He drew up house plans on notebook paper. He built a home for his family on his land by himself except for his 2 yr old son, Hoyt B. (Bert) Ming. Hoyt L. used the wood from the old home he bought and the nails he pulled from the wood when he was dismantling the former house. Hoyt L. and Rozelle lived there until they both passed away—nearly 70 years. The house is still standing and has seen another young family raise children there.

Hoyt Ming and the Pep-Steppers played until the 1930s but retired musically when their family began getting older. Neither played their instruments until the 1970s after being visited by a writer from England who had been searching for them for a while due to their popularity in some circles in England. That incident rekindled the fire in Hoyt L. to play again. He said he went to the back of his land to practice the vocal part of "Indian War Whoop". According to Hoyt L., when he hit those high notes for the first time in 40 years the dogs ran off. The rest is in much of the material I sent.

When we were making our first trip to Washington D. C. for the folk festival on the mall Hoyt L.'s fiddle came unglued on the way to mine and Bert's house in Fayette, AL. He and Bert spent most of the night gluing it back together. All was well by the time we got there to play. He said, "Well, I'll just borrow one if I need to." "What!?!" we all thought. Playing on a fiddle you aren't used to playing? Crazy! Hoyt L., in his quiet way was right as usual. He didn't spend a lot of time worrying about anything except when Rozelle got cancer. His favorite "curse" word was "Good gunnies". Generally used to express shock.

Hoyt L. grew sweet potatoes all his life. He filled orders for plants from all over the US. He had a catfish pond and a lake on his property. He also had Black Angus cows. He provided for his family better than most during the Depression with his family garden, cattle, and family chickens. The whole time I knew them they never bought anything on credit. He and Rozelle always worried that another depression would happen.

Hoyt L. was very soft spoken. Bert told me that in his entire life he never heard his dad raise his voice to anyone. He was a Godly man who loved his Lord and treated everyone kindly. He liked to tease family members and he liked to laugh. His grandchildren loved coming to see him and spent their time taking every step he took.

Rozelle was professionally trained on the violin. The mandolin she played with the Pep-Steppers had been in her family many years and it had been in her family nearly 100 years when she gave it to me. She wanted things played the way they were written and Hoyt L. (as well as Bert) played by ear. It would drive her nuts if he hit a note differently than the composed notes. That was what Hoyt L.'s music unique I think. He put his spin on everything. On the first trip to Washington DC the Pep-Steppers were playing to a crowd of 50,000. Hoyt L. began playing the song when Rozelle suddenly stopped, forgetting about the mic right at her face, and said, "Hoyt, are you going to play in C or D? You said C, but you're playing in D." The crowd went wild. They loved it. She never knew what was so funny. Later in the same set Hoyt L. got really lost in his music and was bending closer and closer to Rozelle. Eventually he was flicking her hair with every down swing of his bow. Again, the crowd lost it. A man came to me the show to see if they wrote their own material because it was so funny. I told him no that was just the Mings. They were always themselves.

Rozelle was a bit high strung and could really get angry. When that happened she would grab her head on each side and unknowingly make the scarf like thing on her head turn sideways. It was always sure to make us laugh. She loved flowers and her yard was a licensed flower nursery. She loved that boy of hers and he was her baby until she died. She would often speak of his love for fig preserves and other happy memories of his growing up. We all loved her even if we butted heads from time-to-time.

She was thin and tall for a woman. She made THE best butter milk biscuits you ever put in your mouth. I loved her cooking even though she never thought of herself as a good cook. She would patiently sit with the love of her life and play music for as long as he wanted.

Rozelle's voice was high pitched and she could call you from the back porch door in a way that could be heard clear to the very back of the farm. Believe me when I say that is a long way. She had a dinner bell but she never used it. She didn't need it. Her funny little quirks endeared her to all of us.

My Bert—he was great. We were married in 1970. Prior to our marriage he worked off shore and loved it. He always loved the sea and ships with sails. In one of my favorite pictures of him he is wearing a ship captain's hat with a distinct swagger. He loved it. He only wore golf caps (driving caps to some).

For 25 years he was a retail store manager. He retired when he was 62. He took very good care of himself by exercising daily and watching what he ate very closely. Bert began playing the guitar by ear when he was about 15. He began the genealogy quest about 2 yr before he retired (1996) and continued until he got sick in 2005, but always loved talking about it to anyone.

His personality was much like his dad's. He could pitch a fit with the best of them. He had to in order to put up with me. We liked sitting up until late just the two of us talking about all sorts of things. He enjoyed teasing me until I was aggravated then he would laugh and say, "Have I got you irritated?" When I said "yes" is a not very nice tone he would laugh and walk away. He could always make me laugh even when I wanted to be angry with him for something he'd done.

He loved to travel and spent lots of time doing just that once he had retired. He and our youngest daughter once started in Northport and traveled Hwy. 43 all the way to Niagara Falls, NY and within 3 miles of the Canadian border. He hiked 30 miles of Appalachian Trail by himself and primitive camping along the way. He wanted to walk the whole thing but his health prevented it.

We enjoyed the weekends together. Saturdays we loved sitting on the back porch and just chatting and admiring the view, which included all the work on the yard Bert did. He got a love for plants from his mother. Sunday mornings we would walk around the yard with a cup of coffee looking at what was newly bloomed and such.

When we first moved in this house I was hanging pictures. After listening to the banging for a while, Bert came in to see what I was up to. What he saw was a perfect circle of holes in the wall where I was trying to get a picture in line with another one. He snatched the hammer out of my hand and told me I was foreboden from ever using the hammer again.

He was a perfectionist like his mother, a wonderful carpenter, and maker of anything from wood I asked him to make. He, like his dad, would draw up his own plans and go for it. He was a very talented artist. His medium was oils and mixed mediums. He would also paint with acrylics on old saw blades. Every picture had water in it somewhere. He loved to hide his signature in the picture so you had to really hunt to find it.

None of this may be what you were wanting from me, but it's my view of some of the Mings I love. My husband was my everything. I miss him every day and will never meet anyone who comes close to being the man he was in my eyes. I will love him forever. He was THE ONE for me. I have enjoyed reminiscing about the unique people who were members of the Pep-Steppers I knew.

Scottie Ming

JUST A FEW OF THE NEWSPAPER AND EVENTS
INVOLVING MING'S PEP STEPPERS

New Victor Record Hit
---by---

Ming's Pep Steppers

Old Red Indian
War Whoops !!

Some real old time fiddling by Lee County Artists.

The first VICTOR Record of any Lee County Orchestra. Don't Miss It. Get Yours Now.

From left: Mr. Hoyt L. Ming, Mrs. Rozelle (née Young) Ming, and Troy Ming, who is standing in for Rozelle Ming's sister. Standing is a (unknown) friend of Hoyts. Hoyt Ming and his Pep Steppers music was used in the 2000 movie, "O Brother where Art Thou?" The movie stared George Clooney, John Turturro, Tim Nelson and John Goodman.

115

Letter

Hoyt L. Ming & Co.
Attn: Hoyt Ming
Route 2, Box 9
Ackerman, Ms. 39735

Dear Hoyt L. Ming & Co.:

Congratulations! You have been recognized as one of Mississippi's finest performers.

The Performing Arts Screening Committee of the Mississippi World's Fair Council takes pleasure in announcing the acceptance of Hoyt L. Ming & Co. to perform at the Mississippi Pavilion at the 1984 Louisiana World Exposition on Tuesday, July 24 through Friday, July 27, 1984.

You, and other performing artists from across the state will entertain the millions of visitors who will experience Mississippi's world class exhibit from May 12 through November 11, 1984.

If for some reason you are not available to perform on this date, please contact the manager of the Encore '84 program immediately at 800-962-1984.

In the near future, you will receive a participant's packet containing detailed information regarding your performance time, the World's Fair and the Mississippi Pavilion. Also included in the packet will be information on housing for entertainers.

Again, congratulations and we look forward to seeing you at the Mississippi Pavilion.

Sincerely,
Carol Palmer, Manager, Encore '84

Countians Return from Festival

Hoyt Ming's Pep Steppers and James Lucas, a wood-carver from Weir were among the Mississippians selected by the Smithsonian Institute in Washington DC to put on a National Folk Festival. The festival closed July 7, and the participants have now returned home.

Approximately 100,000 people each day visited the festival, and heard and saw the participants. A great deal of favorable publicity was generated for the County and State, both in the United States and abroad. The British Broadcasting Company televised some of the program to England.

The Pep Steppers include Mr. and Mrs. Hoyt Ming, Hoyt Ming Jr., James Alford, and Wayne Dawkins. They reported an enjoyable time in Washington.

Arts commission to sponsor theme concert

The first in a series of concerts featuring music of rural Mississippians will be in Jackson on Sunday, October 28, through the cooperation of the Mississippi Agriculture and Forestry Museum and the Mississippi Arts Commission.

Typical of folk tradition, each artist featured in this series has developed a proficiency in a particular musical style without formal training. Included in the concert series will be blue-grass, gospel, blues, sacred harp singing, and string band tunes.

Hoyt Ming and his Pep-Steppers will draw the spotlight with their old-time string band entertainment at the October concert at 3:00 p.m.

Eighty-two year old Ming and his Pep-Steppers, comprised of family and friends, recorded several tunes at the Peabody Hotel in Memphis in 1928. During the 1930s they played for dances and parties throughout northeast Mississippi.

Ming has played at the National Folk Festival in Virginia and at the Festival of American Folk Life in Washington, D. C. His group's musical style has a blues-type quality of drawing the emotional value of each note.

Tom Rankin, director of the Folk Arts Program at the Mississippi Arts Commission, will provide a cultural interpretation for this event.

The Sunday, November 11, musical guests will be James "Son" Thomas and Boyd Rivers for a 3:00 p.m. blues and gospel show.

Thomas has played the blues in Washington, D. C. and Europe. Rivers performs gospel music and spirituals and has played for the Smithsonian Festival of American Folklife in Washington DC.

Southern Grass, formerly known as the Wilson Brothers Band, will play a variety of music from old dance and string band tunes to bluegrass and gospel on Sunday, November 25, at 3:00 p.m.

This band played in north Mississippi during the 1960s and 1970s. They have performed for the Friday night Grand Ole Opry and Ernest Tubb's Mid-Night Jamboree.

To close the series of folk music concerts, on Saturday, December 15, at 1:00 p.m. the Mississippi Sacred Harp Singers will perform seasonal Christmas hymns as well as traditional songs from the Sacred Harp Hymnal.

They will be directed by veteran shape-note leader Hugh Bill McGuire, who is president of the Calhoun County sacred Harp Singing Convention. In Mississippi the tradition of shape-note dates back to the 1860s.

Ming's Pep Steppers To
National Folk Festival

Hoyt Ming's musical group, known as Ming's Pep-Steppers, who were quite famous in the Country Music world back in the 30's, are again in demand. Some of their old records have been revived, and they are being asked to cut more records.

They have been invited to appear in the National Folk Festival July 26–29 at Wolf Trap Farm Park for the Performing Arts. This park is located in Vienna, Va., a suburb of

Washington DC. The Mings will receive all expenses, plus an honorarium of $600.00 for their appearance.

The Ming group has been requested to cut some records of their music while at the Festival. The record companies expect boom sales of the Ming recordings, as country and folk music demand is on the upswing, not only in the south and west, but in the metropolitan centers as well.

- 1984 Jackson Daily News -

Musician from Ackerman has been fiddlin'
By JIM EWING
JACKSON DAILY NEWS Staff Writer

ACKERMAN – Hoyt Ming has a certain pep to his step, a trait he has displayed to hundreds of appreciative, old-time fiddle music audiences.

Ming, 81, formed a group called The Pep-Steppers nearly 60 years ago and they recorded such favorite songs – still played today – as "Indian War Whoop," "Old Red," "White Mule" and the "Tupelo Blues."

"We recorded with (RCA) Victor in February 1928," said Ming, relaxing at his home about two miles north of Ackerman. "They sold pretty good, but they hit right in the Depression," coming out in 1929, precluding any further fame. "But the result of it has been pretty good in the last 10 years."

Ming, who says he has been playing the fiddle since he was 16, formed the group back in the 1920s playing for square dances, sing-a-longs, "just about anywhere you might want to have some" good, peppy dance music.

"We called ourselves the 'Pep Steppers' because we loved fast music, that had a pep to it . . . and it's been that (name) ever since."

The group was composed of his brother Troy Ming, who died about 10 years ago, and his wife of more than 60 years, Rozelle, who died last September.

Ming said the group won the right to record the songs in a contest pitting what were considered to be the best string groups in northeast Mississippi at the time against each other. They recorded in a makeshift studio set up in the Peabody Hotel in Memphis.

But the tunes that were to bear his name did not carry their original names, Ming said.

"White Mule" was originally called "'Woe Mule, Let Me Put the Saddle on You.' But, he (the record producer) called it 'White Mule,'" Ming said, shaking his head disapprovingly. "That sounded like it had too much whiskey in it."

Tupelo Blues was originally called Florida Blues until the producer wanted to give the song a Mississippi flavor.

Even Ming's name came out differently on the records. Instead of Hoyt Ming, as it was clearly spelled on his contract, the final product had the name, Floyd Ming.

"We kept playing until about 1957–58. There was about 15 years I quit playing. I was busy farming and I had a family. And music just didn't seem to be doing much."

118

One day, he said, he picked up his fiddle bow and all the hair was off it, "and the neck was unglued and I just let it set for several years."

But now, Ming is back to playing and it came about in a rather unusual fashion.

A few years back David Freeman, a New York record producer, ran across the old recordings of "Indian War Whoop" and "Tupelo Blues."

"And they'd heard it and they wanted to know if they (the group) was still living," Ming said. "They wanted a picture and then they wanted to re-record some of those old records."

So, in 1973, Freeman visited and heard Ming and his wife play, which led to an appearance at the Wolf Trap Performing Arts Festival in 1973, followed by the American Folklife Festival in Washington DC, in 1974, a stint in the movie 'Ode to Billy Joe" and other play dates elsewhere.

His latest big performances were at the Mid-South Folk Festival in Memphis in 1982 and the New Orleans World's Fair in early June.

Since the death of his wife, Ming has made up his "Pep Steppers" with a few friends: his son, Hoyt Jr., on bass; Harley Burdine of Mathiston on banjo; L. C. Freshouir of Eupora on guitar; and Wayne Dawkins of Starkville.

Although Ming says he never seeks out places to play, he manages to keep busy, mostly at small gatherings and in front of charitable and civic groups.

They play such traditional tunes as "Old Red," "Miss Sawyer," "Monkey in the Dog Cart," "Make me a Pallet on the Floor," "Cripple Coon," and "Wednesday Night Waltz." That's the kind of music, Ming says, he really likes.

"You know, music, it's got to have a feeling in it," he explained. "If it hasn't got a feeling in it, it's not music . . . you've got to feel it and put that feeling in it."

And, he added, "I'm going to play as long as I'm able to draw a bow."

You can go to the www and listen to Hoyt Ming and the Pep Steppers play the Indian War Whoop and Monkey in the Dog Cart etc. This is truely great old-time fiddling by a master.

CHAPTER 5
THE MENG FAMILY OF HOHEN-SÜLZEN, GERMANY (1725)

1225 JAHRE

The Meng-Shamhart book is in the Hohen-Sulzen City Library

The Village of Hohen-Sülzen

The Meng family lived and worshipped in the village of Hohen-Sülzen, which is about 12kms from the major town of Worms and about 26kms from the town of Friedelsheim where the Ellenberger family resided. The first ancestor we can trace to is Johann Stephan Meng who was in the pages of the parish records in the 1740s. Apparently the Meng name does not appear in the 1600s.

In 1991 the community of Hohen-Sülzen celebrated the 1225th anniversary of the first mention of its name in a document. The area has always had rich soil so we can be sure that the history of settlement in the Hohen-Sülzen region extends over the entire 1200 years of documented history. We know very little about the community's earlier centuries. The first sure documented proof is found in the 11th century, when Hohen-Sülzen is found under the names Sülza, Sülzen, Horsülzen, and Sülczen from which through the development of speech patterns today's name became the accepted name of the village. Later the community belonged to the Count of Falkenstein's holdings (about 23 km/14 miles west of Hohen-Sülzen near Kirchheim-Bolanden) and was under Austrian administration until the "Reichsdeputationsausschuss" (major restructuring of Germany's internal and external borders) in 1803. The Austrian emperors carried under their numerous titles that of "Lord of Falkenstein" until the end of the World War I. Later, Hohen-Sülzen participated in the fate of the lands on the left (west) bank of the Rhine.

Today, the Hohen-Sülzen community (of between 500 and 600 people) is partly employed in farming and wine growing, but most residents work in Worms. The citizens are proud of their town and this shows itself in the active agendas of the community associations and the acquisition of public facilities such as the village meeting house and the loving preservation of the historic community Rathaus (town hall). The Hohen-Sülzen church was once used by both Catholic and Lutheran congregations at the same time.

Early Hohen-Sülzen postcard (1898).

Johann Stephan Meng (ca. 1725–?)

Johann Stephan Meng is the first Meng ancestor we know about who had his family in the village of Hohen-Sülzen. It is likely his father was a Johann Meng, possibly Johann Otto Meng from Hohen-Sülzen, but this needs to be proven. Johann Stephan Meng was an Ackersmann or farmer. He married Maria Elisabetha Bohlander in about 1746 and had the following children:

Johanna Catharina Margaretha Meng	(1747-07-17–?)
Johann Peter Meng	(1748-12-04–?)

His first wife must have died as he married Maria Catherina Bertrand in about 1757, and they had the following children:

Maria Christina Meng	(1758-01-11–?)
Johannes Meng	(1760-02-07–?)
Johann Christian Meng	(1762-06-12–1838-03-07)
Johann Martin Meng	(1765-03-17–?)
Peter Jacob Meng	(1767-10-08–?)
Karl Philipp Meng	(1771-06-07–1859-01-22)
Johann Philipp Meng	(1774-03-20–?)

Johann Stephan Meng had Meng relations who are godparents to his children who could possibly be brothers or cousins or one of them even Johann Stephan's father. Their names were Johannes Meng and Maria Elisabetha (wife) from Heppenheim and Johann Adolph Meng and Maria Christina (surname Pabrina?) (wife) from Obrigheim and Johann Jacob Meng from Hohen-Sülzen. Johann Martin Meng and Anna Maria (wife) from Hohen-Sülzen and Johann Otto Meng of Hohen-Sülzen were also godparents to one of Johann Stephan Meng's children, and they also had family in Hohen-Sülzen in the 1760s. There was also a Johannes Meng and Anna Maria (wife) who had children in Hohen-Sülzen around 1738–1749, and are also in the Hohen-Sülzen parish records.

Obrigheim and Heppenheim may be villages that the family originated from, but further records would have to be looked at.

Karl Philipp Meng (1771-06-08–1859?)

Karl (Carl) Philipp Meng was born in Hohen-Sülzen and was named after one of his godparents, Carl Philipp Blaufuß, a Lutheran schoolmaster from Hohen-Sülzen. Karl Meng, an Ackersmann (farmer), married Maria Dorothea Schneider [b. 1771-06-24 in Hohen-Sülzen, daughter of Johann Tobias Schneider, master linen weaver, and Anna Margareta (surname not found in the records)] in 1798 in Hohen-Sülzen, Germany. They had the following children that we know of:

Johannes Meng	(ca. 1794–1799)
Reichard Meng	(1799-11-12–1871-01-22)
Anna Maria Meng	(ca. 1802–?)
Catherina Meng	(ca. 1811–?)
Elizabetha Meng	(?–?)

Margaretha Meng	(?–?)
Elizabeth Meng	(?–1808)

Karl died in 1859 aged 88 years old, and it was listed that he had three children still surviving at his death (names not listed on the record).

Reichard Meng (1799–1871) Finds Two Fourth-Century Roman Stone Coffins and Third-Century "The Vas Diatretum" on His Property in Hohen-Sülzen, Germany

Reichard Meng (1799-11-12–1871-01-22)

Reichard married Maria Eva Dörrschuck (b. 1811-09-03), daughter of Johannes Dörrschuck, farmer, and Anna Barbara Diehl of Grossniedesheim on 1829-03-08 in Hohen-Sülzen, Germany. They had 11 children that we know of as follows:

Johannes Meng	(1830-08-05–1870-07-27)
Christian Meng	(1832-10-29–?)
Karl Philipp Meng	(1834-06-27–1885-08-19)
Margaretha Meng	(1836-02-13–1914-03-09)
Catherine Meng	(1838-06-12–?)
Wilhelm Meng	(1841-04-10–1843-06-??)
Jacob Meng	(1843-05-28–1871-01-03)
Anna Barbara Meng	(1845-04-04–?)
Anna Maria Meng	(1850-01-27–1916-11-08)
Luisa Meng	(1853-02-09–1853-08-02)
Friedrich Meng	(1855-10-05–ca. 1900)

Reichard Meng was a farmer, and owned and leased a lot of land in Hohen-Sülzen, but apparently wasn't rich by any means. The Meng family owned quite a lot of land, but, in general, most families had to share or split it in each generation, so they never became really rich. A book states that in 1869, Reichard Meng found two fourth-century stone coffins in his fields in Hohen-Sülzen (a place called Weil), each with a skeleton inside. In one of these were Roman glasses from the third century. One of the glasses is the famous *vas diatretum*. The glasses were sold to the museum of Mainz. The book also says that not far from this place there were a couple of graves from several centuries. In another website about Hohen-Sülzen, it says that "In 1869, a Dionysus bottle from the third century was unearthed in Hohen-Sülzen. The bottle is 42 cm tall and has figures ground into it. The image was cut into the glass's outside surface in vividly effective deep grinding. The figures' effect was further strengthened by engraving individual body parts. The scene with several figures stems from the wine god Dionysus's milieu. The bottle has been ascribed to the same workshop that made the Lynceus beaker in the Romano-Germanic Museum. This glass was found together with a cage cup, which has been lost since the Second World War. The Hohen-Sülzen bottle now stands as the centrepiece of the Roman glass collection at the *Landesmuseum Mainz* (Inventar Nr. R 6111)."

The following message was given to Belinda Landsley:

1855 J.Meng found the place (on his field) where a large roman villa (Weil) was. Later there was a monastery. R. Meng found the roman sandstone coffins, where the wonderful glasses were discovered. The "netglass" disappeared after World War II, the Americans had to send them back, from a place outside of the town of Mainz, where the museum brought them, before Mainz was bombed down. The other glasses are lost or stolen too. Only "Die Hohensülzer Henkelflasche", called "Dyorissosflasche", which is the most important Roman glass or bottle from our region came back to the museum. There are many figures on it."

Roman artifacts from two Roman sandstone coffins, with two skeletons inside, were found by Richard Meng in 1869 in Hohen-Sülzen. The remains were from the fourth century along with glasses from the third century, including the famous vas diatretum.

Maria Eva Meng (née Dörrschuck) died on 1870-12-30 and Reichard died less than a month later on 1871-01-22, both in Hohen-Sülzen. They are buried with their sons Johannes and Jacob, who all died over a period of one month in Hohen-Sülzen.

Reichard Meng's Children

We know a little now about the Meng family in Hohen-Sülzen, and this includes a couple of Karl Meng's siblings and a cousin or two.

Johannes Meng (1830-08-05–1870-07-27)
Johannes died in 1870 aged 39 and is buried with his parents (Reichard and Maria Eva Meng) and brother (Jacob) in Hohen-Sülzen. We are not sure if he married.

Christian Meng (1832-10-29–?)

Margaretha Meng (1836-02-13–1914-03-09)
Margaretha married into the Velde family (name of husband unknown) and died aged 78. She is buried in the old Hohen-Sülzen graveyard with her sister Anna Maria.

Catherine Meng (1838-06-12–?)

Wilhelm Meng (1841-04-10–1843-06-??)
Wilhelm died young at age two.

Jacob Meng (1843-05-28–1871-01-03)
Jacob died aged 27 and is buried with his parents and brother (Johannes) in Hohen-Sülzen. We are not sure if he married.

Anna Barbara Meng (1845-04-04–?)

Anna Maria Meng (1850-01-27–1916-11-08)
Anna Maria Meng married Jakob Umstadt on 1872-07-02 in Hohen-Sülzen. She is buried with her sister Margaretha in the old Hohen-Sülzen graveyard. One of her direct descendants Helmut Umstadt lives in Germany.

Luisa Meng (1853-02-09–1853-08-02)
Died at about six months old in Hohen-Sülzen.

Friedrich Meng (1855-10-05–ca. 1900)
Friedrich was the youngest son of Reichard Meng and Maria Eva Dörrschuck, and yet he was the one to take over his father's house. This will have been because his elder brothers had either died or moved away. Friedrich was listed as one of the citizens of Hohen-Sülzen and worked as a Landwirt (farmer). In 1881, he had plans drawn up for a new house to replace the very tiny house he grew up in with his parents and siblings. The new house had two floors and an attic area. This house was called house 74 (now Kirchstrasse, 17).

In 1898, there was an election for the town hall, and only one person voted for Friedrich Meng. It was a local joke that perhaps he voted for himself and this was the only vote cast. The son of a former priest in Hohen-Sülzen by the name of Wilhelm Briegleb wrote a small theater book with the title "De Rothausreformader," which is translated as "the man who reforms the town hall." Some names in the book are the original names of the locals and some are changed. One of the persons "Sibille Müller" a.k.a. Friedrich Meng gets only one vote. In reality, there was no female to vote for. In the book that Briegleb wrote, the locals discuss the necessity of getting water for all houses. They fear that this might be too expensive. The village received water in 1909 and electricity in 1913. Canalization (to take the wastewater outside the village) finally came in the year 1989! Then the streets were renovated.

Friedrich married a woman with the surname Stamm (first name unknown) and had seven children as follows:

Magdalene Meng	(ca. 1887–?)
Luise Meng	(1889–1963)
Emelie Meng	(?–?)
Eugen Meng	(?–?)
Richard Meng	(1896–1974)
Johannes (Hans) Meng	(ca. 1898–?)
Daughter Meng	(ca. 1900–ca. 1918)

Friedrich Meng died around 1900 committing suicide—by hanging himself in the stable at the back of his house. His wife was pregnant with their last daughter. This daughter died young at 18.

Friedrich's son Richard went on to have five children: Hans and Kurt (twins), Maria (Maya), Herbert, and Richard. The son Richard born in 1926 was the last Meng living in Hohen-Sülzen until he died in 1976. His house at 17 Kirchstrasse, Hohen-Sülzen, was sold in 1976. Richard's sister Maya Schneider (née Meng) is still alive in Germany in 2011.

Reichard Meng's Uncle and Cousin

Johann Christian Meng (1762-06-13–1838-03-07)

Johann Christian Meng, known as Christian Meng, was a resident of Hohen-Sülzen and the son of Johann Stephan Meng and Maria Catherina Bertrand. He married Katharina Barbara Stahl in Hohen-Sülzen in 1780 and had four children that we know of. Johann Christian was a great-uncle to the younger Karl Philipp Meng and lived in house 26.

One of Johann Christian's sons was named Johannes Meng and was also a resident of Hohen-Sülzen.

The Meng Houses and Land in Hohen-Sülzen

In the Hohen-Sülzen parish records, it appears that Johann Stephan Meng was leasing land off the church as he is one of the names in a list from the 1760s. Since then the Meng family has leased and owned land in the village.

There is a two-page document from the archives in *Worms* which lists the land that the Meng family owned or leased. It is dated 1886 and includes Reichard Meng and other Meng relations. The word "Flur" is on the document and is still used today. It describes where the field is exactly situated. Flur 1 always describes places inside the village, Flur 2, 3, 4, and so on are outside the village. Reichard owned or leased many pieces of land inside and outside of the village. The document is complicated and hard to translate into modern-day figures, but it basically states how many fields each person owned or leased (the fields were usually small), and the figures can also include gardens and cellars. Sometimes the properties were sold or changed with neighbors or split when parents died and so on. Germans had the measurements like meters, square meters, acres, and hectares but also had a measurement called morgen. This is translated to mean "morning" and was the size of a field which a horse could work on in half a day (in a morning). The Meng family owned pigs, rabbits, and chickens, but had no cows, oxen, or horses to help plow the fields.

During the "French period" from 1792 to 1814, all documents relating to Hohen-Sülzen were written in French and all the streets had funny French names with houses having a number in the village. Members of the Meng family lived in houses 18, 22, 74, 31¼, and 26. Three of the houses still exist.

A Meng family home, originally identified as house 18, now identified as house 25 Hauptstrasse in Hohen-Sülzen, Germany.

On house 31 (now Wormestrasse 38) is a stone plaque with "bez. Joh you Cha Meng 1833" written in it. It means Johannes and wife built the house in 1833. This was Johannes Meng and Katharina Barth. Johannes Meng was the son of Johann Christian Meng (1762–1838).

128

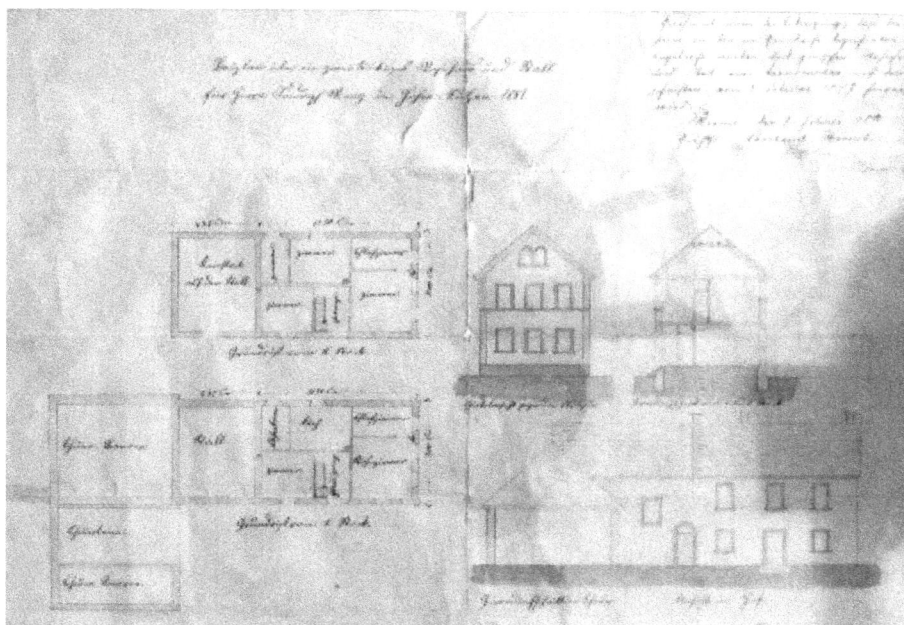

The original 1881 floor plan of the Friedrich Meng Haus, originally identified as house 74, now house 17 Kirchstrasse in Hohen-Sülzen, Germany.

Built in 1881.

Loam and clay diggers in a pit in Hohen-Sülzen. This became the main occupation from the 1870s for quite a while and made some residents a lot of money so that they could build bigger houses. This may have been why Friedrich Meng could build himself a much bigger house in 1881.

Clay diggers in Hohen-Sülzen. They used flat heavy iron shovels and even children did the work.

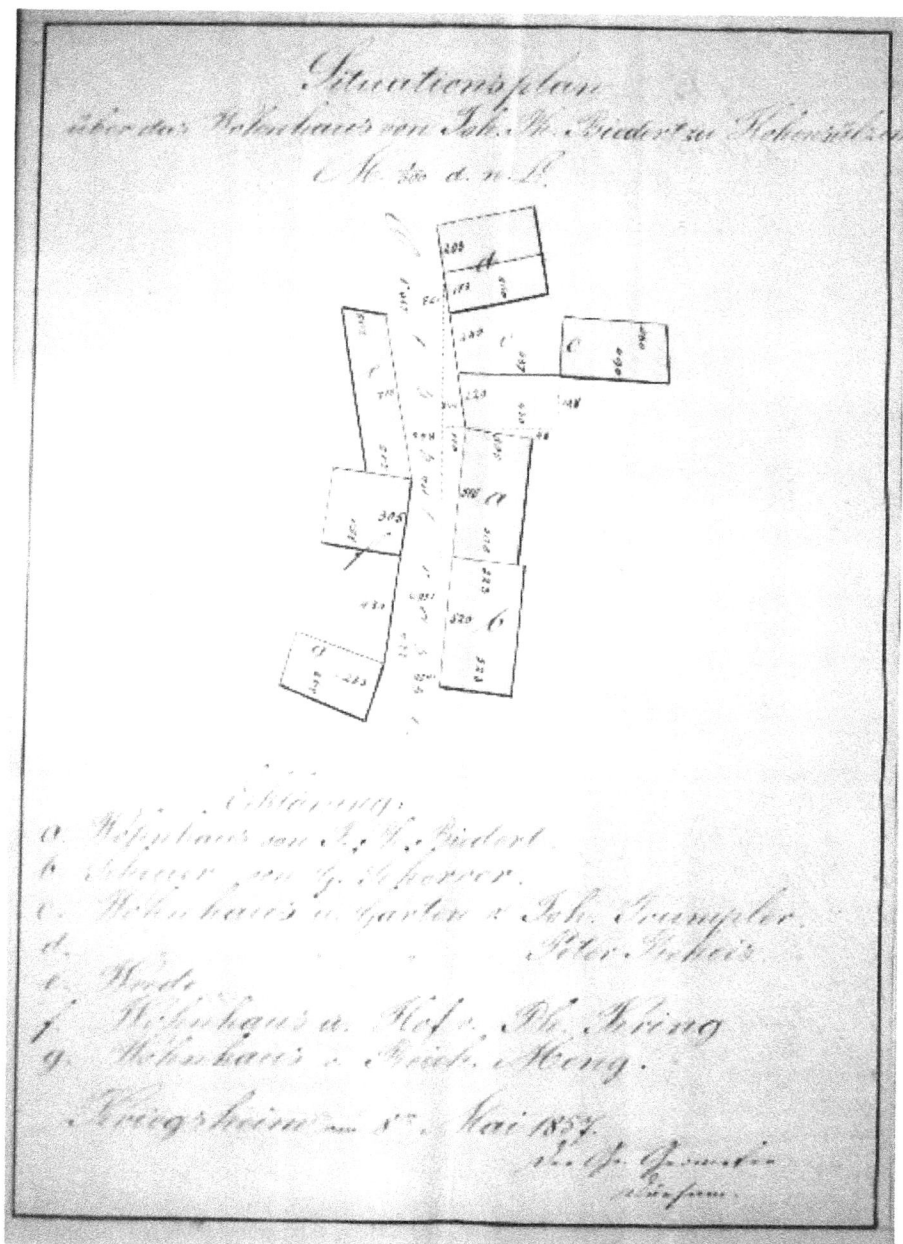

Townhall on Hauptstr. no. 22 (since demolished) in Hohen-Sülzen, Germany.

Johannes Meng (1795–1873-07-13)

Johannes (a first cousin once removed to Karl Philipp Meng) married Katharina Barth on 1830-06-27 in Hohen-Sülzen. They lived at house 31 (now Wormerstrasse 38). On the building is carved in stone "Built by Joh and Cha Meng 1833."

Johannes was an Ackersmann (farmer), and in 1855, Johannes Meng found in his field a Roman coin (Konstantin), rests of lances, and large iron rings from Roman wagons. The lances were destroyed by touching them.

Johannes Meng had four children still alive when he died in 1873. Johannes Meng's son Philipp Meng emigrated to America in 1886.

Marriage of Reichard Meng and Maria Eva Dörrschuck.

Marriage of Johannes Meng and Katharine Barth.

Im Jahr, eintausend achthundert und dreißig den *[handwritten]* vor mir *[handwritten]* Civilstands-Beamten der Gemeinde von *[handwritten]* Kanton *[handwritten]* sind erschienen *[handwritten]*

großjähriger Sohn von *[handwritten]*

hiebei gegenwärtig *[handwritten]*

welche Erschienene mich ersucht haben zur feierlichen Vollziehung ihrer vorhabenden Heirath zu schreiten und von welcher die Verkündigung vor der Hauptthüre des Gemeindehauses, nämlich die erste den *[handwritten]* des Monats *[handwritten]* eintausend achthundert *[handwritten]* um *[handwritten]* Uhr des *[handwritten]* und die zweite den *[handwritten]* des Monats *[handwritten]* um zwölf Uhr des Mittags *[handwritten]*

gemacht worden sind.

Da mir kein Einspruch gegen die Heirath notifizirt worden, und indem ich derselben Ersuchen Recht widerfahren lasse, und oben gemeldete Schriften, so wie das sechste Kapitel des Civilgesetzbuchs, betitelt: Von der Ehe, vorgelesen habe, und den zukünftigen Ehemann und die zukünftige Ehefrau gefragt, ob dieselben sich für Mann und Frau nehmen wollen, und ein jedes von ihnen besonders solches bejahet; so erkläre ich im Namen des Gesetzes, daß *[handwritten]* und die *[handwritten]* durch die Ehe verbunden sind.

Worüber ich gegenwärtigen Akt geführt in Gegenwart von *[handwritten]*

welche nach geschehener Vorlesung gegenwärtigen Akt mit mir und den kontrahirenden Theilen unterschrieben haben. *[handwritten]*

Johannes Meng (son of Reichard Meng) [b. 5 Aug 1830–d. 27 Dec 1870], at 35 years of age, married Katharine (née Barth) who was 25 years old.

Jacob Meng (son of Reichard Meng) [b. 28 May 1843–d. 3 Jan 1871].

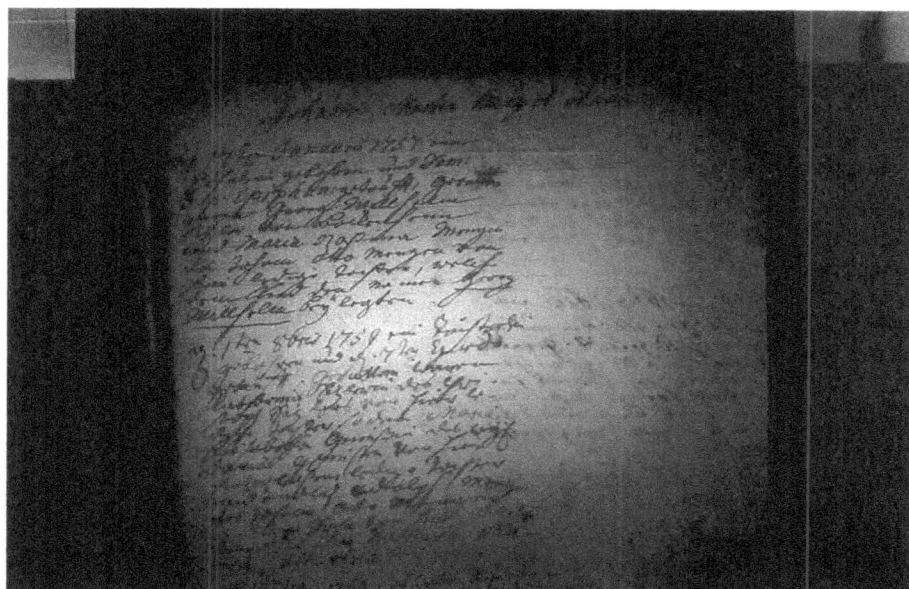

Copy of church record of Johann Martin (son of Johann Stephen Meng) and Anna Meng having a son, Georg Wilhelm Meng (b. 17 Jan 1757).

Johann Martin Meng and Anna Maria had a boy on January 17, 1757, which was christened on the third Sunday after Epiphany. The godparents were Georg Wilhelm Sitzler from Bockenheim and Rosina Mengen, daughter of Johann Mengen, from Hohen-Sülzen. She was unmarried. They gave the child the name of Georg Wilhelm. The family broke tradition of the first name Johann Martin probably because of the godparents.

We have a resident list from Hohen-Sülzen from 1654. There are no Mengs in our village after the lasting war in middle Europe (1618–1648).

1854

An interesting document signed by the mayor of Hohen-Sülzen, Christopher Stamm II, with the signatures of Johannes Meng and Reichard Meng, who were on the local government council. On page 1 of the documents is a list of men born in 1834 who were required to serve in the German army. However, not everyone served. Some would pay the government not to join.

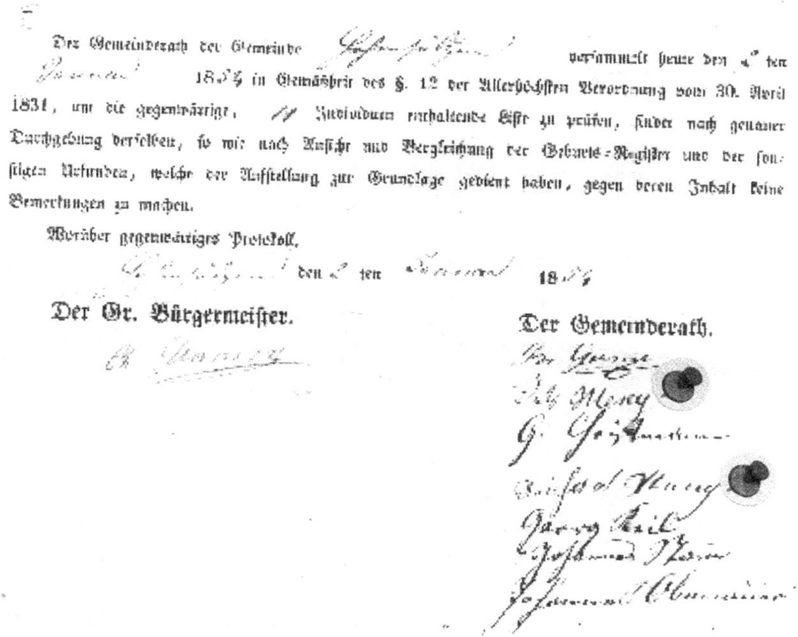

Der Gemeinderath der Gemeinde [illegible] versammelt heute den 2ten [illegible] 18[illegible] in Gemäßheit des §. 12 der Allerhöchsten Verordnung vom 30. April 1831, um die gegenwärtige, 11 Individuen enthaltende Liste zu prüfen, findet nach genauer Durchgehung derselben, so wie nach Ansicht und Vergleichung der Geburts-Register und der sonstigen Urkunden, welche der Aufstellung zur Grundlage gedient haben, gegen deren Inhalt keine Bemerkungen zu machen.

Worüber gegenwärtiges Protokoll.

[illegible] den 2 ten [illegible] 18[illegible]

Der Gr. Bürgermeister.

Der Gemeinderath.

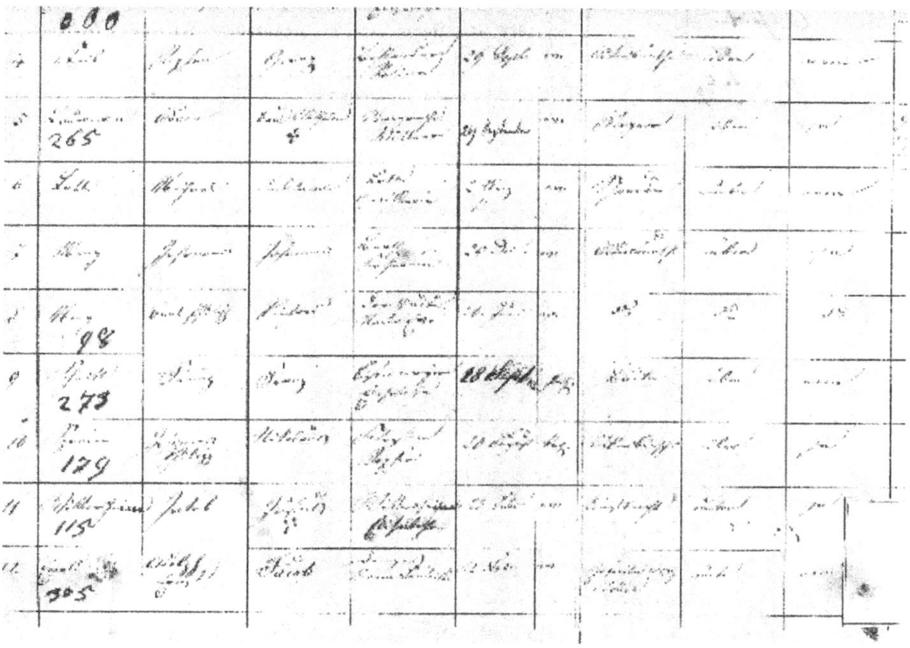

4	[illegible]								
5	265								
6	[illegible]								
7	Meng								
8	98								
9	273								
10	179								
11	115								
12	305								

HOHEN-SÜLZEN'S MILITARY PAST

Hohen-Sülzen under Nazi regime.

Military deaths during World War I (1916–1918) of soldiers from Hohen-Sülzen. Soldier 10 is A. Meng (row two). Richard Meng, also from Hohen-Sülzen, survived the war.

Kellerbesuch bei Bürgermeister Sitzler
Hohen-Sülzen 23.September 1910

*Although not Mengs, this picture certainly looks like
the Meng ancestors solving world problems 1910.*

The Crew that brought running water to Hohen-Sülzen in 1909.

Sources

[1] The Hohen-Sülzen information is the product of the gracious contribution of Werner Schabbehard, a Shamhart relative from Bielefeld, Germany. Additional information and historic pictures of Hohen-Sülzen have been offered by Belinda Lansley, from her family book collection. Belinda is another newly found Meng relative. We are very thankful to all for their contributions and to our expanded understanding Meng history.

CHAPTER 6
THE NEW ZEALAND BRANCH OF THE
MENG GENEALOGICAL TREE (1771)[3]

Karl Phillip Meng (1834–1885) Leaves Hohen-Sülzen, Germany, for Australia in 1863; Ends up in Ashley, New Zealand

Karl Philipp Meng (1834-06-27–1885-08-19)

Karl Philipp Meng (also known as Carl or Charles Meng) was born in Hohen-Sülzen, Germany, to parents Reichard and Maria Eva (née Dörrschuck). He was named after his grandfather who was a godparent at his christening. There is a family story that Karl was a lieutenant in the German army and that he emigrated from his residence of Hohen-Sülzen, Palatinate, Germany, on 1862-12-12 to get away from the army. After talking to a local historian, he thinks this is highly unlikely and that he would have left due to poverty. In the year 1857, it was so dry in the region that people were suffering. In the following years, they were poor, usually had many children and couldn't feed them. It would have been the same for the Meng family as they had a lot of children, and they lived in a very small house. Karl was probably not a lieutenant. Officers in the villages were rare, and the German army had very few officers. He may have also been escaping from compulsory army service as a soldier.

In the Hohen-Sülzen Protestant church book, it is written that Karl Meng left for Australia in the year 1863. With him was Georg Schmitt, whose parents knew nothing of his leaving. A third person with the name Schneider was with them. The third person was Peter Schneider, a friend of Karl's. Karl and Peter came to New Zealand and not Australia. We don't know about Georg Schmitt, but some Schmitt still live in the same house in Hohen-Sülzen to this day. They are not related to the former Schmitt family.

We believe Karl was on the ship *Sebastopol* which arrived in 1863, named as single man Jacob Menges, a farm laborer aged 27. This is the boat that the Ellenberger family was on, and Elise Katharina was wrongly named as Maria Ellenberger, domestic servant aged 24. The errors could have been due to their lack of English language skills when asked to give their name. A researcher of the German church in Christchurch also believes that Karl and Elise were these people on the *Sebastopol* as a whole lot of people from their area of Germany were recruited to sail out on this ship by a man Phillip Tische who was already in New Zealand. Tisch went back to Germany when his father died in 1862 and encouraged other Germans to come with him. Most of the people on the ship were Lutheran or Reformed and this ensured the German church in Christchurch would get its promised subscriptions.

"ARRIVAL OF SEBASTOPOL" *The Press, May 23rd 1863*

"The ship *Sebastopol*, Captain D Taylor, arrived in Lyttelton harbour, from London, on Thursday evening about 5 p.m., after a protracted passage of over 100 days. She left Gravesend on the 17th January, and did not clear the land until the 9th February, experiencing heavy gales all the time. Her passenger list includes 17 in the 1st, and 27 in the 2nd cabin, besides 205 assisted Government emigrants. The passengers speak highly of the Captain, surgeon, and officers, and a few days before arrival presented them with testimonials, the one given to the Captain consisting of a purse of sovereigns and an address containing 230 signatures. This ship has been exceedingly free from sickness, no deaths having occurred during the voyage, but 3 births and one marriage."

On 1865-09-08, Karl purchased 100 acres of land in the Ashley district (RS 8471) from W. S. Blunt worth 300 pounds. He sold a small part of it to James Carnegy Lock on 1865-09-21 and the rest on the 1869-10-13. Karl paid 50 pounds of his own money and had a mortgage of 250 pounds at 10% interest. This piece of land was situated on the corner of Cones Road and Boundary Road, just north of Ashley Township. Whether he ever farmed it or leased it out is unknown. At the same time, he owned this land the family actually lived in Rangiora for a while and at Tuahiwi on the Maori Reserve. Apparently, the Maori Reserve was Maori land, but the local Maori often leased pieces to Europeans as they couldn't be bothered farming it themselves. It was highly sought-after land and some of the best farming land in Canterbury. Karl may have leased the land there as there is no record of him owning any land in Tuahiwi.

Karl later owned a farm at Mill Road, Ohoka, which was close to 100 acres [RS 9449 and Pt 2685 (bought on 1873-08-01)]. It was later owned by his son-in-law Edwin Lord in 1896. Karl married Elise Katharina Ellenberger on 1866-07-05 at St. Peter's Riccarton, Christchurch, and they had seven daughters. Only three survived to maturity.

Hellene Barbara Meng	(1867-06-23–1869-08-03)
Elise Mary Meng	(1868-11-02–1881-07-05)
Mary Meng	(1870-05-21–1937-02-27)
Katherina Meng	(1872-10-23–1969-05-14)
Emma Magdalena Meng	(1875–1931-09-24)
Lina Amelia Meng	(1877-10-08–1878-03-19)
Amelia Wihelmina Meng	(1877-10-08–1878-02-23)

None of these children were baptized as they are not in the Christchurch parish records. This makes sense as the Ellenberger family was Mennonite and did not believe in baptizing children. Mennonites believed that baptisms should take place when the person was old enough to make their own decision. Karl Meng attended the Lutheran

Church in Hohen-Sülzen, Germany, like his ancestors before him, and may not have been Mennonite.

It appears that Karl was a laborer living in Rangiora when his first child Hellene was born in 1867. Whether this was on his piece of land in Ashley, or laboring for someone else, we are not sure. He was listed as a farmer residing in Rangiora on Elise Mary's birth certificate in 1868. A year later, they were resided at the Maori Reserve at Woodend.

INQUEST INTO DEATH OF HELLENE BARBARA MENG (1869)

Their oldest child, Hellene Barbara Meng, drowned in Woodend at about the age of two years and one month. It seems Elise left her daughter outside for about five minutes and then realized she couldn't hear her and went to look for her. Hellene had followed a furrow on a freshly ploughed field on the property and fell into a six-foot-deep water hole. A full transcription of the inquest is further on in this book. The following extract was in *The Press* dated Thursday, August 5, 1869.

> *An inquest was held on Wednesday last at Woodend before C. Dudley Esq, coroner, on the body of a child, daughter of Mr Meng, residing near the bush. It appears that on Monday evening the child (two years and a month old) was found drowned in a pool of water in a paddock near where it parents resided. A verdict of Accidentally Drowned was returned.*

The *Lyttelton Times* and the *Star* had this extract published August 5, 1869.

> *Inquest—An inquest was held yesterday at Woodend, on the body of Helena Barbara Meng, whose parents reside on the Maori Reserve. The child had left the house the day previous and was found drowned. The evidence of the mother and a neighbour named David Stuart was taken and the jury returned a verdict of "Accidental Death".*

In the inquest, Elise went to see Reverend Stack for help so the family likely went to St.Stephen's Church, Tuahiwi, for a while before they moved to Ohoka. It was a couple of months after Hellene's tragic death that Karl sold his land at Ashley (Oct 1869).

In November 1869, Karl was awarded 20 pounds compensation for cattle destroyed at the Maori Reserve (under proclamation) as they had pleuropneumonia. From *The Star*, it seems that there were many people in the area affected by this disease. On April 17, 1871, Karl was compensated again for cattle destroyed on the Maori Reserve, this time 18 pounds. This may have encouraged Karl to finally leave the Native Reserve and move to Ohoka in about 1871, but we are not sure about this. Reverend Stack and his family also left the area and moved to Kaiapoi after his cottage burned down on May 5, 1870. The Meng family's support from the local reverend in Tuahiwi was now gone.

Mary Meng was born in Woodend in 1870 while Katherina Meng was born at Ohoka in 1872, so the family moved during this time period. The twins Lina and Amelia Meng were born in 1877 and died in 1878 in Ohoka after illnesses from birth. Lina appears to have had inanition from birth (lack of nutrition) and died at five months old while Amelia had general atrophy from birth and died at about four months old. On Amelia's inquest, she had been sick on the Saturday and Karl Meng had gone to Christchurch to buy a double perambulator for his girls. While away, Amelia died as

Elise had nobody to send for a doctor. She probably would have died anyway as she was in a very poor state nutritionally.

Ohoka in 1871 would have been a fairly hard place to live. Despite the main drain being dug in 1860 and 1861, the land was still very wet and "the settlers were frequently prisoners during the winter months." Phillip Threlkeld, an Ohoka identity, commented that "there would be little exaggeration in saying that the land was knee-deep in water." The settlers were frequently completely isolated during the winter months until the railway came in the mid-1870s. Even then the Ohoka section of the railway was known as The Ohoka Punt. The railway was a great step forward for the Meng family, and they didn't have to wait long for it to arrive. A two-story hotel opened in Ohoka in April 1871 and, a year later, a store was opened diagonally opposite the hotel. By 1874, there was a post office facility at the store.

The sheep records show that Karl had 43 sheep in 1880 and 22 sheep in 1881 on the property at Ohoka. On the farm, Karl used to carry on the German tradition of curing his own bacon and making sausages, according to his granddaughter Dorothy Lord, so it looks like he may have had some pigs as well. We don't know what other animals were on the farm or whether he had crops as well.

Karl and Elise went to the Deutsche Kirche or German Church which opened in 1874 on the corner or Montreal Street and Worcester Street (now the site of the Christchurch Art Gallery). At the anniversary of opening, 400 people were present and "Mesdame Meng" was one of many ladies mentioned who presided over the supper tables. In 1877, Karl Meng paid one pound as a first payment of two for subscription to the Oxford Church, for Pastor Lohr's services there. The pastor traveled to the Oxford area for those who couldn't always make it into Christchurch every Sunday. Oxford apparently had a large German Lutheran population.

At the death of Karl's wife, Elise Katharina, in 1879, he had four girls to look after. One of his daughters, Elizabeth, later died in 1881 at the age of 12 of acute pneumonia. He remarried on January 28, 1882, to a widow Sarah Winfield Potts (née Brown). She looked after his three remaining daughters. Whether Karl married Sarah Potts specifically so she could look after the girls is unknown but could have been a possibility. Once married, it is possible he moved straight to Christchurch and lived at 30 Antigua Street with his second wife Sarah, or ???

Karl Meng's sister's
(Anna Maria Umstadt)
gravestone.

Reichard Meng [b. 12 Nov 1799–d. 22 Jan 1871]. Reichard was married to
Maria Eva (née Dorrschuck) (1811–1870). On December 12, 1862, Reichard's
son, Karl Meng, emigrated from Hohen-Sülzen, Germany, to New Zealand
and started a new branch of the family tree in another country.

Mary Meng (ca. 1890)

Emma Meng (ca. 1890)

Katherina Meng (ca. 1890)

Elise Katharina Meng (née Ellenberger) with children Elise Mary Meng on the left and Mary Meng in 1873 (taken by Rangiora photographer E. Barnard.) She is seen here gripping her children; the memory of losing Hellene four years earlier would still be fresh in her mind.

St. Stephen's Church, Tuahiwi, which the Meng family would have attended whilst living near the Church Bush. Elise ran for Rev. James Stack, who preached there when her daughter Hellene was drowned.

SARAH WINFIELD POTTS MARRIES WIDOWER KARL PHILLIP MENG (1882)

The Meng Children's Stepmother

Sarah Winfield Potts (née Brown) (1830–1904-06-20)

Even though Sarah is not a blood relation, she is a very interesting lady. She was christened at Dorking, Surrey, England, on September 19, 1830 to parents James Brown and Mary Ann Weller. She came to New Zealand aboard the *Gananoque* which sailed on February 9, 1860, and arrived on May 9, 1860, and is listed as a domestic servant/matron aged 27. She must have followed James Potts (who she married on 11 Jun. 1860 at St. Michael's, Christchurch) to New Zealand as she married him soon after arriving in Christchurch. They had two stillborn children and two children who survived the birth but didn't live very long.

James Potts died on October 25, 1879, leaving Sarah a childless widow. It must have been very heartbreaking for her. She married Karl Philipp Meng on January 28, 1882. This may have been a marriage of convenience so that Sarah could look after Karl's three daughters (Mary, Katherina, and Emma Magdalena) and also give to herself some security, however it may have been love. We will never know.

Once Sarah married Karl Meng, the Meng and Lord families had a close connection. In the early days, James and Sarah Potts lived out in Courtenay near to where the Lords lived, and they would have known each other. The Lords included Sarah in their family, and she was legally family after Mary Meng and Edwin Lord married in 1893. She is even in a family photo of the Lords dated between 1900 and 1904. There exists a Christmas card that was sent from Mrs. Meng to Mrs. Anderton, Edwin Lord's aunt.

Katherina Fraser (née Meng) told her children that stories about wicked stepmothers were not always true. Sarah must have been a wonderful stepmother to the three girls who had lost their real mother at such a young age.

Sarah and Karl Meng lived at 30 Antigua Street and both died there. Sarah owned a piece of land on the corner of Halkett and Antigua Streets when she died in 1904. This was where she lived originally in the 1860s with James Potts, and they rented out furnished apartments before moving to the Halkett area. She split the land into three sections and gave one to each of her three stepdaughters. Mary Lord still owned her place in the 1911 electoral roll. All Sarah's personal belongings, such as household furniture, clothing, jewelry, and ornaments, went to her three stepdaughters. She also left some money to relatives in England.

Sarah Winfield Meng is buried in Addington Cemetery with her first husband James Potts and four children.

Emma Elise Meng.

Kate Meng as a child.

Sarah Winfield Meng
(formerly Potts, née Brown).

Sarah Winfield Meng (formerly Potts, née Brown) (c. 1880).

149

Maybe they moved when he became ill with cancer in 1883. He appeared at a meeting for the German Church in 1883, now living much closer to the church. He must have leased his farm at Ohoka as he still owned it when he died. Karl Meng died on August 19, 1885, after a long and painful illness. It appears he had cancer for two years. He was living at 30 Antigua Street in Christchurch. An extract from his will follows:

> *... upon trust in the first place to pay to my wife Sarah Wingfield Meng the sum of one hundred pounds for her sole and separate use and benefit absolutely and to hold in trust for my said wife all the shares which I now possess in the Colonial Bank of New Zealand and all dividends and sums of money if any now and payable in respect thereof for her absolute use and benefit. My real and personal estate and effects and all sum and sums of money coming to the hands of my said trustees under by virtue of this my Will and the yearly produce thereof upon trust for my three children Mary, Katherina and Emma on their respectively attaining the age of twenty-one years in equal shares. They are to be paid 40 pounds per year respectively out of the income of the presumptive share or shares of such dividends when under the age of 21 ...*

Karl Meng's estate consisted of the following items:

98 ac 24 per of farm land with house thereon at Ohoka	1650
16 shares in the Kaiapoi Woollen Factory	400
40 shares in the Colonial Bank	84
Cash in bank	100/8/0
Fixed deposit Colonial Bank	100
An IOU	26/17/6
Household furniture	40
	2400/18/2
Credit	723/8/5

Karl Meng's will took a long time to sort out, and the executors, Mr. Peter Schneider and Mr. Heinrich Kissell, received 1,885 pounds for administration. This was a large cut of the will. Heinrich Kissell was on the same ship coming out to New Zealand as Karl and Elise and was from Grosskarlbach about 11 km from where Karl grew up. Heinrich went to the Deutsche Church in Christchurch as well, so was probably a close friend. According to researcher Ian Arnst, Peter Schneider was also from Hohen-Sülzen and, if this is the case, is possibly related to Karl as Karl's grandmother was a Schneider from the same village. It appears Karl and Elise had a fairly hard and tragic life in New Zealand. They are buried in the Flaxton Cemetery along with their daughters Elizabeth, Lina Amelia, and Amelia Wilhelmina Meng. It is likely that Hellene is buried in the Kaiapoi Anglican Cemetery as it was "the burial place for all bodies on which inquests was held in the district between the Waimakariri and the Hurunui" according to the Waimakariri District Council. The records are not complete for this cemetery as Hellene's name cannot be found.

1866
Karl Philipp Meng and his wife Elise Katharina (née Ellenberger) Meng.

DESCENDANTS OF JOHANN STEPHAN MENG

The NZ Connection

1 Johann Stephan Meng (b. ca. 1727) in Germany

....+ Maria Elisabetha Bohlander

....2 Johanna Catharina Margaretha Meng (b. 19 Jul 1747) in Hohen-Sülzen, Pfalz, Bayern, Germany

....2 Johann Peter Meng (b. 4 Dec 1748) in Hohen-Sülzen, Pfalz, Bayern, Germany

*2nd Wife of Johann Stephan Meng:

....+ Maria Catherina Bertrand (m. ca. 1757) in Pfalz, Bayern, Germany

....2 Maria Christina Meng (b. 11 Jan 1758) in Hohen-Sülzen, Pfalz, Bayern, Germany (christ. 15 Jan 1758) Hohen-Sülzen, Pfalz, Bayern, Germany

....2 Johannes Meng (b. 7 Feb 1760) in Hohen-Sülzen, Pfalz, Bayern, Germany (christ. 10 Feb 1760) Hohen-Sülzen, Pfalz, Bayern, Germany

....2 Johann Christian Meng (b. 12 Jun 1762) in Hohen-Sülzen, Pfalz, Bayern, Germany (d. 7 Mar 1838) in Hohen-Sülzen, Pfalz, Bayern, Germany

........+ Katharina Barbara Stahl (b. ca. Mar 1765) in Germany (d. 31 May 1853) in Hohen-Sülzen, Pfalz, Bayern, Germany m: 1780 in Hohen-Sülzen, Pfalz, Bayern, Germany

........3 Maria Katharina Meng

........3 Marie Magdeleine Meng

........3 Martin Meng

........3 Philipp Meng (d. 2 Nov 1846) in Hohen-Sülzen, Pfalz, Bayern, Germany

........+ Elizabetha?

........3 Johannes Meng (b. 1795) in Hohen-Sülzen, Pfalz, Bayern, Germany (d. 13 Jul 1873) in Hohen-Sülzen, Pfalz, Bayern, Germany

............+ Katherina Barth (b. 1804–d. 1875) in Hohen-Sülzen, Pfalz, Bayern, Germany (m. 27 Jun 1830) in Hohen-Sülzen, Pfalz, Bayern, Germany

............4 Sophia Meng (b. 23 Jan 1831) in Hohen-Sülzen, Pfalz, Bayern, Germany

............4 Johannes Meng (b. 29 Dec 1834) in Hohen-Sülzen, Pfalz, Bayern, Germany

............4 Katherina Wendeline Meng (b. 1837) in Hohen-Sülzen, Pfalz, Bayern, Germany

............4 David Meng (b. 1838) in Hohen-Sülzen, Pfalz, Bayern, Germany (d. 1839) in Hohen-Sülzen, Pfalz, Bayern, Germany

............4 Friedrich Meng (b. 2 Mar 1840) in Hohen-Sülzen, Pfalz, Bayern, Germany

............4 Philipp Meng (b. 22 Feb 1847) in Hohen-Sülzen, Pfalz, Bayern, Germany

...............+ Margaretha Trumpler (m. 7 Oct 1873) in Hohen-Sülzen, Pfalz, Bayern, Germany

............*2nd Wife of Philipp Meng:

.... + Teresa ? (b. ca. 1857) in Germany (m. 1881) in Hohen-Sülzen, Pfalz, Bayern, Germany

.... 5 Barbara Meng (b. ca. 1882) in Hohen-Sülzen, Pfalz, Bayern, Germany

.... 5 William J Meng (b. ca. 1890) in Pennsylvania, United States of America

.... 4 Anna Elisabetha Meng (b. 3 Mar 1843) in Hohen-Sülzen, Pfalz, Bayern, Germany

.... + Michael Meurer (m. 1868) in Hohen-Sülzen, Pfalz, Bayern, Germany

.... 4 Maria Magdalena Meng (b. 22 Jul 1833)

.... 3 Anna Elisabetha Meng (b. 10 Feb 1797) in Hohen-Sülzen, Pfalz, Bayern, Germany (d. 25 May 1884) in Hohen-Sülzen, Pfalz, Bayern, Germany

.... 3 Wendeline Meng (b. 1810)

.... 3 Anne Marie Meng (b. 1812)

....2 Johann Martin Meng (b. 17 Mar 1765) in Hohen-Sülzen, Pfalz, Bayern, Germany (bapt. 22 Mar 1765) Hohen-Sülzen, Pfalz, Bayern, Germany

....2 Peter Jacob Meng (b. 8 Oct 1767) in Hohen-Sülzen, Pfalz, Bayern, Germany (bapt. 9 Oct 1767) Hohen-Sülzen, Pfalz, Bayern, Germany

....2 Karl Philipp Meng (b. 7 Jun 1771) in Hohen-Sülzen, Pfalz, Bayern, Germany (d. 22 Jan 1859) in Hohen-Sülzen, Pfalz, Bayern, Germany (bapt. 8 June 1771 Hohen-Sülzen, Pfalz, Bayern, Germany

.... + Maria Dorothea Schneider (b. 24 Jun 1771) in Hohen-Sülzen, Pfalz, Bayern, Germany (m. 1798) in Hohen-Sülzen, Pfalz, Bayern, Germany

.... 3 Elisabeth Meng (d. 1808) in Hohen-Sülzen, Pfalz, Bayern, Germany

.... 3 Elizabetha Meng

.... + Wilhelm Gottler (m. 19 Aug 1832) in Hohen-Sülzen, Pfalz, Bayern, Germany

.... 3 Margaretha Meng

.... + Jakob?

.... 3 Johannes Meng (b. ca. 1794) in Hohen-Sülzen, Pfalz, Bayern, Germany (d. 1799) in Hohen-Sülzen, Pfalz, Bayern, Germany

.... 3 Reichard Meng (b. 12 Nov 1799) in Hohen-Sülzen, Pfalz, Bayern, Germany (d. 22 Jan 1871) in Hohen-Sülzen, Pfalz, Bayern, Germany

.... + Maria Eva Dörrschuck (b. 3 Sep 1811) in Hohen-Sülzen, Pfalz, Bayern, Germany (d. 30 Dec 1870) in Hohen-Sülzen, Pfalz, Bayern, Germany (m. 8 Nov 1829) in Hohen-Sülzen, Pfalz, Bayern, Germany

.... 4 Johannes Meng (b. 5 Aug 1830) in Hohen-Sülzen, Pfalz, Bayern, Germany (d. 27 Dec 1870) in Hohen-Sülzen, Pfalz, Bayern, Germany

.... 4 Christian Meng (b. 29 Oct 1832) in Hohen-Sülzen, Pfalz, Bayern, Germany

.... 4 Karl Philipp Meng (b. 27 Jun 1834) in Hohen-Sülzen, Pfalz, Bayern, Germany (d. 19 Aug 1885) in 30 Antigua St., Christchurch, New Zealand (christ. 29 Jun 1834) Hohen-Sülzen, Pfalz, Bayern, Germany

.... + Elise Katharina Ellenberger (b. 19 Nov 1839) in Friedelsheim, Palatinate, Germany (d. 29 Mar 1879) in Ohoka, North Canterbury, New Zealand (m. 5 Jul 1866) in St. Peter's Anglican Church, Riccarton, Christchurch, New Zealand

.... 5 Hellene Barbara Meng (b. 23 Jun 1867) in Rangiora, New Zealand (d. 3 Aug 1869) in Church Bush, Tuahiwi, New Zealand

.... 5 Elise Mary Meng (b. 2 Nov 1868) in Ohoka, North Canterbury, New Zealand (d. 2 Jul 1881) in Ohoka, North Canterbury, New Zealand

.... 5 Mary Meng (b. 21 May 1870) in Woodend, North Canterbury, New Zealand (d. 27 Feb 1937) in Christchurch, New Zealand

....................+ Edwin Lord (b. 31 Mar 1865) in Halkett, New Zealand (d. 17 Jul 1944) in Christchurch, New Zealand (m. 5 Apr 1893) in St. Michael's and All Angels, Christchurch, New Zealand

...................6 Elise May Lord (b. 5 May 1896) in Ohoka, North Canterbury, New Zealand (d. 8 Dec 1962) in Little River, Banks Peninsula, New Zealand

...................+ Unknown

...................*2nd Husband of Elise May Lord:

...................+ John Lewis Grant (b. 1897) in New Zealand (d. 1968) in New Zealand (m. 6 Jan 1926) in Knox Presbyterian Church, Christchurch, New Zealand

...................6 Catherine Emma Lord (b. 1899) in Ohoka, North Canterbury, New Zealand (d. 1899) in Ohoka, North Canterbury, New Zealand

...................6 Dorothy Wingfield Lord (b. 25 Oct 1900) in Ohoka, North Canterbury, New Zealand (d. 25 Apr 1997) in Auckenflower Rest Home, Bishopdale, Christchurch, New Zealand

...................+ Arthur Cyril Pearce (b. 26 Oct 1899) in Christchurch, New Zealand (d. 16 May 1981) in Christchurch, New Zealand (m. 20 Jan 1926) in St. Paul's Anglican Church, Papanui, Christchurch, New Zealand

...................6 Carl Edwin Lord (b. 7 Nov 1902) in Ohoka, North Canterbury, New Zealand (d. 12 Aug 1910) in Ohoka, North Canterbury, New Zealand

.... 5 Katherina Meng (b. 23 Oct 1872) in Ohoka, North Canterbury, New Zealand (d. ca. 14 May 1969) in Wellington, New Zealand

...................+ William Alexander Fraser (b. 1872) in Otago, New Zealand (d. ca. 17 Nov 1945) in Wellington, New Zealand (m. 3 Jan 1899) in St. Michael's and All Angels, Christchurch, New Zealand

...................6 Charles William Fraser (b. 16 Nov 1899; d. 1987)

...................+ Stella Gordon (m. 6 Dec 1927) in their residence, "Ngaio", Opotiki, NZ

...................6 Alexander Douglass Fraser (b. 14 Feb 1901) in Ohingaiti, New Zealand (d. 1994)

...................+ Freda Rose Somerville (m. 1924) in New Zealand

...................6 Allan Austin Fraser (b. 14 Feb 1901) in Ohingaiti, New Zealand (d. 20 Mar 1981)

...................+ Lilian Robina Day (m. 1927) in New Zealand

...................6 John Andrew Fraser (b. 1902; d. 1903)

...................6 Margaret Ruth Fraser (b. 30 Aug 1904; d. 2002)

...................6 Edward Percy Fraser (b. 6 Dec 1907; d. 1997)

....................6 Wilfred Robert Fraser (b. 1909; d. 1909) in died in infancy aged three
weeks

....................6 Marion Faith Fraser (b. 1 Sep 1914) in New Zealand (d. 2005) in New
Zealand

.........................+ Alexander McCormack (m. 20 May 1939) in St. Aidan's Church,
Miramar, New Zealand

....................6 Esther Fraser

.........................+ ? Harris

.... 5 Emma Magdalena Meng (b. 1875) in Ohoka, North Canterbury, New
Zealand (d. 23 Sep 1931) in Dunedin, New Zealand

....................+ Thomas Henry Dalton (b. 1867) in Rangiora, North Canterbury, New
Zealand (d. 27 Aug 1943) in Christchurch, New Zealand (m. 1 Jan 1902)
in St. Michael's and All Angels, Christchurch, New Zealand

.... 5 Lina Amelia Meng (b. 8 Oct 1877) in Ohoka, North Canterbury, New
Zealand (d. 17 Mar 1878) in Ohoka, North Canterbury, New Zealand

.... 5 Amelia Wihelmina Meng (b. 8 Oct 1877) in Ohoka, North Canterbury, New
Zealand (d. 23 Feb 1878) in Ohoka, North Canterbury, New Zealand

.... *2nd Wife of Karl Philipp Meng:

.... + Sarah Winfield Brown (b. 19 Sep 1830) in Dorking, Surrey, England (d. 20
Jun 1904) in 30 Antigua St., Christchurch, New Zealand (m. 28 Jan 1882)
in St. Matthews, St. Albans, Christchurch

.... 4 Margaretha (Margarete) Meng (b. 13 Feb 1836) in Hohen-Sülzen, Pfalz,
Bayern, Germany (d. 9 Mar 1914) in Hohen-Sülzen, Pfalz, Bayern, Germany
(christ. 21 Feb 1836) Hohen-Sülzen, Pfalz, Bayern, Germany

.... + ? Velde

.... 4 Catherine Meng (b. 12 Jun 1838) in Hohen-Sülzen, Pfalz, Bayern, Germany

.... 4 Jacob Meng (b. 28 May 1843) in Hohen-Sülzen, Pfalz, Bayern, Germany (d. 3
Jan 1871) in Hohen-Sülzen, Pfalz, Bayern, Germany

.... 4 Wilhelm Meng (b. 10 Apr 1841) in Hohen-Sülzen, Pfalz, Bayern, Germany (d.
Jun 1843) in Hohen-Sülzen, Pfalz, Bayern, Germany

.... 4 Anna Barbara Meng (b. 4 Apr 1845) in Hohen-Sülzen, Ffalz, Bayern, Germany

.... 4 Anna Maria Meng (b. 27 Jan 1850) in Hohen-Sülzen, Pfalz, Bayern, Germany
(d. 8 Nov 1916) in Hohen-Sülzen, Pfalz, Bayern, Germany (bapt. 3 Feb 1850)
Hohen-Sülzen, Pfalz, Bayern, Germany

.... + Jakob Umstadt (b. 13 Nov 1847) in Hohen-Sülzen, Pfalz, Bayern, Germany
(d. 22 Sep 1891) in Hohen-Sülzen, Pfalz, Bayern, Germany (m. 2 Jul 1872)
in Hohen-Sülzen, Pfalz, Bayern, Germany

.... 4 Luisa Meng (b. 9 Feb 1853) in Hohen-Sülzen, Pfalz, Bayern, Germany (d. 2
Aug 1853) in Hohen-Sülzen, Pfalz, Bayern, Germany

.... 4 Friedrich Meng (b. 5 Oct 1855) in Hohen-Sülzen, Pfalz, Bayern, Germany (d.
31 Aug 1903) in Hohen-Sülzen, Pfalz, Bayern, Germany

.... + Katharina Stamm

.... 5 Magdalene Meng (b. ca. 1887)

....................+ ?

....................6 Luise?

....................6 Magdalena? (b. 1914)

....................6 Elisabeth?

....................6 Karl?

.... 5 Luise Meng (b. 1889) in Hohen-Sülzen, Pfalz, Bayern, Germany (d. 1963) in Germany

....................+ ?

....................6 Georg?

....................6 August?

....................6 Elisabeth? (b. ca. 1938) in Germany

....................+ Ernst Schneider

.... 5 Emelie Meng

....................+ Franz Breier

....................6 Hilde Breier

....................6 Ema Breier

.... 5 Eugen Meng

....................6 Friedrich (Fritz) Meng (d. bet. 1939 and 1945) died in World War II

....................6 Eugen Meng

....................+ Katharina?

....................6 Marga Meng

.... 5 Richard Meng (b. 1896) in Hohen-Sülzen, Pfalz, Bayern, Germany (d. 1974) in Hohen-Sülzen, Pfalz, Bayern, Germany

....................+ Katharina Sutter (b. 1893) in Germany (d. 1963) in Hohen-Sülzen, Pfalz, Bayern, Germany (m. ca. 1922) in Germany

....................6 Maria (Maya) Meng (b. 4 May 1923) in Wachenheim, Pfalz, Bayern, Germany

....................+ Manfred Schneider

....................*2nd Husband of Maria (Maya) Meng:

....................+ ?

....................6 Richard Johannes (Hans) Meng (b. 11 Dec 1924) in Monsheim, Pfalz, Bayern, Germany (d. 28 Jan 2010) in Germany

....................+ Hella?

....................6 Kurt Meng (b. 11 Dec 1924) in Monsheim, Pfalz, Bayern, Germany (d. Mar 1945) and shot in World War II, Heilgenteil/Ostpeussen, Germany

....................6 Richard Meng (b. 15 Jul 1926) in Hohen-Sülzen, Pfalz, Bayern, Germany (d. 1976) in Germany

....................6 Herbert Meng (b. 10 Mar 1931) in Worms-Pfeddersheim, Pfalz, Bayern, Germany

.... 5 Hans Meng (b. ca. 1898)

....................+ ?

....................6 Alma Meng

....................6 Renate Meng

....................6 Anita Meng

....................6 Amelie Meng

....................6 Hans? Meng

.... 5 Elisabetha Margareta Meng (b. 19 Aug 1903)

........3 Anna Maria Meng (b. ca. 1802) in Hohen-Sülzen, Pfalz, Bayern, Germany

.... + Jacob Scherrer (m. 1821) in Hohen-Sülzen, Pfalz, Bayern, Germany

........3 Catherina Meng (b. ca. 1811)

.... + Gottfried Schneider (m. 19 May 1829) in Hohen-Sülzen, Pfalz, Bayern, Germany

....2 Johann Philipp Meng (b. 20 Mar 1774) in Hohen-Sülzen, Pfalz, Bayern, Germany

........+ Margaretha Trumpler?

Sources

[1] The Ashley, New Zealand, information is the product of the gracious contribution again, of Werner Schabbehard. Belinda Lansley has also accomplished extensive research connecting Karl and Elsie (née Ellenberger) Meng's (ca. 1866) marriage in New Zealand with the Meng family in Hohen-Sülzen, Germany. Belinda's information on the New Zealand Meng–Ellenberger families, remains a work that is still in progress. These newly found connections exemplify one of the rewards of investigating family history and meeting new friends like Werner and Belinda.

The Meng-Shamhart book is in the Christchurch City Library

One of the many rewards of preparing this book, was the ability to converse and share documentation with relatives in Germany via the computer. One such computer relative was Armin Kurt Meng who had earlier helped with the books content but surprisingly came to the U.S. in 2018 to chaperone a group of German exchange students to a local university. This event allowed Armin and I to have a very pleasant in person discussion of Meng family history and relationships in both the U.S. and Germany. Subsequently, Armin has extended the Meng family history with the following.

Meng-family from Hohen-Sülzen – Monsheim – Worms – Darmstadt

Nuno Maximilian Meng (*2018-10-04 in Frankfurt) son of **Kristina Meng** (*1983-11-02 in Kassel, Hessen, Ger.) and **Peter Hartmann**

Jannis Meng (*1988-01-26 in Darmstadt, Ger.) and **Alina Adam**

Silvia Meng, nee Lohrbach

Armin Meng (*1954-07-20 in Worms, Rheinland-Pfalz, Ger.)

Meng family, Peter, Kristina, Alina, Jannis, Silvia, Armin and Opa Herbert Lohrbach

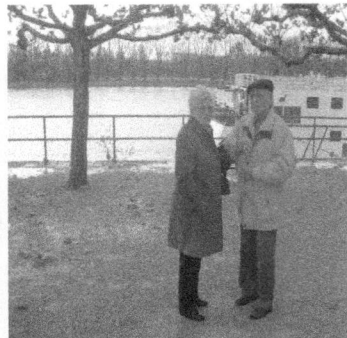

Richard Johannes (Hans) Meng (*1924-12-11 in Hohen Sülzen, Rheinland-Pfalz, Ger. † 2010-01-28 in Worms) and **Hella Meng**, nee Strack (*1928-10-13 in Monsheim, Rheinland-Pfalz, Ger. † 2018-03-20 in Worms) parents of Armin Meng

Meng-family from Hohen-Sülzen – Monsheim – Worms – Darmstadt

Richard Meng	+	Katharina Sutter	Hohen-Sülzen
1896-06-08 / 1974-12-23		1983-12-14 / 1963-07-07	

↓

Maria Meng (Schneider)	+	Manfred Schneider	Hohen-Sülzen
1923-05-07 / 2015-			
Richard Johannes (Hans) Meng	+	Hella Meng, nee Strack	Hohen-Sülzen
1924-12-11 / 2010-01-28		1928-10-13 / 2018-05-20	Monsheim
Kurt Meng			Hohen-Sülzen
1924-12-11 / 1945-March		shot in WorldWarII	
Richard Meng			Hohen-Sülzen
1926-07-15 / 1987-03-12			Monsheim
Herbert Meng	+	Hedy Meng	Hohen-Sülzen
1931-03-10 / 2012			Worms

↓

Gabriele Meng
ca. 1960 – 1976

Armin Kurt Meng	+	Silvia, nee Lohrbach	Worms / Kassel
1954-07-20		1954-08-04	

↓

Jannis Christopher Meng	+	Alina Adam	Darmstadt
1988-01-26		1987-07-13	
Kristina Nadine Meng	+	Peter Hartmann	Kassel
1983-11-02		1979-06-21	

↓

2018-10-04	Frankfurt/Main

Karl Philipp Meng (ca.1880)

CHAPTER 7
THE ILLINOIS BRANCH OF THE MENG GENEALOGICAL TREE MONSHEIM, GERMANY (1834)

The first of the Illinois branch of the Meng that landed on American shores originated with Conrad (sometimes spelled Konrad) Meng. The first marriage of Conrad Meng (age 24 years and 4 months) was to Jeanne Elizabeth Hofmann from Wachenheim, age 21 years and 11 months, on December 5, 1808, in Monsheim, Germany. Children born of this marriage were Wilhelm Meng (20 Oct 1810), Heinrich Meng (8 Sep 1812), Appolonia Meng (25 Feb 1814), Johann Conrad Meng (22 Feb 1816), and Ludwig Meng (27 Oct 1818). Elizabeth Meng (née Hofmann) died on December 5, 1818, in Monsheim. Conrad's second marriage occurred on May 28, 1819, when he was 34 years 10 months of age to Elizabeth Muller who was 31 years and 3 months old. This wedding also occurred in Monsheim, Germany. Children born of this marriage include Elizabeth Meng (17 Jul 1820), Katharina Meng (22 Jan 1823), and Johannes Meng (19 Mar 1825). At the time of Conrad's immigration to America, on August 1, 1837, he was 52 years old and a farmer. His passport number was 933; arriving from Germany in the port of New York, New York, with his second wife, Elizabeth (née Mueller), and eight of their nine children, Guillaume (Heinrich) Meng, William Meng, Conrad Meng, Louis Meng, Elizabeth Meng, Catharine Meng, John Meng, and Frederick Meng. The Conrad Meng family crossed the Atlantic Ocean on the ship *Manchester* who sailed from Le Havre, France.

Conrad and Elizabeth's ninth child, Wilhelm, married Marie Schreiber in Eberstsheim, Pfatz, Bayern, Germany. They had three children: Louis Meng (22 Feb 1837), Christina Meng (11 Apr 1842), and Christian Meng (1838). The Wilhelm and Marie Meng family crossed the Atlantic to America on January 22, 1848, on the ship *Asia*, arriving in the port of New Orleans, Louisiana.

The complete line of the Illinois branch of the Meng from Wilhelm Meng through Jacob Shamhart (Meng) Cochran (born in the USA) will follow. Although this information is in the appropriate German Language, the data contained within can easily be interpreted with very little effort.

Monsheim

Coat of arms

The Meng-Shamhart book is in the Monsheim City Library

NACHKOMMEN VON WILHELM MENG (1755–2005)

Erste Generation

1. Wilhelm Meng

> Quelle/source: Standesamt (civil registry office) der Verbandsgemeinde Monsheim Alzeyer Str. 15 67590 +49 06243 1809-34. Auf der Sterbeurkunde seines Sohnes sind er und seine Frau vermerkt.

Wilhelm heiratete NN Schiffmann.

> Quelle/source: Standesamt (civil registry office) der Verbandsgemeinde Monsheim Alzeyer Str. 15 67590 +49 06243 1809-34. Auf der Sterbeurkunde ihres Sohnes sind und ihr Mann vermerkt.

Wilhelm und NN hatten die folgenden Kinder:

2 M   i. George Wilhelm Meng wurde 1755 geboren. Erb starb am 02. Juni 1822.

Zweite Generation

2. George Wilhelm Meng (Wilhelm) wurde 1755 in Hohen-Sülzen geboren. Er starb am 02. Juni 1822 in Monsheim, Rheinland-Pfalz.

George war Ackersmann in Monsheim, Bornstr. Nr. 80.

Stirbt im Alter von 67 Jahren

> Quelle/source: Death certificate of Standesamt (civil registry office) der Verbandsgemeinde Monsheim Alzeyer Str. 15 67590 +49 06243 1809-34

George heiratete Appolonia Hofmann am 23. Mai 1784 in Monsheim, Rheinland-Pfalz[1].

Appolonia wurde 1755 in Hohen-Sülzen, Rheiland-Pfalz geboren. Sie starb am 25. Januar 1811 in Monsheim, Rheinland-Pfalz.

Stirbt im Alter von 56 Jahren

> Quelle/source: Death certificate of Standesamt (civil registry office) der Verbandsgemeinde Monsheim Alzeyer Str. 15 67590 +49 06243 1809-34

George und Appolonia hatten die folgenden Kinder:

3 M   i. Conrad Meng wurde am 09. Juli 1784 geboren. Er starb 1842.

Dritte Generation

3. Conrad Meng[2,3,4] (Georg Wilhelm, Wilhelm) wurde am 09. Juli 1784 in Monsheim, Rheinland-Pfalz geboren. Er wurde am 10. Juli 1784 in Monsheim, Rheinland-Pfalz getauft. Er starb 1842 in United States.

    Conrad war Ackersmann in Monsheim, Bornstr. Nr. 80.

    > Quelle/source: Meng, James Leroy, St. Louis, Missouri
    > Quelle/source: Zentralarchiv, Evangelische Kirche in Hessen Nassau

    Conrad heiratete Jeanne Elisabeth Hofmann[5] Tochter von Johann Jacob Hofmann und Maria Margaretha Spindler am 05. Dezember 1808 in Monsheim, Rheinland-Pfalz[6] (1). Jeanne wurde 1786 in Wachenheim geboren. Sie starb am 05. Dezember 1818 in Monsheim.

    > Quelle/source: Standesbeamter Stefan Lösch, Verbandsgemeindeverwaltung Monsheim Alzeyer Str. 15 67590 Monsheim

    Ihren Tod zeigen an: Ludwig Hofmann, alt 30 Jahr, einer Profession Schreiner, Vetter der Verstorbenen, wohnhaft zu Monsheim und Peter Jacob Scheuer, alt 67 Jahre, Nachbar der Verstorbenen, wohnhaft zu Monsheim

    Conrad und Jeanne hatten die folgenden Kinder:

    4 M   i.   Wilhelm Meng wurde am 27. Juli 1810 geboren. Er starb am 16. Dezember 1850.

    5 M   ii.   Heinrich Meng[7] wurde am 08. September 1812 in Monsheim, Rheinland-Pfalz geboren.

    > Quelle/source: Standesamt (civil registry office) der Verbandsgemeinde Monsheim Alzeyer Str. 15 67590 +49 06243 1809-34

    6 W   iii. Apolonia Meng[8] wurde am 25. Februar 1814 in Monsheim, Rheinland-Pfalz geboren.

    > Quelle/source: Standesamt (civil registry office) der Verbandsgemeinde Monsheim Alzeyer Str. 15 67590 +49 06243 1809-34

    7 M   iv.   Johann Conrad Meng[9] wurde am 22. Februar 1816 in Monsheim, Rheinland-Pfalz geboren.

    > Quelle/source: Standesamt (civil registry office) der Verbandsgemeinde Monsheim Alzeyer Str. 15 67590 +49 06243 1809-34

    8 M   v.   Meng[10] wurde am 27. Oktober 1818 in Monsheim, Rheinland-Pfalz geboren.

    > Quelle/source: Standesamt (civil registry office) der Verbandsgemeinde Monsheim Alzeyer Str. 15 67590 +49 06243 1809-34

Conrad heiratete Anna Elisabetha Müller[11,12,13] Tochter von Wilhelm Müller und Barbara Geyer am 28. Mai 1819 in Monsheim, Rheinland-Pfalz[14] (2). Anna wurde am 02. Februar 1793 in Monsheim, Rheinland-Pfalz geboren.

> Quelle/source: Meng, James Leroy, St. Louis, Missouri
> Quelle/source: Standesamt (civil registry office) der Verbandsgemeinde Monsheim Alzeyer Str. 15 67590 +49 06243 1809-34

Conrad und Anna hatten die folgenden Kinder:

9 W   vi.   Elisabeth Meng[15] wurde am 17. Juli 1820 in Monsheim, Rheinland-Pfalz geboren.

> Quelle/source: Standesamt (civil registry office) der Verbandsgemeinde Monsheim Alzeyer Str. 15 67590 +49 06243 1809-34

10 W vii. Katharina Meng[16] wurde am 22. Januar 1823 in Monsheim, Rheinland-Pfalz geboren.

> Quelle/source: Standesamt (civil registry office) der Verbandsgemeinde Monsheim Alzeyer Str. 15 67590 +49 06243 1809-34

11 M viii. Johannes Meng[17] wurde am 19. März 1825 in Monsheim, Rheinland-Pfalz geboren.

> Quelle/source: Standesamt (civil registry office) der Verbandsgemeinde Monsheim Alzeyer Str. 15 67590 +49 06243 1809-34

Vierte Generation

4.   Wilhelm Meng[18,19] (Conrad, Georg Wilhelm, Wilhelm) wurde am 27. Juli 1810 in Monsheim, Rheinland-Pfalz geboren. Er starb am 16. Dezember 1850 in St. Clair County, Illinois.

> Quelle/source: Standesamt (civil registry office) der Verbandsgemeinde Monsheim Alzeyer Str. 15 67590 +49 06243 1809-34

> Quelle/source: Meng, James Leroy, St. Louis, Missouri

Wilhelm William George MENG (my great-great-great-grandfather) born 1810 in Mertesheim, State: Rheinland-Pfalz, County: Bad Duerkheim: Region: Rheinhessen-Pfalz Germany (January 1847–March 1849) St. Clair County, Illinois; died 16 Dec 1850 in St. Clair County, Illinois. He was son of Conrad Meng and Elizabeth Mueller. He married Anna Maria Schreiber on May 31, 1837 in Evangelish, Ebertsheim, Rheinland-Pfalz, Bad Duerkeim County: Rheinhessen-Pfalz region Bayern.

Wilhelm heiratete Marie Schreiber[20] Tochter von George Schreiber und Catharin NN am 31. Mai 1837 in Ebertsheim, Pfalz, Bayern[21] (1). Marie wurde 1818 geboren.

Died between 1845 and 1846 in May

Quelle/source: Meng, James Leroy, St. Louis, Missouri

Wilhelm und Marie hatten die folgenden Kinder:

12 M i. Louis Meng wurde am 22. Februar 1837 geboren. Er starb am 06. Juli 1882.

13 M ii. Christian Meng[22] wurde 1838 geboren.

Quelle/source: Meng, James Leroy, St. Louis, Missouri

14 W iii. Christina Meng[23] wurde am 16. März 1841 in Mertesheim, Hessen Darmstadt geboren. Sie starb am 22. Mai 1913 in Belleville, St. Clair County, Illinois.

Quelle/source: Meng, James Leroy, St. Louis, Missouri

Christina heiratete Martin Darmstatter[24] am 26. Februar 1860 in St. Clair County, Illinois[25,26]. Martin wurde 1840 geboren.

Quelle/source: Meng, James Leroy, St. Louis, Missouri

15 M iv. Friedrich Meng[27] wurde am 28. Mai 1844 geboren. Er wurde am 02. Juni 1844 in Evangelisch, Ebertsheim, Pfalz, Bayern getauft.

FamilySearch™
FRIEDRICH MENG
Birth: 28 MAY 1844
Christening: 02 JUN 1844 Evangelisch, Ebertsheim, Pfalz, Bayern
Father: WILHELM MENG
Mother: ANNA MARIA SCHREIBER
C982651 - 1694 - 1875 - 0193832

Wilhelm heiratete Henriette Seybert am 03. Januar 1847 in Evangelisch, Ebertsheim, Pfalz, Bayern[28] (2).

Sie hatten die folgenden Kinder:

16 W v. Katharina Meng[29] wurde am 31. März 1847 geboren. Sie wurde am 18. April 1847 in Evangelisch, Ebertsheim, Pfalz, Bayern getauft.

FamilySearch™
KATHARINA MENG
Birth: 31 MAR 1847
Christening: 18 APR 1847 Evangelisch, Ebertsheim, Pfalz, Bayern
Father: WILHELM MENG
Mother: HENRIETTA SEIBERT
C982651 - 1694 - 1875 - 0193832

Fünfte Generation

5. Louis Meng[30,31] (Wilhelm, Conrad, Georg Wilhelm, Wilhelm) wurde am 22. Februar 1837 in Evangelisch, Ebertsheim, Pfalz, Bayern geboren. Er starb am 06. Juli 1882 in Freeburg, St. Clair County, Illinois.

> Quelle/source: Meng, James Leroy, St. Louis, Missouri

Louis Meng, born February 22, 1837 in Ebertsheim, Pfalz, Germany Aug 1, 1837, USA. 1848 St. Clair, County Illinois; died July 6, 1882 in Freeburg, St. Clair co., Illinois. He was the son of Wilhelm William George Meng and Anna Marie Schreiber. He married Christina Borger April 1859

> FamilySearch™
> LOUIS MENG
> Birth: 22 FEB 1837 Evangelisch, Ebertsheim, Pfalz, Bayern
> Father: WILHELM MENG
> Mother: MARIE SCHREIBER
> C982651 - 1694 - 1875 - 0193832

Louis heiratete Christine Borger[32] Tochter von George Borger und Elisabeth B. NN am 11. April 1859 in Freeburg, St. Clair County, Illinois[33]. Christine wurde am 11. April 1842 in Family homestead south of Freeburg, Illinois geboren. Sie starb am 29. Mai 1902 in Freeburg, St. Clair County, Illinois.

> Quelle/source: Meng, James Leroy, St. Louis, Missouri

Christina "Christine" BORGER, born 11 Apr 1842 in Family homestead 1 mile south of Freeburg, St. Clair Co IL; died 29 May 1902 in Freeburg, St. Clair Co IL. She was the daughter of George BORGER Sr. and Elizabeth B.(?) BORGER

Louis und Christine hatten die folgenden Kinder:

17 M i. George W. Meng[34] wurde am 24. Oktober 1860 in Freeburg, St. Clair County, Illinois geboren. Er starb am 11. Mai 1953 in Freeburg, St. Clair County, Illinois.

> Quelle/source: Meng, James Leroy, St. Louis, Missouri

George heiratete Margaret Bernhart[35] am 20. November 1889 in St. Clair County, Illinois[36]. Margaret wurde am 25. Dezember 1866 in Germany geboren. Sie starb am 25. August 1954 in Freeburg, St. Clair County, Illinois.

> Quelle/source: Meng, James Leroy, St. Louis, Missouri

18 M ii. Martin Meng[37] wurde am 26. September 1862 geboren. Er starb am 26. September 1862.

> Quelle/source: Meng, James Leroy, St. Louis, Missouri

19 M iii. Friederich Fred Fritz Meng wurde am 11. Oktober 1863 geboren. Er starb am 23. Januar 1913.

20 M iv. Martin Meng[38] wurde im Juni 1865 in Freeburg, St. Clair County, Illinois geboren. Er starb am 17. Oktober 1947 in Belleville, St. Clair County, Illinois.

Quelle/source: Meng, James Leroy, St. Louis, Missouri

21 M v. Kondrad Meng[39] wurde 1868/1869 in Freeburg, Twp, Freeburg St. Clair County, Illinois geboren. Er starb 1953 in Freeburg St. Clair County, Illinois.

Quelle/source: Meng, James Leroy, St. Louis, Missouri

5-Conrad Konrad "Coonie" MENG, born Bet. May 1868-May 1869 in Freeburg Twp, Freeburg, St. Clair Co, IL; died Bet. 12 May- 31 May 1953 in Freeburg, ST.

Clair Co, IL; married Josephine A "Josie" FRITZ on 26 Oct 1899 in Freeburg, St. Clair Co, IL; born Sep 1878 in New Athens Twp, Freeburg, St. Clair Co, IL; died 17 Aug 1945 in Freeburg, St. Clair Co, IL.

Konrad heiratete Josephine Fritz[40] am 26. Oktober 1899 in Freeburg St. Clair County, Illinois[41,42]. Josephine wurde im September 1878 in New Athens, St. Clair County, Illinois geboren. Sie starb am 17. August 1945 in Freeburg St. Clair County, Illinois.

Quelle/source: Meng, James Leroy, St. Louis, Missouri

22 W vi. Mary E. Meng[43] wurde am 22. Dezember 1869/1870 in Freeburg St. Clair County, Illinois geboren. Sie starb am 26. Januar 1926 in Belleville, St. Clair County, Illinois

Quelle/source: Meng, James Leroy, St. Louis, Missouri

6-Mary E. MENG born bet. 22 Dec 1869 - 1870 in Freeburg, St. Clair Co, IL; died 26 January 1926 in Belleville, St. Clair Co, IL

23 W vii. Elizabeth B. Meng[44] wurde am 28. Februar 1872 in Freeburg St. Clair County, Illinois geboren. Sie starb am 24. April 1975 in Freeburg St. Clair County, Illinois.

Quelle/source: Meng, James Leroy, St. Louis, Missouri

Elizabeth heiratete George H. Kilian[45] im Juni 1898 in St. Clair County, Illinois[46]. George wurde 1872 in High Prarie, Illinois geboren. Er starb 1935. Er wurde in Elmwood, Cemetery, Freeburg, Illinois bestattet.

Quelle/source: Meng, James Leroy, St. Louis, Missouri

24 W viii. Kathryn I. Meng[47] wurde am 17. Februar 1878 in Belleville, St. Clair County, Illinois geboren. Sie starb am 21. Juli 1954 in Freeburg St. Clair County, Illinois.

Quelle/source: Meng, James Leroy, St. Louis, Missouri

25 M viii. Dr. William L. Wilhelm Meng[48] wurde im Juli 1880 in Belleville, St. Clair County, Illinois geboren. Er starb am 10. Januar 1945. Er wurde in Perry Point, Cecil Copunty, MD bestattet.

Quelle/source: Meng, James Leroy, St. Louis, Missouri

William heiratete Eleanor L. Lovejoy[49] am 10. Februar 1912[50]. Eleanor wurde 1880 geboren. Sie starb nach 1931. Sie wurde in Perry Point, Cecil Copunty, MD bestattet.

24 W viii. Kathryn I. Meng[47] wurde am 17. Februar 1878 in Belleville, St. Clair County, Illinois geboren. Sie starb am 21. Juli 1954 in Freeburg St. Clair County, Illinois.

Quelle/source: Meng, James Leroy, St. Louis, Missouri

Sechste Generation

6. Friedrich Fred Fritz Meng[51] (Louis, Wilhelm, Conrad, Georg Wilhelm, Wilhelm) wurde am 11. Oktober 1863 in Freeburg, St. Clair County, Illinois geboren. Er starb am 23. Januar 1913 in New Athens, St. Clair County, Illinois.

Quelle/source: Meng, James Leroy, St. Louis, Missouri

Friederich heiratete Elisabeth Margaret Koesterer[52] Tochter von Berthold Bartley Koesterer und Katharina Reinheimer am 23. November 1892 in St. Clair County, Illinois[53]. Elisabeth wurde am 29. Mai 1869 in Freeburg St. Clair County, Illinois geboren. Sie starb am 12. Mai 1947 in Granite City, Madison County, Illinois.

Quelle/source: Meng, James Leroy, St. Louis, Missouri

Friederich und Elisabeth hatten die folgenden Kinder:

26 M i. Friedrich Martin Meng[54] wurde am 05. Oktober 1893 in New Athens, St. Clair County, Illinois geboren. Er starb am 15. April 1985 in St. Elisabeth Hospital, Granite City, Madison County, Illinois.

Quelle/source: Meng, James Leroy, St. Louis, Missouri

Friedrich heiratete Sarah Agnes Roseberry[55] am 28. Juni 1931 in Alhambra, Madison County, Illinois[56]. Sarah wurde am 14. Juni 1902 in Wanda, Russel TWP, Madison County, Illinois geboren. Sie starb am 15. März 1986 in 2107 Monroe, Granite City, Illinois.

Quelle/source: Meng, James Leroy, St. Louis, Missouri

27 M ii. Elmer Joe Meng[57] wurde am 26. Februar 1895 in Freeburg St. Clair County, Illinois geboren. Er starb am 23. Dezember 1900 in Freeburg St. Clair County, Illinois.

Quelle/source: Meng, James Leroy, St. Louis, Missouri

28 W iii. Frieda Marie Meng[58] wurde am 29. November 1896 in Freeburg St. Clair County, Illinois geboren. Sie starb am 20. September 1987 in Granite City, Madison County, Illinois

Quelle/source: Meng, James Leroy, St. Louis, Missouri

Frieda heiratete Roy Bennington[59] am 03. Mai 1958 in St. Peter's Evangelical United Church of Christ, Granite City, IL. Roy wurde am 22. Oktober 1898 in LaHarpe, Illinois geboren. Er starb am 11. Februar 1991 in Granite City, Madison County, Illinois.

Quelle/source: Meng, James Leroy, St. Louis, Missouri

29 M iv. Walter George Meng[60] wurde am 13. Dezember 1898 in Freeburg St. Clair County, Illinois geboren. Er starb am 22. Juni 1986 in Alton, Madison County, Illinois.

Quelle/source: Meng, James Leroy, St. Louis, Missouri

Walter heiratete Helen C. Schneider[61] am 06. Oktober 1937[62]. Helen wurde am 04. Oktober 1901 geboren. Sie starb am 23. February 1990 in Alton, Madison County, Illinois.

Quelle/source: Meng, James Leroy, St. Louis, Missouri

30 M v. Ervin B. Meng[63] wurde am 30. November 1900 in St. Clair County, Illinois geboren. Er starb am 24. Dezember 1900 in St. Clair County, Illinois.

Quelle/source: Meng, James Leroy, St. Louis, Missouri

31 M vi. Edward John Meng wurde am 04. Dezember 1901 geboren. Er starb am 01. April 1983.

32 M vii. Wilmer Walter Meng[64] wurde am 21. Dezember 1903 in Freeburg St. Clair County, Illinois geboren. Er starb am 11. Januar 1995 in Fullerton, Orange County, CA.

Quelle/source: Meng, James Leroy, St. Louis, Missouri

Wilmer heiratete Thelda Cooper (1).

Quelle/source: Meng, James Leroy, St. Louis, Missouri

Wilmer Walter "Wil" MENG born 21 Dec. 1903 in Freeburg, St. Clair Co, IL; died 11 Jan 1995 in Fullerton, Orange Co, CA; married (1) Thelda COOPER; born 20 Aug;

Wilmer heiratete Iris Ligett[65] am 30. Juni 1937 in Idaho[66] (2). Iris wurde am 15. August 1912 in Milltown, IN geboren. Sie starb am 02. September 1964 in Fullerton, Orange County, CA.

Quelle/source: Meng, James Leroy, St. Louis, Missouri

Wilmer heiratete Vaughnille Vonnie Joseph[67] 1965 in Los Angeles, CA[68] (3). Vaughnille wurde am 28. August 1912 geboren. Sie starb nach 1999 in CA.

Quelle/source: Meng, James Leroy, St. Louis, Missouri

33 M viii. Oscar Jerome Meng[69] wurde am 25. Januar 1906 in Freeburg St. Clair County, Illinois geboren. Er starb am 20. März 1970 in Kansas City, KS.

Quelle/source: Meng, James Leroy, St. Louis, Missouri

Oscar heiratete Elma Leone Cooper[70] am 21. Februar 1933[71]. Elma wurde am 19. Juli 1912 in Wood River, Madison County, Illinois geboren. Sie starb am 15. April 1993 in Kansas City, KS.

Quelle/source: Meng, James Leroy, St. Louis, Missouri

34 W ix. Elsa E. Meng[72] wurde am 21. Mai 1908 in New Athens, St. Clair County, Illinois geboren. Sie starb am 27. Dezember 1908 in New Athens, St. Clair County, Illinois.

Quelle/source: Meng, James Leroy, St. Louis, Missouri

Siebte Generation

7. Edward John Meng[73] (Friederich Fred Fritz, Louis, Wilhelm, Conrad, Georg Wilhelm, Wilhelm) wurde am 04. Dezember 1901 in Freeburg St. Clair County, Illinois geboren. Er starb am 01. April 1983 in St. Louis County, Missouri.

Quelle/source: Meng, James Leroy, St. Louis, Missouri

Edward heiratete Jessie Frances Shamhart[74] Tochter von Wilmer W Shamhart und Olive Foster am 12. September 1928[75]. Jessie wurde am 02. Juli 1903 in Newton, Jasper County, Illinois geboren. Sie starb am 18. Februar 1978 in Granite City, Madison County, Illinois.

Quelle/source: Meng, James Leroy, St. Louis, Missouri

Edward und Jessie hatten die folgenden Kinder:

35 M i. Edward Shamhart Meng[76] wurde am 19. Juni 1933 in Granite City, Madison County, Illinois geboren. Er starb am 1ᵉ. September 1989 in Richland, Columbia, South Carolina.

36 M ii. James Leroy Meng wurde am USA geboren.

Achte Generation

8. James Leroy Meng[77] (Edward John, Friederich Fred Fritz, Louis, Wilhelm, Conrad, George Wilhelm, Wilhelm) wurde am USA

Quelle/source: Meng, James Leroy, St. Louis, Missouri

James heiratete Beverly Ann Lewis[78] Tochter von Noyle Keith Lewis und Velma Viola Logan am USA [79]. Beverly wurde am USA

Quelle/source: Meng, James Leroy, St. Louis, Missouri

James und Beverly hatten die folgenden Kinder:

37 W i. Heather Andrea Meng wurde am USA geboren.

38 M ii. Erik James Meng[80] wurde am USA geboren.

Quelle/source: Meng, James Leroy, St. Louis, Missouri

Neunte Generation

9. Heather Andrea Meng[81] (James Leroy, Edward John, Friederich Fred Fritz, Louis, Wilhelm, Conrad, Georg Wilhelm, Wilhelm) wurde am USA

Quelle/source: Meng, James Leroy, USA. Heather Andrea MENG, born in USA; married David W Cochran; divorced.

Heather heiratete David Wistar Cochran in USA [82].

Sie hatten de folgender Kinder:

39 M i. Alexander David Cochran[83] USA geboren.

Quelle/source: Meng, James Leroy, St. Louis, Missouri

40 M ii. Jacob Shamhart Cochran[84] USA geboren.

Quelle/source: Meng, James Leroy, St. Louis, Missouri

Anhang A - Quellen

1. Zentralarchiv der Evangelischen Kirche in Hessen und Nassau.
2. Meng, James Leroy.
3. Family Search, Compact Disc 42 Pin 905556.
4. Zentralarchiv der Evangelischen Kirche in Hessen und Nassau.
5. Standesamt Monsheim.
6. Standesamt Monsheim.
7. Standesamt Monsheim.
8. Standesamt Monsheim.
9. Standesamt Monsheim.
10. Standesamt Monsheim.
11. Meng, James Leroy.
12. Family Search, Submission Search: 648630-0318102131451.
13. Standesamt Monsheim.
14. Standesamt Monsheim.
15. Standesamt Monsheim.
16. Standesamt Monsheim.
17. Standesamt Monsheim.
18. Family Search, M982651 - 1694 - 1885 - 0193832.
19. Standesamt Monsheim.
20. Meng, James Leroy.
21. Family Search, M982651 - 1694 - 1885 - 0193832.
22. Meng, James Leroy.
23. Meng, James Leroy.
24. Meng, James Leroy.
25. Meng, James Leroy.
26. Family Search, Record submitted after 1991 by a member of the LDS Church.
27. Family Search, C982651 - 1694 - 1885 - 0193832.
28. Family Search, M982651 - 1694 - 1885 - 0193832.
29. Family Search, C982651 - 1694 - 1885 - 0193832.
30. Family Search, C982651 - 1694 - 1885 - 0193832.
31. Thru 84, Meng, James Leroy.

WHY THE MENGS, KOESTERERS, SHAMHARTS AND OTHER FAMILIES CAME TO AMERICA?

Living in Germany during the 1800s was very difficult for the common person. The fall of Napoleon in 1815 resulted in the French king Louis Phillippe to abdicate his crown. The minister of the monarchial system of the Habsburg monarchy in Germany was subsequently driven into exile by the then Habsburg ruling family. The people of Germany started demanding liberal changes to their constitutions. There was growing conflict between the conservative German North Kingdom of Prussia, ruled by King Friedrich Wilhelm IV, an anti liberal, and the liberals in Southern Germany centered in Baden. In an attempt to gain formal consent to raise new (more) taxes, the first assembly of representatives from all of the Prussian provinces was convened by King William. William opposed any relationship between his royalty and the common man. This attitude continued to foster discontent among Germans. By 1848, the seeds of revolution had spread throughout the country to street riots in Berlin, where it failed.

While there was growing unrest between the conservatives and liberals of German, there was rise in immigration to America. What started out to be 10,000 immigrants to America in 1832, about one million Germans, nicknamed "48ers" escaped the harsh political situation during this revolution. Once established in their new homeland, such as St. Clair County, Illinois, these immigrants wrote to their families back in Germany describing the opportunities, the freedoms, and rich farmland that was available in their new country. These letters were circulated among friends and reprinted in German newspapers prompting "chain immigrations." The typical, common German family who remained in Germany was forced to endure land seizures, subjected to high unemployment, and repercussions of the failed German Revolution of 1848. With the advent of steamships and steam-operated trains, the movement of immigrants to the various ports and even to English ports became much easier and safer. Consequently, the prospect of going to America for a better future became even more attractive. As a result, almost five million Germans had now immigrated to this new country called America and more were coming. Among these immigrants were the Meng's, Koesterer's, Borger's, Reinheimer's, Mueller's, Weber's, Vogt's, and their friends and neighbors.

The following "direct" air miles (not sailing miles) reflect the distances that the Meng immigrants traveled to their respective destinations. Think of this trip in terms of what it would have been like having given up your homeland, friends, relatives, and possessions to travel to a new and virtually undiscovered land. Then think of what it would have been like making this voyage cramped with hundreds of other travelers for months in a small sailing ship and then, at best, an early steamship. These were very brave people!

It is highly recommended that you read the informative 1985 book titled, *Lets go to America!* The path of emigrants from Eastern Westphalia from Eastern Westphalia to the USA by Karl Sieveking, Chairman of the Heimatverein Lohile, and Gerhard Bartling, Study Group for Heimatpfleg Bad Oeynhausen. This book describes just who these emigrants were, why they left Germany and the terrible conditions on the so called death ships like the" Leibnitz", a sailing ship where 100 of the 542 passengers died of cholera during the crossing. These ships averaged one to three per cent deaths during their crossing to America. For example, they had only one toilet per fifty passengers, almost undrinkable water, rancid food, moldy bread etc... The average voyage on a sailing ship took 45 days from Brenerhaven to New York, 51 days to Baltimore, and 59 days to new Orleans, many times sleeping out in the open air during winter. When steamships became available, the time to cross with all the unpleasantness was reduced by a third.

Included in all these conditions, was a Meng grandmother, Mary Angeline Devault, to be illustrated later in this chapter. She was born at sea in 1834 with no Doctors on board, one very tough young lady!

Burial of an emigrant on the h igh seas - lithography by Theudnr Hoseman n, 1855 - in F. Gerstacker: Off to America - Leipzig, 1855

Flight distances

- Speyer, Germany, to Philadelphia, Pennsylvania, United States = 3,998.47 miles
- Hohen-Sülzen, Germany, to Ashley, New Zealand = 11,583.66 miles
- Monsheim, Germany, to Freeburg, Illinois, United States = 4,625.33 miles

Ellis Island, aboard ship.
Courtesy of the Library of Congress, LC-USZ62-7307—photograph by Wm. H. Rau, 1902.

Courtesy of the Library of Congress, LC-USZ62-11202.

WHAT DID THE MENG, KOESTERER, SHAMHART AND OTHER FAMILIES CONFRONT AFTER ARRIVING IN AMERICA?

As one of the predominant immigrant groups in the nineteenth century, the Germans adapted to their new country while, at the same time, continued many of their German customs from their homeland. These customs included a strong commitment to education. German immigrants in St. Louis, Missouri, started the first kindergarten in America, based upon the kindergartens in Germany. Germans also introduced physical education and vocational education, plus the inclusion of gymnasiums in school buildings. Equally important, the Germans were responsible for introducing, a new idea to America at the time, universal education. German customs were soon adopted by others in their new country.

The Christmas tree was introduced to America by a Pennsylvania Dutch family in Lancaster while German cartoonist, Thomas Nast, created the image of Santa Claus (and Uncle Sam) as we know it today. A bunny that delivers eggs at Easter was a tradition in Germany. The two-day weekend to go to church and have picnics and family outings was initiated by these new immigrants. The list of adopted German customs in America goes on and on.

As the German farmers moved west, many ended up in the urban areas of the larger cities such as Milwaukee, Cincinnati, and St. Louis. While the communities surrounding these towns, such as in St. Clair County near St. Louis, where land was cheap and fertile, attracted many farming immigrants. "Ben" Koesterer was an example of a very successful German farmer in Freeburg, Illinois. Ben bought many acres of fertile bottom land with the philosophy that ". . . if the land does not pay for itself in 5 years, then do not buy it." He practiced what he preached and paid cash for all of his property. This area of St. Clair County soon had towns with German names like Freeburg, Millstadt, New Baden, and Frankfort, etc. Even the Bellville High School mascot is named "Dutchmen" and in Edwardsville, Illinois, there is a street named Mengstrasse. Many of the German Americans immigrants were store owners, like Conrad Meng in Freeburg who sold appliances and Louis Meng in Lementon, Illinois, who was a dealer in dry goods, groceries, hardwares, whiskey, and tobacco products. The new immigrants were also employed in the skilled trades that they had learned in their homeland, particularly as carpenters, as bakers, as butchers, as cigar makers, as distillers, as machinist, and as tailors. Obviously, a major German business in America was in the beer industry. Meanwhile, many of the German women, who normally did not work in the factories, were employed as janitors, nurses, saloon keepers, and tailors.

Many of the "48ers" were well-educated intellectuals who contributed greatly to their new country. The Germans soon entered the American factories and founded many new industries such as John Bausch and Henry Lomb; Steinway, Knabe and

Schnabel; Rockefeller; Studebaker; Chrysler; H. J. Heinz; Frederick Weyerhaeuser; and John Jacob Astor.

Not all German Americans were united. Divisions occurred based upon geography and resistance to ideology before 1871, during the push for German unification. Not all Germans felt pride in their fatherland and its achievements. American Germans at first identified themselves with the southern liberal part of Germany as Bavarians, Württenbergers, or Saxons. However, with the dream of a more democratic Germany encompassing both the Bismarckian and liberals, Germans soon became united in a feeling of pride as German Americans.

However, religious differences between German Americans continued. Most of the German immigrants were Protestants with Lutheranism by far, the most dominate. Consequently, conflict soon developed within the German Lutheran churches that had been Americanized by using English in all or part of their services. These German American Lutherans also adopted a new constitution in which all references to the Augsburg Confession had disappeared. The newer German immigrants, after 1847, wanted to maintain the old-style doctrine and organized the Missouri Synod. Today the Missouri Synod remains the foundation for the more conservative American Lutherans.

All was not easy for the German Americans with the coming of World War I. A backlash developed against the German culture occurred in the United States. When the United States declared war against Germany in 1917, anti-German sentiment became popular. The names of schools, foods, streets, and towns were often changed. Even the music of Wagner (including the traditional wedding march) and Mendelssohn were removed from concerts. German American businesses and homes were vandalized. "Pro-Germans" were tarred and feathered.

The most pervasive and lasting damage occurred to the German language and education. Many German-language newspapers were either run out of business or quietly closed their doors. One such paper was the *Belleville Zeitung* (pronounced *tys-loong*, which means newspaper). The *Zeitung* was eventually merged with the *Post*, a St. Louis newspaper. From 1890 to 1910, the *Post* and *Zeitung* was at its circulation peak. However, with the advent of World War I, many efforts were made to stop the circulation of German newspapers and interest. The *Zeitung* would have been the paper that my father, Edward J. Meng, and his brothers and sister would have had to read in front of their grade school class in New Athens, Illinois, every Friday. This act was demonstrated to the teacher that he was learning to read and speak German. Dad complained about this practice because he never knew what paragraph he would be required to read, thus could not prepare in advance.

During this time period, President Woodrow Wilson did not approve of "hyphenated Americans" whose loyalty he declared was divided. It was said, "Every citizen must declare himself American, or traitor." I believed President Wilson was right! Although it is interesting to note that Wilson did choose a German American, John J. Pershing, to lead the American efforts in World War I even though the Perishing family had earlier changed their American name from Pfoerschin to Pershing.

Some German Americans during World War I even changed their family names or the names of their businesses in an attempt to conceal their German heritage. One such example was the *king*. No, not the king of Germany, but Elvis Presley, who would have been known as Elvis Pressler had his family name not been changed by his father.

The anti-German feelings rose again during World War II, but not as strong as during World War I. Dwight Eisenhower, a descendant of the Pennsylvania Dutch, led the American efforts in World War II, assisted by fellow German Americans: Adm. Chester Nimitz of the navy and Gen. Carl Spaatz of the army air corps.

In my personal situation, and being born in 1939 and of German heritage, I was never taught to speak German. This seems odd today since my entire family spoke fluid German. I regret that decision even today. However, I believe it may partly reflect the sentiment toward people of German heritage during World War II.

COPIES OF MENG FAMILY DOCUMENTS FROM GERMANY

The following are some of the official church documents obtained in Germany supporting the Illinois branch of the Meng genealogical tree.

Henry Meng's Birth Certificate 8 Sept 1812

Conrad Meng's Birth Certificate 9 July 1784

Wilhelm Meng and Appolonia Hoffmann's marriage (1784).

oo Georg Wilhelm Meng and Appolonia Hofmann
Source: Zentralarchiv der Evangelischen Kirche in Hessen Nassau, Ahastr. 5a
64276 Darmstadt Tel.: + 49 6151/3663-94 Dr. Marcus Stippack

THE FIRST MARRIAGE OF CONRAD MENG, AGE 24 AND 4 MONTHS WITH
JEANNE ELIZABETH HOFMAN, 21 YEARS AND 11 MONTHS. JEANNE WAS
FROM WACHENHEIM, GERMANY. THE MARRIAGE OCCURRED ON 5 DEC
1808 IN MONSHEIM.

* Conrad Meng
Source: Zentralarchiv der Evangelischen Kirche in Hessen Nassau, Ahastr. 5a
64276 Darmstadt Dr. Marcus Stippack

oo Conrad Meng and Jeanne Elisabeth Hofmann
Source: Standesamt (civil registry office) der Verbandsgemeinde Monsheim
Alzeyer Str. 15 67590   +49 06243 1809-34

Conrad's parents were George Wilhelm Meng and Appolonia (née Hoffman) Meng.
Conrad was born on July 9, 1784, and baptized on July 10, 1784. His godparents were
Conrad Emmert from Hohen-Sülzen with his unwed bride Catherine Meng, who was
Georg Wilhelm Meng's sister, also from Hohen-Sülzen.

For all the children of Conrad Meng in the two marriages the source is:
Standesamt (civil registry office) der Verbandsgemeinde Monsheim Alzeyer
Str. 15 67590 +49 06243 1809-34
--
Herzliche Grüße aus Bielefeld
Werner Schabbehard

Birth certificate of Guillaume (Wilhelm) Meng 27 July 1810.
Translated from the French form into English by Werner Schabbehard.

In the year one thousand and eight hundred and ten, on the twenty seventh of July at ten o'clock in the morning before me, serving Adam Ernest. Mayor Civilstand's official of the municipality of Monsheim, canton of Pfeddersheim, department du Mont-Tonnerre est. comparu le Mister CONRAD MENG, of twenty seven years, farmer living in Monsheim, who presented us a child of masculine gende:, born on the twenty seventh of July at four o'clock in the afternoon he declared that he and his wife Misses ELISABETH nee HOFMANN, and whom he declared to give him the first name of GUILLAUME (WILHELM).

Aforementioned statement and presentation made in the presence of first witness Mister CHRETIN HOFMANN, age fifty three years, MENNIFRIER and second witness Mister PIERRE JACQUES SCHEUER, age fifty nine years, farmer, living in Monsheim.

And the father and the witnesses with me have signed the present natal act, after the same has been read out to them.

CONRAD MENG, father,
CHRISTIAN HOFMANN, witness
PETER JACOB SCHEUER, witness

Serving

Death certificate of Apolonia Hofmann * around 1755 +24. Jan 1811
translated from the French form into Englisch by
Werner Schabbehard on the 01. Dec 2010

In the year one thousand and eight hundred and eleven, on the twenty-fifth of January at eight o'clock in the morning before me, Adam Ernest Loving, Mayor and Civilstand's official of the municipality of Monsheim canton of Pfeddersheim, dèpartment du Mont-Tonnerre, appeared George Paul Scheuer Sergeant de Police resident of Monsheim and Christian Hofmann mennifrier resident of Monsheim who declared us that on the twenty-fourth of the month of January at nine o'clock in the morning Anne Appolonie nee Hoffmann, wife of (Conrad) corrected into Guillaume (Wilhelm) Meng, farmer at the age of fifty six years

Loving

died on the twenty fourth of the month of January at nine o'clock in the morning in the house no.-----road said Borngasse and signed the explanation with us of the present act, after a reading was made to them.

Christian Hofmann   George Paul Scheuer

Loving

Heinrich Meng's Birth Certificate 9 Sept 1812

In the year of 1812 on the 9TH of the month of September at ten o'clock in the morning before Adam Ernest Sevin, Major and officer of the civil register office of the village of Monsheim parish of Pfeddersheim, department of Mont-Tonnere, has appeared Conrad Meng, age 28 demeurant and farmer of Monsheim who is registered to us a child of male gender born on the ninth of month of September at night at 10 o'clock and whom he and his wife, nee Hoffmann have given the first name Henry (Heinrich).

Aforementioned statement and presentation made in the presence of Christian Hofmann, age 54 years Menusier demeurant of Monsheim and of Michel Scheuer age 46 years . . . of Monsheim and father and witness have signed with us the present birth certificate, after it had been provided.

Conrad Meng
Christian Hofmann
Johann Michael Scheuer

Birth certificate of APOLON (APPOLONIA) 25 February 1814. Translated from the French form into English by Werner Schabbehard.

In the year one thousand and eight hundred and fourteen, on the twenty fifth of February at nine o'clock in the morning before me, ADAM ERNEST Seving, Mayor and official of the municipality of Monsheim, canton of Pfeddersheim, department du Mont-Tonnerre, est comparu le CONRAD MENG, age thirty years, farmer living in Monsheim, who presented us a child of feminine gender, born on the twenty fifth of the month of February at nine o'clock in the evening he declared that he and his wife ELISABETH born HOFMANN and to whom he declared to give her the first name APOLON (APPOLONIA).

Aforementioned statement and presentation made in the presence of MICHEL SCHEUER, age thirty six, Jourmalier (journalist) . . . ? and of GUILLAUME JULLMANN age forty three years, Taylor both, living in Monsheim.

And the father and the witnesses with me have signed the present natal act, after the same has been read out to them.

CONRAD MENG
MICHEL SCHEUER
WILHELM JULLMANN

Serving

Geburtsurkunde von Johann Konrad Meng * 22. Februar 1816

Im Jahre eintausendachthundert und sechszehn, den zweiundzwanzigsten des Monats Februar um drei Uhr Nachmittags erschien vor mir Johannes Krämer .... official of the municipality of Monsheim, Kanton Pfeddersheim Donnersburger department Konrad Meng alt einunddreißig Jahre, Landwirt, wohnhaft in Monsheim, welcher mir erklärte, daß ihm am zweiundzwanzigsten Februar um zwölf Uhr Mittags von seiner Ehefrau Elisabetha geborene Hofmann ein Kind männlichen Geschlechts geboren worden sei und welchem er die Vornamen Johann Konrad zu geben gesonnen ist.

Obige Erklärung geschah in Gegenwart von Wilhelm Jullmann alt dreiundzwanzig Jahre, Ackersmann, wohnhaft in Monsheim, und Michael Scheuer alt achtunddreißig Jahre, Taglöhner, wohnhaft in Monsheim, welche nach Vorlesung des gegenwärtigen Aktes mit dem Anzeiger und mir unterschrieben haben.

Conrad Meng

Wilhelm Jullmann Michael Scheuer

Kraemer

Birth certificate of Johann Konrad Meng * 22. February 1816 translated from the German form into Englisch by Werner Schabbehard on the 01. Nov 2010

In the year eighteen hundred and sixteen, the twenty second of the month of February at three o'clock in the afternoon, Johannes Krämer, appear before me ... official of the municipality of Monsheim, canton Pfeddersheim, Donnersburger department, Konrad Meng, old thirtyone years, farmer, resident of Monsheim who explained to me that a child of masculine gender was born to him of his wife Elisabetha born Hofmann on the twenty-second of February at twelve o'clock at midday and to which he is reflected to give the first names Johann Konrad.

The above explanation happened in the presence of Wilhelm Jullmann, old twenty three years, farmer, resident Monsheim, and Michael Scheuer, old thirty eight years, day-laborer, resident in Monsheim, who have signed after reading the present act with the indicator and me.

Conrad Meng
Wilhelm Jullmann Michael Scheuer

Kraemer

Birth certificate of Ludwig Meng * 27. Oct 1818
translated from the German form into Englisch by
Werner Schabbehard on the 30. Oct 2010

In the year one thousand and eighthundred and eighteen, on the twenty-seventh of October at five o'clock in the afternoon has appeared before me, Johannes Krämer, Civilstand's official of the municipality of Monsheim, canton of Pfeddersheim, Konrad Meng, old thirtyfour years, farmer in Monsheim, who explained to me that on the twenty-seventh of October at two o'clock in the afternoon a child of masculin gender was born and which child the same has shown to me, declared to give him the first name Ludwig and himself for the father of this child, which he has generated with his wife Elisabetha nee Hofmann; that the child was born in the situated house of Borngasse no. 80.

This explanation and exhibition has happened in the presence of the witnesses Philipp Sartorius, age thirtytwo years and of schoolteacher occupation resident in Monsheim and Burghard Schalck fiftysix years old, resident of Monsheim, and the father and the witnesses with me have signed the present natal act, after the same has been read out to them.

Conrad Meng, Philipp Satoriu Burkhard
Schlack

Kraemer

CONRAD MENG'S first wife, JEANNE ELIZABETH HOFMANN MENG died ON 5 DEC 1818 IN MONSHEIM, GERMANY. The following is a copy of Jeanne's death certificate.

Second marriage of Conrad Meng 28th of May 1819 Anna Elisabetha Müller translated from the German form into Englisch by Werner Schabbehard on the 03. of Nov 2010

In the year one thousand eight hundred and nineteen before me, the eighth of May, John Krämer mayor, civil status = officials of the community of Monsheim, State of Pfeddersheim appeared: Conrad Meng, old thirty-four years ten months of its state a farmer, born and residing in Monsheim, widower of deceased Elizabeth Hofmann, son of Georg Wilhelm Meng, farmer . . . Monsheim, on this occasion, currently and his approval giving and his faded wife ----- Apolonia nee Hofmann and lie the current-death certificates and birth certificate, --- and the Anna Elisabetha Müller, thirty-one years and three months old, without status, was born and living in Monsheim grown-up daughter of Weiland Wilhelm Müller in his lifetime farmer and his wife Barbara nee Geyer sogleich verstorben (at this time also dead, can't better translate) which appearing have asked me for the solemn execution of its projects be marriage to proceed and in which the announcements before the main door of the village hall, namely the first to the ninth of the month May one thousand eight hundred and nineteen at one o'clock in the afternoon and the second one on the fifteenth of the month of May of the year at one o'clock in the afternoon have been made.

Since I have now notified no objection to the marriage, and as I leave the same request again go ---, and I red up journals and reported the sixth chapter of the Civil Code be --- from the marriage, and the future husband and future wife have asked whether the same want to take themselves for man and woman and each of them especially those affirm so I declare on behalf of the law that Conrad Meng and the Anna Elisabetha Müller are connected by the marriage.

Whereby I have done the present act in the presence of Heinrich Ludwig Weinheimer, forty-six years old, neighbor of the bridegroom and Johannes Sch-----.thirtytwo years old and neighbor of the bridegroom and Philip Schindler, old---years, good friend of the bride and as the fourth witness Philipp Satorius, thirtythree years old,---good friend of the bride all resident of Monsheim which have signed present act with me and the contracting parts after happened lecture.

Conrad Meng   Anna Elisabetha Müllerin
Georg Wilhelm Meng   Heinrich Ludwig Weinheimer   Johannes Sch--

Birth certificate of Elisabeth Meng * 17. July 1820
translated from the German form into Englisch by
Werner Schabbehard on the 30. Oct 2010

In the year one thousand and eighthundred and twenty, on the seventh of July at nine o'clock in the morning has appeared before me, Johannes Krämer, Civilstand's official of the municipality of Monsheim, canton of Pfeddersheim, Konrad Meng, old thirtysix years, occupation farmer and resident in Monsheim, who explained to me that on the seventeenth of July at four o'clock in the morning a child of feminine gender was born and which child the same has shown to me, declared to give him the first name Elisabeth and himself for the father of this child, which he has generated with his wife Anna Elisabetha nee Hofmann; that the child was born in the situated house of Borngasse no. 80.

This explanation and exhibition has happened in the presence of the witnesses Philipp Sartorius, age thirtyfour years and of schoolteacher occupation resident in Monsheim and Burghard Schalck fiftyeight years old, resident of Monsheim, and the father and the witnesses with me have signed the present natal act, after the same has been read out to them.

Conrad Meng,   Philipp Satorius   Burkhard
Schlack

Kraemer

Death certificate
Gerorg Wilhelm Meng
+
02.06.1822
Monsheim

Im Jahr eintausend achthundert zwei und zwanzig, den ... sind vor mir ... Civilstands-Beamten der Gemeinde von ... Kanton von ... erschienen Conrad Meng ...

den ... um ... Uhr des ... in dem Hause Nro. ... in der ... Straße ... gestorben ist, und haben die Erklärenden gegenwärtigen Akt, nachdem solcher ihnen vorgelesen worden, mit mir unterschrieben.

Deathcertificate
Georg Wilhelm Meng
+
02.06.1822
Monsheim

Deathcertificate
Georg Wilhelm Meng
+
02.06.1822
Monsheim

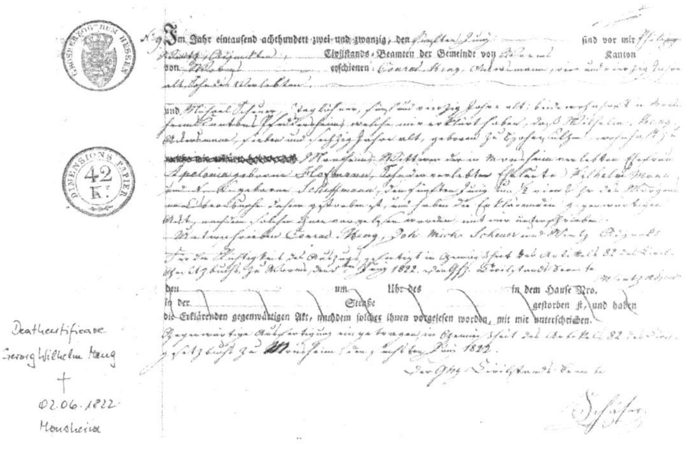

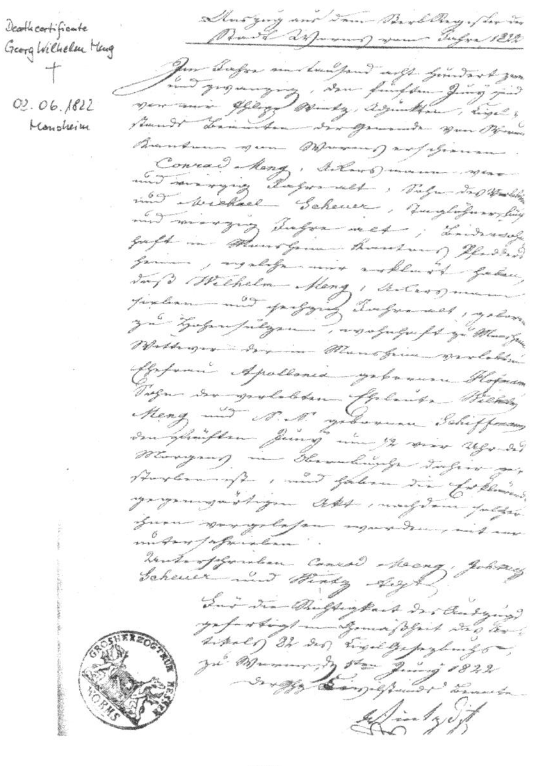

Birth certificate of Katharina Meng * 21 January 1823
translated from the German form into Englisch by
Werner Schabbehard on the 30 Oct 2010

In the year one thousand and eighthundred and twentythree, on the twenty-second of January at one o'clock in the afternoon has appeared before me, the Mayor, Civilstand's official of the municipality of Monsheim, canton of Pfeddersheim, Konrad Meng, fourty years old, farmer in Monsheim, who explained to me that on the twenty-first of January at three o'clock in the afternoon a child of feminine gender was born and which child the same has shown to me, declared to give him the first name Katharina and himself for the father of this child, which he has generated with his wife Anna Elisabetha, nee Müller; that the child was born in the situated house of Borngasse no. 80.

This explanation and exhibition has happened in the presence of the witnesses Philipp Sartorius, age thirtyseven years and of schoolteacher occupation resident in Monsheim and Burghard Schalck sixtyone years old, Mayor thereat and resident of Monsheim, and the father and the witnesses with me have signed the present natal act, after the same has been read out to them.

Conrad Meng,   Philipp Satorius   Burkhard
(Schlack)

Sch

(alck)

It looks like Burkhard Schalck is Mayor at this time of Monsheim and possble married to a Meng daughter.

Birth certificate of Johannes Meng * 19. March 1825
translated from the German form into Englisch by
Werner Schabbehard on the 30 Oct 2010

In the year one thousandeighthundred and twentyfive, on the nineteenth of March at one o'clock in the afternoon has appeared before me, the Mayor, Civilstand's official of the municipality of Monsheim, canton of Pfeddersheim, Konrad Meng, fourty years old, occupation a farmer living in Monsheim, who explained to me that on the nineteenth of March at ten o'clock in the morning a child of masculine gender was born and which child the same has shown to me, declared to give him the first name Johannes and himself for the father of this child, which he has generated with his wife Anna Elisabetha, nee Müller; that the child was born in the situated house of Borngasse no. 80.

This explanation and exhibition has happened in the presence of the witnesses Philipp Sartorius, age thirtynine years and of schoolteacher occupation resident in Monsheim and Burghard Schalck sixtythree years old, Mayor clerc thereat and resident of Monsheim, and the father and the witnesses with me have signed the present natal act, after the same has been read out to them.

Conrad Meng,   Philipp Satorius   Burkhard
(Schlack)

(Pleiharl?)

Here is Burkhard Schalk no longer Mayor

191

New York Passenger Lists, 1820-1957 record for Conrad Meng

Record Index

Name:	Conrad Meng
Arrival Date:	1 Aug 1837
Birth Year:	abt 1785
Age:	52
Gender:	Male
Port of Departure:	Le Havre, France
Port of Arrival:	New York, New York
Ship Name:	Manchester

Christening of Louis Meng 22 Feb 1837

Parents Wilhelm and Maria Meng both from Monsheim.
This child has been christened legally by the Catholic priest Hoffman.

Marriage of Wilhelm Meng and Maria Scheiber 31 May 1837

Wilhelm, single son of farmer Conrad Meng and Marie Scheiber, a single daughter
of Nicola Scheiber and Elizabeth, nee Hofmann, both from Morsheim have been
ecclesiastically confirmed without ceremony by the Catholic priest Hofmann.

New Orleans Passenger Lists, 1820-1945 record of Wilhelm Meng

List of Passengers taken on Board the *Am. Ship Asia* whereof *P. Wensor* is Master, at the Port of Havre and bound for New-Orleans.

Name: Wilhelm Meng
Arrival Date: 22 Jan 1848
Age: 35
Gender: Male
Port of Departure: Le Havre, France
Ship Name: Asia
Port of Arrival: New Orleans, Louisiana
Birthplace: Baden
National Archives' Series Number: M259_28

Marriage of Wilhelm Meng and Henriette Seiberg 03 Jan 1846

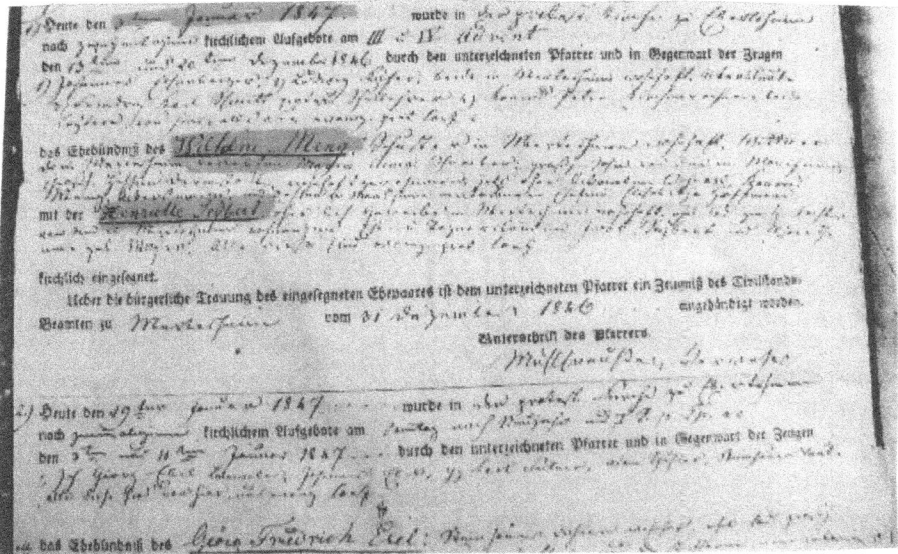

Marriage of Wilhelm Meng and Henriette Seibert 03 Jan 1846

In the church of Ebertsheim, signed priest and in the present of Johannes Eisenberger, Ludwig Kafer both Mertesheim resident farmers and teacher Friedrich Karl Schmitt of evangelic protestant denomination, the marriage of Wilhelm Meng, a shoemaker and resident in Mertesheim and widower of the Mertesheim deceased Maria Anna Schreiber. Conrad Meng farmer and his late wife from Monsheim, Elisabeth Hoffmann with Henrietta Seybert of Mertesheim, daughter of the day laborer Jacob Seybert, Elisabeth nee Mayer, all of evangelical protestant denomination...

Signature of the priest
Muhlhauser, "Verweser"

Christening of Katharina Meng 18 Apr 1847

Today, the 18th of April 1847, received in the Protestant church in Ebertsheim by the signing priest and the presents of Godmother Katherine Seibert from Mannheim, conjugal single adult daughter in Mertesheim married couple and day laborer Jacob Seibert and Elizabeth, nee Meyer, of evangelic protestant denomination. The inauguration of the baptism remedial to Katharina Meng, born 31st of March 1847 at 8 o'clock in the morning at Mertesheim, the conjugal little daughter of Henriette, nee Seibert, of evangelic protestant denomination.

The birth of this child is according to the certificate delivered to the signing priest of the civil servant from 31st of March 1847 as recorded in the natal registers of the municipality of Mertesheim.

Signature of the Priest

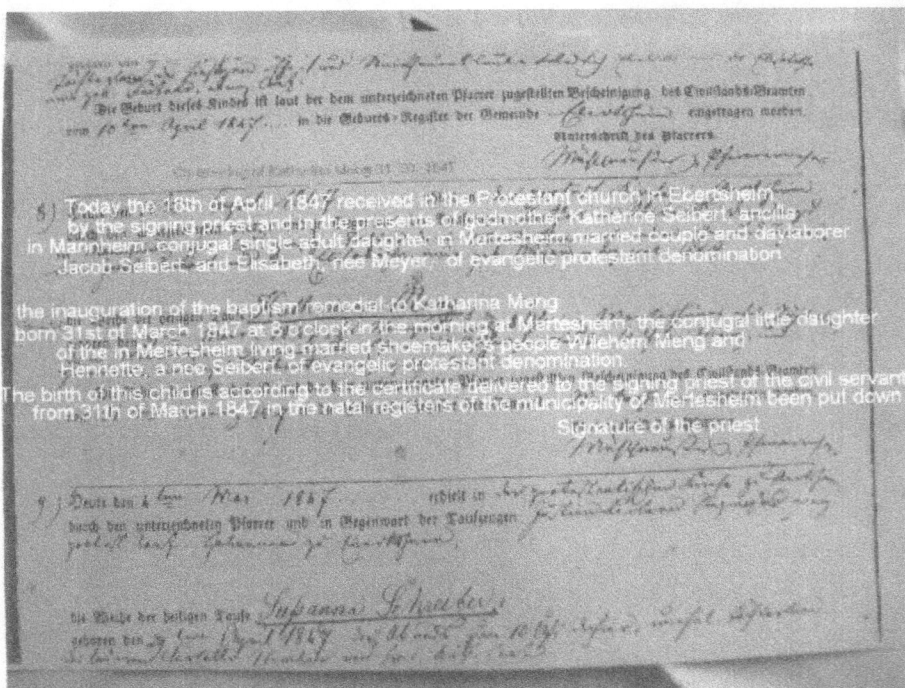

CHAPTER 8
LOUIS AND CHRISTINA (BORGER) MENG IN FREEBURG, ILLINOIS

Freeburg History

Freeburg lies in the fertile and rolling southern Illinois plains between the Kaskaskia and Mississippi Rivers. It was platted in 1836 as the town of Urbana by immigrants to this area from Virginia around 1800. The first European settlers of Freeburg were of English and Irish ancestry.

There were five migratory Indian tribes that crisscrossed each other in Illinois; the Peorias, Cahokias, Kaskaskias, Tamaroas, and Michiganics. It is said that Turkey Hill north of town was a popular Indian campground that also attracted many early settlers because of the view it provided of the surrounding countryside. The last Indian tribes left this area by 1820.

The big German migrations to this area started around 1830 and continued quite strong for the rest of the century. Obviously, the abundance of coal, the availability of cheap fertile farm land, as well as the proximity to the frontier city of St. Louis, only 20 miles to the northwest, are what attracted settlers to Freeburg. In 1848, Louis Meng arrived in Freeburg as a member of the "48ers".

The old "Plank Road" was built in the 1850s and for 35 cents travelers could ride from Belleville to Freeburg in "comfort" without potholes on what is now known as the old Freeburg Road. Abe Lincoln is said to have used this road on at least one occasion.

In 1851, the post office came, and when it was found that there was another town of Urbana in Illinois, the city fathers changed the name in 1859 to Freeburg after the beautiful city of Freiburg in the state of Baden, Germany, from which some of the early settlers had come.

The town was incorporated in 1867 with 808 residents. The railroad came in 1869 and exchanged owners several times before being sold to the Illinois Central.

In the heyday of independent coal mines, as many as 1500 miners lived here, and in 1874, there were 10 hotels for them to choose from if they could not find more permanent lodging. With the closing of the Peabody River King Mine just east of Freeburg in 1989, coal no longer played a dominant role in the local economy.

Today, Freeburg remains a conservative community with a highly diversified business economy that also serves as a bedroom community for Belleville and the St. Louis metroplex, while still providing essential services needed in any small community.

A Meng grandmother, Mary Angeline Devault (Kinney), born at sea in 1834 coming to America from Prussia.

Mary Angeline (Devault) Borger (Kinney)

Mary married Phillip Borger, father of Christina Borger who married Louis Meng.

:

Their son, Friederich Meng, married Elizabeth Koesterer.

:

Friederich was the father of Edward John Meng who married Jessie Shamhart.

:

Edward and Jessie were the father and mother of
Edward Shamhart Meng
and
James Leroy Meng.

Louis Meng

Arrival Date: 22 Jan 1848
Age: 9
Gender: Male
Port of Departure: Le Havre, France
Ship Name: Asia
Port of Arrival: New Orleans,
Louisiana
Birthplace: Baden
National Archives Series Number:
M259_28

Louis Meng—New Orleans Passenger Lists (1820–1945)

199

THE LOUIS MENG AND CHRISTINA NEE BORGER MENG FAMILY.

The following is a copy of the business ledger of the general merchandise store owned and operated by Louis Meng, husband of Christina Meng. The store was located in Lementon, Illinois (12 Mile Prairie). The ledger reflects the names of many of the residents in the area from 1870 to 1900.

LOUIS MENG,
Lementon, Ill.

Dealer in
DRY GOODS AND GROCERIES, HARDWARE, &C.

INDEX
NAMES APPEARING IN THE STORE LEDGER OF LOUIS MENG,
12 MILE PRAIRIE/LEMENTON, ILLINOIS (1870–1900)

A

Adams, Wm.
Adames, Wash.
Antherson or Antheson,
    James
Anthony, A.
Anthony, Wm.
Appleton Voges & Co.
Arenz, Wm.
Arnold, John Baptist.

B

B. & J.F. Slevin & Co.
Baker, J. H.
Balcha, Geo.
Baltz, Wm.
Baumgartner, Geo.
Beaky, James
Becker, V.
Berker, H.
Blisch, Martin
Boger, Dan

Borger, Geo.
Borger, Henry
Breoh, John
Bumellmann, Frantz

C

Carde, Chas
Cunlach, Ph.
Cunrath, Henkel

D

Dan Baltz Bros.
Darmstatter, Christina
Darmstatter, Fritz
Darmstatter, Geo
Darmstatter, Louis
Darmstatter, M.
Diedrich, John
Dielweber, John
Duglas, Mrfs.
Dunken, A.
Dunken, Dest. or West.

Duttenhaver, Geo.
?D..ink blot.. llmann, Joseph

E

Eberhard, Aug.
Ebert, Fritz
Edelson, A.
Elend, Chas.
Espenheim & Feifs & Co.

F

Fehler, Melcher
Felzner, Casper
Ferdinand, A.
Feurer, John
Feurer, Wm.
Fisher, A.
Fitz, Wm.
Fohmer, Dan
Frefs, Nic
Funke, A.

G

*Gusloitz or Gauloitz, Gustav
Genther, E.
Germann, Adam
Gerrmann, Fred
Gilbert, H. and Henry
*Goelitz, Gust.
Groh, Nic

H

Halb, Gust
Hamill, James
Hardman & Bros.
Hermann, Ph.
Hill, A. S.
Hiller, Mary
Hilsinger, Mike
Hoerner or Horner, Henry
Hood, James
Houff or Hauff, Chas.
Huppert, Gust.

J

Joachim, Jac
John Koch Bros.
Joseph, H.
Joseph, John
Jung, Frank

K

Karlein, H. & Henry
Keberlin, Fred
Kehler, Melcher
Keller, Ph.
Kircher, Joseph
Kling, E.
Knight, Fiske
Knoche, Chris

L

L. Barthel & Co.
Lentz, A.
Lie, Nic
Lively, James
Lortz, A.
Lortz, John
Lortz, Mary

Lortz, Geo.
Lortz, Louis
Lorts, Ph.
Ludwig, Johanes

M

Mattis, John
Maur, Chas.
Maurer, Chas.
Maurer, Chathrina
Maurer, Ph.
Mcgee, H.
Mcgee, Henry
Meng, Conrad
Meng, Henry
Meng, John
Meyer, Chas. F.
Meyer, Julius
Miller, Elick
Miller, Jac
Miller, Louis
Miller, Wm.
Miller, Theo.
Mitchell, Edward
Mitchell, John

N

Niehold, Louis
Nierath, Chas
Neuhouse Krite & Co.

O

Obergin, Wils.
Oldendorf, H.

P

Pate, Pat
Peter, A.
Peter, Peter
Petre, Geo.
Philip Bonman & Co.
Pilhan, Louis
Pitz, Wm.

R

Räder, Jac
Räder, Ph.
Reice, Geo

Reifs (Reife?), Geo.
Reppel, John
Ricks, Adolph
Rippermann, H. and Henry
Roth, Jac.
Rovergel?, Lisabeda

S

S. J. Wilderman Bros.
Schaffer, C.
Schanz, Fred
Schanz, Geo.
Schmith, D.
Schmitknecht, Wm.
Schultz, Jac.
Seibert, Jac
Seldner, H. & Hermann
Skear, Ph.
Short, J. S.
Short, S.
Sneibel?, Geo.
Senibel?, Ph.
Stekmager, John
Stitzelbercher, Jac.
Stroh, Ph.
Stuntz, L. D.
Swortz, Wm.
Sydow, Ferd & Ferdinand
     (also written as
     "Sedow" and
     "Sidow")

T

Talbert, M.
Thilemann or Thillmann,
     Fred
Tholsheimer, A. (possibly
     Thalsheimer)
Thomson, Chathrin

U

Underberger, H.
Underberger, J.

V

Varnez, A.
Vogel, H.
Vogt, Dona

W

Warm or Worm, Joel
Weber, Fred
Weigert?, Dietrich
Weimer, Geo
Weppler, Nic
Wicks or Kicks, Margaret
Wilderman, Wm.
Winder, Louis
Winkler, Nic. C. L.
Wiscomp, Henry (also
      written as "Wiscamp)
Wiscamp, Louis
Woods, B. F.
Wunderlig, Peter

Z

Zinsel, Geo.

The above was transcribed
from the original script
to print on May 1, 1995
by Bev Meng's friend and
genealogist, Janet Flynn.

Lemonton, Ill April 12th 1873

Mr Frantz Bumelman?

In Account with **LOUIS MENG,**
Dealer in

1873 DRY GOODS AND GROCERIES, HARDWARE, &C.

Jan	1	To	Ballance	15 50
	6	"	Sundries?	20
Feb	3	"	"	2 95
	20	"	"	15
March 14	"	"	23
"	17	"	"	6 75
"	20	"	"	20
"	26	"	"	50

Lemonton, Ill, _____ 187

M

In Account with **LOUIS MENG,**
Dealer in

DRY GOODS AND GROCERIES, HARDWARE, &C.

Lemonton, Ill, _____ 187

M

In Account with **LOUIS MENG,**
Dealer in

DRY GOODS AND GROCERIES, HARDWARE, &C.

28.25
7 00

Lemonton, Ill, Aug 31 187

M

In Account with **LOUIS MENG,**
Dealer in

DRY GOODS AND GROCERIES, HARDWARE, &C.

LOUIS AND CHRISTINA MENG'S NINE CHILDREN

Louis and Christina's first child.

Two Martin Mengs

Louis and Christina Meng's second child was named Martin Meng who was born and died on 26 Sept 1862. His grave is in the Meng (a.k.a. Meng-Joseph) Cemetery between Freeburg and New Athens, Illinois. His headstone reads in part: "We are united with God together . . ." The grave is located directly in front of his grandfather Wilhelm Meng 1810-1850.

Subsequently, Louis and Christina had a fourth child which they also named Martin. The second Martin Meng's grave (1865–1947) is located in Elmwood Cemetery in Freeburg, Illinois.

Louis and Christina's second child.   *Louis and Christina's fourth child.*

Louis and Christina's third child. (James L. Meng's grandparents)

Louis and Christina's fifth child.

Conrad and Christina Meng

Louis and Christina's sixth child.
Mary died of asphyxiation (failed love affair).

200 years with Santa

Two residents of the St. Paul Nursing Home, 1021 West E. St., Belleville, who will observe their 100th birthdays shortly after the new year begins, agree a chat with Santa is a treat at any age. Mrs. Elizabeth Kilian, left, will be 100 on Feb. 28, while Mrs. Allie Self will observe her birthday Jan. 16.

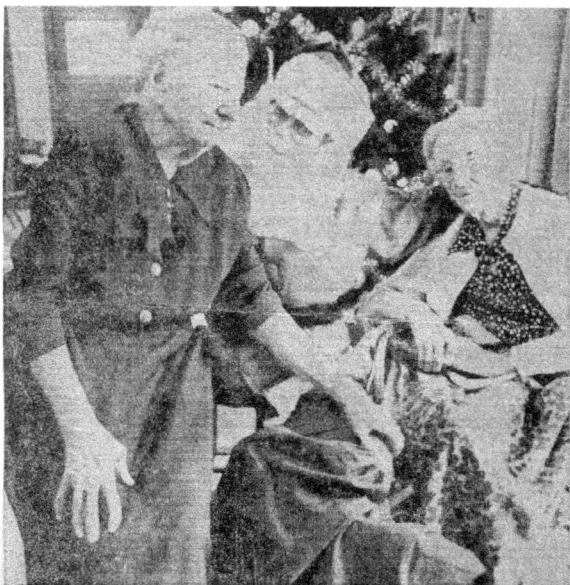

By Al Macas, Metro-East Journal staff

Party marks 103rd birthday

Mrs. Elizabeth Meng Kilian today celebrated her 103rd birthday with a party at St. Paul's Home in Belleville where she has been a resident for the past 18 years.

Seven nieces and nephews, ranging in age from 67 to 83, and her pastor, the Rev. Robert A. Krause of Union United Methodist Church of Belleville, attended the party.

Featured was a giant cake, covered with pink candy rosebuds.

tificate is written in German employes at the home said.

She was a school teacher before she married the late George Kilian and they moved to his farm on Smithton Road south of Belleville where they spent most of their married life.

Asked if she has any plans for the coming year, Mrs. Kilian replied, "That remains with God."

She is alert and until recently when she developed problems with her eyes she was

Louis and Christina's seventh child.

Taught Area's First
End of Summer School Brings Fond Memories
Belleville News Democrat

The end of the current summer school session brings fond memories for Mrs. Elizabeth B. Killian, nee Meng, formerly of Freeburg and now a resident of St. Paul Home.

When Mrs. Killian taught summer school in 1886 she went to work by train and if the train was late, she walked. That was the practical thing to do 86 years ago. Mrs. Killian doesn't ride trains anymore and as for walking, she prefers the comfort of her favorite rocking chair.

Now 100 years old, Mrs. Killian began her teaching career at the age of 14. "Little Lizzie" as she was called by friends and neighbors, earned $32 per month conducting the area's first summer school at the original Turkey Hill Grange Hall. Her charges were 32 farm children who needed to "catch up", because many of the youngsters missed regular classes during the winter due to bad roads.

"I heard that the children were unruly but I didn't have any discipline problems" said Mrs. Killian.

It was fitting that Mrs. Killian became a teacher. When she was small, she was eager to learn.

"I remember hurting my leg when I was three years old and I was unable to walk until I was six," Mrs. Killian said. "I had my brothers carry me to the schoolhouse and I would just sit there and listen. I was younger than the other pupils but I just let everything flow in."

Her disability grew worse and eventually she could not attend school. The county doctor came to the Meng home and warned the family that Elizabeth would die if he did not amputate the leg.

"I told him no because I was too young to know what death meant," said Mrs. Killian. Her leg healed after a few months despite the physician's warning.

Mrs. Killian, who reached the 100 year milestone last February, does not plan to ride any more trains. And as for as dying is concerned, Mrs. Killian says: "I'm still too young to know what death means." Mrs. Elizabeth Killian, a resident of St. Paul Home, will be 100 years of age on Monday.

The "Egg" Haviland
J. L. Meng

Elizabeth B. Kilian Meng, who lived in Belleville, gave Ed and Jessie Meng a 12-place setting (total 103 pieces) of Haviland china.

I was with my parents when these dishes were given to them. On that visit, we all went out to her garage where she had them stored in a big wooden barrel that had shredded fiber-like material for packing. Elizabeth said she would sell her chicken eggs in town until there was enough money to buy the dishes. I could tell that she didn't want to give up the dishes, but she wanted them to remain in the family.

The night she gave my parents the Haviland, Elizabeth also gave me a lead crystal toothpick holder. I believe she gave me the crystal holder because at the time, I was taking piano lessons and was required to play with each visit. I was not any good but these command performances were with each visit. At this point in time, Elizabeth's husband, George H. Kilian (1872–1935), had already died, and she was living with her sister, Katheryn I. Meng (1878–1954). They both "said" they liked my piano playing, but I think they were both just being nice.

One incidental memory about our visits, which were frequent, was that they were the only people I knew who had a doorbell located in the center of their front door that you would twist. (It was an old Victorian bell.) All I knew was that it was different, and I was in charge of announcing our presence with a good hard twist. I'm sure Elizabeth and Katheryn appreciated my door ringing abilities.

My parents were very proud of the Haviland; however, it was never used except on the holidays or on some special occasion like graduations and the day my parents met my wife. The event had to be big.

The Haviland was then passed on to my wife and me who have continued the tradition that the occasion had to be big, or no Haviland. This also means no dishwasher, hand wash only. When Beverly and I are finished using Elizabeth B. Kilian Meng's Haviland, they go to our daughter, Heather Andrea Meng. It will then be her responsibility to continue the protection of these very fragile but beautiful dishes that were originally bought with chicken egg money.

The pattern on the china is a light green flowering plant with light pink flowers spread intermittently on each dish. The edges of the bowls, saucers, plates, etc., are scalloped with gold accents at the base of each scallop. On some items like the gravy bowl, there is a gold wreath, open at the top with two bell-like figures at the base of the wreath. The handle on the water pitcher also has gold accents. The plates seem small in comparison to today's standards.

The bottom of each item is marked Haviland, France in large green letters and Haviland & Co. Limoges in red. *Apple blossoms*—Green mark *Haviland France* Dated 1889–1893 blank no. 5 scalloped edge with raised embossed white zigzag ridges all around. Gold thumb print daubs on edge no. 216. Pattern—small pink flowers, white larger flowers, green branchy leaves.

Elizabeth Kilian Meng's hundredth birthday—
the last time Jim and Bev visited with her. She lived to 103!

The "Egg Haviland"

Louis and Christina's eight child

Kathryn Meng, 76, Retired Teacher, Dies from Heat
Taught English at Junior High School for Many Years
Belleville News Democrat

Miss Kathryn I. Meng, 76, veteran retired teacher in local public schools, died suddenly at her home 617 East A Street, 15 7:30 last night, the victim of a heat stroke, according to her physician. Mrs. Elizabeth B. Kilian, a sister with whom Miss Meng lived, told police that a short time before she told her that she was not feeling well and wanted to lie down. Mrs. Kilian said that her sister slipped to the floor and remarked calmly, "Let me rest here for a while." A few minutes later she had expired.

Miss Meng began her teaching career in the Freeburg grade school in 1897. After teaching there two years she taught one year at Belle Valley School. In 1900 she returned to Freeburg and on May 31, 1901, she was appointed to the Belleville grade school system (one of Kathryn Meng's students was Christian Rudolph Ebsen Jr. a.k.a. Buddy Ebsen, actor and dancer of TV, Broadway and movie fame). Miss Meng was best known as an English teacher at Junior High until her retirement June 18, 1943.

She was born in Freeburg on Feb. 17, 1878, a daughter of the late Louis and Christina Borger Meng. A brother, Conrad Meng, who preceded her in death, was a funeral director at Freeburg. She was a member of the First Baptist church here, the Missionary society of that church, and the Illinois Teachers Association. Besides Conrad Meng, she was preceded in death by four other brothers and one sister. Funeral services will be held at 2 o'clock Friday afternoon at the Gundlach and Company funeral home. Rev. Seide B. Janssen will officiate. Interment will be in Elmwood cemetery, Freeburg.

William L. Meng was the ninth child of Louis and Christina Borger Meng.

Funeral is Held
Belleville News Democrat

The funeral of Dr. William L. Meng, above, formerly of Belleville and Freeburg, was held at the Barnard funeral home, Fergus Falls, Minnesota. Rev. William Van Dyken, officiating. Dr. Meng was buried at Oak Grove cemetery, where Masonic bodies and the American Legion took part.

In 1913 Dr. Meng went to Fergus Falls, where he was a member of the state hospital staff for 18 months, but returned to Belleville to enter private practice. When the First World War broke out, he offered his services and went overseas with the Jefferson Base Hospital unit, stationed at Nantes, France. As a soldier, he ranked as major. In 1921 he returned to Fergus Falls where he served on the hospital staff for six years, before entering the Veterans Administration Service where he was a psychiatrist for 16 years, serving at Marion, Indiana, and Perry Point, Maryland, when he retired.

Owing to the shortage of physicians, Dr. and Mrs. Meng, who is also a physician returned to Fergus Falls to take places on the state hospital staff to devote time helping out on the home front. About the middle of last September, Dr. Meng was taken ill and had to relinquish his duties.

Dr. Meng was a man of high principles, devoting his life to alleviate the sufferings of his fellowman. His death is mourned by his widow, Dr. Eleanor Lovejoy Meng, and son, Lt. Ralph H. Meng, also a physician, and a host of friends.

He is buried in Perry Point, Maryland.

State of Illinois,
St. Clair) County.

The Physician who attended any person in a last illness should immediately return this Certificate, accurately filled out, to the **County Clerk.** *Penalty $10.00, if not returned within 30 days.*

STATE BOARD OF HEALTH.

Name *Louis Meng* — Sex *male* Color *white*
Age *48* years *2* months *9* days. Occupation *police Magistrate*
Date of death *July 6th* *4* hour *P.M.*, Single, Married, *Widower, Wide*
Nationality and place where born *German Mattespeim Bavaria*
How long resident in this State *37 years*
Place of death† *Freeburg*
Cause of death‡ *Phthysis pulmonalis* — Complications *fistula in ano*

Duration of disease *8 months* *Duration of Complication* *4 years*
Place and date of burial *Freeburg village Cemetery July 8th*
Name and place of Undertaker *Chas. Weber Freeburg*
'ed at *Freeburg July 6th* 1882 — *Fred Koeberlin* M. D.
Residence *Freeburg*

erase such of these as are not required.
ity—No., Street and Ward ; same in towns that have them ; township or precinct.
ate primary and immediate cause of death, and examine the list of diseases printed on cover of this book, and law pertaining to Coroner's inquests

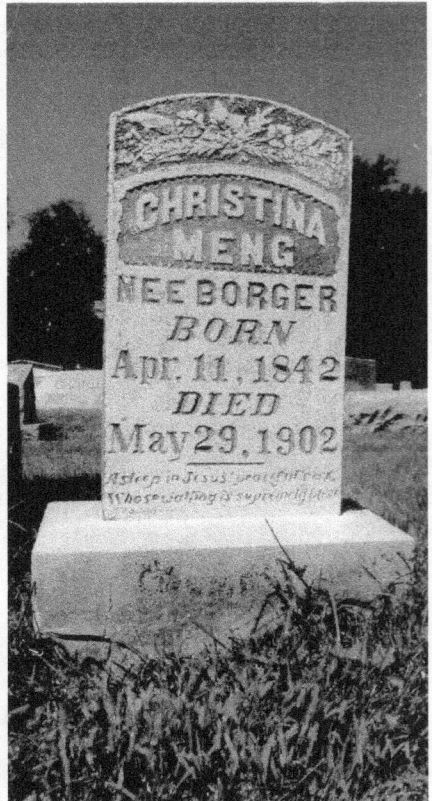

Meng Cemetery

In 2004, James and Marvin Meng visited the Meng Cemetery which is located halfway between Freeburg and New Athens, Illinois. The cemetery is approximately one and a half mile off the road located on a small hill overlooking a valley. The cemetery was overgrown with brush, trees, and downed tree limbs. Many of the headstones were down with an equal number covered with dirt and grass. With chain saws in hand and several bonfires to eliminate unwanted brush, the area was once again opened up; however, many headstones remain down. Martin Meng's headstone (b. and d. 26 Sep 1862) was reset in concrete with a small metal "cowboy riding a horse" imbedded in the new concrete base. This cemetery also known as the Meng-Joseph cemetery still needs a lot of work as of 2009.

The following is from the St. Clair County *Genealogical Society Quarterly*, 1987, Vol. 1; page 40.

MENG CEMETERY

Located in the W 1/2 of the NW 1/4 of Section 16 in the angle between Survey 387 & 388, Township 2 South, Range 7 West, New Athens Township, St. Clair Co., IL. Located east of Ruh Road south of Five Forks Road East. Copied 14 Mar 1983 by Martha Mae SCHMIDT.

Barbara dau of
Georg & Mar. BORGER
31 Mar 1861
6 Nov 1864

Henry son of John &
Gertrude FEURER
10 Apr 1851
1 Jan 1863
11 yr 8 mo 21 d

Jerome son of Dan'l
& Caroline FULLMER
28 Feb 1875
27 Mar 1875

John L. son of Dan'l
& Caroline FULLMER
13 July 1873
31 July 1874

Andreas JOSEPH
28 Nov 1811
3 Oct 1885

Anna Margaret wife
of Andrew JOSEPH
11 July 1815
2 June 1869

John JOSEPH
4 Feb 1846
14 Jan 1873

Lelia Alethea dau of
William & Sarah LORTZ
15 May 1882
17 Dec 1884

Martin son of
Lu's & Chs MENG
b & d 26 Sept 1862

Wilhelm MENG
b. 1810
d. 16 Dec 1850

Ida dau of
A. & K. WILDGRUBE
15 Feb 1877
9 Apr 1877

Johnny son of
A. & K. WILDGRUBE
14 July 1878
3 Aug 1878

Turkey Hill Grange is one of the agricultural cooperatives established to assist and educate farmers. Going to the Grange Meeting was often mentioned on the TV series *Little House on the Prairie* which represented life in 1870s and 1880s. Elizabeth Killian (nee Meng) taught school at the original Turkey Hill Grange when she was 14 years old.

Turkey Hill Grange

Invites You to Our Annual

WURSTMARKT

Route 15 & Greenmount Road, Belleville, IL

Sunday, October 30, 2011

10:30 a.m.-3:00 p.m.

Perfect Pork Sausage

Green Beans, Homemade Mashed Potatoes & Gravy, Sauerkraut, Cranberry Sauce, Homemade Apple Sauce, Pies and Cakes!

James L. Meng has attended this Wurstmart on Halloween weekend since at least 1945 or for 66 years. The Meng and Koesterer families have been officially connected to the Turkey Hill Grange organization for many years. Conrad Meng's name and business continues to be shown on the stage screen. Heather Meng's children continue the family tradition, a fourth generation of Wurstmarters!

- **Dr Ronald L. Meng's 2006 obituary from the Chicago Tribune. An Outstanding Life cut way too short.**

Dr. Ronald L. Meng, leading cardiothoracic and vascular surgeon, Decatur, IL. Dr. Ronald L. Meng, born in Belleville, IL, died January 15, 2006, at the age of 55, after a brief battle with gastric cancer. He is survived by his wife Rochelle, nee Robinson; daughter Laura and son Christopher; their dog Daisy; sister Peggy (Robert) Kaiser;...and aunt Delores Meng of Belleville, IL; ... He was preceded in death by his parents, Leslie and Verna (Parini) Meng. In 1968, Meng graduated as valedictorian of his class at Waukegan Township High School...Meng's legacy continues in the lives of his children and the myriad of people he helped through his great talents, energy and compassion. Widely recognized as a leading practitioner of cardiothoracic and vascular surgery and an authority on the treatment of adult and pediatric vascular disease,... Meng began practicing medicine in 1974, and most recently, in 2002, started a cardiac surgical services program at Decatur Memorial Hospital's Heart and Lung Institute. He was the first cardiac surgeon to serve Macon County, IL. Prior to his work at Decatur Memorial, Meng spent more than a decade at Lutheran General Hospital in Park Ridge, IL. In addition to his surgical work at Lutheran General, Meng held a wide variety of administrative posts, including Director of the Surgical Intensive Care Unit, Chairman of the Cardiac Surgery Division, and Chairman of the Pediatric Cardiac Surgery Section. During that time, Meng was also an attending physician at Holy Family Medical Center in Des Plaines, IL, and Condell Medical Center in Libertyville, IL. From 1982-1988, he was an attending physician at the University of Iowa Hospitals, Iowa City, IA, and the Veterans Administration Medical Center, also in Iowa City. Throughout his career, Meng received numerous accolades and prestigious awards, including being named a "Top Doctor in Chicago" by the Donnelly Press, and a "Top Doctor in America" by the Center for the Study of Services in Washington, D.C. Meng was affiliated with a wide variety of professional organizations, including the American College of Surgeons, the Society of Critical Care Medicine, the American Medical Association, the International Society for Heart Transplantation, the American College of Chest Physicians, the American College of Cardiology, and the International Society for Minimally Invasive Cardiac Surgery. Meng received his B.S. from the University of Illinois, Champaign Urbana in 1971, graduating Phi Beta Kappa. He received his M.D. in 1974 from the University of Illinois, Chicago and completed his residency in General Surgery in 1979 at Rush-Presbyterian-St. Luke's Medical Center, Chicago, IL. He received an M.S. in Surgery in 1977 from the University of Illinois, Chicago. From 1979-81, he was a Fellow, Thoracic Surgery, Rush-Presbyterian-St. Luke's Medical Center, Chicago, IL. He was certified by the American Board of Surgery, the American Board of Thoracic Surgery, and the American Board of Surgery, Special Qualification in General Vascular Surgery. Meng received several academic appointments at various colleges and institutions, including Rush Medical School, Chicago, IL, University of Iowa College of Medicine, Iowa City, IA, University of Chicago College of Medicine, Chicago, IL, and the University of Illinois College of Medicine, Chicago, IL... In addition to his work in medicine, Meng was an accomplished professional trumpet player, performing with a broad range of artists, including Elvis Presley, Frank Sinatra, Tommy Dorsey, Jimmy Dorsey, Sonny and Cher, Mel Torme, and Glen Campbell....

CHAPTER 9
FRIEDERICH AND ELIZABETH (KOESTERER) MENG AND THEIR NINE CHILDREN

Fredrich Meng

Birth: 11 Oct 1863 in Freeburg, St. Clair , Illinois
Death: 21 Jan 1913 in New Athens, St Clair, Illinois
Other Spouses:
Parents: Louis Meng & Christina Borger

Elizabeth Margaret Koesterer

Birth: 29 May 1869 in Freeburg, St Clair, Illinois
Death: 12 May 1947 in Granite City, Madison, Illinois (2707 Madison Ave.)
Other Spouses:
Parents: Berthold Koesterer & Katharina Reinheimer

Marriage 23 Nov 1892 in , St. Clair, IL

CHILDREN	SEX	BIRTH	SPOUSE	MARRIAGE	DEATH
Friedrich Martin Meng	M	5 Oct 1893 in New Athens, St Clair, Illinois	Sarah Agnes Roseberry	Aug 1933	15 Apr 1985 in Granite City, Madison, Illinois
Elmer Joe Meng	M	26 Feb 1895 in Freeburg, St Clair, Illinois			23 Dec 1900 in Freeburg, St Clair, Illinois
Frieda Marie Meng	F	29 Nov 1896 in Freeburg, St Clair, Illinois	Roy Keith Bennington	3 May 1958 in Granite City, Madison, Illinois	20 Sep 1987 in Granite City, Madison, Illinois
Walter George Meng	M	13 Dec 1898 in Freeburg, St Clair, Illinois	Helen C. Schneider	6 Oct 1937	22 Jun 1986 in A ton, Madison, Illinois
Ervin B. Meng	M	30 Nov 1900 in , St. Clair, IL			Dec 1900 in , St. Clair, IL.
Edward John Meng	M	4 Dec 1901 in Freeburg, St Clair, Illinois	Jessie Frances Shamhart	12 Sep 1928	1 Apr 1983 in St. Louis, St. Louis Co., MO
Wilmer Walter Meng	M	21 Dec 1903 in Freeburg, St Clair, Illinois	Thelda Cooper		11 Jan 1995 in Fullerton, Orange, CA
Oscar Jerome Meng	M	25 Jan 1906 in Freeburg, St Clair, Illinois	Alma Cooper	21 Feb 1933	20 Mar 1970 in Kansas City, Wyandotte, Kansas
Elsie E. Meng	F	21 May 1908 in New Athens, St Clair, Illinois			27 Dec 1908 in New Athens, St. Clair, Illinois

FREDRICH MENG—Family Group Sheet

CERTIFICATION OF VITAL RECORD

ST. CLAIR COUNTY, ILLINOIS

No. 1702

MARRIAGE LICENSE.

ADULT.

Mr. _Fred Meng_

with

Miss _Lizzie Koestner_

Issued _November 22d_ 189_2_

Married _____ 189_

Filed _____ 189_

County Clerk

DEC 1 1892

Phillip Rhine
County Clerk

Registered _____ 18_

Marriage Register _____ Page _

John Horris Company, Printers, Chicago.

CERTIFIED COPY OF VITAL RECORDS

CERTIFICATION OF VITAL RECORD

ST. CLAIR COUNTY, ILLINOIS

MARRIAGE LICENSE

STATE OF ILLINOIS — COUNTY OF ST. CLAIR

THE PEOPLE OF THE STATE OF ILLINOIS

To any person legally authorized to solemnize Marriage

GREETING

Marriage may be celebrated

Between Mr. Fred Meng of Freeburg in the County of St. Clair and State of Illinois of the age of Twenty Nine years and Miss Lizzie Koester of Freeburg in the County of St. Clair and State of Illinois of the age of Twenty Three years

Witness Phillip Rhein, County Clerk and the seal of said County at his Office in Belleville in said County this 22 day of November A.D. 1892

Phillip Rhein County Clerk

By J.O. Fleischbein Deputy

State of Illinois } ss
ST. CLAIR COUNTY

I Anton Werthfvereisk a German Ev. Prot. Priest hereby certify that Mr. Fred Meng were united in Marriage by me at Miss Lizzie Koester Freeburg in the County of St. Clair and State of Illinois, on the 23th day of November A.D. 1892

Anton Werthfvereisk
R.M.

It is the duty of the person celebrating the Marriage to fill out and sign the above Certificate and to return the same, together with the License, to the County Clerk within thirty days after the Marriage is solemnized. ONE HUNDRED DOLLARS PENALTY For FAILING SO TO DO.

CERTIFIED COPY OF VITAL RECORDS

STATE OF ILLINOIS
COUNTY OF ST. CLAIR } ss

DATE ISSUED   OCT 26 2009

I, Bob Delaney, St. Clair County Clerk, do hereby certify that this document is a true and correct copy of the original record which is on file in the office of the COUNTY CLERK, ST. CLAIR COUNTY, BELLEVILLE, ILLINOIS.

Bob Delaney
BOB DELANEY
COUNTY CLERK

Not valid without the embossed seal of St. Clair County.

ANY ALTERATION OR ERASURE VOIDS THIS CERTIFICATE

CERTIFICATION OF VITAL RECORD

ST. CLAIR COUNTY, ILLINOIS

ILLINOIS STATE BOARD OF HEALTH.

Return of a Marriage to County Clerk.

1. Full Name of GROOM *Fredric Meng*
2. Place of Residence *Freeburg Ills.*
3. Occupation *Engineer*
4. Age next Birthday *30* years. Color *White* Race *Caucasian*
5. Place of Birth *Dutch miles Prairie*
6. Father's Name *Louis Meng*
7. Mother's Maiden Name *Christina Borger*
8. Number of Groom's Marriage *first*
9. Full Name of BRIDE *Elisabeth Margar Kosterer*
   Maiden Name, if a Widow
10. Place of Residence *Freeburg Ills.*
11. Age next Birthday *24* years. Color *White* Race *Caucasian*
12. Place of Birth *Freeburg Ills.*
13. Father's Name *Bernhard Kosterer*
14. Mother's Maiden Name *Katharina Rheinheimer*
15. Number of Bride's Marriage *first*
16. Married at *Freeburg* in the County of
    St. Clair and State of Illinois, the *23th*
    day of *November* 1892.
17. Witnesses to Marriage *Joseph Koesterer Jr.*
    Mary E. Meng

N. B.—At Nos. 8 and 15 state whether 1st, 2d, 3d, &c., Marriage of each.
17 give names of subscribing witnesses to the Marriage Certificate. If no subscribing witnesses give names of two persons who witnessed the ceremony.

Freeburg Ills. Nov. 23 1892

We Hereby Certify that the information above given is correct to the best of our knowledge and belief.

Fredric Meng (Groom.)
Lizzie Koesterer (Bride.)

I Hereby Certify that the above is a correct return of a Marriage solemnized by me.

Anton Fritz Korens
Roman Catl. Priest

Dated at *Freeburg Ills.* this *23th*
day of *November* 1892.

CERTIFIED COPY OF VITAL RECORDS

STATE OF ILLINOIS } ss.
COUNTY OF ST. CLAIR

DATE ISSUED

OCT 26 2009

I, Bob Delaney, St. Clair County Clerk, do hereby certify that this document is a true and correct copy of the original record which is on file in the office of the COUNTY CLERK, ST. CLAIR COUNTY, BELLEVILLE, ILLINOIS.

Bob Delaney
BOB DELANEY
COUNTY CLERK

Not valid without the embossed seal of St. Clair County.

ANY ALTERATION OR ERASURE VOIDS THIS CERTIFICATE

Friederich (Frederick) Meng was the son of Louis Meng and Christina (née Borger) Meng. Friederich married Elizabeth Margaret (née Koesterer) on November 23, 1892.

Freeburg, Ill., Dec 4 1903

Mr Fred Meng

BOUGHT OF **PHILLIP CONRATH,**

Dealer in STOVES, HOLLOW-WARE, GUNS, PISTOLS, AMMUNITION, CUTLERY, ETC.,

— AND MANUFACTURER OF —

Tin, Copper and Sheet Iron Ware

Roofing, Guttering Spouting and Jobbing done on short notice.

FULL LINE OF STAPLE AND FANCY GROCERIES.

Dec 4 To Balance 6 19

Pleas and settel this bill and get it off the Books

If not called for in Five Days return to

P. H. CONRATH,

FREEBURG, ILL.

Dealer in GROCERIES, STOVES,
HARDWARE, Etc.

Mr Fred. Meng

Freeburg

Ill

Funeral notes referencing Friederich Meng death as written by Friedrich Martin Meng, the eldest son

Fred MENG
aka: Friederich (Frederick) MENG

Notes

As described by his son, Fred: Brawny, a fighter if he had a couple beers. He never hurt anyone, but no one ever beat him. He had brown eyes, black hair. It turned gray, and he was bald in center. He could drink more beer than anyone else.

The reason he had no religion was that he thought ministers should earn their money with their hands like everybody else. He was strong headed—the best guy in the world if you agreed with him.

Signed autograph book of Lizzy Koesterer Meng, his wife.

Bill for his funeral from Gundlach and Company Livery, Boarding, Undertaking, Belleville, Illinois, January 27, 1913.
January 25: Funeral expenses for Fred Meng, dec'd.

Casket, box, etc.	$75.00
Embalming and work with body	$12.00
Suit	$18.00
Hearse	$10.00
Pall Coach	$6.00
5 carriages	$30.00
Gloves and Crepe	$2.50
Candles	$.75
Delivering box to cemetery	$3.00
Total	$107.25

MENG Cemetery is in the W 1/2 of the NW 1/4 of Sec 14 off Ruh Road off Five Fork Road east of Route 13. It is the wedge between Survey 387 and 388. This cemetery is in very bad condition with many stones buried and very overgrown. Burials range from 1850–1885. (History of St. Clair County, Vol. I)

SONS AND DAUGHTER OF FRED AND ELIZABETH MENG.

OSCAR J. MENG FRED M. MENG WALTER G. MENG

WILMER W. MENG FRIEDA M. MENG ELIZABETH M. MENG EDWARD J. MENG

OSCAR ALMA OJ JR AND FRANCES WILMER AND IRIS FRED, AGNES AND JANET MOM AND FRIEDA WALTER AND HELEN ED, JESSIE, JAMES AND ED JR

1939 FAMILIES:

226

SEVENTIETH BIRTHDAY
ANNIVERSARY

Mrs. Elizabeth Meng, 2707 Madison avenue, was honored with a surprise birthday party and family reunion in celebration of her seventieth birthday anniversary yesterday.

Out-of-town guests were Mr. and Mrs. Walter G. Meng and Mrs. Johanna Snyder of Alton, Mr. and Mrs. Wilmer Meng of Kooskia, Idaho, Mr. and Mrs. O. J. Meng and children of Kansas City, Kan., and Miss Viola Brendle of St. Louis, and from this city those present included Mr. and Mrs. Fred Meng and daughter, Janet; Mark Roseberry, Miss Frieda Meng, and Mr. and Mrs. Edward Meng and sons, Edward and James.

Elizabeth M. Meng and daughter, Frieda M. Meng, on back porch steps of their home at 2707 Madison Ave., Granite City, IL. Not shown are the strawberry plants growing on each side of the walk and (white) grape arbor.

1. PLACE OF DEATH.	Registration Dist. No. 617
County of Madison	
Granite City	Township / Primary Dist. No. 3447
Street and Number, No. 2707 Madison Ave	Registered No. 124

49093 STATE OF ILLINOIS — COUNTY CLERK'S RECORD
DWIGHT H. GREEN, Governor
DEPARTMENT OF PUBLIC HEALTH
CERTIFICATE OF DEATH

LENGTH OF TIME AT PLACE WHERE DEATH OCCURRED ... yrs. ... mos. ... ds.

2. PLACE OF RESIDENCE: STATE Illinois County Madison Township Granite City Road Dist.
City or Village Granite City Street and Number 2707 Madison Avenue

3. (a) FULL NAME Elizabeth Margaret Meng
3. (b) If Veteran name war. no No. none 3. (c) Social Security

MEDICAL CERTIFICATE OF DEATH

4. Sex Female 5. Color or race White 6.(a) Single, widowed, married, divorced Widowed
20. Date of death: Month May day 12 year 1947 hour 5 minute 45 AM
6. (b) Name of husband or wife Fred 6.(c) Age of husband or wife if alive 20
21. I hereby certify that I attended the deceased from August 1946 May 12 1947; that I saw h. alive on May 10 1947;
7. Birth date of deceased May 29 1869
8. AGE: Years 77 Months 11 Days 23
Immediate cause of death Myocarditis — Duration 1 yr.
9. Birthplace Freeburg, Illinois
Associated diseases
10. Usual occupation Housewife
11. Industry or business Own Home
Other conditions Hypertension — 3 yrs.
FATHER 12. Name Berthold Koesterer
13. Birthplace Germany
22. Was an operation performed? No Date of. For what disease or injury? xx Was there an autopsy? No Findings? xx
MOTHER 14. Maiden name Katherine Reimeheimer
15. Birthplace Freeburg, Illinois
23. If a communicable disease; where contracted? xx
16. INFORMANT Fred Meng P.O. Address Granite City, Illinois
Was disease in any way related to occupation of deceased? no If so, specify how:
17. PLACE OF BURIAL (a) Cemetery Elmwood (b) DATE 5 14 47
Location Freeburg County St.Clair State Illinois
24. (Signed) E.M.Arnovitz M.D. Address 1915 Delmar, Granite City, Ill Date May 12 1947
All cases of death from "violence, casualty, or any undue means" must be referred to the coroner. See Section 10 Coroner's Act.
18. Funeral director Ferd Pieper Pieper Funeral Home ADDRESS Granite City, Ill 4128
25. May 13 1947 A.L.Stevens Registrar. P.O. Address Granite City, Ill

This is a true and correct copy of the official record filed in the office of the county clerk of Madison County (for genealogical purposes only).

The following chapters report the nine children of Friederich and Elizabeth Meng including their great and great-great-grandchildren.

Friedrich Martin Meng (1893–1985), chapter 10
Elmer J. Meng (1895–1900), chapter 9
Frieda Marie Meng (1896–1987), chapter 11
Walter George Meng (1898-1986), chapter 12
Ervin B. Meng (1900–1900), chapter 9
Edward John Meng (1901–1983), chapter 13
Wilmer Walter Meng (1903–1995), chapter 19
Oscar Jerome Meng (1906–1970), chapter 20
Elsie E. Meng (1908–1908), chapter 9

Friederich and Elizabeth Meng lost three children, their second, fifth, and ninth

Elmer J. Meng (26 Feb 1895–23 Dec 1900)
Ervin B. Meng (30 Nov 1900–Dec 1900)
Elsie E. Meng (21 May 1908–27 Dec 1908)

Elmer J. Meng, Ervin B. Meng, and Elsie were children of Fred and Elizabeth Meng. Elmer J. Meng died in December 1900. When Elmer died, Elizabeth was nursing Ervin. It is said the shock of Elmer's death poisoned Elizabeth's milk causing Ervin's death. The following picture was taken while they lay in state in the family parlor. They were buried together. Elsie E. Meng also died in December. My father, Edward J. Meng, who was born on December 4th, often referenced these three deaths during the Christmas holidays, which in turn affected his Christmas emotions the rest of his life.

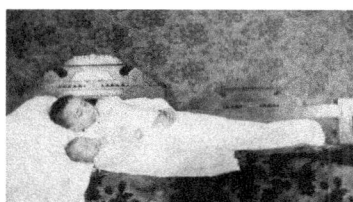

Elmwood Cemetery., Freeburg, St. Clair, IL.

229

A brief summary of the Meng connections to music.

Our family has always participated in and enjoyed a wide range of music over the years ranging from, to Dixie Land, to Sinatra, to Andre Reiu and to our favorite, Richard Wagner's *Tannhauser Pilgrim's Chorus*. Each generation has been involved in some form of music as illustrated in the following family summary below.

-In 1928, Hoyt Lester Ming recorded the *Indian War Whoop* on the Victor label which was used in the movie *O Brother where Art Though* staring George Clooney, John Goodman while in 1975, Hoyt Ming recorded th sound track for the movie *Ode to Billy Joe*. His recording is now in the Smithsonian. Hoyt's son Hoyt Bertrand Ming continued the family tradition in music with the Pep Steppers who also preformed the *Indian War Whoop, Old Red, White Mule, Tupelo Blues* at the Worlds Fair, Wolf Trap and at the National Folk Festival etc.. Go to the www to listen to this very talented master.

-The Vaughncille Joseph Meng Concert Hall at California State University in Fullerton California is named after the wife of Wilmer W. Meng. Vonnie was a tremendous piano player certainly at the concert level. While her husband, Wilmer W. Meng loved playing the ukulele for various events.

- Edward J. Meng played the clarinet and tenor sax in dance bands in the 1930's and the 1940's. He and my mom thoroughly enjoyed music which always filled our home.

- Agnes Meng played great rag time and her rendition of any of Scott Joplin's music especially *Maple Leaf Rag* was certainly at a professional level. Agnes played for a variety of local organizations while her husband Fred, played the trumpet, drums and was a U.S. Army bugler during WWI.

-Edward S. Meng was a very good tenor. He sang in all high school choirs and with the Central Methodist University A Cappela choir under the notable direction of the Mr. Luther T. Spayde.

-Beverly Meng has sung for over sixty years in various church choirs, has directed the Twin Oaks Presbyterian English Hand bell choir for ten years was the church pianist and currently plays the piano for nursing homes.

- Heather Meng played piano as a youth and won a competition trophy. Even played some "mean" boogie woogie that was accidentally heard in the funeral parlor at Jessie Meng's wake much to the delight of all the attendees and I suspect, my mom, Jessie.

-DR. Ronald L. Meng not only was a world renown medical doctor but was also an accomplished professional trumpet player, performing with a broad range of artist, including Elvis Presley, Frank Sinatra, Tommy Dorsey, Jimmy Dorsey, Sonny and Cher, Mel Torme, and Glen Campbell.

-James L. Meng took piano lessons for six years and cannot pay a note!

CHAPTER 10
FRIEDERICH AND AGNES (ROSEBERRY) MENG

Friederich Martin Meng (1893–1985)
Just who were Fred and Agnes Meng?
J. L. Meng (nephew)

Of all my aunts and uncles, I grew up being around the Fred Meng family the most, not only did they live close, but their children, Marvin and Janet, were approximately the same age as me. Fredric Martin Meng and his wife Agnes lived in Granite City, Illinois, at 2107 Monroe Avenue. Knowing Fred and Agnes was an experience every child should have. Fred was a very colorful person and master at making "things," be it Boy Scout projects or instruments made out of various kitchen utensils for Agnes' (kazoo) kitchen band. He was a man of many talents and could do anything. He was even the neighborhood barber who would cut all the kids' hair, including the traditional Mohawk, to many moms' chagrin, at the end of the school year. At Christmas, he and the neighborhood kids would make a large rabbit out of snow approximately six feet high complete with colored eggs. A picture of the rabbit would always end up in the local paper. He was also a bugler during World War I and played the drums for enjoyment.

Fred liked to cook. He enjoyed making a "sunshine" cake, which, during Easter, he would decorate with marshmallow bunnies that he would cut with a scissors and then add red eyes with food coloring using a toothpick. He would bake his cake in his kitchen which he often referred to as a "one ass kitchen" because it was quite narrow. Narrow it was, but realistically, more than one person could occupy the room. But then again, Fred's description was much more colorful.

During frequent picnic outings to his brother's (Edward J. Meng) 26-acre farm in Edwardsville, Fred was always in charge of the barbecue. The fire had to be just right, plenty of coals but not too hot. Some of the finest ribs in the world came from the direction of Fred Meng. During one such picnic, Fred decided what this place really needed is an outhouse. Without any further discussion, saws, levels, and hammers came out of the trunks of the cars (I don't know why anyone would carry these items with them) and plans were being drawn on an old grocery bag. The event was so big, that an 8-mm camera was used to record the excitement of the construction from its beginning through to its completion. (His son, Marvin Meng, has the movies of the outhouse project.) After a multitude of arguments and curse words over dimensions involving the slope of the roof, how much space was needed to occupy the outhouse and still close the door and, of course, the size of the hole in the seat, the project was complete. Everyone was then invited to raise the structure into place. There it was, a true miracle, one of the finest buildings in Madison County engineered by Fred Meng and brothers and built without a federally funded environmental impact study! This marvel had to be the envy of the free world and definitely a challenge to the St Louis arch. The only problem was no one ever used it. It seems that wasps also appreciated the building and moved in. The prospect of being in a confined space with a bare rear end and wasps just wasn't that amusing to us city folks.

Fred, like all the rest of us, also had a small garden at the Edwardsville farm. One year, we had a problem with crows eating the young plants, so Fred shot some crows, hung them upside down on long poles placed throughout the planted area. During one picnic, Fred noticed that one of the poles was leaning over, so he went to correct the problem. Keep in mind, this old crow had been hanging there in the hot sun for over a week. After he straightened the pole, he learned over and jammed the pole into the ground. The old rotten crow came loose and hit him in the back of the neck. Curse words flew like I never heard before. All of this while performing a very animated dance and ripping his shirt off. It was quite a sight to see pieces of a white shirt and buttons flying into the air. Definitely one of those *Kodak moments*.

As custom in our family, when anyone of our relatives came to visit, they knock once on the door, enter the home, and holler "Is any one home?" This was an accepted standard procedure. One time, when I was a child of about six years old, Fred stopped in during the day and proceeded with the normal family entrance. Unfortunately, my pet black chow named "Tang" did not approve of Fred's entrance and immediately chased him up the stairs to the second floor of our home. As Fred would take one step down the stairs, Tang would take one step up the stairs, growl, and show his teeth. In full retreat, Fred went to our bathroom window to holler down to my mom who was hanging wash in the backyard, "Get that G*@ D@## dog out of here!" She did, and Fred came down the stairs, saying, "I'd kill that s*@ of a b**## dog." Shortly thereafter, my mom caught me holding Tang's mane with my face pressed against the dog's saying, "Tang, you SOB. Tang, you SOB." Of course, I didn't get in any trouble, because I had no idea what I was saying, but Fred was scolded for corrupting a seven year old kids mind. It may have been my imagination, but ever since the stair incident, it seemed that whenever Tang and Fred were in the same room, they always watched one another out of the corners of their eyes.

Curse words and Fred Meng came in the same package. This language, never demeaning or intended literally, was just part of his normal vocabulary. Agnes would attempt to correct Fred, but this, we all knew, was a futile attempt.

Fred also liked Fords. It seemed that every two years, he would buy a new car, a Ford. One time, I bought a new 1962 Studebaker Hawk, 4-speed, bright red. Knowing Fred's propensity toward Fords, I deliberately drove my Hawk to his house to show it off. I began my tour of the car with the statement, "This will beat any damn Ford on the street." Fred's only comment was "Like hell it will. It's a Studebaker." Getting the expected response, anything else would have been "abnormal," I returned home with a grin.

Agnes was heavyset. She was an outstanding piano player with an uncanny talent to play ragtime music. She had a 1904 Baldwin baby grand piano that she had purchased in her youth. She started her piano playing as a young girl in the 5 & 10 Cent Stores. Although she did not play professionally, her talent level was such that, with some direction, she certainly could have reached this status. She received numerous comments from fellow musicians who were professionally trained as to her ability and "feel" for ragtime. To hear her play *Maple Leaf Rag, Dark Town Strutter's Ball*, or any other music of that era was a total treat. She did play piano for several organizations in town, including Mrs. Green's tap dance school, and was often featured on the admiral riverboat, the Fox Theater in St. Louis, Missouri, and the Rebecca's organization, etc.

On one visit, when my children (Heather and Erik) were seven and five years old, Agnes sat down at her piano and started playing her normal ragtime music. As stated earlier, Agnes did carry a few extra pounds. Fred, who was also a drummer, immediately got up and commenced patting Agnes on her rear end in perfect time with the music. Agnes never flinched and neither did I because this type behavior was considered normal. However, my kids were astonished. Their eyes got big as they looked in wonderment at me as if to say, do you see what he is doing? Is this proper adult behavior? Is this what is in my gene pool? Later, I found out that my wife (Beverly) was equally astonished wondering what kind of family had she married into.

The outhouse project, the crow, and the rear end drumming are only a few examples of growing up around Fred and Agnes Meng. These events were routine and frequent. Agnes' devotion to Fred and her futile attempt to keep him in line was admirable, a full-time job, and the source of many fond memories.

Fred Meng looked like all the Mengs: gray haired with a large nose. His physical appearance in later years was very similar to Arthur Fiedler, the director of the Boston Pops, white hair combed straight back, a white mustache, and a tan, wrinkled face. He was extremely colorful, dependable, and the type of uncle everyone should experience.

PRESS-RECORD, Thursday, June 19, 1980–17

MR. AND MRS. FRED MENG, 2107 Monroe Ave., will celebrate their golden wedding anniversary at an open house reception Saturday, June 28, at St. Peter Evangelical United Church of Christ, from 2 to 4 p.m.

Mr., Mrs. Fred Meng to mark anniversary

Mr. and Mrs. Fred Meng, 2107 Monroe Ave., will be guests of honor at an open house reception Saturday, June 28, in observance of their 50th wedding anniversary.

The affair, hosted by their children and grandchildren, will be held at St. Peter Evangelical United Church of Christ, 2103 Cleveland Blvd.

Guests will be received from 2 to 4 p.m.

Mr. Meng and his wife Agnes were married on June 28, 1930 in the parsonage of St. Peter Church in Alhambra.

He had resided in the New Athens and Freeburg area prior to their marriage. Mr. Meng was employed by John Hancock Insurance Co. for 32 years prior to his retirement in 1960. He is a member of World War I Veterans, Barracks 34.

Mrs. Meng worked as cashier and bookkeeper for the former Davis Grocery Store for 12 years before she retired. She was a member of the Juanita Rebekah Lodge where she served as noble grand officer and is currently holding the office of musician for DelRay Rebekah Lodge.

Mr. and Mrs. Meng are the parents of a daughter, Mrs. Janet Holtzscher of Findlay, Ohio, and one son, Marvin Meng of Edwardsville. They also have six grandchildren.

Fred and Agnes Meng attending James Meng's college graduation in 1961. Having an aunt and uncle like Fred and Agnes support throughout life was like having two sets of parents.

Fred and Agnes were very proud of their
children, Janet and Marvin Meng

THE LORD'S PRAYER

My Jesus have mercy on the soul of

Agnes S. Meng
June 14, 1902
March 15, 1986

"The Lord's Prayer"

Our Father who art in heaven,
hallowed be thy name.
Thy kingdom come. Thy will be
done on earth as it is in
heaven.
Give us this day our daily
bread.
And forgive us our trespasses
as we forgive those who
trespass against us.
And lead us not into tempta-
tion, but deliver us from
evil. Amen.

Fred Meng's One Ass Kitchen

While growing up, we would visit Uncle Fred and Aunt Agnes' home at 2107 Monroe Avenue in Granite City. They were like second parents. These visits also allowed me to see my cousins, Janet and Marvin Meng, who were of same age. The kitchen in Fred and Agnes' home was narrow, what some call a "Galley Kitchen." Every now and then, when someone would come into the kitchen while he was in there, Fred would announce, "This is a One Ass Kitchen." Knowing Fred's past colorful language, you just passed his announcement off as just another routine day on Monroe Avenue.

Many years later, we lived in Seven Pines Subdivision in St. Louis County. Frequently I would follow this unknown station wagon out of our subdivision. Its license plate read "9ASWAGN." Having grown up around Fred Meng and his kitchen, I read the license plate as "9ass wagon." You know, 3 people in the front seat, 3 people in the middle seat and 3 people in the rear seat. Add them up! I also thought this unknown person must have known, worked with, or had a DNA relationship with Fred. This went on for years until one day Bev was with me and this 9ASWGN pulled out in front of my car. I immediately explained to Bev the meaning of the license plate. Bev said, "Oh no," that means *Nina's wagon*, which is my boss's wife's name who lives close to us. Indecently, Bev's boss was the chief general counsel for Mallinckrodt Medical Co. in St Louis. Later that year, I met Bev's boss and Nina at a Christmas party where I explained my misinterpretation of her license plates, due to having grown up around Fred Meng. They both had a good laugh over my interpretation adding that they would like to have met Fred.

THE
GRANITE CITY
JR. CHAMBER OF COMMERCE
presents the
"MISS GRANITE CITY"
PAGEANT OF 1956-57

Granite City High School
June 9, 1956
An Official Preliminary Miss America Contest

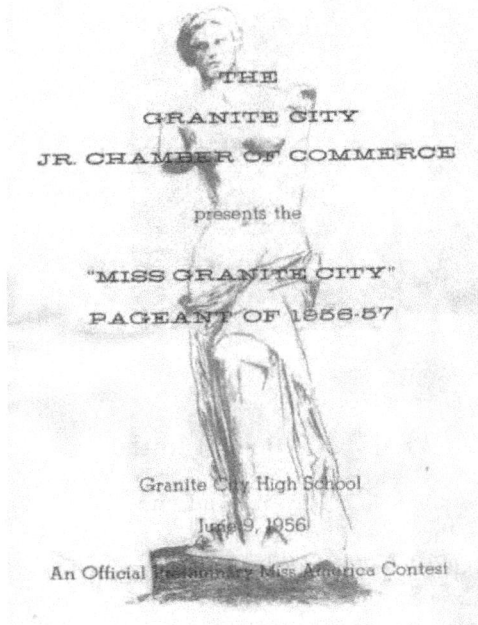

Janet A. Meng was always very friendly, popular and very pretty. She was not only a good student, but a finalist in the Miss Granite City beauty contest. The contest was held by the local news paper, The Granite City Press Record which also sponsored the winner in the Miss Illinois pageant.

Miss Marilyn Champion
SPONSORED BY
Ranft's Bottling Company

Miss Carol Johnson
SPONSORED BY
Ford's Flowers

Miss Pat Nega
SPONSORED BY
Cochrane Realty

Miss Janet Meng
SPONSORED BY
Ranft's Bottling Company

Miss Audrey Lancaster
SPONSORED BY
Ford's Flowers

Miss Nancy Tucker
SPONSORED BY
Community Coach Co.

Miss Barbara McCullough
SPONSORED BY
Cochrane Realty

Miss Diane Neuboff
SPONSORED BY
Community Coach Co.

Granite City Press Record will sponsor the entry
of Miss Granite City into the State
Contest

CHAPTER 11
FRIEDA (MENG) AND ROY BENNINGTON

Frieda Marie Meng (1896–1987)
Who was Frieda Meng Bennington?
J. L. Meng (nephew)

Frieda Meng was born in Freeburg, Illinois. She then moved with the family to 2707 Madison Avenue in Granite City, Madison County, Illinois. My father (Edward J.) often said that Frieda became a substitute mother for her five brothers who were not the tamest young men in town (a major understatement). Frieda did all the baking for the family including great coffee cakes, pies, and breads. She made clothing such as shirts for her brothers and packed their daily lunches as they came and went all hours while working the different shifts in the steel mills. Frieda devoted her early life to her brothers. When her mother Elizabeth Meng became ill, she devoted considerable time taking care of her until her death in 1947.

As a child, I remember visiting my grandmother Meng and Frieda who lived just one block from my house. She always gave me bologna sandwiches with mustard and coffee cake which she would have sitting on the counter covered with a cloth. She also baked great gingerbread men and molasses cookies at Christmas and stored them (I should say hid them) upstairs so they would become soft to eat. Cookies simply cannot be hidden from someone like me and my cousin Marvin. We would raid her cookie batch and nearly break our teeth on these tasty but brick-like goodies.

In addition to giving up half of her personal life for the benefit of others in the family, Aunt Frieda also worked for Curlee Clothing in St. Louis, Missouri, as seamstress until retirement. One time in 1950, after being without family responsibilities, she bought a new green Chevrolet two-door which she drove until 1956. In 1956, she decided to buy another new car, trading in her total "cream puff" 1950 for a 1956 power-packed two-toned hard top. Frieda's top speed was about 45 mph. However, the engine in her new power-packed '56 was so powerful that her brother Fred had to drive it frequently to blow out the carbon. The family often said that the salesman really saw her coming. It was an extremely neat car, but come to think about it, her car was much faster than any of her brothers, which I think everyone knew.

I remember one time Frieda took me to Kemoll's Italian Restaurant in north St. Louis when I was about 10 to eat a new food, recently introduced to St. Louis called pizza. I had heard about pizza but never had seen one. My first, a personal milestone, was delivered by Frieda Meng.

Each Christmas and Easter, I am also reminded of Frieda Meng. When I was 10 years old, Frieda escorted me on the church bus to Bloomington, Illinois. The purpose of the trip was to hear Handel's *Messiah*, performed by a group of churches in that area. At 10 years old, having to wear a coat and tie on a long bus ride to hear something titled Handel's *Messiah* was a little bit heavy. After all, at that point in time, I was more interested in playing "Cowboys and Indians" and beginning to like rock and roll. I had never heard of this guy named Handel, but I survived the trip to Bloomington. However, the *Messiah* has since become one of my favorite performances and a must hear at Christmas and Easter. So when we rise to hear the Hallelujah Chorus, I always think of Frieda and thank her for taking this stupid little kid to hear Handel's great work. Think of it, my first pizza and Handel's *Messiah*, what a legacy!

On May 3, 1958, at the age of 62, Frieda married a widower named Roy Bennington, a local jeweler in town. Bennington Jewelry was thought of as the best jewelry store in town. Roy was a small-framed person and an avid Cardinal baseball fan. Frieda and Roy lived at 2856 Iowa in Granite City, Madison County, Illinois. Each Sunday, they would attend the Central Christian Church for services and then go out for a fried chicken dinner. Frieda was always, and I mean always, very neat and well dressed. She was solidly built but would not think of going anywhere without being dressed properly. She had her hair done every Friday at the local beauty shop. Frieda and Roy made a nice-looking couple, both well-dressed, driving a black four-door Plymouth.

An interesting sidelight to Roy occurred with my father who worked in the Granite City Post Office. The government sent instructions to the post office to destroy all the weight-driven windup clocks. My father had difficulty destroying these items which he thought were attractive and valuable, so he attempted to give them away. They were all Seth Thomas number "twos." However, no one wanted them except for one local jeweler named Roy Bennington. Roy took the clock and had it running in his store when

he met and married Aunt Frieda. They then had the clock hanging on their breakfast area wall. Later on, when Roy and Frieda passed on, this same clock was returned to me where it now ticks away in our home.

Frieda Meng in her drum
and bugle corps in 1937.

Frieda at a young age in New Athens, IL.

Frieda Meng's power-packed 1956 Chevy.
Did the salesman see her coming?

Frieda's "cream puff" 1950 Chevy.

Frieda Marie Meng in front of Elizabeth M. Meng's home at 2707 Madison Ave., Granite City, IL.

Elizabeth M. Meng and daughter Frieda M. Meng on back porch steps of their home. Not shown are the strawberry plants growing on each side of the walk and (white) grape arbor.

1953

Frieda had no children.

Frieda and Fred Meng

241

Frieda (Meng) and Roy Bennington

Frieda had an exceptional family reputation for being an excellent cook and baker. Every year, around Thanksgiving time, she would make molasses cookies that needed to rest in her attic for about a month before they were soft and ready to bake. Unknown to Frieda, or maybe known, Marvin and James Meng knew of her attic hiding location. The cookies which started out as hard as a brick in their early stage of curing always tasted exceptionally good. Visits to Frieda's home always resulted in a piece of fresh coffee cake, cookies, and anything else that could be put into an oven.

Cookie eaters

Frieda nee Meng Bennington
Granite City Press Record

Frieda M. (Meng) Bennington, 90, of 2856 Iowa St., ill for two years, died at 3:15 a.m. Sunday, Sept 20, 1987, at the Madison County Nursing Home, Edwardsville, where she was a patient for two weeks.

She was born in Freeburg, Ill., and moved to this area in 1919. Mrs. Bennington was employed as a sleeve setter for the Curlee Clothing Co. factory, St. Louis, for 25 years before retiring.

A member of St. Peter Evangelical United Church of Christ, she also was a member of the FAC Class and Evening Guild of the church.

Survivors include her husband, Roy Bennington; one brother, Wilmer Meng of Fullerton, Calif.; and nieces and nephews.

Visitation started at 6 p.m. Tuesday at Irwin Chapel for Funerals, 2801 Madison Ave., will officiate at 10 a.m. services Wednesday. Burial will be at a cemetery in Freeburg.

THE LORD'S PRAYER

My Jesus have mercy on the soul of

Frieda Marie Bennington
November 29, 1896
September 20, 1987
"The Lord's Prayer"

Frieda was buried in Freeburg, IL., with a small flat headstone. Her husband Roy, who died a few years later, was buried with his first wife. Frieda, who had spent her entire life talking care of her brothers, her mother and others, once again was by herself. Some things in life are just not as they should be.

CHAPTER 12
WALTER AND HELEN (SCHNEIDER) MENG

Walter George Meng 1898-1986
Who were Walter and Helen Meng?
J. L. Meng (nephew)

Walter George Meng married Helen C. (née Schneider) on October 6, 1937. They were my aunt and uncle and lived in Alton, Illinois. Walter was a journeyman machinist for the Laclede Steel Co. in Alton. His hobbies in vegetable gardening, rose growing, and the stock market gave him great success and delight. On visits to their home, Walter's impressive gardens were quite large and productive. During his frequent visits to Granite City, he would deliver full grocery bags loaded with produce from his garden to his sister, Frieda Meng, and his brothers, Fred Meng and my dad, Edward J. Meng. I think one of his specialties was growing sweet potatoes, for it is this food that I remember him bringing most often. These potatoes were quite big, and Uncle Walter made a point of expressing just how big they really were. And, he was right and they were good!

Walter also bought and sold common stocks frequently. He always told me to watch the people who ran the company. If they were solid and had a good track record, then buy the stock; the company would do well. If they were unproven, then stay away or sell the stock. One of his favorite companies was the Granite City Steel Co. (National Steel). I believe he would study and buy and sell this one particular stock frequently to great success. If you wanted to spend a full hour discussing investments, all you had to do was find Walter Meng. And if you didn't find him, he would find you.

Uncle Walter was of average height and weight with the typical Meng "nose" just like all his brothers. Helen was of small frame and very quiet. She never said too much, perhaps because when Walter and his brothers all got together, there was very little room for anyone to say anything.

As mentioned above, Walter Meng's expertise in cultivating roses and gardening were well known throughout the community. A newspaper article discussing his gardening talents follows.

Wedding picture of Walter George Meng (left) and Helen C. Schneider (sitting) (6 Oct 1937). Standing behind Walter and Helen are Helen's twin sister Bertha and her husband, Henry Maul.

Walter Meng and his roses. He had several hundred roses which he cultivated.

83-year-old Alton gardener
knows no strangers

By Mary Ann Mazenko
Family Page Editor

Gardeners know no strangers, they say, and Walter Meng of Alton may prove the saying is so.

Since a *Telegraph* article in August about Meng's skill at starting new rose bushes from cuttings of established plants, he's had impromptu visits from numerous area residents interested in having cuttings from his plants.

Meng not only gave his surprise visitors the requested cuttings, he proffered advice as well — a natural state of affairs

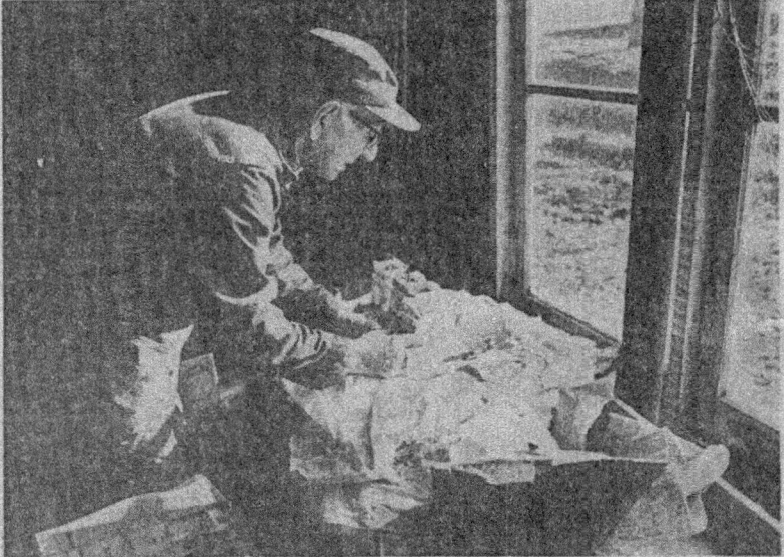

GROWING NEW ROSES FROM OLD PLANTS IS A BREEZE FOR WALTER MENG—The Alton gardener starts tiny new rosebushes from established plants by breaking off "slips" from bushes in the large rose garden behind his upper Alton home. Meng checks the cuttings he is rooting in small milk cartons to see if they are ready to transplant to his garden, where he'll cover them with glass jars "like grandmother used to do." By spring, the miniature plants should be established and ready to blossom into full-blown rose bushes. (Photos by John Badman)

247

when one gardener talks to another.

"I've given out about 200 rose 'slips' to people I never saw before — perfect strangers," Meng said.

"I'm glad somebody is making use of them. Next spring, when I trim back my rosebushes, I'd throw them away anyway," he said good naturedly.

The 83-year-old Altonian has a rose garden with 50 bushes in the backyard of his home on Worden Avenue in upper Alton.

Only two of his 50 plants were purchased. Others, he started by his method of rooting "slips" or cuttings broken from the mother plant.

"I'm using a new method this fall. I break off a two-inch portion of the older bush — a small branch with a sprout on it. Then I plant it in a little half-pint milk carton filled with dirt."

When the tiny plants are established and the sprouts are green and growing, he slits the carton and sets the baby bushes out in his garden with a glass jar over them to serve as a miniature greenhouse for the winter.

Besides cultivating his roses, Meng keeps up an extensive garden at the rear of his home, supplying friends and neighbors with fresh produce until

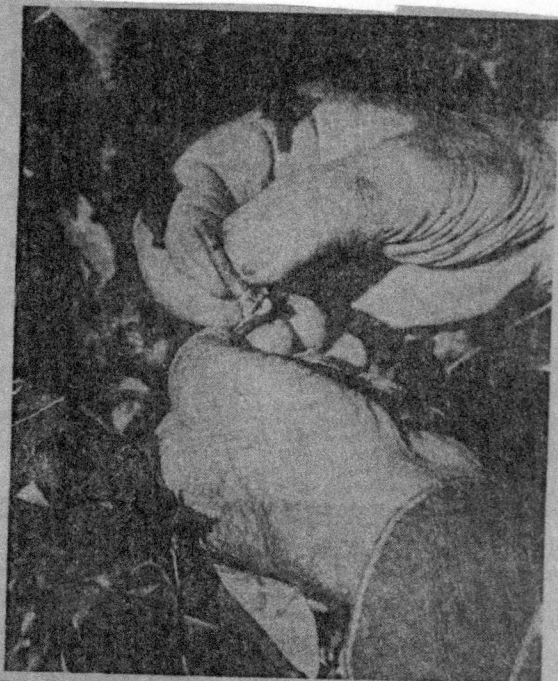

THE SURE HANDS OF A SKILLED GARDENER—break off a tiny rose branch with a new sprout, as Walter Meng prepares to root new plants for his rose garden next spring.

the first frost.

Is he planning to sit by the fire and relax for the next few months, now that this year's gardening season is over?

Not Walter Meng. "I'll move indoors now and work in my basement workshop until spring," he said.

"And recently I received my first 1983 garden catalog in the mail," he said, with dreams of next year's garden twinkling in his eyes.

The Busiest Retiree We Know!

Walter Meng [above and at right, in his rose garden]

What does a tea rose and a turret have in common? In some instances, both have been nurtured and produced by an innovative gentleman. His name? Walter Meng.

Walter Meng, a machinist at Laclede Steel for 15 years, gives the same creative effort to caring for his gardens, full of roses and every vegetable imaginable, that he gave to producing "just the right" design for the war effort or the many machines he improved and modified during his working career.

Meng, 83, was born in Freeburg, Illinois and was raised in New Athens. "I knew what hard work meant by the time I was twelve," he said, "then my dad died, so I had to quit school in the sixth grade and work to help support my family. I did a little bit of everything. We raised our own food and depended on the Kaskaskia River for an oc-casional fish dinner."

In 1919, Meng went to work for Western Cartridge, and soon set production records for heading .22 shells. He went on to Granite City Steel, working while he attended Renken Trade School at night. The son of a machinist, he went to school with a natural aptitude for the basic skills, and soon developed the innovative and questioning energies that led him to change, experiment and improve in his 40 years as a machinist.

Meng and his work have had far-reaching impact. While at Sterling Aluminum, during World War II, he made the holders (racks) that carried atomic bombs. At Emerson Electric, Meng designed and built the tail gunners' turrets for bomber planes that "saved 100 lives a day on the battlefield", he was told.

"The strangest job of my entire life was quilting", Meng claimed. "I was assigned to a special project at Emerson and it was sure a challenge. After designing the thing, we decided it had to be quilted. So, I just got out the needle and thread and did it".

"I like to experiment", commented Meng recently. "I like to do things that haven't been done before". This attitude is undoubtedly what led him to develop one of the finest gardens in the area.

BUSIEST RETIREE [Cont.]

When Meng and his wife Helen moved to their present home, many years ago, the back of the lot was choked with sky-high weeds and all kinds of refuse washed down through their yard from a storm sewer opening. "Made rich, fertile ground," Meng said, "and I've grown great vegetable crops here in this same spot for years and years." He designed a concrete walkway over the storm sewer, and has good access to all of his crops.

The rose garden contains some 50 bushes, of many colors and varieties. The blooms are huge and their fragrance fills the air. Meng is proud of the fact that this past winter he lost only two plants to the bad weather. "I'll tell you my secret," Meng said. "I cover my plants with leaf mulch, and, contrary to what the experts tell you, I leave it on year after year." This practice, he believes, provides all the protection and fertilizer needed.

More active than men half his age, Meng and his wife lead a busy, happy retired life. He is a student of the stock market, and never misses a Wall Street Journal. He builds a variety of things in his well-equipped basement workshop during the winter, including lamps with bases made of five different woods.

The Mengs have been married forty-five years, and have two children and grandchildren. They have good things to say about the credit union movement in general and Laclede Credit Union in particular.

"I started out working for just a few cents an hour", says Meng. "I had to learn to spend my money wisely and save whatever I could. Laclede Credit Union is a great place to save, and borrow, and to learn about family finances."

Upper Alton News

GETS 21½ POUNDS OF POTATOES OFF PLANT

Walter Meng of 1719 Worden Ave. has what he calls a surprising harvest this year with one plant yielding 21½ pounds of sweet potatoes.

The Laclede Steel Co. employe uprooted the more than a dozen potatoes Thursday. Some of them were eight inches long.

Mrs. Meng says that one would be plenty for a meal for four people. Which gives the Meng family 12 meals off of one potato plant.

The entire crop is a good one, she says. The back yard will yield enough to keep the Meng family and friends in stock.

Mrs. Meng says her husband grows other truck crops, most of which he gives away.

His green thumb considerably out-produces the food consuming potential of the Meng family.

Mrs. Meng said that to get 15 pounds of potatoes off of one plant is way above average. Their 21½ pounds is in the world beater class.

In Loving Memory of

Walter G. Meng

Date of Birth: December 13, 1898
Date of Death: June 22, 1986

In Loving Memory of

Helen C. Meng

Date of Birth: October 4, 1901
Date of Death: February 23, 1990

Walter and Helen Meng were very proud of their children, Mary and Bill

CHAPTER 13
EDWARD J. AND JESSIE F. (SHAMHART) MENG

Edward John Meng (1901–1983)
Who were Edward J. and Jessie F. Meng?
James L. Meng (youngest son)

Who were Ed and Jessie Meng? The answer is simple; they were my parents, my heroes. Let me explain. My mother's parents moved from Newton, Illinois, to Granite City, where her father, Wilmer Shamhart, became a business agent for the Carpenters Union representing Granite City, Madison, and Venice. Dad's mom, sister, and brothers moved to Granite City from Freeburg, Illinois. Dad said his mom's only advice was, "I don't care what you do, Son, as long as you're not a social miner like your dad." Fortunately, Granite City had a lot of industry: Granite City Steel, Laclede Steel, Nesco, General Steel Industries (Commonwealth plant), etc. While attending the Commonwealth school at nights, Dad operated an overhead crane in the plant during the day. He was subsequently fired from this position after throwing a pie at one of his friends on the floor, while passing overhead in the crane. Cured of pie throwing, he then moved on to the post office where he started a 40-year career, initially as a letter carrier.

Mom was working for the Federal Reserve Bank in St. Louis when she met Dad. Jessie was very attractive. While at the bank, she entered a beauty contest and won first place. Her prize was a sterling silver marcasite watch which I eventually inherited.

Shortly before Mom and Dad got married, they bought a 1½-story stucco-covered home at 2612 Madison Avenue in Granite City. The home was the only one on the block at that time. Surrounded by open fields, the next house going east on Madison Avenue was grandmother Meng's in the next block at 2707. After more homes were built, the address on our home was then changed from 2612 to 2624. The stucco was eventually replaced with cedar shingles, which were unfortunately painted with oil base paint. Dad admitted the painting of the shingles was a mistake since the house had to be repainted every five years. Ed and Jessie Meng lived in this home until their death, 55 years later.

Dad finished his education; after the Commonwealth school, he then went on to Washington University in St. Louis at nights studying accounting. He attended through his junior year, but with the birth of my brother, marriage and the expenses associated with a new home, he could not afford to finish. It was at this same time that Dad had to also give up his clarinet lessons. He was a serious musician, playing both clarinet and saxophone. He had played with John Tates' band, which was featured in local dance halls, outdoor concerts, and parades. Another reason why he quit was because his fingers had gotten too big and he could not operate the keys on his instruments. I still have his instruments and much of his music. After Dad passed away, I inherited his 32 degree Masonic ring. When I took it to the jewelers to have it made smaller, the jeweler put the ring on a graduated piece of steel to determine its size. His ring slid completely off the measuring device! They had not seen a ring that size. As a 32 degree Mason myself, I now wear his Masonic ring.

The environment at home was positive and very cheerful. Neither Mom nor Dad used any four letter words, although Dad would occasionally use the word "dammit" and would tell some off-colored jokes with male companions. Ed and Jessie also did not argue with one another. Disagree, yes, but argue, no. As Dad gave the outward appearance of being stubborn and determined in his ways, he was actually a marshmallow on the inside. My mom knew it and handled him in such a way that she almost always got her way. Dad also knew if Jessie wanted to do something, it was automatically okay with him. They were a team. The radio was always on at home playing music. Since I was born in 1939, the big band music of the 1940s played while I scooted around on the floor learning to talk by singing "Don't Fence Me In" and other such songs. *Queen for a Day*, Arthur Godfrey, or some soaps were played during the day. At night, Dad listened to Gabriel Heater and Walter Winchell for the news and ". . . all the ships at sea." Dad constantly read the newspaper. He was very well informed on all local and international events. Frequently, he would read me the "funnies." His breath smelled of coffee and he would take great delight in rubbing the stubble of his beard on my face. Later, my mom would put me to bed and say my prayers while my dad would come in later and tell me to stretch to see how big I had grown.

The neighborhood along Madison Avenue was also alive with activity when I was growing up. None of the moms worked and therefore people were out in their yards working in their gardens, hanging wash or talking to each other over the fence. The Watkins' man would come to our front door to sell cough syrup, etc.; the iceman would stop at our neighbors to deliver ice (all the kids would get slivers of ice to eat); the rag man would push his cart down the alley collecting old rags; the "huckster" would stop in front of the house selling fresh produce to all the neighbors, and a strange-looking truck would drive down the street ringing a bell indicating that he was available to sharpen knives and scissors. In addition, to all of these folks, was the milkman, the mailman, and the gas, water, and electric company meter readers. There was a lot of going on, and Mom was actively involved as we played Cowboys and Indians throughout the neighborhood. At night, it was time to catch fireflies.

Jessie and her parents, Wilmer and Olive Shamhart, were, like my dad and his parents, of German ancestry. They all belonged to the Central Christian Church. However, Dad was raised Catholic and attended Catholic schools in New Athens and Freeburg when he grew up. His father died when he was a young boy. According to Dad, he was raised Catholic because the Catholic Church started at a different time than the Lutheran Church. Therefore, in order to have someone around the house and to work on the farm, his mom sent some of the kids off to the Catholic Church and others off to the Lutheran Church. According to Uncle Fred, the oldest children in the family were raised Protestant because at the time, their father, Fred Sr., was still alive. After he died, the younger children were raised Catholic.

Dad and all his brothers worked for Ben Koesterer, who was a very successful farmer. I remember his telling that they would put a cabbage leaf under their hat to keep them cool while working in the fields. I also remember him saying that his job as a child was to close the outside window shutters on the house at sundown during the winter. While in grade school, Ed got into a big argument with a nun over the infallibility of the pope. The nun stated the pope was infallible. But Dad took the position that he was like any other human who makes mistakes. He told me the nun beat him with a ruler. But it was to no avail. The one thing you never, and I mean never ever, want to do is try to force Ed Meng to change his opinion when he doesn't want to (Mom excluded). The nun finally broke her ruler and gave up. He never did change his position on the pope. Another significant event occurred when my parents got married. A Catholic priest wanted Mom and Dad to sign some kind of document indicating that their future children would be brought up Catholic—big mistake for the priest, as he too tried to force Dad into a decision that he was not ready to make. Dad broke away from the Catholic religion at that point and both my brother and I were raised Protestant, in the Central Christian Church, the church that Wilmer and Oliver Shamhart attended and Mom and Dad joined. I was baptized in the same church in 1956.

As Mom kept house, Dad worked long hours at the post office. At Christmas time, he would come home very late because they had to have all the mail processed by the end of the day. He could not get excited about Christmas like the rest of us did. Besides putting in long hours at the post office, there were several deaths in his family during the Christmas season while he was growing up. Consequently, he never seemed to get into the spirit of the season.

Mom was born with a serious birth defect, a hole (later found to be the size of a half dollar) in her heart. Because of this condition, she would have to take afternoon naps. And it is perhaps because of this condition that she always carried a buckeye in her purse for good luck. A maid also had to be hired to do the heavy house cleaning. As a child, I knew things were not right and was kept uninformed. Although at my young age, I'm not sure if I would have understood any more had I been told. Our home had a one car garage which my grandfather and dad then converted into a bedroom with a half bath. This was done just in case my mom couldn't go up the stairs to their bedroom. Although finished, the downstairs bedroom was never used.

On February 18, 1973, at the age of 76, an attempt was made to close the hole in Mom's heart. At that point in time, she was the oldest patient in Barnes Hospital in St. Louis history to have this type of operation. The operation was a failure; the hole was too large. Mom died exactly five years later from the date of the surgery on February 18, 1978.

In 1950, Mom became our Cub Scout den mother, Troop 6. All my friends joined our troop which met in our living room once a week. This was a big deal. Mom was very artistic and came up with a lot of craft ideas. She made me the den chief, my first and only political appointment.

Her artistic talents also were exhibited with numerous oil paintings. She attended night school at Granite City High School with her friends developing this hobby. In 1964, she took second place in oils in a contest sponsored by the Granite City Artist Guild. There were a total of 77 entries in this contest in the various categories. Her winning painting was that of the bridge at Bennett Springs State Park in Lebanon,

Missouri. This painting was the result of a one week vacation that Mom, Dad, and I took when I came home from the Air Force Technical School in 1964. We currently have many of her pictures in our home, including the Bennett Springs bridge painting.

Another one of Mom's favorite hobbies was shopping. She would drag me to downtown St. Louis to Stix, Baer and Fuller (now Dillards) and Famous-Barr (now Macy's) and Scruggs department stores and occasionally to Knickerbockers to shop. One sale day, she would be in front of the department store before it opened, with me pressed up against the glass door. My instructions were to hang on to her hand because once the door opened, all these women would start pushing and running inside to a specific location. This event was frequent and I knew the routine well. Of course, a small bribe to eat lunch at the Forum Cafeteria after shopping, to eat Chinese chow mein certainly helped my willingness to participate.

Throughout childhood and into adult life, my parents allowed me to have a variety of pets, all of which stayed inside the house. One reason for these pets was to teach responsibility. Another reason was that they enjoyed pets, perhaps because of their farm background. Yet another reason was because Mom was soft-hearted and would take in strays.

As mentioned earlier, both Mom and Dad grew up on a farm. Consequently, they continued to be interested in keeping their hands in the soil. Dad often quoted Ben Koesterer, his mom's brother, who said, "If the ground can pay for itself in five years, it's a good buy." Following this advice, my parents bought a 30-acre, a 40-acre and an 80-acre farm in Newton, Jasper County, Illinois, where Mom had been raised. Soybeans were grown on a one-third for us and two-third for the farmer basis. These farms were soon clear of any indebtedness and sold one at a time. The 80-acre farm was the last to sell in 1958. All three farms had no buildings, only open fields of beans. As a child, we would monitor the farms and visit the relatives by driving to Newton in my grandfather's (Wilmer M. Shamhart) 1939 four-door black Oldsmobile. I remember his cigars and how "green" I would be upon arrival in Newton. After grandfather died, we bought his car and would continue our visits to watch the combine harvest the crop. It was interesting to listen to all the projections as to what seed would produce the best crop, how big the yield would be, and how close the nearest oil well was to our property. (There were several oil wells around Newton, but none were ever drilled on our property.)

Some of the money from the sale of the farms was used to purchase a 26.39-acre farm in Edwardsville, Madison County, Illinois, and a new "pink" Chrysler Imperial. Edwardsville was only a 20-minute drive from Granite City as opposed to a four-hour drive (no interstates) to Newton, Illinois. The Edwardsville farm seemed to go through a variety of stages. At first, it was pure recreation, which meant there was a lot of grass to cut.

Then one year, it was decided to grow tomatoes for profit. Big, big mistake! Mom and Dad along with captive child labor, me, (my brother was six years older and off doing other things) planted, cultivated, sprayed, hoed, picked, picked, and picked six acres of tomatoes. The first year of this project was with Milton and Cybil Fisher; their children, Richard and Max were also involved. Unfortunately, Milton died of cancer during the second year of this project, so our production staff was reduced. The third and final year, only our family and four acres was involved: same number of tomatoes, but only three pickers. By the time we would get finished with one end of the field, the tomatoes needed something at the other end—be it picking or hoeing. And we would start all over again. My pay was a soda at the end of the day, which was actually a treat since we never had soda around the house.

My parents sold these tomatoes by the big truck load to the Brooks ketchup people in Collinsville, Illinois, and to A&P, Kroger, and Tri-City grocery companies in Granite City by the bushels. We also took tomatoes to Farmers Market in St. Louis, where we sold them out of the back of our 1946 "woody" Ford station wagon.

I never thought a frost could be so beautiful: six acres of dead plants, no picking, no hoeing, nothing. It was a pretty sight; my revenge and Mom and Dad's relief. As Yogi Berra would say, "It's déjà vu all over again." The thought that four acres would somehow make the job easier was wrong. Finally, another beautiful frost arrived and that was the end of the tomato project. I was never told if they made any money off the tomatoes. I suspect it was a little better than cost proposition. Mom and her captive labor, me, would then pick blackberries all day in the hot sun, along with ticks, chiggers, and an occasional black snake. Although this was not that pleasant, it sure beat tomatoes. Besides, blackberry cobblers taste a lot better than stewed tomatoes.

It was then decided that there was money in pine trees. Dad bought about 4,500 little 10" pine seedlings from the state. These sticks had to have their roots covered with a mud solution and stuck in the ground. Uncle Fred made a special spade that had a 4" blade that we used and all were soon planted. We now had a registered tree farm. I really didn't mind this project, since wherever a pine was planted, no one could plant one of those damn tomato plants. The pines were never harvested although we did end up with free Christmas trees for several years.

Dad then decided to return to farming crops. By this time, he was a supervisor in the post office five days a week and a farmer on weekends and occasionally in the evenings. To accomplish this task, he bought Ben Koesterer's Oliver 70 Row Crop tractor along with all the implements. The only problem was that after we planted all the pines, there were only about six acres left that were tillable. And with the size of Uncle Ben's equipment, after working two hours tops, Dad was finished doing whatever he was supposed to do in the fields. The rest of the time was then spent developing a family garden. Mom would then can the garden's products. I can still see her in the kitchen sterilizing bottles, cooking tomatoes, corn, peaches, blackberries, pickles, apples, etc., with all the steam and large pots and also heating paraffin to seal the tomato preserves and listening to the lids of the canned vegetables pop as they completed their sealing process. The tomato preserves were excellent; some had lemon rind in them while others had a touch of anise. Either way, the preserves were unique and outstanding.

One of my fondest memories of the Edwardsville farm was the numerous picnics we would have. Almost every weekend, my aunts and uncles and their families would meet at the farm. Uncle Fred was in charge of barbecuing the ribs. He was excellent! The best ribs in the world came from the hands of Fred M. Meng. After the meal was over and everyone was as full as a tick, the men would sit around the fire while the women played canasta and gossiped. As a kid, sitting listening to adults talk about everything from buried treasure to lost ships, to their lives growing up, or to whether or not there are people on the moon, was a real treat. The stories and topics had no boundaries. What made these sessions so great was the experience and intelligence of the people involved. All of my uncles were successful, but in different areas. Parry Schippers (not an uncle), who was a dentist married to Lillian Vogt, liked to talk about the supernatural and outer space. As a kid with the fire flickering and all these serious stories being told, it was better than any book or movie. These sessions would occasionally last until 1 or 2 a.m. Then, a week or two later, we would all meet again with more ribs and more stories.

I suspect that the real purpose behind the Edwardsville farm and all of its projects was that it was therapeutic for Dad. He worked behind a desk balancing figures all day. He was under constant pressure with his job and other community involvement. He had a nerve condition in which he would later become very ill and have to lie down for several hours. These events or attacks occurred more frequently when he became older, resulting in the use of all his sick leave just prior to his retirement in the post office with 40 years of service. The various farming projects presented an escape from his daily pressures and the hard physical work probably extended his life. In retrospect, the tomato and pine projects really were not that bad, and I would do it again for this purpose. The road leading to this farm was named Mengstrasse in 1992 in memory of Ed and Jessie and all the relatives who attended these gatherings. We now wonder what these people would say today about the road's name if they were here, sitting around one of those campfires. I suspect they would say, "Damn good job, James!"

Mom began working in the information booth in the mid-1950s at Stix, Baer and Fuller at their St. Louis downtown store. She would cut out their newspaper advertisements every day to take to work so she could answer the customer questions as to what was on sale. She did this for 20 years. Although she didn't make much, she spent her money on bargains for the family, using her 15%–20% employee discount to buy all of our clothes. As the farm was my dad's escape, Stix became my mother's escape. She made many friends with her associates who would alert her as to when things would go on sale. One of her more noticeable habits was to buy items that were on sale even though we didn't need it—for example, a large pipe rack when no one smoked a pipe. I currently have six place settings of sterling silver, none of which match but the price was right, so she bought them. We even used non-matching sterling for our everyday utensils. I remember this because Mom would get upset if I left mustard on a knife, which would tarnish its surface. Again, she would buy this stuff only because the price was right, like $2-$5.

Originally, she would take the streetcar (Illinois Traction, Alton car) that passed in front of our house to work. When they stopped services, she took the bus.

Dad would pick her up at night at the employee entrance. This routine was so common that the corner policeman directing traffic knew Dad on a first name basis, allowing him to illegally park while waiting for Mom.

As Mom was painting with her oils and shopping at Stix, Dad, with no tomatoes to pick, became very active in the community. He was president of the Postal Clerks Union, president of the Postal Supervisors, State of Illinois vice president of Postal Supervisors, president of the school board, and president of the Parents Club (an organization made up of parents who had children in the Granite City school district).

Dad was also a member of Lodge 877 AF & AM Scottish Rite Bodies (32°), Tri-City Shrine Club and a member of Ainad Temple, AAONMS of East St. Louis, Illinois. An interesting sidelight to Dad's Masonic activity was that he was, as mentioned earlier, raised in the Catholic faith and I signed his blue lodge petition. Normally, the father recommends his son to become a member. In this case, the son recommended the father to become a member.

In addition, Dad was on the Salvation Army board and a member of both the Boy and Girl Scout Councils. The Boy Scouts gave their highest award, the Silver Beaver Award, to Dad for his volunteer efforts. He was also a 17-year member of the Civil Service Board.

However, of all the activities he was involved in, his most single long-term commitment, other than his wife and family, was to Rotary International. He was the Granite City Rotary Club president while Mom was the president of the Rotary Anns. Dad ran for Rotary district governor position for the state of Illinois but lost by only a few votes. He also accumulated 36 years of perfect attendance in Rotary, 36 years! When considering Rotary met once a week, that translates into 1,872 consecutive meetings. Sprinkled in the 1,872 meetings were six foreign countries where he attended Rotary. He also received the Paul Harris award from Rotary International, the highest award given. Incidentally, his brother Wilmer W. Meng who was also active in the Rotary Club in Fullerton, California, also received the Paul Harris Award but was never club president.

After Dad's death on April 1, 1983, the city council of Granite City passed a resolution declaring January 18 as Edward J. Meng Day, in honor of his past civic contributions to the community. The council's vote on the resolution was unanimous.

Granite City with all its industry was a strong union and Democratic town. He was the president of two postal unions before going on to management. Dad voted 100% Democratic throughout his life. He took this position because he rose from letter carrier to assistant postmaster. He was to be the next postmaster. Then, Dwight Eisenhower, a Republican, was elected president. At that time, the postmaster was a patronized position and another person, a Republican who had never been in a post office except to buy stamps in the lobby, was appointed over Dad. This was a major disappointment, one which he viewed as a personal failure. But nothing could be done even with the help of a personal friend's, Democratic Congressmen Mel Price and Paul Simon. A postmaster today is no longer a patronized position.

What is interesting in Dad's political situation was that he didn't believe in any of the liberal positions the Democrats took. He was a conservative in every way, believing people make their own choices and must take full responsibility for the results of their choices. No handouts, no special privileges, and most of all, no excuses. Even when Beverly and I got married and bought our first home in Granite City, Mom and Dad loaned us $3,000.00 for the down payment. However, true to form, we were also charged 8% interest and put on monthly payments. There were no free rides for me. He passed this philosophy on to me not in statements like "Jim, sit down. I want to tell you what I think and how to vote," but by example. He recognized that I had my own life to live and relied on my ability and his example to make the right decisions. His philosophy and example worked. Everything I do today and try to instill in my children are the product of what my father and mother taught me, only not always with success. Mom, on the other hand, voted split tickets. She didn't care what political party the candidate belonged to as long as he or she was a conservative.

After retirement, they traveled considerably. They enjoyed the West, spending much time in Arizona where Mom would find scenery to paint. They drove to these destinations in a blue Volkswagen Beetle. One time, they got caught in a sandstorm which removed all of the car's paint while etching the headlights and windshield. They also traveled to Puerto Rico and the Grecian Isles, then on to Germany, Austria, and Switzerland.

They both constantly supported my endeavors even when they didn't fully understand what or why I was doing something. (On many occasions, I didn't know why I did things either.) When I started playing football in high school over my mom's objections, they would go to the games just to listen to what my fellow students would say about me. Dad never participated in athletics like his brothers; he was too serious. So even though Mom and Dad were at my games, they didn't really understand what was happening. All Mom knew was that I was putting on a lot of weight, up to 190, and none of my clothes would fit. The coach told Dad I should eat a lot of protein––enter six eggs a day and steak, but only when it was payday. That wasn't too bad, but a three egg glass of eggnog every morning was a bit much.

Another example of unquestioned support was when I bought a new Corvette, 1968, 327, 350 HP, 4 speed, blue convertible with a white top. I told Dad that I bought a Corvette. His response was, "isn't that the car with an engine in the rear?" I replied, "No, that's a Corvair. They're different." Nothing more was said, but mom smiled and gave a big wink.

After graduation from college in 1962, I joined the Missouri Air National Guard. There was nothing going on in the world at this period of time, but the Cuban missile crisis did develop when I was in basic training. When I told my parents what I did, all that was said was great––who is the Air National Guard? What do they do? (Dad was too young for the World War I and too old for World War II.)

It seemed that whatever decision I would make, I knew in advance that Mom and Dad would agree that it was the proper decision and would stand behind me. I knew there was support. In return, I wanted to do anything I could make them proud of me, be it athletics, graduating from college, getting a master's degree, and marrying a very lovely wife. One special event occurred while I was in the Air Guard at summer camp. A plane (T-33) caught fire and I put it out. For this, I was given an award. More importantly, the Guard unit had a parade for me (and two others) with my parents present. It was on the local TV and radio stations, in a national military magazine, and published in the newspapers. It was payback time to the parents who nourished me with food and thought, taught me the difference from right and wrong, and supported me on into adulthood.

Mom and Dad then became grandparents to Heather and Erik Meng, our kids.

Mom would say how beautiful Heather was and how big and handsome Erik was going to be. They were as proud of these two as they could be, passing up no opportunity to inform others.

Unfortunately, both were gone when Heather graduated from Baylor University and Erik grew to a strong, good-looking 6' 2" man.

So, all of this and much, much more is who Edward J. and Jessie F. Meng were. They were neither perfect nor saints. But they were my parents and certainly my heroes.

CERTIFIED COPY OF BIRTH REPORT

STATE OF ILLINOIS,)
) ss.
County of St. Clair.)

N⁰ 17732

STATE BOARD OF HEALTH

1. Full Name of Child _____ Edward J. Meng _____ 2. Sex _____ Male _____

3. No. of Child to this Mother _____ 6th _____ 4. Color _____ White _____

5. Date of Birth December 4, 1901 _____ 6. Place _____ Freeburg, Illinois _____

7. Father's Nationality _____ German _____ 8. Father's Place of Birth _____ Freeburg, Ill. _____

9. Age _____ 38 _____ Years. 10. Mother's Nationality _____ German _____

11. Mother's Place of Birth _____ Freeburg, Ill. _____ 12. Age _____ 32 _____ Years.

13. Mother's Name _____ Lizzie Meng _____ 14. Mother's Maiden Name _____ Lizzie _____ Koesterer _____ 15. Mother's Residence _____ Freeburg, Ill. _____

16. Name of Father _____ Frederick Meng _____ 17. Father's Occupation _____ Minor _____ 18. Name of Medical or other Attendant and Address:

Name _____ T. Winterbauer _____ Address _____ Freeburg, Illinois

Dated: Jan. 9, 1902 _____

STATE OF ILLINOIS,)
) ss.
County of St. Clair.)

I, _____ Elmer Touchette _____, County Clerk in and for the County and State aforesaid, and keeper of the files and records of said office, do hereby certify the above and foregoing to be a full and complete copy of a report of the birth of _____ Edward J. Meng _____ as the same appears from the files and records in my office remaining.

IN WITNESS WHEREOF, I have hereunto set my hand and affixed the seal of my office at Belleville, this _____ 9th _____ day of _____ June _____ A. D., 19 60

_____ Elmer Touchette _____
County Clerk.

By _____ Deputy

St. Agatha's Church

Rev. M. Walterbosch

New Athens, Ill., *April 26th* **191/7**

To whom it may Concern, this is to certify. that Edward John Meng, son of Fred Meng and Elisabeth nee Koesterer was born on the 4th day of December 1901, and was baptized in our Church by me on the 19th day of Dec 1912 In testimony thereof I sign my name and press the seal on it of St Agatha Church New Athens Ill.

M. Walterbosch.

Award of Honor

This Certifies That

Eddie Meng

of New Athens Public School, District No. 62, St. Clair County, Illinois, having received four monthly Certificates of Perfect Attendance for being

Neither Absent Nor Tardy

is commended for good attendance and punctuality, and is therefore awarded this Testimonial.

Given at Belleville, Illinois, this 31st day of March 1941.

Irma E. Batdorf
TEACHER

H. A. Hough
COUNTY SUPERINTENDENT

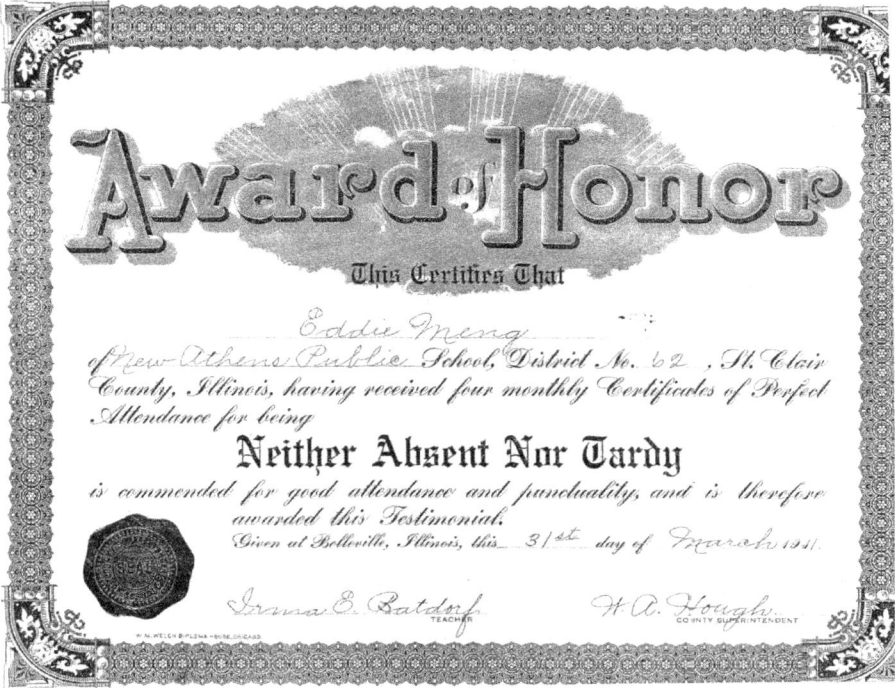

TRANSCRIPTION

OF

RECORD

of

COMMUNITY

HIGH SCHOOL

GRANITE CITY, ILL.

From.

Wilmer at 12 years, Edward at 14 years, and Oscar at 10 years.

CHS Form 114 8-29-1M

Granite City, Ill., Date 3/21/33

Name Meng Edward

Entered this school Sept '29

Left this school

or

Graduated from this school Jan 13, 1933

WITH THE FOLLOWING CREDIT COMPLETED

FIRST YEAR

SUBJECTS	YR OF SUB IN COURSE	WKS.	REC. PER WEEK	GRADE	UNITS
Eng	1 + 2			85.5	1.0
Alg	1 + 2			72.5	1.0
Gen Sci				95.0	.5
Physical				93.0	.5
Shop				Cr	1.0

EXPLANATION

THIRD YEAR

| French | 1 | 20 | 5 | B | ½ |

The example shows the French taken to have been that regularly given in first year, that this pupil took it in third and shows allowance of ½ unit is withheld till subject is completed.

½ under recitation per week, signifies 3 recitations, 4 laboratory (2 double) periods; 5 signifies exercises including laboratory.

One unit is credit for five periods per week for one year of 40 weeks unless otherwise stated. Two periods of shop work are, in this report, the equivalent of one period of recitation. Length of period excluding passing...........minutes.

GRADES A—Excellent Grade

B—High Grade

C—College Recommendation

D—Passing E—Poor F—Failure

Work accepted from other schools entered in red.

SECOND YEAR

SUBJECTS	YR OF SUB IN COURSE	WKS.	REC. PER WEEK	GRADE	UNITS
Eng	3 + 4			89.0	1.0
Geom	1 + 2			72.5	1.0
Physics	1 + 2			93.0	1.0
Shop				Cr	1.0

THIRD YEAR

SUBJECTS	YR OF SUB IN COURSE	WKS.	REC. PER WEEK	GRADE	UNITS
Eng	5 + 6			94.0	1.0
Gem	3			90.0	.5
U.S. Hist	1 + 2			82.5	1.0
Ind Hist				93.0	.5
Civics				90.0	.5
Economics				92.0	.5

FOURTH YEAR

SUBJECTS	YR OF SUB IN COURSE	WKS.	REC. PER WEEK	GRADE	UNITS
Eng	7 + 8			93.5	1.0
Alg	3			92.0	.5
Trig				72.0	.5
Ercl Hist	1 + 2			83.0	1.0
Coml Law				92.0	.5
Coml Geog				97.0	.5

Most of this work was completed at the Commonwealth Steel Company's division of the Granite City Community High School

SPECIAL REPORT

Attendance

Passing Grade 75%

Record in Athletics, etc.

Literary

Class or other

Activities

Remarks

SCHOOL IS ACCREDITED AT

North Central Assn.

University of Illinois

Signed Bert Alderman Secretary to Principal

262

This Certifies That

Edward J. Meng

Having completed the requirements for graduation from the Granite City Community High School as prescribed by the Faculty and approved by the Board of Education is entitled to this

Diploma

Given at Granite City, Illinois, this 13th day of January, 1933.

For the Board of Education and Faculty

President

Secretary

Superintendent

Principal

Washington University

University College

Graduate

This is to certify that

Edward John Meng

as a student in the University College has creditably completed the three year course for the

Certificate in

Accounting

Signed this sixth day of June, 1939

Chancellor

Dean, University College

EDWARD J. MENG

Edward J. Meng, clerk in the Granite City post office, who received his certificate in accounting at Washington University College last Tuesday, June 6. He is a graduate of the Commonwealth school here and continued his education at night in St. Louis.

Edward J. Meng, clerk in the Granite City post office, who received his certificate in accounting at Washington University College last Tuesday, June 6. He is a graduate of the Commonwealth school here and continued his education at night in St. Louis.

Doctors Birth Record of Jessie F. Shamhart.

Part of page torn from Dr. Reason Henry Shamhart's, (Jessie Frances Shamhart's uncle) birth delivery book indicating Olive Shamhart giving birth to Jessie on July 2, 1908.

Report card — NEWTON PUBLIC SCHOOLS

REPORT OF _____
Room ____ Class __

1917 -1918	First Quarter	Second Quarter	Third Quarter	Fourth Quarter	Average
Reading		B.	B	a²	92
Writing		C.	C	a	88
Spelling		a+	A	C.	76
Arithmetic		C.	B	A	88
Language		a+	a	B	85
Geography		a+	A	a	91
History		a+	a	a+	99
Numbers					
Drawing					80
Physiology		a.			87
Music					
Civics			a+		
Deportment		a+	a	B	
Days Present		41	39	40	
Days Absent		1	6	2	
Times Tardy		1	2	2	

_____ Teacher.

Sybil and Jessie Shamhart in Newton, IL.

*The class of May 4, 1911, Newton, IL. Jessie F. Shamhart
is the fifth student from the left in the front row.*

JESSIE FRANCES SHAMHART

FEDERAL RESERVE BANK

OF

ST. LOUIS

March 6, 1933.

PRESIDENT'S PROCLAMATION

To All Banks in District No. 8:

Whereas there have been heavy and unwarranted withdrawals of gold and currency from our banking institutions for the purpose of hoarding; and,

Whereas continuous and increasingly extensive speculative activity abroad in foreign exchange has resulted in severe drains on the nation's stocks of gold; and,

Whereas these conditions have created a national emergency; and,

Whereas it is in the best interests of all bank depositors that a period of respite be provided with a view to preventing further hoarding of coin, bullion or currency or speculation in foreign exchange and permitting the application of appropriate measures to protect the interests of our people; and,

Whereas it is provided in section 5 (b) of the act of October 6, 1917 (40 stat. 1. 411) as amended, "that the President may investigate, regulate, or prohibit, under such rules and regulations as he may prescribe, by means of license or otherwise, any transactions in foreign exchange and the export, hoarding, melting or earmarking of gold or silver coin or bullion or currency, * * *" and,

Whereas it is provided in section 16 of the said act "that whoever shall willfully violate any of the provisions of this act or of any license, rule, or regulation issued thereunder, and whoever shall willfully violate, neglect, or refuse to comply with any order of the President issued in compliance with the provisions of this act, shall, upon conviction, be fined not more than $10,000, or, if a natural person, imprisoned for not more than ten years, or both, * * *".

Now, therefore, I, Franklin D. Roosevelt, President of the United States of America, in view of such national emergency and by virtue of the authority vested in me by said act and in order to prevent the export, hoarding, or earmarking of gold or silver coin or bullion or currency, do hereby proclaim, order, direct and declare that from Monday, the sixth day of March, to Thursday, the ninth day of March, nineteen hundred and thirty-three, both dates inclusive, there shall be maintained and observed by all banking institutions and all branches thereof located in the United States of America, including the territories and insular possessions, a bank holiday, and that during said period all banking transactions shall be suspended. During such holiday, excepting as hereinafter provided, no such banking institution or branch shall pay out, export, earmark or permit the withdrawal or transfer in any manner or by any device whatsoever, of any gold or silver coin or bullion or currency or take any other action which might facilitate the hoarding thereof; nor shall any such banking institution or branch pay out deposits, make loans or discounts, deal in foreign exchange, transfer credits from the United States to any place abroad, or transact any other banking business whatsoever.

During such holiday, the Secretary of the Treasury, with the approval of the President and under such regulations as he may prescribe, is authorized and empowered (A) to permit any or all of such banking institutions to perform any or all of the usual banking functions, (B) to direct, require or permit the issuance of clearing house certificates or other evidences of claims against assets of banking institutions, and (C) to authorize and direct the creation in such banking institutions of special trust accounts for the receipt of new deposits which shall be subject to withdrawal on demand without any restriction or limitation and shall be kept separately in cash or on deposit in Federal reserve banks or invested in obligations of the United States.

As used in this order the term "banking institutions" shall include all Federal reserve banks, national banking associations, banks, trust companies, savings banks, building and loan associations, credit unions, or other corporations, partnerships, associations or persons engaged in the business of receiving deposits, making loans, discounting business paper, or transacting any other form of banking business.

In witness whereof, I have hereunto set my hand and caused the seal of the United States to be affixed.

Done in the City of Washington the sixth day of March, 1 A. M. in the year of our Lord one thousand nine hundred and thirty-three.

(Seal)   FRANKLIN D. ROOSEVELT.

By the President:
    Cordell Hull,
        Secretary of State.

Jessie F. Shamhart was employed by the Federal Reserve Bank in St. Louis, MO, when she met and married Ed Meng. This proclamation was a sign of the difficult times.

Edward and Jessie Meng's wedding picture.

269

Ed and Jessie Meng's home
(2624 Madison Ave., Granite City, IL).

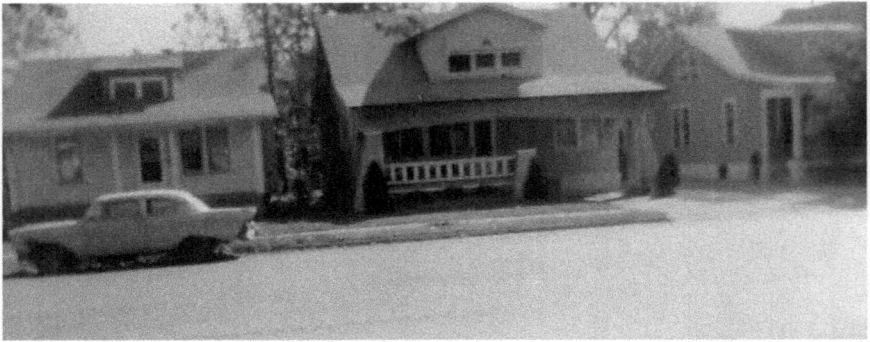

EDWARD AND JESSIE MENG'S MARRIAGE

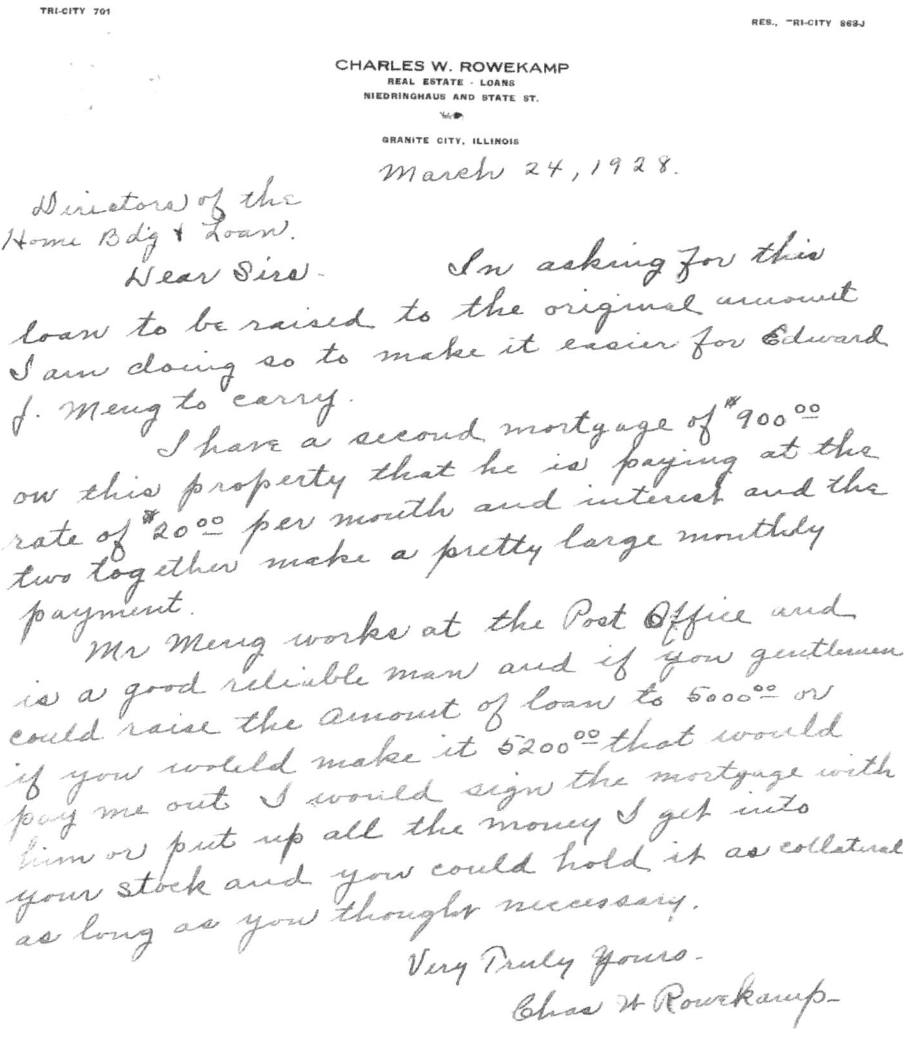

TRI-CITY 701

RES., TRI-CITY 863-J

CHARLES W. ROWEKAMP
REAL ESTATE - LOANS
NIEDRINGHAUS AND STATE ST.

GRANITE CITY, ILLINOIS

March 24, 1928.

Directors of the
Home Bldg & Loan.

Dear Sirs - In asking for this loan to be raised to the original amount I am doing so to make it easier for Edward J. Meng to carry.

I have a second mortgage of $900.00 on this property that he is paying at the rate of $20.00 per month and interest and the two together make a pretty large monthly payment.

Mr Meng works at the Post Office and is a good reliable man and if you gentlemen could raise the amount of loan to $5000.00 or if you would make it $5200.00 that would pay me out I would sign the mortgage with him or put up all the money I get into your stock and you could hold it as collateral as long as you thought necessary.

Very Truly Yours -

Chas H Rowekamp -

Character statement to support purchase of Madison Avenue home (pre marriage).

271

Edward J. Meng, Jessie F. Meng, Edward S. Meng, James L. Meng (1944)

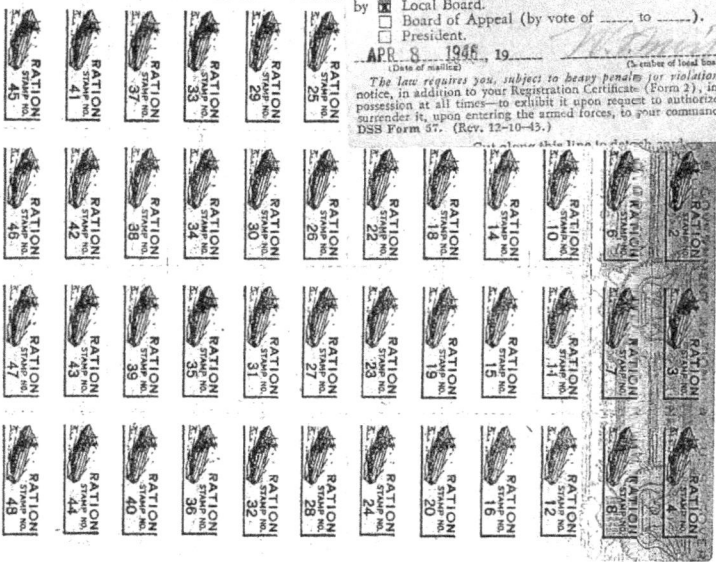

A sign of the times.

Instrument of Surrender

of

All German armed forces in HOLLAND, in
northwest Germany including all islands,
and in DENMARK.

1. The German Command agrees to the surrender of all German armed
Forces in HOLLAND, in northwest GERMANY including the FRISIAN
ISLANDS and HELIGOLAND and all other islands, in SCHLESWIG-
HOLSTEIN, and in DENMARK, to the C.-in-C. 21 Army Group.
This to include all naval ships in these areas.
These forces to lay down their arms and to surrender unconditionally.

2. All hostilities on land, on sea, or in the air by German forces
in the above areas to cease at 0800 hrs. British Double Summer Time
on Saturday 5 May 1945.

3. The German command to carry out at once, and without argument or
comment, all further orders that will be issued by the Allied
Powers on any subject.

4. Disobedience of orders, or failure to comply with them, will be
regarded as a breach of these surrender terms and will be dealt
with by the Allied Powers in accordance with the accepted laws
and usages of war.

5. This instrument of surrender is independent of, without prejudice
to, and will be superseded by any general instrument of surrender
imposed by or on behalf of the Allied Powers and applicable to Germany
and the German armed forces as a whole.

6. This instrument of surrender is written in English and in German.

The English version is the authentic text.

7. The decision of the Allied Powers will be final if any doubt or
dispute arises as to the meaning or interpretation of the surrender
terms.

German signatories:
Grand Admiral v. Friedeburg
General Kinzel
Rear Admiral Wagner
Colonel Poleck
Major Friedel

Copy of First Instrument of Surrender by Germany on May 5, 1945. This instrument was superseded by the Rheims instrument of May 7, 1945, and the Berlin instrument of May 8, 1945. A major success of our ancestors provided by US Army Sgt. Earl Sandweg, a neighbor of Jim and Bev Meng. Sgt Sandweg was a survivor of the D-Day invasion on Omaha Beach, France. The Sgt also gave a D Day history lesson to the Jim and Bev Meng grandchildren.

Copy of Japan's surrender agreement signed September 2, 1945, on the USS Missouri to end World War II in the Pacific. A major success of our ancestors.

Christmas (1947)

Ralph T Shamhart
B: abt 1893 Missouri
M:
D: AUG 31,1963

Henry Shamhart
B: Dec, 2 1794
D: Dec.19,1859 Illinois, USA

Catherine Overly
B: 24 Jul 1804 Pennsylvania, USA
D: 11 Mar 1896 Noble Co, OH

Simon H Schamhardt aka Shamh
B: Dec 2 1792 Germany
M:
D: Dec 19 1857 Beaver, Ohio, USA

Manda G Shamhart
B: abt 1893 Kansas
M:
D:

Wilmer Weston Shamhart
B: 7 Aug 1878 Jasper County, Illinois
M: 12 Apr 1899
D: Granite City, Madison, Illinois

Jessie Frances Shamhart
B: 2 Jul 1903 Newton, Jasper, Illinois
M: 12 Sep 1928
D: 18 Feb 1978 Granite City, Madison, Illinois (

Thomas Foster
B: 12-29-1816 Kentucky, USA
M:
D: 12-28-1860 Kentucky, USA

Foster
B:
D:

William Foster
B: 8-25-1838 , Jackson, Ohio, USA
M:
D: 2-10-1884 , Oregon, USA

Mary Trexler
B: 22 Jun 1824 Kentucky
M:
D: 24 Oct 1883 Greenton, Missou

JONATHAN Trexler
B: 11-4-1791 Pennsylvania, USA
D: 1-29-1880 Illinois, USA

RACHEL MARTIN
B: 5-13-1795 West Virginia, USA
D: 12-26-1859 Illinois, USA

Olive Foster
B: 25 Nov 1876 Newton, Jasper, Illinois
M: 12 Apr 1899
D: 27 Oct 1962 Madison, Illinois

Henrietta Crail
B: 4-6-1843 United States
M:
D: 1-2-1933 United States

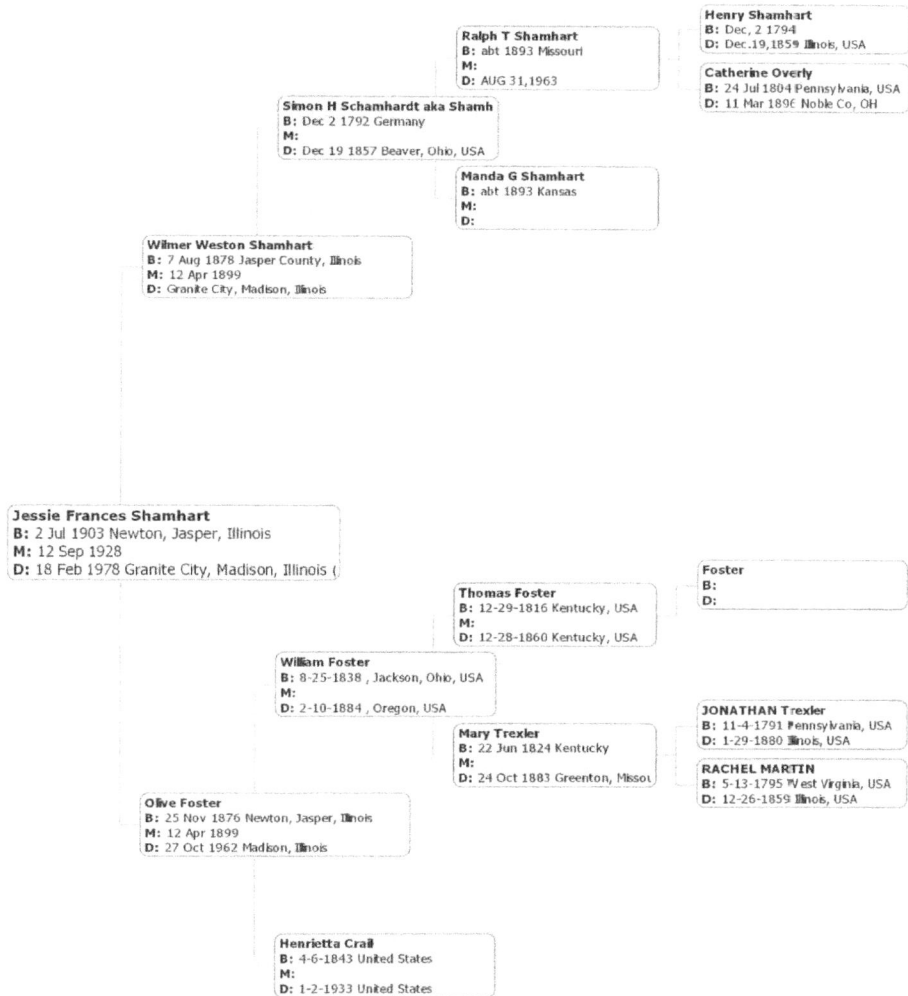

Meng family in America.

277

GRANITE CITY ART SHOW contest winners pictured (left to right) are Teresa Killian, second place, water colors; Carl Foster, first place, pastels; Brenda Dusek, first, oil painting; Jessie Meng, second, oils; Arleen Naglich, second, ink drawing; and Edith McGee, honorable mention, oils. Not shown are Roy Hormann, first, water colors; Edith Schaefer, first, ink; Marian Shelton and Lorraine Paladin, honorable mention, oils; and Katherine Maloney, second, pastels. Some of the 77 entries in judging sponsored by the Granite City Artist Guild are visible along the wall.

Jessie's winning oil painting was the stone bridge at
Bennett Springs State Park, Lebanon, MO (1964).

77 Art Show Entries Judged, Four Winners

Brenda Dusek placed first in the oil division, Roy Hormann in water colors, and Edith Schaefer in ink, and Carl Foster in the pastel division of an art contest sponsored by the Granite City Artrist Guild. The 77 entries were judged Saturday by Eugene Aiassi, Miss Marguerite Barker and Mrs. Joyce Blair and were shown Saturday and Sunday.

Paintings judged included expressionistic abstracts, impressionistic portraits, delicate-textured water colors, precise ink drawings and scenery works described as flowing and colorful. There were 29 contestants, some submitting more than one artwork.

Awards are to be presented Thursday evening. Winners included: oils, Jessie Meng, second, and Marion Shelton, Edith McGee, Gil Singleton and Lorraine Paladin, honorable mention; water colors, Teresa Killian, second; ink, Arlene Naglich, second; and pastels, Katherine Maloney, second.

Den Mother Jessie with neighborhood crew.

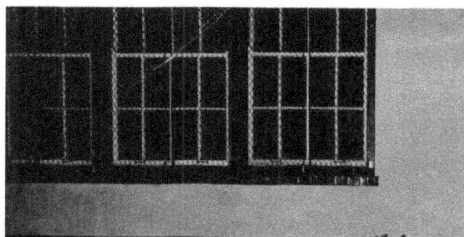

(Left to right) Jessie with her sisters Sybil
Shamhart Fischer and Lois Shamhart Cox.

Easter bonnets in 1968. Jessie Meng (L) with good friend Maxine Anderson (R).

(Rear left to right) James L. Meng, Edward S. Meng, Edward J. Meng, Heather A. Meng, Beverly A. Meng, Jessie F. Meng, and Erik J. Meng (1976)

EDWARD JOHN MENG'S 40-YEAR US POST OFFICE CAREER
EDWARD J. MENG HAVING FUN DOCUMENTING AIRMAIL HISTORY.

Edward J. Meng was a devoted family man, but he also enjoyed working for the US Postal Service, which he did for 40 years. Dad also enjoyed using the US mail to acquire interesting treasures, whether valuable stamps, first-day issues, or postmarks which some day would become historic in nature and for his grandchildren.

For example, he sent a letter on the first flight airmail from the United States to Germany addressed to President Von Hindenburg, Berlin, Germany. As planned, his letter was returned with all the proper official *Graf Zeppelin* a.k.a. LZ 127 stamps/marks etc., indicating the significance of this flight. See the following.

Dad also sent letters to other destinations including a first-day airmail issue also on the German airship, *The Graf Zeppelin*, inaugurating the first airmail service from Europe to Pan-America. See the following.

While another very interesting treasure is that Ed Meng had his letter, properly documented or postmarked, etc., on the *Graf Zeppelin* as it traveled around the world. Information on this special round-the-world flight and a copy of his letter follows.

Another one of Ed Meng's *Graf Zeppelin* letters was sent and returned from the Soviet icebreaker *Malygin* in the Arctic. Originally, this *Zeppelin* trip was to rendezvous with the ill-fated *Nautilus* submarine. See the following.

Edward J. Meng's 40-year post office career starts as a mail carrier.

Dad also had two of his letters travel on the luxury liner, the SS *Ile de France*, again returned properly stamped with the proper identifications. The *Ile de France* provided the fastest airmail service to Europe with its seaplane catapults in 1928. Incidentally, The *Isle de France* had a major role in the rescue after the collision of the SS *Andrea Doria* and MS *Stockholm* in 1956.

Still another letter was sent to Tampico, in the Mexican State of Tamaulipas in 1929. He received a reply from the postmaster, Mr. Ernest E Querra, in Tampico stating the following:

> "Dear sir, your envelope arrived too late owing to rebels' atrocities on the rail road lines . . . Yours truly, . . ." See the following.

Ed Meng then had his letters on Col. Charles Lindberg's last flight on February

20, 1928, from Chicago, Illinois, to St. Louis, Missouri. See following love letter to his future wife, Jessie.

However, Ed Meng sent many first-day issue airmail letters to a variety of other destinations, all returned with the proper documentation postmarks. These destinations included first flight airmail service from Chicago to Atlanta; New Orleans to Houston; Miami to Nassau; St. Johns, Canada, to Montreal; United States to the Canal Zone; St. Louis to Omaha; Albany to Buffalo; etc.

There was the Ed Meng trick of sending selected people a letter, or in my case a Christmas card, around the world. This was done by sending the card halfway around the world as general delivery. If the card is not picked up, it will be returned via the shortest route. Consequently, the shortest route meant that the letter or card would then continue to travel the rest of the way around the world resulting in the card being properly stamped as it passes through every post office! See the following.

Then there are the stamps. Lots! Including many pre–World War II German stamps.

Yes, Ed Meng enjoyed working in the post office participating in historical events. I am thoroughly impressed with Dad's ingenuity! All of the above and more are to remain in the Meng family for future generations.

LZ 127 Graf Zeppelin
From Wikipedia, the Free Encyclopedia

LZ 127 *Graf Zeppelin* (Deutsches Luftschiff Zeppelin #127; Registration: D-LZ 127) was a large German passenger-carrying hydrogen-filled rigid airship which operated commercially from 1928 to 1937. It was named after the German pioneer of airships, Ferdinand von Zeppelin, who held the rank of Graf or Count in the German nobility. During its operating life the great airship

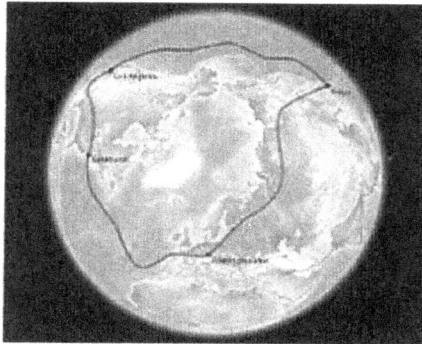

Route of *Graf Zeppelin*'s round-the-world flight.
Germany: 47.654°N 9.479°E47.654°N
9.479°E USA: 40.033°N
74.3536°W40.033°N 74.3536°W
Germany: 47.654°N 9.479°E Japan: 36.05°N
140.217°E 36.05°N 140.217°E
USA: 33.9425°N 118.408°W33.9425°N
118.408°W41.8675°N
87.6243°W40.033°N 74.3536°W
Germany: 47.654°N 9.479°E

made 590 flights, covering more than a million miles.

Round-the-world flight

The growing popularity of the "giant of the air" made it easy for Zeppelin company chief Dr. Hugo Eckener to find sponsors for a "Round-the-World" flight. One of these was the American press tycoon William Randolph Hearst, who requested the tour to officially start at Lakehurst Naval Air Station, NJ.[17] As with the October, 1928, flight to New York, Hearst had placed a reporter, Grace Marguerite Hay Drummond-Hay, on board,[17] who thereby became the first woman to circumnavigate the globe by air. The other passengers were also journalists, except one who paid for his ticket himself and two US naval officers.

Starting there on August 8, 1929, *Graf Zeppelin* flew back across the Atlantic to Friedrichshafen to refuel before continuing on August 15 across the vastness of Siberia to Tokyo (Kasumigaura Naval Air Station), a nonstop leg of 6,988 miles (11,246 km), arriving three days later on August 18.[7] Dr. Eckener believed that some of the lands they crossed in Siberia had never before been seen by modern explorers. After staying in Tokyo for five days, on August 23, the *Graf Zeppelin* continued across the Pacific to California flying first over San Francisco before heading south to stop at Mines Field in Los Angeles for the first ever nonstop flight of any kind

Cover flown on the Graf Zeppelin from Lakehurst to Lakehurst on the round-the-world flight between August 8 and September 4, 1929. Being the dedicated USPS enthusiast, Edward J. Meng observed and once again collected.

285

across the Pacific Ocean. The Pacific leg was 5,998 miles (9,653 km) and took three days.[7] The airship's final leg across the United States took it over Chicago before landing back at Lakehurst NAS on August 29, taking two days and covering 2,996 miles (4,822 km).[7][18]

The flying time for the Lakehurst to Lakehurst legs was 12 days and 11 minutes.[7] The entire voyage took 21 days, 5 hours and 31 minutes including the initial and final trips between Friedrichshafen and NAS Lakehurst during which time the airship traveled 49,618 km (30,831 miles) whereas the distance covered on the designated "Round the World" portion from Lakehurst to Lakehurst was 31,400 km (19,500 miles).

Among the passengers on board the return flight from Lakehurst to Friedrichshafen, which departed on 1 September, were the newly-wed Arctic explorer Sir Hubert Wilkins and his bride Suzanne Bennett. They had married two days earlier and the trip was their wedding gift from Hearst, whom Wilkins had reported for during the initial Around The world trip.

A U.S. franked letter carried on the whole trip from Lakehurst to Lakehurst required $3.55 USD in postage, the equivalent in 2007 of roughly $43 if based on the CPI.[19]

Silver 3-Reichsmark coin (1930A) honoring the Graf Zeppelin's round-the-world flight (Weltflug 1929).

The Graf Zeppelin's Polar Flight and Postmarks

Flown USSR picture postcard delivered by the Graf Zeppelin to the Soviet icebreaker Malygin on the "Polar Flight" 1931.

The ship pursued another spectacular destination in July, 1931, with a research trip to the Arctic; this had already been a dream of Count Zeppelin 20 years earlier, which could not, however, be realized at the time due to the outbreak of war.[20]

In July, 1930, Hugo Eckener had already piloted the *Graf* on a three-day trip to Norway and Spitsbergen, in order to determine its performance in this region. Shortly after this, Eckener made a three-day flight to Iceland; both trips were completed without technical problems.[5]

The initial idea was to rendezvous with the ill-fated *Nautilus*, the submarine of polar researcher George Hubert Wilkins, who was attempting a trip under the ice. This plan was abandoned when the submarine encountered recurring technical problems, leading to its eventual scuttling in a Bergen fjord.[21]

Eckener instead began to plan a rendezvous with a surface vessel. He intended funding to be secured by delivering mail post to the ship. After advertising, around fifty thousand letters were collected from around the world weighing a total of about 300 kilograms. The rendezvous vessel, the Russian icebreaker *Malygin*, on which the Italian air shipman and polar explorer Umberto Nobile was a guest, required another 120 kilograms of post. The major costs of the expedition were met solely by sale of postage stamps.[5] The rest of the funding came from Aeroarctic and the Ullstein-Verlag in exchange for exclusive reporting rights.

The polar flight took one week from July 24–31, 1931. The *Graf* traveled about 10,600 kilometers; the longest leg without refueling was 8,600 kilometers. The average speed was 88 km/h.

Germany issued this stamp commemorating the Graf polar trip which was also collected by Edward J. Meng

SS Île de France

The SS *Ile de France* was a French ocean liner built in Saint-Nazaire, France, for the Compagnie Générale Transatlantique. The ship was the first major ocean liner built after the conclusion of World War I and was the first liner ever to be decorated entirely with designs associated with the Art Deco style. It was neither the largest ship nor the fastest ship, but was considered the most beautifully decorated ship built by the Compagnie Générale Transatlantique (CGT, known also as the "French Line") until the *Normandie*.

SS Ile de France

287

Even though the *Ile de France* was not the fastest vessel in the world, it was used briefly for the quickest mail system between Europe and the United States. During July 1928, a seaplane catapult was installed at the ship's stern for trials with two CAMS 37 flying boats that launched when the ship was within 200 miles, which decreased the mail delivery time by one day. This practice proved too costly, however, and during October 1930, the catapult was removed and the service discontinued.

Springfield Ill
Feb. 18-28

Dear Friend
While passing through
this city this morning I was
thinking of you and the good
times which we have had
together.
I saw in the paper that
Col. Lindbergh was making his
last flight over his old air mail
route on the 20th of Feb. and thought
you would like to have one of his
letters as a souvenir.
Your Friend

Ar Edward J.
Meng love letter
to his future
wife. Dedication
and love!

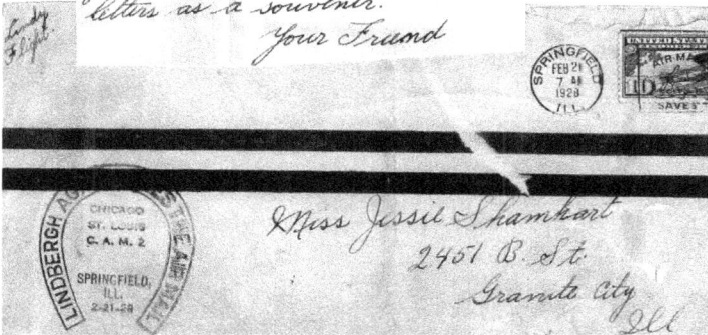

Miss Jessie Shamhart
2451 C. St.
Granite City
Ill

289

All I ask, is for a smile and a kind thought!

Edward J. Meng enjoyed doing things out of the ordinary. Since he was working in the post office and enjoyed stamps, he would send a letter, general delivery, to a destination (i.e., South Africa) halfway around the world, with the instructions, "if this letter is not delivered after 30 days, forward to another destination (i.e., somewhere in China), a little further around the world. If not delivered after 30 days at the second destination, return to sender, which was him. When the letter was returned, it had the official stamp of each destination indicating his letter had traveled around the world. Although technically illegal, he sent many of these letters for his children and friends.

As a postal employee, he obviously enjoyed collecting stamps. He collected German stamps, Zeppelin stamps, and many first-day issues. He also had letters with the special stamp, Lindbergh's last airmail flight. These stamps and letters are in the possession of J. L. Meng, his son.

Another post office incident occurred one day when Ed was working at the "window" in the Granite City office. On this day, a woman approached the window to put her money in postal savings. She completed her postal form but left the beneficiary line blank. When Ed called the woman's attention to this omission, she replied, "Oh, sorry, I don't know anyone, just put your name on it." Ed replied he couldn't—that would be illegal. But standing behind this women was another customer with a young girl. Ed suggested that the woman put the young girl's name as beneficiary, which she did.

Many years later, a young woman came to the post office and asked to see Mr. Meng. The woman was the young girl who was designated as the beneficiary on the postal savings account years earlier. The young woman said she just wanted to thank him for what he had done, because she had just inherited $10,000. Dad replied, "All I ask is for a smile and a kind thought".

AIR MAIL
UNITED STATES POSTAGE
25

2624 Maa
Granite City Ill
U.S.A.

Received at New York, N. Y.
under cover from Post
Office at Granite City, Ill.

James L Meng
Elizabeth town
South Africa

GRANITE CITY
DEC 2
530PM
1952
ILL.

If not called for in 3 days
forward to Gen Del Manila P.I.

WASHINGTON. D. C.
FEB 13
1 - PM
53

BUILD YOUR FUTURE
WISELY, SAFELY
U.S. SAVINGS BONDS

PORT ELIZABETH

C.V.K.R. LO. CAPE

The Illusive US Postmaster Position

Edward J. Meng was a documented and active member of the Democratic political party. However, when the postmaster's position in Granite City became open due to a retirement, the country had just elected Dwight D. Eisenhower, a Republican. At this point in our history, the postmaster's position was a "political patronage" position. Therefore, Ed, the active assistant postmaster and a Democrat, was taken out of the rational progression to be promoted to postmaster. This was done in spite of concerted efforts by all the Democratic congressmen of Illinois.

As an achiever throughout his life, Ed viewed this event, even though it was totally out of his control, as a personal failure. This perceived failure precipitated a nervous condition that led to his disability and retirement after 40 years of dedicated service. Thankfully, after two (2) years of retirement and away from the post office, the nervous condition dissipated.

Ed Meng was of the highest character and integrity and a dedicated civil servant; however, any kind of failure whether perceived or not was not in Ed Meng's DNA.

The use of the "political patronage system" to fill the postmaster's position was eventually discontinued.

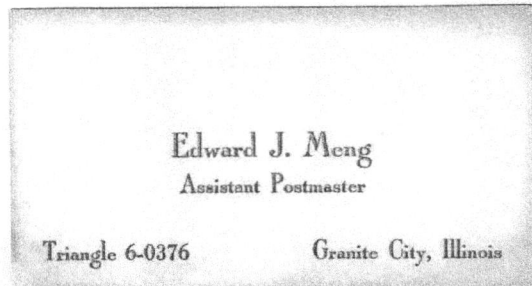

Edward J. Meng expressing the virtues of the US Postal Service at the Home Show in Granite City.

MELVIN PRICE
24TH ILLINOIS DISTRICT

WASHINGTON, D.C., ADDRESS:
1234 NEW HOUSE OFFICE BUILDING

HOME ADDRESS:
426 N. EIGHTH ST.
EAST ST. LOUIS, ILL. 62201

MEMBER COMMITTEE ON
ARMED SERVICES

JOINT COMMITTEE ON
ATOMIC ENERGY

Congress of the United States
House of Representatives
Washington, D.C. 20515

Janauary 31, 1964

Mr. Edward J. Meng
Assistant Postmaster
Granite City, Illinois

Dear Ed:

   May I again express my regrets that I will not be
able to return to the district to join you many friends to
honor you on the occasion of your retirement from the postal
service.

   The tribute paid you by your co-workers is well-
deserved and results from your dedicated and loyal service,
and your conscientious efforts to provide efficient service
to the patrons of the Post Office. I am confident you will
look back with pride at your accomplishments.

   While I know your poor health makes it necessary for
you to retire, I hope that without the daily pressures and
responsibilities of your work, your health will improve and
you will have many pleasant and satisfying years of retirement.

   Best wishes.

                              Sincerely,

                              Melvin Price
                              Member of Congress

MP:gth

MEMBER OF COMMITTEES ON :
   CONSERVATION
   EDUCATION
   PUBLIC WELFARE
   REVENUE

CHAIRMAN
SOUTHWESTERN ILLINOIS
AREA STUDY COMMISSION

GENERAL ASSEMBLY

STATE OF ILLINOIS
PAUL SIMON

STATE SENATOR 47TH DISTRICT
TROY, ILLINOIS

September 27, 1963

Mr. Edward J. Meng
2624 Madison
Granite City, Illinois

Dear Ed:

Just a note to join the many others who are wishing you
the very best for your retirement.

I know you have a host of friends who join me in all
good wishes.

Sincerely,

Paul Simon

PS:ee

Post Office Department

Honorary Recognition

is accorded

EDWARD J. MENG

for devotion to duty in the course of an honorable career in the

United States Postal Service

This citation, tendered upon the occasion of retirement from active duty, conveys official commendation and an expression of esteem from coworkers.

Date of retirement: December 30, 1963

W. T. Ouerbeck,
Postmaster

John A. Gronouski
Postmaster General

295

EDWARD JOHN MENG: THE CIVIC LEADER

No, it's not the Mafia. (Left to right) Paul Grigsby, superintendent of Granite City school system; Edward J. Meng, president of the school board; and Vascil Eftimoff (1953 at a school board convention in Atlantic City, NJ).

Ed Meng's Schoolhouse bell from a rural school in Granite City, IL. Used many times in Shriner and Rotary parades. Is now used on New Years eve and on special occasions by James L Meng and grandchildren.

As a School Board member, Edward J. Meng presented both sons, Edward S. Meng and James L. Meng their High School Diplomas during graduation ceremonies.

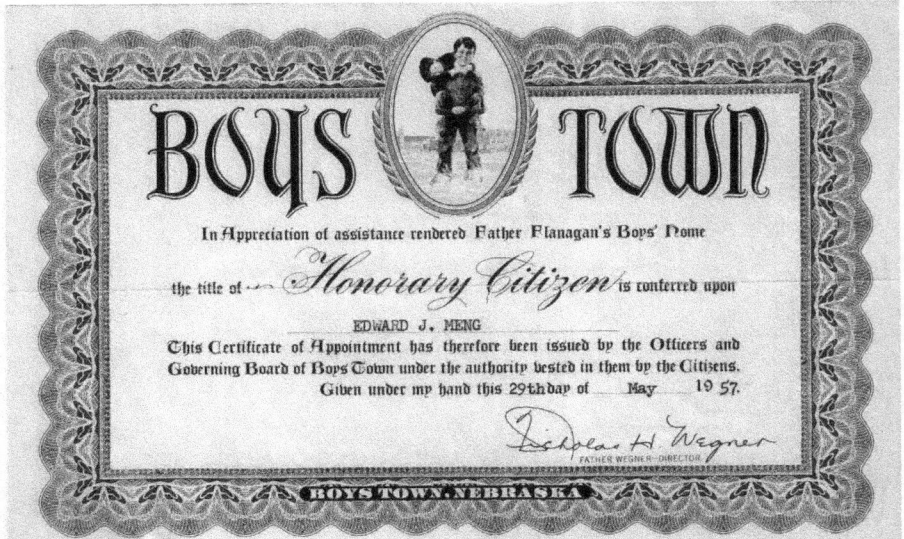

BOYS TOWN

In Appreciation of assistance rendered Father Flanagan's Boys' Home

the title of *Honorary Citizen* is conferred upon

EDWARD J. MENG

This Certificate of Appointment has therefore been issued by the Officers and Governing Board of Boys Town under the authority vested in them by the Citizens. Given under my hand this 29th day of May 1957.

FATHER WEGNER—DIRECTOR

BOYS TOWN, NEBRASKA

EDW. MENG HEADS CHS DADS' CLUB

Edw. Meng, local postal official, was elected president of the Community high school Dad's Club at the organization meeting held Thursday night at the school.

Other new officers are M. E. Anderson, vice-president; George Butler, treasurer; W. L. Sholts, secretary; Ed Hunt, historian. Board members elected were Roy Berves, Robert Flader, Louis Branding and David Bergfield.

Coffee and doughnuts were served to the 20 fathers present and the group voted to meet regularly at the school on the third Thursday of each month at 7:30 p. m. A program is to be planned for the next meeting.

Purpose of the Dad's Club is to promote and take an active interest in student affairs at the school.

PAUL GRIGSBY ADDRESSES PARENTS' CLUB

An interesting talk on "Educational Needs" was given by Paul A. Grigsby, superintendent of schools, was given Thursday evening before the Parents' Club of the Granite City high school at a meeting in the school cafeteria.

Murl Anderson, president, presided and a short movie starring W. C. Fields was presented. Mrs. E. Conreaux was in charge of entertainment.

The first half of the student contest in a membership drive for the Parents' Club with Mrs. Roy Berves as chairman was won by the top junior class, Bob Lawson, president, and a prize of $25 will be presented to the class during the next assembly period.

Harry Sher was appointed chairman of the committee for the soft drink booth the club will sponsor at the Shriners circus to be held on the fotoball field July 9th, and plans were completed for the presentation of the a cappella choir of Central College of Fayette, Mo., in the high school auditorium Apr. 25. Mrs. Ed Meng is chairman of this project and tickets are now on sale.

A fair for the close of the school year was also discussed and Mrs. Conreaux was named chairman.

Refreshments were served by Mrs. Fred Schuman and Mrs. Harold Fischer.

New members enrolled were Mr. and Mrs. Harry Sher, Mr. and Mrs. F. W. Bigb, Mr. and Mrs. Don Williams, Mr. and Mrs. Fred Nichols, Mr. and Mrs. D. Wade and Mr. and Mrs. J. Walker.

The next meeting will be held Apr. 17 in the school cafeteria.

THE BOY SCOUTS OF AMERICA

EXPRESSES ITS APPRECIATION TO

MR. EDWARD MENG

FOR HELP AND COOPERATION IN THE

SUCCESSFUL OPERATION OF THE THIRD

NATIONAL JAMBOREE AT IRVINE

RANCH, CALIFORNIA, JULY 17-23, 1953

PRESIDENT   CHAIRMAN, JAMBOREE COMMITTEE

CHIEF SCOUT EXECUTIVE

MENG PROPOSED AS ROTARY
DISTRICT GOVERNOR IN 1969
Granite City PRESS-RECORD
Thurs., Feb. 23, 1967

EDWARD J. MENG
Rotary Candidate

Edward J. Meng, 2624 Madison Avenue, was proposed as 1969-70 governor of Rotary District 646 in a resolution adopted by Granite City Rotarians at their weekly luncheon Tuesday. The district conference will be sought for this area in the spring of 1969.

Meng, a past president of the club, serves as a director and as public information committee chairman. He has been publicity chairman for annual benefit Rotary horse shows and was assistant Granite City postmaster until retiring.

Rev. Alfred Buls, pastor of Hope Lutheran Church, served as moderator for Tuesday's program, which featured explanations of the role of churches in the Quad-Cities.

Rev. Paul Sims, pastor of Niedringhaus Methodist Church, discussed ministers' duties as administrators of their church staffs and facilities, and Salvation Army Lieut. Donald Wisor spoke of churches' community service and leadership.

Rev. David B. Maxton, pastor of the First United Presbyterian Church of Granite City, reviewed efforts by churches to serve the needs of parishioners, including those encountering problems in their lives.

President William Thoelke presided and Edwin G. Schmitt thanked the club for surprise activities honoring him, at its Valentine dinner party February 14.

NEW ROTARIAN OFFICERS of the Granite City club installed at a banquet recently are, left to right, William Haedebecke, sergeant-at-arms; Dean Moberly, second vice-president; Glenn Abernath, director; Edward Meng, president; Alfred Gehlert, director; Roy Rufler (seated), secretary; and Stanley Bell, assistant sergeant-at-arms. Officers not shown are Jerry Broadway, first vice-president; Elmer Klocaid, assistant secretary; Al [...] treasurer; James Louis, assistant treasurer; and Loren Davis, director.

Granite City Rotary Club

1969 · 1970

DISTRICT 646

PROUDLY PRESENTS

for

DISTRICT GOVERNOR NOMINEE

Edward J. Meng

PAST PRESIDENT

of

GRANITE CITY, ILL.

EDWARD J. MENG

ROTARY EXPERIENCE

Member of Granite City Rotary Club for twenty years, perfect attendance, served as chairman on the Budget, Club Service, Community Service, Scholarship and Awards, Vocational Service, Four Way Test, and International Service committees; member of the Board of Directors for nine years; Chairman of Annual Horse Show Publicity Committee; Associate Editor of weekly news bulletin; Past President of Granite City club.

EDUCATION

Graduate of Granite City High School; holds three-year Certificate in Accounting from Washington University, St. Louis, Missouri; completed Psychology of Foremanship course at the University of Illinois.

WORK EXPERIENCE

Employed by U. S. Postal Service for forty years, retired; President of Postal Clerks; President of Postal Supervisors; State Vice President Postal Supervisors; member of Civil Service Board for seventeen years; Assistant Postmaster for eighteen years.

COMMUNITY ACTIVITIES

President Granite City High School Parents' Club for ten years; member of Granite City Girl Scout Board; Granite City Boy Scout Commissioner; member of Granite City School Board, School District #9 or five years; member A. F. & A. M Masonic Lodge 877, Granite City.

PERSONAL

Age 65; resident of Granite City, Illinois for forty-eight years; wife's name, Jessie Shamhart Meng; two sons, Edward S. Meng, Scottsdale, Arizona, and James L. Meng, Granite City, Illinois.

SPECIFIC QUALIFICATIONS FOR OFFICE OF GOVERNOR

President of the Granite City Club for the .961-62 Rotary year; and as panel moderator, he has appeared before District 646 Assemblies and Institutes, has attended an International Convention and many annual conferences.

Edward J. Meng has all the qualifications for the office of District Governor. He is of high business standing and executive ability.

He can give the time necessary for his Rotary work. Being retired, he can devote full time to the duties of the Governor.

He is an active member in good standing, with a proper classification, with twenty years active service on club committees, holding offices including club president. He has the esteem and confidence of his own club.

He is willing and able, physically and otherwise to fulfill this office and agrees to attend the International assembly in full, and the International Convention.

He has a good knowledge of Rotary and is able to discuss fluently any phase of Rotary in a convincing manner.

Edward J. Meng's campaign literature for district governor of Rotary International

Rotary Club president Edward J. Meng. His gavel is in possession of James L. Meng (1961).

ROTARY CLUB ⚙ ROTARIËRKLUB

LUNCHEON THURSDAYS 12.45   NOENMAAL DONDERDAE 12.45

GOODWOOD HOTEL, GOODWOOD   P.O. BOX 22 POSBUS   GOODWOOD HOTEL, GOODWOOD

CAPE PROVINCE, SOUTH AFRICA   **GOODWOOD**   KAAP PROVINSIE, SUID-AFRIKA

President: CAPE PROVINCE   Secretary:
Tel.:   REPUBLIC OF SOUTH AFRICA   Sekretaris:
     Tel.:

JWC/CDC.

22nd June, 1967.

Rotarian Edward J. Meng,
2624, Madison Avenue,
GRANITE CITY. ILL.
United States of America.

Dear Edward,

How delighted we all were to receive your letter of
May 25th and to hear that you have been proposed as
District Governor for 1969. Everyone in the Goodwood
Club sends their heartiest congratulations and very
best wishes, and we feel that we have come to know you
a little through your letters and are sure you will
have a wonderfully successful and rewarding year.

We are also interested in what you told us about your
area and are sending you two brochures - one on Cape Town
and one issued by a local bank, giving details of our
country.

As you will appreciate, our Docks are now packed to
overflowing with all the ships diverted around the Cape
because of the Middle East crisis and, from my home, I
can see several dozen large ships, mainly huge tankers,
waiting out in the Bay for a berth.

We hope that the stones have now arrived and are suitable
and, once again, kindest regards from us all.

Yours sincerely,

JACK CLIFFORD.

BROCHURES ORDINARY MAIL.

THE ROTARY FOUNDATION
OF
ROTARY INTERNATIONAL

1600 RIDGE AVENUE   EVANSTON, ILL. 60201, U.S.A.

1 June, 1977

Mr. Edward Meng
Member, The Rotary Club
Granite City, Illinois

Dear Edward:

Congratulations on becoming a PAUL HARRIS FELLOW. The generous gift given to The Rotary Foundation in your honor by the Rotary Club of Granite City will help to further the Foundation's objective of international understanding among the peoples of the world. In addition, it is a fitting and lasting tribute to you for your dedication to the ideals and goals of Rotary.

Since the first Graduate Fellows were awarded in 1947, thousands of young men and women have gone abroad under the Foundation's programs to act as ambassadors of good will and through their contacts, have made significant strides in understanding and appreciating their fellow man - his beliefs, practices and traditions. Without thoughtful gifts such as the one given in your honor, the Foundation and its programs would cease to exist.

On behalf of the trustees of The Rotary Foundation, congratulations on this complimentary recognition which has been bestowed on you.

Sincerely,

Jerry

Gerald C. Keeler
Assistant Secretary

"A CONTRIBUTION TO THE FOUNDATION IS AN INVESTMENT IN THE FUTURE."

303

1974

J. MENG

Stix Baer & Fuller

For 20 years, as a part-time information booth employee in the Downtown STL store, loved every minute.

*Edward J. Meng and Jessie F. Meng receiving the
Paul Harris Award from Rotary International (1977).*

Edward Meng to Receive Rotary Award

Edward J. Meng, 2624 Madison, will receive the Paul Harris Fellowship Award at Friday's dinner meeting of the Granite City Rotary Club.

The meeting will be held at Sunset Hills Country Club on Route 157 near Edwardsville. Cocktails will be served at 6 00 p.m. and dinner will be at seven.

The Paul Harris Fellowship Award, one of the highest in the Rotary organization, will be given to Meng in recognition of outstanding attendance and service to the club.

Meng has been president of Rotary Club, has held numerous other offices, has served on many committees, and has a perfect attendance record that stretches for more than 30 years.

Meng is retired from the US Post Office. He and his wife, Jessie Shamhart Meng, have two sons: Edward S. Meng, Laguna Beach, California; and James L. Meng, Granite City.

THE ROTARY FOUNDATION OF ROTARY INTERNATIONAL

Edward J. Meng

is hereby named a

PAUL HARRIS FELLOW

in appreciation of tangible and significant assistance given for the furtherance

of better understanding and friendly relations between peoples of the world.

The Trustees of The Rotary Foundation

CHAIRMAN

The Imperial Council

of the
Ancient Arabic Order
of the

Nobles of the Mystic Shrine

for North America

To all True and Faithful Nobles of the Mystic Shrine:
Know Ye that the Worthy Noble

EDWARD J. MENG

was regularly Received, Admitted and Constituted
A Noble of the Mystic Shrine in

AINAD   Temple of EAST ST. LOUIS, ILLINOIS

On the 4TH day of NOVEMBER, 1967 and that he is duly
Enrolled as such upon the Records of the Order.

In Testimony Whereof We have hereunto
subscribed our Names, and affixed the Seal of
The Imperial Council for North America.

Imperial Recorder   Imperial Potentate

AINAD   Temple

Recorder

306

E. J. Meng, Masonic Lodge 877 AF&AM, the Scottish Rite Bodies, Tri-City Shrine Club, and Ainad Temple. Normally, it's the father who recommends the son to the Masonic order. In this instance, the son, James, recommended the father (1967).

AFTER RETIREMENT

Ed and Jessie purchased the Boze Mill cabin on the Eleven Point River (near Alton, MO), and then rebuilt the entire structure. The cabin became air-conditioned, with a 42" stone fireplace, with two new bedrooms, a gas furnace and water heater, carpet, a glass wall facing the river, and a custom-built shower and kitchen. The Eleven Point River was a clear spring-fed river with trout and white water which was great for floating. Ed and Jessie enjoyed this escape from Granite City and would stay at the cabin for months.

The city of Alton wanted Ed to run for sheriff of Oregon County, but he declined. Ed and Jessie, along with 10 other full-time retired residents of Boze Mill, were forced to sell their properties under fair market value to the US Forest Service.

When dad complained that the real estate appraisals did not match the government's offer to pay, the Forest Service told dad, "If you do not like our price, sue us." There is no need to record Ed's very descriptive and appropriate reply to the Forest Service. Ed also had a very heated and colorful conversation with then US senator Tom Eagleton (D), who was suspected to have personal problems, supported the government takeover of the Eleven Point River. More on the Boze Mill experience will follow.

"The cabin" as it appeared when purchased (1965) at
Boze Mill near Alton, MO on the Eleven Point River

The "Boze Mill cabin" after a "little" work by James Meng and his good friend, James O'Master.

Why the Boze Mill cabin was purchased?

The Boze Mill Spring. The dark line going into the spring branch is the water line to supply the cabin. Wow, was it ever cold taking a shower! The old mill is gone.

Jessie Meng and Sybil Shamhart Fischer after some trout in the Eleven Point river.

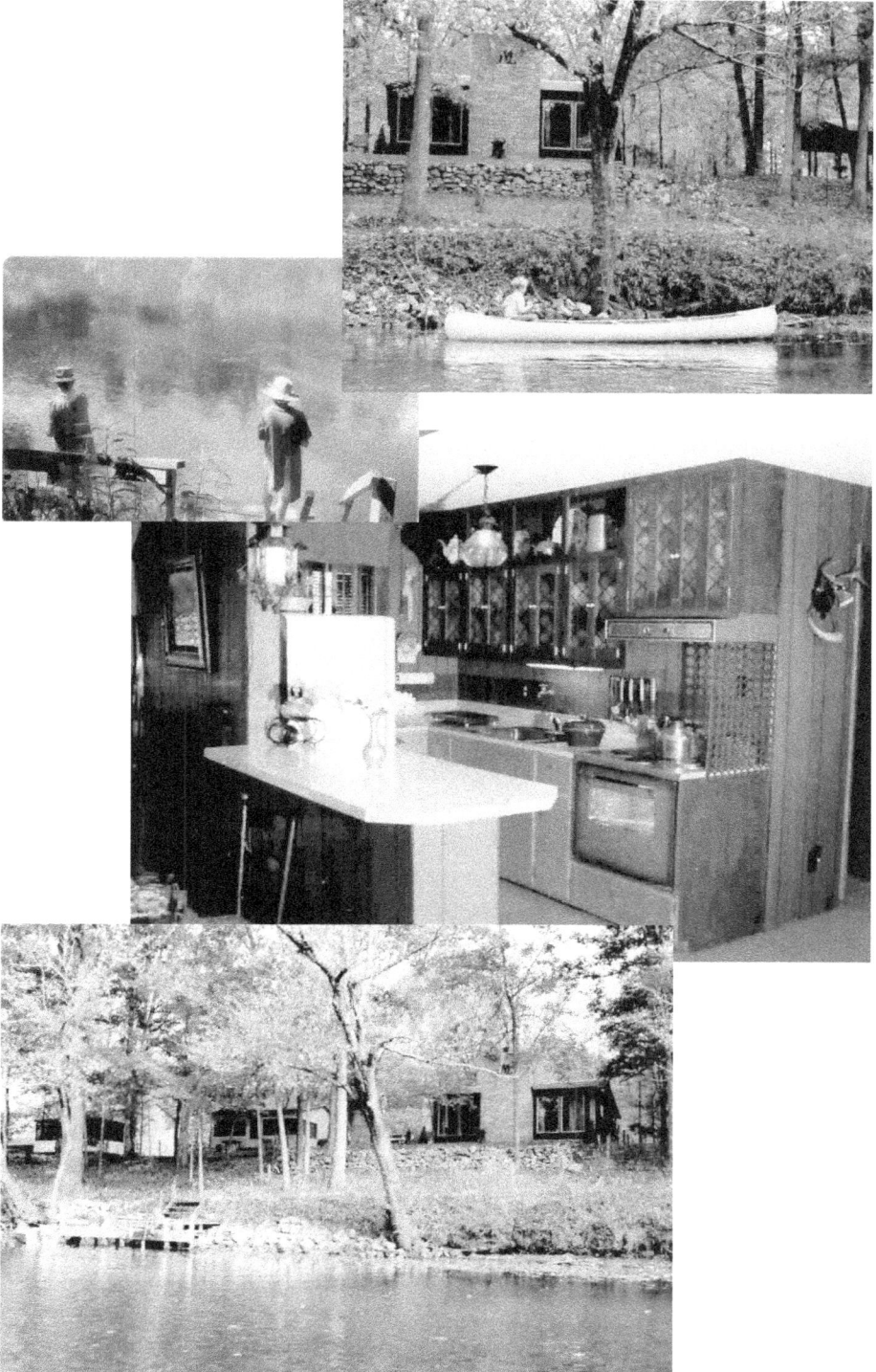

More on Boze Mill, Missouri

The Boze Mill community was an active and resourceful community of residents who lived, enjoyed and monitored the Eleven Point River. Although the old mill was long gone, the very active spring continues to flow. When my mom and dad discovered Boze Mill and decided to purchase a summer home, they were unsuspectedly interviewed by two residents to determine if they were of such character to have them as neighbors. Mom shared a small cake with the two families during their interviews. They indeed passed the local inquisition, because after the second interview they were told who to contact to make their purchase.

Boze Mill had the sort of residents whom we could call and say we would be arriving from St Louis Friday night. Upon arrival, we would find all the electric blankets on our beds turned on and a fire in the fireplace. Both, a welcome sight after a long four-hour drive. On Saturday morning, we would hear a knock at our door with someone in a squeaky voice saying, *yoo-hoo, are you up, yoo-hoo?* It would be one of our neighbors with homemade jelly for breakfast! All were solid, delightful people (the salt of the earth type) whom you just enjoyed knowing and being near.

The residents of Boze Mill also took great pride in the monitoring the condition of the river. There was always a spring clean up involving the removal of brush and trees that had fallen into the river over the winter that made it difficult and dangerous for the canoes. In some instances, the trees were so large that one of our neighbors, who owned a Ford dealership in Alton, would use his wrecker to remove the trees. There were also frequent inspections of the river by the Boze Mill residents to remove broken Styrofoam coolers, bread wrappers and basic junk left behind by the floater's who where frequently drunk. Rescue missions were performed where the "city folk campers" would pitch their tents and sleeping bags next to the babbling river only to have an upstream rainstorm flood their campground. Consequently, our neighbors would tell of events of rescuing flooded families from trees or provide telephone service or medical supplies.

During the hot summer months many of the residents, including the Mengs, would don their swim suits and sit in the river on a gravel bar facing down stream. As the cool, clear spring water would travel over your shoulders, a discussion of the day's events would occur. Although we all resembled a bunch of mud hens sitting in the river, it was definitely not something we did in the city. The entire Meng family enjoyed Boze Mill and all it had to offer, including Heather who would take her nightly bath in the kitchen sink.

The US Forest Service thought it would be just great to run over these people under the disguise of the Scenic Rivers Act of 1968. With their take our low offers, sue us attitude and condemnation threats, they ended up bulldozing all the homes. Many like my parents were retired and on fixed incomes. The liberal bureaucrats were now very happy with 14,195 acres and a 44.4-mile stretch of river totally under government control.

Boze Mill is now nothing more than a weed and brush patch, copper head snakes, ticks and chiggers. Every weekend there are now 100-200 canoes jamming, sometimes by required reservations, to put in at Hwy 19 or Greer Springs to begin their float. An abundance of trash from the canoes remains in the once pristine water with only a token effort by the Forest Service to maintain the river's integrity.

More could be written about the government's actions in destroying Boze Mill and its residents. This whole process was nothing more than a typical land grab of liberal bureaucrats who had no idea what they were doing. Shame on them all!

Boze Mill existence and disappearance is reminiscent of the mystical town of *Brigadoon*.

The Farm
The Edward and Jessie Meng 26.39-acre farm in Edwardsville, Illinois.

The farm was not only for recreation, but a release from the stresses of everyday life. Small gardens containing your basic vegetables were grown, canned, and enjoyed throughout the year. The Fred Meng family also had several small gardens. The spring rains provided sassafras roots for tea, an abundance of morel mushrooms, while the hot July sun provided blackberries and the best blackberry custard pies and cobblers. Of course, there were also plenty of tics, chiggers, and black snakes to keep everyone busy.

On two occasions, Ed and Jessie decided to plant five acres of tomatoes for fun and profit. These tomatoes were then sold to local grocery stores and to the "Brooks Catsup" Company in Collinsville, Illinois. In Jim Meng's eyes, this was a very bad idea. Being in junior high school, he was just right to be child labor. After you finished picking your way through the five acres, the beginning of the field was again ripened and ready to start the picking process all over again. Did I say it gets hot and humid during the summer? Well, it does, very hot! The picking, hoeing, and the carrying out bushels of heavy tomatoes never seemed to end. However, if there was any joy in this process, anyone who was bent over while Jim had a tomato in his hand, did so at their own risk.

1939 FORD 9 N, "TURBO CHARGED" (NOT).
Used to cut grass and brush after Jim and Bev bought the farm.
Unfortunately, not available for the tomato project

American Tree Farm System

THIS CERTIFIES THAT THE FOREST LANDS OF

Edward J. Meng

as described on the reverse of this certificate are being managed in a manner which will assure continuous production of commercial forest crops in accordance with forestry practices approved by American Forest Products Industries, Inc. and the Illinois Forest Industries Committee.

In recognition thereof, these lands are hereby designated a TREE FARM and so to remain as long as the owner complies with the said approved standards of forest practices.

112
Tree Farm No.

Chairman, Tree Farm Committee

Date Certified **1/28/59**

Chairman, Forest Industries Committee

Another family picnic at the Meng's Edwardsville farm. What a great time full of memories.

At the Edwardsville, IL, farm. (Left to right) Ben Koesterer, Elizabeth Koesterer, Frieda M. Meng, Fred M. Meng, Wilmer W. Meng, Edward J. Meng, and Lillian Voght Schippers. (Front) Walter Meng and Edward Voght. The bell is from a schoolhouse in rural Granite City and is currently in possession of James L. Meng.

Another gathering at the farm.

Edward J. Meng with James L. Mengs, 1968 Vette that originally thought was a Corvair

At the Edwardsville farm. (Left to right) Janet Meng, unknown, Walter Meng, Ben Koesterer, Edward J. Meng, and Fred M. Meng (1956?)

JESSIE MENG ELECTED ROTARY ANNS PRESIDENT

SPRING THEME FOR ROTARY ANNS
Granite City PRESS-RECORD Thurs., April 9, 1964

The Rotary Anns were entertained at the Rose Bowl Tuesday by Mrs. William Hoedebecke, Mrs. G.W. Hoelscher and Mrs. Arthur Koerper.

Luncheon was served at 12:30 at tables bedecked with spring blossoms. Twenty-two were seated, including two guests, Mrs. Gladys Welch and Mrs. Carl Ranft.

Mrs. Edward Meng conducted the business meeting and appointed a nominating committee to select new officers. Those named were Mrs. E.G. Schmitt, Mrs. Harvey Balke and Mrs. Murl Anderson.

ROTARY ANNS ELECT OFFICERS
AT SEASON'S OPENING MEETING
Granite City PRESS-RECORD, 1965

Officers for the remaining season were elected Tuesday at the first full meeting of the Rotary Ann's at the country house of Mrs. Edward Meng near Edwardsville.

Mrs. William Hoedebeck, whose husband is president of the Rotary Club, was named president; Mrs. Bernard Finney is the new secretary; and Mrs. Homer Huber was elected treasurer. Mrs. Lorraine Decatur is the retiring president.

An outdoor picnic luncheon, a tradition at the opening meeting of the fall, is held each year at the Meng home and the hostess committee serving with Mrs. Meng consisted of Mrs. Warren Decatur, Mrs. Eugene Coe and Mrs. Loren Davis. The business session followed and at its close the program was provided by Mrs. Sonia Scharf, widow of Dr. Hal Scharf, who exhibited pictures of Paris and other parts of France taken on her recent trip there.

Other members attending the meeting were Mesdames Glenn Abenroth, Murl Anderson, Elwood Ackerman, Harvey Balke, Carl Mathias and Howard Wellman. Guests present were Laura Dyer, Kathy Coe and Anna Balke.

One of the many Rotary Ann Meetings held at Jessie Meng's Edwardsville farm. Guest were always given a bundle of bittersweet to take home.

ROTARY ANNS PLAN CHRISTMAS PARTY

Mrs. Irvin Wiesman, assisted by Mrs. Lena Rouland, Mrs. Sadie Linder and Mrs. Mignon Abenroth, entertained the Rotary Anns Monday evening in her home, 1106 Twenty-Seventh Street.

Mrs. Jessie Meng, president, was in charge and during the business hour plans were furthered for a Christmas party Dec. 4 in the home of Mrs. Ann Schmitt, 2408 Cleveland Boulevard. There will be a pot luck supper in connection with the party and a gift exchange among the members, each of whom will bring la toy to be distributed to needy children.

Entertainment Monday evening was furnished by a group of young people, members at the high school glee club, and there was bridge and canasta. The young people who sang were Misses Barbara Matthews, Marcella Wood, Charlene Biggs, Betty Stubblefield, Max Anderson, Gerald McGowan and Edward Meng.

Refreshments were served from attractively decorated tables and favors were chrysanthemum nut cups. Approximately 25 attended and prizes at cards went to Mrs. Dorothy Kerch, Mrs. Reva Helman and Mrs. Mae Holescher. The hospitality committee for the Christmas party will consist of Mrs. Schmitt, Mrs. Thelma Baker, Mrs. Elsie Balke and Mrs. Vivian Johnson.

An oil painting of the "shed" at the Edwardsville Farm by Perry Schippers (1950s).

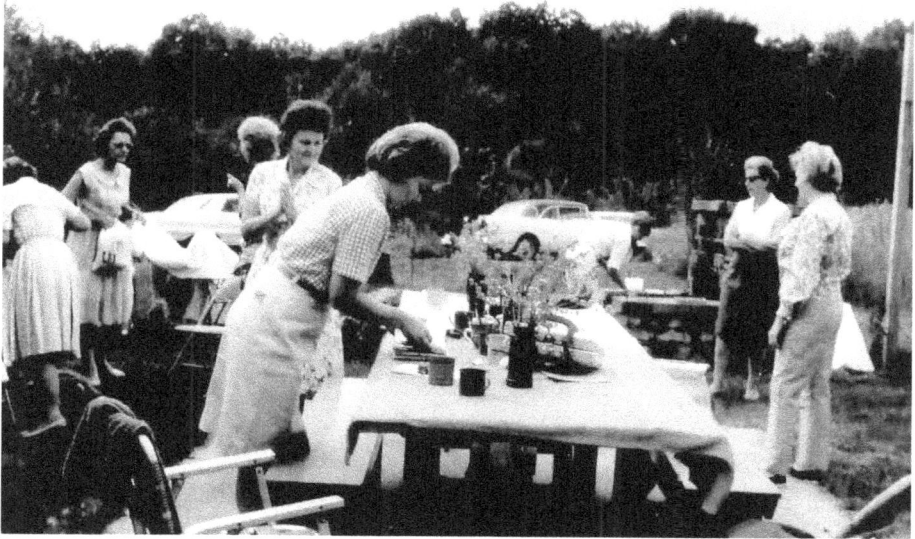

Granite City Rotary Anns at the Edwardsville farm. Jessie Meng
was president. Note: Fabled outhouse in rear of bottom picture.

Introducing

4031 Mengstrasse

Features:

- 26.39 +/- Acres
- Potential Estate Home(s)
- Flat and Rolling Terrain
- City Water/ Sewer Connections
- Full Mineral Rights (plus)
- Highway Access
- Mature Pine Groves
- Lake site-small creek
- Edwardsville Schools
- 2003 Real Estate Taxes $744
- Adjoins Timber Lake Sub.
- Seller reserves the right to name streets
- Got a horse?

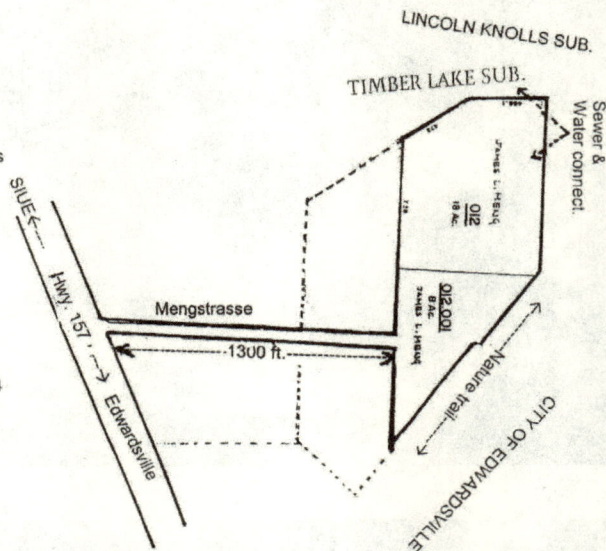

Timber includes many hardwoods and pine trees. Conveniently located near a grade school, middle school, two high schools and Southern Illinois University. A prime location close to the Madison County Court House, YMCA, Country Club, shopping and parks. Only 20 minutes from downtown St. Louis, 30 minutes to Lambert International and Mid America airports. Property adjoins a nature trail. This is an exceptionally beautiful piece of property. An estate that awaits the discriminating buyer.

This information is believed to be accurate but is not warranted.

Did you know there is another Mengstrasse in Lübeck, Germany? I wonder what the history is behind the Lübeck, Mengstrasse?

The Meng Farm Is Sold but the Family Names Remain

DEED RESTRICTION TO HONOR ALL PAST, PRESENT AND FUTURE MENG'S WITH THE PERPETUAL RETENTION OF A STREET NAMED "MENGSTRASSE".

RESTRICTION ON USE OF PROPERTY

JAMES L. MENG, Trustee of the JAMES L. MENG Revocable Trust Dated February 18, 2002, and BEVERLY A. MENG, Trustee of the BEVERLY A. MENG Revocable Trust Dated February 18, 2002, impose the following restriction on the use of the real property, the legal description of which is attached hereto as Exhibit "A".

There exists upon such property, or portions thereof, a roadway located in Sections 10 and 15 of Township 4 North, Range 8 West of the Third Principal Meridian, Madison County, Illinois and extending from the center of St. Louis Road, commonly known as Highway 157 to and part of the property described in Exhibit "A".

The roadway located on such property has been known as "Mengstrasse". The purpose of this restriction is to further restrict the use of the land described in Exhibit "A" so that the name of the road shall remain "Mengstrasse" in perpetuity. This restriction also applies to any roadway used in general as the entry road to the property from St. Louis Road even if such roadway right-of-way is enlarged in width or extended in length further into the property.

This restriction is binding on all of the heirs, personal representatives, successors, grantees and assigns of the grantors of this restriction. The power to revoke this restriction is specifically reserved to the grantors and further conveyed to JAMES L. MENG and BEVERLY A. MENG, personally. This restriction may only be revoked by joint action of both JAMES L. MENG and BEVERLY A. MENG, acting individually, and not as trustees of the aforementioned trust.

JAMES L. MENG, Trustee of the JAMES L. MENG Trust
Dated February 18, 2002

DON'T YOU KNOW THERE IS A GROUP OF LITTLE MENG ANGELS IN HEAVEN SITTING ON THE EDGE OF A CLOUD PLAYING THEIR HARPS SMILING AT THIS EVENT!

Mrs. Meng, 74, dies at home

Mrs. Jessie F. (Shamhart) Meng, 74, of 2624 Madison Avenue, was pronounced dead at home at 8:30 a.m. Saturday by William Sternberg, Madison County deputy coroner.

She was a member of Central Christian Church, a past president, and active member of the Rotary Anns, and also belonged to the Parents' Club at the high school. Mrs. Meng also was a den leader with a Cub Scout pack.

Born in Newton, Illinois, Mrs. Meng resided in this area for 59 years.

She was employed 18 years at the information desk at Stix, Baer and Fuller Store, St. Louis, prior to her retirement.

Mrs. Meng is survived by her husband, Edward J. Meng, formerly assistant postmaster in the Granite City Post Office; two sons, James L. Meng of St. Louis and Edward S. Meng of Laguna Beach, California; two sisters, Mrs. Robert (Lois) Cox of Granite City and Mrs. Sybil Fischer of Oklahoma City, Oklahoma; and two grandchildren.

Funeral arrangements are given in the obituary column.

Obituaries

MENG, MRS. JESSIE F. (Shamhart), 2624 Madison Ave. Entered into rest 8:30 a.m. Saturday, Feb. 18, 1978, at home.

Beloved wife of Edward J. Meng; dear mother of James L. and Edward S. Meng; dear sister of Mrs. Lois Cox and Mrs. Sybil Fischer; dear grandmother.

Jessie F. Meng's Funeral Program

A CELEBRATION OF LIFE
in loving memory of
JESSIE FRANCIS MENG
July 2, 1903   February 18, 1978

The Order of Worship

The Prelude	Betty Grote
Call to Worship	The Pastor
*Hymn (by Congregation)	"The Old Rugged Cross"
*The Invocation	The Pastor

In Memoriam

The Scripture Reading   John 14:1 - 6
Romans 8:28, 29   I Corinthians 15:52,57

THE MEDITATION: "T O B E C O N T I N U E D"
Text: "Jesus said to her, 'I am the resurrection and
the life, he who believes in me, though he die, yet
shall he live...'"   John 11:25, 26

*Hymn (by Congregation)   "Abide with Me"
*The Benediction   The Pastor

*Indicates that Congregation is to stand

Jessie Francis Meng, daughter of Wilmar & Olive Shamhart, was born in Newton, Illinois. They moved to Granite City where she met Ed and married Sept. 12, 1928.

The Mengs began 50 years of marriage in their present
Madison Ave. home. They were blessed by Edward Shamhart on June 19, 1933 and James Leroy on April 25,1939.

Jessie was employed by the Federal Reserve Bank for
8 years and Stix, Baer, & Fuller for 18 years. She was
twice President of the Rotary Anns; served as a Cub Scout
Den mother, and was a member of the Parents' Club.

Our Lord graciously called her to a higher life at
74 years of age quietly in her sleep. Jessie is survived by her husband Edward, two sons, and grandchildren
Heather and Erik,t and sisters Lois and Sybil.

"HE WILL SWALLOW UP DEATH IN VICTORY."   Isaiah 25:8

THE OLD RUGGED CROSS

On a hill far away stood an old rugged cross,
The emblem of suff'ring and shame,
And I love that old cross where the dearest and best
For a world of lost sinners was slain.

CHORUS
    So I'll cherish the old rugged cross,
    Till my trophies at last I lay down;
    I will cling to the old rugged cross,
    And exchange it some day for a crown.

Oh, that old rugged cross, so despised by the world,
Has a wondrous attraction for me,
For the dear Lamb of God left His glory above,
To bear it to dark Calvary.

CHORUS (see above)

To the old rugged cross I will ever be true,
Its shame and reproach gladly bear;
Then He'll call me some day to my home far away,
Where His glory forever I'll share.

CHORUS (see above)
+ + + + + + + + + + + + + + + + + + + +

ABIDE WITH ME

Abide with me: fast falls the eventide;
The darkness deepens; Lord, with me abide;
When other helpers fail, and comforts flee;
Help of the helpless, O abide with me.

I fear no foe, with Thee at hand to bless;
Ills have no weight, and tears no bitterness;
Where is death's sting? Where, grave, thy victory?
I triumph still, if Thou abide with me.

Arrangements by the Davis Funeral Home
The Rev. Don F. Pierson, Pastor

The Pallbearers: Past Presidents of G.C. Rotary Club

Burial at Sunset Hills, Edwardsville

"I AM THE WAY, THE TRUTH, AND THE LIFE"

Funeral services 1 p.m. Tuesday, Feb. 21, at DAVIS FUNERAL HOME Chapel, 21st Street and Cleveland Boulevard. Interment Sunset Hill Cemetery, Edwardsville Township. Visitation after noon today.

While at my mom's funeral, two women came up to me and said, "Your mom was a classy lady". A comment that was not only accurate but greatly appreciated.

Edward Meng, former civic leader, dies

Edward J. Meng, 81, of 2624 Madison Avenue, a longtime resident and active in civic and community events, died at 2 a.m. Friday, April 1, 1983, at Clayton House Center in Clayton, Missouri.

Mr. Meng was a 40-year employee at the Granite City Post

Office and 18 years of that time he served as assistant postmaster. He was a past president of the Postal Clerks, president of the Postal Supervisors, and state vice president of the Postal Supervisors.

A member of Nameoki United Methodist Church, Mr. Meng also held membership in Masonic Lodge 877, AF&AM, Scottish Rite Bodies, Tri-City Shrine Club, and Ainad Temple.

He was a former Granite City Board of Education member, treasurer and board member of the Salvation Army, and former member of both the Boy and Girl Scout Councils, and was recipient of the Silver Beaver Award, Boy Scouting's highest award for a volunteer.

Mr. Meng had 36 years of perfect attendance in the Granite City Rotary Club with attendance at meetings in six foreign countries. He was a 17-year member of the Civil Service Board and received the Paul Harris Award from the Rotary Club.

During the years, Mr. Meng attended the University of Illinois and Washington University, where he majored in accounting.

The city council of Granite City passed a resolution this year declaring January 18 as Edward Meng Day, in honor of his past civic contributions to the community. The formal statement was read by Second Ward Alderman Sam Whitmer and approved unanimously by the council.

Mr. Meng and his wife, Mrs. Jessie Meng, who died February 18, 1978, made their home at the Madison Avenue address for 55 years. He was born in Freeburg, Illinois. His son has temporarily moved into his father's home.

Edward Meng

Edward J. Meng, 81, of 2624 Madison Avenue, a retired Granite City postal employee, died at 2 a.m. Friday, April 1, 1983, at Clayton House Care Center in Clayton, Missouri.

He was employed at the Granite City Post Office for 40 years, with 18 years of that time serving as assistant postmaster.

Mr. Meng was a member of Nameoki United Methodist Church and held membership in many other civic and community organizations. A related story on his life appears elsewhere in today's issue.

His wife, Mrs. Jessie Meng, died on February 18, 1978.

Survivors include two sons, Edward S. Meng and James L. Meng, both of St. Louis; three brothers, Fred Meng of Granite City, Walter Meng of Alton, and Wilmer of Fullerton, California; one sister, Mrs. Roy (Frieda) Bennington, Granite City, and two grandchildren.

Visitation was at Davis Funeral Home, Twenty-First Street and Cleveland Boulelvard, where Masonic services were conducted at 8 p.m. Sunday. The Reverend Eugene Seaman will officiate at 1 p.m. funeral services today, April 4, at the funeral home with burial in Sunset Hill.

-EULOGY-

ED MENG   APRIL 4, 1983   DAVIS FUNERAL HOME

ED MENG DIED PEACEFULLY IN HIS SLEEP AT CLAYTON HOUSE NURSING CARE APRIL 1, 1983. ED SUFFERED FROM AN ENLARGING CANCEROUS CONDITION FOR NEARLY 3 YEARS . . . HE HAD BEEN UNDER CONTINUOUS CARE FOR SOMETIME . . . ALL OF THIS WE KNEW . . . ED HAD THE PRIVILEGE OF WALKING TO THE BOUNDRIES OF LIFE AND HAD BEEN GIVEN A REPRIEVE TO REFLECT UPON HIS JOURNEY . . . "WHEN THE HOUR COMES, I WILL BE READY," HE HAD SAID . . . AS THE MONTHS PASSED WE SAW HIM DETERIORATE EACH DAY . . . IN THE EARLY WINTER WE HAD SEEN HIM GAIN STRENGTH AND HAD HOPED HE WOULD BE ABLE TO RESUME A SOMEWHAT NORMAL EXISTANCE . . . BUT IT WAS NOT TO BE SO . . . SO TODAY WE GATHER TO PAY TRIBUTE TO HIS EXISTANCE . . . WE WILL NOT PRETEND WE WISH HE COULD HAVE LIVED FOR MANY MORE YEARS . . . BUT WE KNOW THAT ED HAD ATTAINED THE AGE OF 81 YEARS . . . IT WAS A LONG AND FRUITFUL LIFE . . . WE ARE MADE SAD BY HIS DEATH . . . BUT NOT ONE OF US HERE COULD HAVE WISHED EVEN ONE MORE DAY UPON HIM . . . SO TODAY WE REMEMBER WHO HE WAS TO US . . .

CHILDHOOD: ED WAS BORN AT FREEBURG, ILLINOIS, ON THE 4TH DAY OF DECEMBER 1901 . . . THE TURN OF THE CENTURY FOUND AMERICA ENTERING THE INDUS-TRIAL AGE WITH A RUSH . . . ED'S PARENTS, FRED AND ELIZABETH (KEESTER) MENG WITH THEIR FOUR CHIL-DREN, MOVED TO GRANITE CITY TO PARTAKE OF THE NEWLY INDUSTRIALIZED COMMUNITY . . . MANY WILL REMEMBER THOSE EARLY YEARS . . . THE OLD STEAM POWER THAT WAS PREVELANT THE ELECTRIC STREET CARS . . . GAS LIGHTS . . . HORSES PULLING GREAT DRAY WAGONS . . . RACY SULKIES . . . AND THE OCCASIONAL PUT-PUT OF THE NEW HORSELESS BUGGIES . . . THE CLOUDS OF WAR WERE GATHERING OVER EUROPE AND WE SANG,

"WE WON'T BE BACK TILL ITS OVER OVER THERE," WHEN
OUR BOYS MARCHED AWAY TO ARMED CONFLICT . . .

HUSBAND-FATHER; ED MOVED HERE WITH HIS PAR-
ENTS . . . WHEN HE WAS A YOUNGSTER . . . WAS EDUCATED
IN THE PUBLIC SCHOOL SYSTEM HERE AND WENT ON
TO COLLEGE AT THE UNIVERSITY OF ILLINOIS AND
WASHINGTON UNIVERSITY IN ST. LOUIS . . . HE MET AND
FELL IN LOVE WITH A PRETTY YOUNG GIRL AND WAS
MARRIED IN THE PARSONAGE OF THE OLD METHODIST
EPISCOPAL CHURCH TO JESSIE SHEMHART WHO PRE-
CEEDED HIM IN DEATH . . . THEY WERE THE PARENTS
OF TWO FINE YOUNG MEN JAMES AND EDWARD HE WAS
VERY PROUD OF BOTH OF YOU AND PLEASE PUT AWAY
THOSE THINGS THAT WERE LESS THAN THEY SHOULD
BE AND IMMULATE HIS GOOD QUALITIES REMEMBER-
ING THAT YOUR FATHER WAS A VERY HUMAN PERSON . . .
HE WAS NOT PRETENTIOUS ONE COULD SEE THROUGH
HIM AS IF HE WERE CELLOPHANE.

COMMUNITY: ED PULLED A LOT OF WEIGHT IN HIS
COMMUNITY . . . HE OBTAINED A JOB WITH THE POST OF-
FICE DEPARTMENT AND WORKED HIS WAY UP TO SUPER-
VISOR . . . HE WAS THE SENIOR POST OFFICE EMPLOYED
AMONG US . . . HE RETIRED IN 1966 AND HAD REALLY
ENJOYED RETIREMENT . . . LIFE HOWEVER SEEMED TO
TAKE ON NEW MEANING FOR HIM WHEN HE LOST HIS
LIFE LONG MATE . . . IT WAS DIFFICULT FOR HIM TO COPE
WITH LIFE ALONG AFTER THAT . . . HE HAD SPOKEN IN
CONFIDENCE MANY TIMES OF THE DRASTIC CHANGE IT
HAD WROUGHT IN HIS APPROACH TO LIFE . . . MANY OF
THOUGHT HE HAD LOST HIS WILL TO GO ON . . .

GRANDPARENT: ED WAS EVERYTHING GOOD THAT
BELONGS TO THE STEROTYPE OF THE GRANDPARENT . . .
HE WAS INCAPABLE OF CONCEALING HIS JOY ABOUT
YOU AND WASTED NO OPPORTUNITY TO EXTROLL THE
LATEST ANTICS IN YOUR LIVES . . . LIFE OUT HIS GOOD
QUALITIES IN HIS LIFE AND PUT AWAY THOSE THINGS
THAT WILL BE HURTFUL . . .

ED WAS A WILLING WORKER IN HIS COMMUNITY
HE HAS A LONG AND PRESTIGEOUS RECORD IN THE
CIVIC ORGINAZATIONS . . . MASONS LODGE #877, SHRINE
CLUB . . . AINAID SHRINE, CIVIL SERVICE BOARD . . . RO-
TARY . . . RECIPIENT OF PAUL HARRIS AWARD FOR CIVIC
DUTY . . . 36 YEARS OF PERFECT ATTENDANCE IN AMERICA
AND SIX FOREIGN COUNTRIES . . . MEMBER OF GRANITE

CITY UNITED METHODIST CHURCH...SCHOOL BOARD MEMBER... THE LIST COULD GO ON AND ON... BUT IN THE FACE OF DEATH IT SOMEHOW SEEMS UN-IMPORTANT... IT ONLY MATTERS THAT HE WAS... HE WAS WARM CARING INDIVIDUAL SO TENDER INSIDE THAT HE HAD TO MASK THE OUTSIDE WITH A GRUFF AND HARD SHELL WE COULD TELL OF THE SILVER BEAVER AWARD FROM SCOUTING...AND HIS TENURE IN GIRL AS WELL AS BOY SCOUT ACTIVITIES...HE WAS NEIGHBOR: CITIZEN: A STRONG COMPETITOR: THE LIST COULD GO ON AND ON... IN FACT THE LIST IS INCOMPLETE... ED WAS A PERSON SHY AT HEART... AND ALTHOUGH HE WORKED OUT FRONT HE WAS REALLY A HESITANT PERSON NO ONE EVER HAD TO WONDER WHERE HE STOOD WITH ED...AND WITH HIS VERY COLORFUL LANGUAGE HE DESCRIBED SITUATIONS HE DISLIKED AS WELL AS WHAT HE LIKED...HE WAS NOT QUICK TO OPINIONATE ABOUT THINGS... WANTED TO HEAR OUT OTHERS... AND ALTHOUGH HE MIGHT VEHEMENTLY DISAGREE HE RESPECTED OTHER RIGHT TO THEIR OPINIONS... HE COULD DIG IN HIS HEELS WHEN HE FELT PRINCIPLE WAS AT STAKE... AND BE VERY RECESSIVE IF IT WERE NOT... HE COULD TAKE HIS PLACE WITH ANY ONE IN THE ELEVATOR AND GAINER PUBLIC OPINION... HE WAS A MANS MAN... COULD STAND UP TO WRONG... BUT COULD GIVE GROUND WHEN FEELINGS WERE AT STAKE...ED LIVED HIS LIFE ON THE PROPOSITION THAT MAN HAD INTRINSIC WORTH. HE WAS TENDER ALMOST TO A FAULT...HE KEPT HIS DISTANCE FROM DENOMINATIONAL AFFILLIATION FOR MANY YEARS...IT WAS NOT THAT HE WAS ANTI-RELIGIOUS FOR HE AND HIS WIFE ATTENDED CHURCH...IT WAS SIMPLY THAT HE OBSERVED THAT THOSE WHO SPEAK THE MOST ABOUT CHURCH OFTEN EXIBIT THE LEAST CHRISTIAN ATTITUDES... HE HAD ASKED ABOUT MEMBERSHIP IN CHURCH LAST YEAR AND WE WERE HAPPY TO MAKE HIM A MEMBER... HE WONDERED IF A STAMP WAS NEEDED FOR ENTRY INTO THE KINGDOM WHEN WE ASSURED HIM IT WAS NOT HE HAD SAID..."WELL I WANT IT ANY HOW..."

HE HAD TAKEN TO READING THE BIBLE AFTER HIS WIFE HAD PASSED...HE READ THAT GOD ADMONISHED US "TO BE TENDERHEARTED ONE TO ANOTHER... FORGIVING OTHERS AS GOD HAS FORGIVEN US"...

HE HAD OBSERVED THAT THIS IS EASIER SAID THAN
DONE . . . FOR THERE WERE A FEW DEMOCRATS AND RE-
PUBLICANS HE HAD TO EXTRICATE FROM HIS CRAW . . .
BUT HE GOT THE JOB DONE SOMEHOW . . . AND IN HIS IMI-
TATABLE LANGUAGE . . . HAD FORGIVEN THEM . . . IN THE
CHECKLIST IN HIS MIND HE THOUGHT HE HAD TOUCHED
ALL THE BASES AND NOW HE WAS READY TO GO.

WOULD ED HAVE APPROVED OF THE THINGS WE
HAVE WRITTEN HERE? . . . PERHAPS NOT . . . HE WOULD
HAVE OBSERVED THEY WERE VOID OF IMPERFECTION . . .
HE KNEW HE WAS NO PERFECT PERSON . . . HE WOULD
HAVE BEEN EMBARRASSED BY ALL THE COMMOTION . .
BUT WHAT WE HAVE SAID HERE TODAY WE BELIEVE TO
BE TRUE AND JUST . . . AND COULD HAVE BEEN SPOKEN
BY ANY ONE HERE . . . PERHAPS WE CAN END WITH HIS
OWN WORDS . . . "PREACHER, I DID MY BEST . . . I TRIED
MY HARDEST . . ." AND WE ALL KNOW THAT HE DID IN-
DEED . . . FAREWELL OLD FRIEND . . . WE WILL MISS YOU . . .

SKWEEK (news letter) FOR THE WEEK OF APRIL 12, 1983

ROTARY BOARD MEETING 11:15 AM SHARP AT THE "Y"...

VISITING ROTARIANS AND GUESTS: WILL MENG, ED S.
MENG, SCOTTY THOMPSON (GUEST OF JACK DEMPSEY),
MIKE KULIER (GUEST OF EARL DOTZAUER), JOHN R.
SMITH, EDWARDSVILLE...

...WE WERE ALL UPSET BY THE SUDDEN DEATH OF ED
MENG AND EXTEND OUR SYMPATHY TO HIS FAMILY A
SPECIAL THANKS TO THE SIX MEN FROM ROTARY (DICK
WEST, DEAN MABERRY, RICH SUESS, GLEN ABENROTH,
LOUIE MEEK, AND JOE HASSLER) WHO WERE THE PALL-
BEARERS. IT WAS ED'S WISH THAT ROTARIANS BE HIS
PALLBEARERS. ED WAS A LOYAL ROTARIAN FOR MANY
YEARS AND HAD 36 YEARS OF PERFECT ATTENDANCE.
HE WILL BE MISSED BY US ALL...

DEVOTION, RANDALL IRWIN, SPEAKER.)

Council Resolution Honors Edward Meng

Edward J. Meng, former Granite City assistant postmaster, has been
honored by the Granite City Council with a resolution recognizing
his past civic contributions. The resolution declared January 18 as
Edward Meng Day in the city.

The formal statement was read by Second Ward Alderman Sam Whitmer and approved unanimously by the Granite City Council on Tuesday night.

Mayor Paul Schuler sited Meng's willingness "always to serve well" and praised his good citizenship.

The resolution listed Meng's accomplishments as a former Granite City Board of Education member, treasurer and board member of the Salvation Army, and former member on both the Boy and Girl Scout councils in the area.

Meng also was a longtime member of the Granite City Rotary and a participant in several other area organizations.

He is a former Granite City resident and now resides at the Clayton House care institution, where he is being nursed for a serious illness. He was a member of the community here since 1917.

Friends are being invited to write or visit Meng at the Clayton House, 1251 Clayton Road, Manchester, Missouri, 63011.

His son, Edward S. Meng, also a former resident, has temporarily moved into his father's home at 2624 Madison Avenue.

JANUARY 19, 1983
DECLARED AS EDWARD J MENG DAY IN GRANITE CITY, IL.

RESOLUTIONS

WHEREAS, Edward Meng served faithfully and dilligently as Assistant Postmaster of Granite City; and

WHEREAS, Edward Meng served as a Member of the Granite City School Board; and

WHEREAS, Edward Meng served as a Member of the Salvation Army Board, Granite City Rotary Club and both the Boy Scouts and Girl Scouts of America Councils; therefore

Be It Resolved, that Wednesday, January 19, 1983 be declared as EDWARD MENG DAY in recognition of his many years of service to his fellow Granite Cityans.

Paul Schuler
Mayor

ATTEST: _Robert W Stevens_
City Clerk

Sunset Hills, Edwardsville, IL

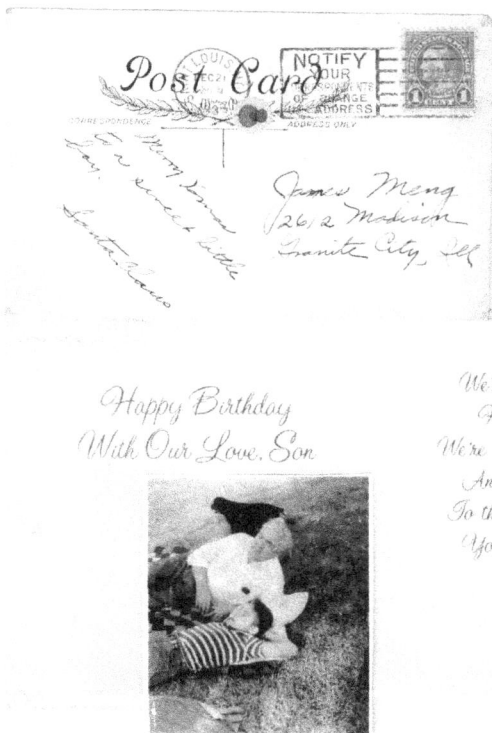

James L Meng at 8 months old, received his first Christmas card from Santa Clause, a.k.a. Dad, on December 21, 1939. Forty-two years later, two years before Dad's death, James received the following birthday card. What more could a son want from a great father, who continues to be missed every day.

Vaughncille Joseph Meng Concert Hall

Recognition

An engraved brass name plate bearing the name

Jessie Frances Meng

has been placed on one of the seats in row M in the
Vaughncille Joseph Meng Concert Hall
in the Performing Arts Center at
California State University, Fullerton
a gift from
James and Beverly Meng
December 25, 2006

Vaughncille Joseph Meng Concert Hall

Recognition

An engraved brass name plate bearing the name

Edward John Meng

has been placed on one of the seats in row M in the
Vaughncille Joseph Meng Concert Hall
in the Performing Arts Center at
California State University, Fullerton
a gift from
James and Beverly Meng
December 25, 2006

CHAPTER 14
EDWARD SHAMHART MENG
SON OF EDWARD AND JESSIE MENG

Who Was Edward Shamhart Meng?
By James L. Meng (brother)

Edward S. Meng was six years older than I; consequently, his friends and my friends had different interests. We were not close. This was apparent with our likes and dislikes. I enjoyed scouts and all kinds of sports, etc.; he wanted nothing to do with these activities. This separation was also evident with the normal household chores, from doing the dishes to cutting and raking grass, to taking out the clinkers from our coal-fired furnace every spring. Some of these events were just an elder brother taking advantage of a younger brother. Right or wrong, I viewed his actions as being more than just an age difference. However, I also recognize that I could have been misinterpreting the relationship. Unfortunately, my many attempts at reconciliation all failed.

Edward enjoyed singing in the various choirs in high school and was a member of the a-capella choir in college. He was quite good. As he graduated from college in May 1957, I entered the same college in September. We were both in the same social fraternity.

In the 1950s, while in the US Army, he was stationed in Germany and drove a 2½-ton truck. His big purchase while in Germany was a 1935 Daimler Benz limousine that he bought from a hospital for $300 for back taxes. The car was in perfect condition and even had directional's. That is right, directional's on a 1935 car (we never got directional's in the US until 1950's) Ed also had the original owner's manual for his car written in German. This car was a true classic in every sense of the word. It had front side mounts for its spare tires, running lights, and big headlights with a metal bracket behind each light to hold a small German flag. Inside the car were black leather seats, a sliding glass window separating the front and back seats, fold down limo seats, pull down shades on all the rear window, cigar lighters. Edward's limo was the only registered 1935 Daimler Benz in the United States. He drove the car all over Germany and, on occasion, would put it on a flatbed railcar for transport to another country.

When the army brought the car to New York, he started driving to Granite City. However, he ran into some mechanical problems halfway home, so he bought an old LaSalle to tow the Benz. Unfortunately, Edward never kept the Benz in running condition. But that did not keep me from sneaking out in the LaSalle or Benz (when it was running) to do a little cruising.

He also bought a 9-mil German Luger pistol that had never been fired, with all matching numbers and swastikas. When I sold him my 1962 Studebaker Hawk at a very, very low price, he never paid me. I told him I would keep the Luger which I did.

Edward taught school in Granite City before he went to Southern California to buy a real estate company. He was quite successful in this endeavor Fro what I would hear, since I was away in college at this time, he was also a good teacher having his grade school students reading and reporting on stories in the Wall Street Journal.

Edward was, kind, generous and always viewed as very intelligent, as evidenced by receiving good grades throughout school. I always hated it when my teachers would say, "Jim, why don't you get good grades like your brother?" I never had a reply. Edward Shamhart Meng was a good man! He was born on June 19, 1933 in Granite City and died on September 14, 1989 in South Carolina. He was cremated at his request and buried at the foot of his mother

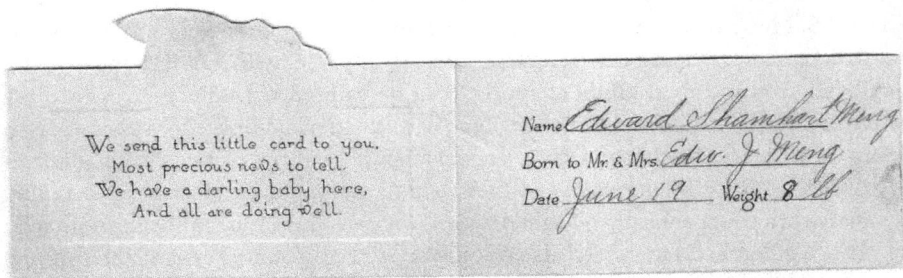

We send this little card to you.
Most precious news to tell.
We have a darling baby here,
And all are doing well.

Name Edward Shamhart Meng
Born to Mr. & Mrs. Edw. J. Meng
Date June 19   Weight 8 lb

1951

Edward Shamhart Meng, eldest son of Edward J. and Jessie F. Meng.

Certificate of Membership

Edward Shamhart Meng II

Phi Mu Alpha

Sinfonia Fraternity

of America

Beta Mu

March 8, 1952

Chapter

National President

National Secretary

Chapter President

By Press-Record Staff Photographer.
INDUCTED INTO THE ARMY yesterday, six Quad-Cityans are shown at the Edwardsville selective service office. Kneeling, left to right, are Edward Takmajian, Edward Koonce and Neil Winters, and standing, left to right, are Ed Meng, Horst Quante and Ronald Awalt. aug 12-53

Honorable Discharge

from the Armed Forces of the United States of America

This is to certify that

PFC MENG EDWARD S   ER55427771   AT-USAR

was Honorably Discharged from the

Army of the United States

on the 31 day of AUG 1961 This certificate is awarded
as a testimonial of Honest and Faithful Service

R. L. WADE
CAPT   TC

Jim, Dad, and Edward standing in front of Edward's Mercedes at Central College. Both James and Edward graduated from Central College.

The Edward J. Meng family at Christmas. Jessie in the background, Edward J., Edward S. and James L. Meng.

CENTRAL COLLEGE A CAPELLA CHOIR of Fayette, Mo., which will present a program of music here at 8 p. m. Saturday in the Niedringhaus Memorial Church. The choir of 41 mixed voices is under the direction of Dean Luther T. Spayde of the Swinney Conservatory of Music at the college. It will present a concert of classical, modern and spiritual numbers.

DEAN LUTHER T. SPAYDE, widely known organist and choral director who organized the choir in 1932 and has been its conductor ever since.

Central College Choir To Give Program Saturday

The 41-voice Central College A Cappela choir will present a program at 8 p.m. Saturday in the Niedringhaus Memorial Church under the direction of Dean Luther T. Spayde of the Swinney Conservatory of Music at Central College, Fayette, Mo.

A member of the choir is Tenor Edward Meng jr., son of Mr. and Mrs. Edward J. Meng, 2624 Madison avenue.

The choir, which is making its second appearance here in four years, has been recognized for its balanced interpretation of a widely-varying concert repertoire. The concert is designed to please all and includes classical, modern and spiritual numbers.

For the first time the choir will present the women and the men as separate choral groups. One of the featured numbers by the women's chorus will be "The Lord's Prayer" by Malotte. "The Prodigal Son," taken from James Weldon Johnson's "God's Trombones," and set to music in a contemporary style by Robert Elmore will be sung by the male chorus.

The appearance of the choir here will be its only performance in this state. There will be no admission charge, but a good will offering will be taken to defray the expenses of the choir.

1951 THE CENTRAL COLLEGE A CAPELLA CHOIR, directed by Prof. Luther T. Spayde, began its new year Sunday, Sept. 23, at the Paul H. Linn Memorial Methodist church, participating in the morning worship service there.

PRINT	LAST	FIRST	MIDDLE	
FULL NAME	MENG	EDWARD	S. (only)	
LEGAL ADDRESS			CODE	

THIS IS YOUR IDENTIFICATION CARD. KEEP IT.

2624 MADISON AVE

CITY OR TOWN	ZONE	TOWNSHIP	COUNTY	
GRANITE CITY		GRANITE CITY	MADISON	ILL.

NAME OF CAR	YEAR MODEL	BODY STYLE	NO. CYL	HORSE POWER
DAIMLER BENZ	1935	4 Dr. Sedan	6	23

FACTORY OR SERIAL NO.

101617138

IDENTIFICATION CARD

WRITTEN SIGNATURE of Owner _ Edward S. Meng

STATE OF ILLINOIS
CHARLES F. CARPENTIER, Secretary of State
This license expires Dec. 31, 1959

1959

Edward S. Meng's 1935 Daimler Benz. A grass fire from a locomotive traveled about one mile, got under the car and burned it up. Totaled. Edward purchased this car in Germany, while in the army, for $300 for taxes from a hospital who owed back taxes. It was the only registered 1935 limousine in the United States. A complete total with no insurance—-what a major tragedy!

345

SHIELDS REAL ESTATE NAME DROPS LAST 'S'
Granite City PRESS-RECORD Monday, June 2, 1975

LAGUNA BEACH - On May 1 a well-known Laguna Beach real estate firm underwent a minor name change and a major organizational change.

Shields Real Estate became Shield Real Estate, Inc., and its new owners Edward Meng and Hermes Serrano, took over. Richard Martin is vice president of the new setup.

Meng is the operating Broker of the corporation. He came to Shields Real Estate in 1974 after beginning his real estate career with Art Leitch Realtors in San Diego four years ago. A graduate of Central Methodist College, Fayette, Missouri, he taught elementary school for five years and was a textbook publisher's representative.

Hermes Serrano, new secretary-treasurer for Shield Real Estate, holds a masters degree from the University of New York. He was an instructor at the University in Bogota, Columbia.

Marie Thomas has been appointed office manager. She came to Laguna in 1967 from Buffalo, New York via Las Vegas. She has been active in Real Estate for nearly three years. Thomas has devoted much time to fund-raising projects for South County Community Hospital and she served as president of the Silver and Gold Chapter of the Auxiliary. For the past four years she has been cochairman of St. Catherines-St. Nicholas School Bus Transportation.

Mrs. Thomas has just been awarded an honorary membership in the Laguna Beach Museum of Art. She is also a member of the Mater Dei High School Parents Guild and of the Special Activities Committee for the Laguna Beach Board of Realtors.

NEW PRESIDENT. Edward S. Meng, son of Mr. md Mrs. Edward J. Meng of 2624 Madison Ave., has been elected president of Shield Real Estate, Inc., at Laguna Beach, Calif. Meng graduated from Granite City High School in June 1951 and received his B.A. degree from Central Methodist College, Fayette, Mo., in 1957. He is a former elementary teacher in Granite City and Los Angeles. Meng has been in California real estate for three years, beginning his career in San Diego. In March 1974 he joined Shields in Laguna Beach, an art colony of 15,000 population on the Pacific Ocean 50 miles south of Los Angeles, where the average price of a home is $88,000. Meng's partner is Hermes Serrano, a native of Colombia, South America, and a former instructor of Los Angeles University in Bogota.

346

A NEW SHIELD — Edward Meng and Marie Thomas erect a new shield symbolic of the name-change for a well-known Laguna Beach real estate firm. Effective May 1, Shields Real Estate became Shield Real Estate, Inc. Weng is co-owner and president of the recently re-organized firm. Hermes Serrano is the other owner, and Richard Martin back — —

EDWARD MENG
ENTERTAINS SCHOOLMA—

Edward Meng, a son of Assi—
nt Postmaster and Mrs. Edward
. Meng, 2624 Madison averue,
ho is studying for his masters
egree at the University of Mis-
ouri, was at home for the
hanksgiving holidays accom-
anied by two fellow studer ts,
akhruddin Abdulhadi, of Da-
iascus, Syria, and Wing Lam of
ong Kong, China, both mem-
rs of International House
here Meng is president.
While here the visitors toured
e local steel plants and other
aces of interest in the area.
m is doing post graduate work
the university and Abdulhadi
a student in the School of En—

NEW YEAR'S EVE PARTY
OR FRATERNITY

Pvt. Edward S. Meng who ha
just completed basic training a
Camp Kilmer, N. J., and is a
home for a visit with his parents
Mr. and Mrs. Edward J. Men
2624 Madison avenue, before leav
ing for overseas duty, was hos
New Year's Eve at a party for Al
pha Phi Gamma social fraternit
of Central College at Fayette
Mo., where he was a student fo
two years.
Among those present were Sam
Barco of Faye te, formerly of this
city; Miss Dorna Littrell of Men
don, Mo.; Tom Kauffman o
Thayer, Mo.; Miss Jerue Yoder o
Webster Groves, Mo., fraternit
sweetheart; Relton Spotts of th
city a past president of the frat
ernity, and several additiona
guests. The latter were Miss Joan
Bofinger of Maplewood, Miss Lyn
Munger, Normandy, Mo.; Wayn
Bloomquist and Bob Wilson o
Granite City.
The evening was spent dancin
and a late supper was served t—

347

BURIAL – REMOVAL – TRANSIT PERMIT
and
DEATH NOTIFICATION

31763
PERMIT NUMBER

SOUTH CAROLINA
DEPT. OF HEALTH and ENV'. CONTROL
OFFICE OF VITAL RECORDS AND PUBLIC HEALTH STATISTICS

RICHLAND
COUNTY

Death Certificate Attached ☒Yes ☐ No

Name of Deceased	Date of Death	Hour of Death	Fetal Death
EDWARD S. MENG	Sept. 14,1989	7:03A.M.	☐ Yes ☒No

Place of Death (Hospital or Street & Number)	City or Town	If Hospital Death	
VAH, COLA,SC	COLUMBIA	☐ D.O.A. ☒ In-Patient ☐ Emer. Rm. ☐ Out-Patient	

Attending Physician, Med. Exam or Coroner	Address	Autopsy	Coroner/Medical Examiner Notified
R..M. CHAPMAN,M.D.	COLUMBIA, SC	☐ Yes ☒ No	☐ Yes ☒ No

Funeral Home First Assuming Custody of Body

Name DUNBAR FUNERAL HOME Address COLUMBIA, SC Phone

Name and Address of Funeral Home Handling Final Disposition if other than Funeral Home Named Above

Permission is hereby granted to remove this body and upon compliance with the requirements of the laws of this state to dispose of the remains. If disposal is by cremation or burial at sea, a certified copy of the death certificate and, when required by law, an authorization by the medical examiner must be attached to this permit prior to disposition.

Michael Ratcliff
MICHAEL W. RATCLIFF   9-14-89

Signature of Registrar or other authorized issuing officer	Date Issued	Name and Address of Cemetery or Crematory
Date of Disposition		Signature of Sexton or Person in Charge

DHEC Form 076 (Rev. 10/86)   THIS COPY FOR FUNERAL DIRECTOR

CERTIFICATE OF CREMATION

September 15 , 19 89

This is To Certify That The Remains Of   Edward Shamhart Meng

Have This Day Been Cremated At Dunbar Crematory Services, Inc. Subject To Its Rules Or Regulations And All Legal Requirements.

By _____

Dunbar Crematory Services, Inc.
1527 Gervais Street
Columbia, South Carolina 29201
Telephone (803) 771-7990

Vaughncille Joseph Meng

Concert Hall

Recognition

An engraved brass name plate bearing the name

Edward Shamhart Meng

has been placed on one of the seats in row M in the
Vaughncille Joseph Meng Concert Hall
in the Performing Arts Center at
California State University, Fullerton
a gift from
James and Beverly Meng
December 25, 2006

CHAPTER 15
JAMES L. AND BEVERLY A. NEE LEWIS MENG
SON OF EDWARD AND JESSIE MENG

James L. Meng's Early Life Influences

The Influences of Granite City While Growing Up and Later in Life

Included in this exercise are memories of growing up in the 1940s and 1950s in the blue-collar steel town of Granite City, Illinois. These events included World War II ending, ration stamps, stay-at-home moms, radio serials and introduction of TV, flattops, polio, rock and roll music, etc. This was, without a doubt, the best possible time to be a child and to be molded into an adult.

It seems as if all the residents of Granite City (except my dad, who worked in the post office) worked in the steel industry, including myself. Granite City Steel, A. O. Smith, General Steel Industries, Laclede Steel, American Steel, and supporting industries all flourished. These companies were also good civic partners.

My friends and neighbors in Granite City were from all economic levels, all the product of solid American families. For example, my wife's dad was not only a proud family man but a proud welder, retiring from General Steel Industries in Granite. Many of my friend's parents had a strong foreign accent, but no one cared. Some of my friends lived in Lincoln Place, a foreign part of town, while others lived on Twenty-Seventh Street across from Wilson Park, a higher economic part of town, but again, no one cared. I was certainly blessed going from kindergarten through high school with the same friends and neighbors of Granite. Every morning in school, we all stood and said the pledge of allegiance to the American flag before school began and also said a group prayer before every football game. Those were standard practices, the same as playing and singing and standing for the national anthem with your hand over your heart before all major events.

Our childhood activities included Cub Scouts, toy trains, Boy Scouts, swimming at Wilson Park (a great city park), DeMolays, Junior Achievement, HS athletics, band or choral concerts, school plays or Gilbert and Sullivan operettas, Christmas caroling, proms, riding the Illinois Terminal streetcar to St. Louis to go shopping in St. Louis, family gatherings, the annual school boat on the S.S. Admiral etc. On Friday nights, it was Teen Town at the YMCA with an occasional sock hop in Granite and Madison Teen Town on Saturdays. In the summer months, it was the Wilson Park swimming pool pavilion every night and ROCA on Wednesday nights.

On dates, we went to the "show" at The Washington, The City, and The KEN theaters in Granite and The Fox, The Missouri, The Lowes State, The Ambassador, etc., in St. Louis, in a coat and tie making sure the guy walked near the curb. Why, we did not know just that our parents told us to do that. We had pizza afterwards at Roses Italian Restaurant at Tenth and Franklin Avenue in St. Louis, hung out at Tony's Pizza place on Collinsville Road, and occasionally watched submarine races at the Chain of Rocks canal!

There were parades down Madison Avenue (right in front of my house) every Memorial Day, Fourth of July, and Labor Day with bands, marching US Army soldiers and equipment, Shriners riding horses, driving funny cars, clowns acting silly, Amvets, the Black Knights (an excellent DeMolay drum and bugle corps from Belleville, Il.), a variety of other marching organizations and floats which threw out candy to us kids, even convertibles with pretty girls. It was a Norman Rockwell type of town, only with a touch of steel and the smell of "the Coke Plant" in the air. One of my friends, Sarki Nighohossian lived in Lincoln Place. He was of Armenian heritage. His parents owned Sammy's Tavern which had its walls painted pink and power blue. The customers would sit at their small tables, drinking their beverages and speak in a variety of foreign languages. I had no way of knowing what they were saying but they seemed very happy. Sarki was in our wedding and became a scientist and while his brother, Casper, became a lawyer. It seemed that regardless of ones economic status or ability to speak proper English, all strived to be successful in their chosen endeavors and raise successful families.

According to the May 8, 2014 St. Louis Post Dispatch, Hollywood may produce a movie of one of the former 1940's Lincoln Place residents named Andy Phillips. Andy led the G.C.H.S. and the University of Illinois basketball teams to State and National Championships. Andy went on to play in the NBA and entered the N.B.A. Basketball Hall of Fame. The title of the movie is said to be The Boys of Lincoln Place. William Hurt and Sally Field are reported to star in this movie.

One life time friend from kindergarten through high school was Allan Wolff, who became a prominent medical doctor in Chicago. His parents, Harry and Ann Wolff, operated the National Automobile Supply store in town and were like an additional set of parents. Another good friend in high school was Jim O'Master. He was also our best man in our wedding. We were both on the football team while in the spring, I participated in track and Jim was a catcher and co captain on a championship baseball team. Unfotunately, Jim, now a Purchasing Agent with a major steel co. died at 33 years of age of a heart attack. Jim was so good that he was offered a tryout with the Pittsburg Pirates professional baseball team. The other co captain on Jim's team was Dal Maxville. Dal went on to play shortstop for the World Champion, St Louis Cardinal Baseball team winning a Gold Glove for his efforts. He then became The Cardinal's General Manger. Both Jim O'Master and Dal Maxville also had the accurate high school reputations of being very nice guys, which they were.

There were also many other notable alumni of Granite City, included but not limited to: John Bischoff, catcher for the Chicago White Sox; Harry Boyles, pitcher for the Chicago White Sox; Owen Friend second baseman for the St Louis Browns; Andrew Goodpaster, former Supreme Allied Commander and four star U. S. Army General; Kevin Green, former N. F. L. linebacker; Ruben Mendoza two time world cup team member; Ralph Smith Senator etc. The G.C.H.S. soccer teams won 11 state championships between 1972 and 2011 while the schools wrestling team was state co-champions in 1965 and has won more duel meets than any other team in America.

In addition to all the successful athletics, many Granite City alumni were also very successful in other fields. For example, Gib Singleton became a world famous sculpture noted for his bronze cross that he sculptured for Pope John II, crosier. His cross is included in the permanent collection in the Vatican while his other sculptures are on display in the Cowboy Hall of Fame. My classmates from kindergarten through high school were also successful. One became a Circuit and Administrative Judge in St. Louis while others became Teachers; School Administrators; Medical Doctors; Nurses; Military Professionals; Coaches; Lawyers; Steel Company executives; various Journeymen in Industry and Business Owners. One friend bought/operated a major winery in Missouri. A Vice president of a major steel company married one of my kindergarten classmates, while another kindergarten classmate became the lawyer representing the Freda Meng/ Bennington's estate. These were the same people and others to numerous to mention, that I was fortunate to know, go to school and socialize with while growing up in Granite City, Illinois.

It should be also noted that Granite City was appropriately awarded the National Civic Leagues All-American City Award in 1958 for outstanding civic accomplishments. I firmly believe that people like my parents, my heroes, Jessie and Edward J. Meng, referenced earlier in chapter 13, were major contributors to this tribute.

What high school did you go to?

I have since moved to St. Louis, were just like other communities accross the nation, has its own local customs and preferred foods. In the St. Louis area, it is common to BBQ pork steaks and bratwurst, eat Gooey Butter cakes and deep fried, breaded, beef Ravioli and then ask that all encompassing, very, very important question, "What high school did you go to?" It's a very important unique St. Louis Question.

Your answer will determine the inquisitor your economic background, social status, and whether or not you are allowed to even have children! When I proudly answer Granite City, I can see their uninformed minds analyzing my answer as if to say "you poor guy." Well, if they could read my mind, knowing what I know of my past life in Granite City, they would certainly not appreciate my appropriate reply.

Again, I am including the above history to show the times that many in my referenced generation experienced and were ultimately influenced in later life. I know I was influenced, being very thankful of the lessons learned and friends known in Granite City, Illinois.

~ Kindergarten in Granite City, IL.1945 ~

The recital program from Bessie Morgan Reese's kindergarten class of June 1945 in which James L. Meng started his formal education. This event illustrates one of the advantages of growing up in a smaller town (45,000). Many of the kids you met and went to school with as early as kindergarten became your classmates and friends all the way through high school and life. One kindergarten classmate became my fraternity brother in college while another friend turned out to be my future wife's cousin. Note the patriotic readings and songs in the program including the program's close with the entire ensemble and audience singing God Bless America! Incidentally, the first kindergarten in America was established in St. Louis, MO. by German immigrants.

```
                    R E C I T A L

                    By Pupils of

                BESSIE  MORGAN  REESE

Central Auditorium          -   -           June 12, 1945 - 8:00P.M.

                     PART ONE

            PLAYLET - AN AFTERNOON TEA.

                    Characters

        Mrs. Bland     -   Helen Roseman
        Mrs. Monger    -   Dora Marie Hilliard
        Miss Butterwort-   ElDonna Oyler
        Mrs. True      -   Peggy Daugherty
        Miss Prim      -   Betty Stoecklin
        Red Cross Nurse -  Marilyn Francis
        Boy Scouts -  Thane Earny - Earl Branding

                    PROGRAM

Let's Remember Pearl Harbor )
When The Lights Go On Again  )  -   -   -   -   Junior Group
Reading - "The Lost Ponny"   -   -   -   -  Peggy Daugherty
Carolina Moon    -   -   -   -   -   -  Suzanne Mainor

Songs My Mother Taught Me  - D'Vorak   -   -   Senior Group

Reading - "A Little Girl Goes To Market"   -   -   Betty Stoocklin
I Passed By Your Window - Braho    -    -   -  Thane Earny
Blue Birds Over The White Cliffs of Dover"  Kont -  Entire Group

Reading  "Uncle Tom's Cabin"  -   -   -   El Donna Oyler
O What a Beautiful Morning - -  -  "Oklahoma"  -  Junior Group
I Had A Little Talk With the Lord -  "Mezzy"  -  -  Holen Roseman
Reading - " A Soldier Speaks"  -.  -   -   -  Earl Branding
Coming in On A Wing and a Prayor  -  McHugh   Helen Roseman and Entire Group
```

354

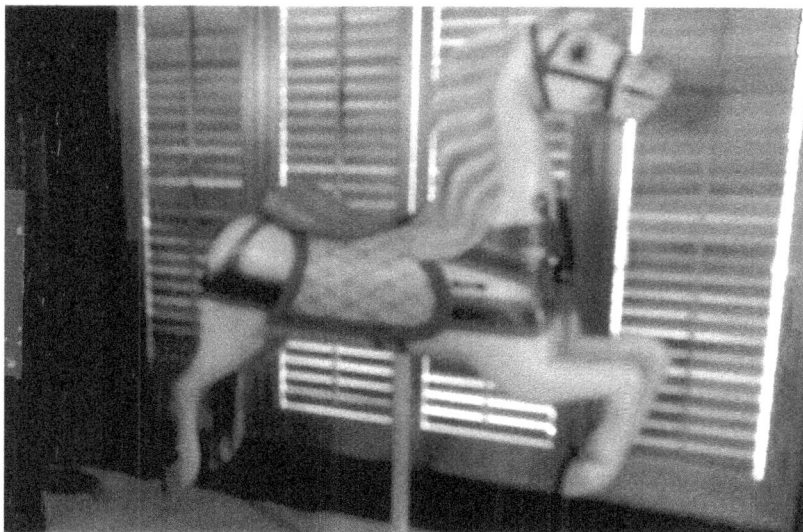

One of two "Dare" made carousel horses bought by Ed and Jessie Meng in the early 1950s when a traveling carnival went broke in Pontoon Beach, Illinois. Total cost for both horses was $15.00. It is hand carved by German and Italian immigrants, etc., made in the late 1880s before carousel horses went up and down (a "Dare" carousel horse has a real horse hair tail, an eagle saddle, and glass eyes with a cherub face). It is willed to Heather Meng.

It was ridden by Jim Meng and friends in basement of Madison Avenue home while playing Cowboys and Indians. The horse was refinished by Judy and Carlos Sardina. A second horse belonged to Edward S. Meng, who donated the horse to a church.

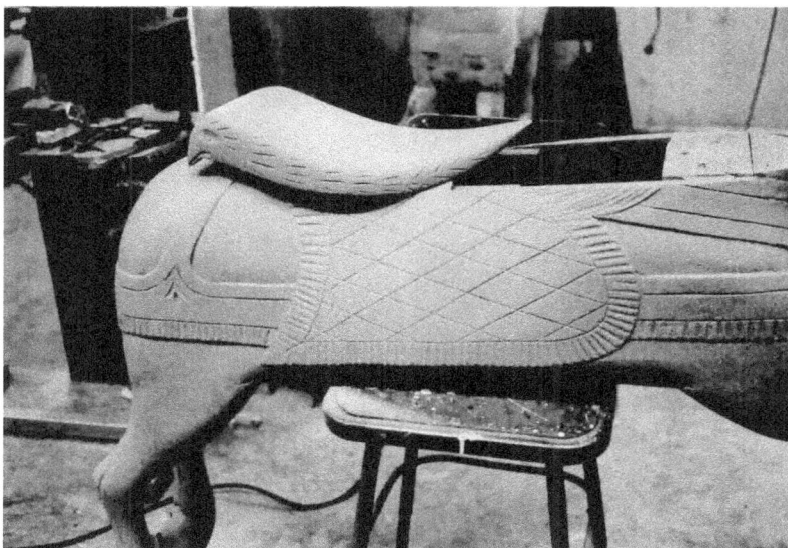

MEMBERS OF THE JUNIOR GROUP: Gloria Evans, Joan Foote, Judith Hogg, Eddie Koch, Carol Henson, Julia Maples, James Mong, Tony Miller, Linda Mozier, Carol Oonk, Nancy Lowell, Judy Stainton, Ernest Stainton, Cleon Statton, Dennis Slate, Phylis Streheide, Susan Walters.

PART TWO. - PIANO

The Shoemaker	Old Dance Tune	Shiela Holt
Drifting	Williams	Carolyn Kent
Floral Parade	Martin	Martha Gribben
Idle Moments	Lichner	Patsy Hawks
Melody	F.Thome	Patsy Lee Townsend
Etholinda	Greenwald	Helen Roseman
Dolls Dream	Oesten	Carol Johnson
The Bells	Williams	Betty Ruth Denley
Sweet Kiss - Polka	Kinkel	Norma Jean Jachino
Waltz	Gurlitt	Shirley Foote
*** The Brook	Holst	Joannine Roman
LaCzarine	Ganne	Patsy Mahon
Rose Fay	Hoins	Patsy Strole
The Fountain	Bohm	Marian Detmer
Romance Paroles	Streabog	Shirley Harshany
Glide	Vanderbeck	Myra Tapp
Nightingales Trill	Fischer	Dora Marie Hilliard
Fuer Elise	Beethoven	Barbara Mathews
Butterfly	Lege	Ruth Lovett
Butterfly	Merkel	Billy Smith
La Cascade	Hoins	Gerald Harshany
Pomponnette	Durand	Joan Hawks
Idilio	Lack	Betty Bea Hedaller
Valse Arabesque	Lack	Lois Johnson
Polish Dance	Scharwenka	James Wade
A La Bien Aimee	Schutt	Dorothy Lou Buenger
Duet - Qui Vive	Ganz	}Dorothy L. Buenger }Bessie Morgan Reese

God Bless America - Entire Ensemble and Audience.

*** Gertrudes Waltz - Beethoven - Rudolph Martin

Jim Meng
My New Friend in the Philippines (1947)

When I was seven years old, we had C.A.R.E. boxes located in my school, Webster Grade School, in Granite City, Illinois. The small personalized boxes were placed in the window of our classroom. Our teacher asked us to bring personal supplies to send to the people of the Philippines who were recovering from the ravages of World War II. My mom slipped my name and address inside the wrapper of a bar of Palmolive soap.

I then received the following letter from an appreciative family in the Philippines who had found my mom's note. I corresponded for several years with Ena; then my mom corresponded for several more years with Maura. We subsequently lost contact.

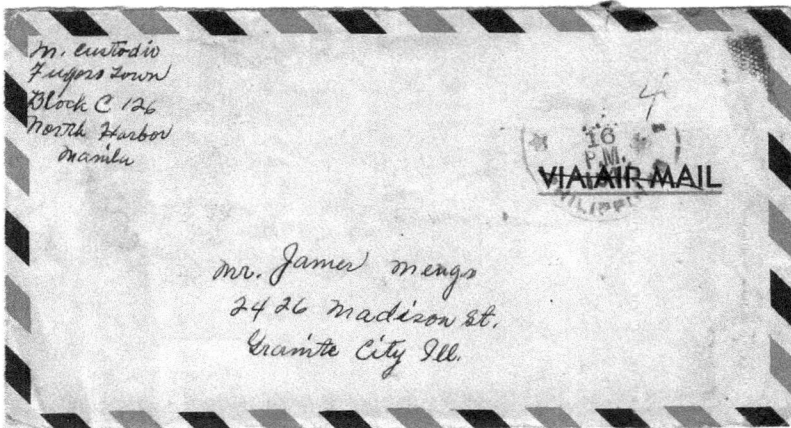

A parent's lesson to a child that there are other children, countries, and cultures in the world.

Manila P.I.
Mar. 30, 1947

Hello Mrs. Meng,

Perhaps you will be surprise to recieve a letter from an unknown friend. I am Maura Custodio of Manila. I am five feet high, brown complexion my favorite hobbies are reading stories such as true romance and holly wood screen.

During the deleberation I was in the province of Leyte. Later on I come to Manila to look for some works. To tell you frankly Mrs. Meng, I have two kids both girls. One is seven yrs. old. The other is almost one year and three month.

Mrs. Meng, I want to hear news from a distant place. How would you like to exchange words of friendship among us.

Lastly Mrs. Meng, I will end my stories now. I extend my best regards to you and your family.

I hope to hear your sweet reply soon.

Your new friend,
Maura

P.S. I am the mother of Ema a seven yrs. old girl who wants to be a pen pal of your boy.

Manila, P.I.
Mar. 30, 1947

Hello James,

I hope you will recieve my short letter.

I am Ena Custodio of manila who wants to be a pen pal. I have a friend who happen to introduce you to me, and I was glad to know your name even thow I have never written to you.

I am a mere first grade pupil only, and I dont know yet how to write. You supposed to excuse me of writing a few sentence.

My mother is the one who has written for me. You know a first grade can't write yet.

Lastly James, I want to hear your sweet reply very soon. Please give this letter to your mama. Thanks.

Your new friend,
Ena

Webster Grade School, Granite City, Illinois.

1946

1947

1948

1949

1951

High School. Granite City, Ill.

The Granite City High School pictured above in the 1920s became Central Junior High School (seventh and eighth grades). James Meng attended this Junior High in 1952-1953. However, the school has since been torn down.

Central Junior High School, Granite City, Illinois.

1952

1953

Boy Scouts of America

I started in scouting as a Cub Scout under the leadership of my mom, Jessie Meng. After Cub Scouts, I joined Troop 6 located at the Lutheran Church in Granite City, where I reached the rank of "star." Having interest in the American Indian, I then joined Post 48 in Collinsville, Illinois, which was exclusively involved in Indian lore. Post 48 was led by an exceptional leader, Mr. Frank Acardi. Mr Arcardi was a man that we all admired.

Post 48 copied Indian dances and performed in various parades, the Illinois State Fair, school and church functions, and in an Indian ceremonial conducted each spring. Our troop was also on local TV, specifically NBC's local affiliate channel 5. We were on the Charlotte Peters Show. As a member of this troop, we made our own costumes involving beadwork, headdresses, and copied the various Indian dances like the devil dance, eagle dance, snake dances, etc. These dances were exact copies of the Plains Indians in North America. Just prior to me joining Post 48, a former member became Chief Illiniwek, the mascot and official symbol of the University of Illinois.

Each summer, Post 48 would drive our own converted stretch limousine to Colorado and other destinations in the American West. We would visit La Junta, Colorado, each year to practice with the Koshare Indians, another scout organization, only with a much larger budget and full city support. The Koshare organization was very well known, large enough to travel and perform in Europe and on many college campuses in the United States. They had their own personal Greyhound type, air conditioned bus!

When traveling, we slept in "pup tents" and cooked our own meals. We would travel to all, and I mean all, the federal parks in the west. One day in 1953, my mom asked me if I wanted to use my savings from my postal savings account to help pay for a trip to their annual national jamboree in California. I said yes, so off we went on a six-week journey. I was 14 years old at the time. We traveled to Rapid City, South Dakota, and performed with the Sioux Indians in their ceremonials. The Sioux Indians were very proud of their heritage and were gracious host. We felt honored to be with them as they taught us their customs. We traveled to the states of Montana, Washington, Idaho, California, New Mexico, Colorado, and Nevada sleeping in pup tents in federal and state parks. While in Arizona at the Grand Canyon, we walked from the top of the north rim to the bottom, which wasn't that bad.

But walking back to the top of the canyon was a little different. Hot sun, at least 100 degrees, limited shade, numerous mule trains passing us on a dusty narrow canyon trail (from guided tours) passing gas and pooping every 20 steps as they slowly walked by wasn't cool. Of course, the warm water in our canteens that we drank was about 105 degrees which did not help. But we did it!

The jamboree was certainly different: 45,000 Boy Scouts from all over the world living in tents. There were movie stars everywhere, including Roy Rogers and Dale Evans, James Stewart, Dottie Lamore, Danny Kay, Lash La Rue, Bob Hope, Debbie Reynolds, Preston Foster, and even Mitzi Gaynor stopped by our tent and had lunch with us. She was exceptionally friendly and to a 14-year-old; very pretty.

President Dwight D. Eisenhower gave his greetings while Vice President Nixon was the convention speaker. There were pageants regarding how our country came to be, that is, Columbus, the Pilgrims, Valley Forge, Alamo, Spanish Conquistadors, etc. Every day, the flags of all the attending nations were raised and lowered to the sounds of scout drum and bugle corps. Even Scottish bagpipers were in dress and played frequently.

Our troop Post 48 was selected to perform Indian dances on national television, which made us quite proud. We were one of five Indian dance troops to be selected. Just prior to going on stage, a man grabbed my arm and said, "Hi, dog bones." It was Mr. Pershall from Tri City Grocery Company who would give me "dog bones" for my pet from behind the meat counter at their store on Twenty-Seventh and Madison Avenue in Granite City, and best, at no charge. I was glad to see him since he was a real friend and a friendly face from home.

I made my parents very happy when I came home with a "horned toad." I thought it was really neat. It was kept on our back porch in a washtub filled with sand. Then one day, it disappeared? My dad said a cat must have gotten it. I was never sure about the toad's demise; I think my dad just may have been the cat.

The entire scouting experience from Cub Scouts through the jamboree and beyond was an unforgettable experience. As I entered high school, I dropped scouting and moved onto other interests.

Boy Scout National Jamboree, Irvine Ranch Calif. 1953

Local contingent of Boy Scouts and leaders at the triennial International Boy Scout Jamboree, held at Irvine Ranch, 40 miles south of Los Angeles, within a mile of the Pacific Ocean.

Row one (sitting): Milford Simons, Collinsville; Ronald Foster, Glen Carbon; Gene Rinehardt, Granite City; James Kapp, Highland; Gerald Warren, Granite City; James Davis, Greenville; and Jack Spindler, Highland.

Row two (kneeling): *James Meng, Granite City*; Robert Lux, Madison; Leonard Zobrist, Highland; David Jenkins, Collinsville; Dale Cook, Collinsville; Jerry Hug, Highland.

Row three (standing): Robert Schutte, Collinsville; Vernon Deason, Collinsville; Jerry Adams, Collinsville; Howard Schutte, Collinsville; Marline Kreider, Collinsville; Carl Kreider, Collinsville; Wilmer Cook, scoutmaster of the combined "troop," Collinsville; Lyn Nash, Granite City; Fred Serfas, Edwardsville; Art Wetzel, assistant scoutmaster, Edwardsville; Richard Wiedey, Edwardsville; David Ochs, Edwardsville; Frank Acardi, assistant scoutmaster, Collinsville; Dick Pinkel, Collinsville; Thomas Gibbons, Edwardsville; Thomas Wetzel, Edwardsville; and Joel Connely, Greenville.

Explorer Scout Indian dancers who performed on Saturday before 500 persons in a jamboree program sponsored by the Granite City high school Parents' Club. (Front row, left to right): Don Rivenburg of Granite City, Bob Schuette, Don Allwell, Sunny Schoder, and Frank Acardi. (Second row): Richard Momphard and Ted Mussell of Granite City, Milford Simons, Larry Niepert, and James Meng of Granite City. (Third row): Gene Reinhardt and Bob Pope of Granite City, Carl Kreider, Jerry Adams, and David Jenkins.

Explorer Posts 48 Scouts in front of their "Stretch Limo" traveling all over the American west, sleeping in pup tents and cooking all their own meals. Trips occurred each summer, lasting anywhere from two weeks to six weeks in length. Activities included walking to the bottom of the Grand Canyon, the National Scout Jamboree in California, participating in ceremonies with the Sioux Indians in Rapid City and visiting all the National Parks in the west.

FORTY-FIVE THOUSAND BOY SCOUTS stood shoulder-to-shoulder Friday night at a huge outdoor pageant climaxing the first day of their National Jamboree at Irvine Ranch, Cal. Seven thousand Scouts took part in scenes depicting American historical incidents and then heard a transcribed message from President Eisenhower over loudspeakers.

Collinsville Scouts Stage Indian Dance at Jamboree

Denny Donnell Jr., of Green-ville, was the top Illinois win-ner in the Globe-Democrat Boy Scout Reporter Contest last spring. His award was an ex-pense-paid trip to the National Boy Scout Jamboree.

By DENNY DONNELL, JR.

IRVINE RANCH, CAL, July 18 —A group of Scouts from Collins-ville, Ill, put on an Indian dance in a variety show in one of the campfire arenas here last night.

Frank Azzidi of Collinsville was the leader.

Taking part in the dance were Carl Kreider, Milford Stiemke, Howard and Ron Schnette, Jerry Adams and David Junkins of Col-linsville, James Ming and Dave Reinhardt of Granite City, and Ronny Foster of Glen Carbon. They appeared on a television show tonight.

Fifty thousand Boy Scouts last night marched into the Arena to be welcomed by high Scout offi-cials and distinguished guests for the formal opening of the Jam-boree. Lanny Ross led in singing of camp songs.

The Scouts were entertained today with a show by Roy Rogers, cowboy movie star. When he stepped on the stage he hesitated one moment and then said he had never faced so many cameras be-fore in his life.

Roy then did some fancy shoot-ing and Dale Evans sang.

President Eisenhower by means of a recording gave a message of welcome to the assembled Scouts and assured them they would learn some important lessons in living from the Jamboree.

The opening proceedings began with a flag ceremony using 1200 flags, one from each troop en-camped in the Jamboree area.

NATIONAL JAMBOREE IRVINE RANCH CALIF. 1953 BOY SCOUTS OF AMERICA

TOUR GROUP NO.	SECTION NO.
733	36
TROOP NO.	COUNCIL NO.
26	128

HOME ADDRESS

NAME Cahokia Mound Council #128
STREET BOY SCOUTS OF AMERICA
1338a Niedringhaus Ave.
CITY Granite City, Illinois
STATE

367

The Lincoln Trail Hike

(EST. 1926)

Sponsored by

Abraham Lincoln Council Boy Scouts of America

Boy Scout Award

Scout James L. Meng, at 13 years old, walked 21 miles in one day from Salem, Illinois, to Springfield, Illinois, in Abraham Lincoln's footsteps, on August 13, 1952.

The Lincoln Trail Hike

In 1926, R. Allan Stephens, a former Scout commissioner of Springfield, Illinois, originated the idea of a Lincoln Trail Hike. At that time, there were no official Boy Scout trails in the United States. Mr. Stephens believed that Boy Scouts would acquire a greater appreciation of the obstacles Abraham Lincoln overcame in his rise to the presidency if they also walked the same 20-mile route followed by Lincoln from New Salem to Springfield…

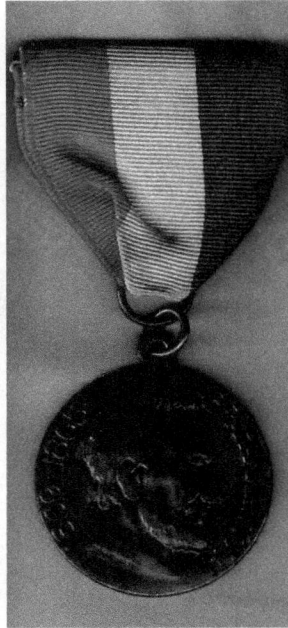

The Grand Council of the

Order of DeMolay

Greeting   Number 1189283

Know ye that Brother

JAMES LEROY MENG

Whose signature appears in the margin hereof, is a member of the Order of DeMolay, initiated by.

GRANITE CITY CHAPTER
GRANITE CITY, ILLINOIS

He is known and recognized by us, of our obedience and is entitled to be received and welcomed as such everywhere, having been invested with the degrees on the dates as indicated hereon, and attested by the signatures below.

Initiatory Degree   DeMolay Degree

November 3, 1953   December 1, 1953

Scribe   Master Councilor

Advisor from Advisory Council   Chairman Advisory Council

Issued by The Grand Council of the Order of DeMolay whose See is at Kansas City, in the State of Missouri, United States of America.

In Testimony Whereof, we have hereunto set our hands and caused the seal of the Grand Council to be affixed.

Secretary General   Grand Master

When 14 years old, James Meng joined the "Order of DeMolay." Interest in this Masonic organization continued on through memberships in Lodge 877 in Granite City, obtaining the thirty-second degree level in the consistory and a member of Ainad Temple AAONMS, Shrine.

369

October 19, 1954

In the October, 18, 1956 issue of Life magazine, the U.S. Masons were featured with the Granite City, Illinois Chapter of the Order of DeMolay on the magazine's cover. The cover picture showed the flower talk ceremony in a Granite City chapter meeting. Each candidate is given the motherhood talk where a flower is given. This talk is impressive. As I write this entry, I remember, after 56 years, just how appropriate it was. Both the De Molay's and Job's Daughter's, a young woman's Masonic order, are certainly very worthwhile organizations.

Supreme Council
Sovereign Grand Inspectors General

WHEREAS, the Supreme Council of the Ancient Accepted Scottish Rite for the Northern Masonic Jurisdiction of the United States of America is celebrating its 204th year; and

WHEREAS, he has faithfully adhered to the tenets of his profession as a Master Mason; and

WHEREAS, he has steadfastly adhered to the highest tenets of Scottish Rite Freemasonry and has demonstrated his devotion to the Rite; and

WHEREAS, he has devotedly maintained a patriotic affirmation in his duty to country; and

WHEREAS, he has faithfully maintained his membership in the Valley of Southern Illinois;

NOW, THEREFORE, I, John Wm. McNaughton, Sovereign Grand Commander, recognize

James L. Meng 32°
For his 50 Years of Membership

IN TESTIMONY WHEREOF, I HAVE HEREUNTO SET MY HAND AND CAUSED TO BE AFFIXED THE SEAL OF THE SUPREME COUNCIL ON THIS 31st DAY OF AUGUST IN THE YEAR 2016.

JOHN WM. MCNAUGHTON,
SOVEREIGN GRAND COMMANDER

Junior Achievement

The Junior Achievement organization was a big deal in high school. The purpose of the organization was to teach kids how to start up and run a business or a manufacturing organization. All the companies in the St. Louis metropolitan area would sponsor a specific miniature company that actually produced a service or product.

There was an annual ball with the crowning of a queen and her court. A Granite City girl, Murna Tucker, was crowned Queen. Dancing and entertainment followed including the popular 1950s singing group, "The Crew Cuts," and a visit by movie star Kirk Douglas, who autographed their pictures.

THE CREW-CUTS   Exclusiv
HIPPODROME BUILDING, CLEVELAND, OHIO

This is to certify that
James Meng
is an accredited member of
JUNIOR ACHIEVEMENT
and has earned the designation of
ADVANCED ACHIEVER

Jan 9, 1957
Date   Executive Director

THE CHRISTIAN CHURCH

At GRANITE CITY, IL

To the Christian Church, At_____Greeting:

THIS IS TO CERTIFY

That the bearer, JAMES MENG

is a member of this congregation and, having requested transfer of membership, is cordially commended to your Christian love and fellowship. BAPTIZED 12-2-56

By order of the Church, this_____day of_____19___

NOTE—The Church receiving the bearer of this letter is requested to notify us at once in order that our records may be completed.

Rev. V. Davis Ruthlege

THE BETHANY PRESS, ST. LOUIS, MO. 63166

RECOGNITION OF
PROMOTION
FOR

James Meng

TO 2nd YEAR WORK IN THE

Junior DEPARTMENT

IS HEREBY GIVEN.

Dolores M. Todd
DEPT. SUPT.

F. G. Gruen
GEN. SUPT.

Central Christian Church
SUNDAY SCHOOL

Mason Gregg
PASTOR

—Hoffmann

NO. 226 © 1941 THE BETHANY PRESS

PRINTED IN U.S.A.

Athletics

James L. Meng loved athletics, with repeated school letters in both football and track in high school and college. At that point in time in football, it was common to play "both ways," that is, the starters were expected to play both offense and defense. James was always on the first team, starting at right tackle when on offense and left tackle when the team was on defense. Of course, the same players were also expected to be on the kickoff and punt return teams. In short, players of that era never left the field except for halftime or the end of the game. In addition, up until 1956, no face guards were used and no energy drinks like Gatorade. James with the typical large Meng nose received three breaks, which resulted in rhinoplasty in 1970 to correct.

Another sport that was equally enjoyable was track and field, which had many of the football players from other schools participating. James lettered in the shot put or discus in both high school and college while adding the javelin at the college level. In this sport, you were able meet and talk to many of the same football players who were your adversaries in the fall.

Granite City, 1957, Southwestern Track and Field Champions

The Granite City track team won the southwestern track and field meet held in East St. Louis. The Southwestern Illinois Athletic Conference is composed of Granite City, East St. Louis, Alton, Edwardsville, Collinsville, Woodriver, and Bellville.

Track coach Jack Richardson (like football line coach Al Lewis) was an outstanding leader and adult role model for the team. Each day before going out to practice, the team would stop by the coach's office to pick up an individualized workout schedule tailored specifically to the needs of the individual. Richardson was a "class act."

Coach Richardson scheduled meets such as the Normal, Illinois, Invitational which had 61 entries (Granite won third place), the Maplewood, Missouri, relays with 31 Missouri and Illinois schools (Granite tied for first place), the East St. Louis relays with all the large schools from St. Louis and Eastern Illinois, (Granite took third place), the Madison County meet with all the schools from Madison County, Illinois (Granite took first place). The few duel and triangular meets that were scheduled were all won by Granite. The team had many good athletes, such as Joe Schroeder and Pete Roberson in the mile, Rich Kacera in the high jump, Tom Skubish in the pole vault, Sheridan Dutchik and Harry Basen anchoring all the relays, etc. Jim Meng won first place in the shot put at the Madison County meet, and second place in the SW conference meet. Jim Meng's nemesis, an All-American from Collinsville, Illinois named Tom Jackson, beat Jim in every head-to-head meeting in the shot and discus.

A few years later, Coach Richardson left GCHS to become the successful head track coach of Southern Illinois University in Carbondale, Illinois, where he coached several Olympic champions. We were a very good team with an excellent coach.

Fifty-year High School Class Reunion, 2004

Top: J. Meng, S. Dutchik, H. Basan, G. Crane, Coach and Mrs. Richardson, J. Schroeder, and P. Roberson.

Out of Shape and Breaking Training Rules
H. Basan, Coach Richardson, J. Meng, and G. Crane.

August 22, 2002
Dear Jim:

I thought I'd drop you a line to let you know how pleased I was to see you at the reunion. It doesn't seem possible that the great season you fellows made happen was 45 years ago. I have followed Granite City track via the St. Louis Post Dispatch. They have had several outstanding individuals but, I don't believe that any subsequent GCHS team has come close to achieving the team results that you fellows managed in 57. I coached track at S.I.U. after leaving Granite and I had some gifted atheletes who achieved national and international recognition, but I feel that coaching that 57 GCHS squad was my most satisfying accomplishment. You fellow were team oriented and willing to work hard.

It was a pleasure to be your coach—you fellows were and still are an important part of my life.

> Best Wishes
> Jack Richardson
> Granite City High School Track Coach, 1957

377

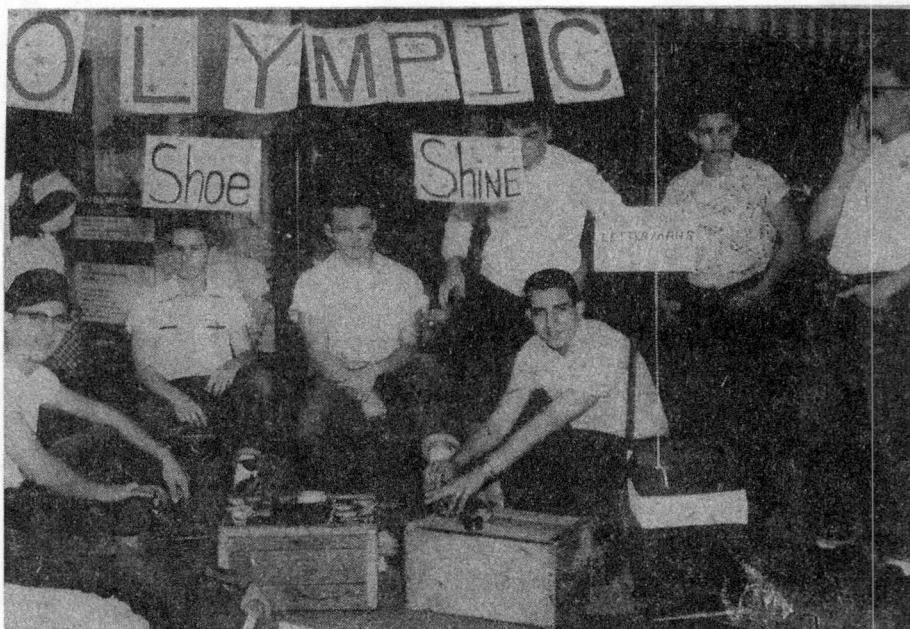

Meng and Sekora Named Linemen; Linhart and Hampton Named Backs of Week

John Sekora of Madison and Jim Meng of Granite City were selected as the linemen of the week on their school football teams, while Joe Linhart of Granite City and Charles Hampton of Madison were named as the backs of the week by their coaches.

Meng, a 195-pound senior tackle, was personally responsible for 16 of 22 yards lost by Pana ball carriers, as his top defensive play stymied Pana's scoring threats. He had a dozen tackles, leading the Pana coach to comment that he was one of the toughest tacklers that he had seen all season. The coach also noted that Meng had faced the strongest part of the Pana line.

He wasn't alone in consideration for the honor of the week as his coaches pointed out that teammate Harold Boyles also played an outstanding defensive game. Meng is in his fourth season on Warrior grid teams.

Linhart, a 165-pound senior quarterback, is in only his first year on the Warrior football team but he was promoted to first-string quarterback after showing steady signal calling and passing ability. One of his passes last Friday night, to end Jerry Wilson, helped set up a touchdown that enabled the Warriors to tie the Pana team.

   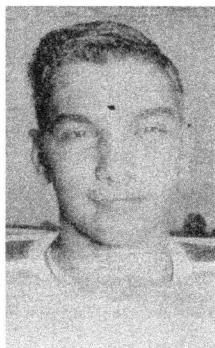

JOE LINHART   JIM MENG   CHARLES HAMPTON   JOHN SEKORA

When the football season ended, Jim was offered two football scholarships: one from Missouri Valley College in Marshall, Missouri (complements of Mr. James Steward, GCHS teacher and college scout), the other from Eastern Illinois University. a Division 1 school, in Charleston, Illinois. Although there was some interest in Missouri Valley, an immature, foolish decision was made to attend Central with all his friends and not to attend Eastern was one of Jim's few, regrettable decisions.

K. Parker, J. Fedora, A. Lewis, coaches.

(Row 1): S. Dutchik, R. Hutchings, R. Sigite, G. Davis, W. Baumeyer, C. Nighohossian, R. Wade, G. Crane, J. Meng, and J. Wilson. (Row 2): J. O'Master, S. Szadai, R. Ruppel, D. Wallace, D. Hall, R. Rich, J. Roberts, D. Slate, J. Bledsoe, C. Statton, H. Basan, and D. Kraus. (Row 3): N. Brokaw, P. Cline, E. Jackson, J. Linhart, B. Patrick, W. Puhse, W. Garrard, J. Lorentz, J. McClintock, A. Becerra, J. Donley, and G. Carstens. (Row 4): Coach Rice, L. Rider, T. Hughes, H. Thurau, E. Ford, R. Craycraft, R. Jachino, R. Mitchell, T. Sparks, J. Lybarger, R. Chapman, and C. Soliday. (Row 5): Coach Parker, Coach Lewis, D. Withers, J. Chepley, B. Oliver, L. Morgan, B. Chapman, E. Dickey, Coach Fedora, and Coach Richardson.

June 1957

FOOTBALL

(50 FT)

"The Stinky"

To a fine boy and a great prospecto to athlete your friend + coach Mr. Parker

R. Craycraft, J. Roberts, J. Bledsoe.

R. Sigite, J. Meng, G. Davis, G. Crane, R. Hutchings, J. O'Master, E. Jackson.

1958 Central College, Fayette, MO.

Granite City PRESS-RECORD
Thurs., Oct. 17, 1957

FORMER WARRIOR GRIDDERS now playing football with the
Central College team at Fayette, Mo. Posing with Head Coach Sam
Nakaso (right) and Assistant Coach Bob Brasher are Barry Gushleff
(left), son of Mr. and Mrs. William Gushleff, 3244 Carlson, and
Jim Meng, son of Mr. and Mrs. Edward J. Meng, 2624 Madison
avenue. Gushleff, a sophomore pre-medical student, is a 165-pound
end. Barry is a member of Alpha Phi Gamma social fraternity. At
Granite City high school he lettered three years in football, track and
wrestling. Meng, a freshman, is 6 feet, 1 inch, weighs 210 pounds and
is starting at tackle, the same position he played for the Warriors. He
also lettered in both football and in track here. His brother, Edward S.
Meng, an economics major, was graduated from Central in August.

381

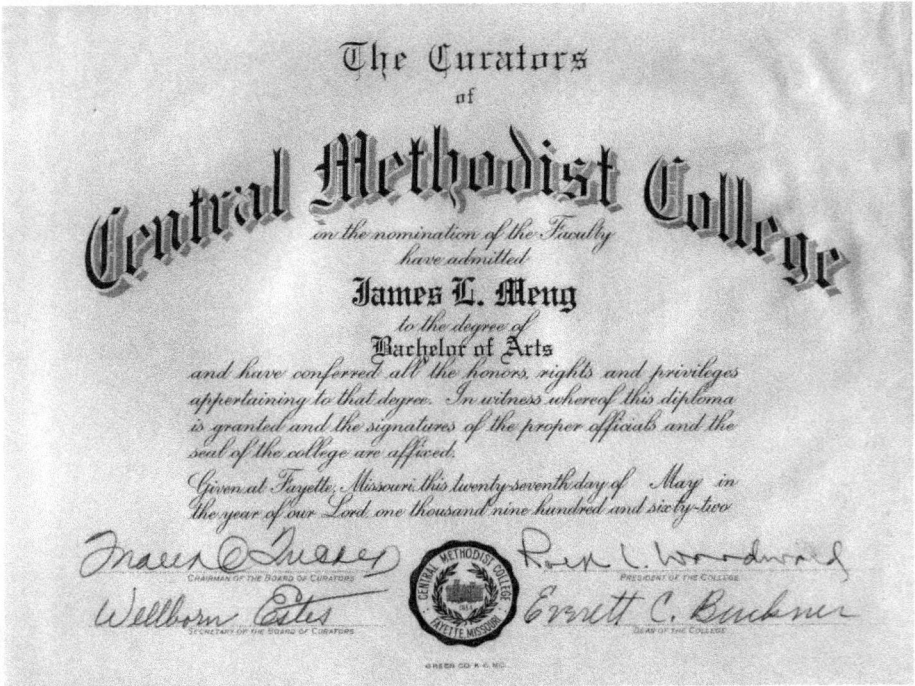

Now known as Central Methodist University.
Major: Business Administration. Minors: Chemistry and Economics.

Central Methodist University

Established	1854
Type	Private
Religious affiliation	United Methodist Church[1]
Endowment	31.4million[2]
President	Dr. Marianne E. Inman
Students	3,382[3]
Undergraduates	1,172 (Main Campus) 2,209 (Graduate and Extended Studies)[4]
Location	Fayette, Missouri, USA
Campus	Rural, 55 acres (22.3 ha)
Fonner names	Central Methodist College
Colors	Green and White
Athletics	HAAC (NAIA DI)
Nickname	Eagles
Website	http://www.centralmethodist.edu/

The Meng and Shamhart book is in the Smiley Memorial Library at C.M.U.

382

JAMES L. MENG IN THE MISSOURI AIR NATIONAL GUARD

North American F-100 Super Saber. The 110th Tactical Fighter Squadron received its first F-100 in September 1962 (Missouri National Guard Photo). For more images of the Super Saber F-100C in action with 110th Fighter Squadron, see the Missouri Air National Guard.

Upon graduation from college, it was time to serve my country. I joined the Missouri Air National Guard based at Lambert International Airport, St. Louis, Missouri. This is the same unit that Charles A. Lindbergh (Lucky Lindy) was a member. The obligation was for six years. The experience began in San Antonio, Texas, for basic training and continued to Amarillo, Texas, for Jet Engine Mechanics School one and two engines. Incidentally, Amarillo is not a pleasant part of our country. After graduating tech school, I was reassigned to my home base in St. Louis. It was peacetime although the Cuban missile crisis did occur while in basic training which could have started World War III.

We were required to attend a two-week summer camp at Volk Air Field located in Wisconsin every year. While in the Air Guard, I made several lifetime friends which I continue to have today. They are Jerry Van Deven, John Murphy, Jim Bledsoe, and Richard Brown. These same friends were in our wedding in 1969.

3377th School Squadron
3320th Technical School (ATC)
UNITED STATES AIR FORCE
Amarillo Air Force Base, Texas

REPLY TO   19 March 1963
ATTN OF: TS-T

SUBJECT: Letter of Appreciation

TO: A3C James L. Meng
      3377th School Squadron
      Amarillo Air Force Base, Texas

1. It gives me great pleasure to take this opportunity to express my
appreciation for the outstanding manner in which you performed your
duties while assigned to this organization.

2. During your assignment, you demonstrated your ability to lead, this
resulted in your being selected as a Flight Leader in support of the
Student Leadership Program. It was indeed gratifying to note your
willingness to accept additional responsibilities and the excellent
manner in which you performed these duties.

3. Your personal appearance and military bearing was outstanding and
you set an outstanding example for your men. You were responsible for
the morale, discipline and conduct of approximately 100 airmen and the
cleanliness and uniformity of their barracks and area.

4. You gave unstintingly of your time in improving the health and
welfare of your students and maintained excellent control at all times.
The job you performed, contributed materially, to the success of the
squadron operation and reflects most favorably on you as a potential
leader.

5. Again, I wish to commend you for your excellent performance of duty
while assigned to my squadron and I wish you well as you progress in
your Air Force career.

JAMES M. CUNNINGHAM
2ndLt, USAF
Commander

384

AIR TRAINING COMMAND

United States Air Force

To all to whom these presents shall come ... Greeting.
Whereas

A/3c James L. Meng AF 27538382

Is awarded this certificate for

Outstanding duty and performance as Student Leader

Whereupon, by virtue of authority, this recognition
is conferred this 20 th day of March   in the year of
our Lord one thousand nine hundred and sixty three

Rosco R. Garcia, 2nd Lt, USAF

Administrative Officer 3377 School Squadron

James M. Cunningham, 2nd Lt, USAF

COMMANDER 3377 th School Squadron

ATC FORM 154, AUG 62

AIRMAN JAMES MENG TO
GET MEDAL IN CEREMONY SUNDAY
Granite City PRESS-RECORD, Thursday, May 13, 1965

In special ceremonies at 1 p.m. Sunday at the Robertson Air National Guard Base, Lambert-St. Louis Municipal Airport, Airman Second Class James LeRoy Meng of Granite City will receive the Airman's Medal for exemplary courage and heroism in helping to avert a possible aircraft explosion last July.

A member of the Missouri Air National Guard, Meng, 26, is unmarried and resides with his parents, Mr. and Mrs. Edward Meng, 2624 Madison Avenue.

Lt. Col. Frank Crooks, commanding officer of the 131st Materiel Squadron, attached the 131st Tactical Fighter Wing, said the local serviceman and another enlisted aircrew member will receive the citations during the weekend training assembly.

The action in which Airman Meng distinguished himself involved voluntary risk of life at Volk Air National Guard Base, Wisconsin, on July 22, 1964. He was servicing the oxygen system of a T-33 aircraft when a fire was discovered in the area of the oxygen filler valve.

The citation reads in part "with complete disregard for his own safety, Airman Meng, despite the hazard of explosion, unhesitantly began extinguishing the fire while the oxygen servicing equipment was being removed from the aircraft. The exemplary courage and heroism displayed by Airman Meng reflect great credit upon himself and the United States Air Force."

Meng attended Granite City High School and received a Bachelor of Arts degree at Central Methodist College, Fayette, Missouri, in 1962. In June of the same year, he enlisted in the 239th Mobile Communications Flight, Missouri Air National Guard.

After basic military traing, Meng was selected to attend technical training school at Amarillo AFB, Texas, as an apprentice. He is currently employed at A.O. Smith Corporation.

One of those significant times in life where parents are rewarded by a son.

THE UNITED STATES OF AMERICA

TO ALL WHO SHALL SEE THESE PRESENTS, GREETING:

THIS IS TO CERTIFY THAT
THE PRESIDENT OF THE UNITED STATES OF AMERICA
AUTHORIZED BY ACT OF CONGRESS JULY 2, 1926
HAS AWARDED

THE AIRMAN'S MEDAL

TO

AIRMAN SECOND CLASS JAMES L. MENG
UNITED STATES AIR FORCE

FOR

HEROISM

AT VOLK AIR NATIONAL GUARD BASE, WISCONSIN ON 22 JULY 1964

GIVEN UNDER MY HAND IN THE CITY OF WASHINGTON
THIS   30TH   DAY OF   APRIL   1965

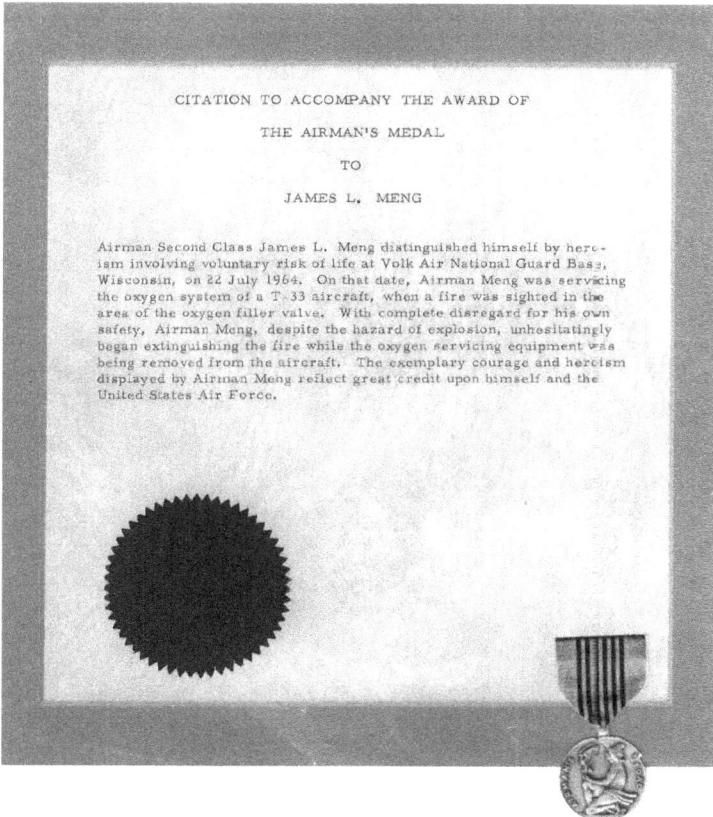

CITATION TO ACCOMPANY THE AWARD OF

THE AIRMAN'S MEDAL

TO

JAMES L. MENG

Airman Second Class James L. Meng distinguished himself by heroism involving voluntary risk of life at Volk Air National Guard Base,
Wisconsin, on 22 July 1964. On that date, Airman Meng was servicing
the oxygen system of a T-33 aircraft, when a fire was sighted in the
area of the oxygen filler valve. With complete disregard for his own
safety, Airman Meng, despite the hazard of explosion, unhesitatingly
began extinguishing the fire while the oxygen servicing equipment was
being removed from the aircraft. The exemplary courage and heroism
displayed by Airman Meng reflect great credit upon himself and the
United States Air Force.

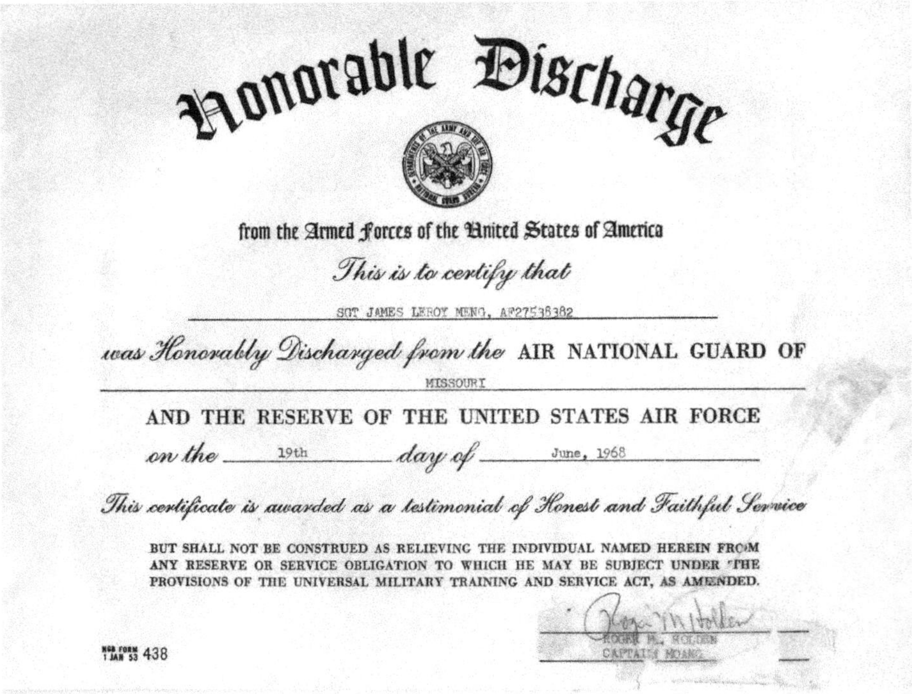

Honorable Discharge

from the Armed Forces of the United States of America

This is to certify that

SGT JAMES LEROY MENG, AF27538382

was Honorably Discharged from the AIR NATIONAL GUARD OF

MISSOURI

AND THE RESERVE OF THE UNITED STATES AIR FORCE

on the _____19th_____ day of _____June, 1968_____

This certificate is awarded as a testimonial of Honest and Faithful Service

BUT SHALL NOT BE CONSTRUED AS RELIEVING THE INDIVIDUAL NAMED HEREIN FROM
ANY RESERVE OR SERVICE OBLIGATION TO WHICH HE MAY BE SUBJECT UNDER THE
PROVISIONS OF THE UNIVERSAL MILITARY TRAINING AND SERVICE ACT, AS AMENDED.

ROGER M. HOLDEN
CAPTAIN MOANG

NGB FORM
1 JAN 53 438

Jim Meng's pre marriage activities.

Model "A" Ford that James Meng bought from Charlie and Mary Shamhart in 1958. Car was subsequently repainted by Fred Meng, was a great car for college, and was fun to drive had it not been for the plate glass, friction brakes, dim headlights, top heavy, and a gas tank sitting in your front lap!

Planned/scheduled Kodiak Bear hunt to Kodiak Island, Alaska and planned cross country flight to complete pilots licenses cancelled due to engagement?. Hey, where is my new Corvette convertable, 327, with 4 on the floor?

JAMES L. MENG AND BEVERLY A.
(NÉE LEWIS) MENG EARLY MARRIAGE

Jim and Bev met at the Starlight Room in the Chase Park Plaza Hotel, which is located on Kingshighway in St. Louis, Missouri, at a dance sponsored by the Collegiate Club. After a few dances, we adjourned to the rooftop terrace and talked about many things, that is, current events, life, etc. Several months of dating passed when Jim asked Bev if she wanted to get married. There was no reply. Another month goes by, and Jim asked her again to which she replied that she was not saying no but wanted to be sure, because she had just broken an engagement. More time goes by and she finally said yes.

At the time Jim was driving a new 1968 Corvette convertible, blue with a white top, 327 cu. in., four on the floor, etc. Between engagement and our honeymoon, Jim's Corvette was traded for a 1969 VW bug, which we drove to Monterrey, Mexico. Jim's former boss at A. O. Smith became plant manager of the plant in Monterrey. Consequently, he took care of us and paid for our Hotel Ancira, including troubadours beneath our window. On the return trip, we had no money except a Phillip's gas card. However, we had a care package from home that contained a can of Spam, summer sausage, and crackers. I was fine, but Bev refused to eat Spam and sang, "Mama said there'd be days like these!"

Our first home which we bought before we were married was located in Granite City, Illinois. This was a precut 900-square-foot slab with a shallow gravel roof. We paid $9,000 with an assumed 4½% GI loan. We added $4,000 to update everything. When we moved in, we had a TV, a couch, and a popcorn popper. Bev was teaching English at Ritenour's Hoech junior high. Jim was a process control engineer at the A. O. Smith Corporation in Granite City.

Our neighborhood during this time period was rather unique. The guy across the street parked his motorcycle in his front room. Each night, we would see him moving the cycle through his front door. In addition, his neighbor always seemed to have a lot of friends, considering the number of cars parked on the street. However, we later discovered that the woman living there was running a "cathouse." It was also interesting coming home from work, only to see another neighbor swapping out his car engine in his front yard. Then, our next-door neighbor had an old car parked between our houses which he used as a "doghouse." Each night he would call his dog and open the car door, and the dog would hop in. Also there was another memorable event when Bev was pregnant with Erik and babysitting a neighbor's toddler daughter. Suddenly, Bev noticed the toddler dunking Heather's head (who was only one-and-half-year-old) in the toilet. You would not believe the amount of screaming and commotion that produced. I know all of this sounds bad, but when you're in love, in your own home and the rest of the neighbors were very friendly and good, it made no difference.

Bev never did like Granite City because of all the smells and dirt from the steel mills. Since Jim grew up in Granite, he thought everything was normal and said he did not trust air that he could not see.

Saving their money, Jim and Bev eventually bought a one-acre lot in north St. Louis County with intentions to build. This idea was then discarded with the idea that we wanted to live in west St. Louis County. Heather and Erik were both born while we lived in Granite. Bev quit teaching when Heather was born to stay home with the kids. Heather was three and Erik was one and a half when we sold the lot with a profit to buy a home in west St. Louis County. Our new home, a two-story, was in Seven Pines subdivision. This house had 2,400 square feet with a real basement and closets. Although a track home in a 400-home subdivision, it was a perfect place to raise children. The subdivision had a swim club used for swim meets and diving competitions, Fourth of July parades with floats, bikes, antique cars, fire trucks, and pets. In preparation for one parade, Erik left the house with our family pet, a cairn terrier named Bambi. She was the best pet anyone could have and was given to us by Karen and Marvin Meng. The parade theme was sports. Bambi wore Erik's baseball T-shirt with white shorts. Bev and Jim went to meet Erik at the parade starting line, only to find Erik returning home holding Bambi's shorts, crying that Bambi pooped in his white shorts. The subdivision also sponsored Easter egg hunts, pumpkin carving contests, garden clubs, and the Parkway North high school homecoming parade.

On one anniversary, Bev told Jim not to buy her cut roses, but a rosebush. Jim found a sale and bought five bushes. Consequently, a rose garden was born and soon there were 40 hybrid tea rose bushes in our backyard. Bev then joined the St. Louis Rose Society. On one Memorial weekend, Bev entered her roses in the competition. The only problem was that both kids had a baseball and softball game on that day and it was raining. Bev complained, so Jim picked three roses in various stages of bloom (bud, half open, and fully open) and shook the rain off the blooms and stuck them in an old fruit jar. We then delivered the roses to the Missouri Botanical Gardens for the contest, and continued on to the kids' games. The next day after church, Bev and her mom, Velma Lewis, went to the Gardens to view the rose displays. Bev was very upset since her roses were not where she had placed them, plus someone had taken her old jar. With a slow burn, she started looking for someone to report the theft. Suddenly, she noticed her roses on the winners' table, "First Place for Roses in Three Stages of Bloom," a major and difficult category to win. A large traveling sterling vase, approximately 18" in height, with her name and date inscribed was presented at a dinner. Since the trophy was to be returned the next year, a picture of the vase award was professionally photographed, framed, and hung in our foyer.

When the Rose Society had their awards banquet to present Bev with her sterling vase, another conflict with baseball and softball occurred. In our rush to get the kids to their games and dress for the award banquet, Bev did not notice that she was wearing two different pairs of sandals. You have to picture the banquet with 100-plus rose people, the newspapers, trophies, and Bev walking across the stage with shoes that didn't even come close to matching.

Shoe problems were also a problem with the kids. At first, we had one pair of baseball cleats. Heather would wear them to her game, come home, and give the same shoes to Erik for his game and vice versa. This resulted in several scheduling conflicts until Santa bought a second pair of cleats.

Heather and Erik never broke any bones nor had any serious injuries while growing up. However, there were three events that are memorable. The first event occurred when

Uncle Wilmer visited from California for a visit. Consequently, Bev was a preparing a large special meal for Wilmer and Jim's Dad, Edward Meng, who just had his birthday. While Wilmer and Ed were talking in the dining room, our pet Bambi came in from the yard, stinking of whatever she had rolled in. Wilmer would say, "Ed, your dog smells!" My dad would reply, "Oh, she is okay." This conversation kept repeating itself over and over. Bev, upon smelling the dog, discovered Bambi had indeed rolled in some undesirable "stuff," resulting in the poor dog being rapidly placed in the basement. Wilmer then proceeded to show Heather how he could make a quarter disappear. This was also known as Wilmer's famous disappearing quarter trick. Heather asked if she could try it. She did and swallowed the quarter! It was 4:31 p.m.; the pediatrician's office had closed. Now what? Jim was called out of a grievance meeting at work and rushed Heather to the emergency room. As Jim pulled out of the driveway, Erik, who was sitting in the dining room with Wilmer and Ed, then fell backwards from the table in his chair, resulting in a large hole in the drywall and a damaged chair. Bev is now all frustrated with Heather's problem, the dog smelling, Erik knocking a hole in the wall, a damaged chair, and her dinner that she was working on all day, in jeopardy.

The doctor eventually met with Jim in the waiting room and gave him the removed quarter. Jim argued that Heather had swallowed a Krugerrand, but to no avail. The quarter was subsequently framed and inscribed with the date, event, and amount of the doctor's bill, and has hung in Heather's bedroom and dorm room and now in her home (see chapter 16 for a picture of the famous quarter).

The second event occurred when Heather visited the emergency room when she had her ears pierced. She was wearing starter studs. However, one ear became infected and very swollen. Dr. Jim said not to worry; he could remove that earring using his needle nose pliers to pull the back of the stud. Unfortunately, the stud was pulled and disappeared into Heather's ear lobe, that's right; the stud had disappeared into her earlobe! Rats! It was off to the emergency room again.

The third event occurred when Erik had only one occasion to meet the fine doctors and nurses in the emergency room who were now calling us by our first name. He returned from a weekend scouting adventure consisting of spending two nights sleeping in an old cave. Erik came home with the ripe smell of bat pooh, smoke, and dirt. He also didn't think it was necessary to shower, or put on a clean shirt, or change underwear. He was one dirty, smelly mess and kept complaining that his side hurt. Dr. Jim kept telling Erik to quit complaining, that it was probably food poisoning from their campfire food or bat pooh. As the evening progressed, Erik was now rolling around on the floor, crying and holding his side. Reluctantly, Dr. Jim and Bev took Erik to St. John's Hospital. This extremely dirty kid is now lying on the sterile white hospital bed diagnosed with appendicitis. We had to wait until 4:00 a.m. until another specialist could arrive. Erik continued to make unintelligible moaning noises lying on the bed, but became concerned when Dr Wood, who was on his fourth appendectomy that evening, arrived in street clothes with his hair all messed, looking like Albert Einstein or the white-haired guy in the movie Back to the Future, and mumbling when he talked. Erik, thinking Dr. Woods must be the janitor, kept pulling away from the doctor while asking, "Mom, Dad, why is the janitor poking me?" Why is he in here? The good doctor, who was on his fourth appendectomy that night, with two more scheduled, blamed it on the full moon. Erik finally disappeared to the operating room about 5:30 a.m. with hospital personnel wearing mask and a big bottle of disinfectant. We all survived!

The fourth event was by far the most significant with Bev's diagnosis of breast cancer in 1996. This traumatic news scared the entire family. After evaluation, she decided to have a single mastectomy and reconstruction. This decision has proven to be correct since she has been a cancer survivor for 15 years and still counting! This event painfully places the three previous medical episodes in perspective.

The Early Years

Bev Meng's first Easter Bonnet!

Jim Meng's first "Thunder Mug"!

Beverly (née Lewis) Meng

Beverly Ann Lewis was born in the USA. She grew up on 4113 Laclede Avenue (south St. Louis City) and lived next door to her cousin, Donna Gaston. They were both only children, but were like sisters having the same dolls, buggies, doll clothes, etc. They were inseparable.

Bev accepted Christ as her Lord and Savior on March 21, 1955. She was baptized by Dr. O. R. Shields, pastor of Lafayette Park Baptist Church. Her parents were very active in the church with her dad, Keith Lewis, a church deacon and her mother, Velma Lewis, always a Sunday school teacher. The Lewis' moved to Baden when Bev was in fourth grade. She attended Beaumont High School, because she lived nine blocks from the county line. Bev graduated on June 1963, ranking eleventh place in a class of 450 students. After graduation, Bev attended Southwest Baptist College in Bolivar, Missouri. She was transferred to Samford University in Birmingham, Alabama, and received her BA degree in English secondary education.

Her first job was teaching seventh grade English in Ritenour school district. After two years, she married, moved to Granite City, Illinois, and transferred to Kirby Junior High School in Hazelwood school district. After two and half years, she left teaching and had two children, Heather Andrea and Erik James. She was always carpooling the kids to baseball and softball practices, piano lessons, scouts, and Ross elementary school.

Once the children were in first and second grade, she sought to reenter the teaching field; however, no openings were available. This led to Bev's secretarial career. Bev became a legal secretary, working three-plus years at Citicorp. She was employed at Mallinckrodt Medical in the Patent Department. Tyco Inc. bought out Mallinckrodt, so Bev took the "early retirement" package after 10 long years working for attorneys.

Bev asked Jim to buy a rosebush for Mother's Day instead of a bouquet. He bought her four hybrid tea roses. This sparked an interest and increased to a 40-rosebush garden. She joined the American Rose Society. Her first year in this organization she entered a rose (Futura) in the three stages of bloom category. She won a traveling trophy. A few years later, she won Queen of Small Garden Roses and received a trophy.

Bev's dad had Parkinson's disease and Alzheimer's disease in his sixties. Bev joined the Alzheimer's Association and became active in the lecturing programs and the advocacy program. She testified before the Senate subcommittee on the Homestead Act, allowing the well spouse to remain in her own home after income was spent. This bill became a law. She also testified regarding the Bed Stay policy. Whenever a patient was sent to the hospital, the nursing home would not reserve their bed unless daily payment was made during their absence. This became a partial success, granting some leniency.

Bev began singing in the sanctuary choir during her senior year in high school and has continued some 40-plus years. She was church pianist at Calvary Baptist Church and also a Sunday school teacher. She learned to play handbells and was in Parkway Baptist Church's choir for three years, which resulted in directing handbells for 10 years at Twin Oaks Presbyterian Church.

Samford University

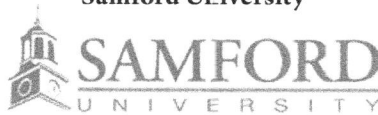

Upon the recommendation of the Faculty of

Howard College

The Trustees of the University hereby confer upon

Beverly Ann Lewis

the degree of

Bachelor of Arts

with all the rights, honors and privileges pertaining thereunto.
In Witness Whereof we have caused to be affixed hereunto the Seal of the University and the signatures of the duly authorized officers of the Trustees and of the Faculty.

Given in Birmingham in the State of Alabama, this twenty-seventh day of May, in the year of Our Lord nineteen hundred and sixty-seven, and of this University the one hundred and twenty-sixth.

Major: English- Secondary Education

Samford University

SAMFORD
UNIVERSITY

Motto	For God. For Learning, Forever
Established	1841 (as Howard College)
Type	Private
Religious affiliation	Alabama Baptist Convention
Endowment	$249.5 million[1]
President	Andrew Westmoreland
Academic staff	264
Undergraduates	2,882
Postgraduates	1,558
Location	Homewood, Alabama, US
Campus	Suburban 180 acres (0.7 km²)
Athletics	13 varsity teams
Colors	Red and Blue
Nickname	Bulldogs
Affiliations	Southern Conference
Website	samford.edu

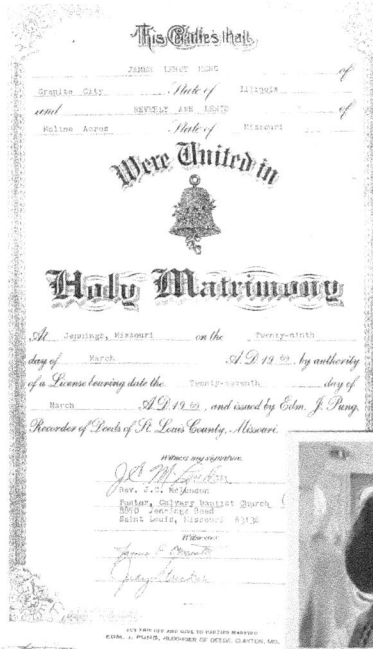

This Certifies that

JAMES LEROY MENG of
Granite City State of Illinois
and BEVERLY ANN LEWIS of
Moline Acres State of Missouri

Were United in

Holy Matrimony

At Jennings, Missouri on the Twenty-ninth
day of March A.D. 19 69 by authority
of a License bearing date the Twenty-seventh day of
March A.D. 19 69 , and issued by Edw. J. Pang,
Recorder of Deeds of St. Louis County, Missouri.

Rev. J.C. McKinnon
Pastor, Calvary Baptist Church
8440 Jennings Road
Saint Louis, Missouri 63136

395

Marriage Record

Bev Lewis and *Jim Meng*

Joined In Holy Matrimony

Witnessed By

Judy Stricker
Maid Of Honor

Jim O'Master
Best Man

Bride's Maids

Cindy Fry
Donna Paston
Terri Rich
Sandy Campbell

Groom's Ushers

Jackie Nighthawn
Jerry Van Deven
Vern Schaeffer
Bruce Lewis
Rich Brown
Jim Bledsoe
John Murphy

Flower Girl

Brenda Krewson

Ring Bearer

Kenny Krewson

Vocalist

Pat Gates

Organist

Glenna Wandling
Bill Linck
Photographer

Upon seeing this photo, mom got all upset for not having her gloves on. She kept saying, how could I forget that? She was always very particular as to the way she was dressed.

Before Marriage

After Marriage

Honeymoon in Mexico

Granite City PRESS-RECORD
Page 36

SPRING BRIDE. Mrs. James L. Meng, the former Beverly Ann Lewis, a daughter of Mr. and Mrs. Keith Lewis, Moline Acres, St. Louis, who was married at Calvary Baptist Church, St. Louis. The bridegroom's parents are former Assistant Postmaster Edward Meng and Mrs. Meng, 2624 Madison avenue. After a honeymoon in Mexico, the couple will reside here.

Southern Illinois University

Graduate School

On recommendation of the President and Faculty,
the Board of Trustees, by virtue of the authority vested in them,
have conferred on

James Leroy Meng

the degree of

Master of Science in Education

and have granted this Diploma as evidence
this thirteenth day of June, 1970

Major: Counselor Education. Thesis titled: Grievants in a Midwestern Metal Fabricating Industry. (A study of grievances submitted by the U.A.W. to the A.O. Smith Corporation).

Southern Illinois University Edwardsville

Established	1957
Type	Public
Endowment	US$16.4 million[1]
Chancellor	Julie Furst-Bowe
President	Glenn Poshard
Academic staff	1,003[2]
Admin. staff	2,437.[2]
Students	14,235.[3]
Undergraduates	11,428[3]
Postgraduates	2,807[3]
Doctoral students	518[3]
Location	Edwardsville, Illinois, USA
Campus	Suburban, 2,660 acres (1,076.5 ha)
Colors	Red and White
Nickname	Cougars
Mascot	Eddie the Cougar
Affiliations	NCAA Division I; Ohio Valley Conference

The Meng and Shamhart book is in the Elijah P. Lovejoy Library at Southern Illinois University

Ivy Productions

Jim Meng and a friend, Jim Solari, formed an "S" corporation named "Ivy Productions" with Meng as president. The company professionally wrote and produced a 20-min video with professional actors. The video discussed the frequently misunderstood poison ivy, oak, and sumac plants. An 87-page, fully illustrated book accomplished the video which sold as a package for $300. Clients included water, electric, gas, and construction companies from across the nation and to the St. Louis public library system. One of the more interesting sales was to a nudist group in California. Hum!

The video and book were advertised in trade magazines, during a PBS TV auction, the National Safety Council, etc. Page 4 of the book had a picture of the Shamharts. The company folded with the company's typist, Bev Meng, still not being paid.

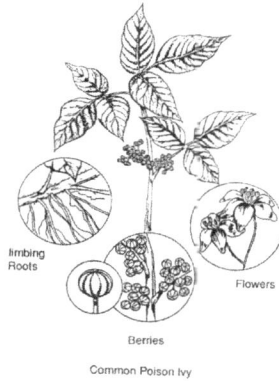

Our forefathers had no herbicides, no brush hogs, and no power mowers to eradicate poison ivy and poison oak. But they did have four-legged weed eaters who could eat the lush foliage of these plants with no ill effects.

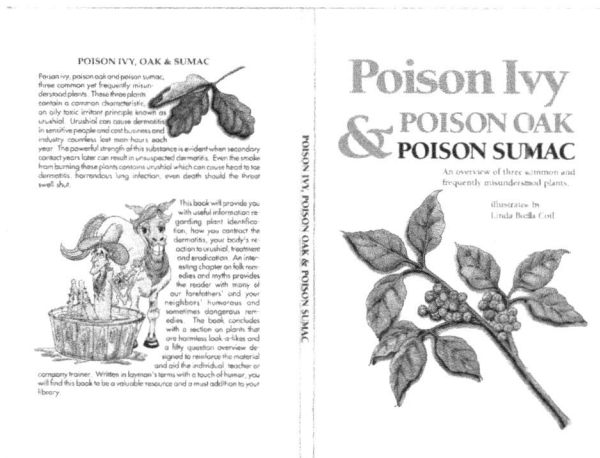

JAMES L. MENG'S EMPLOYMENT

I attended Central Methodist College in Fayette, Missouri, with a major in business administration and economics with a minor in chemistry, receiving a BA in 1962. Upon graduation, I entered the Missouri Air National Guard, which after successfully completing basic training, received an Illinois Military Scholarship. I then enrolled in graduate school at Southern Illinois University at Edwardsville in the field of education. This was done with the misconception that, three months off during the school year to trout fish and all the holidays and snow days would be attractive. Upon course completion and a reevaluation of my interest, I met with my advisor just prior to writing my required thesis. I told my advisor that I wanted nothing to do with teaching or counseling, believing it would be excessively dull. The advisor, based upon my manufacturing background, recommended a change to the field of labor relations. Consequently, a thesis titled "A One-Year Study of Grievant in a Midwest Metal Fabricating Industry" based upon UAW Grievants in the A. O. Smith Corporation was prepared, submitted, and approved. This resulted in an MS degree dated 1970. At this point in time, I had been employed by the A. O. Smith Corporation for eight years as a process control engineer.

I was then employed by the Chrysler Corporation Automobile Assembly Car Plant in Fenton, Missouri, as a labor relations representative. I then became the corporate personnel director for Central Hardware, an INTERCO Co., then with Gould Inc., then with Barry Wehmueller, and then on to retirement after 20 years as a labor arbitrator for the state of Missouri for the American Water Company where I prepared, presented, and briefed labor arbitrations. My work performance resulted in my name being place in the "Who's Who in Finance and Industry 20th edition 1977-1978" record.

Throughout my labor experience, I have negotiated with a variety of Union's, that is, ... Teamsters locals 688 (warehouse); Teamster Local 688 (office); Teamsters Local 688 (Foundry); Teamster Local 682 (warehouse); Teamster local 610 (truck drivers); Painters District Council 2; United Food and Commercial Workers Union Local 35, 219, 575, 435, and 655; Service Workers Union Local 50; Carpenters District Council of St. Louis; Boilermaker and Helpers Union Lodge 27; International Association of Machinist and Aerospace Workers District 9; United Automobile Workers of America Local 136; Utility Workers Union of America both Physical Union and Office Unions Local 335 in St. Louis, Physical Unions St. Charles, Joplin and St. Joseph, Missouri. Some of these negotiating sessions lasted around the clock while others were done in a local bar. Additional responsibilities included procedure and policy writing, benefit analysis, and Union avoidance in Ohio, Indiana, and Kentucky, covering 3000 employees while Corporate Personnel Director with Central Hardware.

Involvement in labor relations has also produced some notable exciting experiences such as walkouts, slowdowns, wildcat strikes, being shot at (using a .22 cal, shot a mercury vapor light over our heads while protecting the plant during a UAW strike at the A. O. Smith Corporation, which was before I was even in labor relations), windows broken out of my car, numerous flat tires from union nails being spread across the plant entrances during strikes, breaking up employee fights using angle irons, an armed escort to my car for two weeks after a touchy discharge, unlisted home telephone numbers, entering a large angry union crowd in a public parking lot (with many drunks) to get them back into the plant after a two-day wildcat, pickets with signs marching in front of my home which was not appreciated by any of my neighbors, etc.

It was also exciting to hear the St. Louis police tell me that our plant guard's murder case was still open (Gould Inc.) just after being hired. We also had two armed robberies inside the same plant by a person in a ski mask and a sawed-off shotgun. Both robberies were in the plant's shower room with one victim sitting on a toilet with his pants around his ankles and then, six months later, when another employee was standing on a bench naked, drying off after a shower. These events led to the St. Louis police department putting undercover officers both inside and outside the plant. The robber was never caught. I was also advised and complied with my predecessor's request to carry a two-foot club with a rubber handle next to me in the front seat of my car. Luckily, I never had a need to use this and passed the club to my replacement when I left the company. Of course, there were other events like taking a shower at the plant and hearing a noise on the roof. Upon investigation, it was discovered that while in the shower, someone had ripped the copper guttering off the roof. They were never caught. On another occasion, a supervisor and an employee were observed and caught on the plant roof having sex. Then there was the time when the furnace blew up, and the time 10 Chrysler engines were damaged by sabotage, cars being "keyed," or the time someone tried to burn down the plant, twice. There were also drug cases, plenty of your basic drunks, falsification of documents, etc.

One theft case required me to testify in front of the grand jury and then on to trial in downtown St. Louis. This event involved a $250,000 theft of aluminum from the plant. The employee was not convicted, but months later, I observed on the five o'clock news, the suspected thief shot and lay on the street, after trying to rob a Quick Shop.

Of course, I was on a first name basis with investigators from the EEOC, OSHA, NISH, ICE, FMCS, and NLRB. Numerous charges were filed, but the unions won none, zero. However, the Machinist Union, District 9, in St. Louis, Missouri, made me an honorary union steward, stating I had always been fair and honest when dealing with their union. After all that you go through, I was very proud of this gesture. This union card was framed and hung in my office for years. Other unions just sent me Mother's Day cards. All of this activity contradicts my father's past, who was a union president in the post office, and my grandfather, Wilmer Shamhart, who was a Carpenter's Union Business Agent for Granite City, Madison, and Venice, Illinois.

The above sounds a little crazy, but nothing serious ever happened. Labor relations proved very, very interesting, plus a lot of fun as well as being rewarding. With this job assignment, I normally dealt with the 5%–8% of the deviates that are in all companies. However, I was also fortunate to work firsthand with a lot of very fine, hardworking people of all colors, shapes, sizes, and backgrounds who wanted no more than to provide for their families. Many of the union business agents were professional and fun to deal with. Other agents resembled the south end of a horse going north. However, like the games of chess, poker, or bridge, a challenge was always available.

403

Labor relations proved, I think, to be a lot more interesting and rewarding than any school teaching job would ever have been. The only difference with labor was that between all of the above events, I had to wait until my scheduled vacation to do any trout fishing.

However, as exciting as labor relations proved to be, my most enjoyable and best employment by far paid $0.75 per hour, with 12-hour work days, six days a week. This job was that as a lifeguard at the Wilson Park Swimming Pool in Granite City, Illinois, the best job I ever had.

While with the A. O. Smith Corp. during a UAW strike, I got a brick thrown through my (parked) car window. This was the same week that they shot a mercury vapor light out over our heads and ruined all four of my tires with roofing nails. Thugs!

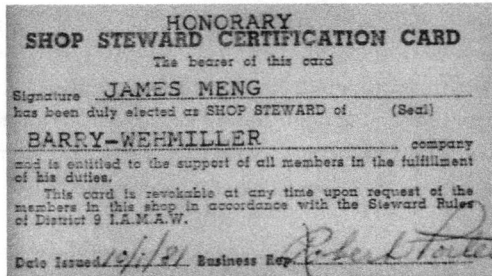

After stopping a two-day wildcat strike at The Barry-Wehmiller Co., the union made me an honorary chief steward. My actions actually saved the union a lot of money and court cost (unauthorized) which also proved that I was not always a horse's butt.

Not all encounters with the Unions were serious or life threatening. Labor Relations was always interesting and sometimes actually fun. For example, the day I met the U.A.W. for the first time.

With a last name of Meng, I grew up with a few new acquaintances asking if I was Chinese. I would simply reply, "No, I am 100% German" and the conversation would continue. To finish my Masters degree, I wrote my thesis on Labor Relations using data from my current employer, the A.O. Smith Cooperation where I was a Process Control Engineer. With thesis in hand, I applied and was hired as a Labor Relations Reprehensive by the Chrysler Corporation at the Fenton, Missouri Car assembly plant. This was a 6000 employee plant that was joined by a Chrysler truck plant with 5000 additional employees.

During my first week of employment at Chrysler, my supervisor had me join him to attend a meeting with all the car plant's U.A.W. Committeemen. These are U.A.W. union representatives who have come up through the ranks to the committeeman position. They were loud, intimidating and all smoking cigars. After about 5 minutes, my supervisor said he had to make a phone call and left me in the room by myself with the committee.

They were all blowing cigar smoke directly in my face. Suddenly, a very loud voice said, "What the hell kind of name is Meng?" I replied, "Chinese". Suddenly, another loud voice said, "You look more like a damn American Indian" I replied, "Well, I am half Indian, my great, great grandfather was working out west building the railroads and married and Indian squaw." A loud voice came out of the abundant cigar smoke and said. "You're a real Mess!" There was considerable foot stomping and fist pounding on the table throughout the meeting as I explained my alleged Indian heritage, I replied that I had their wedding picture of my grandfather with his new bride. She had a single feather sticking upward out her hair". Another loud voice shouted, "I'll be dammed, you are a real big mess!" This comment was then followed by a very loud question, "Where the hell did you work before coming to Chrysler?" I replied "Burger King." They all started shuffling their feet and throwing papers in the air when another loud voice came out of the cigar smoke filled room and shouted, "What the hell did you do at Burger King?" I replied, "I flipped burgers but sometimes I was on fries" The room erupted again with all kinds of nasty comments. A loud statement was then shouted, "What the hell is this company doing hiring people for labor relations from Burger King?" My supervisor then returned to the completely cigar smoke filled room and the meeting began. For several months after this meeting, I would be walking through the plant and would hear a committeeman shout, "Hey Burger Helper". I would just wave at them and keep going.

I was always big as evidenced by playing the right offensive and the left defensive tackle in both High School and in College football. Once while going through the plant cafeteria line at Chrysler, I heard a loud voice come from the sitting area saying, "He is the biggest G ... D ... Chinaman that I have ever seen".

These committeemen were always vocal, intimidating but under all the huff and puff they were OK but with an agenda that was at times contrary to the company's interest. But make no doubt; they did have a major influence on Company operations. In balance, Chrysler was a very good company made up of a lot of good employees. It was all fun. Unfortunately, the Company has since moved its assembly operations from Fenton, MO.

BEVERLY A. MENG WINS CHALLENGE TROPHY IN ROSE SHOW

Bev Meng Wins the Fred J. Blum Challenge Trophy!

Bev Meng wins the 1986 competition for the Fred J. Blum Trophy, a classification open to all rose gardens in the American Rose Society of Greater St. Louis. Her entry, "The Futura Hybrid Tea," was presented in three stages of bloom: one bud, one exhibition bloom, and one open bloom, all shown in one vase. The highly prized, highly competitive Blum trophy, a traveling trophy (pictured) had Bev's name engraved and presented to Bev at the Society's annual dinner.

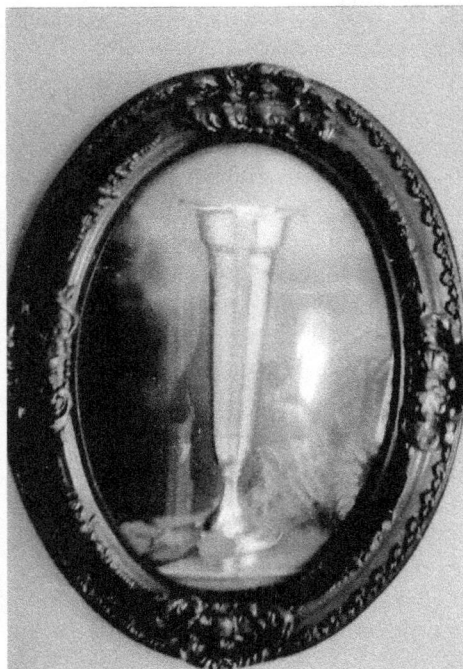

Futura's tulip shaped buds are pure rich orange, with a deeper coral-orange reverse. It has a good fragrance and vigorous growth.

News Release . . .

BEVERLY MENG WINS, AGAIN, AT THE ROSE SHOW

Beverly Meng won the "Queen of the Show" award for rose gardens with less than 40 rose bushes during the Spring Rose Show at the Missouri Botanical Gardens. The show was held on May 23rd and 24th and was sponsored by the Rose Society of Greater St. Louis and was open to their members and members of the American Rose Society. Beverly has been a member of both Societies for the past five years. She will receive the "Luer" Trophy for the best small garden hybrid tea rose during a dinner meeting late in June.

Her winning rose was a "Futura" which is a light orange colored hybrid tea. This was the same rose that won her the "Fred J. Blum" Trophy in the "Challenge Class" during the Spring Show of 1986. The Blum Trophy was open to rose gardens of all sizes and involved three hybrid teas of the same variety, shown in three stages of bloom—one bud, one exhibition bloom, and one open bloom all shown in one vase.

Beverly has entered the competition for the past two years and has won major awards both times. Her biggest problem in growing roses in Seven Pines is not bugs or black spot, but baseballs and softballs that occasionally land in the garden as her two children, Heather and Erik, practice in the backyard. They too have won their share of trophies but they also know that it is in their best interest to stay out of Mom's rose garden.

Beverly Meng won the "Queen of the Show" award for rose gardens with less than 40 rosebushes during the Spring Rose Show at the Missouri Botanical Gardens. The show, held on May 23 and 24, was open to members of the American Rose Society. Her winning rose was a "Futura," which is a dark orange-colored hybrid tea. This was the same rose that won her a trophy in the "Challenge Class" during last year's competition. Bev will receive the "Luer" trophy during a dinner meeting late in June.

Twin Oaks Presbyterian Church Handbells

Bev Meng began and directed an English handbell choir at Twin Oaks Presbyterian Church (PCA) in St. Louis for 10 years. As director, she recruited, trained, and selected the music to be played for preludes and offertories. In addition to an annual Christmas concert, Bev also initiated a "pop" spring concert, which included songs such as "Elephant Walk," "The Pink Panther," "Phantom of the Opera," "Beauty and the Beast," and others. This was great fun and definitely far removed from church music. The Christmas concerts included approximately 10 numbers. Bev's choir played difficult level of bell music. Occasionally, the handbell choir would accompany a guest artist, that is, a professional clarinetist. He played "A Closer Walk with Thee" in true Dixieland style. The music begins with a funeral dirge and then "goes" swinging Dixie. The performance "brought the house down" with clapping, unusual for Presbyterians!

Bev's group played for weddings, nursing homes, and other churches in the area. The choir wore white tops and black bottoms for a nursing home performance, therefore a man asked one of the ringers for a Bud (Budweiser). Apparently, the day before, the home had just been visited by a group who served them beer. The bell choir was never asked that question again! The choir was invited to Powell Symphony Hall to perform before the orchestral music, but unfortunately, several choir members could not attend.

Bev also bought a full three-octave set of hand chimes for the choir and then initiated a hand chime youth choir. In addition, Bev also purchased the fourth and fifth octaves of handbells for the church.

The choir required a great amount of work and time, but was worth it. Several in the congregation would praise that the music had blessed them.

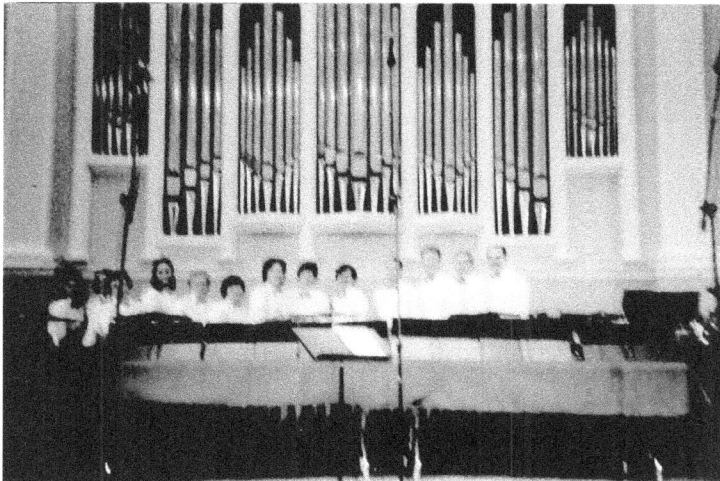

PROGRAM

Let Heaven and Nature Ring!

Prelude	What Child Is This?	arr. David Lanz
	Junia Haas, piano	

Procession of Praise — arr. Arnold Sherman

Adeste Fidelis — arr. Cynthia Dobrinski

We Three Kings — arr. Arnold Sherman
Jubilant Ringers

The Christmas Angels — arr. Michael Helman
Median Ringers

O Come, O Come Emmanuel — arr. Janet Van Valey and Susan Berry
Ring! Jr.

West Indies Carol — folk tune of the West Indies arr. Hart Morris
Jubilant Ringers

Ukrainian Bell Carol — arr. Hart Morris
Median Ringers

Joy To The World — arr. Martha L. Thompson
Ring! Jr.

Away In A Manger — arr. Valerie Stephenson
Kelly Monroe & Vickie Loveall

O Come, O Come, Emmanuel — arr. Valerie Stephenson
Jill Monroe, Kelly Monroe & Vickie Loveall

Offertory

I Heard The Bells On Christmas Day — arr. C. Dobrinski

While By My Sheep — arr. Cynthia Dobrinski
Jubilant Ringers

Processional Alleluia — arr. Kevin McChesney
Good King Wencelas — arr. Barbara Kinyon
Median Ringers

God With Us For All Time — arr. Betty Garee
Veni Emmanuel

Masters in This Hall — arr. Arnold Sherman
Jubilant Ringers

What Child Is This? — arr. Martha L. Thompson
Ring! Jr.

"Merry" Mallets — arr. Kirtsy Mitchell
Median Ringers

Troika (from "Lt. Kije") — Sergei Prokifiev arr. Kevin McChesney

Stille Nacht — arr. Betty Garee
Jubilant Ringers

Jim and Bev's Homes from 1969 thru 2009

House #1

House #2

House #3

The Meng family

The Lewis family

A proud grandpa

Happy birthday

JAMES AND BEVERLY MENG'S POLITICS

Jim and Bev were very active in national politics at the local level. Bev hosted a "tea and crumpet" party with friends and neighbors (including Lillian Shippers) at their home for then congressman James Talent. Talent spoke on the day's issues and why he should be elected to the US House of Representatives. Jim and Bev also worked at the polls for the congressman and attended campaign dinners and the election return night parties. While Talent was running for his two terms in the US House and one term in the US Senate, Jim drove Talent, using Bev's, convertible, in all the local parades.

Jim also worked for Senator Phil Gramm's presidential campaign in 2000 by traveling to the Iowa Caucus on a campaign bus and participating in all of the Gramm's president activities. The Senator and his family were very gracious to those who were working in his behalf. Taking part in all the floor demonstrations and watching and hearing all the Republican candidates close up was a lot of fun. Meeting Charlton Heston (a.k.a. Moses) and listening to him speak was also quite an experience.

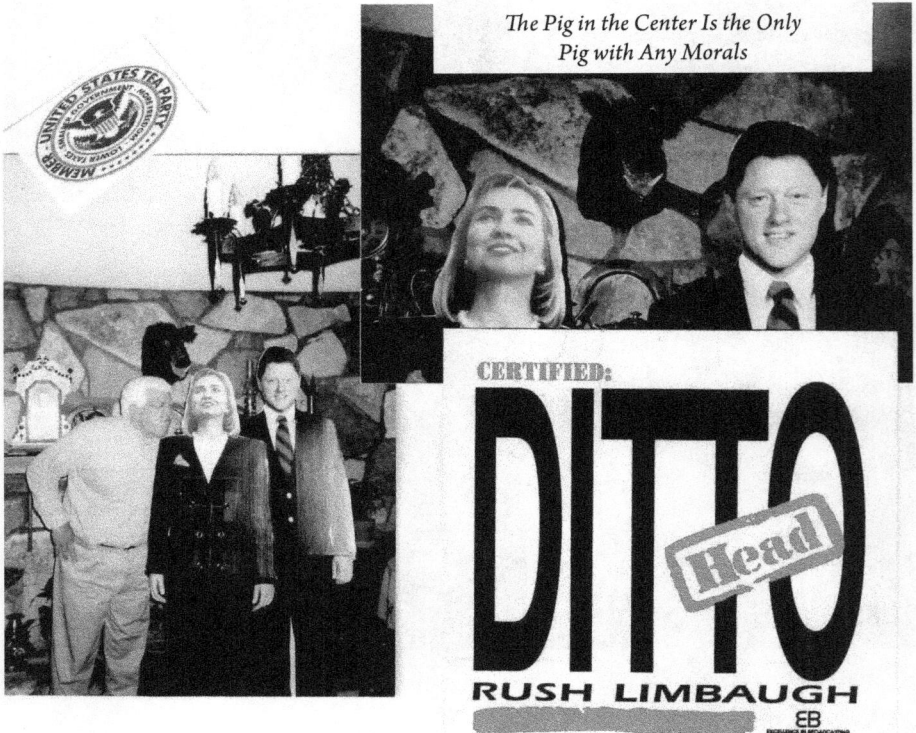

The Pig in the Center Is the Only Pig with Any Morals

CERTIFIED: DITTO Head

RUSH LIMBAUGH

PHIL GRAMM
UNITED STATES SENATOR

November 1, 1995

Dear Jim:

It was a pleasure seeing you during my recent trip to Saint Louis. The meeting on October 20th was a great success and I appreciate you taking the time to attend.

As the race for the Republican presidential nomination intensifies and the primary season approaches, I cannot overestimate the importance of supporters like you. My campaign continues to gain strength as my message resonates with voters nationwide. The citizens of the United States have demanded a change in our nation's direction and as your next President, I will provide the leadership necessary to make America a place of less government and more freedom.

Again, I appreciate your support. I look forward to seeing you on the campaign trail and if I can ever be of service, please let me know.

Yours respectfully,

PHIL GRAMM
United States Senator

PG:jlb

P.O. BOX 33119, WASHINGTON, D.C. 20033-0119
PAID FOR BY PHIL GRAMM FOR PRESIDENT, INC.

413

Participating in and representing U.S. Congressman Phil Gramm
in the 1995 Republican Presidential Straw Poll in Iowa.

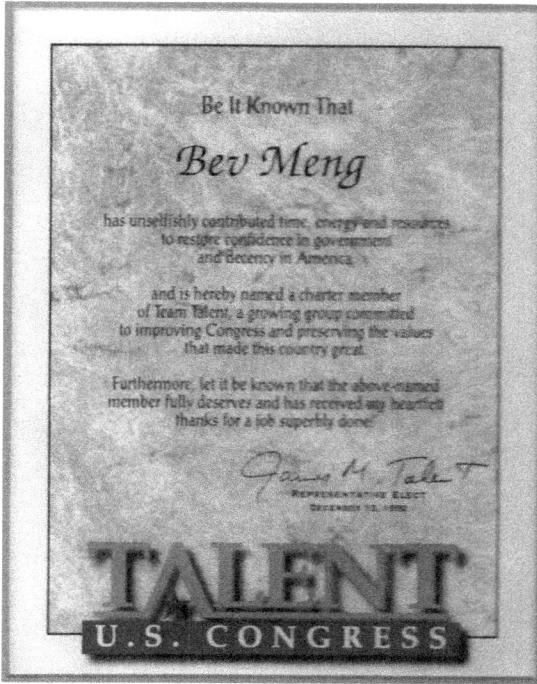

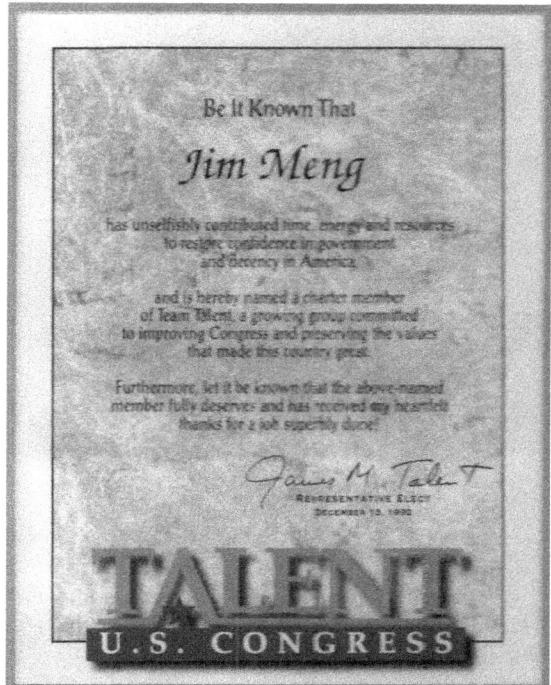

A little political fun by MS Rags P. Pooch, Security Technician

PRESIDENTIAL LEGAL EXPENSE TRUST

1111 19th Street, N.W., Suite 608 · Washington, D.C. 20036
Telephone (202) 463-8423 · Telefax (202) 463-8426

Ms. Rags P. Pooch
Security Technician

April 2, 1997

Dear Ms. Pooch:

Thank you for your recent contribution of $5.00 to the Presidential Legal Expense Trust. On behalf of our fellow Trustees, we express our appreciation for your generosity and support.

Contributions to the Trust will be used to pay legal expenses incurred by President and Mrs. Clinton after January 20, 1993 in connection with any legal proceedings involving them. Payment of these expenses by the Trust will allow the President to remain focused on his responsibilities as Chief Executive of our nation.

President and Mrs. Clinton have asked that we convey their gratitude for your gift.

As we impart our appreciation to you, we also extend our best wishes.

Sincerely,

(Rev.) Theodore M. Hesburgh, C.S.C.   Nicholas deB. Katzenbach
Co-Chair   Co-Chair

Five dollars was sent to President Bill Clinton's legal defense fund as a joke and to get in the Clinton's money grubbing database. The letter was signed by Ms. Rags P. Pooch, security technician. Rags was our pet cairn terrier! Rags picture was then attached to a copy of the letter which was then sent to the Rush Limbaugh radio show. Several days later, Rush announced on his show that "even the cats and dogs are contributing to Clinton's Defense." Many additional letters have also been received by Ms. Rags requesting more money . . .

In Celebration of
the 55th American Presidential Inaugural
the National Republican Congressional Committee
requests the presence of

Mr. James L. Meng

to attend and participate in the Inauguration of

George W. Bush

as President of the United States of America
and

Dick Cheney

as Vice President of the United States of America
on Thursday the twentieth of January
two thousand five
in the City of Washington, D. C.

The Committee for
The Presidential Inaugural
requests the honor of your presence
to attend and participate in the Inauguration of

Donald John Trump

as President of the United States of America

and

Michael Richard Pence

as Vice President of the United States of America

on Friday, the twentieth of January

two thousand and seventeen

in the City of Washington

Presidential Inaugural Committee
Commemorative Invitation
1789 - 2017

On January 20, 2017, our nation honored the 58th inauguration of the President and Vice President of the United States of America. This special occasion celebrated the triumph of our democracy with a peaceful transition of power and the shared ideal that make its continuance possible.

Please accept this invitation as our gift to commemorate the inauguration of Donald John Trump as the 45th President of the United States of America and Michael Richard Pence as 48th Vice President of the United States of America.

The 58th Presidential Inaugural Committee
Thomas J. Barrack, Jr.
Chairman

PAID FOR BY THE 58TH PRESIDENTIAL INAUGURAL COMMITTEE

Could the future King and Queen of England use a toaster?

SUZANNE PLUNKETT/AFP/GETTY IMAGES
A Coat of Arms for Kate Middleton's family.

Upon hearing that Prince William and Miss Middleton were getting married, I immediately thought we thought we should send them a toaster for a wedding gift which is a common practice in America. However, after a brief discussion with my wife, Beverly, on the merits of me behaving, I decided otherwise. Non the less, they seemed so nice and such a credit to the future of England, I wanted to do something. Therefore, I mailed them a very nice letter meant every word in our letter. I subsequently receive a very gracious "Thank You" for the Meng family gift. Prince William's and Miss Middleton's reply will follow.

March 31, 2011

Dear Prince William and Catherine Middleton,
    You will receive numerous gifts more expensive and perhaps more important than this. However, no gifts will possess more best wishes for a long and blissful marriage than the enclosed. There will be times during your marriage that you will want to be by yourselves, to get away from all the attention or just to go behind closed doors, relax and enjoy one another. During these times, we hope you will use the enclosed to have a couple cups of your favorite tea and think of two unimportant Americans who wish you both the very best for a long and happy marriage.

Sincerely,

ST JAMES'S PALACE

From: The Office of HRH Prince William of Wales and HRH Prince Henry of Wales

Private and Confidential

12th April, 2011

Dear Mr. and Mrs. Meng,

Prince William and Miss Catherine Middleton have asked me to thank you most sincerely for the delightful tea set, which you so generously sent to mark the occasion of their Wedding.

The Prince and Miss Middleton very much appreciated your incredibly kind thought, and were so touched that you took the trouble to send a gift.

The couple regret that they are unable to respond personally to the many letters and gifts which they have received. They would, however, have me send you their warmest thanks and very best wishes.

Yours sincerely,

Mrs. Claudia Holloway

Mr. and Mrs. Jim Meng

Look out, Red Baron! Here comes Bev Meng on her thirty-sixth birthday, 1981, in her bi-wing fighter with good friend John Murphy (pilot).

Bev Meng in her first glider ride.

Heather and Erik Meng watching Jim and Bev lift off in a hot air balloon with good friend Mel Hanson as the pilot.

Bev and Jim's "Been There and Done That" experiences, illustrating a strong desire for adventure, to travel, see, and experience the history of the world.

United States
Switzerland
Netherlands
Norway (2)
Denmark (2)
Finland
Spain
Estonia
Sweden
Italy
Russia
Canada (6)
Mexico (2)
Bahamas
England (5)
Scotland (2)
Wales
Ireland (2)
Lichtenstein
Belgium (2)
Germany (4)
France
Austria (4)
Monte Carlo
Majorca

*Beverly Meng with a Mint Julip at
the 2012 Kentucky Derby*

What have Bev and Jim Meng been doing?

In addition to raising two outstanding children and surviving essential employment, Bev and Jim also reserved the time to travel all over the U.S./Canada/Mexico and 23 western European countries walking in world history and meeting a lot of very good and interesting people! Some of Bev and Jim's uncorrelated, incomplete and unescorted adventures, plus a few incidental activities, commenced with a honeymoon in the historic Gran Hotel Ancira, Monterrey, Mexico. Following the history theme, we:

- Sang *Silent Night* in Oderndorf where the song was written; rode to the top of the Zugspitze; sat on Hadrian's Wall; toured King Ludwig' Neuschwanstein castle viewing Richard Wagner's gold piano then off to tour his Linderhof castle; toured Kings College at Cambridge and the London Tower including the Crown Jewels; toured Parliament, watched changing of the Guard in London and Edinburgh; viewed the Declaration of Independence in Williamsburg and the Magna Carta in Yorkshire; took the tube to see the plays *Wicket/Phantom of the Opera (3)/ Oliver; Les Miserables, Miss Saigon* and *Chicago*; visited home of the 1936 winter in Garmisch-Partenkirchen and 1980 winter Olympics in Lake Placid; turned the Golden Ring at Schoner Brunner 3 times in Nuremburg and made a wish, then, just to make sure, made another wish and tossed three coins in the Trevi Fountain in Rome.

- Just like the song, *I (we) Lost my Heart in Heidelberg* with *The Student Prince*; ate great chocolate in Brugge and again in Hershey; visited the Little Mermaid statue in Copenhagen harbor; visited the 1560 Federicksburg Palace/ Castle; toured the First's Conway Castle; took the ghost walk in Tenby, Wales; attended/sang/partied at the real "Oktoberfest" in Munich; attended the St. Petersburg Symphony Orchestra (with dinner and champagne} in the Hermitage; attended a Berlinier Philharmoniker concert in Berlin; visited Wales and all their sheep.

-Afternoon tea at the Fairmont Empress Hotel in Victoria, B.C., then off to the Butchart Gardens and a stay at Painter's Lodge to catch salmon; ate great quiche in Quebec City; drove around Newfoundland looking at lighthouses; stood in the ruins of the Roman Senate, Roman Coliseum and Stonehenge; stopped in Gibraltar for some VAT free shopping then off to Marjorca to purchase Majorca pearls; drove to the Isle of Skye for a taste of haggis; drove up Pikes Peak; took the Cog Railroad up Mount Washington; rode the Chattanooga Choo Choo; took a short trip on the Norfolk and Western's steamer; #611; visited Shakespeare's Stratford-upon-Avon home and Anne Hathaway's cottage; rode in a bi-wing (Stearman), hot air balloon, a glider and a hydrofoil from England to France; went punting in Cambridge; did not see a wallow at Capistrano; ate cheese and dank wine in the home towns of Edam and Gouda; walked the Edinburgh Royal Mile twice and walked the Boston Freedom Trail; toured the Hummel figurine, Waterford Crystal, Spode, Dresden, Wedgwood, and Delft china factories; visited the actual *A Bridge Too Far* location in Arnhem; ate great lobster in the town where the picture Carousel was filmed in Booth Bay Harbor; viewed Sir William Wallace's *Braveheart* Stirling Castle; toured Trexlertown's 1760 house in a P.A., a town founded by a relative.

- Toured the Royal Albert Hall; toured the Fragonard perfume factory in Grasse, France; toured Ottawa; received a "Thank You" letter from the future King and Queen of England, Prince William and Kate Middleton, for a letter and wedding gift; invited to the White House for the inauguration of George W. Bush and Dick Cheney; drank beer and sang in the famous Hofbrauhaus then walked to the Marienplaz to watch the Glockenspiel; toured the *inside* of Buckingham Palace; viewed the play *Oliver* at the Palladium; toured the Dachau concentration camp; drank *smoked beer* in Bamberg.; Swayed to good music in several German beer gardens singing the old American favorite *Rosamunde* (Roll Out the Barrel); walked the Ringstrasse viewing the Palace Schonbrunn listening to the great music of Vienna including attending waltz concerts in Johan Strauss' music hall; visited the Grand Canyon, Bryce Zion, Monument Valley.

- Then off to Capitol Reef, Arches, and Canyon lands National Parks, Dead Horse Point State Park, Grand Staircase-Escalante, Rainbow Bridge National Monuments, Lake Powell, Monument Valley, Glacier, Yellowstone and other national parks; toured the salt mines in Berchtesgarden and drove the ex-silver mining tunnels o Guanajuato; toured Sir Winston Churchill's War Room and museum; toured Cape Canaveral; listed for the nightingale to sing in Berkeley Square; viewed the Book of Kells at Trinity College.

- Cruised on Cunard's Queen Victoria, Queen Elizabeth and Queen Mary 2, had lunch on the Queen Mary 1; walked across Lucerne's Chapel Bridge; kissed the Blarney Stone; walked in Hitler's Eagles Nest; unknowingly spent the night in a former ex-Gestapo headquarters; climbed to the top of the Aztec Pyramid of the Sun, Teotihuacan, toured the Aztec history museum then toured the Mayan ruins; took a great boat ride on the Konigsee; attended the Kentucky Derby wearing a large hat; walked on the deck of the 1797 USS Constitution, a.k.a. *Old Ironsides* then off to the site of the 1692 Salem Witch Trials; walked the Piazza ella Signoria square; viewed the White Cliffs of Dover and the beautiful Cliffs of Moher; toured Barcelona; viewed Check Point Charlie; cruised the gorgeous Norwegian Fjords and saw a troll under a bridge wearing a pantsuit that looked just like Hillary Clinton!; spent the night in a relative's hometown, Crail, Scotland, then visited the St. Andrews Golf course; skipped around on one of the pillars of The Brandenburg Gate; Bev sang *I am 16...* while jumping from bench to bench in the actual gazebo used in the film Sound of Music, Salzburg; toured the Hermitage and the Peterhof Grand Palace; visited the beautiful windmills in Kinderdijk; toured the Hofburg and Schonbrunn palaces; ate the world's best pastry and chocolate in Demel's in Vienna (established 1786); spent a day with the other half in Monte Carlo; hopped on a red double-decker bus to go shopping at Harrods; viewed Bev's uncle Lee Roy Logan's name in London's St. Paul Cathedral's American Chapel book; rode the railway in Bourton On The Water in the beautiful Cotswold's; sat on the Singing Bench of Tallinn, Estonia; strolled the Piazza del Duomo in Florence.

- Drove the entire Rhine Valley plus the Romantic Road including time in the beautiful town of Rothenburg with its wall and Christmas shops; toured and remembered the Alamo; both Heather and Erik are sent to a one year course at the

German Language school; Heather is sent to Germany in a H.S. exchange program for three weeks; Jim names a city street in Edwardsville, IL. *Mengstrasse* in perpetuity, in honor of his parents, Edward and Jessie Meng; Jim's Y-DNA matches American patriot John Hanson, the First President of the Continental Congress 1781-1782.

- Attended Sunday services in the 1156 St. Michael's church in Schwabish Hall and watched its absolutely fascinating annual hunting ceremonies; visited Fort Sumter where it all began; spent the night (25th wedding anniversary) in the Sleeping Beauty turret tower of the Brothers Grimm's Deornroschenschloss in Sababurg, of Red Riding Hood and Sleeping Beauty fame; rested in warm sands on the Bermuda, Puerto Vallarta and Vero, Florida beaches; visited the Gatlinburg battlefield; toured Andrew Jackson's Hermitage; plus the homes of John Knox, Mozart, J. S. Bach, Beethoven, and stood in Martin Luther's room in the Wartburg castle (where he hid translating the Bible from Latin to high German); visited Rasputin's actual room in St. Petersburg (where he died, died and died); toured West Point and the U.S. Air Force Academy.

Then there were music events:

- Attended concerts of Luciano Pavarotte, Andrea Bocelli, Tony Bennett, Glenn Miller (in the Starlight room where we met), Sissel, the Beach Boys, Kenny Rogers, Straight No chasers, Celtic women, Ambassadors of Harmony, the Grand Ole Opera (featuring Merle Haggard and Dolly Parton), Jerry Lee Lewis, Ballet Folkorico, frequent the St. Louis Symphony and St. Louis Muny Opera, concert at the Mormon Tabernacle in Salt Lake, Andre Reiu, Manheim Steamroller; attended the dedication of *The Meng Concert Hall* at California State University, Fullerton, CA, purchasing 7 family named seats in row "M" then met and had dinner with the gracious movie star Carol Channing.

When not walking in the footsteps of history or going to music concerts, we:

- Took numerous 21 mile canoe floats on the scenic 11 Point River, Boze Mill; fished Rockbridge for trout; Bev directs the hand bell choir and sings in the *Twin Oaks Presbyterian* church choir; watched Cubs vs. Cards at Wrigley and Cards vs. Cubs in St. Louis, more Cardinals, Rams, Blues in St. louis; Bev wins two major first place trophies in the St. Louis American Rose Societies competition for hybrid tea roses; Bev testifies before the Missouri Senate subcommittee on the Homestead Act (and won!) then testifies in Jefferson City against the Bed Hold Policy of nursing homes (and won!); Jim becomes U.S. Congressman James Talent's parade chauffer and represented U.S. Senator Phil Gramm at the 1995 Iowa Straw Political Caucus, meeting Charleston Heston a.k.a. Moses/Ben Hur; played at Disney World; Jim coaches little league baseball; published a 690 page book on family history back to 1147 on his mother's side and 1630 on his father's side which is now in five German City Archives and many libraries in the U.S. including the Daughters of the American Revolution plus Crail, Scotland and Christchurch, New Zealand, www James L Meng book; Jim receives two

U.S. Patents for a roof gutter cleaner named *The Gutter Dragon and Celebration Patio Light Gel Bags*; passes the 50 year membership milestone in Freemasonry, Scottish Rite (32 degree) and Shriner's.

In love on 1968, married, and still going!

Deutschland über alles...

CUNARD

Queen Mary 2

MAIDEN CALL IN IRELAND

Dunmore East - Friday 17 June 2005

Today, Cunard's flagship Queen Mary 2 makes her maiden call at Dunmore East
becoming the largest passenger liner ever to visit this country.

Cunard is proud of its continued links with Ireland and is delighted to
commemorate your participation in this special event with this certificate.

Signed *Commodore Darioek* Master of Queen Mary 2

THE MOST FAMOUS OCEAN LINERS IN THE WORLD

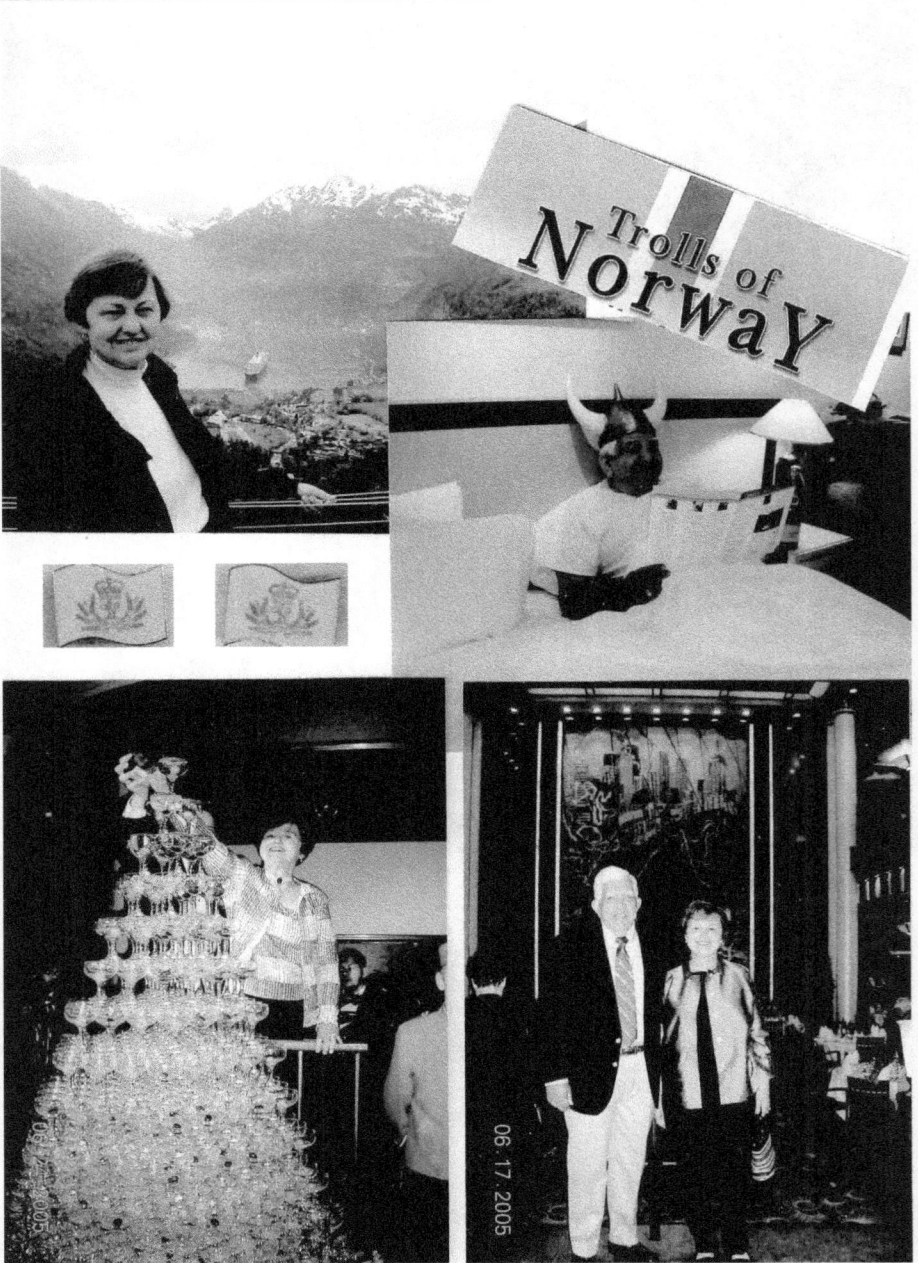

Jim and Bev Meng cruised on Cunard's Queen Mary II *in 2005, the* Queen Victoria I *in 2009, and the* Queen Elizabeth III *in 2011. We also had lunch on the* Queen Mary I *in Long Beach, California in 2005.*

QUEEN
VICTORIA℠
CUNARD®
THE MOST FAMOUS OCEAN LINERS IN THE WORLD ℠

| ABSTRACT OF THE LOG OF |
| QUEEN VICTORIA |
| Mediterranean Medley |
| 17th August 2009 – 30th August 2009 |

In Command: Captain Paul Wright
Staff Captain: Hamish Suthers
Chief Officer: Aseem Hoshmi
Navigator: Chetan Sawyer
Snr Second Officer: Andrew Foote
Second Officer: Aaron Wood
Third Officer: David Johnson
Third Officer: Ned Tutton

Date	Port Of Call	Noon Position	Distance (nautical miles)	Average Speed (Knots)	Arrival/Departure (Local Time)
Monday 17th	Southampton		-	-	1658
Tuesday 18th	at sea	47'10.3'N 007'10.2'W	325	20.3	
Wednesday 19th	at sea	39'44.5'N 010'06.5'W	528	22.6	
Thursday 20th	at sea	36'15.1'N 003'06.1'W	531	22.1	
Friday 21st	Barcelona		1772	21.0	0750/1833
Saturday 22nd	Monte Carlo		282.7	23.1	0817/1846
Sunday 23rd	Livorno		125	11.4	0616/1830
Monday 24th	Civitavecchia		135	12.6	0709/1853
Tuesday 25th	Alghero		218	19.4	0651/1702
Wednesday 26th	Palma		280	21.1	0754/1174
Thursday 27th	Gibraltar		450	21.7	1420/1845
Friday 28th	at sea	39'17.9'N 009'50.7'W	354	20.8	
Saturday 29th	at sea	47'03'N 006'57.3'W	351	22.1	
Sunday 30th	Southampton		1188*	21.0*	0700*
		Total Distance	4399*		

Happy Anniversary
40 Great Years
Wishing you a memorable celebration.
onboard Queen Victoria.

Master

Entertainment Director

Social Hostess

World Club
CUNARD®

SILVER

BEVERLY MENG
598755874B

World Club
CUNARD®

SILVER

JAMES MENG
598755874A

Jim and Bev celebrate their fortieth wedding anniversary, with some Nectar of the Gods!

Garmisch-Partenkirchen

Where Heather Meng participated in a student exchange program as a senior in High School. Jim and Bev also visited this beautiful town staying with Heather's hosting family and touring the site of the 1936 Winter Olympic Games. Lunch on top of the Zugspitze, the tallest mountain in Germany, was absolutely beautiful!

CHAPTER 16
HEATHER A. MENG

Heather Andrea Meng, daughter of James and Beverly Meng

NATIONAL SOCIETY OF THE

Children of the American Revolution

Be it known that

Heather Andrea Meng

has been duly admitted a member of this Society by
right of descent from

Emanuel Trexler

who aided the cause of American Independence
Given under our hands and the Seal of the
National Society this 22nd day of April, 1982.

National Number
126127

Admitted
February 8, 1982

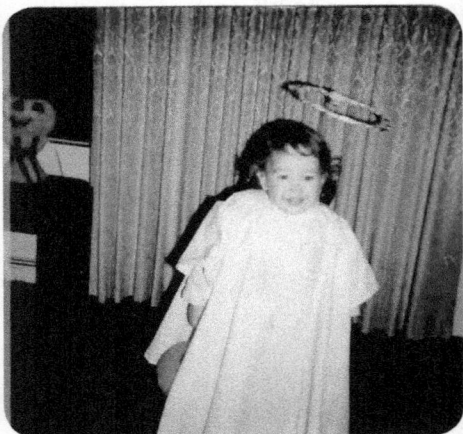

Heather, an angel at times while
not so angelic at other times

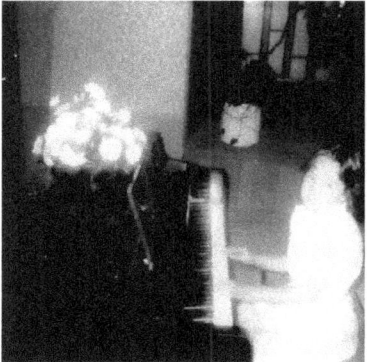

NATIONAL FEDERATION OF MUSIC CLUBS

This is to certify that

_____

Member of the _____ Club

Received _____ Rating

in the

NATIONAL FEDERATION JUNIOR FESTIVALS

held under the auspices of the

_____ FEDERATION OF MUSIC CLUBS

| Event | Class | Year |

Chairman   State President

NATIONAL FEDERATION OF MUSIC CLUBS

RATING SHEET FOR JUNIOR FESTIVALS

Name _Heather Meng_ or Number _158_

Event _Piano Solo_ Class _MD 2_

Arabesque Sentimentale – _Gillock_
(Required Composition) (Composer)

Sailor's Song – _Grieg_
(Choice Composition) (Composer)

INSTRUCTIONS FOR JUDGE: (See Bulletin, page 3, rules 7, 8)
Festival Entrants do not compete against each other, but rather, each is rated on his own merits-as a student and not a professional performer. Natural talent and potential ability should be given special consideration as well as the present performance, the good points of which should always be mentioned when giving suggestions for improvement. General factors to be considered are: talent, musicianship, technique, poise, intonation, and diction. Ratings: Superior, Excellent, Very Good,
JUDGE'S COMMENTS:

REQUIRED: _A very fine performance; quiet flow, attention to markings. I really enjoyed your interpretation m. 12-rest!!_

CHOICE: _Rests were observed, but ♪'s just before them were shortened too much; be sure to hold full value._

RATING _Superior_ _Jane McDaniel_
Judge's Signature

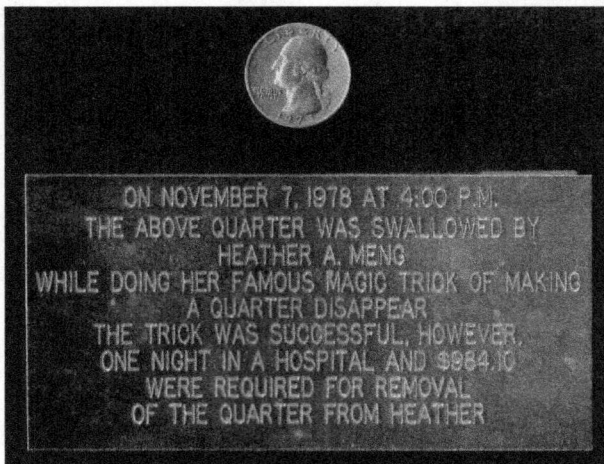

What the above plaque does not say, is that Uncle Wilmer W. Meng was the one who was showing Heather how to do his famous disappearing quarter trick!

[8]

The new guard?
Young Maniacs get the better of older clubs with 37-21 record

By Parker Oliver
Journal correspondent

The County Athletic Association, the largest area organization for girls fast-pitch softball, finds itself loaded with local talent, and there's a new team in the National League level of the Debutante Division—the association's highest classification—that figures to run wild with a little more experience.

Manchester Maniacs Coach Darryl Williams knows his young team is capable, and is pleasantly surprised with his club's 37-21 record.

"We're the new girls on the block," he said. "All of our girls are 16 playing in an 18-and-under league. So we thought that a .500 season was an optimistic prediction when the season started. To be playing the way we are is just great."

Williams, who has been coaching these girls for the last five years, expects his team to improve and possibly break onto the national scene.

"The softball in this area is great," he said. "You will see a number of teams from St. Louis in the national tournament in the next few years."

The Maniacs field a 16-player roster and Williams says every player contributes to the team's success.

"We have a core group of about seven girls that are the heart and soul of the team, but everyone does their part," Williams said.

The Maniacs' offense is powered by by Melissa Williams, Tiffany Heick and Lisa Bailey. They are the leaders in all offensive categories. Williams is batting .362 with 20 runs batted in. Heick, tops in both categories, is hitting .379 with 40 RBI. Bailey is batting .343 with 39 RBI. The 99 runs that they have produced constitute 45 percent of the Maniacs' total runs.

The pitching duties fall on Heather Meng and Melissa Williams. They split time on the mound, each serving as reliever for the other. Together, they have combined for an earned run average under 2.50 in 58 games.

The Maniacs began their season in mid-May and will conclude with the CAA tournament next week. All told, these girls will have played more than 70 games in 2½ months.

"Some of these girls are among the best around," Williams said. "I wouldn't be surprised if they received full rides to college to play softball."

Last weekend the Maniacs finished a disappointing sixth in the Metro Tournament, missing a chance to qualify for the regional tournament, which accepts only the top four teams.

"The team that won that tournament will probably go on to nationals," Williams said. "The second and third-place teams we had already beaten twice this season. So I guess I'm a little unhappy about the way things turned out."

MANIACS—1988

437

SPORTS
Wednesday, November 11, 1987 - *West Citizen Journal* IF

Vikings dominate all-South softball team

It's no surprise that conference champion Parkway North dominates this year's all-Suburban South softball team.

Six Vikings are on the first team, including pitchers Heather Meng and Sheil Aden, catcher Jen Cherye, first baseman Micki Schenbert, third baseman Dorie Sher and outfielder Wendy Adelstein. Aden also was the coaches' choice at shortstop.

Other first-round picks include Eureka first baseman Kathy Mosley, Park South second baseman Dianne Risher, designated hitter Michelle Biggs and outfielders Thelonda Malone of Eureka, Kristi Kordonowy of Parkway South and Lorri Hoppi of Oakville.

The second team lineup includes pitchers Gibbs and Allie Powers of Parkway South; catchers Joanna Coibon of Oakville, Stacy Beck ofParkway South and Tonya Ross of University City; second baseman Windy Cottrell of Eureka; third baseman Lisa Bailey of Parkway South; shortstops Latoya Branscomb of Eureka and Wendy Anzalone of Oaville; outfielders Dawn Graves of Parkway North, Barb McGhee of University City, Lesli Wickers of Parkway South and Tracy Kaufman of Parkway North.

The honorable mention list includes Tammy Bunton of Parkway North.

Heather Meng at age 14 on an earlier team with a wicked curve ball.

Meng lifts Maniacs
Page 8B - July 22, 1988 - *West Citizen Journal*

In a sense, the Manchester Maniacs girls softball team has strong-armed its way to a 37-21 record. And one of the team's strongest arms belongs to pitcher Heather Meng.

Meng is no stranger to pitching success. As a sophomore at Parkway North, Meng hurled her way to a 9-2 record with a 1.57 earned run average. Her efforts were good enough to earn her All-Suburban South Conference honors.

Meng has been a Maniac for the last two

Manchester Maniacs hurler Heather Meng takes the sign.

years, and has carried the brunt of the pitching duties. This season Meng has a 22-11 record with a 1.66 ERA. Her control is impeccable. With 92 strikeouts, Meng has fanned nearly one-fifth of the batters she has faced.

"Heather is very effective when she gets her breaking ball across," Maniac Coach Darryl Williams said. "She has a good fastball, good change-up and a great riser. She has been our No. 1 pitcher this season and last."

Having pitched since she was in sixth grade, Meng has honed her skill into an art. With good concentration, she seems capable of putting the ball anywhere she wants. Since fast-pitch softball puts very little strain on a pitcher's arm, Williams has the luxury of putting Meng on the hill nearly every night.

"I have been alternating Missy (Williams) and Heather on the mound just to give the girls a rest, but Heather has been our most effective and No. 1 pitcher all year," Williams said. At only 16, Meng has solidified her role as the top pitcher on both the Parkway North Vikings and the Maniacs. "We're all just 26 playing against 18-year olds," she said. "I know we're as good; we just lack experience."

Athletes of the month
West Citizen Journal, 1989

Heather Meng

Meng, a senior pitcher for the Parkway North softball team, has been a workhorse for the Vikings this season, pitching every inning this season. Through games of September 29, Meng has a 7-7 record, but had a 1.64 ERA in 98 innings. Meng has struck out 52 batters while walking just 28.

"The key to her success is that she throws strikes and doesn't hurt herself with walks," Parkway North Coach Bob Robben said. "She changes speeds well and moves the ball in and out and up and down. She has good velocity, although she's not overpowering. She lets her defense help her."

Meng is the only senior on a team that returned just three players from last season, Robben said. Meng is providing plenty of leadership this season.

"The team has come together partially because of Heather," Robben said.

Also mentioned in the newspaper as athlete of the month was Andy Bailey, a senior defensive back at Parkway West.

Heather Meng
Parkway North
softball pitcher

Heather Meng, a Parkway North
High School exchange student to
Garmisch-Partenkirchen, Germany.

Heather Meng at Busch Stadium playing an exhibition
game before a regular Cardinal baseball game.

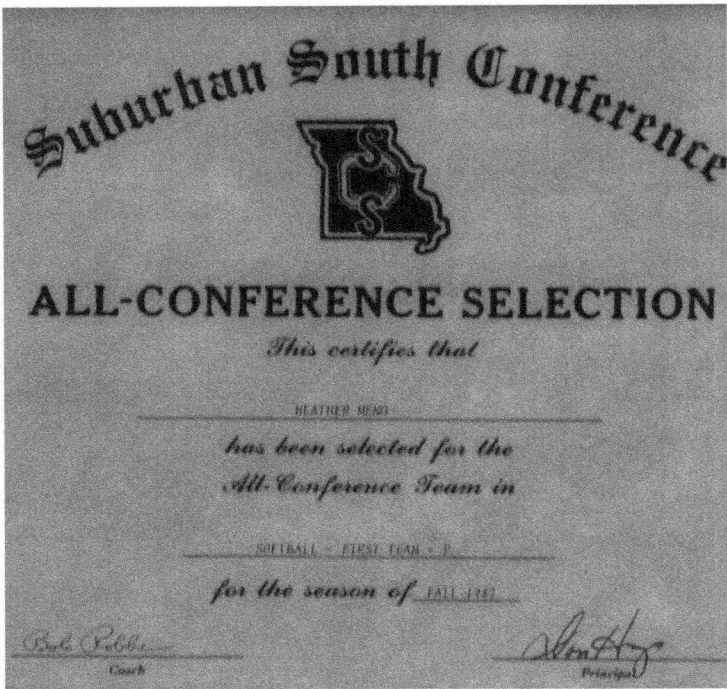

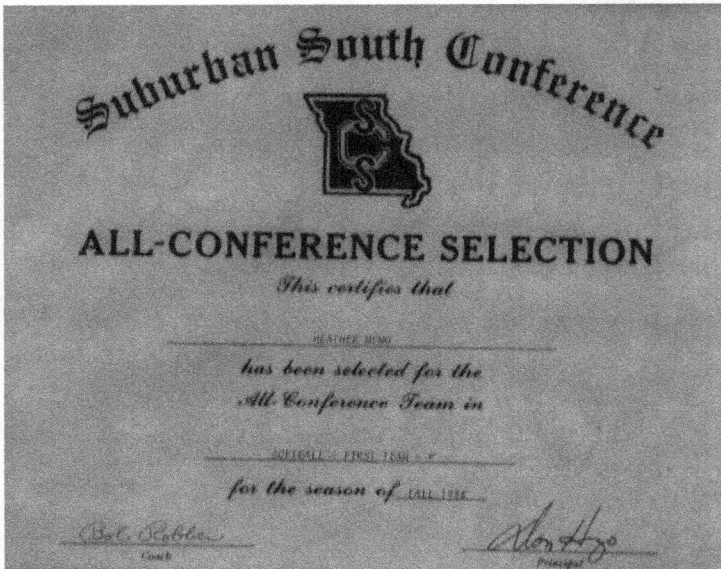

Heather A. Meng was voted the First Team All-Conference pitcher in the Suburban South Conference in her sophomore, junior and senior years in high school. She also qualified as a first team pitcher during her freshman year but was denied the honor because she was a freshman. These awards and others generated considerable interest from division one Universities.

Meng dynasty ends after 4 record varsity seasons
by Jason Sklar
Norsestar Sports Editor,
Wednesday, November 29, 1989

In our lives, dominated by mediocrity, the emergence of a true champion is a rarity. Senior Heather Meng is the epitome of such a champion and her four year softball career supports such top billings.

The recording of the final out by the girl's varsity softball team against McClure not only marked the end of the game, it marked the end of an era. Heather Meng four year varsity star threw her final pitch in a Viking uniform. Even though she won't play for the team again, she will not be forgotten by her teammates, coaches and fans.

Although the face of the team itself has been an ever changing variable over four years, there has been one constant in the equation—Heather. In her four year career, she's been a part of teams that have compiled in a 25-1 conference record, with three conference championships and one district championship ('86) of which to speak.

Heather herself has earned numerous honors. She's been selected to first team all conference for four years in a row. She has compiled a career record of 41-9 in her four years here. And she pitched every inning, except one, in every game this season for the Varsity squad.

Heather, however, is not a one dimensional player; she sparked the team offensively as well. She led the team in RBI's with 25, a number only surpassed in by Wendy Adelstein, twice. She was also team captain and second on the team with a batting average of .341.

Her leadership has been silent but strong. "She led by example," said Robben.

Obviously, Heather had a very successful softball career. As she approached her high school graduation, she received three (3) unsolicited scholarship offers to continue her softball pitching career. These offers came from St. Louis University, Indiana University and Samford University. Heather made the decision that she had successfully conquered this endeavor and it was time to "hang up her cleats", pack away all the trophies, and move on to the next challenge. She then attended and graduated from Baylor University in Waco, Texas.

You are cordially invited to attend
Parkway North High School
Honors Evening
Wednesday May 2, 1990
in the Gymnasium at 7:30 in the evening

Honoree: *Heather A. Meng*

Reception immediately following the ceremony

Jim and Bev are broke!

From an extremely proud grandfather, Edward J. Meng, a.k.a. Santa Clause, to his first grandchild, Heather Andrea Meng. Wow, was he and grandmother Jessie F. Meng proud!

Hi Heather:

You sure gave me a scare, I dropped in on your home on Yellow Ave and found the house vacant. The other evening I was making my rounds and checking on little girls and boys and I heard a little girl crying very hard so I looked in the window and there was my little girl Heather whom I thought I had lost in Granite City. I could not believe my ears she was crying because she had to go to bed. Now that is how little girls do but not a big one like you; and I did not see you kiss your Mother and Daddy good night; shame on you.

I saw you help your little brother several times and that is fine, all big girls help their little brother, and you help your Mother a lot in the kitchen, drying the dishes and sweeping the floor and help her make cookies. That little brother of yours is getting to be some boy. You take good care of him; oh! I almost forgot I saw you push him down, which I don't think was very nice for a big girl.

I saw you at your Grandma's home, you always have a good time there, but be a little more gentle with that old cat, I have seen that old cat around for many years.

Well I must close and check on a lot of other girls and boys, I will be back and check on you and your brother again before Christmas. Be good and I will bring you a lot of toys

Sincerely

Santa Claus.

'975

Project Management Institute

THIS IS TO CERTIFY THAT

Heather Meng

HAS BEEN FORMALLY EVALUATED FOR DEMONSTRATED EXPERIENCE,
KNOWLEDGE AND SKILLS TO LEAD AND DIRECT PROJECT TEAMS AND IS HEREBY
BESTOWED THE GLOBAL CREDENTIAL

Project Management Professional

IN TESTIMONY WHEREOF, WE HAVE SUBSCRIBED OUR SIGNATURES UNDER THE SEAL OF THE INSTITUTE.

Beth Parleton · Chair, Board of Directors

Mark A. Langley · President and Chief Executive Officer

PMP® Number **1419757**

PMP® Original Grant Date **22 June 2011**

PMP® Expiration Date **21 June 2014**

Project Management Institute

ALEXANDER DAVID COCHRAN AND JACOB SHAMHART COCHRAN

Children of Heather A. Meng*

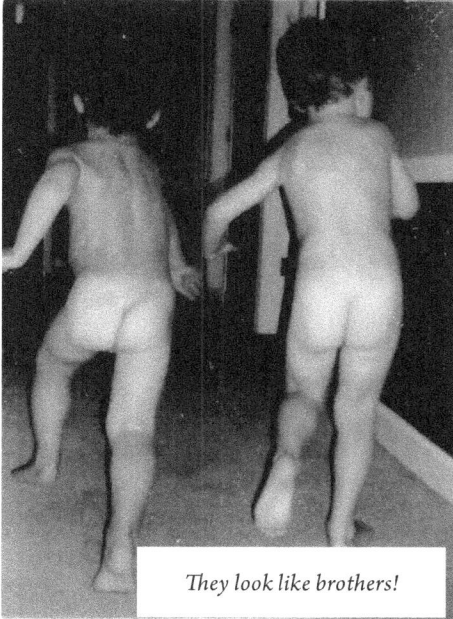

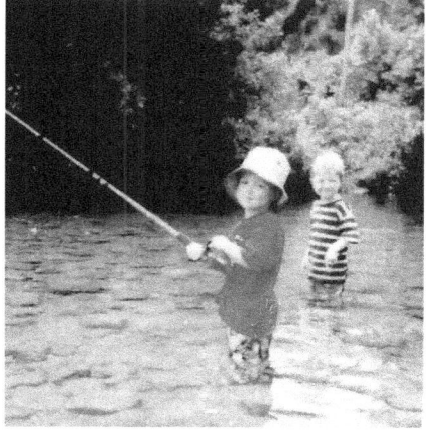

They look like brothers!

Both Alexander and
Jacob are members of
The National Society
of the Children of the
American Revolution. This
connection is to the Patriot
Emanuel Trexler who is
referenced in Chapter 29.

---

* Heather divorced David Cochran, retained custody of both children and regained her maiden
name of Meng. Heather subsequently married Timm Schowalter who had two children, Ryan
and Kristin, from an earlier marriage.

Family tree for Jacob and Alexander David Cochran
Produced by Werner Schabbehard 2010-09-18

First Generation

1. Jacob Shamhart Cochran[1] was born in the USA

1. Alexander David Cochran[1] was born in the USA

> Source: Meng, James Leroy, St. Louis, Missouri

Second Generation

2. David W. Cochran marries Heather Andrea Meng, they divorce.

3. Heather Andrea Meng[3] was born in the USA
    (Heather's brother, Erik James Meng was born in the USA and is unmarried as of 2012).

> Source: Meng, James Leroy, St. Louis, Missouri

6. James Leroy Meng[4] was born in the USA
    He married Beverly Ann Lewis in the USA

> Source: James Leroy, Meng, St. Louis, Missouri

7. Beverly Ann Lewis[6] was born in the USA

> Source: James Leroy, Meng, St. Louis, Missouri

Fourth Generation

12. Edward John Meng[7] was born on December 4, 1901, in Freeburg, St. Clair County, Illinois, and died on April 1, 1983, in St. Louis County, Missouri. He married Jessie Frances Shamhart on September 12, 1928[8].

> Source: James Leroy, Meng, St. Louis, Missouri

13. Jessie Frances Shamhart[9] was born on July 2, 1903, in Newton, Jasper County, Illinois, and died on February 18, 1978.

> Source: James Leroy, Meng, St. Louis, Missouri

Fifth Generation

24. Friederich Fred Fritz Meng[10] was born on October 11, 1863, in Freeburg, St. Clair County, Illinois, and died on January 23, 1913, in New Athens, St. Clair County, Illinois. He married Elisabeth Margaret Koesterer on November 23, 1892, in St. Clair County, Illinois[11].

> Source: Meng, James Leroy, St. Louis, Missouri

25. Elisabeth Margaret Koesterer[12] was born on May 29, 1869 in Freeburg, St. Clair County, Illinois, and died on May 12, 1947, in Granite City, Madison County, Illinois.

   Source: Meng, James Leroy, St. Louis, Missouri

26. Wilmer W Shamhart[13] was born on August 7, 1878, in Jasper County, Illinois, and died on December 28, 1947. He married Oliver Foster on April 12, 1899[14].

   Source: either Shamhart, Carl—Shamhart, Bruce, Ray—Shamhart, John Shamhart—Elizabeth McPherson

27. Oliver Foster[15,16] was born on November 25, 1876, in Newton, Jasper County, Illinois, and died on October 27, 1962, in Granite City, Madison County, Illinois.

   Source: Meng, James Leroy, St. Louis, Missouri

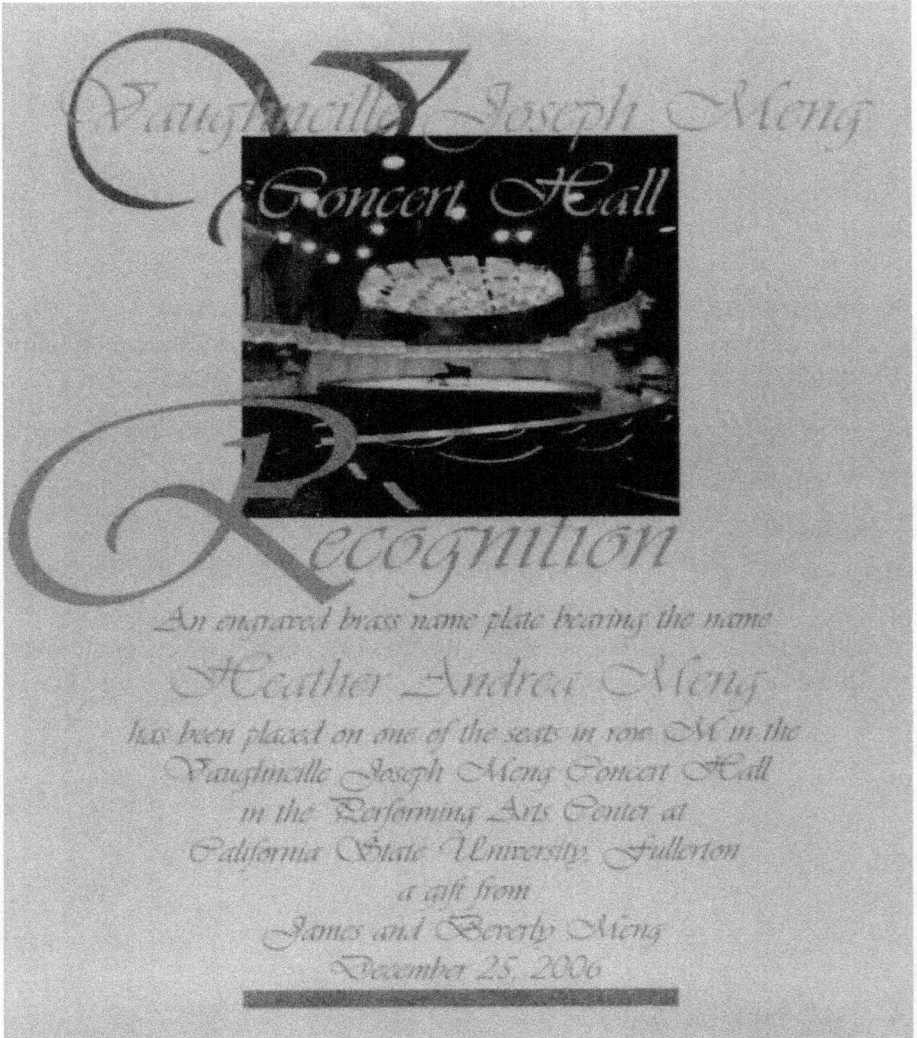

Vaughncille Joseph Meng Concert Hall

Recognition

An engraved brass name plate bearing the name

Heather Andrea Meng

has been placed on one of the seats in row M in the Vaughncille Joseph Meng Concert Hall in the Performing Arts Center at California State University, Fullerton a gift from James and Beverly Meng December 25, 2006

Alex and Jake, the early years

First Santa

First pumpkin hunt

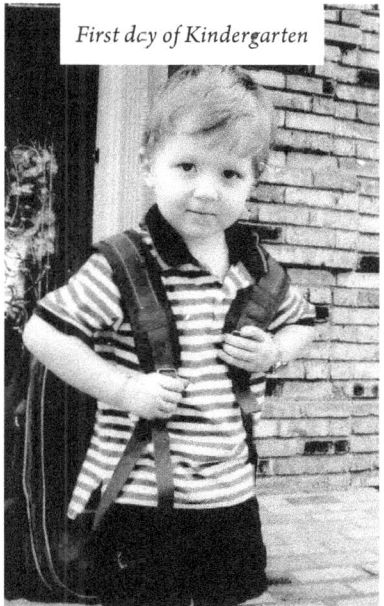

First dcy of Kindergarten

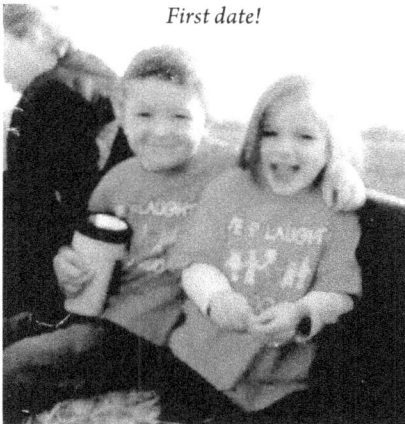

First date!

The Timm and Heather (nee Meng) Schowalter Family

*Ryan, Kristin, Heather, Timm,
Jacob and Alexander*

Pastor Bill Myers

James and Beverly Meng's grandchildren

Kristin Schowalter, Ryan Schowalter, Alex Cochran, and Jacob Cochran

CHAPTER 17
ERIK J. MENG

Erik James Meng, son of James and Beverly Meng

NATIONAL SOCIETY OF THE

Children of the American Revolution

Be it known that

Erik James Meng

has been duly admitted a member of this Society by right of descent from

Emanuel Trexler

who aided the cause of American Independence. Given under our hands and the Seal of the National Society this 22nd day of April, 1982.

National Number:
126128

Admitted:
February 8, 1982

455

Erik graduated from Parkway North High School in St. Louis, MO. He is employed as a journeyman painter at the FPL Nuclear Power Plant in Ft. Pierce, Florida. Keep in mind this is the same kid that when told to clean our basement, he used a gas-powered leaf blower!

September, 1987

SEVEN PINES IMPROVEMENT ASSOCIATION

forest flashes

On Monday, August 10, 1987, the Creve Coeur Cougars, a C.C.A.A. baseball team composed of 7th grade boys from the Seven Pines area played an exhibition baseball game with Belgium. the Belgian team was a National all-star team from Antwerp, 3 years older than the Cougars, and were similar to our legion teams. Belgium won.

The Mayor of Creve Coeur, Mrs. Peggy Vickroy proclaimed this day as Creve Coeur Cougar/Antwerp Eagles Baseball Day in the City of Creve Coeur and donated a City flag that was presented to the Belgian team during the pregame ceremonies. Mayor Vickroy also provided special Creve Coeur lapel pins for the Belgian players and framed, personalized, certificates of appreciation to each of the Cougar players for participating in this event.

The Cougars have been a successful team in meeting their objective of winning 80% of their games over the past three years. They have also taken first or second places in local tournaments in Manchester, Ballwin, Chesterfield, Pond, and Creve Coeur. Early this season, the Cougars and their parents traveled to Cape Girardeau where they won 2 out of 3 games against the Cape Girardeau all-star teams. The Cougar roster includes Erik Meng and Norm Bilow of Seven Pines, Chris Webb from the Village, Jason Tilly and Aaron Wilkins from Old Farm, plus Phillip Chazen, Brian Houchin, Jason Leath, Al Plucinski, Tom Scott, David Werner, Phil Wright and Eric Peterson from other subdivisions.

After the game, a pool party and chicken dinner was held at the Seven Pines swimming pool in honor of the Belgium team. The pool was decorated with U.S. and Belgium Flags plus red, white and blue banners. It is important to recognize the special consideration provided these two teams by the Trustees of Seven Pines in arranging for the use of the pool facilities. A special thanks to Mr. Max Malz and his associates who helped arrange for the pool. A special thanks is also extended to the Pool Manager and Lifeguards who were on duty during the party. they were outstanding and certainly did an excellent job in representing Seven Pines. The Belgians were thoroughly impressed with our facilities and the hospitality displayed by the Cougar team and the representatives of the Seven Pines Subdivision.

Erik did not continue his baseball career, electing to become a trout fisherman instead. As such, he became well known as a terrific rainbow trout fisherman.

West Chesterfield County News
August 13   Vol. 5 No. 15

Creve Coeur Cougars Host Belgium Baseball Team

The Creve Coeur Cougars, a Creve Coeur Athletic Association baseball team composed of seventh grade boys, was defeated by the Eagles from Antwerp, Belgium, 22–5 in an exhibition game earlier this week.

Creve Coeur Mayor Peggy Vickroy honored the event by donating a Creve Coeur city flag which was presented to the team manager and special lapel pins for the players. Special recognition awards were given to each of the Cougar players.

Following the exhibition game, a chicken dinner and swim party was held for the two teams at the Seven Pines subdivision swimming pool.

The Cougars have been a successful team, meeting their objectives of winning 80 percent of their games in the past three years. They have also taken first or second places in the local tournaments in Manchester, Ballwin, Chesterfield, Pond and Creve Coeur.

Cougar members are Norm Bilow, Phillip Chazen, Brian Houchin, Jason Leath, Erik Meng, Eric Peterson, Allen Plucinski, Tom Scott, Jason Tilly, Chris Webb, David Werner, Aaron Wilkins, and Phil Wright.

Creve Coeur truce[8]
Pool party is the "war booty" for Belgians, local boys after game

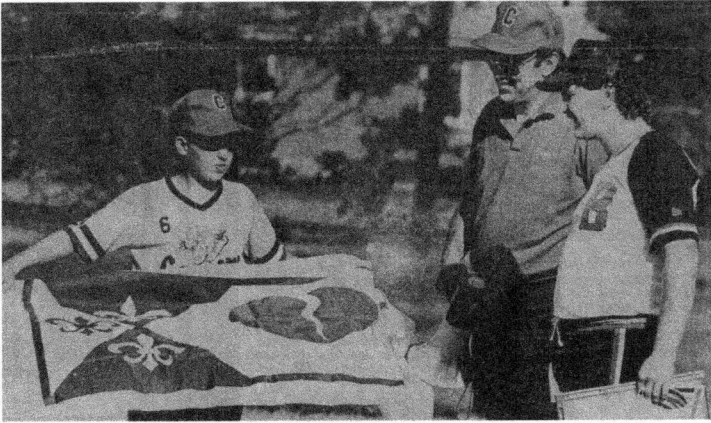

Erik Meng of the Creve Coeur Cougars (left) presents the Creve Coeur city flag to Coach Tony Ilegems (right) of the visiting Belgian team as Creve Coeur coach Larry Tilly looks on. The clubs played each other in a baseball game Monday at ABC Park and then headed out together for a swim party.

Page 2E––July 20, 1988––Press Journal
Journal correspondent

On June 18, 1815, Napoleon's military career came to an abrupt halt about 40 miles south of Brussels, Belgium in the town of Waterloo.

In Monday's exhibition baseball game at ABC Park, the Creve Coeur Cougars met their own Waterloo, 24–6, against a determined Belgian force. But in this instance, there was immediate peace between the two groups once the battle had ended.

A Seven Pines pool party arranged by Gail Chazen, mother of second baseman Phillip Chazen, helped close the distance and age gaps (the Belgian boys, at 15, are two years older than the Americans) between the teams. Since Antwerp is the world's third largest port, it was no surprise that love for the water was just as apparent for the Antwerp-based contingency as for their American counterparts. Naturally, there were other similarities.

"On the way here, we discovered that we like the same kind of music," said Phillip Chazen. "And we're all interested in girls. One of their players said there's a good-looking girl at 9 o'clock."

Although the Belgians displayed signs of Whiteyball in stealing bases and successfully executing countless bunt attempts, they admit that their brand of baseball––which developed from watching touring Japanese and American teams in the 1950s—is a far cry from that of the United States.

"We don't have nearly as many people interested in baseball because we don't see it much on TV or in the newspapers," said Belgian head coach Tony Ilegems. "Also, localized sports are not transmitted in Brussels. Because of that, we can't get any sponsors."

But considering the fortunes of a few of Ilegems' own players, Belgium's youth just may change the stagnant "country club sport" image that baseball has projected in that country.

"Not everyone there considers it very exciting but I really like it," said Filip Jacobs. "I started in school and they asked me to come back and play again if I liked it. It's an original kind of thing for me and I've made a lot of friends through it. Now I'm in my eighth year."

"Baseball's not nearly as well known in Belgium," said team captain Willem Gabriels. "There aren't many teams and we only play about 20 games. But it's growing. I started playing with a friend and at first I was bored with the game. After I learned to play better it was good fun, especially when we win."

But former Creve Coeur Coach Jim Meng, who worked through the International Athletic Foundation in arranging Monday's game, said long before the contest that winning and losing was not important here.

"We don't care about the score," he said. "It's a chance for members of our team to meet kids from a totally different culture and background. It's a breakaway from our regular season pattern of trying to score runs. When they come over, we'll be the U.S. first and baseball players second. Hopefully, their kids will look back and say that Americans treated us well and are good people."

City of Creve Coeur

Certificate of Appreciation

Presented to

Erik Meng

Who has rendered extraordinary service and assistance to the City of Creve Coeur.
With grateful appreciation and recognition of your superior performance,
this certificate is presented this ___9th___ day of _August_ 19_87_

_____
Mayor

COUGARS #1

Creve Coeur, MO

CHESTERFIELD TOURNAMENT
BASEBALL BANTAM II
COUGARS
1985
CHAMPIONS

1985 CAA TOURNAMENT
SECOND PLACE

CREVE COEUR TOURNAMENT
COUGARS
MIDGET I
1986
FIRST PLACE

10 TEAM POND TOURNAMENT
COUGARS
MIDGET I
1986
SECOND PLACE

Fishing at an early age

The Difference between Men and Boys Is the
Price of Their Toys, Trains, and More Trains

Erik Meng became a model train collector and operator at an early age. Somehow, Santa, the Easter bunny, and birthday fairy brought Erik Lionel and American Flyer toy trains. With a large train layout in the basement with elevated tracks and tunnels, Erik became an excellent operator. The age of the trains ranged from 1929 to 1980. He has collected approximately 100 model trains, all in running condition. Erik even held one birthday party among the real trains at the Missouri Transportation Museum.

The pictures below are Erik and Heather in the cab of the Norfolk and Western Number 611, one of the last steamers in existence. The last steam driven train to travel was a special round-trip excursion from St. Louis to Moberly, Missouri. Erik added the Lionel version of the "611" to his collection.

Heather and Erik Meng at Bruce and Mary Lewis's wedding. Good looking kids!

Parkway North High School

St. Louis Co.  Missouri

This Certifies That

Erik James Meng

has satisfactorily completed the Course of Study prescribed by the Board of Education for the High School and is therefore entitled to this

Diploma

Given at St. Louis County, Missouri, this 31st day of May, 1992.

Richard B. Wells
PRESIDENT

Gretchen Fleming
PRINCIPAL

Carol A. Orlando
SECRETARY

John Smith
SUPERINTENDENT

**International Union of Painters and Allied Trades-AFL-CIO,CLC
Joint Apprenticeship & Training Fund**

**Certificate of Completion
Of Apprenticeship**
Know All Concerned that this certifies

Erik J. Meng

has fulfilled the terms of the Apprenticeship Agreement entered into in accordance with the national standards for

Painter / Decorator / Drywall Finisher

under a program duly registered with the U.S. Department of Labor, Bureau of Apprenticeship and Training
and is hereby recognized as a qualified skilled journeyperson with all opportunities and responsibilities which pertain thereto.

given this 23rd day of July 2011

Joint Apprenticeship and Training Committee Co-Chairman

General President, Union of Painters and Allied Trades

Joint Apprenticeship and Training Committee Co-Chairman

Atlantic Technical Center

This certifies that

ERIK J. MENG

has met the requirements of a program of training in

Painting & Decorating

*as prescribed by the Florida Department of Education, and
The School Board of Broward County, Florida
and is hereby presented this Certificate of Program Completion*

Given this 16th day of June 2011

Director

Instructor

On July 23, 2011, Erik Meng completed a three-year apprenticeship program and was promoted to a journeyman painter and intermediate supervisor at the Florida Power and Light Company's Nuclear Power Plant in Port St. Lucie, Florida.

Port St. Lucie Nuclear Power Plant

Erik worked as a first responder, electrical, during hurricanes Matthew in 2016 and Irma in 2017 while working for Wilco Electric in Florida. Tired of seeing alligators, snakes and fish that would kill you plus an occasional dead body, Erik said good bye to these attractions and their annual hurricanes and returned to St. Louis MO. in 2018. After all, there is nothing like enjoying four seasons, a white Christmas and good baseball.

The adventures of Erik J. Meng

Bungee jumping from a crane
(Oct. 30, 2009, Orlando, FL).

Received certification as deep diver, at 100 ft
(Dec. 24, 2011, Singer Island, FL).

Sky diving at 16,000 ft
(Jul. 8, 2009, Sebastain, FL).

469

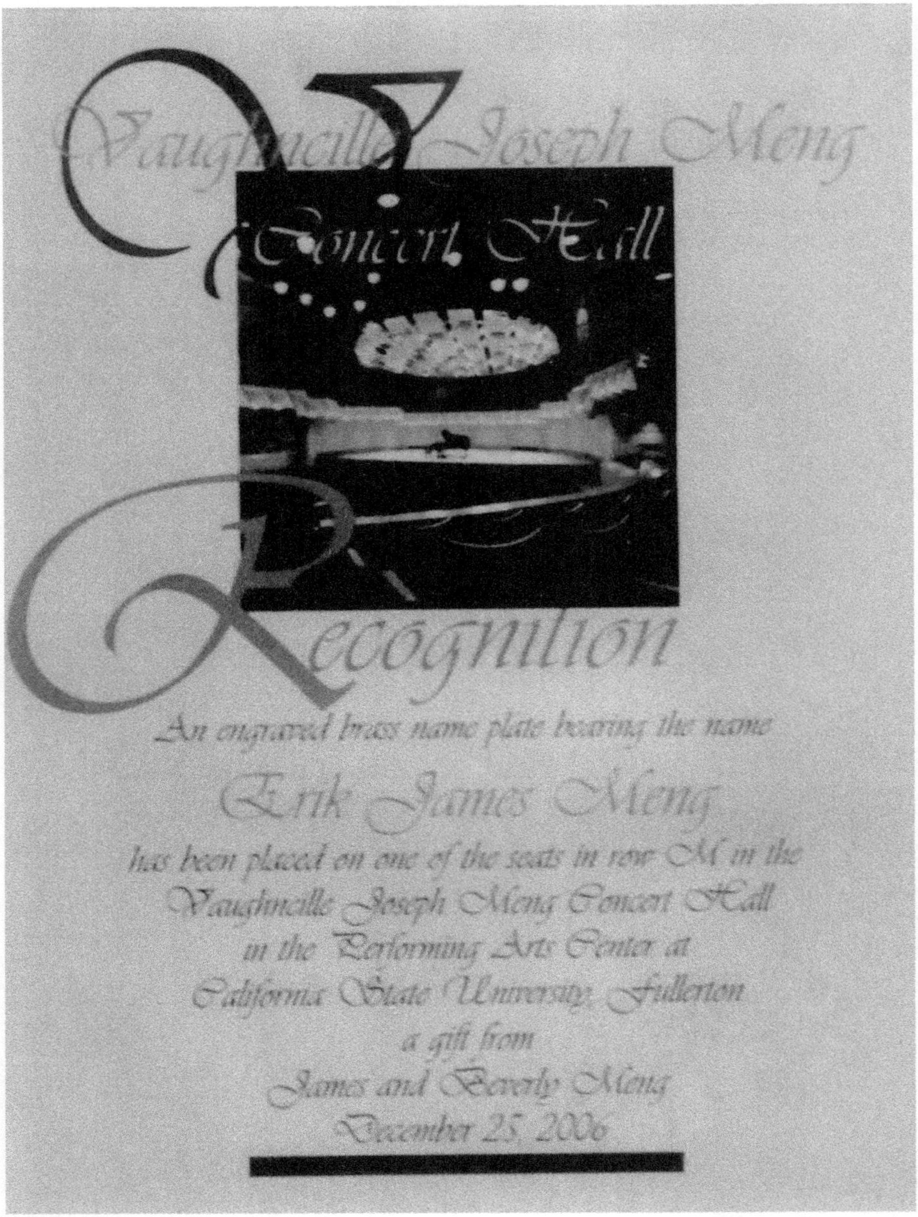

Vaughncille Joseph Meng
Concert Hall

Recognition

An engraved brass name plate bearing the name

Erik James Meng

has been placed on one of the seats in row M in the
Vaughncille Joseph Meng Concert Hall
in the Performing Arts Center at
California State University, Fullerton
a gift from
James and Beverly Meng
December 25, 2006

An interesting Development!

While visiting Erik in Florida, we noticed a pile of rusty items located in his garage. When asked what they were, Erik said a previous owner had collected them (about 6 in total) from the beach. We decided they looked like WWII sea mines. A quick call to the Sheriffs Department resulted in the St Lucie County Bomb Disposal Squad arriving with their lights and sirens and a specialized truck that had x ray capabilities. People were then evacuated. As it turned out, these rusty items were in fact WWII sea mines that had washed ashore but they were not thought to be active! The mines were hauled away very slowly. Keep in mind Erik's bedroom was on the other side of the wall from these mines. The bomb squad told us that had these mines been active and were detonated, they would have taken out the entire city block! Apparently, their existence and collection by some uninformed residents is common in Florida. That being said, Erik loves Florida and it is beautiful.

Erik J. Meng, married Robyn Roschelle Bruce, 2018. Robyn had one child, Christopher Michael Durette from a previous marriage.

CHAPTER 18
NOYLE (KEITH) AND VELMA VIOLA (LOGAN) LEWIS

The Beverly (née Lewis) Meng family

*1943 Wedding day
This is my beautiful wedding
dress in navy, and those are
felt flowers on the front.*

Velma Viola (née Logan) Lewis

Keith and Velma Logan Lewis (1943)

Keith's birthday (1987, 67 years old)

1946

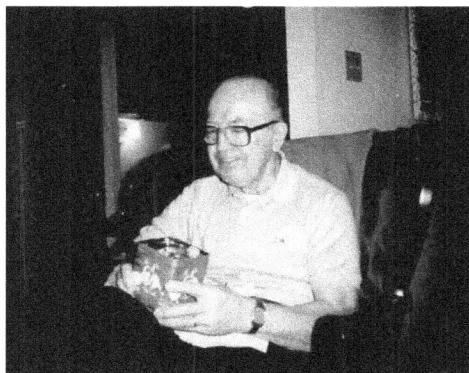

Rosie the Riveter a.k.a. Velma Viola Lewis

On a quiet Sunday morning on December 7, 1941, 183 Japanese warplanes attacked Hickam field, in Pearl Harbor, Hawaii. This attack resulted in 2,433 American deaths, destruction of 18 US warships and 188 US airplanes. This event resulted in America entering World War II.

With the American men enlisting in the war effort, American women, mothers, daughters, wives, and schoolgirls entered the workforce to replace the men who were off to war. More than six million first-time female workers helped to build planes, bombs, tanks, and other weapons of war. One such facility in this war effort was the *Richmond Shipyards* in Richmond, California. This shipyard constructed more ships during World War II than any other shipyard in America.

The Richmond Shipyard is where the term *Rosie the Riveter* originated and also is the home of the Rosie the Riveter memorial. This memorial is listed on the National Register of Historic Places. Originally known as Wendy the Welders in the shipyards, they soon became known as Rosies. The term *Rosie the Riveter* was first used in 1942 in a song of the same name written by Redd Evans and John Loeb and made popular by big band leader Kay Kyser. The song was a national hit.

One of the Rosie the Riveters working in the Richmond shipyards was Velma Lewis, from Raymondville, Missouri. She was a welder, wore leather overalls, hair covered with a bandanna, welding hood, steel-toed shoes, lunch bucket, and all. She used an arc welder to fuse metal plates in the fabrication of American warships. Throughout her life, Velma was extremely, and I mean extremely, particular in everything she did. Knowing Velma, her welds just had to be as perfect as possible and, I am sure, much to the satisfaction of our sailors and the US Navy.

During Velma's tour of duty in the shipyards, she was also accompanied by her husband Keith, a certified welder by occupation. Keith had flat feet, so he could not enter the armed services; however, Keith, like many others, served his country in another manner. They lived together in housing that was provided specifically for the shipyard workers.

At this point in time, Pearl and Dean Krewson lived in California. Grandma Mae Logan and Evelyn Logan joined Dean in California. Pearl was also a *Rosie* in the Richmond yards . . .

Me in my work clothes before I started on my job (Richmond, CA). My hair had to be covered with a bandanna before I put on my welding hood, then leather overalls over my jeans, and then steel-toed safety shoes.

476

Both Velma and Keith talked about this experience in later years, not only their responsible duty as an American, but they enjoyed their work and many new friends.

Both Keith and Velma and Pearl received a *letter of appreciation for a job well done* from the Richmond Shipyards operator, Permanente Metals, which is part of Kaiser Shipyards.

A *"Wendy the Welder"* at
the Richmond Shipyards

Norman Rockwell's Saturday
Evening Post cover featuring
Rosie the Riveter

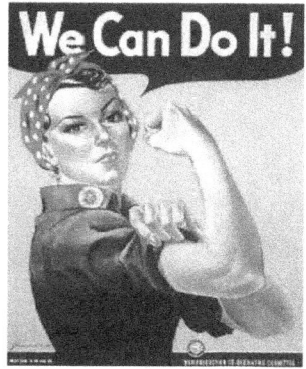

J. Howard Miller's "We Can
Do It!"—commonly referred
to as Rosie the Riveter

(Richmond, CA) Dressed in
work clothes before started
welding had to wear welding
hood. He has on his steel-toed
safety shoes. Men only had to
work leather jackets and no
leather overalls if they so chose

Noyle Keith Lewis, Richard,
California, May 1944.

The last of 519 Liberty ships from the Permanente Metals Corporation joins the fleet.

ST. PAUL'S CATHEDRAL

At the east end of the Cathedral behind the high altar is the American Memorial Chapel. This part of the building was destroyed during the Blitz and, when rebuilt in the 1950s, formed a chapel funded by the British people to commemorate the members of the US forces based in Britain who gave their lives defending liberty during World War II.

The Chapel is also known as the Jesus Chapel, as the space was known prior to World War II.

In a case behind the high altar is an illuminated book of remembrance: the *American Roll of Honour*, presented by General Eisenhower in 1951, in which their 28,000 names are inscribed.

	Sgt.	U.S.A.A.F.	Lombardo, P.P.	S/Sgt. U.S.A.A.F.
Logan, G.H.Jr.	1st.Lt.	U.S.A.A.F.	Lomden, G.S.	Sgt. U.S.A.A.F.
Logan, J.A.	2nd.Lt.	U.S.A.A.F.	Lonchar, P.M.	Capt. U.S.A.A.F.
Logan, J.A.	Cmctr.	U.S.N.R.	Londo, V.J.Jr	WT1. U.S.C.G.
Logan, J.C.	CMM.	U.S.N.	London, D.A.	1st.Lt. U.S.A.A.F.
Logan, L.R.L.	S/Sgt.	U.S.A.A.F.	London, E.	F/O U.S.A.A.F.
Logan, N.G.	2nd.Lt.	U.S.A.A.F.	London, K.F.	2nd.Lt. U.S.A.A.F.
Logan, P.F.	S/Sgt.	U.S.A.A.F.	Lone, N.R.	ChMate U.S.M.M.
			Long, A.D.	

*Bev Meng's uncle or Bev's mom's brother is Leroy Logan,
listed in the book titled American Roll of Honor, 1941–1945.
The book is left open for the public to see and be reminded of
their sacrifice. One page is turned daily to a new list of names.*

Logue, H.W.	Wpr.	U.S.M.M.	Long, E.A.	Sgt. U.S.A.A.F.
Logue, R.J.	Sgt.	U.S.A.	Long, E.W.	Pvt. U.S.A.
Logue, S.C.	Ens.	U.S.C.G.	Long, G.M.	F/O U.S.A.A.F.
Loguidice, A.C.	Cpl.	U.S.A.A.F.	Long, H.D	Pfc. U.S.A.
Lohlein, G.B.	2nd.Lt.	U.S.A.A.F.	Long, H.E.Jr	2nd.Lt. U.S.A.A.F.
Lohman, C.M.	T/Sgt.	U.S.A.A.F.	Long, H.O.Jr	S/Sgt. U.S.A.A.F.
Lohmann, W.L.	2nd.Lt.	U.S.A.A.F.	Long, H.W.	1st.Lt. U.S.A.A.F.
Lohmeyer, M.E.	2nd.Lt.	U.S.A.A.F.	Long, J.A.	Capt. U.S.A.A.F.
Lohneis, J.C.	Sgt.	U.S.A.A.F.	Long, J.B.	1st.Lt. U.S.A.A.F.
Loholdt, C.A.	Sgt.	U.S.A.A.F.	Long, J.D.	Pvt. U.S.A.
Loija, R.A.	T/Sgt.	U.S.A.A.F.	Long, J.M.	S/Sgt. U.S.A.A.F.
Lojewski, T.	1st.Lt.	U.S.A.A.F.	Long, M.D	Pfc. U.S.A.A.F.
Loken, R.C.	S/Sgt.	U.S.A.A.F.	Long, M.M.	Pvt. U.S.A.
Lolley, L.W.	Capt.	U.S.A.A.F.	Long, M.R.	2nd.Lt. U.S.A.A.F.
Lomax, S.H.	LtCol.	U.S.A.	Long, R.C.	2nd.Lt. U.S.A.A.F.
Lombardi, J.D.	MM3.	U.S.N.R.	Long, R.E.	S/Sgt. U.S.A.A.F.
Lombardi, J.M.	T/Sgt.	U.S.A.A.F.	Long, R.H.Jr	Pvt. U.S.A.
Lombardo, A.J.	T/Sgt.	U.S.A.A.F.	Long, R.L.	Sgt. U.S.A.A.F.
Lombardo, L.J.	Sgt.	U.S.A.A.F.	Long, R.M.	S/Sgt. U.S.A.A.F.

479

Professional bean snapping Mae Logan (Velma's mother)

A Mom's final touch

Bev's wedding

Heather's wedding

In loving Memory of
Keith N. Lewis
February 28, 1920
April 20, 1992

A sad day

In Loving Memory of
Velma Viola (nee Logan) Lewis
May 31, 1922
July 13, 2010

Velma Viola (née Logan) Lewis

483

As Told by Bev's Mom Velma Lewis to Granddaughter Heather Meng

I, Velma (Logan) Lewis, was born at Raymondville, Missouri, on May 31, 1922. My father was Joseph G. Logan, born November 10, 1879, in Marion County, Arkansas. He died on January 8, 1946, at Rolla Hospital at the age of 67. My dad worked the timber business in Washington State for about 10 years. My mother was Mae Nola Courtney, born November 1896 at Greenfield, Missouri. She died on February 23, 1980, at Cabool Nursing Home. They were married at Ink, Missouri, on September 13, 1913, and the next day left for the state of Washington. Afterward, they returned to Raymondville.

On May 31, 1922, their greatest treasure was born—me! I'm the only Missourian in the bunch. My three sisters and only brother were born in the state of Washington. Pearl was born on August 23, 1914, and died on October 19, 2000. Lauretta was born on April 5, 1916, and died on October 16, 1997. Evelyn Logan was born on June 21, 1918, and died on August 27, 1988. Leroy Logan was born on January 9, 1920. He was enlisted in the US Army Air Force on June 4, 1942, and trained in several camps in the States before being assigned overseas as an aerial gunner in February 1944. He died in England during World War II on April 21, 1944. (See the American Memorial Chapel remembrance book in St. Paul's Cathedral referenced earlier).

On May 9, 1943, Noyle Keith Lewis and I were married. We met on a blind date. We moved to California the next day because there were jobs there. We welded on the large battleships for World War II. Both Pearl and I were welders.

Two years later, we returned to St. Louis where Beverly Ann Lewis was born.

Your mom was married at age 23 and had you at age 26. I was at your mom's house when she called your dad from work and told him it was time for her to go the hospital. When I went to the hospital to see you, you were in the room for feeding time. I picked you up in my arms, and to me, you were the most beautiful thing in the world. I had to look fast because a nurse came in and booted you out instead of me.

MISSOURI DEPARTMENT OF HEALTH AND SENIOR SERVICES

STATE FILE NUMBER

124 -

CERTIFICATE OF DEATH

VS 300 MO 580-2211 (1-10)

1. DECEDENT'S LEGAL NAME (Include AKA's if any) (First, Middle, Last, Suffix)			2. SEX	3. IF FEMALE, LAST NAME PRIOR TO FIRST MARRIAGE	4. ACTUAL OR PRESUMED DATE OF DEATH (Month, Day, Year)
Velma Viola Lewis			Female	Logan	July 13, 2010

5. SOCIAL SECURITY NUMBER	6a. AGE- Last Birthday (Years)	6b. UNDER 1 YEAR		6c. UNDER 1 DAY		7. DATE OF BIRTH (Month, Day, Year)	8. BIRTHPLACE (City and State or Foreign Country)
558-32-5681	88	Months	Days	Hours	Min/Yrs	May 31, 1922	Raymondville, Missouri

9a. RESIDENCE (COUNTRY)	9b. STATE, TERRITORY or PROVINCE	9c. COUNTY	9d. CITY, TOWN, OR LOCATION		
United States	Missouri	St. Louis	St. Louis		

9e. STREET AND NUMBER			9f. APARTMENT NO.	9. ZIP CODE	9h. INSIDE CITY LIMITS?
10024 Kennerly Road				63128	☐ Yes ☒ No

10. WAS DECEDENT EVER IN U.S. ARMED FORCES?	11. MARITAL STATUS AT TIME OF DEATH		12. SURVIVING SPOUSE'S NAME (If wife, give name prior to first marriage)
☐ Yes ☒ No	☐ Married ☐ Married, but separated ☒ Widowed ☐ Divorced ☐ Never Married ☐ Unknown		

13. FATHER'S NAME (First, Middle, Last, Suffix)	14. MOTHER'S NAME PRIOR TO FIRST MARRIAGE (First, Middle, Last, Suffix)	
Joseph Logan	Mae N. Courtney	

15a. INFORMANT'S NAME (First, Middle, Last, Suffix)	15b. RELATIONSHIP TO DECEDENT	15c. MAILING ADDRESS (Street and Number, City, State, Zip Code)
Beverly A. Meng	Daughter	76 Meadowbrook Country Club Estates Drive, Ballwin, MO 63011

16. PLACE OF DEATH (Check only one; see instructions.)

IF DEATH OCCURRED IN A HOSPITAL: IF DEATH OCCURRED SOMEWHERE OTHER THAN A HOSPITAL:

☐ Inpatient ☐ Emergency Room/Outpatient ☐ DOA   ☒ Hospice Facility ☐ Nursing Home/Long Term Care Facility ☐ Decedent's Home ☐ Other (Specify)

17. FACILITY NAME (If not institution, give street and number)	18. CITY OR TOWN, STATE AND ZIP CODE	19. COUNTY OF DEATH
DeGreeff Hospice House	St. Louis, Missouri 63128	St. Louis

20a. METHOD OF DISPOSITION	20b. DATE OF DISPOSITION (Month, Day, Year)	21. PLACE OF DISPOSITION (Name of cemetery, crematory, other place)	22. LOCATION (City or Town, State)
☒ Burial ☐ Cremation ☐ Donation ☐ Entombment ☐ Removal from State ☐ Other (Specify)	07/18/2010	Cedar Grove Cemetery	Salem, Missouri

23. NAME AND COMPLETE ADDRESS OF FUNERAL FACILITY	24. SIGNATURE OF FUNERAL SERVICE LICENSEE OR OTHER PERSON ACTING AS SUCH	25. FUNERAL ESTABLISHMENT LICENSE NUMBER
Stygar Florissant Chapel, 13980 New Halls Ferry Road, Florissant, Missouri 63033	▶	2004002788

26. ACTUAL OR PRESUMED TIME OF DEATH	27. WAS MEDICAL EXAMINER/CORONER CONTACTED?
1:25 A.M.	☒ Yes ☐ No

CAUSE OF DEATH (See instructions and examples on handbook)

29. PART I. Enter the chain of events – disease, injuries, or complications – that directly caused the death. DO NOT enter terminal events such as cardiac arrest, respiratory arrest, or ventricular fibrillation without showing the etiology. DO NOT ABBREVIATE. Enter only one cause on a line. Add additional lines if necessary.

IMMEDIATE CAUSE (Final disease or condition resulting in death)	a.	Cervical spine fractures	Due to (or as a consequence of):
Sequentially list conditions, if any, leading to the cause listed on line a. Enter the UNDERLYING CAUSE (Disease or injury that initiated the events resulting in death) LAST.	b.		Due to (or as a consequence of):
	c.		Due to (or as a consequence of):
	d.		

PART II. Enter other significant conditions contributing to death but not resulting in the underlying cause given in PART I.

Hypertensive cardiovascular disease

30. WAS AN AUTOPSY PERFORMED?	☐ Yes ☒ No
30a. WERE AUTOPSY FINDINGS AVAILABLE TO COMPLETE THE CAUSE OF DEATH?	☐ Yes ☐ No

31. DID TOBACCO USE CONTRIBUTE TO DEATH?	32. IF FEMALE	33. MANNER OF DEATH
☐ Yes ☐ No ☐ Probably ☒ Unknown	☒ Not pregnant within past year ☐ Pregnant at time of death ☐ Not pregnant, but pregnant within 42 days of death ☐ Not pregnant, but pregnant 43 days to 1 year before death ☐ Unknown if pregnant within the past year	☐ Natural ☒ Accident ☐ Suicide ☐ Homicide ☐ Pending Investigation ☐ Could not be determined

34. DATE OF INJURY (Month, Day, Year) (Spell Month)	35. TIME OF INJURY	36. PLACE OF INJURY (e.g. decedent's home; construction site; restaurant; wooded area)	37. INJURY AT WORK?
07/08/2010	10:00 A M	Residence	☐ Yes ☒ No

38a. LOCATION OF INJURY - STATE	38b. COUNTY	38c. CITY OR TOWN	38d. STREET AND NUMBER	38e. ZIP CODE
Missouri	St. Louis	Ballwin	76 Meadowbrook Country Club Estates Drive	63011

39. DESCRIBE HOW INJURY OCCURRED	40. IF TRANSPORTATION ACCIDENT, SPECIFY:
Fall	☐ Driver/Operator ☐ Passenger ☐ Pedestrian ☐ Other (Specify)

41. CERTIFIER (CHECK ONLY ONE)

☐ Certifying Physician - To the best of my knowledge, death occurred at the time, date, and place, and due to the cause(s) and manner stated.

☒ Medical Examiner/Coroner - On the basis of examination, and/or investigation, in my opinion, death occurred at the time, date, and place, and due to the cause(s) and manner stated.

SIGNATURE   _Mary E Case_

42. NAME, ADDRESS, AND ZIP CODE OF PERSON COMPLETING CAUSE OF DEATH (Item 29)	43. TITLE OF CERTIFIER
Mary E. Case, M.D. 6039 Helen Avenue, St. Louis, Missouri 63134	Chief Medical Examiner

44. CERTIFIER LICENSE NUMBER	45. CERTIFIER NPI NUMBER	46. DATE CERTIFIED (Month, Day, Year)
32097	n/a	07/22/2010

47. REGISTRAR SIGNATURE	48. FOR REGISTRAR ONLY- DATE FILED (Month, Day, Year)
Celia Spencer	AUG 0 4 2010

49. DECEDENT'S EDUCATION (Check the box that best describes the highest degree or level of school completed at time of death.)	50. DECEDENT OF HISPANIC ORIGIN? (Check the box that best describes whether the decedent is Spanish/Hispanic/Latino. Check the "No" box if decedent is not Spanish/Hispanic/Latino.)	51. DECEDENT'S RACE (Check one or more races to indicate what the decedent considered himself or herself to be.)	
☐ 8th grade or less	☒ No, not Spanish/Hispanic/Latino	☒ White	☐ Other Asian (Specify)
☐ 9th - 12th grade; no diploma	☐ Yes, Mexican, Mexican American, Chicano	☐ Black or African American	☐ Native Hawaiian
☐ High school graduate or GED completed	☐ Yes, Puerto Rican	☐ American Indian or Alaska Native (Name of the enrolled or principal tribe)	☐ Guamanian or Chamorro
☐ Some college credit, but no degree	☐ Yes, Cuban		☐ Samoan
☐ Associate degree (e.g. AA, AS)	☐ Yes, other Spanish/Hispanic/Latino (Specify)	☐ Asian Indian	☐ Other Pacific Islander (Specify)
☐ Bachelor's degree (e.g. BA, AB, BS)		☐ Chinese	☐ Other (Specify)
☐ Master's degree (e.g. MA, MS, MEng, MEd, MSW, MBA)		☐ Filipino	☐ Unknown
☐ Doctorate (e.g. PhD, EdD) or professional degree (e.g. MD, DDS, DVM, LLB, JD)		☐ Japanese	
		☐ Korean	
		☐ Vietnamese	

52. DECEDENT'S USUAL OCCUPATION (Indicate type of work done during most of working life. DO NOT USE "RETIRED".)	53. KIND OF BUSINESS/INDUSTRY
Homemaker	own home X

CHAPTER 19
WILMER AND VAUGHNCILLE (JOSEPH) MENG

Wilmer Walter Meng, (1903–1995)
Who was Wilmer W. Meng?
J. L. Meng (nephew)

Wilmer Walter Meng was married three times. His first marriage was to Thelda Cooper, the sister of O. J. Meng's wife, Elma Cooper. I'm not sure what happened, but I think the marriage was annulled, but I don't know the reason. He lost his second wife, Iris Leggett, to cancer, after being married for 15 years. He then married Vaughncille Vonnie Joseph.

Iris was very attractive. While living in Ashland, Kentucky, and again in California, they were both active in Little Theater. This organization was composed of local people who had a desire to be on the stage.

Wilmer and Iris also enjoyed ballroom dancing and square dancing, quite a combination. They were members of several dance clubs in Anaheim and Long Beach, California.

Wilmer never had any children. Consequently, he more or less adopted all the nephews as his own. This was good for us since it meant a lot of wrestling matches, Christmas gifts, and, most importantly, attention whenever he came to visit. Wilmer was a kid's kind of guy, and we all knew it.

One of my first memories of Uncle Wilmer was when he worked for the federal prison system. As a nine-year-old, his station in life was viewed as exceptionally neat stuff. He even had a gold badge (which I have today) as a symbol of his authority. Think of it, your uncle in charge of people like Black Bart and all the other hardened villains that we were reading in comic books and seeing on Saturday afternoons at the theater. One of his neat prison tricks that he taught us was how to get someone to go through a doorway that they didn't want to go through. With all the nephews acting exceptionally tough, Wilmer with a few simple moves placed us on our back sides, through door. Now this was really serious: this is the kind of stuff you tell all your friends at Webster school the next day. Little did we know that Wilmer was a personnel office, an administrator, and nothing to do with the controlling of hardened criminals. But at nine years of age, a guy who had a gold badge, worked in the prisons, and could put you through a doorway was a definite bona fide hero.

Uncle Wilmer was also a four-year Granite City High School letterman and captain of the football team, a four-year letterman in baseball, and pole vaulted on the track team during the off-season. When the nephews became active in athletics, Wilmer was always there asking questions and listening to our adventures. Even though he retired from the prison system and moved to Fullerton, California, as a hospital administrator, he followed the nephews' athletic careers with more questions and support. He was also an avid fan of the LA Lakers, the Dodgers, and the Rams. Therefore, whenever the St. Louis Cardinals would beat the Dodgers, a frequent occurrence in the 1980s, a phone call was immediately placed to California. For example, in 1985, during the ninth inning of the sixth game of the National League play-offs, the Dodger relief pitcher, Neidenfeur, decided to pitch to Jack Clark of the Cardinals. He shouldn't have. Clark hit a home run. The Dodgers' season abruptly ended with that one pitch and the Cardinals continued to the World Series. As soon as Clark touched home plate, it was time to place a call to Wilmer. He was not a happy camper. However, being the gentleman that he was, he continued to be gracious in defeat, explaining that the Cardinal's third base coach, Hacker, and manager, Whitey Herzog, were both from his hometown of New Athens, Illinois, and that's why St. Louis won. He then started talking about the weather for some reason??

A few years later, on a visit to St. Louis, Uncle Wilmer, my dad (Edward J.), and our family went to a German restaurant named "Eberhards" in Columbia, Illinois. Our kids, Heather and Erik, were about six and eight at the time. While waiting for our dinner, the restaurant was playing German music. Without any hesitation, Wilmer and my dad started singing the song in German. The restaurant came to a halt. The owner, Eberhard, then joined in along with another customer. My wife and kids watched in amazement as Wilmer was at his best. Good food, good beer, must and most importantly, an audience. While in California, Wilmer met Vonnie Joseph, a widow who was originally from Oklahoma. They made a perfect couple with identical interests. Wilmer played the mandolin and Vonnie played the piano. As good as Agnes Meng (Fred's wife) was at playing ragtime, Vonnie was equally good at playing in a professional style on her full-size baby grand. Vonnie's ability was concert quality reflecting her years of professional training. It was interesting to hear Vonnie say how she would like to play ragtime like Agnes, but couldn't, and Agnes say how she would like to play like Vonnie, but couldn't. Both had their own style, products of the musical environment in which they were raised and trained.

Wilmer and Vonnie also played their musical instruments frequently for the Fullerton, California, Rotary Club, which Wilmer was a member. Vonnie was the official pianist for the club and received awards for their many years of service. Wilmer also received the Paul Harris Award from Rotary International, the highest award given by this organization.

Later in life, Wilmer developed glaucoma and eventually lost his eyesight. This was a difficult time for both him and Vonnie. He could no longer enjoy his rose garden, which he constantly bragged about, or the orange trees in his yard. He could no longer look out his backyard and see Catalina Island or the nightly fireworks at Disneyland. However, he continued to enjoy all of his California sports teams on the radio and told the seemingly countless variety of jokes and stories that he had accumulated over the years. Both he and Vonnie made the best of a situation that they had no control over.

After Wilmer passed away, Vonnie also developed glaucoma. She sold their home in Fullerton and moved into a managed care facility. One of the Rotarians who they knew over the years currently assists Vonnie in her daily affairs.

Finally, the Meng family has frequently been accused of a lot of things, especially being "full of hops." If this is true (which I strongly suspect that it is), Wilmer had an overload! He was full of stories and jokes which he loved to tell to anyone who would listen. Besides his fondness for children, Uncle Wilmer's ability to tell jokes one after another cannot be forgotten, for he was excellent and loved sharing these stories with strangers in restaurants, on airplanes, in front of his Rotary Club, in hospitals, etc.-- wherever he could get someone to listen. These stories, "normally" clean, were quite good and representative of a man who, although was professional, always looked on the humorous side of life—always wanting to make people smile--which he did!

At his funeral, one of the eulogies referred to Uncle Wilmer as a man who was proud of his family, his heritage, and wore the map of Germany on his weathered face. This description by his Rotarian friend was most appropriate.

1925 Baseball

The Granite City High School baseball team autographed the team ball after the last out in their 1925 season. The following note shows Wilmer Meng at first base, O. J. Meng in right field, plus the other players (Courtesy: Wilmer Meng).

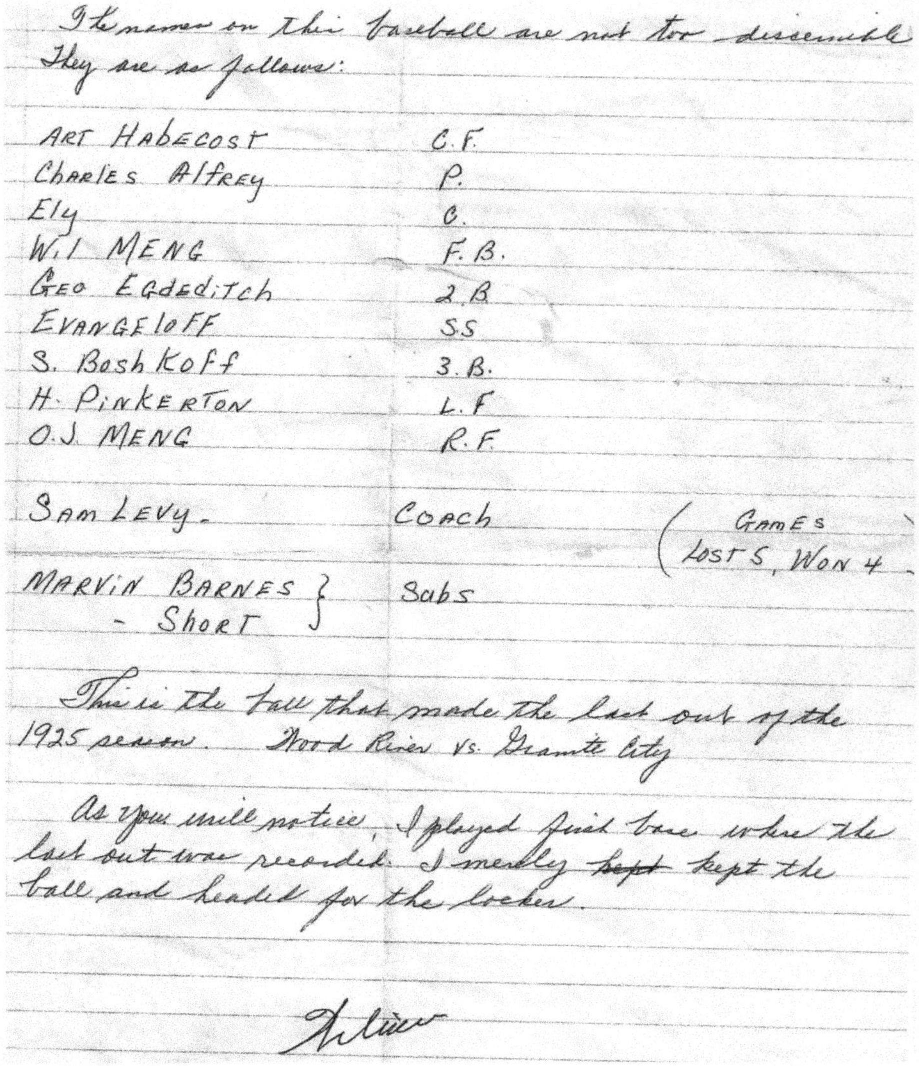

The names on this baseball are not too discernible. They are as follows:

ART HABECOST	C.F.
CHARLES Alfrey	P.
Ely	C.
WIl MENG	F.B.
GEO EQdeditch	2.B
EVANGELOFF	SS
S. Bosh Koff	3.B.
H. PINKERTON	L.F
O.J. MENG	R.F
SAM LEVY.	COACH
MARVIN BARNES } — ShoRT	Subs

(GAMES
LoST 5, WoN 4

This is the ball that made the last out of the 1925 season. Wood River vs. Granite City

As you will notice, I played first base where the last out was recorded. I merely kept kept the ball and headed for the locker.

Wilmer

Mr., Mrs. Meng Are Honored at Dinner Party

Mr. and Mrs. Fred Hamrick, 1509 Morningside Drive, entertained Saturday night with a dinner and bridge party in honor of Mr. and Mrs. Wilmer Meng, who will leave soon to make their home in Long Beach, California. Mr. Meng, who is with the Federal Correctional Institution at Summit, is being transferred to Long Beach.

Decorations for the dinner table carried out the theme "My Old Kentucky Home." A log cabin and figurines in colonial costumes composed the centerpiece, accented by lighted tapers. Lynn, the Hamrick's younger daughter, received guests in a colonial costume.

The two high prizes for bridge went to Mrs. Meng and Mack Kenney.

A gift was presented from the group to Mr. and Mrs. Meng.

Guests included Mr. and Mrs. Meng, William Rice, Mr. and Mrs. Mack Kenney, Mr. and Mrs. Barr Sinnett, Mr. and Mrs. Merrell Davis of Huntington, Mr. and Mrs. Roy Guthrie of Huntington, the hosts, and their daughter, Lynn.

Meng Explains New Routine at Summit

A new type of prison government, undergoing the experimental stage at the Federal Correctional Institution, Summit, was explained to members of the Republican luncheon club by W. W. Meng today.

Meng is associated with the prison and has been on the personnel of the institution for 14 years.

For many years before the war, the majority of prisoners sent to Summit were adults, Meng said. He explained that adult prisoners required different treatment from juveniles, who are in the majority now.

Since the war, Meng declared, juvenile prisoners were increasing and that twice as many prisoners from the ages of 18–22 were being received now.

The director of prisons decided to use the Summit institution as an experimental center for juvenile cases, and Meng said that the personnel was being changed with the idea of coping with the new problems. A psychiatrist, a psychologist, and a sociologist have been added to the staff, and the entire prison routine is being revamped to take care of the new situation.

He said that now a juvenile prisoner may be sentenced to a period of observation at the institution, and, after that time, if prison officials felt that the prisoner could safely be released, he was granted a parole. After the fulfilling of the parole period, if the prisoner has observed the good behavior test, he is given his full freedom.

The Summit institution will soon be known as a diagnostic center. In order to take care of this new program, new buildings will be needed and complete new personnel to deal with the new work will be installed.

Meng was introduced by Max Lively, program chairman.

LITTLE THEATER

Wilmer W. Meng Is New President of Little Theater

Wilmer W. Meng was elected president of the Ashland Little Theater at a meeting of the group on Thursday evening held in the clubroom at the Milner Hotel.

Other new officers are Gerald Osborne, vice-president; Miss Betty Hoffman of Ironton, Ohio, secretary; Bill Hurt, treasurer; and Ms. Camilla Broyles, a member of the board at large.

The Howard Billick "Oscar" awards were received this season by Bill Hurt, male lead for *O Mistress Mine*; Ms. Edith Dickore, female lead for *All My Sons*; Mrs. Bernard Lipsitz, female supporting role for *All My Sons*; and Bob Marzetti, male supporting role for *Finian's Rainbow*.

At Thursday's meeting, a picnic was planned for June 23, to be held on the lawn of the home of Mr. Meng, 3337 Condit Street.

It was announced that a producer will be appointed for each play next season, a change in the previous policy in which one producer was appointed for an entire season.

> The Bishop of Lax" is the part taken by Wilmer Meng in the Little Theater comedy, See How They Run, to be given in the Senior High School auditorium December 8 at 8:15 p.m.
>
> Mr. Meng, who is president of the Ashland Little Theater this year, has appeared in Little Theater productions in the roles of prosecuting attorney in Missing Witness, Dr. Herman Einstein in Arsenic and Old Lace, Lord Oakleigh in Anything Goes, Uncle Willie in Philadelphia Story, and Finian in Finian's Rainbow.

The
Ashland Little Theatre

Presents

PHILLIP KING'S
"SEE HOW THEY RUN"

A Production for the 1951 - 1952 Season

One of Wilmer Meng's play bills from his "Little Theater" activities.

A Message from the President

In behalf of the Ashland Little Theatre
it is my privilege to welcome you to the
first production of the 1951–52 season.
It is with sincere pleasure that we greet
you at the beginning of each season and
with genuine regret that we leave you at
its close. For the past sixteen seasons
we have earnestly endeavored to bring
you the finest entertainment available
in as nearly professional manner as
possible. You have come to expect this
and we feel confident that this, our
seventeenth season, will live up to your
every expectation.

In the past we have brought you entertainment to fit your every
mood. In the tense world situation of today we felt that something
light was needed, hence we open our season with a rollicking,
hilarious farce that should relieve taut nerves and offer an excellent
opportunity to relax.

In these strenuous times relaxation is needed as never before.
The Ashland Little Theatre offers relaxation in a variety of ways, not
just for a few brief moments on the nights the plays are produced,
but throughout the entire season. At the numerous rehearsals and
the myriad other jobs that must be done before a production can be
a success, the cares and worries of day-to-day living disappear in the
satisfaction of doing a worthwhile job in a congenial atmosphere.

We cordially invite each and every one of you to visit our club
room during rehearsals, attend our meetings and, if you care to, join
your neighbors and friends in finding relaxation, good companionship
and an outlet for any talents or creative ability you may have.

We sincerely thank you for your support through the years,
support that has made our success possible, and we hope you will
enjoy the plays we have planned for you during the coming season.

WILMER W. MENG,
President

Picture used on the Little Theater marquee.

A typical Uncle Wilmer Story, told frequently resulting in a room full of laughs

The following "story" was found in a letter from Wilmer W. Meng to Edward J. Meng. The story, which would be followed by load laughter, is typical of one of Uncle Wilmer's notorious tales.

Mrs. George Woods, of Chowan County, now deceased, had a mule, which was named Horace. One evening, she called up Dr. Satterfield in Edenton and said to him, "Horace is sick, Doctor, and I wish you would come and take a look at him."

Dr. Satterfield said, "Oh, Fanny Lamb, it's after six o'clock and I'm eating supper. Give him a dose of mineral oil, and if he isn't all right in the morning, call me, and I'll come out and take a look at him."

"How'll I give it to him?" she inquired.

"Through a funnel."

"But he might bite me," she protested.

"Oh, Fanny Lamb, you're a farm woman and you know about these things. Give it to him through the other end."

So Fanny went out to the barn, and there stood Horace with his head hanging down and moaning and groaning. She looked around for a funnel, but the nearest thing she could see to one was Uncle Bill's foxhunting horn hanging on the wall. A beautiful gold-plated instrument with gold tassels hanging from it. She took the horn and affixed it properly. Horace paid no attention. Then she reached upon the shelf where the medicines for the farm animals was kept, but instead of picking up the mineral oil she picked up the turpentine by mistake and poured a liberal dose of it into the horn.

Horace raised his head with a sudden jerk. He let out a yell that could have been heard a mile away. He reared up on his hind legs, brought his front legs down, knocked out the side of the barn, jumped a five-foot fence, and started down the road at a mad gallop. Now Horace was in pain, and every few jumps he made sure that horn would blow. All the dogs in the neighborhood knew that when that horn was blowing, it meant that Uncle Bill was foxhunting. So out on the highway they went, close behind Horace. It was a marvelous sight. First Horace--running at top speed with the hunting horn in the most unusual position, the mellow notes issuing from there, the tassels waving and the dogs barking joyously.

They passed by the home of Old Harvey Hogan, who was sitting on his front porch. He hadn't drawn a sober breath for 15 years, and he gazed in fascinated amazement at the sight that unfolded itself before his eyes. He couldn't believe what he was seeing. Incidentally, he is now head man in the Alcoholics Anonymous in the Albemarle section of the state.

By the time it was good and dark, Horace and the dogs were approaching the inland waterway. The bridge tender heard the horn blowing and thought it was a boat approaching. He hurried out and uncranked the bridge. Horace went overboard and was drowned. The dogs also went into the water but swam out without much difficulty. Now it so happened that the bridge tender was running for sheriff, but he managed to poll only seven votes. The people figured that any man who couldn't tell the difference between a mule with a horn up his rear and a boat coming down the inland waterway wasn't fit to hold public office.

Movie star Mitzi Gaynor

Another "Little Theater" publicity picture. I think Wilmer enjoyed this!

Woman sues over bolt of lightning[9]

The Ashland Home Telephone Co. was named defendant in a $10,500 personal injury damage suit brought yesterday in Boyd County Circuit Court as the result of lightning striking a telephone wire.

Mrs. Iris L. Meng, plaintiff, claims that she suffered shock that resulted in permanent illness when lightning struck a telephone wire leading into her home during an electrical storm last September 5. It resulted in a flash explosion and fire in the room she was occupying, she claims.

The suit was filed through attorneys P. H. Vincent and John L. Smith.

Telephone Co., Defendant in $10,000 Suit

CATLETTSBURG: The Ashland Home Telephone Company, Inc., is named defendant in a $10,000 personal injury damage suit filed this morning in Boyd Circuit Court by Mrs. Iris L. Meng of 2723 Beech Street, Ashland.

Mrs. Meng alleges in her petition that she suffered serious and permanent physical injury on September 5, this year, when lightning struck telephones wires and entered her home resulting in a flash explosion and fire in the room she was occupying. She charges that the telephone installation was done by the defendant company in a "careless, negligent and improper manner," thus permitting the explosion to occur. In addition to personal injury damages Mrs. Meng seeks $500 compensation for hospital and medical expenses incurred by reason of her injury. Her petition was prepared and filed by Attorney P. H. Vincent of Ashland and John L. Smith of Catlettsburg.

Iris and Wilmer Meng

Iris and Wilmer Meng in their square dance outfits

JAMES MENG

A *Tribute*
Published in the pages of *Daily News Tribune*
Fullerton, California
Sept. 3, 1964

Memorial Obituary

Entered into Eternal Rest
Wednesday, Sept. 2, 1964

Mrs. Meng Dies after Brief Illness

Mrs. Will Meng

Mrs. Iris Meng, 52, of 827 El Dorado Drive, died Wednesday, September 2, 1964, at St. Jude Hospital after an illness of little more than a month. She was the wife of Wilmer W. Meng, director of public relations at St. Jude.

Funeral services will be held at 2 p.m. Saturday at the First Methodist Church of Fullerton. Officiating will be the Rev. Milton Weisshaar. Burial will be at Forest Lawn Memorial Park, Cypress. Walters & McCormick Mortuary is in charge of arrangements.

Mrs. Meng had resided in Fullerton three years, coming here from Long Beach after a residence there of seven years. Mr. and Mrs. Meng moved to Fullerton after he retired from service with the U.S. Department of Justice, and became associated with St. Jude.

She was a member of St. Jude Hospital Guild and the Terpciety Dance Club of Anaheim. She was former secretary of the board of directors of the South Coast Association of Square Dance Clubs, and a former member of the Haylofters Square Dance Club of Long Beach.

Besides her husband, she is survived by her cousin, who was reared in her home, Mrs. Dorothy Keene, Oak Grove, Ore.; her brother, Allen C. Liggett, Royal Oak, Mich.; her sister, Mrs. Martha Jean Ettinger St. Paul, Minn.; and her step-mother, Mrs. J. T. Liggett, Granite City, Ill.

Mrs. Meng was born Aug. 15, 1912, in Milltown, Ind., and grew up on Granite City, Ill. She and her future husband met as high school students in Granite City. They were married June 30, 1937, in Idaho, and came to California in 1955 from Ashland, Ky.

Meng Named to PR Post[10]

Wilmer W. Meng, director of public relations for St. Jude Hospital here, has been installed as vice president of the public relations section of the Hospital Council of Southern California.

Meng, who has been with St. Jude since October 1961, after retiring from the US Department of Justice, Bureau of Prisons, resides with his wife at 827 El Dorado Drive.

New president of the HCSC is Fred Edmunds of St. John's Hospital in Santa Monica, and Don Olson, Glendale Hospital, is secretary.

The Hospital Council of Southern California consists of 167 hospitals. Sr. Jane Frances, St. Jude administrator, recently was named as president-elect of the council.

Wilmer and Vonnie Meng. Although Wilmer was good on the mandolin, Vonnie was excellent on the piano. Her professional training and enjoyment of music was evident.

Close Harmony—Mr. and Mrs. Wilmer Meng play up a storm on electric mandolin and piano in living room of their home, 1237 Longview. Now retired, Mr. Meng was public relations director at St. Jude Hospital for a number of years, rounding out working years which included jobs in a steel mill and a career in the US Bureau of Prisons, among other staring roles in community theater productions an interesting sideline.

RETIREES ON THE GO[10]
Taking Life Slow, Easy No Go for Active Mengs

By SUE CAMPBELL
News Tribune
Women's Staff Writer

"I never had a chance to stagnate," said Wilmer W. Meng, recently retired from a super-active life of such varied activities as steel roller, prison guard, public relations director and sometime actor. One suspects that stagnation isn't on his retirement list either.

Mr. Meng, who resides at 1237 Longview with his musically talented wife Vaughncille, has put to work a portion of his seemingly inexhaustible energies and installed some ironwork on the exterior of their home and built a mirrored wall in the entryway. His future plans also call for some cement work, a few flower beds, some travel and performances on his custom made electric mandolin.

He sees opportunities to improve and serve wherever he goes and with Mrs. Meng's encouragement, he sets about doing something about them.

Born into an economically deprived family in Illinois, he went to work in the steel mills the day he became old enough to work. He began his life as an iron man quite literally, sleeping about four hours of each 24 and carrying a full load of school subjects. He also found time and energy for athletics and was captain of the football team, winning letters in four sports before leaving school one year short of graduation.

"I was the oldest basketball player in Ashland, Ky.," he laughed. "I played in the industrial leagues till I was 39 years old--my hair was getting gray. I really loved that game."

He tried sales work and went into politics during the depression. "To tell the truth, I did public speaking at $5 per speech for tongue-tied politicians. Anything to make a dollar," he said.

He joined the Department of the Interior in 1935 as a guard in the Interstate Commerce Building and transferred to the Bureau of Prisons which paid more. He wound up in North Idaho on the staff of a penal institution amid a primitive wilderness where the deer and the antelope played and also an occasional bear.

In time, he was transferred (as a staffer) to the California Correctional Institute at Terminal Island, from which post he retired after conducting training programs of various kinds.

"Over the years I watched the emphasis shift from purely punitive measures to the much better theory of rehabilitation. States often fall down in these programs because they do not have enough work for the prisoners. Also, state prisons receive those convicted of the heinous crimes such as murder which federal prisons largely do not.

"Government prisons try to train prisoners in some line of useful work and will try more than one trade until the prisoner is learning something he is suited for. An inmate may also obtain a high school diploma from a local school. But the critical period in a man's rehabilitation is the period between his release and that first pay check."

Mr. Meng claims he got into public relations work because the prison warden couldn't make speeches. He got Mr. Meng to write them and speak for him before the organizations requesting such information. So, following his retirement from government service, the by-now accomplished speaker moved into personnel and production work for an engineering concern and eventually joined the public relations staff of St. Jude Hospital from which he retired a year or so ago, this time for good, he says.

According to Mr. Meng, all work and no play makes for a pretty dull life, so he added the spice of community theater to an already full schedule of activities. He began with the Ashland Little Theater and, over the years, has appeared in such productions as "A Man Called Peter," "Seven Year Itch" with Richard Erdman in the lead, "Bad Seed" and "Arsenic and Old Lace."

From the desk of . . .

WILMER W. MENG

Hi! and Merry Christmas:

1981 has been a very eventful year, in a negative sort of way. Vonnie lost her mother on October 29th. We went back for the funeral and the following week her first cousin died and the week after that her mother's brother, and only remaining sibling, died. Three funerals in three weeks.

In July I had surgery for cataract on my left eye. The procedure went haywire and I lost the sight in that eye. Because of glaucoma etc. etc. in my right eye I also have very little vision left in that eye. Consequently I can't drive the car, play music or do many of the things I used to enjoy. However, I'm thankful I can still get around without a white cane.

Had a wonderful trip into nostalgia-land last spring. Visited places where I lived as a boy and also Ashland Kentucky where I spent 15 years just prior to coming to California. It was so great to see and visit with old and dear friends I hadn't seen in years and with one lady I hadn't seen since we were in grade school together, some sixty-odd years ago.

We're hoping 1982 will be a little kinder as we fervently hope you and yours will have a most happy and blessed Christmas and that 1982 will bring you all the things you want most.

As ever

Vonnie and Wilmer Meng

Wilmer W. "Wil" Meng   Irma Vaughncille (Vonnie) Joseph Meng
21 Dec 1903   28 Aug 1912
11 Jan 1995   04 Aug 2007

Notes:

1. Wilmer's first wife was the former Thelda Cooper, the sister of Wilmer's brother, Oscar J. Meng's wife, the former Alma Cooper. This marriage was annulled. Wilmer then married his high school sweetheart, the former Iris Liggett. They were married for 27 years, until Iris died of cancer. Wilmer then married Vaughncille (Vonnie) Joseph on 24 September 1966. Vonnie was originally from Elk City, Beckham, Oklahoma and daughter of Merl Vern Joseph 1892–1987 and Lillian Joseph 1891–1981. Wilmer had no children; consequently, he and Vonnie spent considerable time and effort spoiling all of their nephews and nieces.

2. When my Mom, Jessie F. Meng, passed away, Dad (Edward John Meng was completely devastated. It was interesting to note that Dad flew out to California to be with Uncle Wilmer, partly to get into different surroundings, but also to confide with his brother, Wilmer. They had a lot in common. One of my saddest memories was watching my Dad slowly walk away to board the aircraft.

VAUGHNCILLE JOSEPH MENG'S 800-SEAT CONCERT HALL AT CALIFORNIA STATE UNIVERSITY, FULLERTON

The 800 seat, state of the art Meng Concert Hall in Fullerton, California is an appropriate tribute to Vonnie and Wilmer Meng for they both played and enjoyed music. In addition, having the Meng family name on such a fine edifice makes all the Meng's throughout America, Germany and New Zealand extremely proud. More information on the magnitude of Meng Concert Hall will follow.

In 2005, Jim and Bev Meng visited the Meng Concert Hall at Cal State Fullerton. This event was a rededication of the Hall which opened to the public in 2004.

Jim and Bev purchased seven seats in row "M" inside the hall. The first seat has the name of Vonnie's husband, Wilmer Meng, on a brass plate on the back of the seat. The next seven seats have the names of Edward J Meng, Jessie F. Meng, Edward S. Meng, James L. Meng, Beverly Meng, Heather A. Meng, and Erik J. Meng.

After the rededication, Jim and Bev Meng had the pleasure of meeting with Carol Channing who performed during the ceremonies. She was everything that you would expect from a Broadway and movie star. A black-tie dinner and champagne followed the ceremonies.

Mr. Jim Young and his wife Dottie were Jim and Bev's hosts for the evening. The Youngs were very gracious and had taken care of Vonnie for years while she was in a nursing home. The Rotarians at the table that evening were extremely generous and friendly. They were everything and more than what Wilmer and Vonnie had said

Carol Channing

Think of it this way, Wilmer Meng, a former bilingual resident of the small town of Freeburg, Illinois, with no money ends up with the family name "Meng" on an 800-seat, state-of-the-art concert hall on the other side of the country, in Orange County, California. Congratulations to both Wilmer and Vonnie!

September 5, 2006

Hi Jim Young,
    We mailed the money for the seats and the tickets today. ($7,500)

Dear Jim Meng,
    I received your e-mail and am delighted that the MENG FAMILY will be a part of the beautiful concert hall here. We look forward to seeing you and Beverly at the gala. It will be an outstanding black-tie affair with many dignitaries, a gourmet evening and show.
    As to the seats, I have talked with those in charge at the University and they are going to start making the name plates immediately and as I told you, the seats will be in row "M".
    It occurs to me I have not been in touch with Marvin recently.

It would be nice if the two couples could be here for the gala. I will write him today and send pictures of Vonnie.

Oh, yes! You asked how to write the checks. They would be made out to California State University Philanthropic Foundation.

The Meng family seats in row "M"

Wilmer Walter Meng

James Leroy Meng

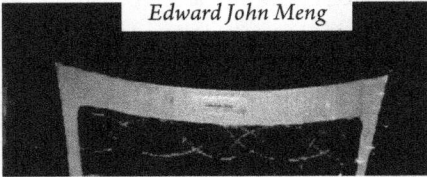
Edward John Meng

Beverly Ann Meng

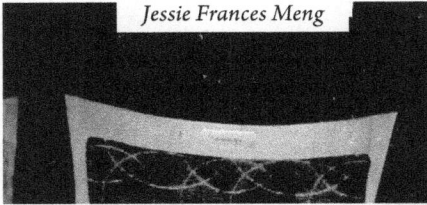
Jessie Frances Meng

Heather Andrea Meng

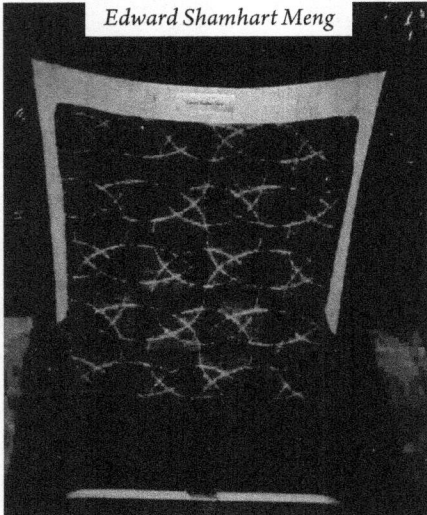
Erik James Meng

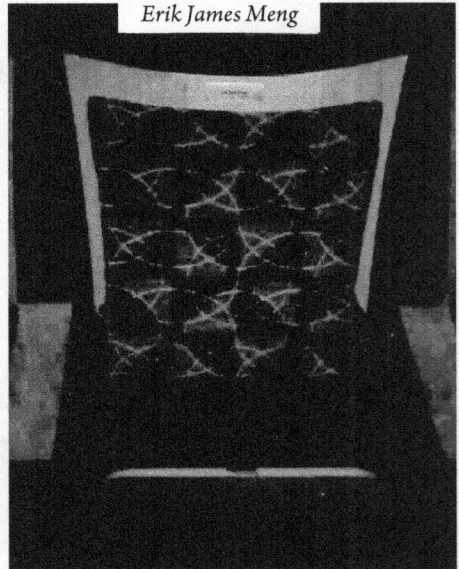
Edward Shamhart Meng

Fullerton, California
October 15, 2005

Mr. & Mrs. Jim Meng

Dear Jim and Beverly:

It is a beautiful October day here in Fullerton. Just thought I'd drop you a note about Vonnie and send you the information on the "Vaughncille Joseph Meng" concert hall at the university. The venue is almost completed now and is a wonderful legacy. Vonnie was so excited about the development of the center and I am hoping she can stay well long enough to enjoy a concert there.

Before she had the strokes, she wanted to attend all the concerts and we took her to everything including student recitals. She did love her music. I still go to see her very day and she seems to be somewhat stabilized physically though she cannot speak. She jabbers and points her finger and raises her eyebrows based on something she wishes to convey. She does not seem frustrated by this failure and even laughs when I say, "Vonnie I know you have a lot to tell me but I am just too stupid to really understand you." She is one of the favored residents because she is so gentle and the nurses all love working with her.

I haven't heard from Jill, Vonnie's brother's daughter, for some time. I know Don is having some very serious health problems too and is being cared for to a great extent by Jill and her brother. Time does take its toll on all of us eventually. It is hard to believe that Wil has been gone since 1995.

We hope all is well with all of you and your families. And that the winder months will be good to you.

Sincere good wishes,
James D. "Jim" Young

The 250 seat James D. Young Theater is also within the Meng preforming arts Concert Hall.

THE GREAT MENG CONCERT HALL

The Meng Concert Hall is the first true concert hall built in Orange County exclusively for the presentation of music - a performance space that clarifies and amplifies the great music of all time. Acoustical Mark Rothermel had the final word on all physical aspects of this space, from the soaring volume of the hall to the smallest detail that would affect the quality of sound produced on the stage.

Angled walls abound and the varied surfaces from hard, smooth, tilted kite walls to the soft drapes and fabric seats create the perfect setting for the sound of music. Adjustable settings for overhead and side curtains and adjustments on the stage canopy create the acoustically ideal environment for orchestra, band, choir, chamber, solo and jazz performances.

Under the zinc roof of this hall are layers of concrete and insulation material to keep out all outside noise. The walls and floor are insulated and glass windows above the stage are constructed with two layers of glass with air space between to isolate the hall from all exterior sound.

The visual elements of the hall were designed to create a warm interior using a bold chromatic chorus of color, texture and form. Cherry wood on the stage floor and seat backs and banisters throughout the hall adds the final touch of richness to the environment. The light pendants float across the open ceiling like Asian inspired lanterns.

Vaugncille Joseph Meng, a music teacher and longtime resident of Fullerton, has set up a significant endowment for the College of the Arts to fund enrichment opportunies in the performing arts and scholarship awards for students in music and theatre. Unfortunately, known to the family as Aunt Vonnie, she was too frail to be at the opening, but she knew that her gift will have direct and positive effect on the lives of music and theatre students and the Meng family far into the future.

Meng Hall is a stunning cultural resource for students and for patrons and friends in surrounding communities. This hall will become a destination for artists and music lovers a center of excellence on the campus of Cal State Fullerton. The Meng Hall is among the finest ever created for love of music performance, all the result of the thoughtfulness of Aunt Vonnie Joseph Meng! A large amount of the above compliments of C.S.U.F.

Jim and Dottie Young were very good friends of both Aunt Vonnie and Uncle Wilmer. Jim was a fellow Rotarian and Paul Harris Fellow with Wilmer. They took very good care of Vonnie while she was in the nursing home with many visits and attending to her special needs. The entire Meng family owes a great deal of gratitude to both Jim and Dottie Young.

A birthday party with the students and faculty from the University. They provided a birthday cake, sang songs, and preformed for Vonnie's eighty-fifth birthday. What a great group and treat for Vonnie!

A summer outing. Vonnie needed no excuse to play "dress up" for any and all events!

California State University, Fullerton

Established 1957
Type Public
Endowment US $32.3 million
Students 37,677 (Fall 2012)

October 30, 2012 8:00 PM.
Vienna Boys Choir at Cal State Fullerton

Meng Concert Hall (map)

MUSIC EVENTS

UNIVERSITY BAND
Mitchell Fennell, director
Wednesday, November 14, 2012, 8pm
Meng Concert Hall
Free admission

UNIVERSITY SYMPHONY ORCHESTRA
Kimo Furumoto, director
Sunday, November 11, 2012, 4pm
Meng Concert Hall

Copland: *Fanfare for the Common Man*
Rossini: Overture from *Barber of Seville*
Bach: Brandenburg Concerto No. 3
Brahms: Symphony No. 2

STRING FESTIVAL CONCERT
Sunday, November 4, 2012, 8pm
Meng Concert Hall

UNIVERSITY SINGERS & CONCERT CHOIR
Robert Istad and Christopher Peterson, directors
Saturday, November 3, 2012, 8pm
Meng Concert Hall

Notable people

Kevin Costner   Tracy Caldwell Dyson

The Meng-Shamhart book is in the Paulina June & George Pollak Library at C.S.U.F.

CHAPTER 20
OSCAR AND ELMA (COOPER) MENG

Oscar Jerome Meng (1906–1970)

Recollections of OJ and Elma Meng as remembered by OJ Jr. (son)

OJ came to Kansas City during the Depression, looking for work. I'm not sure of the date, but I believe it was around 1931 or 1932. He obtained employment at Phillips Oil Co., where he worked until he retired in 1965. Later he sent for Elma, and they were married on February 21, 1933. In 1934, they bought their home at 3000 N Baltimore in KCK, where they lived until they divorced in 1967.

Frances Marie was born on April 20, 1934, and I was born on June 17, 1936.

Dad was a hardworking man that loved to work around the house. He studied building contracting through ICS courses and could do anything around the house. He remodeled it from top to bottom during the time they lived there.

Mom was mostly a housewife in the early years. Like most women of that era, she was there to take care of us kids.

Dad was a very dominating person, and Mom and Dad did not get along that well. They argued most of their married life, which finally led to their divorce in 1967. That aside, there were many good times with the family. When we were young, Dad always did things with us. From taking us to sleigh riding and ice skating to joining in softball games in the street, he was always willing to join in. We took many nice vacations together during our growing up time. Dad liked to visit points of interest and history around the area. We did a lot of camping around the Midwest, which I was not real fond of, trying to pitch a tent, late at night in cold temperatures, but we did get to see a lot of good things in Yellowstone Park, Colorado and Wyoming. I remember, when I was 16, we started out in his '42 Mercury, which I was driving. We pulled a one-wheel trailer behind us that was well overloaded. We were behind a gas truck, and Dad told me to pass. I jerked the steering wheel too fast and, with the load in the trailer, it started to sway the car from one side of the road to the other, out of control. We finally went off the side of the road into a foot of mud. No harm done; we pushed it out and went on our way. I learned to ease the car from one lane to the other so the trailer wouldn't sway the car.

That trailer was a source of fun for us and the neighbor kids. He was always hauling something, and we all got to ride in it. Mom and Dad, during the early years at Christmas, would always wait until Christmas Eve to put up and decorate the tree. It was a real thrill on Christmas morning to see what had taken place the night before. Mom was the one who took care of getting us to school and taking part in that area. I remember reading out loud to her out of my beginning readers while in grade school and her helping me with my schoolwork. She took part in PTA and was room mother many times during my grade school years.

Dad and Mom lived by a wooded area that ran up close to the house. It was an excellent place to play, and both Honey and I spent many a summer day playing there. Dad got permission to make a garden on part of the property. He cleared a large area and planted about every vegetable he could; I spent many hours working in that garden. At the time, it wasn't a lot of fun. However, the vegetables we got from it were very good. We mostly gave away a lot of it to neighbors. I remember though during the summer at lunchtime, we had lunch meat sandwiches with everything on them, fresh from the garden. It is today one of my favorite ways to eat. We also canned a lot of vegetables in those days, which was not a lot of fun. On hot summer days, the whole family was either boiling water, or cutting corn off the cob, or shelling peas.

I know that Dad was a good athlete when he was in high school. He played football, basketball, and baseball. He always told me what a good hitter he was. Well, one day, when a friend of mine and I were playing catch and hitting pop flies to each other behind our garden, Dad came down to tell me something before he went to work. I was 15 and my friend was 16, and a pretty aggressive kid. Dad was 45 at the time and hadn't swung at a hardball for years. Of course my friend claimed he could throw one by Dad. Well, Dad picked up the bat; the kid threw one as hard as he could. With one swing the ball was sent screaming into the air; we never found it. I knew then that Dad was a pretty good hitter.

On that same property, we also had neighborhood wiener roasts with everyone on the block. I used to eat and drink so much pop, I had to lie down and rest before I could continue. Mom and Dad had a lot of friends they would play cards and have dinner with. Both were good bridge players. Mom went to work around 1950 and worked for Folgers coffee until their divorce in 1967. She played bridge every day on the lunch hour and was an excellent player. Jane and I used to play bridge with Mom and Dad when were first married. However, the game was hard to me, since I didn't play that much.

Dad was also a dog lover. He always had beagles, which were part of our family. Dad and I used to hunt a lot, and the beagles made it a lot of fun. Dad was also a Ford man. He would never consider driving anything else. The first car I remember was a gray '37 Ford V-8. He drove it for 11 years. He paid $600 for it, new. He also had a '42 and '51 Mercury and a '54 and two 1960s Lincolns.

I remember, in 1956, he had to have his feet operated on to remove tumors, and he could not drive. I would drive him to Granite City. He would sit in the back seat and drink beer. He told me to keep it under 100, and I did barely. I don't remember anyone passing us on those trips. I always drove Fords and Mercurys as well until 1960 when I bought a Corvette.

Dad had a dominating personality; Mom was secondary in everything. She was easier to get along with because she thought he was hard on us. She was under a good deal of stress during the marriage and had two nervous breakdowns. She had shock treatments, was very resilient, and recovered completely.

Mom's maiden name was Cooper. Her father and mother both died before I was born. Mom had a brother named Ivan, and two sisters--Elizabeth and Shelda (who was married to and divorced from Uncle Wilmer). Ivan died in 1970. Thelda died in 1986. Elizabeth lives in Trenton, Illinois, with her husband Richard Crystal. Mom's father at one time owned a ranch in western Kansas. They couldn't make a go of it and moved back to Illinois. Her mother was accidentally shot by a policeman, got cancer, and died in 1934. Her father was moving furniture and dropped dead in 1933.

L/R: Wilmer, Edward, and O. J. Meng

Nice Hats!
OJ and Wilmer Meng at their
New Athens home

Who Was O. J. Meng and Elma Meng?
J. L. Meng (nephew)

Oscar Meng referred to as O. J. Meng Sr. was born in Freeburg, Illinois, and then moved to Granite City Illinois. OJ was the fullback on the high school football team while his brother Wilmer W. Meng was the quarterback. OJ was apparently quite good, receiving four varsity letters in football and all-conference honors. He then moved to Kansas City, Kansas, where he worked for the Phillips Petroleum Co. in their refinery.

OJ's mannerisms and voice always reminded me of the movie actor Ernie Kovacs, except with a wide bald strip. He was big, smoked cigars, and talked loud with laughter that would fill a room. He even made home brew in his basement. His brewing operation apparently was quite extensive with a variety of gauges, even a small bottling line.

As his brother Fred liked Fords, OJ's car was a Lincoln Continental (at least that's the only kind of car I saw him drive). On visits to St. Louis, he would drink his home brew and smoke his cigars from one side of the state of Missouri to the other side. All of this would put him in a rather "jolly" mood upon his arrival. As his son OJ Jr. became old enough to drive, OJ Sr. would retire to the back seat to drink and smoke while OJ

Jr. would drive. I am sure junior received considerable driving advice during the long journey.

Like his other brothers, OJ loved to tease everyone. As an example, he always made me mad at Christmas time when he would send a gift the first week in December with big letters saying "Don't open until Christmas." I always thought it was a dirty thing to do to a kid who very seldom received anything in the mail, let alone a gift. It was typical OJ. I knew he was laughing, knowing it was bugging the heck out of me.

As big as OJ was, his wife, Aunt Elma, was just as small. Short in stature, attractive, and small boned with a gravel voice. She always smoked cigarettes. One time when visiting our house, Agnes Meng (Fred's wife) played the piano while Elma started dancing the Charleston. It was quite a sight, and the music was so loud that we had people stop in front of our house. We even had a stranger come to our front door asking if they could join the party. As a wide-eyed 10-year-old, I had never seen such commotion by adults, but it was fun to watch.

Perhaps due to the distance between Granite City and Kansas City, I did not see OJ and Elma as frequently as we would have liked. At this period in time, there was no interstate highway system, and it was a long drive––beer or no beer.

OJ and Elma eventually got divorced—the only divorce in our family, neither remarried.

Oscar J. Meng family: (left to right) OJ Jr., Elma, Frances, and OJ Sr.

Sister-in-laws: Elma Meng, Agnes Meng, and Jessie Meng

Meng Cousins
Janet, Frances, Edward, OJ Jr., James, and (unknown pet) and Marvin Meng

517

In Memory of Elma Leone Meng
(1912–1993)

Entered into Rest
April 15, 1993

Elma L. Meng

Elma Leone Meng, 80, died on April 15, 1993, in the St. Joseph Care Center, Kansas City, Kansas, where she lived. Memorial services will be at 7:00 p.m. on Monday at the Highland Park Chapel. The family suggests contributions to the St. Joseph Care Center. Mrs. Meng was born in Wood River, Illinois, and lived in Kansas City, Kansas, most of her life. She was a volunteer for the Foster Grandparents program in Kansas City, Kansas. Survivors include a son, OJ Meng, Kansas City, Kansas; a daughter, Frances Meng, Olathe, Kansas; a sister, Elizabeth Crystal, Trenton, Illinois; and two grandchildren.

Jane and OJ Jr. with children
Jane and OJ Jr. have since moved from Kansas City, Kansas, to Las Vegas.
Frances Meng, OJ Jr.'s elder sister, died in March 2009 after a long illness.

CHAPTER 21
THE KOESTERER FAMILY INCLUDES THE VOGTS AND SCHIPPERS

Louis and Louisa Koesterer's fiftieth wedding

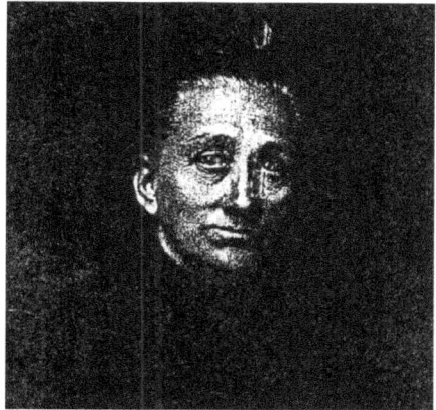

Louis married Louisa Reinheimer on November 25, 1877; they had two children, Robert L. Koesterer (b. 5 Jun. 1881–d. 10 Dec.1882) and Carrie Koesterer (b. 17 Jan. 1893–d. 23 Dec. 1989).

Wedding picture of Benard (Ben) P. Koesterer and Frieda L. Weik

*Frieda Weick Koesterer
1915*

Ben and Frieda going cruising

Wedding picture of Bernard P. Koesterer and Frieda Weik

Bernard Phillip Koesterer born 30 Dec 1879 in Freeburg, Illinois. Died 7 May 1960 in Freeburg, St Clair, Illinois. Parents were Berthold Koesterer 1843-1886 and Katharina Reinheimer 1847-1908. Married Frieda L. Weik 1884-1972.

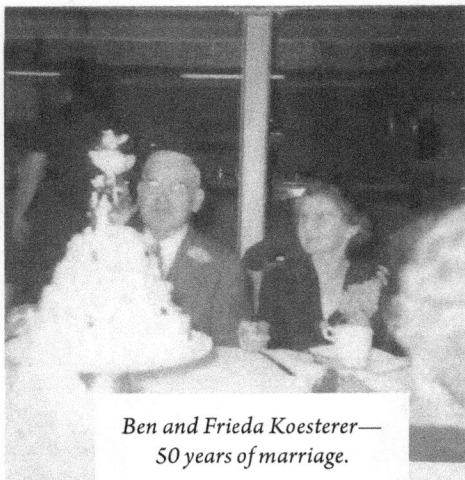

Ben and Frieda Koesterer—
50 years of marriage.

Ben and Frieda. (They had no children.)

522

Emma Koesterer (wife of Adoloh) with Stella

*Stella Koesterer (daughter of
Adolph Koesterer) Wagner*

PARRY AND LILLIAN VOGT SCHIPPERS

Remembering Parry and Lillian Vogt Schippers
James L. Meng

For one, they were both doctors. Parry was a dentist and Lillian had a PhD in education. Parry's dental practice was on South Kingshighway in Afton, Missouri. Lillian held several high positions in education, including the director of language arts for the Afton School District in St. Louis. They owned and lived in a three-family apartment on Southerland Avenue. They had no children.

Lillian's mother, Emma Koesterer, was the sister of my grandmother, Elizabeth Koesterer Meng. My father, Edward J. Meng, and all of his brothers and sister knew Lillian when they were growing up in Freeburg, Illinois.

My first recollection of Parry and Lillian was when I was about six years old when they would visit our home in Granite City. Parry would wrestle me and my cousin, Marvin Meng, on the living room floor. This was great fun since no other adult would partake in such activity. As Marvin and I became older and bigger, these matches eventually stopped.

Parry and Lillian were extremely interesting people. There were many family gatherings at our home and at the Schippers' home. These were rather large dinners with my parents and uncles along with friends of the Schippers. The food was always plentiful and good.

The BBQ area at our farm, referenced earlier on Mengstrasse, had a 15 × 20 concrete pad with a homemade picnic table. Almost every other weekend and on all summer holidays, there was a picnic at the farm. Again, the food was plentiful and good. My uncle Fred M. Meng was always in charge of the BBQ, normally pork ribs. Fred's son Marvin and I would take off to the woods to spend the afternoon, swinging from vines and playing in the creek, getting an abundance of ticks and chiggers. While we were involved with this adventure, Fred and his helpers would start the BBQ fire. This was a major event since all agreed that the BBQ coals had to be just right for the ribs.

While the hunt for firewood and fire building was going on, the women would play cards. Normally, canasta was the game of the day. After the meal, the men would adjourn to the campfire to discuss the world's problems, both real and imagined. This is where Parry would take over with a wide range of subjects.

The BBQ area had large logs sitting on concrete blocks on three sides of the fire pit. As we sat on the logs at night watching the flames of the fire, Parry and others would talk about such things as buried treasure, World War II events, politics, the universe, ancestors and whether or not there was life in outer space etc. It is impossible to describe the variety of subjects discussed. The atmosphere and discussions were intense but always very interesting. The only break in these conversations came when the coals of the fire had to be adjusted or a new log had to be added. These conversations really made you think. They were, without a doubt, one of the highlights of my youth. Unfortunately, my children, Heather and Erik, had no such opportunity when they were growing up since all the original participants in these campfire discussions were much older and these picnics ceased.

Parry and Lillian seemed to be opposites. Lillian gave an air of sophistication, while Parry was like an "old shoe." Parry always had his hair messed up. They even had a cocker spaniel named Dukee who had the hair on the top of his head messed up. They looked alike which always make me wonder if this condition was catching.

Parry enjoyed practical jokes. He would visit trick shops to get the latest gimmick. When you visited their home, you would find a fly in a fake ice cube, a spoon that would collapse, a drinking glass designed to leak, and light bulbs that he could control their functions. When we would leave his home, you never knew what you might find in your car when you arrived home. My Uncle Fred found a women's corset under his car's drive shaft. This brought many chuckles when Fred had his oil changed. Uncle Fred also found women's nylons under his front seat which his wife, Agnes, did not think was too funny.

Parry and Lillian traveled all over the world. Lillian always took old clothes on her travels, unlike most people. When these were dirty, she would throw them away. Parry had a tendency to use Lillian's old clothes in a variety of creative ways. One such occasion was while in Paris, France. Parry tied Lillian's old bra on to the tour bus' antenna. This created quite a stir among the tourist and Parisians. On another trip to Russia, Lillian threw away an old traveling alarm clock and some nylons. Well, the ticking brought on the KGB and one heck of an investigation. However, all were finally cleared and everything returned to normal. That is until after one dinner, a piece of silverware was missing. Again, more KGB and another investigation. The utensil was then found in the kitchen and everyone settled back down.

On another trip to Russia, every time Parry would return to the tour bus, he would drop a rock or rocks into a fellow passenger's bag which he left open in the aisle of the bus. Parry continued the rock activity for several days. His victim hauled these rocks around for days. Once discovered, the victim angrily announced that whoever was putting rocks in his bag should stop, and stop now! Parry told the victim that he was shocked that anyone would do such a childish thing. Lillian would just put her head back and roll her eyes, which she did frequently, and smiled.

When I was growing up, Parry was my dentist. I did not like going to any dentist and would be scared stiff. Once I sat in Parry's dentist chair, he would bring out a large hammer, a large chisel, and a large auger. He would flash and bang these tools around in front of me and say such things as "Let me know if any of this hurts." I would sweat through my clothes.

My mom and dad were very close to Parry and Lillian. They traveled together to Puerto Rico several times to visit Lillian's brother, Elwood Vogt. He worked for the navy department. There were many stories about tropical bugs getting into Lillian's nightgowns. I suspect Parry may have been involved in some manner. They also traveled together to Germany, Austria, Switzerland, and Greece. They had a lot of common interests.

Lillian was very active in the community and in Republican politics. While she was doing these activities, Parry would paint in oils. The painting of the Edwardsville shed under "the Mengs" section of this book. Parry and my mom, Jessie F. Meng, often painted together. Mom was the better painter. Parry's pictures were different, depicting sad faces and subjects that were not too happy. He painted frequently.

Parry and Lillian Schippers were unique and very interesting people. They are both gone at this writing; gone except for the memories of two people that I had the good fortune to know.

Phillip C. Vogt and Emma Koesterer's wedding (Dec. 12, 1896)

Elwood B. Vogt (b. Dec. 10, 1896)

1914, Elwood Benjamin Vogt, age 14, 8th grade graduation

Lillian Vogt, as she graduated high school (1927)

Spring festival at Harris Teachers College (1928)

Saint Louis
Graduates - June 1927

Accounting

DONNA SPATHELF	CARL B. BALTER
CLIFFORD THOMAS AYERS	PAUL MOTCHAN
ALBERT BORAZ	ISADOR HAROLD ROSEN
MAURICE COHEN	HARRY N. ROSENSTROCH
HARRY GOLDER	HARRY TARVIN

Fine Arts

FANNIE FLEISHMAN	MARY ELIZABETH ITTNER
LELA HAGER	ADELE ZEILER

Classical

EDITH EVANGELINE ROY	ELLA M. TROVILLION
	BEN STEIN

General

ELSIE M. ALLEN	SARAH WORTMAN
ANTOINETTE DOCKHORST	EMMA WUESTLING
DOROTHY RUTH BOHNE	JAKE ALTMAN
DOROTHY MAE CHASE	GARLAND KIMBROUGH BASS
VIOLA M. CROWE	CHARLES B. BENNER
SARA VIVIAN DERR	HARRY BORNSTEIN
META CATHERINE FINKLANG	CARL VICTOR DASCHKA
CLARABELLE FIXMAN	HERMAN DREIFKE, JR.
BEULAH BEE GREER	RICHARD E. DUNCAN
MARY JOSEPHINE HENNON	LEON GOLDSTEIN
CLARA HOMO	GILBERT FRANKLIN GROB
LAURA ELEANOR HOUSE	BERNARD GROSSMAN
ONETA RUTH HUMPHREY	GLENNON HARDY
MYRTLE M. IMHOFF	MAURICE HEISKOWITZ
HOPE LAURIE KIEURTZ	QUINN WATKINS KING
EMMA ROSANOVICH	DAVE LITVAG
MARIE E. LEINKER	JOSEPH L. LUCIDO
LULA LORANDOS	KENNETH W. LUEKE
ALMA LUEKE	PAT MARIAM
SYLVIA M. MAGIDSON	VINCENT T. McCARTHY
DOROTHY ELIZABETH MARSHALL	ROLAND ROBERT MENOWN, JR.
MELVINA MILLER	NORMAN C. PARKER
ALICE FRANCES O'GARA	ORVILLE V. PAUL
NATALIE OJEMAN	LOUIS PLAX
LUCILLE VIVIAN OVERBECK	MAHLON R. ROBERTSON
ELSIE KATHERINE PRIEP	ISADORE RUBIN
GERTRUDE SCHEIBLE	EDWARD J. SCHOLLE
ROSE ALROD SHICKMAN	LEWIS CHARLES SCHOLLE
DOROTHY PHYLLIS SINGER	RALPH SCEUDART
EDNA J. SMITH	HENRY W. SIMPSON
EVA STEINBERG	BEN E. SINGER
DORA TORIN	BERNARD I. TUREEN
MABELLE ALICIA VELDE	FRED VAN KRANENBURGH
LILLIAN CATHERINE VOGT	MORRIS B. YATHEMAN
JANE ELIZABETH WELPOTT	RICHARD I. YOUNG

Home Economics

DOROTHY E. BRAUN	JANICE E. PHELPS
HELEN LOU CHASE	ELIZABETH JANE SHELTON

Manual Training

ELMER F. BAUMGARTNER	ALVIN HOLMAN
CLIFFORD W. BLACKSTUN	FRED THOMAS MEYER
CHARLES J. GRAF, JR.	EDWARD T. O'SHAUGHNESSY
WILLARD WILLIAM GRAFEMAN	ARTHUR SAM TOWNE
	HENRY L. VESPY

Scientific

BOZENA J. MILONSKI	JAKE SARASOHN
MEYER L. KATZ	SAMUEL SCHNEIDER
JAMES H. KOCH	SAM TRAUB
LEONARD G. ROSENTHAL	FRANK DALE WELTNER

Stenographic

MEREDITH DOWLING	MINNIE PRESS
BERNICE LANDON	VELMA MARIE RISZ
FLORENCE E. MARTIN	FANNY ROTHMAN
REBECCA PALANT	ABE MANDELKERN

Webster School

THE JUNE CLASS OF 1923

CORDIALLY INVITES YOU TO BE PRESENT

AT THE

Graduating Exercises

THURSDAY, JUNE 14, 1923

AT 10:00 O'CLOCK A. M.

IN THE

AUDITORIUM

PLEASE SEND NO FLOWERS TO THE SCHOOL

Graduates

GIRLS

Helen Anderson
Pearl Bailin
Freada E. Buesking
Marcella R. C. Devinney
Katherine Zelma Gillen
Hilda H. L. Gottwald
Hilda Leona Haase
Genett C. Hunt
Ida May James
Mina Beatrice Jones
Julia Marie Kemper
Selma E. Lindenmeyer
Georgia Irene Matthews
Beulah Belle McBrian
Julia V. Rajewski
Leona A. M. Schlottman
Lelia St. John
Christine Toliver
→ Lillian Catherine Vogt
Priscilla Abigail Wade
Marie Grace Webber

Lillian Vogt Schippers (center) in Writers Club at Central High School, St. Louis, MO.

Wedding picture of Lillian Vogt (daughter of Emma and Adolf) (Sept. 2, 1944, to Parry Schippers.

Parry Schippers, DDS, 1941

To all to whom these presents may come, greetings in the Lord.
We, the President and Board of Trustees of

Saint Louis University

certify that on the recommendation of the Dean and Faculty of the

Graduate School

we have conferred on

Lillian Vogt Schippers

A.B., A.M. in Ed.

the degree of

Doctor of Philosophy

with a major in

Education

with all the rights and privileges pertaining to that degree.

In witness whereof we have signed our names and affixed the Seal of the University to this diploma at Saint Louis, Missouri, on this twenty-sixth day of April in the year of Our Lord nineteen hundred and seventy-four, of the United States of America the one hundred and ninety-eighth, and of the University the one hundred and fifty-sixth.

Daniel C. O'Connell, S.J.
President

William Stauder, S.J.
Dean

J. J. Marletta
Secretary

*Lillian Schippers at St. Louis University Honorary National
Education Society, Pi Lambda Theta (1970)*

529

Athens, Greece, 1970.
L/R: Lillian Schippers, Jessie Meng, Edward Meng, Parry Schippers. Person standing (unknown).

The Mengs and Schippers were very close friends, traveling together, going to dinner at each others home, etc., many BBQ outings at the Meng's Edwardsville farm occurred during the year.

The Mengs and Schippers also traveled together to Puerto Rico several times to visit Lillian's brother Elwood, who worked for the US Navy. They also traveled together to Germany, Austria, and the Greek Isles.

After retirement, Edward J Meng audited a German language class at Southern Illinois University in Edwardsville. This was about 50 years after leaving Freeburg. Much to Ed's and the teacher's surprise, he could still speak the language. This ability became useful when the Mengs and Schippers traveled together to Germany and Austria on vacation. Ed would talk to everyone in German and was very proud of himself and his Freeburg teachers that he could still speak a language from his years as a child.

Lillian Schippers, 82; teacher in Affton Schools, Volunteer

Lillian V. Schippers, a retired teacher in the Affton School District and an active community volunteer and politician, died on Sunday (Dec. 6, 1992) at Jewish Hospital after a brief illness. She was 82 and lived in St. Louis.

Mrs. Schippers retired from Affton schools in 1980. She worked for the district for many years as an administrator of remedial reading and testing programs. She also was director of language arts in Affton. She previously taught at the Ames School in St. Louis and at St. Louis University and Harris–Stowe Teachers College.

Schippers

In 1987 and again last year, Mrs. Schippers ran unsuccessfully on the Republican ballot for alderman in St. Louis' Fourteenth Ward. She also worked on a committee that successfully sought a state audit of the St. Louis School Board.

She has been active for many years in the South Hampton Neighborhood Association and was president of the group for a number of years. She was also active in the Gardenville Community Center, serving as its president in 1985. Mrs. Schippers also worked on the Windsor Community Center board and was currently on the board of directors of Bevo 2001.

A native of St. Louis, she received her bachelor's degree at the former Harris Teachers College, a master's degree in education from Washington University, and a doctorate from St. Louis University.

A funeral service will be held at 10:00 a.m. on Thursday at Hope Lutheran Church, 5218 Neosho Street. Burial will be at Memorial Park Cemetery in Jennings. Visitation will be from 2:00 p.m. to 9:00 p.m. on Wednesday at Hoffmeister Colonial Mortuary, 6464 Chippewa Street.

There are no immediate survivors.

Vogt Relatives?
Top: Aunt Mary; Mother and Father Johnson; Uncle Sam, Uncle Eang and Uncle Kale Galoway
(This picture was given to me by Lillian Vogt Shippers. I am not sure who these people are).

CHAPTER 22
THE SHAMHART MTDNA

(a.k.a. Scapaharda, Oberschabbehard, Schabbehard,
Niederschabbehard, Schabbehar, Shamhart, and Shappard)

Coat of arms of North Rhine-Westfalia.svg

The Shamhart mtDNA

In 2009, James L. Meng, son of Jessie (née Shamhart) Meng, participated in the DNA Ancestry Project with the Genebase Company. These test revealed the male Meng Y-DNA to be R1b. The results of James L Meng and Jessie Shamhart Meng's mtDNA reveal a predicted maternal haplogroup of "H," detected over the past 150,000 years.

However, the female mtDNA, unlike the male Y-DNA, does not remain constant, thus it will mutate over the centuries as it is passed down along maternal lines from mother, to mother, to mother, . . . etc.

mtDNA Haplogroup of James Meng

Based on the SNP marker pattern found in James Meng's HVR-1 markers, James Meng's mtDNA haplogroup can be predicted. The top five mtDNA haplogroup predictions are as follows: (1) H, (2) HV, (3) R0, (4) R, and (5) U.

Section 1: Distribution of James Meng's Haplogroup

Timeline of mtDNA Haplogroup H

James Meng's predicted maternal haplogroup, H, arose from 11 key detectable genetic events over the past 150,000 years. This timeline illustrates how haplogroup H arose and shows the genetic changes that occurred over time, resulting in its present-day form. You can confirm James Meng's membership in haplogroup H through Backbone SNP testing to see if James Meng is positive for the defining SNPs for haplogroup H.

Three examples of famous members of Haplogroup H

Marie Antoinette, Jessie Shamhart Meng of Jasper County, Illinois and Empress Alexandra Feodorovna of Russia.

Marie Antoinette

Jessie Shamhart Meng

Alexandra Feodorovna Empress consort of all the Russians

Section 3: James Meng's Placement in the mtDNA Phylogenetic Tree

Location of mtDNA Haplogroup H in Phylogenetic Tree

DNA studies have shown that all people living today descended from common ancestors who lived in Africa over 100,000 years ago. This genetic association can be plotted into a worldwide "family tree of mankind" called a phylogenetic tree. The phylogenetic tree below is based on the human mtDNA and shows how all human maternal lineages (mtDNA haplogroups) are connected to each other. When scrolling down the tree you find • M9a-d 153, 3394; • H « James Meng (predicted haplogroup) 1438

The Meng-Shamhart book being presented to the village of Varenholz, Germany archivist Ulrich Siekmann by Werner Schabbehard.

Unlike libraries, the archives are a record of German history. To be in the archives, the records, in this instance the book, has been selected for permanent or long-term preservation on the grounds of its enduring cultural, historical, or evidentiary value. In short, it is an honor to have the Meng/Shamhart book accepted into the German archives for the present and future yet unborn children

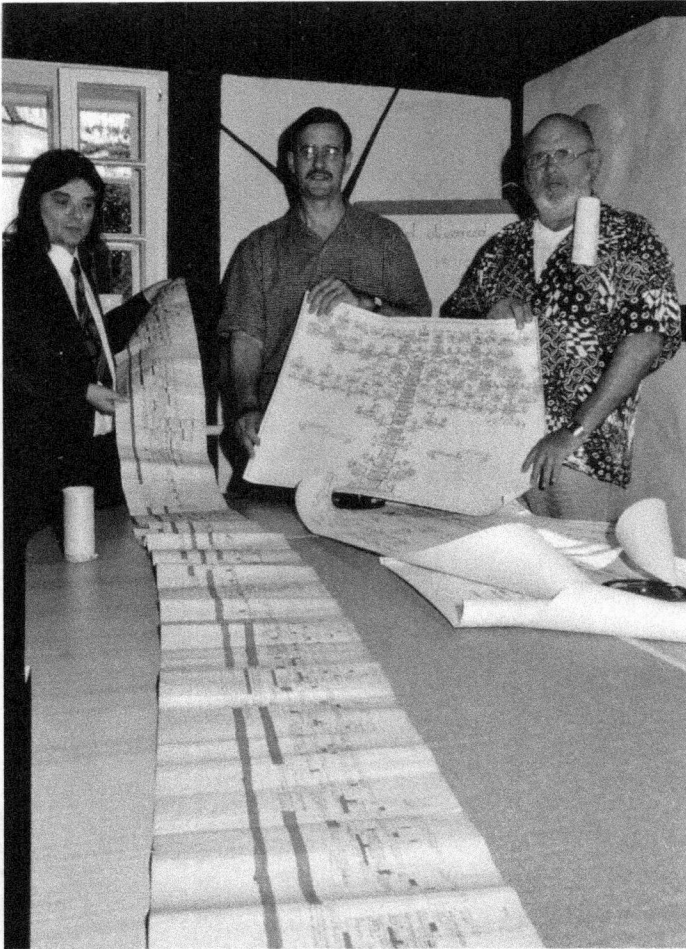

(L/ R) The above picture is of Ulrich Siebrasse during a Schabbehard family reunion in Steinhagen, East Westfalia, Germany on 26.05.2001.Ulrich is displaying his nearly endless family tree. In the middle is Philip Ross Shappard from Chicago, IL.an offspring of Johann Friedrich Wilhelm Schabbehard of Brake, East Westphalia, Germany. On the right is Werner Schabbehard with his extensive family tree. Werner was the organizer of the reunion.

Ulrich Siebrasse was of tremendous help in translating documents that were recorded in old German handwriting into new and a understandable German handwriting. Werner Schabbehard subsequently translated this information into English and communicated these finding to America. Ulrich, a genealogist for more than 40 years, was obviously of great help to *The Meng and Shamhart Family History and Genealogy in Deutschland and America* book. He is also a half cousin of fifth degree to Werner. All the Shamharts and Mengs throughout the world both living and unborn, owe Ulrich, Philip and of course our hero Werner, a great deal of gratitude for their tireless work and generosity!

CHAPTER 23
THE FIRST KNOWN SHAMHART, VARENHOLZ, GERMANY (1147)

There were three significant events that occurred in the year 1147. Undoubtedly, the most significant was the start of the Shamhart a.k.a. Scapaharda family tree. It has been said that this one birth had a tremendous impact on humanity and future world events, thus over shadowing all other events, like the Crusades, of that year.

The second most significant event was the start of the Second Crusade. The Second Crusade (1147–1149) was the second major crusade launched from Europe, was called in 1145, in response to the fall of country of Edessa the previous year to the forces of Zengi. The country had been founded during the First Crusade (1095–1099) by Baldwin of Boulogne in 1098.

The Second Crusade was announced by Pope Eugene III, and was the first of the crusades to be led by European kings, namely Louis VII of France and Conrad III of Germany, with the help of other important European nobles.

The only success of the Second Crusade came unintentionally to a combined force of Flemish, Frisian, Norman, English, Scottish, and German crusaders in 1147. Traveling from England, by ship, to the Holy Land, the army stopped and helped the Portuguese in the capture of Lisbon, expelling its Moorish occupants.

The third most significant event was the start of the Wendish Crusade (Wendenkreuzzug in German) campaign. The Wendish was also part of the Second Crusade, led primarily by the kingdom of Germany inside the Holy Roman Empire and directed against the Polabian Slavs (or "Wends").

The Christian army composed primarily of Saxons and Danes, forced tribute from the pagan Slavs, and affirmed German control of Wagria and Polabia, but failed to convert the bulk of the population.

Obviously, while the Shamhart family tree commenced in 1147, other events, some say of less importance, also occurred: events such as the start of the Second and Wendish Crusades.

The following contribution by Werner Schabbehard connects the Shamharts of Varenholz, Germany and America to the Scapaharda's of Steinhagen, Germany, in 1147.

Schabbehard (Shamhart) Genealogy

In 2000, I received a letter from Philip Shappard, from the Chicago, Illinois, area of the United States. While searching online, he found addresses of all Schabbehards on the Deutsche Telekom website. In a letter to all the Schabbehards, he asked if anyone could help him find a connection to his German family. In an e-mail, I responded that I could help him in the search of his ancestors who had immigrated to America from Germany. I did, and together we found that his ancestors are also descendants from the same ancestors in my family tree. This letter and initial contact with Philip motivated me to continue with the ancestor research. The first documentary, naming our common ancestors, dates from 1147 and mentions the farm Oberschabbehard in Steinhagen No. 3. The farm still exists today after more than 862 years and has changed in the nineteenth century by marriage over to the Steinhage family who are still living there today. In this documentation, I have tried to show a representation of the families Schabbehard from Steinhagen, Shamhart from Varenholz, and Shappard from Brake near Bielefeld of 1147 down to the present day. In the photo above, one may see my grandparents, uncles, aunts, cousins, as well as myself, standing on the right of the children. At that time, my father was in World War II and sadly did not return.

Scapaharda, Oberschabbehard, Niederschabbehard, Schabbehard, Schabbehar, Shamhart, and Shappard—the history of these families

Up to the year 2000, I did not know where my father was born or where my grandparents had their home in the small "Kotten" on the area called Frehen in Bielefeld, at that time belonging to Brake. ("Kotten" is a building in which the farm laborer lived, when they were owned by the landowner, the farmer. Later the people were free, but the name "Kotten" still exists today). By chance, I found a picture of this place in an illustrated book of the city of Bielefeld in the town archive. The reason, why the "Kotten" of my grandparents is illustrated in the book, is because an airplane of the Allies shot down during the World War II fell over Bielefeld directly on the field in front of the "Kotten" of my grandparents and hit the ground. Because my granny and my mother lived only just 15 minutes remotely, we rushed to have a look at the burning airplane. My father was in the war at the time, but he would have said, for certain: "that is the house I was born and raised in as a young child living with my parents." Thus, I stood with my granny there, not knowing that was the "Kotten" where my father was born and my family had lived. After long searches and a piece of luck, I looked after 2000 in the immediate vicinity of the "Kotten," only to find it was gone. However, a witness observed my search and said that someone in a nursery close by would probably remember my grandparents and recommended that I should go to the town archive where the aforesaid picture was found in an illustrated book.

Through the connection to my cousin Philip Ross Shappard from Winfield, Illinois, a Chicago suburb, I learned we had mutual relatives. Carl Henry Shamhart, I found in the American phone book White Pages, gave me the first clues which led to Varenholz. I discovered the Schabbehars recently in the White Pages after renewed search for possible family name bearers in America.

Philip Ross Shappard visited the second time in Bielefeld in 2001, to take part in a family reunion of the Schabbehards, arranged by me in Steinhagen. After we had finished our meeting, together, we started to explore the local native country of our ancestors. Mr. Maschke from Steinhagen took us in the direction of the old homestead of the Oberschabbehards, currently inhabited by the Steinhage family. Mr. Maschke told us new and interesting things about the property, and Mr. Steinhage, the current owner, led us outside and inside about the area and through the old farmhouse.

This is located on the original area of the farm mentioned in the 1147 in the imperial document Scapaharda, the ancestral seat of all Schabbehards, Schabbehars, Schamharts, and Shappards. With Ulrich Siebrasse and some other Schabbehards, we drove even further onto the former Niederschabbehard farm which lies about 1.7 miles from the Oberschabbehard farm. Today's owner is Mr. G., who pursues a respectable horse breeding business on the land.

All Schabbehards, Shamharts, Shappards, and Bistors are descendants according to the 1147 document of Konrad, by divine mercy the second Roman king and emperor who spoke of Oberschabbehard farm No. 3 in Steinhagen, Westphalia, with so-called Scapaharda farm. At that time, according to reports, there was only the farm Scapaharda. Circumstances assumed, possibly, this property was divided in the time around 1270–1333. As a result, in collaboration with the teacher Meise in Steinhagen, it indicates that this division must have taken place in this time era. It was at that time, Steinhagen got its own church, and perhaps, the division is connected with this fact. From 1333, we may suppose that there are the farms Nedderschabbehard (Niederschabbehard) and Oberschabbehard. Oberschabbehard is the place of origin of my ancestors' line; Niederschabbehard, I had not included in my research; however, as new information was discovered, the name of Scapaharda must be considered a likely blood connection. A possibility to let us understand this, perhaps, even today, would exist in a DNA analysis. Still direct descendants of the Niederschabbehards and descendants of the Oberschabbehards are likely related.

The document has among other things the following Latin text: "in the name of the holy and indivisible 3 unity. Konrad, by divine mercy the second Roman king and emperor."

Based on the earliest records available, both families (Niederschabbehard and Oberschabbehard) developed around that time in Steinhagen. From *Scapaharda* occurred *Scepehert, Scapehart, Scapehard*, into *Scapahart* about *de ober Scapehart* and *Oberschabbehard* up to today's manner of writing Schabbehard.

Ulrich Siebrasse, an experienced ancestor researcher with more than 35 years experience, is more than my right hand. He sees the connections, circumstances, and all other interpretations and connections in the name and indexes of names which I have used from church registers and wherever copied and photographed. He recognizes and deciphers the writings on the photos of the documents shot by me and assigns the correct names of the right line. I thank you, dear Ulrich. We became acquainted in 2000 when a long article about our first family meeting had appeared in the local newspaper. He called me and made himself known to me. Now we both know that we are cousins of the fifth degree who are descended together from them on the March 2, 1740, in the Stiftschurch baptized Anne Margarethe Ilsabein Apenbrink. She was married in the first marriage with Johann Hermann Obersiebrasse, Ulrich's ancestor, and in the second marriage with Albert Diederich (Henrich) Schabbehard. And in each case, only one of the children survived, and therefore, we are both also the only legitimate descendants of the Obersiebrasse and the Schabbehard lines.

The history of the families Schabbehard, Shamhart, Shappard, and, perhaps, also of those of Schabbehar goes back to the year 1147 and has its origin in the small municipality of Steinhagen at the past in Westphalia with the farm Scapaharda, to the today's farm Steinhage. The farm Scapaharda was divided formerly into Oberschabbehard (Steinhagen No. 3) and Niederschabbehard (Steinhagen No. 2). In 1333, farm Niederschabbehard is mentioned the first time. I have extended my own ascertained data by the data of Phil Shappard, Carl, Bruce Ray, and John Edwin Shamhart, as well as Irene Raubeson and Ann Brennan and Helen Ann (Nanci) Barnes, born Schabbehar, for the Schabbehar family.

Finally I would still like to mention, that I found in my research in the town archive of Bielefeld a small, simply fixed notebook with the title: CHRONICLE OF THE family Schabbehard i. W. The author was Ob. Reg. Baurat Heinrich Wilhelm Gustav Nieder-Schabbehard from Nuernberg. I looked for the name and found Mr. Jochen Nieder-Schabbehard in Cologne. He showed me the notebook written by a relative and, other, big family trees which had been also provided by this. From the chronicle, I have received suggestions where I could investigate further for my ancestors.

Werner Schabbehard, December 2009

From Schabbehard

Ahnenforschung: The Schabbehard-(Shamhart)-Lines

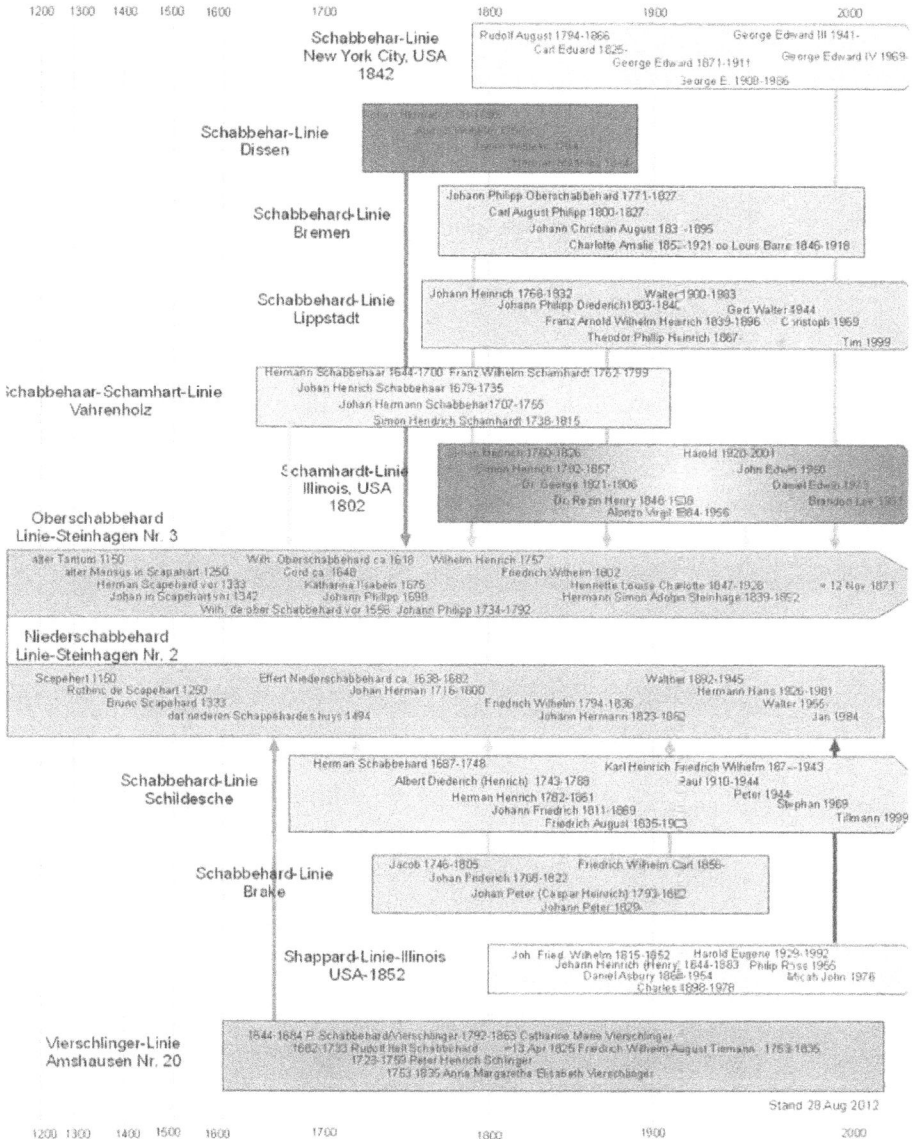

The lines illustrated here reflect the course of the gender "Schabbehard" (Shamhart) down through the centuries. The outgoing mainline on this diagram demonstrates how individual families drifted and migrated. They said their good-byes from Steinhagen and numerous other towns and villages throughout Germany. The towns from which the single families departed to seek their fortunes are provided for your review. The year is also given when these individual family branches acquired modified names and settled in their new home. It is of interest to observe the manner of writing the single family surnames over the course of time.

The diagram above shows the family lines who immigrated to America and some of the known German lines. Most of the families eventually changed their names into either Shappard, or Shamhart, or Schabbehar. It is my desire to connect with all of these families in which there are still living members.

Schabbehard

Documents from 1147 to 1333

The following documents cover the period from 1147 to 1333. First written in the monastery of Herford, they are now located in the state archive in Münster.

Document from 1147
Displayed is a very old document from 1147 in which the name *Scapaharda* is found documented for the very first time. It concerns a so-called imperial document which was written in Latin writing by King Konrad III. King Konrad III (1138–1152), the first Staufer on German throne, signed in March 1147 the document in which the abbess of Herford, Judith von Arnsberg, privileges and possessions of the aristocratic ladies' monastery Herford were guaranteed.

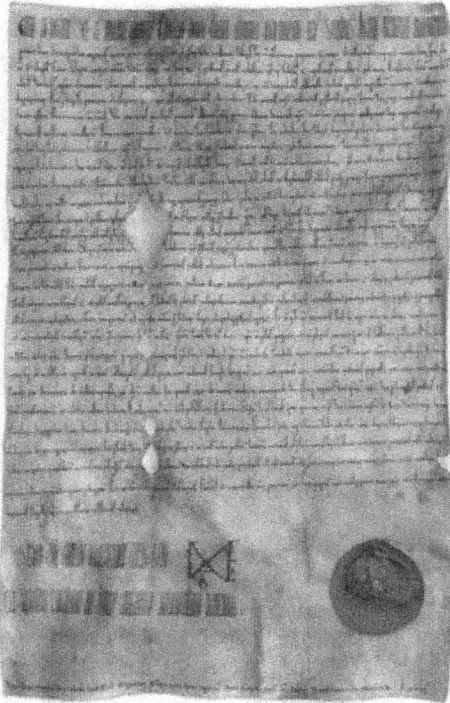

The document of 1147 is issued doubly, because it concerns in it mutual agreements between the abbeys Corvey and Herford. It is printed in "Erhard, Westphalian document book, volume II" and in "Lamey, history of the old counts from Ravensberg." The document has in the translation from the Latin the following text:

In the name of the holy and indivisible 3 unity. Konrad, by divine mercy the second Roman king: It belongs to the generosity of the king's dignity, people who have made themselves well-earned around the state to recompense for their salaries so that they themselves receive the wage of their activity for their continual loyalty, and the others to the fulfillment of their state duties become keen hopeful and (happy). Therefore, the zeal should find out all our future like current faithful that our faithful, dear and venerable abbot Wibold of the cloister of Corvey to our mildness turned with the request that we designed, the privileges of the cloister of Herford at whose head now, as everybody knows, the venerable abbess Judith is, to renew and to confirm.

We granted hearing of his devout request because of his loyal devotion to duty toward ourselves and our rule who is lent us by God, and have taken by the text of this document in our royal protection the place Herford, with all what belongs to it, in it and outdoors, present him with everlasting freedom on grounds of our and all princes power, and confirm by an everlasting law that called the cloister of Herford not come into the power or dominion at all of a person of ecclesiastical or worldly power by a donation at all or exchange, but always should remain under the order and the protection of kings and emperor, and the freedom, which it had up to now in state and appeal as convent, for good should own.

And because two cloisters were built by the emperor Ludwig and were promoted by our ancestors with honor and wealth one a monk monastery, New-Corvey, under the rules of the old Corbie, the other Herforder, however, a convent, similarly of that in Soissons, is decided by them that, who is a present abbot of Corvey the management of the Herforder has, namely in such a way, that he according to the habit of the nuns community after which are in habit to be given provosts according to the ecclesiastical order, in the breeding as well as in all shops, they the nuns according to their gender and their vows not can explain, he their agent and lawyer should be.

Also we follow the tracks of our predecessors and confirm and settle by one for forever remaining decision that all future cloister abbots of Corvey obey the regulations in their management and being under their protection, also against any contradiction, and under protection of the dignity of the abbess where it is of use by the Herforder cloister community. Moreover, the community of the believers should know that the precalled emperor gave as alms of his gender: The cloister of Meppen with all accompanying tenths and possessions, in addition the church of Eresborch, in all directions applying two "Saxon Rastas", to Neu-Corvey. To the Herforder cloister: In the diocese Osnabrück the church to Bünde with subordinated churches to them, in the parish Münster the church of Reni with the belonging churches, namely in such a way that all yields of the tenth and other achievements run toward the precalled cloisters and from them again the tributary people to them in baptism, Communion, burial and confession are supplied, and the priests who have the main churches the office of the archpriests administer to do everything what is in habit to be done by the archpriests of the bishops. And if the bishops themselves must make their visits there, should be given for their lodging how it is prescribed in the orders of our predecessors, namely so much like it is enough. And the bishops should not ask any more and not come with more suite than it can be enough for them. So that they do not ask, however, with the totality of the deliveries owed to the bishops any more than urgently, have decided the bishops of the above mentioned churches, with approval of the church meeting, before our predecessor the emperors Otto and the archbishop Rabanu and the remaining ones who sat with in the church meeting that are given for every church:

4 pigs, each 12 "groschen" worth, or 8 Arieses just as much worth,
4 piglets, 4 geese, 8 chickens, 20 buckets "Meth",
20 buckets honey beer, 60 buckets beer without honey,
120 breads, 100 bushels of oat, 600 "manipuli" (sheaves?).

And it should lie in the power of the bishops whether they want to have from the single churches for a lodging or for two. We also confirm all possessions which this cloister owned up to now undisputedly by which the following are in particular stated:

R e n e (= "Rheine", church since 838). W e t e r i n g e (= "Wettringen", church since 838).
S c o p i n g e (= "Schöppingen"), as well as I b b e n b u r e (= "Ibbenbüren"),
L i g g e r i k e (= "Lengerich"), L i n e n (= "Lienen b. Iburg"), B u n e t h e (= "Bünde" i. W.),
R o t h i n c h u sen (= "Rödinghausen")
S c a p a h a r d a (S c h a b b e h a r d)
U ml o (= "Ummeln"), Bu r d e (= "Borde" later "Steinhagen") and
B e k i n m i n d e n (=?)

Besides, we permit and firmly bet according to the decisions of our predecessors that both places have the free power to select for alle times a personality agreeable to them from theire own cloister community to themselves for theire management for good. And no state judge should have the freedom, to exercise some judicial power against the people who belong to the cloister of Herford; but every legal case should be decided before theire own steward. And in the woods which belong to the cloister or lie besides no higher standing or lower man should dare to go hunting, so that the rest of the servants of God disturbed or theire tenants (coloni) do not come to need.

And with it the permission of our confirmation firmly and unalterable remains in eternity, we have confirmed this document with own-handed signature to see below how and with our printed seal allow to mark.

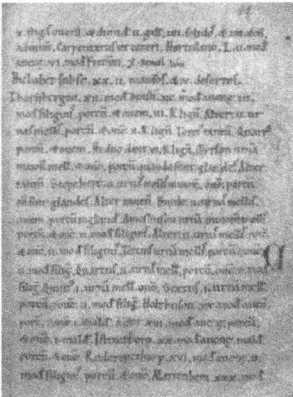

Farm Scepehert, Heberolle (document) from the twelfth century.

Seal of MR. KONRAD, the second Roman king.

I ARNOLD, chancellor, in representation of the arch chancellor Heinrich HEINRICH von MAINT have recognized it. In the year of the incarnation of the Lord in 1147. Under the government KONRADS, second Roman king, in the tenth year of his government. Given to Frankfurt. If it may be luckily. Amen."

These and the following documents which I believe are from the biggest historical value are, I have let send them to me from state archive in Münster as copies.

Document from 1150
Scepehert were obliged to the monastery Herford to the payment of deliveries and taxes and performed other services to the sovereign of Wendt from the year 1556.

Documented in documents of the monastery Herford to be seen in the state archive in Münster.

"Alter Tantum, Scepehert."

The name Scepehert appears in the tenth line as the second word.

Document from the thirteenth century
"Heberolle" of the monastery Herford from thirteenth century which is in the state archive Münster and is printed by Darpe are performed among other things in the administrative district Godesberg the following goods assessable for manor, farms, and heirs:

"Scapehart" were obliged to the monastery Herford to the payment of deliveries and taxes and performed other services and deliveries to the sovereign of Wendt from the year 1556.

Documented in documents of the monastery Herford, to be looked at in the state archive in Münster.

"A Manse is subordinated a medieval name for an unindependent agricultural acquisition unity (court or farm place) which was tenth-liable to a man's court (curtem dominicalis) and this. Mansen were from different size and enclosed as a rule so much civilised country as a great family could manage. In the late mediaeval times the concept Manse or Mansus developed to an economic square measure: 1 Mansus = 4 quarters = 64 Jucherte = 32,683 ha. The name probably comes from in Latin mancipium (= possession) from manus + capio, that is mancipo (= I give to own) or from mansio (= house)." Source: Wikipedia in 2008. In 1150 when reading about "Alter Tantum Scepehert" and "Alter Mansus Scapehart", we must remember that at that point in time, two farms called "Oberschabbehard" and "Niederschabbehard" already existed.

List of the "lehnrührigen" and dependent farms from 1333
The list "Verzeichnis der lehnrührigen und hörigen Höfe aus dem Jahre 1333" brings the following: Officium Godesberg (later Wetere, Werther, called). Scapehard Herman. Scapehard were obliged to the monastery Herford to the payment of deliveries and taxes and performed other services and deliveries to the soverwign von Wendt, from 1556.

From this list is to be recognized that in 1333, two farms existed in Steinhagen. One belonged to the farmer Bruno, to the parish Stenhagen from 1334 belonging, and the other farm owner was Herman Scapehard. In 1338, a correction occurs with that the name Bruno is substituted with Hartwicus. As a result, this indicates that the farmer Bruno Scapehard had passed away in this time and the property had been taken over from his heir Hartwicus Scapehard.

545

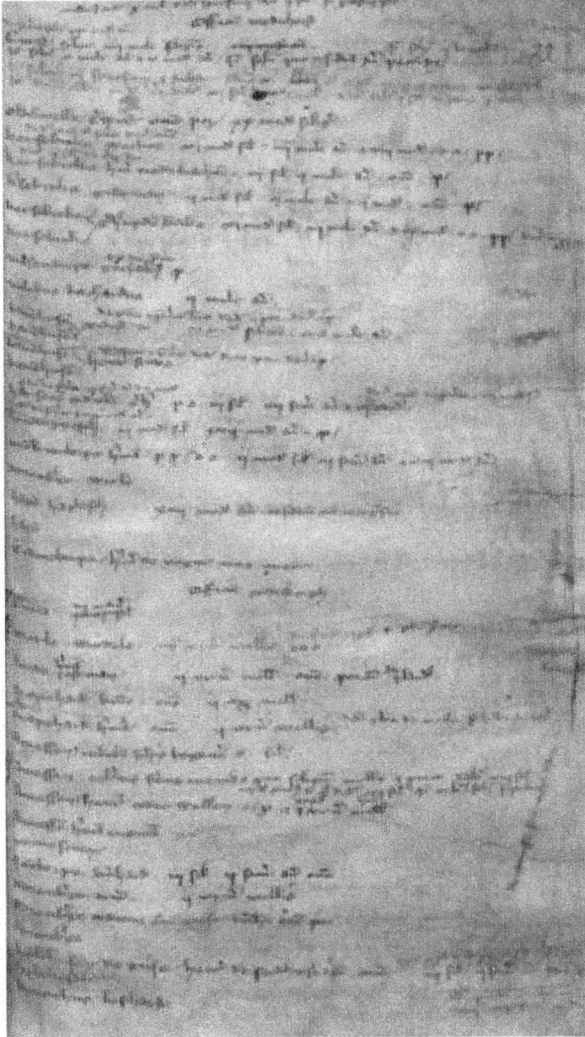

Documented in documents of the monastery Herford, to be looked at in the state archive in Münster.

Note:

See the family tree for James Leroy Meng for connecting his mother, Jessie Frances Shamhart's birth on July 2, 1903, to a Scapaharda's birth before 1147 in Steinhagen, Germany.

In addition, see the Ahnentafel für Wilmer W. Shamhart, Jessie Shamhart's father, to a Scapaharda born before 1147 in Steinhagen, Germany.

Ancestors of
James L. Meng mother's side
Werner Schabbehard father's side
27th of August 2012
by Werner Schabbehard

SCAPAHARDA

A D 1147
East Westphalia
Source: *imperial document from 1147*

Scepehert alter Tantum
before 1150 Steinhagen/East Westphalia
.: *Heberolle (document) from the 12th century*

Scepehert
before 1150 Steinhagen/East Westphalia
Source: *Heberolle (document) from the 12th centu*

Johan de nederschabbehardt
before 1556 Steinhagen/East Westphalia
Source: Ravensberger Urbar von 1556

Wilhelm de ober Schabbeharc
before 1556 Steinhagen/East Westpha
Source: Ravensberger Urbar von 1556

Herman Niederschabbehard
1644 Steinhagen/East Westphalia
Bechtel, Detmold-Staatsarchiv Münster

Wilhelm Oberschabbehard
arround 1618 Steinhagen/East Westphalia
Source: Churchbook of the Ev. Dorfkirche Steinhag

Peter Schabbehard
born 1644 Steinhagen/East Westphalia
Churchbook of the Ev. Dorfkirche Steinhagen

Simon Henrich Schamhardt
born 1760 Varerholz im Kreis Lippe in NRV
Source: Churchbook of the Church in Var,

Paul Schabbehard
22 May 1910 Brake/Bielefeld no. 47 in NRW

Jessie Frances Shamhart
born 02 July 1903 Newton, Jasper County, Ill.

Werner Schabbehard
in Bielefeld in Northrhine- Westphalia

James Leroy Meng
Granite City, Madison County, Illinois

For more information on the historic Shamhart family, go to home.schabbehard.de

CHAPTER 24
THE SHAMHARTS IN AMERICA

Who are the Shamharts and where did they come from and why? First, the name Shamhart a.k.a. Schamhardt is one of many names used over the centuries. Related names include Schabbehard, Shappard, Schabbehar, and Oberschabbehard, our original ancestor.

Jessie Francis (née Shamhart) Meng was the mother to James L. and Edward S. Meng. According to the passenger and immigration list index, 1500s and 1900s, the first Shamhart who came to America was Simon Henrich Schamhardt in 1802. He arrived with his wife and children in Philadelphia, Pennsylvania. This information is sourced in Varenholz, Verdenhalven, Fritz, Die Auswanderer aus dem Fürstentum Lippe (bis 1877).

According to the above records, Simon Henrich Shamhart was born in Varenholz Nordrheim-Westfalen, Germany, on April 13, 1760. Varenholz is located in the northern part of Germany, approximately 31nmE of Hannover. Simon married Amalie Christina Korf (b. 1765) on December 30, 1791. Simon Henrich and Amalie Christina Shamhardt had four children. Amalie Friederike Schamhardt, 1795–1857; Simon Henry Schamhart, 1795–1857; Ernst Gottlieb Schamhardt; and Charlotte Louise Schamhardt 1799–.

Therefore, the question arises—why would Simon and Amalie Schamhardt and the children leave their homeland, friends, and possessions to go to a new, virtually undiscovered land called America? As stated earlier, they came to America in 1802. Therefore, they had to cross the Atlantic in what was probably a small sailing ship, an arduous journey at any time.

However, after comparing the dangers of the sailing to the current and future living conditions in Germany, they obviously decided to sail to the new land. At the time of the Shamhardt's immigration, prices and taxes were very inflated in Germany. These costs were also coupled with high unemployment. A typical large German family lived in crowded conditions without the ability to provide for the family's needs or for their children's future. To complicate these conditions, Germany had a law titled *primogeniture*, which allowed only for the eldest Shamhardt to inherit the family property while all the other siblings in the family inherited nothing! This law was very difficult on large families.

Simon, like many others, wanted to leave for America due to the inflation crisis plaguing the local community. The prices were so high that Simon could not make a living for his family from the making of ropes, alcohol products, and honey from his bees, and other items. Simon then advertised his home in the local newspaper.

Herr Werner Schabbehard, a Shamhart relative, discovered a unique and very rare document relating to this topic in Germany. This document states that Simon Henrich Shamhardt informed his church that he wanted to sell all of his possessions before leaving for America for a better future. However, a "snitcher" or informant within the congregation told the authorities of his intent.

Consequently, the authorities assessed taxes on all of Simon's sales relating to the liquidation of his German estate. This included paying taxes on every chicken, cow, pig, table, bed, rake, etc. A record of these taxes is recorded in Varenholz, Germany.

To further complicate all of the above, an ancient order of distinct social classes existed in Germany. The top class was composed of the notability, followed by the bourgeoisie (town dwellers), and followed by the peasants who owned land, while the peasants who did not own land were at the bottom of the social classes. Incidentally, in 1848, a failed and bloody revolution occurred with the sole purpose of overthrowing the aforementioned four social classes. This failure resulted in a mass exodus from Germany to America. These immigrants were known as the 48ers.

One of the 48ers families was on my father's side of the family, involving Wilhelm Meng, age 35, who came to America from Mertesheim, Germany. Wilhelm arrived on January 22, 1848, with his wife Henrietta, age 28, and their three children: Louis Meng, age 9; Christian Meng, age 8; and Catharine Meng, age 6 months. They arrived in the port of New Orleans in the new country. They then migrated to Freeburg, St. Clair County, Illinois.

The migrating Germans were welcomed in the new states as intelligent, hard workers, especially in the areas of America that needed populating. The land in the Midwestern states became very attractive to these immigrants due to the climate, the fertility of the soil, and the topography that was similar to their German homeland. Areas like Germantown, Pennsylvania; Milwaukee, Wisconsin; Cincinnati and Guernsey County, Ohio; Jasper and St. Clair Counties, Illinois; and St. Louis, Missouri, were most attractive since these Germans, including the Shamharts and Meng families, contained many farmers and tradesmen.

June 10, 1802

The following three pages are the unique documents showing the additional taxes paid by Simon Henrich Shamhardt which resulted from the aforementioned "snitcher" in his church.

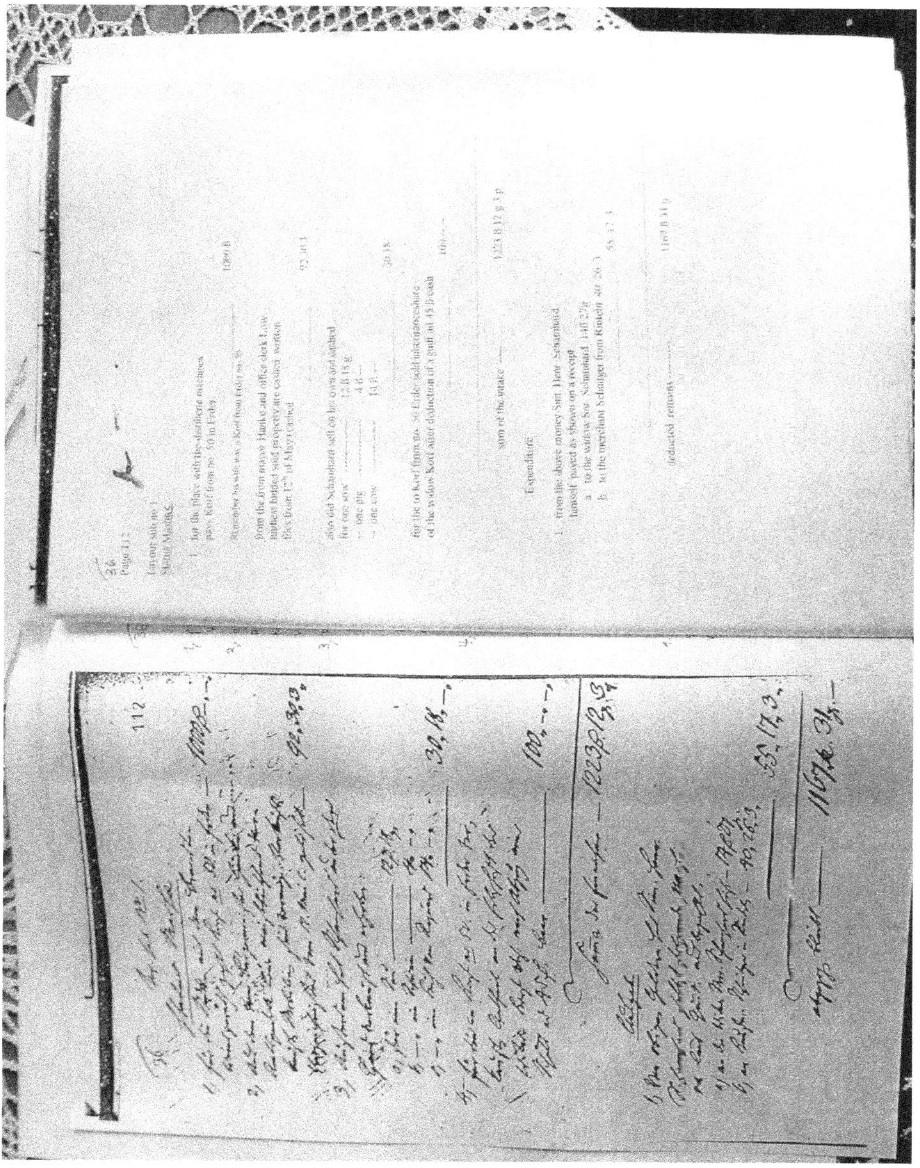

A picture of the restored Schamhardt home in 2010.

Werner Schabbehard and Ulrich Siebrasse standing in front of the
house of Simon Henrich Schamhardt established 1793 in Varenholz

SIMON HENRY SCHAMHARDT'S EXTENDED FAMILY IN AMERICA

SIMON HENRICH SCHAMHARDT

Simon Henrich Schamhardt   married 28 Nov 1820   Catherine Overly
B: Dec 1792   B: 24 July 1804
Varenholz, Nordrhein-Westfalen, Germany   Pennsylvania, US
D: 19 Dec 1857   D: 11 Mar 1896
Beaver, Noble, Ohio, USA   Noble, Noble, Ohio, USA

Children

Name	Birth	Died
George Sylvester Shamhart	13 Jul 1821, Ohio US	17 Jan 1906, Jasper, IL US
Lavenia Shamhart	1823, Guernsey, OH US	
Martha Shamhart	1 Feb 1824, Guernsey, OH US	31 Jul 1905
Ephraim Shamhart	28 Oct 1827, Guernsey, OH US	1906, Ottawa, Franklin, KS US
John Shamhart	28 Oct 1827, Guernsey, OH US	25 Jul 1906, Wade. Jasper, IL US
Elizabeth Anne Shamhart	24 Dec 1829	
Mary Shamhart	1834, Guernsey, Ohio, US	25 Jan 1920
Ephriam W Shamhart	5 July 1837, Guernsey, OH US	6 Apr 1912 Ottawa, Franklin, KS US
Amanda Catherine	18 Aug 1839, OH US	18 Feb 1916, MO City, Ft Bend, TX US
Jane Schamhart	20 Feb 1842	25 Mar 1843
Pheoby Shamhart	20 Feb 1842	17 Mar 1842
Thompson Luther	Jul 1845, OH US	1910
David Shamhart	07 Jan 1849	15 Feb 1849
Reason Alvin Shamhart	27 Apr 1852, OH US	7 Mar 1873

The Oberschabbehard farm on Steinhagen no.3, in Steinhagen, East Westphalia, Germany, the place where Simon Henrich Schamhardt's ancestors originated before moving in the 1600's to Vahrenholz, the tiny little village in the Weser River Valley between Vlotho and Rinteln. The village is located on a hill side of the Lipper Bergland. Simon Herich Schamhardt, who established the Shamhart line in America, was born on 02. Dec 1792 in Varenholz and died on 19. Dec 1857 in Beaver County, Ohio, USA.

Dr. George Shamhart and Leah MacVeay Shamhart

GEORGE SYLVESTER SHAMHART

George Sylvester Schamhart	married 13 Feb 1845	Leah McVey
B: 13 Jul 1821		B: 6 Feb 1825
OH, US		Morris, WA, PA US
D: 17 Jan 1906		D: 20 Jan 1917
Jasper, IL US		N. Muddy, Jasper, IL US

Children

Name	Birth	Died
Reason Henry Shamhart	25 Apr 1846, Guernsey, OH US	19 Feb 1908, Jasper, IL US
Newel B. Shamhart	05 Sep 1849, Guernsey, OH US	08 Dec 1949, OH US
George Sylvester Shamhart	15 Sep 1849, Guernsey, OH US	25 Aug 1879 Jasper, IL US
Alonzo Bailey Shamhart	Mar 1854, Gallia, OH US	
William Willis Shamhart	May 1854, Gallia, OH US	26 Apr 1924, Effingham, Effingham, IL US
John R. Shamhart	Jul 1856, Gallia, OH US	20 Jan 1946, Effingham, Effingham, IL US
Rachel C. Shamhart	03 Nov 1858	20 Nov 1861, OH
Ivan Devore Shamhart	Mar 1861, Gallia, OH US	22 Oct 1916, Phoenix, Maricopa AZ US
Dr. Samuel S. Shamhart	9 Jun 1863, Gallia, OH US	2 Jan 1902, Hyattville, WY US
Leah Nora Shamhart	1869, Jasper, IL US	19 Jan 1946, San Diego, CA US

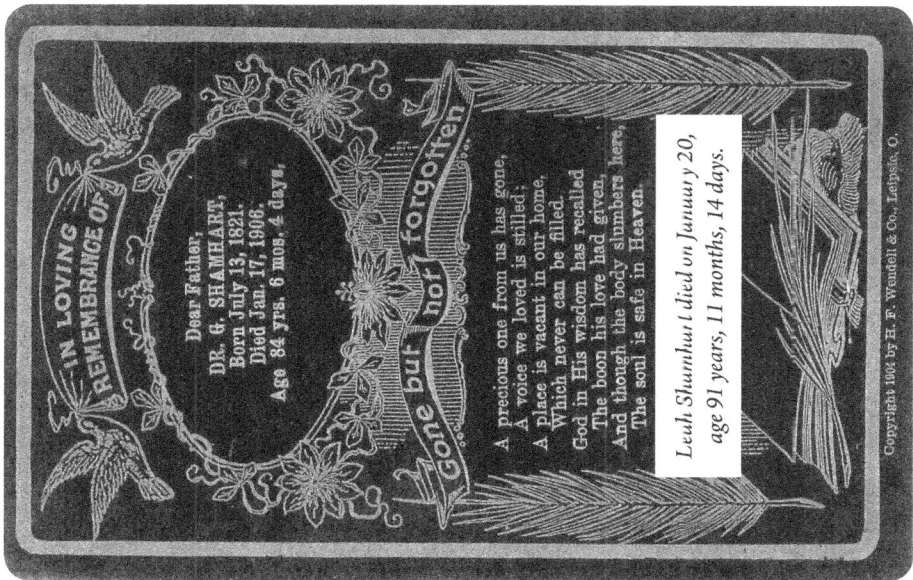

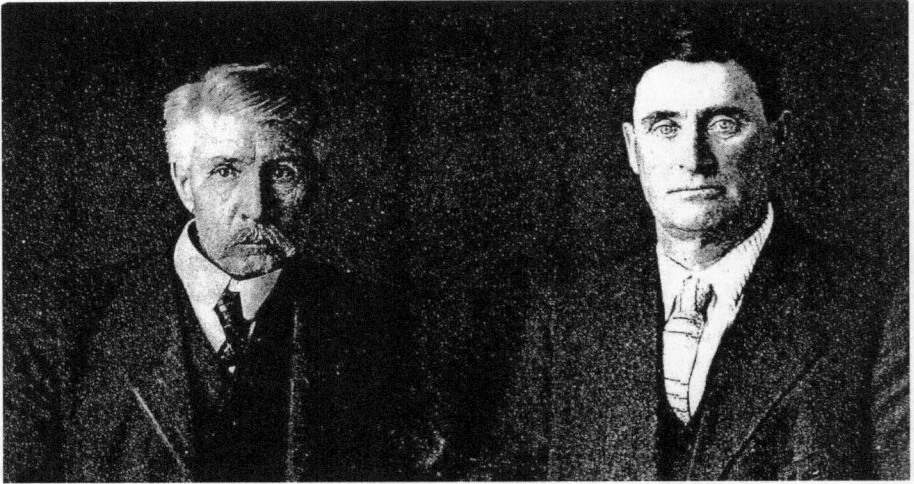

Willis Shamhart with Sherman Wakefield
William Willis Shamhart, 1854–1924, son of George S. Shamhart, Md. and
Leah (née McVey) Shamhart. William Leah were Jessie Meng's aunt and uncle.

Willis and wife Cora

Cora Rife Shamhart (DOB 6/9/1868)
had millinary store in Newton, IL.
Willis and Berl Shamhart families

Family tree for Alex David and Jacob Shamhart Cochran

The following represents the ninth generation connection of (1) Jacob Shamhart Cochran, the youngest and (2) Alexander David Cochran the great-great-grandchildren of Jessie F. (née Shamhart) Meng, back to Simon Henrich Schamhardt (1760).

First Generation

1. Jacob Shamhart Cochran[1] was born in the USA.
    Alexander David Cochran was born in the USA.

    Source: Meng, James Leroy, St. Louis, Missouri

Second Generation

2. David W Cochran David married Heather Andrea Meng, divorced [2].

3. Heather Andrea Meng[3] was born in the USA

    Source: Meng, James Leroy, St. Louis, Missouri

Third Generation

4. James Leroy Meng[4] was born in the USA, He married Beverly Ann Lewis.[5].

    Source: James Leroy, Meng St. Louis, Missouri

5. Beverly Ann Lewis[6] was born in the USA

    Source: James Leroy, Meng St. Louis, Missouri

Fourth Generation

6. Edward John Meng[7] was born on 04. December 1901 in Freeburg St. Clair County, Illinois and died on 01. April 1983 in St. Louis County, Missouri. He married Jessie Frances Shamhart on 12. September 1928[8].

    Source: James Leroy, Meng St. Louis, Missouri

7. Jessie Frances Shamhart [9] was born on 02. July 1903 in Newton, Jasper County, Illinois and died on 18. February 1978.

    Source: James Leroy, Meng St. Louis, Missouri

Fifth Generation

8. Friederich Fred Fritz Meng [10] was born on 11. October 1863 in Freeburg, St. Clair County, Illinois and died on 23. January 1913 in New Athens, St. Clair County,

Illinois. He married Elizabeth Margaret Koesterer on 23. November 1892 in St. Clair County, Illinois[11].

Source: Meng, James Leroy, St. Louis, Missouri

9. Elisabeth Margaret Koesterer [12] was born on 29. May 1869 in Freeburg, St. Clair County, Illinois and died on 12. May 1947 in Granite City, Madison County, Illinois.

    Source: Meng, James Leroy, St. Louis, Missouri

10. Wilmer W Shamhart [13] was born on 07. August 1878 in Jasper County, Illinois and died on 28. December 1947. He married Olive Foster on 12. April 1899[14].

    Source: either Shamhart, Carl - Shamhart, Bruce, Ray - Shamhart, John Shamhart - Elizabeth McPherson

11. Olive Foster [15,16] was born on 25. November 1876 in Newton, Jasper County, Illinois and died on 27. October 1962 in Granite City, Madison County, Illinois.

    Source: Meng, James Leroy, St. Louis, Missouri

Sixth Generation

12. Louis Meng[17,18] was born on 22. February 1837 in Evangelisch, Ebertsheim, Pfalz, Bayern and died on 06. July 1882 in Freeburg, St. Clair County, Illinois. He married Christine Borger am 11. April 1842 in Freeburg, St. Clair County, Illinois[19].

    Source: Meng, James Leroy, St. Louis, Missouri

    Louis Meng, born February 22, 1837 in Ebertsheim, Pfalz, Germany Aug 1, 1837 USA. 1848 St. Clair, County Illinois; died July 6, 1882 in Freeburg, St. Clair co., Illinois. He was the son of Wilhem William George Meng and Anna Marie Schreiber. He married Christina Borger April 1859

    Family Search™
    LOUIS MENG
    Birth: 22 FEB 1837 Evangelisch, Ebertsheim, Pfalz, Bayern
    Father: WILHELM MENG
    Mother: MARIE SCHREIBER
    C982651 - 1694 - 1875 - 0193832

13. Christine Borger[20] was born on 11. April 1842 and died on 29. May 1902 in Freeburg, St. Clair County, Illinois.

    Source: Meng, James Leroy, St. Louis, Missouri

    Christina "Christine" BORGER, born 11 Apr 1842 in Family homestead 1 mile south of Freeburg, St. Clair CO IL; died 29 May 1902 in Freeburg, St. Clair Co IL. She was the daughter of George BORGER Sr. and Elizabeth B.(?) BORGER

14. Berthold Bartley Koesterer[21]. Berthold married Katharina Reinheimer.

> Source: Meng, James Leroy, St. Louis, Missouri

15. Katharina Reinheimer.

> Source: Meng, James Leroy, St. Louis, Missouri

16. John Rufus Shamhart[22] was born on 22. July 1856 and died on 20. June 1946. He married Mollie E Johnson.

> Source: either Shamhart, Carl - Shamhart, Bruce, Ray - Shamhart, John Shamhart - Elizabeth McPherson

17. Mollie E Johnson[23].

> Source: either Shamhart, Carl - Shamhart, Bruce, Ray - Shamhart, John Shamhart - Elizabeth McPherson

Seventh Generation

18. Wilhelm William George Meng[24] was born 1810 in Mertesheim, Germany, and died on 16. December 1850 in St. Clair County, Illinois. He married Marie Schreiber on 31. May 1837 in Ebertsheim, Pfalz, Bayern[25].

> FamilySearch™
> WILHELM MENG
> Spouse: MARIE SCHREIBER
> Marriage: 31 MAY 1837 Evangelisch, Ebertsheim, Pfalz, Bayern
> M982651 - 1694 - 1885 - 0193832

> Source: Meng, James Leroy, St. Louis, Missouri

Wilhelm William George MENG (my great, great, great grandfather) born 1810 in Mertesheim, State: Rheinland Pfalz, County: Bad Duerkheim: Region: Rheinhessen-Pfalz Germany>January 1847-March 1849 St. Clair County, Illinois; died 16 Dec 1850 in St. Clair County, Illinois. He was son of Conrad Meng and Elizabeth Mueller. He married Anna Maria Schreiber on 31 May 1837 in Evangelisch, Ebertsheim, Rheinland-Pfalz, Bad Duerkeim County: Rheinhessen-Pfalz region Bayern.

19. Marie Schreiber[26] was born 1818 and died between 1845-1846 in May.

> Source: Meng, James Leroy, St. Louis, Missouri

20. George Borger[27] George married Elisabeth B. NN.

> Source: Meng, James Leroy, St. Louis, Missouri

Christina "Christine" BORGER, born 11 Apr 1842 in Family homestead 1 mile south of Freeburg, St. Clair Co IL; died 29 May 1902 in Freeburg, St. Clair Co IL. She was the daughter of George BORGER Sr. and Elizabeth B.(?) BORGER

21. Elisabeth B. NN[28].

> Source: Meng, James Leroy, St. Louis, Missouri

22. Dr. George Shamhart[29] was born on 13. July 1821 in Guernsey County, Ohio and died on 17. January 1906 in Jasper County, Illinois. He married Leah MC Vey on 13. February 1845 in Ohio.

More about Dr. George Shamhart:
Burial: Trexler Cemetery, Jasper County, Illinois
Occupation: Doctor
Residence: 1865 Came to North Muddy Township from Gallipolis, Gallia County, Ohio

> Source: either Shamhart, Carl - Shamhart, Bruce, Ray - Shamhart, John Shamhart - Elizabeth McPherson

23. Leah MC Vey[30] was born on 06. February 1825 and died on 20. January 1917 in Jasper County, Illinois.

More about Leah MC Vey:
Trexler Cemetery, Jasper County Illinois

> Source: either Shamhart, Carl - Shamhart, Bruce, Ray - Shamhart, John Shamhart - Elizabeth McPherson

Eight Generation

24. Conrad Meng[31] Conrad married Elisabeth Mueller.

> Source: Meng, James Leroy, St. Louis, Missouri

25. Elisabeth Mueller[32]

> Source: Meng, James Leroy, St. Louis, Missouri

26. George Schreiber George married Catharin NN.

27. Catharin NN.

28. Simon Henrich Schamhardt[33,34] was born on 02. December 1792 in Varenholz and died on 19. December 1857 in Beaver County, Ohio. He married Catherine Overly on 28. November 1820 in USA[35].

> Source: I, Werner Schabbehard, have copied with Ulrich Siebrasse at the state archive

in Detmold the possible church register entries as well as we have copied data from the Verkartung (a special Church file).

29. Catherine Overly[36] was born on 24. July 1804 in PA and died on 11. March 1896 in Noble County, near St. Johns Church, Ohio, USA.

> Source: either Shamhart, Carl - Shamhart, Bruce, Ray - Shamhart, John Shamhart - Elizabeth McPherson

Ninth Generation

30. Simon Henrich Schamhardt[37,38] was born on 13. April 1760 in Varenholz and died on 27. October 1826 in USA. He married Amalie Christina Korf on 30. December 1791 in Varenholz[39].

> Godfathers: Simon Henrich Schamhard und Conrad Everding

> Source: I, Werner Schabbehard, have copied with Ulrich Siebrasse at the state archive in Detmold the possible church register entries as well as we have copied data from the Verkartung (a special Church file).

> Source: either Shamhart, Carl - Shamhart, Bruce, Ray - Shamhart, John Shamhart - Elizabeth McPherson

31. Amalie Christina Korf[40,41] was born on 20. March 1765 in Erder and died in USA.

> Source: I, Werner Schabbehard, have copied with Ulrich Siebrasse at the state archive in Detmold the possible church register entries as well as we have copied data from the Verkartung (a special Church file).

Anhang A - Quellen

1 Thru 12 Meng, James Leroy.
   32. Shamharts in Amerika.
   33. Meng, James Leroy.
   34. Shamharts in Amerika.
   35. Meng, James Leroy.
   36. Family Search, C982651 - 1694 - 1875 - 0193832.

18 Thru 21 Meng, James Leroy.
   37. Offspring des Schamhardt, Simon Henrich b 13 Apr 1760 aus Varenholz migrated to USA.
   38. Offspring des Schamhardt, Simon Henrich b 13 Apr 1760 aus Varenholz migrated to USA.
   39. Family Search, M982651 - 1694 - 1885 - 0193832.
   40. Family Search, M982651 - 1694 - 1885 - 0193832.

26 Thru 28 Meng, James Leroy.

41. Offspring des Schamhardt, Simon Henrich b 13 Apr 1760 aus Varenholz migrated to USA.
42. Shamharts in Amerika.
43. Meng, James Leroy.
44. Meng, James Leroy.
45. Kirchenbuch (Churchbook) der Kirche in Varenholz.
46. Shamharts in Amerika.
47. Shamharts in Amerika.
48. Shamharts in Amerika.
49. Kirchenbuch (Churchbook) der Kirche in Varenholz.
50. Shamharts in Amerika.

Back row: Olive Shamhart, Wilmer Shamhart, Sybil Fischer,
Charlie and Mary Shamhart, Ed and Jessie Meng. Sitting: J R and Mary Shamhart.
Front row: John, Richard, Shirley, Max Fischer. Sybil (née Shamhart) Fischer.

(Left to right) Willis Shamhart, John R. Shamhart, Jessie
Shamhart Meng's grandfather. Willis and John were brothers.

565

John Rufus Shamhart, a.k.a. JR, 1856–1946

John Rufus Shamhart was the father of Wilmer W and Charlie M Shamhart, grandfather of Jessie F. Shamhart Meng.

Front sitting: John Rufus Shamhart, a.k.a. JR (1856–1946), son of George S. Shamhart (1821–1906) and Leah McVey (1825–1917), and John's wife, Mary E. Johnson (1859–1942). Back/left: Olive Foster (1876–1962) with husband Wilmer W. Shamhart (1878–1947). Charles M. Shamhart (1880–1958) with wife Mary Smylda Clagg (1857–). Wilmer and Charles were brothers.

John and Mollie (Mary) Shamhart

John Shamhart

Charlie, John, and Molly Shamhart (this picture was used in the Poison Ivy book by J. L. Meng).

John R. and Mary Elizabeth (née Johnson) Shamhart

Galloway and Johnson families. Left side standing: Mary Elizabeth Johnson (b. 13 Jun. 1858–d. 9 Jan. 1942). Father was Isaac Johnson and Mother Esther Galloway who also had children named Ida, Rosalie, Leona, Etta, Anise, Dell, Eva, and Alva.

Mary Elizabeth Johnson married John R. Shamhart on 23 Sept. 1877. Children born of this marriage were Wilmer W. Shamhart and Charles Mansel Shamhart.

Source: Funeral Memory Book of Mary Elizabeth Shamhart.

DEATH OF JUDGE SHAMHART

Judge Ivan Devore Shamhart (1861–1916) was the son of George S. Shamhart (1821–1906) and Leah McVey (1825–1917). Ivan was Jessie F Meng's uncle. An account of the judge's death, written by his son Claud S Shamhart, is below.

The Newton Press
Official Paper of Jasper County[7]
TUESDAY, NOVEMBER 7, 1816

JUDGE IVAN D. SHAMHART

Particulars as to His Recent Death

The following is a letter to John Kasserman from Claud Shamhart, and the clipping from a Phoenix, Arizona, newspaper, give an account of the death of Judge Ivan D. Shamhart, formerly of this city, where he served on the bench of the county court of Jasper county.

Phoenix, Arizona, Oct. 31, 1916
Mr. John Kasserman,
Newton, Illinois.

Dear Sir:--
    I promised to write you further particulars concerning the death of father, but have been quite busy catching up the threads of the business where father left them. Every thing is in best order possible in such a case. You know he expected to go in just this way, and he always kept things up to the minute.
    Father had been in the best of health lately, having almost entirely recovered from the strain incident to his campaign two years ago. On Friday night before his death, we had been over to the house until quite late and my father had been romping with the kid, in whom he always showed the greatest interest. We had talked on the following morning about how much better he looked and how he had gained in flesh. He looked better than I had seen him for some time. I left that afternoon for Mesa on a hunting trip. On our return to Mesa about 7:00 p. m., Sunday we were informed of his death and did not reach Phoenix until almost 8. I therefore was not present when he died but mother told me as best she could.
    It seems that he had an engagement to speak at a municipal

569

ownership meeting on Sunday afternoon. He had worked all morning about the place and told mother that his back hurt him a little and that if he hadn't promised to go, he'd have stayed at home for a rest. She wanted to hear him and went with him to the City Hall Plaza. He was in the best of spirits and apparently felt refreshed from the ride down on the car. He was the second speaker on the list and talked about twenty minutes (according to the papers). He concluded a statement with the words "And that is not all"; turned, took some water, faced the audience, passed his hand over his face in the way he often did; put out his hand and slowly fell forward. Mother reached him before he finally passed on and when she spoke to him he turned his head and looked at her, but could not speak. He was barely able to put up his lips to be kissed and then passed on. There was apparently no agony or struggle. We went just as he often said he wanted to go. Breathed easily two or three times.

Everyone was and is just lovely to us and mother continues to hold up wonderfully well. Clifford Love was the only one from back home with us and he was certainly a great help.

The Federal, Supreme and Superior Courts stood at recess during the funeral and the flags on the Capitol, Court House and City Hall were and are at half mast for him. The Governor was a great friend of my father and father had done some campaigning for him, traveling with him and his party. He sent a large floral offering, as did the Military Department, the State and County Democratic Central Committees, the Young Men's League, the Maricopa County Bar Association and hosts of friends, clients and neighbors.

He was buried as he wished in Greenwood Cemetery at this place.

We appreciate your expression of sympathy.

Claud S. Shamhart.

TUESDAY, NOVEMBER 7, 1916
Ivan Devore Shamhart
From the Phoenix, Arizona Republican

The funeral of Judge I. D. Shamhart whose sudden death shocked the community last Sunday afternoon, was held yesterday from the mortuary of Moore and McLellan.

There was a large attendance, for though Judge Shamhart had lived a quiet life during his residence of six years in Phoenix, he had made many friends, and those who knew him held him in the highest esteem, both as a lawyer and a man. His character was a most lovable one. Hon L. F. Vaughn and Charles DeSales Wheeler, who had been associated with him in his office for some years, said that he had become peculiarly endeared to them.

He had come to care little for worldly wealth or for professional success, his chief desire being to be helpful to those with whom he came in contact.

The funeral was under the direction of the Odd Fellows. Rev. Marquis read the service.

Besides the stricken widow there were present at the funeral his son, Lieutenant Claud Shamhart and wife.

The estimation in which Judge Shamhart was held by the bar is set forth in the following resolutions, which will be presented at a meeting of the bar today.

To the Bar Association of Maricopa County:

Mr. President—Your committee appointed to prepare and present resolutions commemorative of the life and death of Ivan D. Shamhart, recently deceased, beg leave to report:

Whereas. The death of Ivan D. Shamhart, late member of this association, occurred Sunday, October 22nd, 1916. Be it

Resolved. By the Bar Association of Maricopa county, especially assembled on the 24th day of October, 1916, for that purpose, we deplore his untimely death.

Mr. Shamhart has resided in this Maricopa county for six years last past, during which period he was engaged in the practice of his profession; he was a learned and good lawyer, dignified, courteous and considerate to his brother associates at the bar, to the court and towards his clients, devoted and loyal.

His private life was unexceptional, and association with his fellow men kindly, hospitable and genial; his sympathies were broad and practical and the essential force in him was progressive as to expression and character.

Naturally he was of reserved disposition and those who knew him intimately appreciated the noble qualities of his character; that he, throughout life, was the type of men of whom it may well be said, that the "world is better because he lived."

He has passed from this life, and if his kindly spirit is not re-absorbed by the ocean of universal life, but remains a distinct individual entity, as in this life, then we feel that the benefit of his work here will not be lost to him.

We feel profoundly his absence and desire as the expression of this bar, our sorrow, admiration and affection, and as a token of our grief and our respect, that these resolutions be recorded as a part of the records of the supreme court of the state, and the superior court of Maricopa county and the United States district court of America, and a copy transmitted to the family of deceased. Respectfully,

J. B. Woodard,
Chas. B. Ward,
Loren F. Vaughn.

Claud, Anna and Ralph Shamhart. Claud is the son of Ivan Devore Shamhart and Emma E. (née Daily) Shamhart. Ralph had a daughter named Eileen (née Shamhart) Jones.

John Shamhart (1827–1906)

Child:	John Shamhart
Born:	28 Oct 1827
in:	Guernsey, Ohio, USA
Died:	25 Jul 1906
in:	Wade, Jasper, Illinois, USA
Relationship with Father:	Simon Henrich Schamhardt - Natural
Relationship with Mother:	Catherine Overly - Natural
Reference number:	108

Emigration:	Apr 1864
	Jasper, Illinois, United States
Source:	Public Family Tree - Trista's Family Tree.
Residence:	1860
	Millwood, Guernsey, Ohio, United States
Source:	1860 Federal Census Missouri.

Address and Phone(s)	

Medical

Old Settlers'

ASSOCIATION

——OF——

JASPER COUNTY

Organized August 17 1901

Twenty-second Annual Reunion

PETERSON PARK,

NEWTON, ILLINOIS

Saturday, Sept. 30

1922

Dr. Reason Henry Shamhart (1846–1908) and Louisa A. (née Chestnut) Shamhart. Reason was the son of George Sylvester and Leah McVey Shamhart, aunt and uncle of Jessie F. Meng.

Dr. Reason Henry Shamhart delivered James L. Meng's mother, Jessie Frances Shamhart, on July 2, 1908.

C. L. Foster.

U.S. World War II Draft Registration Cards, 1942 record for Rezen George Shamhart

U.S. World War II Draft Registration Cards, 1917-1918 record for Rezen George Shamhart

Leah Shamhart

Leah May Shamhart (1906–1978) was the daughter of Rezen G. Shamhart (1882–1956) and Anna May, née Hazelton (1886–1970). Leah May Shamhart married Luther Sylvanis Baker.

Leah May Shamhart Baker (1906–1978), daughter of Rezen G. Shamhart (1882–1956) and Anna May Hazelton Shamhart (1886–1970).

1. FULL NAME OF GROOM: Luther S. Baker

2. PLACE OF RESIDENCE: Decatur, Ills.

3. OCCUPATION: Laborer   4. D.O.B. : ----------------   (Next Birthday) 5 AGE: 28

6. PLACE OF BIRTH: Jasper County, IL   7. RACE: White

8. FATHER'S NAME: John Baker   # OF GROOMS MARRIAGE: 1

10. MOTHER'S MAIDEN NAME: Dora L. Murphy

FULL NAME OF BRIDE: Leah M. Shamhart

MAIDEN NAME: ----------------

PLACE OF RESIDENCE: Winterrowd

D.O.B : ----------------   5. AGE: (Next Birthday) 19   6. RACE: White

PLACE OF BIRTH: Jasper County, IL

FATHER'S NAME: George Shamhart

MOTHER'S MAIDEN NAME: May Hazelton

0. NUMBER OF BRIDE'S MARRIAGE: 1

Married at My Residence in the County of Jasper,

State of Illinois the 25th day of April . 1925

Witnessed by Pearl Ervin and Elbert Ervin

Ceremony performed by A. J. Ervin J. P. Wheeler, Ill

Date of return was the 25th day of April . 1925

Linda Huth, JASPER COUNTY CLERK
204 W Washington
NEWTON, ILLINOIS 62448

CERTIFICATION OF VITAL RECORD

JASPER COUNTY, ILLINOIS

STATE OF ILLINOIS

STATE FILE NUMBER

REGISTRATION DISTRICT NO. 80.0

REGISTERED NUMBER 277

MEDICAL CERTIFICATE OF DEATH

DECEASED—NAME	FIRST	MIDDLE	LAST	SEX	DATE OF DEATH (MONTH, DAY, YEAR)
1.	Luther	S.	Baker	2. Male	3. Oct. 24, 1972

RACE WHITE, NEGRO, AMERICAN INDIAN, ETC. (SPECIFY)	AGE—LAST BIRTHDAY (YRS.)	UNDER 1 YEAR		UNDER 1 DAY		DATE OF BIRTH (MONTH, DAY, YEAR)	PLACE OF DEATH	COUNTY
		MOS.	DAYS	HOURS	MIN.			
4. White	5a. 75	5b.		5c.		6. Apr. 25, 1897	7a. Richland	

CITY, TOWN, TWP. OR ROAD DISTRICT NUMBER	INSIDE CITY (YES/NO)	HOSPITAL OR OTHER INSTITUTION—NAME (IF NOT IN EITHER, GIVE STREET AND NUMBER)
7b. Olney	7c. Yes	7d. Richland Memorial Hospital

BIRTHPLACE STATE OR FOREIGN COUNTRY	CITIZEN OF WHAT COUNTRY	MARRIED, NEVER MARRIED, WIDOWED, DIVORCED (SPECIFY)	NAME OF SURVIVING SPOUSE (IF WIFE, GIVE MAIDEN NAME)
8. Illinois	9. United States	10. Married	11. Leah Shamhart

SOCIAL SECURITY NUMBER	USUAL OCCUPATION	KIND OF BUSINESS OR INDUSTRY	U.S. WAR VETERAN (YES/NO)	WAR OR DATES OF SERVICE
12. 324-14-8019	13a. Farmer	13b. Farming	13c. No	13d. None

RESIDENCE	STATE	COUNTY	CITY, TOWN, TWP, OR ROAD DISTRICT NO.	INSIDE CITY (YES/NO)	STREET AND NUMBER
14a. Illinois		14b. Jasper	14c. Newton	14d. No	14e. RFD # 4

FATHER—NAME FIRST	MIDDLE	LAST	MOTHER—MAIDEN NAME FIRST	MIDDLE	LAST
15. John Baker			16. Dora Murphy		

INFORMANT'S SIGNATURE	RELATIONSHIP	MAILING ADDRESS (STREET AND NO. OR R. F. D. CITY OR TOWN, STATE, ZIP)
17a. Leah Baker	17b. Wife	17c. RFD # 4, Newton, Illinois 62448

PART I. DEATH WAS CAUSED BY: [ENTER ONLY ONE CAUSE PER LINE FOR (a), (b), AND (c)]

APPROXIMATE INTERVAL BETWEEN ONSET AND DEATH

18.	IMMEDIATE CAUSE		
	(a) CARDIOGENIC SHOCK		1.30 Hours
CONDITIONS, IF ANY WHICH GAVE RISE TO IMMEDIATE CAUSE (a) STATING THE UNDERLYING CAUSE LAST.	DUE TO OR AS A CONSEQUENCE OF (b) ACUTE MYOCARDIAL INFARCTION		12 Hours approx
	DUE TO OR AS A CONSEQUENCE OF: (c) ARTERIOSCLEROTIC HEART DISEASE		unknown

PART II. OTHER SIGNIFICANT CONDITIONS: CONDITIONS CONTRIBUTING TO DEATH BUT NOT RELATED TO CAUSE GIVEN IN PART I (a)	AUTOPSY (YES/NO)	IF YES, WERE FINDINGS CONSIDERED IN DETERMINING CAUSE OF DEATH
DIABETES MELLITUS	19a. No	19b.

DATE OF OPERATION, IF ANY	MAJOR FINDINGS OF OPERATION
20a.	20b.

21. I CERTIFY THAT TO THE BEST OF MY KNOWLEDGE THIS DEATH OCCURRED AT 3:37 A.M. ON THE DATE, AT THE PLACE AND FROM THE CAUSE(S) STATED

NOTE: IF AN INJURY WAS INVOLVED IN THIS DEATH, THE CORONER MUST BE NOTIFIED.

I ATTENDED THE DECEASED FROM:	MONTH	DAY	YEAR	TO	MONTH	DAY	YEAR	AND LAST SAW HIM/HER ALIVE ON:	MONTH	DAY	YEAR
21a.	3	6	68	21b.	10	24	72	21c.	10	24	72

SIGNATURE	DATE SIGNED (MONTH, DAY, YEAR)	ILLINOIS LICENSE NUMBER
22a.	22b. 10-24-72	22c. 36 39391

MAILING ADDRESS—CERTIFIER	STREET AND NUMBER OR R. F. D.	CITY OR TOWN	STATE	ZIP
23. 521 West Jourdan		Newton	Illinois	62448

BURIAL, CREMATION, REMOVAL (SPECIFY)	CEMETERY OR CREMATORY—NAME	LOCATION CITY OR TOWN	STATE	DATE (MONTH, DAY, YEAR)
24a. Burial	24b. Trexler	24c. Newton Illinois		24d. Oct. 26, 197

FUNERAL HOME	STREET AND NUMBER OR R. F. D.	CITY OR TOWN	STATE	ZIP
25a. Marshall Funeral Chapel, 306 S. Van Buren, Newton, Illinois 62448				

FUNERAL DIRECTOR'S SIGNATURE	FUNERAL DIRECTOR'S ILLINOIS LICENSE NUMBER
25b. Richard J. Yokeley	25c. 7287

LOCAL REGISTRAR'S SIGNATURE	DATE REC'D. BY LOCAL REGISTRAR (MONTH, DAY, YEAR)
26a.	26b. October 25, 1972

SP 200-1 (1968)

ILLINOIS DEPARTMENT OF PUBLIC HEALTH — BUREAU OF STATISTICS

(BASED ON 1968 U. S. STANDARD CERTIFICATE)

CERTIFIED COPY OF VITAL RECORDS

STATE OF ILLINOIS

COUNTY OF JASPER

SS

DATE ISSUED: 4-7-09

This is a true and exact reproduction of the document officially registered and placed on file in the office of JASPER COUNTY CLERK, ILLINOIS

Linda Huth, cu

COUNTY CLERK

JASPER COUNTY, ILLINOIS

CERTIFICATION OF VITAL RECORD

MEDICAL CERTIFICATE OF DEATH

STATE OF ILLINOIS

REGISTRATION DISTRICT NO. 40.0
REGISTERED NUMBER 2-10-78

1. DECEASED NAME: Leah May Baker
2. SEX: Female
3. DATE OF DEATH: February 11, 1928
4a. RACE: White 4b. American 5. AGE: 71 6. DATE OF BIRTH: May 3, 1906 7a. COUNTY OF DEATH: Jasper
7b. Newton 7c. Newton Rest Haven Nursing Home
8. STATE OF BIRTH: Illinois 9. U S A 10. Widowed
12. SOCIAL SECURITY NUMBER: 343-23-5269 13a. Housewife 13b. Home 13c. No
14a. 402 N Maple St 14b. Newton 14d. Yes 14d. Jasper 14e. Illinois
15. FATHER: George Shamhart 16. MOTHER: Anna May Hazelton
17b. Son 17c. R R # 4, Newton, Illinois 62448

PART I
(a) Brain Tumor — 7 months
PART II: Arteriosclerous Heart Disease, Hypertension
19. AUTOPSY: No
20a. DATE OF OPERATION: 12-16-77 20b. Gangrene right foot
21a. 9/3/1968 21b. 2/11/1978 21c. 2/11/1978 HOUR OF DEATH 10:00 A.M.
22. DATE SIGNED 2/13/78
22c. 507 W. Washington, Newton, Illinois 62448 22d. 36-39391
24a. Burial 24b. Trexler 24c. North Muddy Twp, Jasper Co, Ill 24d. Feb 13, 1978
25a. Pulliam Funeral Homes P C,, 304 S Van Buren St, Newton, Ill 62448
25b. 31-8007
26b. Feb 15 1978

CHAPTER 25
REMEMBERING WILMER AND OLIVE SHAMHART

Wilmer Weston Shamhart (1878-1947) and Olive Foster Shamhart (1876-1962) were the parents of Jessie Meng, Sybil Fischer, Wayne Shamhart and Lois Cox

AHNENTAFEL FÜR WILMER W SHAMHART
EIGHTEEN GENERATIONS FROM 1878 TO 1147

Erste Generation

1. Wilmer W Shamhart[1] wurde am 07. August 1878 geboren. Er starb am 28. Dezember 1947.

    > Quelle/source: Entweder/either: Shamhart, Carl - Shamhart, Bruce, Ray - Shamhart, John Shamhart - Elizabeth McPherson

    Wilmer heiratete Olive Foster[2]. Olive wurde in Newton geboren.

Zweite Generation

2. John Rufus Shamhart[3] wurde am 22. Juli 1856 geboren. Er starb am 20. Juni 1946. Er heiratete Mollie E Johnson.

    > Quelle/source: Entweder/either: Shamhart, Carl - Shamhart, Bruce, Ray - Shamhart, John Shamhart - Elizabeth McPherson

3. Mollie E Johnson[4].

Dritte Generation

4. Dr. George Shamhart[5] wurde am 13. Juli 1821 in Guernsey County, Ohio geboren. Er starb am 17. Januar 1906 in Jasper County, Illinois. Er heiratete Leah MC Vey am 13. Februar 1845 in Ohio.

    More about Dr. George Shamhart:
    Burial: Trxler Cemetery, Jasper County, Illinois
    Occupation: Doctor
    Residence: 1865 Came to North Meddy Township from Gallipolis, County, Ohio

    > Quelle/source: Entweder/either: Shamhart, Carl - Shamhart, Bruce, Ray - Shamhart, John Shamhart - Elizabeth McPherson

5. Leah MC Vey[6] wurde am 06. Februar 1825 geboren. Sie starb am 20. Januar 1917 in Jasper County, Illinois.

    More about Leah MC Vey:
    Trexler Cemetery, Jasper County Illinois

Quelle/source: Entweder/either: Shamhart, Carl - Shamhart, Bruce, Ray - Shamhart, John Shamhart - Elizabeth McPherson

Vierte Generation

6. Simon Henrich Schamhardt[7,8] wurde am 02. Dezember 1792 in Varenholz geboren. Er starb am 19. Dezember 1857 in Beaver County, Ohio. Er heiratete Catherine Overly am 28. November 1820 in USA[9].

> Quelle: Ich, Werner Schabbehard, habe mit Ulrich Siebrasse beim Staatsarchiv in Detmold die in Frage kommenden Kirchenbucheinträge abgeschrieben sowie Daten aus der Verkartung mit übernommen.
> Source: I, Werner Schabbehard, have copied with Ulrich Siebrasse at the state archive in Detmold the possible church register entries as well as we have copied data from the Verkartung (a special Church file).

7. Catherine Overly[10] wurde am 24. Juli 1804 in PA geboren. Sie starb am 11. März 1896 in Noble County, near St. Johns Church, Ohio, USA.

> Quelle/source: Schamhards in Amerika

Fünfte Generation

8. Simon Henrich Schamhardt[11,12] wurde am 13. April 1760 in Varenholz geboren. Er starb am 27. Oktober 1826 in USA. Er heiratete Amalie Christina Korf am 30. Dezember 1791 in Varenholz[13].

Paten/godparents: Simon Henrich Schamhard und Conrad Everding

> Quelle: Ich, Werner Schabbehard, habe mit Ulrich Siebrasse beim Staatsarchiv in Detmold die in Frage kommenden Kirchenbucheinträge abgeschrieben sowie Daten aus der Verkartung mit übernommen.
> Source: I, Werner Schabbehard, have copied with Ulrich Siebrasse at the state archive in Detmold the possible church register entries as well as we have copied data from the Verkartung (a special Church file).

> Quelle/source: Entweder/either: Shamhart, Carl - Shamhart, Bruce, Ray - Shamhart, John Shamhart - Elizabeth McPherson

9. Amalie Christina Korf[14,15] wurde am 20. März 1765 in Erder geboren. Sie starb in USA.

> Quelle: Ich, Werner Schabbehard, habe mit Ulrich Siebrasse beim Staatsarchiv in Detmold die in Frage kommenden Kirchenbucheinträge abgeschrieben sowie Daten aus der Verkartung mit übernommen.
> Source: I, Werner Schabbehard, have copied with Ulrich Siebrasse at the state archive in Detmold the possible church register entries as well as we have copied data from the Verkartung (a special Church file).

Sechste Generation

10. Simon Hendrich Schamhardt [16] wurde am 19. Oktober 1738 in Varenholz geboren. Er starb am 10. März 1815 in Varenholz. Er heiratete Maria IIsabein Beucken am 30. Oktober 1757 in Varenholz[17].

> Quelle: Ich, Werner Schabbehard, habe mit Ulrich Siebrasse beim Staatsarchiv in Detmold die in Frage kommenden Kirchenbucheinträge abgeschrieben sowie Daten aus der Verkartung mit übernommen.
> Source: I, Werner Schabbehard, have copied with Ulrich Siebrasse at the state archive in Detmold the possible church register entries as well as we have copiedr data from the Verkartung (a special Church file).

11. Maria IIsabein Beucken[18].

> Quelle: Ich, Werner Schabbehard, habe mit Ulrich Siebrasse beim Staatsarchiv in Detmold die in Frage kommenden Kirchenbucheinträge abgeschrieben sowie Daten aus der Verkartung mit übernommen.
> Source: I, Werner Schabbehard, have copied with Ulrich Siebrasse at the state archive in Detmold the possible church register entries as well as we have copiedr data from the Verkartung (a special Church file).

Siebte Generation

12. Johan Hermann Schabbehar[19] wurde am 26. Juni 1707 in Varenholz geboren. Er starb am 27. Februar 1755 in Varenholz. Er heiratete Anne Maria Boeken am 15. August 1728 in Varenholz[20].

Johan Hermann Schabbehart starb / died 47 Jahre alt / old
Kirchenbuch / churchbook: Varenholz
Er wurde als Schabbehar geboren, he was born as Schabbehar
Er heiratete als Schabbehahrt, he married as Schabbehahrt
Er starb als Schamhardt, he died as Schamhardt

> Quelle: Ich, Werner Schabbehard, habe mit Ulrich Siebrasse beim Staatsarchiv in Detmold die in Frage kommenden Kirchenbucheinträge abgeschrieben sowie Daten aus der Verkartung mit übernommen.
> Source: I, Werner Schabbehard, have copied with Ulrich Siebrasse at the state archive in Detmold the possible church register entries as well as we have copiedr data from the Verkartung (a special Church file).

13. Anne Maria Boeken[21].

Sie stammt aus Stemmen, she is from Stemmen

> Quelle: Ich, Werner Schabbehard, habe mit Ulrich Siebrasse beim Staatsarchiv in Detmold die in Frage kommenden Kirchenbucheinträge abgeschrieben sowie Daten aus der Verkartung mit übernommen.
> Source: I, Werner Schabbehard, have copied with Ulrich Siebrasse at the state archive

in Detmold the possible church register entries as well as we have copied data from the
Verkartung (a special Church file).

Achte Generation

14. Johan Henrich Schabbehaar[22] wurde 1679 in Varenholz geboren. Er starb am
28. April 1735 in Varenholz. Er heiratete Anna Maria Boven am 14. Juni 1705 in
Varenholz[23].

> Quelle: Ich, Werner Schabbehard, habe mit Ulrich Siebrasse beim Staatsarchiv in Detmold
> die in Frage kommenden Kirchenbucheinträge abgeschrieben sowie Daten aus der
> Verkartung mit übernommen.
> Source: I, Werner Schabbehard, have copied with Ulrich Siebrasse at the state archive
> in Detmold the possible church register entries as well as we have copiedr data from the
> Verkartung (a special Church file).

15. Anna Maria Boven[24].

> Quelle: Ich, Werner Schabbehard, habe mit Ulrich Siebrasse beim Staatsarchiv in Detmold
> die in Frage kommenden Kirchenbucheinträge abgeschrieben sowie Daten aus der
> Verkartung mit übernommen.
> Source: I, Werner Schabbehard, have copied with Ulrich Siebrasse at the state archive
> in Detmold the possible church register entries as well as we have copied data from the
> Verkartung (a special Church file).

Neunte Generation

16. Hermann Schabbehaar[25] wurde 1644 geboren. Er starb am 21. Dezember 1700 in
Varenholz. Er heiratete Cathrine Maria NN 1675 in Varenholz[26].

Herman Schabbehard starb im 57ten Jahr, he died in his 57th year of live.

> Quelle: Ich, Werner Schabbehard, habe mit Ulrich Siebrasse beim Staatsarchiv in Detmold
> die in Frage kommenden Kirchenbucheinträge abgeschrieben sowie Daten aus der
> Verkartung mit übernommen.
> Source: I, Werner Schabbehard, have copied with Ulrich Siebrasse at the state archive
> in Detmold the possible church register entries as well as we have copied data from the
> Verkartung (a special Church file).

17. Cathrine Maria NN[27] wurde 1650 geboren. Sie starb am 19. März 1716 in
Varenholz.

Cathrine Maria starb im 66ten Jahr in Vahrenholz. She died in her 66th year of
live in Varenholz.

> Quelle: Ich, Werner Schabbehard, habe mit Ulrich Siebrasse beim Staatsarchiv in Detmold
> die in Frage kommenden Kirchenbucheinträge abgeschrieben sowie Daten aus der
> Verkartung mit übernommen.
> Source: I, Werner Schabbehard, have copied with Ulrich Siebrasse at the state archive

in Detmold the possible church register entries as well as we have copiedr data from the Verkartung (a special Church file).

Zehnte Generation

18. Wilhelm Oberschabbehard[28] wurde 1618 in Steinhagen Nr. 3 geboren. Er starb am 28. November 1695 in Steinhagen Nr. 3. Er wurde in Steinhagen bestattet. Er heiratete Meyer zu Allerdißen? 1643 in Steinhagen, Evangelische Dorfkirche[29].

Wilhelm war Anerbe und Colon in Steinhagen Nr. 3. Er wohnte in Steinhagen.

Sein Name als Pate von Cord Oberschabbehard's erstem Kind Johan Herm von 1671 ist im Kirchenbuch von Steinhagen als Wilm der uberSchabbehard aufgeführt. In seinem Sterbedokument wird er als Wilhelm Oberschabbehard aufgeführt

His name as godfather of Cord Oberschabbehard's first child Johan Herm from 1671 is listed in the churchbook of Steinhagen as Wilm der uber Schabbehard In his death certificate he was named Wilhelm Oberschabbehard.

Weitere Paten für Johan Herm Oberschabbehard sind:
Herm zu Allerdissen (Meyer zu Olderdissen, Quelle Nr 1)
Anna Margretha Polmanns

Further godparents to Johan Herm Oberschabbehard are:
Herm zu Allerdissen (Meyer zu Olderdissen, Quelle no. 1)
Anna Margretha Polmanns

> Quelle/source: Kirchenbuch der Evangelischen Dorfkirche Steinhagen, einsichtbar auf dem Landeskirchenamt in Bielefeld.
> Ich, Schabbehard, Werner, habe das original Kirchenbuch von Steinhagen im Landeskirchenamt in Bielefeld, abfotografiert und die Bilder Ulrich Siebrasse der Handschrift wegen, auswerten lassen.

19. Meyer zu Allerdißen?[30].

> Quelle/source: Siebrasse, Ulrich-Ahnenforschung

Elfte Generation

20. NN Oberschabbehard[31] wurde 1590 in Steinhagen Nr. 3 geboren. Er starb in Steinhagen Nr 3.

NN war Colon (ein Halbspänner) in Steinhagen Nr. 3. Er wohnte seit 1590 in Steinhagen.

> Quelle/Source: Siebrasse, Ulrich-Ahnenforschung

Zwölfte Generation

21. NN Oberschabbehard[32] wurde 1560 in Steinhagen Nr. 3 geboren.

> Quelle/Source: Siebrasse, Ulrich-Ahnenforschung

13. Generation

22. Wilhelm de ober Schabbehardt[33] wurde 1556 in Steinhagen Nr. 3, Nennung im Ravensberger Urbar 1556 geboren.

Wilhelm war Anerbe und Colon in Steinhagen Nr. 3. Er wohnte seit 1550 in Neder-Steinhagen.

Nennung des Hofes unserer Vorfahren im Ravensberger Urbar von 1550.

Es ist dies ein Verzeichnis der dem Landesherrn zinspflichtigen Höfe und Ländereien der Grafschaft Ravensberg, auf Pergament, auch für den Laien gut leserlich geschrieben, von denen die in Frage kommenden Blätter, als Fotokopien, originalgetreu in natürlicher Grösse vom Staatsarchiv Münster angefertigt, im Anhang.......beigefügt sind. Es heisst auf Blatt 252:

Laufende Urbar Nr. 862.

23. Wilhelm de Ober Schabbehardt gehoret Frantzen dem Wende eigen mit wief und kindern. Hait von Meinem Gnedigen Hern nichts dann eine marckewisch. Gibt Meinem Gnedigen Hern davon 3 schillinge.

Wilhelm de ober Schabbehardt, Neder-Steinhagen

Paid taxes to von Wendt

ANNO 1550 means documentation of to whom the farmer had to pay taxes either in money or in natural produce. Witten in a documentation called Urbar der Grafschaft Ravensberg.

Leistete Abgaben an die Familie von Wendt

ANNO 1550 dokumentiert in einer vorliegenden Urkunde an wen der Bauer Abgaben in Form von Geld, Naturalien oder Leiharbeit zahlen oder leisten musste. Dieses Dokument heisst: Urbar der Grafschaft Ravensberg.

14. Generation

24. Johan in Scapehart[34] wurde 1342 in Steinhagen Nr. 3, Register der Abgabepflichtigen geboren.

Johan wohnte seit 1342 in Steinhagen. Er war Anerbe und Colon in Steinhagen Nr. 3.

Im Register des Jahres 1342 wird ein Namensträger unter den Abgabepflichtigen erwähnt:

Johan in Scapehart.
Dieser Johan in Scapehart ist wahrscheinlich der Nachfolger auf dem Hofe des 1333 genannten Bauern Herman Scapehart, der mittlerweile gestorben war und den Hof diesem, seinem Anerben Johan, überlassen hat.

Paid taxes to Stift Herford
Leistete Abgaben an die Familie von Wendt

Documented in books of the Stift Herford (Abbey Herford)
Dokumentiert in Urkunden des Stiftes Herford

15. Generation

25. Herman Scapehard wurde 1333 in Steinhagen Nr. 3, im Verzeichnis der lehnrührigen und hörigen Höfe geboren.

Herman war Anerbe und Colon in Steinhagen Nr. 3. Er wohnte seit 1333 in Steinhagen.

Nennung des Hofes unserer Vorfahren in der vorliegenden Urkunde:
Das Verzeichnis der lehnrührigen und hörigen Höfe aus dem Jahre 1333 bringt folgendes:
Officium Godesberg (später Wetere, Werther, genannt).
Scapehard Herman

Paid taxes to Stift Herford
Leistete Abgaben an die Familie von Wendt

Documented in books of the Stift Herford (Abbey Herford)
Dokumentiert in Urkunden des Stiftes Herford

16. Generation

26. Scapehart wurde 1250 in Steinhagen Nr. 3 geboren.

Scapehart war Anerbe und Colon in Steinhagen Nr. 3. Er wohnte seit 1250 in Steinhagen.

Nennung des Hofes unserer Vorfahren in der vorliegenden Urkunde:
Heberolle / document der Abtei Herford aus dem / from the 13ten Jahrhundert, /

century die sich im Staatsarchiv Münster befindet und bei Darpe abgedruckt ist, werden u. a. im Amtsbezirk Godesberg folgende abgabepflichtigen Güter, Höfe und Erben aufgeführt:

Paid taxes to Stift Herford
Leistete Abgaben / paid duties an die Familie von Wendt

Documented in books of the Stift Herford (Abbey Herford)
Dokumentiert in Urkunden des Stiftes Herford

"alter Mansus" bedeutet Fronhof von dem Wasserschloss Holtfeld, dessen Besitzer Wendt.

"Eine Manse ist eine mittelalterliche Bezeichnung für eine unselbstständige landwirtschaftliche Erwerbseinheit (Hof oder Bauernstelle), die einem Herrenhof (curtem dominicalis) untergeordnet und diesem zehntpflichtig war. Mansen waren von unterschiedlicher Größe und umfaßten in der Regel soviel Kulturland, wie eine Großfamilie bewirtschaften konnte.
Im späten Mittelalter entwickelte sich der Begriff Manse oder Mansus zu einem betriebswirtschaftlichen Flächenmaß:
1 Mansus = 4 Viertel = 64 Jucherte = 32,683 ha
Der Name kommt wahrscheinlich von lateinisch mancipium (= Besitz) von manus + capio, das heißt mancipo (= ich gebe zu eigen) oder von mansio (= Haus)." Quelle: Wikipedia 2008

17. Generation

27. Scepehert wurde 1150 in Steinhagen, Heberolle 12. Jahrhundert geboren.

Scepehert wohnte seit 1150 in Steinhagen. Er war Anerbe und Colon in Steinhagen Nr. 3.

Nennung des Hofes unserer Vorfahren in der vorliegenden Urkunde:
Hof / farm Scepehert, Heberolle aus dem 12 ten Jahrhundert.

Paid taxes to Stift / Abbey Herford
Leistete Abgaben / paid dutie an die Familie / family von Wendt

Documented in books of the Stift Herford (Abbey Herford)
Dokumentiert in Urkunden des Stiftes Herford

Alter Tantum, Scepehert ANNO 1150. "alter Tantum" bedeutet "wie der Vorherige"

18. Generation

28. Scapaharda wurde 1147 in Steinhagen, Kaiserurkunde geboren.

Scapaharda war Anerbe und Colon in Steinhagen Nr. 3. Er wohnte seit 1147 in Steinhagen.

Hier wird zum ersten Mal in der so genannten "Kaiser Urkunde" der Urahn der Schabbehards, Schamharts und Shappards und auch der nach Amerika ausgewanderten Schabbehars erwähnt.

Hof Scapaharda im Wessagau (weißer Gau) mit dem Hauptort Herford, 9. Jahrhundert,

Zahlten Steuern / paid taxes to Stift / Abbey Herford
Leistete Abgaben / paid duties an die Familie von Wendt

Documented in books of the Stift Herford (Abbey Herford)
Dokumentiert in Urkunden des Stiftes / Abbey Herford

Die Urkunde von 1147 ist zweifach ausgestellt, da es sich darin um gegenseitige Abmachungen zwischen den Abteien Corvey und Herford handelt. Sie ist abgedruckt in "Erhard, Westfälisches Urkundenbuch, Band II" und in "Lamey, Geschichte der alten Grafen von Ravensberg".

Die Urkunde hat in der Übersetzung aus dem Lateinischen folgenden Wortlaut: "Im Namen der heiligen und unteilbaren Dreieinigkeit. Konrad, durch göttliche Gnade der zweite römische König und Kaiser".

Anhang A - Quellen

1. Shamharts in Amerika.
2. Shamharts in Amerika.
3. Nachkommen/Offspring des Schamhardt, Simon Henrich geb. 13 Apr 1760 aus Vahrenholz ausgewandert nach USA.
4. Nachkommen/Offspring des Schamhardt, Simon Henrich geb. 13 Apr 1760 aus Vahrenholz ausgewandert nach USA.
5. Nachkommen/Offspring des Schamhardt, Simon Henrich geb. 13 Apr 1760 aus Varenholz ausgewandert nach USA.
6. Shamharts in Amerika.
7. Kirchenbuch (Churchbook) der Kirche in Varenholz.
8. Shamharts in Amerika.
9. Shamharts in Amerika.
10. Shamharts in Amerika.
11. Kirchenbuch (Churchbook) der Kirche in Varenholz.
12. Shamharts in Amerika.

13. Kirchenbuch (Churchbook) der Kirche in Varenholz.
14. Shamharts in Amerika.
15. Kirchenbuch (Churchbook) der Kirche in Varenholz.
16. Kirchenbuch (Churchbook) der Kirche in Varenholz.
17. Kirchenbuch (Churchbook) der Kirche in Varenholz.
18. Kirchenbuch (Churchbook) der Kirche in Varenholz.
19. Kirchenbuch (Churchbook) der Kirche in Varenholz.
20. Kirchenbuch (Churchbook) der Kirche in Varenholz.
21. Kirchenbuch (Churchbook) der Kirche in Varenholz.
22. Kirchenbuch (Churchbook) der Kirche in Varenholz.
23. Kirchenbuch (Churchbook) der Kirche in Varenholz.
24. Kirchenbuch (Churchbook) der Kirche in Varenholz.
25. Kirchenbuch (Churchbook) der Kirche in Varenholz.
26. Kirchenbuch (Churchbook) der Kirche in Varenholz.
27. Kirchenbuch (Churchbook) der Kirche in Varenholz.
28. Kirchenbuch der Evangelischen Dorfkirche Steinhagen, einsichtbar auf dem Landeskirchenamt in Bielefeld.
29. Siebrasse, Ulrich, Ahnenforschung.
30. Siebrasse, Ulrich, Ahnenforschung.
31. Siebrasse, Ulrich, Ahnenforschung.
32. Siebrasse, Ulrich, Ahnenforschung.
33. Ravensberger Urbar von 1550.
34. Ravensberger Urbar von 1550.

Remembering Wilmer and Olive Shamhart
James L. Meng (grandson)

A visit to Wilmer and Olive Shamhart, my grandparents, at 2304 Washington Avenue in Granite City was an experience. Grandpa smoked Dutch Master cigars while rocking in his Windsor rocker. We now have his rocker. Their home was a one-and-a-half-story frame. Inside, the staircase going to the upstairs had a small landing about quarter of the way up it made a left turn. On this landing was a leaded glass window with red tulips in a straight line on a light green background. As a child, I would stare at this window wondering how they made it and intrigued with a light green glow the window give to the room. We had nothing like it and neither did any of our other relatives. Several years ago, I stopped in and visited with the current residents of my grandparents' home. I asked if I could buy the window with the tulips, replacing it with a thermo pane modern energy-efficient unit. Fortunately, they agreed. We now have Olive and Wilmer's stained glass living room window with the red tulips hanging in our home. It is as fascinating today as it was 50 years ago when I was a child.

Grandpa Shamhart (often referred to as Shammy) died of a heart ailment when I was quite young. I remember being at the house when he died. There was a lot of expressed grief on that day. I was immediately sent to Fred and Agnes' home. It was not a good experience. But what I do remember of grandpa was all positive; he frequently sang "Jimmy Cracked Corn," the old Burl Ives' song to me. Burl Ives was from my grandparents' hometown, Newton, Illinois, and the way my grandparents talked, Burl apparently liked his spirits. Grandpa also took me fishing at Horseshoe Lake, a small lake outside of town. At the point in time, the lake wasn't much, but what does a kid know; there was water and bluegills. He was the only person who could take me fishing during the day, and for that I was grateful. He also taught me how to drive a nail through a board. Since he was a carpenter, he would show me how to hold the hammer and, with one hit, put the nail through the board. This was a big deal. No commercial toys, just old boards from the produce boxes thrown away by the Tri-City Grocery Store located across the street, nails and a hammer. One day while he was cleaning out his garage, he gave me a brass carriage light that operated on carbide. I have since had the light professionally cleaned, polished, and sealed. It too is on a shelf in our home. Since Grandpa smoked cigars, he smelled like cigars, his house smelled like cigars, and his 1939 four-door black Oldsmobile smelled like cigars. When we would drive to Newton to visit relatives, I would ride in the back seat. There were no interstates, so the trip took about three hours. I would turn "blue" from all the cigar smoke by the time we arrived in Newton. It was not pleasant, especially during winter trips.

Olive Shamhart lived on for many years after grandpa's death. Her house was always a mess, and I don't mean just "lived in"—I mean a mess. She was the only person I knew who save little pieces of string by rolling them into a little ball. She saved everything and her house showed it. Since she had limited income, she would also make her own dresses from flour sacks. She would buy certain sacks because of the pattern on the sack. When empty, she would wash the cloth, iron it, and "Walla"—a dress. She also sewed aprons which were quite nice. Again, the material for these aprons came from her bag of flour. These aprons then became gifts. She was a very talented seamstress, having learned her trade sewing wedding dresses. She was very, very good. Did I say she baked a lot of good biscuits?

She also had chickens in her backyard. Her yard was divided in half with the rear half being a chicken yard. Remember, this was in the city, and chickens? I'm sure her neighbors appreciated her barnyard. Anyway, it was neat to feed the birds and collect the eggs from the hen house. She even put old light bulbs in their nest to fake out the chickens, expecting them to lay more eggs.

She also liked cats, and there were always plenty around. I don't know how the cats and chickens got along, but I don't remember any fights. As I got older (about the fifth grade), I was charged with cutting her grass with a push mower. This was definitely not fun since she had a small terrace in her front yard. I was also drafted to move her coal from one side of the basement to the other side. For some unknown reason, when she had coal (large chunks) delivered, they put the coal through a basement window that was on the opposite side of the coal bin. (I viewed this as a major design flaw, but said nothing.) Apparently, a truck could not get to the other side of the house due to a neighbor's rather large fence to deliver the coal properly. I think there may have been a connection between her chicken flock and the neighbors' fence. Anyway, I was drafted and performed as a good grandson was (required) to do, and moved the coal.

Olive was interesting, but I think her life was difficult after Grandfather died. She liked flowers, particularly petunias which grew on each side of the walk leading to her front porch steps. I was also assigned weed removal from this garden. Fortunately, she liked to go to the show (Washington Theater), so I was again drafted. One of her favorite movies was Disney's *Song of the South*. She would sing the song "Zippity Doo Da" from this movie for months. Grandma's interest in going to the show also provided an opportunity for me to see a particular movie. However, I don't think Grandma really enjoyed the *Bowery Boys, Bud and Lou Costello*, or *Tarzan* and ten cartoons as much as I did. I think she just tolerated those events. Her favorite saying was "Land negoshuns, child." This was said whenever I got in trouble. One such event was when she did the wash. She had a clothesline attached close to the basement steps. I sat on the basement steps and used a knife to cut the line. All of her wet sheets that she had just hung hit the floor. I ran and hid behind the couch. She ran up the steps, hollering, "Where is he?" Grandpa said, "Behind the couch." She grabbed me by the arm and pulled me out into the room where I got a good (and deserved) spanking. I also heard her saying, "Land negoshuns, child!"

Her clock, a kitchen-style mantel clock that sat on top of her upright piano in the living room, now resides with us. As a kid, the ticking of this clock during a sleepover would prevent me from sleeping. I would lie on the coach (no bed available) counting each tick. Of course, they would go to bed as soon as it got dark, which didn't help. Today, the clock just keeps on ticking in our home, but somehow I no longer hear it.

Grandma Shamhart would often talk of her grandma, Henrietta Crail. Apparently, Henrietta was a favorite of hers and my mom's since they both referred to her frequently. Grandma said the Crails came from Crail, Scotland, which is located just 10 miles south of St. Andrews (for the golfing folks) on the eastern coast. One of the papers passed on to my mom, and then to me, was an interesting 1932 letter from a California congressman Joe Crail, referencing the Crail ancestry. This letter indicated a family connection to the Duke of Argyll and the Duke of Marlborough. I always thought it to be a contradiction to talk of ancestors of royalty when all of the relatives I observed seemed poor. But again, I would just question the logic, but say nothing. In 1996, my wife Beverly and I had the opportunity to travel to Scotland with copies of Grandma's famous documents. We drove to Crail. It is a picturesque town on the coast, noted for lobsters. We gave copies of the Crail information to their museum. No one in town is named Crail anymore. Apparently, they had left for the New World a long time ago when their economic times were bad. The original Crail stone house which is quite large is still there and occupied. It is shown on all of their postcards from the town and is so marked on the attached pictures in the Crail section of this book.

Nonetheless, Grandma was very proud of this lineage. In fact, the entire Shamhart family was also very proud and close. I have approximately 100 postcards of when they wrote each other. Many cards only discussed their gardens, the weather, how is your health, we saw so and so last week, when you coming to visit, etc. It was just interesting to see the number of repetitive postcards that just said the same thing over and over. However, these cards also provided a physical reminder that they were thinking of one another.

Another interesting aspect of Olive's past was that her maiden name was Foster. Grandpa Shamhart was of German ancestry, having had his name Shamhart changed from Shaparda, Oberschabbehard, Schabbehard, Schabbehar, and Shappard. Stephen Foster was from Ohio, where some of the Fosters originated. I do not have any family information to substantiate the songwriter's connection, but it is often referred to in family as fact. This could be worthy of research in the future.

Later in life, Olive was confined to a bed and then with oxygen. This lasted for years. Aunt Sybil (Fisher) stayed with her during these difficult times. Sybil was a widow, having lost her husband Milton to cancer. Sybil was a saint giving up her life to care for her mother. When Olive passed on, all the old stuff in her house, the Crail, Foster, Shamhart, Trexler information, etc., that I thought created such a mess, has now become valued family documents (pictures, and letters postcards as to who the Shamharts were, their lives, and my heritage). The mess that I perceived in Grandma's house has since been transferred to our house and someday my grandchildren will write something saying what a mess we have in our house!

As mentioned earlier, Wilmer Shamhart died when I was very young. It seemed that I was just getting old enough to do things with him when he was lost. He was the only grandfather that I knew since the grandfather on my dad's side, Fred Meng, died before I was born. I've always felt "short changed" by having no grandfather to do things with while growing up. Of course, I knew Grandma Shamhart more since she was around much longer.

Olive was always there to play games and make my visits fun. Unfortunately, there was always coal to move, grass to cut, weeds to pull, furniture to polish, and the vacuum to run. Wilmer and Olive Shamhart were good grandparents—spoiling me in every way they could, the same as all good grandparents are supposed to do!

W. W. Shamhart

College Hill School[7]

This picture of College Hill School, two miles west of Bogota, was taken in about 1898

First row: Gertie Harlow, Etta Richards, Lena (Richards) Lytle, Ben Crouse, Trace Crouse, Harry Diffenderfer, Ross Lancaster, Olen Worthey, Ben Worthey.
Second row: Lora Divine, Esther Worthey, Lora Cline, Viola Reed, Retta Lambird, Ina (Foreman) Brown, ---, Toby Kincade, Dillard Green, Alva Lambird, Walter Lambird.
Third row: -- Edwards, Edgar Tate, Vance Lambird, Bessie Whaley, Abi Green, Rex Lambird, Earl Worthey, Iva Lancaster, Stella Harlow, Delpha Green, Ida Tate, Lilly Reed, Eska Russell, Floyd Monahan.
Fourth row: Johnny Reed, Everett Russell, ---, Nora (Foreman) Watt, Bertha Lancaster, Minnie Cline, Nelle Clark, teacher, Lottie Worthey, Cindy Reed, Willie Smallwood.
Fifth row: Nora Foreman, Elizabeth Whaley, Pearl Crouse, Elmer Reed, Arthur Lambird, John Divine, Chester Reed, Ethan Worthey.
Sixth row: Charlie McKinney, Cassie Whaley, Robert McKinney, Flossie Monahan, Willey McKinney, Lavonia Crouse and Bertha Kincade.

The picture is owned by Mrs. Cora Richards of Newton. The original was made by W.W. Shamhart, old-time Newton professional photographer.
[Contributed to Genealogy Trails by Rhonda; transcribed by K. Torp]

Union School[7]
1899

This is a picture of the Union School, better known as "Cornbread," taken in 1899. It was located two miles south of Latona.

First row: Robert Tarr, Elihu Clagg, Orph Fields, Joe Matlock, Eugene Cornwell Harrison Meeks, Hal Cornwell, Everett Baker, Bernie Vandergrift.
Second row: Ura (Baker) Sparks, Lizzie Tarr, Oma (Rife) Postle, Eliza Clagg, Bernice Adkins, Nellie Meeks, Nettie Murphy, Addie Meeks, Fannie (Rife) Postle, Rosa (Pickering) Sparks, Ora Rife.
Third row: --- Marker, Frank Hicks, Eddie Pickering, Rebecca Clagg, Frankie Marker, Tillie Meeks, Jennie Williams, Maude (Murphy) Fields, Maude (Cornwell) Clagg, Gertie (Workman) Clagg, Edna (Matlock) Fields, Nora (Cornwell) Wetherholt, Grace Baker.
Fourth row: -- Meeks, Elba Adkins, Merritt Murphy, Dell (Adkins) Brackney, Ann (Bruner) Johnson, Eliza Meeks, Semore Knepper, teacher, Zula Vandergrift, Kate (Bruner) Evans, Grace (Clagg) Bailey, Bill Adkins.
Fifth Row: Noah Clagg, Jim Clagg, Lee Adkins, Tom Cook, Wilmer Shamhart, Dave Buck, Arthur Foster, Charlie Shamhart, Charlie Fields, Gus Baker, Homer Gosnell.

The picture belongs to Mr. and Mrs. Ross Sparks of Ithaca, Mich. They enjoy the paper very much also the school pictures. Mr. and Mrs. Sparks were reared in Jasper county.

Wedding Picture of Wilmer W. and Olive Shamhart
Wilber and Olive Shamhart had four children: Sybil (1901–1989);
Jessie (1903–1978); Wayne (1912–1933), and Lois (1914–1992).

BOOK E Page 58

CERTIFIED COPY OF RETURN OF MARRIAGE TO COUNTY CLERK—ILLINOIS OFFICE SUPPLY C ., OTTAWA, ILL.   1108

STATE OF ILLINOIS,

COUNTY OF....Jasper........ }ss.

STATE BOARD OF HEALTH
RETURN OF MARRIAGE TO COUNTY CLERK

1. Full name of GROOM.............Wilmer W. Shamhart........
2. Place of Residence....Latona............   3. Occupation....Farmer....
   next birthday   White
4. Age 21 Date of Birth....----.. Color.... Race....----.   5. Place of Birth..Jasper......
6. Father's Name....John Shamhart..........   7. Mother's Maiden Name..Mary E. Johnson..
8. Number of Groom's Marriage........one.........
9. Full name of BRIDE.....Ollie Foster..........

Maiden name, if a Widow.....---------...........   10. Place of Residence....Latona....
11. Age 23 Date of Birth....---...... Color..White.. Race..----.   12. Place of Birth..Latona, Ills..
    next birthday
13. Father's Name...Wm. Foster............   14. Mother's Maiden Name....Hennrietta Crail
15. Number of Bride's Marriage........one.........   16. Married at..home of bride.. in the County
of....Jasper.........and State of Illinois, the....12th...day of.....April 1899 19XX..
17. Witnesses to Marriage....G. E. Kirkham, Mary Clagg..........
Dated...........April 12, 1899 19XX....   S. A. Walker, M. G.......

STATE OF ILLINOIS,

COUNTY OF......Jasper..... }ss.
                            I,..............Alma LeFever.............
County Clerk in and for said County, do hereby certify that the foregoing is a true and
correct copy of the return of marriage as certified by...........................
.......S. A. Walker, M. G............................and full faith and credit is due
to all his official acts.
            IN TESTIMONY WHEREOF, I have set my hand and affixed my Official Seal
this..........4th...............day of........December.........A. D. 1931

                              Alma LeFever
                                         County Clerk.

                              57

The Wilmer W. and Olive (Foster) Shamhart wedding (Apr. 2, 1899).

Olive Foster

W. W. Shamhart

Olive Foster Shamhart

This picture of the Trexler school was taken in 1912 when Harry Jones was the teacher. It was furnished by Delbert Smith.[7]

First row, left to right: Anna (Howell) Knepper, Harold Jones, *Jessie Shamhart*, *Mildred (Clagg) Davis*, May (Jones) Heitz, *Sybil Shamhart*, and Gladys (Whitehurst) Clark.

Second row: Nina (Kibler) Swank, Nina (Whitehurst) Keagle, Guy French, F. (Jones) Blankmier, and *Fay Trexler*.

Third row: Bernard Jones, Glen Kibler, Burl Davis, Ralph French, Leland Corbin, Ada (French) Clark, Etta (Clagg) Foltz, Mary (Smith) Marriott, and Toni (Whitehurst) Wetherholt.

Fourth row: Bill Miller, *Marie (Corbin) Kirkham*, *Leonard Trexler*, and Ethel (Whitehurst) Bower.

Fifth row: Albert Miller, Mabel (Davis) King, *Charlene (Trexler) Rymer*, Delbert Smith, Wilber Corbin, and Ed Miller.

Jessie F. Shamhart and Sybil Shamhart as students
(Also some Trexlers) in 1912

Wilmer W. Shamhart. Head coach of the Central Christian Church in Granite City, IL.
Milton Fisher, Sybil Shamhart's husband, second from left in back row.

603

W. W. SHAMHART
REPRESENTATIVE
CARPENTERS, MILLWRIGHTS, MILLMEN
LOCAL 633

2451 BENTON STREET

GRANITE CITY, ILLINOIS

Heart Attack Is Fatal To W. W. Shamheart, 69, Retired Carpenter[5]

Wilmer Shamhart, 69, of 2304 Washington avenue, died of a heart attack at his home at 1 p. m. Sunday. He had suffered the first in a series of four attacks on Dec. 17.

Shamhart a native of Jasper County, Ill., had lived in Granite City 29 years. A retired carpenter, he was formerly the business agent for AFL Carpenters' Local 633.

He is survived by his wife, Olive; three daughters, Mrs. Jessie Meng and Mrs. Lois Cox, both of this city, and Mrs. Sybil Fischer of St. Louis; one brother, Charles Shamhart, of Dietrich, Ill.; six grandchildren and two great-grandchildren.

Announcement of the time and place of the funeral is made in the obituary column of this issue.

Christian Church, Granite City, Ill.
1918
The Shamharts and Mengs attended this church

IN LOVING MEMORY

* * *

Blessed are the pure in heart
for they shall see God.

Mrs. Olive Shamhart Dies; Rites Tuesday

Mrs. Olive Shamhart, 85, of 2304 Washington Ave., Granite City,
died at 9:30 a. m. Saturday following a three year illness.

Services will be held at 10 a. m. Tuesday in the Central Christian
Church, Granite City. Burial will be in Trexler Cemetery, Newton,
Ill. Friends may call at the Mercer Funeral Home, Granite City.

Mrs. Shamhart was born in Newton and had lived in Granite
City since 1918. She was a member of the Central Christian Church.
Her husband Wilmer died in 1947.

Surviving are three daughters Mrs. Sybil Fischer, Mrs. Jessie
Meng, and Mrs. Lois Cox, all of Granite City; six grandchildren, and
16 great-grandchildren.

Died Saturday, Oct. 27, 1962

Gravestone for Wilmer Shamhart and Olive Foster Shamhart in the Trexler Cemetery.

Mrs. Zelphia Goode, Dies at Age 68

Mrs. Zelphia M. Goode, 68, of Rural Route 2, Collinsville, a former
Granite City resident for 60 years, was found dead in her bed by her
husband at 1:45 a.m. Friday. She had been ill four months and under
medical care.

Born in Jasper County, Ill., Mrs. Goode and her husband had
resided at 2622 Edwards St. during their residence here. They moved
to the Collinsville address three months ago.

Mrs. Goode was a member of the Church of Christ, 2130 Clark
Ave.

In addition to her husband, she is survived by two sons, Duane and Wallace Goode, both of Granite City, and five grandchildren.

Funeral services were held today. Details are given in the obituary column.

GOODE, MRS. ZELPHIA M., Rural Route Two, Box 847, Collinsville. Entered into rest 1:45 a.m. Friday, Jan. 14, 1972, at home.

Beloved wife of Norman H. Goode; dear mother of Duane and Wallace Goode; dear grandmother.

Funeral services were held at 1 p.m. today, Jan. 17, at MERCER MORTUARY Chapel, 1416 Niedringhaus Ave. Interment Sunset Hill Cemetery, Edwardsville Township.

Wallace Goode was a good friend and classmate of James L. Meng throughout the school years. Wallace was an exceptional talent in art and was a very pleasant person.

WILMER WESTON AND OLIVE FOSTER SHAMHART'S CHILDREN
SYBIL 1901-1989; JESSIE 1903-1978; WAYNE 1912-1933; LOIS 1914-1992.

Wayne Shamhart, age 4, and Lois Shamhart, age 6 (1918).

Sybil Shamhart Fischer's Family

Sybil is daughter of W. W. and Olive Foster Shamhart, sister of Jessie Meng, Wayne Shamhart and Lois Cox

Sybil Shamhart

Wayne Shamhart

1930 REVISION V.S. 5	MARK VON NIDA, MADISON COUNTY CLERK		COUNTY CLERK'S RECORD

STATE OF ILLINOIS
Department of Public Health – Division of Vital Statistics
STANDARD CERTIFICATE OF DEATH

1. PLACE OF DEATH
County of Madison
Registered No. 617
Dist. No. 3147
Granite City
Street and Number, No.
(If death occurred in a hospital or institution, give its NAME instead of street and number) St. Elizabeth's Hospital
Registered No. 44

Length of residence in city or town where death occurred 15 yrs. mos. ds. How long in U. S. if of foreign birth? yrs. mos. ds.

2. FULL NAME Howard Wayne Shamhart
(a) Residence. No. 261 Madison Ave. Ward. (If non-resident give city or town and State)
(Usual place of abode)

PERSONAL AND STATISTICAL PARTICULARS

3. SEX Male
4. COLOR OR RACE white
5. Single, Married, Widowed, or Divorced (write the word) single

5a. If married, widowed, or divorced HUSBAND of (or) WIFE of

6. DATE OF BIRTH (month, day, and year) Feb 4 1912
7. AGE Years 22 Months 9 Days If LESS than 1 day, hrs. or min.

8. Trade, profession, or particular kind of work done, as spinner, sawyer, bookkeeper, etc. Student
9. Industry or business in which work was done, as silk mill, saw mill, bank, etc.
10. Date deceased last worked at this occupation (month and year)
11. Total time (years) spent in this occupation

12. BIRTHPLACE (city or town) (State or country) Newton Ill.

FATHER
13. NAME W. A. Shamhart
14. BIRTHPLACE (city or town) (State or country) Newton Ill.

MOTHER
15. MAIDEN NAME Olive Foster
16. BIRTHPLACE (city or town) (State or country) Newton Ill.

17. INFORMANT Jessie Meng
(personal signature, with pen and ink)
P. O. Address 261 Madison Ave.

18. PLACE OF BURIAL, Cremation or Removal
Cemetery Newton (Kedron)
Location Newton (Township, Road Dist., Village or City) Jasper
19. DATE Feb 28, 1933
County Jasper State Ill.

20. UNDERTAKER Mercer
(personal signature with pen and ink)
ADDRESS Granite City Ill.
(firm name, if any)

MEDICAL CERTIFICATE OF DEATH

21. DATE OF DEATH (month, day, and year) Feb 26 1933
22. I HEREBY CERTIFY, That I attended deceased from Feb 23 1933 to Feb 26 1933
I last saw him alive on Feb 25 1933; death is said to have occurred on the date stated above, at 12-30A
*The principal cause of death and related causes of importance were as follows: Chronic Nephritis Date of onset 6 yrs

Other contributory causes of importance: myocarditis 6 months

23. Where was disease contracted, if not at place of death?
(Was an operation performed? no Date of
For what disease or injury?
Was there an autopsy? yes
What test confirmed diagnosis? clinical & autopsy
24. Was disease in any way related to occupation of deceased?
If so, specify
(Signed) S. E. Arnovitz M. D.
Address Granite City Ill.
Date Feb 28 1933 (9) Telephone TG1676

*N. B.—State the disease causing death. All cases of death from "violence," casualty, or any undue means" must be referred to the coroner. See Section to Coroner's Act.

25. Filed Feb 27 1933 Edwin Wiga Registrar
P. O. Address Granite City Ill.

CERTIFIED COPY OF VITAL RECORDS

Milton Fischer, Sybil Shamhart's husband, holding daughter, Shirley.

Sybil Shamhart

Remembering Sybil (née Shamhart) Fischer
by James L Meng

Sybil Fischer was always a good friend to me and for that I have always been very grateful. Although she lost her husband Milton to cancer, they were a very dynamic family. Richard, John, and Hank served honorably in World War II in the Pacific theater. Hank was a legitimate war hero, the type of Marine that movies are made of. John Fisher lived in Indianapolis, Indiana, and worked in the electronics field. His wife's name was Ruby. Max Fischer lived and worked in Oklahoma City, Oklahoma, with his wife and children. Shirley lived in St. Louis County, where Hank was in the concrete business. One of their children, Chris Fisher, served in Vietnam as a helicopter pilot.

Sybil and my mom were very close. I remember both sitting at our dining room table for hours, days, weeks, painting with oils. They were very talented. A picture of one of Sybil's oil paintings that she painted for my wife's parents follows.

This family definitely needs to be researched and included; however, attempts to contact Shirley Fischer have all failed.

Sybil Shamhart and Milton Fischer had three children, Richard, Shirley and Max

Milton Fischer

Sybil Fischer

Richard and Shirley

John Fischer

Both Richard and John served in the U S Army in the Pacific during World War II

613

Lois (a.k.a. Elouis) Shamhart Cox

Lois

Lois (née Shamhart) Cox and her husband Bob. They had no children.

Three Shamhart sisters: Lois, Sybil, and Jessie

Jessie and Sybil Shamhart

Jessie F. Shamhart Meng

Detailed information on Jessie (née Shamhart) Meng can be found in the Meng section of this book.

615

One of the many historic heroes of Newton, Jasper County, Illinois

Sybil Shamhart b. 1901, Jessie Shamhart b. 1908, Wayne Shamhart b. 1912, Louis Shamhart b. 1914, Burl Ives b. 1909, all attended the Newton, Illinois schools together. Burl, a 33 degree Mason, actor, writer and folk singer was internationally known.

Burl Ives songs were frequently sung in the Shamhart and Meng homes, even today. My grandfather, Wilmer W. Shamhart would often sing one of Burl's hit songs, *The Blue Tail Fly (Jimmy Crack Corn)* to me. Today, we and my grand children all watch and sing Burl's songs Silver and Gold, Rudolph the Red Nosed Reindeer, A Holly Jolly Christmas etc. The world continues to enjoy the music and movies of this very talented man from Jasper County, Illinois. An American hero!

The following monument to Burl Ives is located in Jasper County.

Probably, the inscription on the Burl Ives monument in Mound Cemetery, Jasper County, Illinois, best summarizes the life and accomplishments of this great man and Mason. It reads:

One of America's legendary entertainers
whose career spanned more than a half century
crossing all international borders.
Equally at home before the royalty of Europe
and the farm folk of Midwestern U.S.A.
A performer whose unique style adapted to all media
Literary, Radio, Movies, Recordings, Night Clubs
Broadway and Concert Stage
Carl Sandburg hailed him
"The mightiest ballad singer
of this or any other century."
He lives on through his art.
June 14, 1909-April 14, 1995

The Johson family linage is offered by Ms Barabra Johnson, a newly found friend and Shamhart relative.

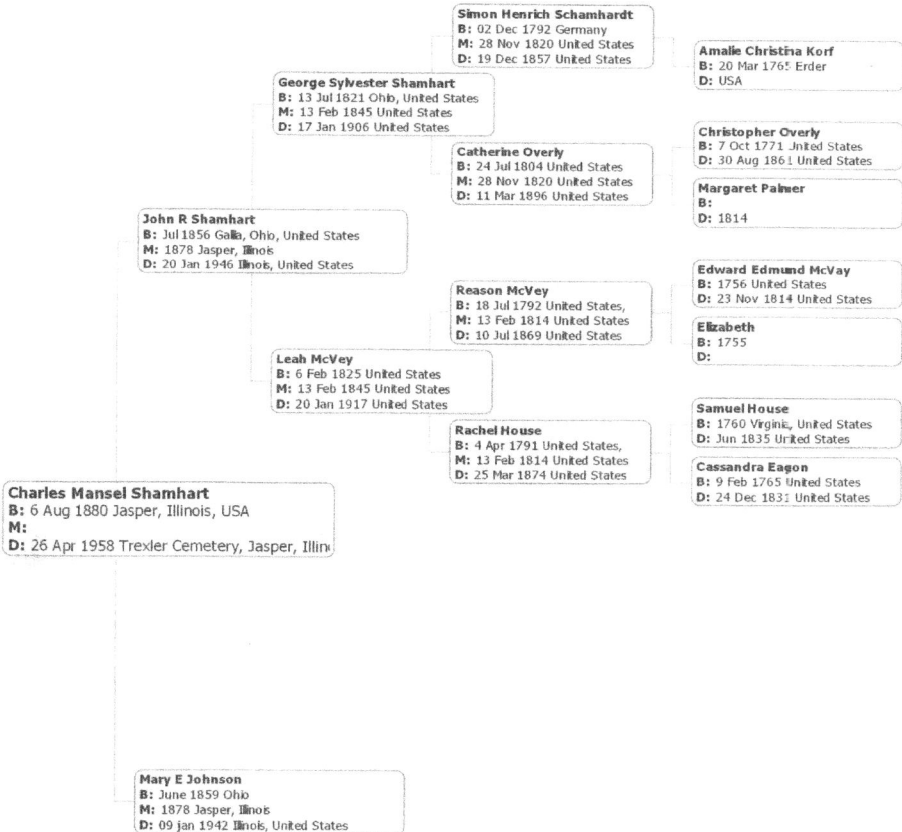

Simon Henrich Schamhardt
B: 02 Dec 1792 Germany
M: 28 Nov 1820 United States
D: 19 Dec 1857 United States

Amalie Christina Korf
B: 20 Mar 1765 Erder
D: USA

George Sylvester Shamhart
B: 13 Jul 1821 Ohio, United States
M: 13 Feb 1845 United States
D: 17 Jan 1906 United States

Christopher Overly
B: 7 Oct 1771 United States
D: 30 Aug 1861 United States

Catherine Overly
B: 24 Jul 1804 United States
M: 28 Nov 1820 United States
D: 11 Mar 1896 United States

Margaret Palmer
B:
D: 1814

John R Shamhart
B: Jul 1856 Galia, Ohio, United States
M: 1878 Jasper, Illinois
D: 20 Jan 1946 Illinois, United States

Edward Edmund McVay
B: 1756 United States
D: 23 Nov 1814 United States

Reason McVey
B: 18 Jul 1792 United States,
M: 13 Feb 1814 United States
D: 10 Jul 1869 United States

Elizabeth
B: 1755
D:

Leah McVey
B: 6 Feb 1825 United States
M: 13 Feb 1845 United States
D: 20 Jan 1917 United States

Samuel House
B: 1760 Virginia, United States
D: Jun 1835 United States

Rachel House
B: 4 Apr 1791 United States,
M: 13 Feb 1814 United States
D: 25 Mar 1874 United States

Cassandra Eagon
B: 9 Feb 1765 United States
D: 24 Dec 1831 United States

Charles Mansel Shamhart
B: 6 Aug 1880 Jasper, Illinois, USA
M:
D: 26 Apr 1958 Trexler Cemetery, Jasper, Illinois

Mary E Johnson
B: June 1859 Ohio
M: 1878 Jasper, Illinois
D: 09 jan 1942 Illinois, United States

617

Remembering Charlie, Mary Shamhart, Dee and Cecil Shamhart
James L. Meng (nephew)

When we would travel to Newton, Illinois, we would stay with either Charlie and Mary Shamhart or with Dee and Cecil Shamhart; these relatives seemed to be my mom's favorite relatives. These excursions were approximately every two months. Both families lived out in rural Jasper County, about a four-hour drive from our home in Granite City, Illinois.

If we were going to stay with Charlie and Mary, we would have to call in advance, to Dee's to see how much rain they had received. This phone call was necessary to find the condition of the one-mile dirt road leading to Charlie and Mary's. On some occasions, our trip had to be canceled or adjusted to Dee's because Charlie's road would be pure mud. We would often pass Charlie's Model A Ford stuck up to its axles in the mud close to his house. When I was a freshman in college, my parents bought me Charlie and Mary's Model A. It was my first car, and a big hit on campus.

Charlie and Mary's house was rather rustic; a one-story farm resembling the real McCoy's house with no electricity and no indoor toilet. Their heat consisted of a black potbellied stove that sat in their living room. They also had an old pump organ in their back room that I used to play with. In the morning, you would have to wash your face in a bowl of cold water that sat on a dry sink. On their back porch was a hand cranked washing machine and large cast-iron pots that they used to make soap. They had only kerosene lamps which gave the house a particular odor. Mary had a large wood burning stove in the kitchen that she used for cooking. I thought it was different; in that, after breakfast, she would rest a few minutes and then start preparing the next meal. All food was handmade, coming from their storage in the fruit cellar under the house. There was no refrigeration or ice. I also remember that Mary would leave many of the utensils, jelly, and foods on the table after each meal, covering them with a large piece of cloth. This was definitely different, and they were our only relatives who did this. Due to their economic status, my parents always brought food with us when we visited. We also bought 12 dozen eggs from Mary with each visit, bringing these eggs home in a special egg crate that I still have. Fortunately, our family loved fruit custard pies which require a lot of eggs. Eggs were also given to all our friends in Granite City.

Mary was heavyset and wore round-horned rim glasses. Her hair was put into a large knot on top of her head. Charlie was tall, raw boned like Abe Lincoln. He also had a large "bump" on the left side of his forehead. He was on a military disability. As a supplement, he also raised and trained hunting dogs for clients in Chicago who would come to Newton to hunt game. Outside of his home, Charlie had about 15 doghouses. In the evenings, he would take five dogs at a time off on separate leashes for walks. Charlie smoked a pipe and talked real slow (similar to Pa Kettle in *The Egg and I*, only with a deep voice). He also rolled his own cigarettes and had a rocking chair that he apparently liked because the only time he would leave it was to eat or to get a bucket of water from the well in their front yard. His only communication with the outside world was an old radio sitting on a table next to his rocker. I thought it was different that he would listen to Chicago stations. Different because we lived next to St. Louis and we only listened to St. Louis stations. In spite of their lack of modern conveniences and a totally different way of life than what I was used to in the big city, visits to Charlie and Mary Shamhart were a lot of fun. Although I could never get over their outhouse, they were content, didn't seem to worry too much, were happy just taking one day at a time.

Dee and Cecil Shamhart had different living conditions, a small brick home on an all-weather road, on a big farm with lots of well-kept buildings. They had an indoor toilet, running water, and electricity––even a fireplace. They had a son much older than I, named Bob. Dee looked similar to Charlie Shamhart, while Cecil was small but as tough as they come. Dee was the game warden for Jasper County. So we had plenty of meals of pheasant, quail, and deer during visits. Cecil would also go out in her backyard and run down a couple of her chickens and wring their necks with one hand. As a kid looking at a chicken being swung around in a circle like that, you just knew you didn't want to get in her way. People just didn't behave like that in the big city. We were more civilized; we bought our dead chickens in the store.

Both Dee and Cecil Shamhart always went overboard in making us feel at home. There was nothing they wouldn't do. Recently, while going through old pictures and letters belong to my parents, I found a congratulations card addressed to my mom who was in the St. Elizabeth Hospital in Granite City. The card was dated April 26, 1939. I was born on April 25, 1939. There were three names written on the card––Dee Meng, John Meng, and James Leroy Meng. The writing belonged to Mom, who apparently was selecting my name while in the hospital. Obviously, had I been named Dee (heaven forbid), I would have been named after Dee Shamhart. My only remaining question was: where did she get the name Leroy? She would never tell but she did say had I been a girl, I would have been named "Molly" after Molly Crail. Thank goodness I was a boy making the name Leroy a little, but not by much, more tolerable

In 1990, I wrote a small book titled *Poison Ivy, Poison Oak and Poison Sumac*. The book was about poison ivy. In a section regarding frontier life and poison ivy, I put in a picture of the Shamharts on page four, my mom's great-grandfather, great–grandmother, and Charlie, holding up sheep in front of them. I don't know why they posed like this, but the picture fit the script––so I used it. Three copies of the book are in the Newton library, seven copies in the St. Louis public library, with others being sold throughout the country.

To visit the Shamhart homes was a step back in time to a way of life that we will no longer experience. Although they did not have many material "things," the "things" we believe are important today, they were all content: content with who they were, and content with what they had. The Shamharts of Jasper County were proud and very gracious people. They and their simple life are missed!

The Charlie and Mary Shamhart family

Charlie Shamhart

L/R: Mary Shamhart, Olive Shamhart, Ed Meng, Charlie Shamhart, and Jessie Shamhart Meng

In Memory of

Mary Elizabeth Shamhart

Birthplace

Guernsey Co, Ohio.

June, 13, 1858
Date

Departed This Life

January, 9, 1942
Date

Dietrich, Illinois.
Place

Age

83 _Years_   6 _Months_   27 _Days_

Interment

Kedron   Jan. 11, 1942
Place   _Date_

_____   _____
Lot   _Section_

_____   Illinois.
City   _State_

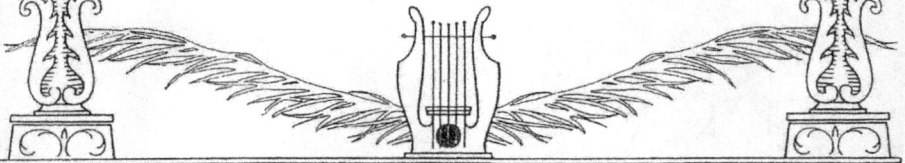

Family Record

	Born	Died

Father's Parents: *Isaac Johnson.*

Mother's Parents: *Esther Galloway.*

Father: *Isaac Johnson*

Mother: *Esther Galloway*

Deceased:

Married to:

Children: *Mary E, Ida, Rosalie, Leona, Etta, Anise, Dell. Eva, Alva*

Biography

Mary Elizabeth Johnson
was born June 13, 1858
Died January, 9, 1942.
She was united in
Marriage Sept. 23, 1877
to John R. Shamhart.
Children were:
Wilmer Weston.
Charles Mansel.
She lived all her
life in Jasper Co. Except
the first 3 or 4 she spent
in Ohio before Coming
to Illinois.

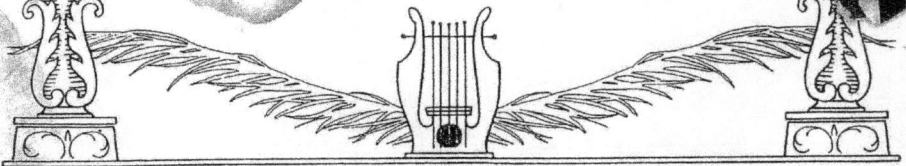

Pall Bearers

Mansel Shamhart

Dale Shamhart

Lavern Dodge

Milton Fisher

Max Fisher

Elw. Meng.

Richard Fischer

John Fischer

Fraternal Organizations

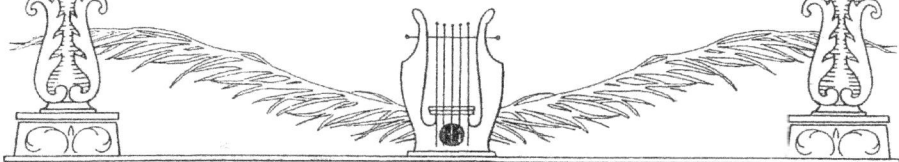

Mary Shamhart, Olive Shamhart, Ed Meng, Charlie Shamhart, Jessie Shamhart Meng

Samuel Dee Shamhart (b. 17 Jan. 1900–d. 16 Jul. 1966) was the son of Reason Henry Shamhart, M. D. Samuel married Cecile C. Evert.

IN MEMORY OF
Samuel Dee Shamhart
DATE OF BIRTH
July 17, 1900
DATE OF DEATH
July 14, 1966
PLACE AND TIME OF SERVICES
Wright's Chapel
Dieterich, Ill.
2:30 P. M.   July 16, 1966
CLERGYMAN
Rev. T. E. Davis
and Rev. Scott Teaford
PLACE OF INTERMENT
Trexler Cemetery
with Masonic service,
Newton Lodge 216
ARRANGEMENTS BY
Wright's Funeral Home
Dieterich, Illinois

Dee, Bob, and Cecil Shamhart

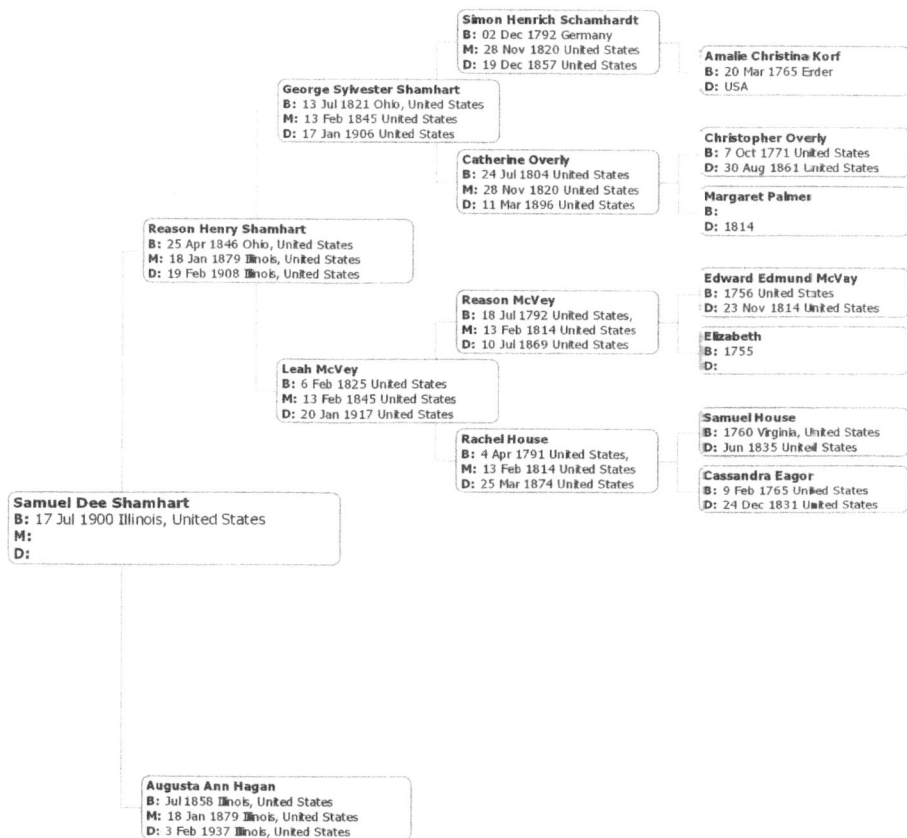

Simon Henrich Schamhardt
B: 02 Dec 1792 Germany
M: 28 Nov 1820 United States
D: 19 Dec 1857 United States

Amalie Christina Korf
B: 20 Mar 1765 Erder
D: USA

George Sylvester Shamhart
B: 13 Jul 1821 Ohio, United States
M: 13 Feb 1845 United States
D: 17 Jan 1906 United States

Christopher Overly
B: 7 Oct 1771 United States
D: 30 Aug 1861 United States

Catherine Overly
B: 24 Jul 1804 United States
M: 28 Nov 1820 United States
D: 11 Mar 1896 United States

Margaret Palmer
B:
D: 1814

Reason Henry Shamhart
B: 25 Apr 1846 Ohio, United States
M: 18 Jan 1879 Illinois, United States
D: 19 Feb 1908 Illinois, United States

Edward Edmund McVay
B: 1756 United States
D: 23 Nov 1814 United States

Reason McVey
B: 18 Jul 1792 United States,
M: 13 Feb 1814 United States
D: 10 Jul 1869 United States

Elizabeth
B: 1755
D:

Leah McVey
B: 6 Feb 1825 United States
M: 13 Feb 1845 United States
D: 20 Jan 1917 United States

Samuel House
B: 1760 Virginia, United States
D: Jun 1835 United States

Rachel House
B: 4 Apr 1791 United States,
M: 13 Feb 1814 United States
D: 25 Mar 1874 United States

Cassandra Eagor
B: 9 Feb 1765 United States
D: 24 Dec 1831 United States

Samuel Dee Shamhart
B: 17 Jul 1900 Illinois, United States
M:
D:

Augusta Ann Hagan
B: Jul 1858 Illinois, United States
M: 18 Jan 1879 Illinois, United States
D: 3 Feb 1937 Illinois, United States

Note:

One of my mom's favorite relatives was Dee and Cecil Shamhart. A congratulatory birth card to my mom, Jessie Meng, dated on the day I was born, had several trial names written on the card's envelope. One name written on the envelope was Dee Meng. However, she passed on that name and decided on James Leroy Meng. "Leroy" as I found out in writing this book is the middle name of Samuel Dee and Cecil Shamhart's son, Bobby! The mystery of the origin my middle name, "Leroy" was finally solved. But like my secretary said, I ended up with a white first name, a black middle name, and a Chinese last name. Your a mess!

CHAPTER 27
THE SHAMHART INVOLVEMENT IN THE WAR OF
1812 AND THE AMERICAN CIVIL WAR

The following Shamhart involvement in the early American wars is not all inclusive, since many other Shamharts also played an active role in our countries history. The following documents and unique daily log provide an excellent example of family information that should be shared with all friends and relatives. For example, William Foster (1838–1884), Olive Foster Shamhart's father, served honorably as a union sergeant in the Civil War. However, much more research into the Shamhart Civil War past is certainly warranted.

In addition to the Meng families involvement in the American Revolutionary War referenced in chapter 3, the Shamhart–Trexler connection via Jessie Shamhart, also reflects a connection to Emanuel Trexler, another Revolutionary War patriot noted in chapter 29. Thus, both the Meng and Shamharts both have a definitive family connection to our countries founding.

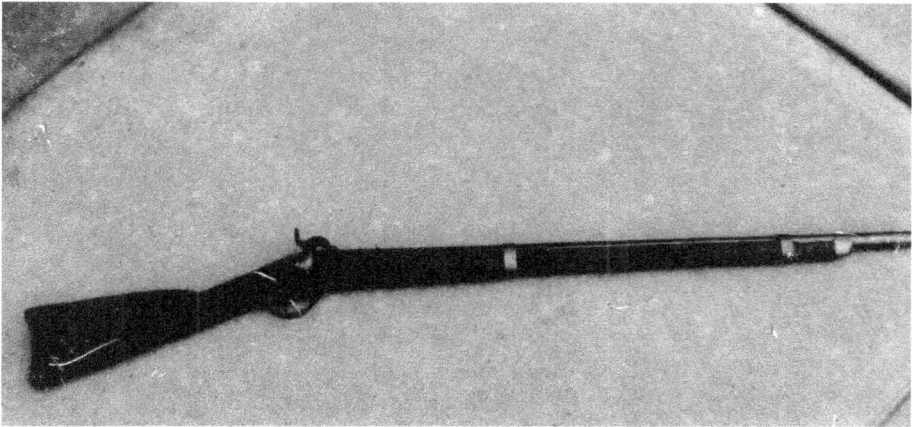

It is believed that the above rifle was originally in the possession of Judge Ivan Devore Shamhart, given to his son Claud Shamhart, and then given to Jessie (née Shamhart) Meng. The rifle will now being passed on to the grandchildren of James L. Meng. The rifle is identified: CSA, 1864, Fayetteville.

Shamharts in the War of 1812

Another problem facing the German families in 1802 was mandatory service in the German army. This service was especially hard on farm families who had several sons who were needed at home and worked on their farm. Once on duty, these soldiers were not allowed to return home until the end of their tour of duty. Therefore, many German families suffered hardships and immigrated to America to avoid the military.

Commodore Perry's Ensign

However, the immigrants who arrived on Americas shores in the early 1800s soon found themselves involved in one of the strangest and yet most controversial wars in American history, the War of 1812.

The British Empire formally recognized the independence of the United States with the Treaty of Paris in 1783 but tensions remained. President James Madison asked the US Congress to declare war on the British Empire for their defiant disregard of the American flag on the high seas, violation of territorial sovereignty in trading, and a perceived security need to run the British out of Canada followed by annexation, etc.

During the War of 1812, Henry (Henrich) Shamhart was a private in the Maryland Militia under Captain Williams. Henry had married Catherine Overly. Upon Henry Shamhart's death, Catherine received a service pension from the War of 1812 because of his military service. Those of us who grew up in the 1950's listened to and sang Johnny Horton's 1959 hit titled, *The Battle Of New Orleans*. This catchy song provided us with a miniscule awareness of the War of 1812.

A partial copy of Catherine Shamhart's War of 1812 "widow's brief" and pension documents follows.

Francis Scott Key was inspired during the War of 1812 to write the song, Star-Bangled Banner, which became the American national anthem.

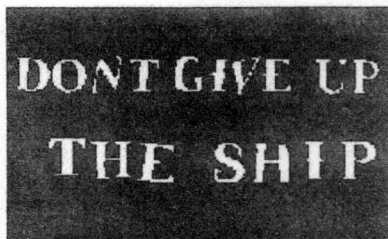

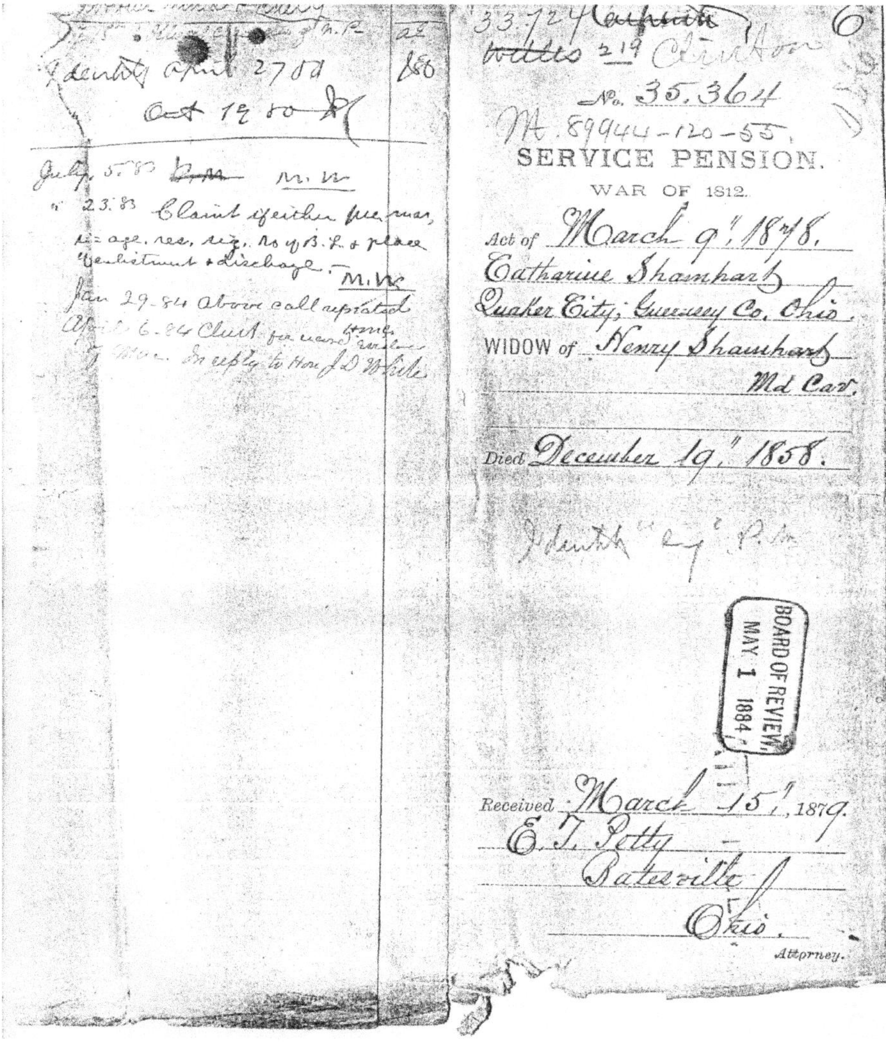

33.724 Captain 6
Willis 219 Clinton
No. 35.364
M. 89944-120-55.
SERVICE PENSION.
WAR OF 1812.
Act of March 9th 1878.
Catharine Shamhart
Quaker City, Guernsey Co. Ohio.
WIDOW of Henry Shamhart
Md Cav.
Died December 19th 1858.
BOARD OF REVIEW. MAY 1 1884.
Received March 15th, 1879.
E. T. Petty
Batesville
Ohio.
Attorney.

Identity April 27 80
Oct 19 80
July 5. 83 M. W.
" 23. 83 Claimt if either pre. mar., age, res., reg., No. of B. L. & place of enlistment & discharge. M. W.
Jan 29-84 Above call repeated
April 6. 84 Claimt for [illegible] In reply to Hon J D White

FAMILY RECORD.

MARRIAGES.	MARRIAGES.

Henry Shambartt
and Katharine
his Wife was
maried November
the 28th A:d 1820

Please return this
to Mrs Catharine
Shambart Quaker City
Guernsey Co Ohio

William Henry Shamber
and Rachel William
was maried the 30 th
of may 1857

John Shambart and
Mary Catharine Brill
was maried the 27 of
April 1857

George Belton and
Amanda Catharine
Shambart was maried
the 1st of August 1855

FAMILY RECORD.

DEATHS.

Childrens deaths
Henry Shamhartt
departed this life October
the 27th A d 1826
Pheby Shamhartt depa
rted this life March
the 17th A d 1842,
Jane Shamhartt de
parted this life March
the 25th A d 1843,
David Shamhart
departed this life
February the 15 A D 1847

DEATHS

fathers Death
Age 69 years 16 days
Death the year of 1857
December th 19
Henry Shamhart

William Henry Shamh.
Died April the 27th 1863
aged 23 years three mon..

Rezin Olein Shamhart
Died March 7th 1873
Aged 20 yrs. 10 month &
10 days

SUMMARY OF PROOF.

Marriage.
Date Nov. 28. 1820 of Henry Shambach to Catherine Overly &
Claimants averment — Asbury Knouff and George J. Long
testify to their knowledge of said parties living together as man
& wife since 1828. March 1870. Wm & Nancy A. Forsyth testify to their

Proof as to capacity to marry.
knowledge of claimant & soldier living & cohabiting together for so
lived within ten miles of them. April 16 1884. Claimant alleges
unable to furnish record evidence of marriage. Also avers that neither
the soldier nor herself had been previously married.

Death of soldier.
Date Oct. 19. 1858. Asbury Knouff and George J. Long testify
to being present at the funeral. — The same witnesses testify
to continued widowhood

Widowhood.
James Dr Long testifies to continued widowhood Apr. 12 18

INCIDENTAL MATTER.

Claimant files family record of marriage certified as to its
genuineness.

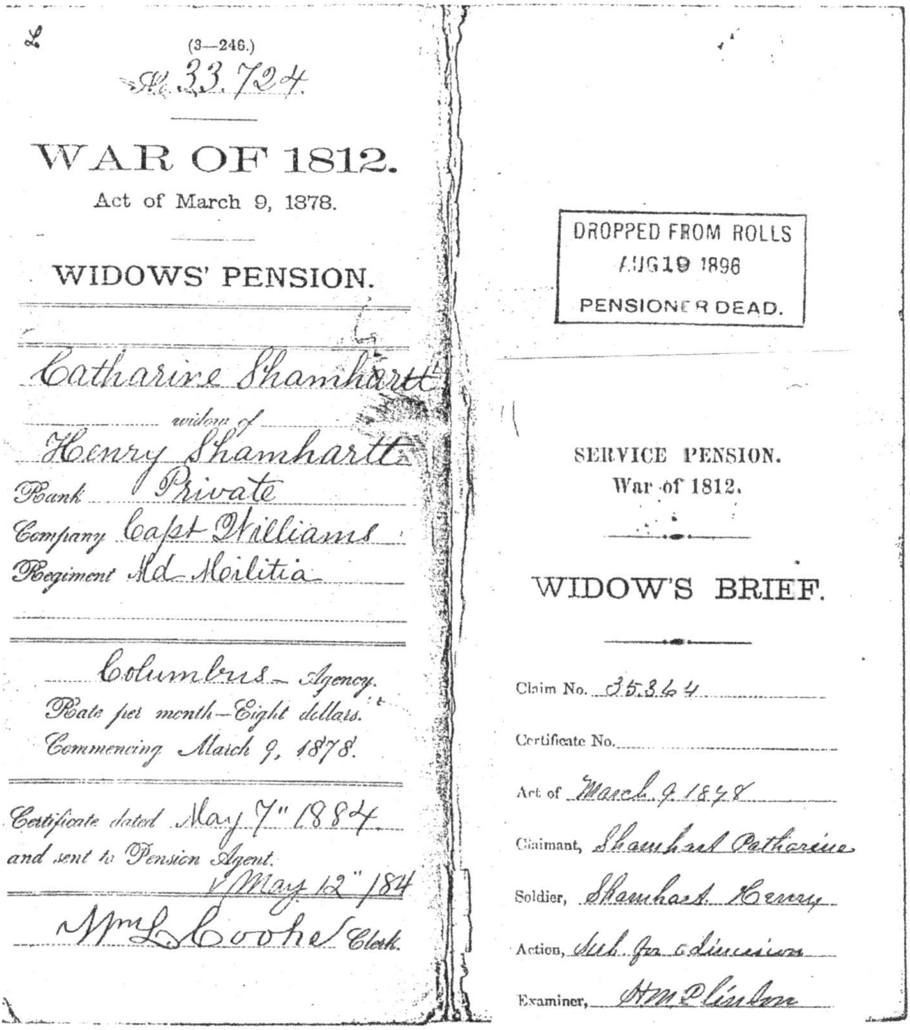

(3—246.)

A. 33.724

WAR OF 1812.

Act of March 9, 1878.

WIDOWS' PENSION.

Catharine Shamhartt

widow of

Henry Shamhartt

Rank *Private*

Company *Capt Williams*

Regiment *Md Meilitia*

Columbus Agency.
Rate per month—Eight dollars.
Commencing March 9, 1878.

Certificate dated May 7" 1884
and sent to Pension Agent.
May 12" 184

Wm L Cooke Clerk.

DROPPED FROM ROLLS
AUG 19 1896
PENSIONER DEAD.

SERVICE PENSION.
War of 1812.

WIDOW'S BRIEF.

Claim No. *35364*

Certificate No.

Act of *March 9 1878*

Claimant, *Shamhart Catharine*

Soldier, *Shamhart Henry*

Action, *Sub for admission*

Examiner, *Hm Plinton*

The American Civil War (1861–1865)

The German families immigrating to America in 1848 after their Revolution and to avoid forced military training in Germany soon found their sons involved in a Civil War in their new country. They served and served well. One such example is illustrated in the following unique record that has been graciously provided by Mr. Phil Schappard in Winfield, Illinois. This diary accurately reflects the daily life of a Union soldier, Jonann Heinrich Schappard, involved in this conflict.

Bev Meng at Fort Sumter in Charleston Harbor, South Carolina, where it all began in on January 9, 1861, when the cadets from the citadel, the Military College of South Carolina, fired the first shots at the steamer, Star of the West.

The Shappards of Pope and Massac County, Illinois

Johann Heinrich Schabbehard (Henry Shappard) was born on July 2, 1844, in Brake, Germany, to Johann Friedrich "Fritz" Schabbehard and Hanne Wilhelmine Beckmann. Young Heinrich was the second of four surviving children. Other siblings included Friedrich Wilhelm (William Shappard) (b. 1841), Hanne Luise (Annie Shappard) (b. 1847), and Friederike Wilhelmine (Lizzie Shappard) (b. 1851).

As tenant farmers in the years following the Revolution of 1848, they were victims of the economic and political pressures that were forcing many Germans to leave their country. Family history tells us both William and Henry at the ages of eight and six were sent ahead of the family to America to escape forced military training. Their parents and sisters were to follow later.

The earliest record of the family in America is Fritz's October 1, 1852, death recorded in the St. James Lutheran Church books in Quincy, Illinois. Now widowed, Hanne became a member of St. James five weeks later on November 8, 1852, and stayed in Quincy for two years until moving to Pope County, Illinois, where she married Friedrich Wilhelm Obermark on May 25, 1854. Friedrich Obermark, also of Brake, Germany, emigrated in late 1853 and lost his first wife Hanne either on the journey or shortly after arriving in the United States. Friedrich Obermark and Hanne Shappard had one child together, Caroline Justine, born on January 27, 1859. The Federal Census one year later lists this family without a mother, possibly meaning Hanne either died giving birth to Carrie or from sickness between 1859 and 1860.

On their own now as robust young men, William and Henry Shappard heeded the call of President Lincoln in the summer of 1861, leaving the farm in Pope County for Metropolis on August 1, where they enlisted in the US Army as privates in the newly mustered Company K of the Twenty-Ninth Illinois Infantry Volunteers.

Ironically, these brothers, who as little boys were sent away from their fatherland to escape forced military service, were now picking up arms in the beginning of the war between States. Now 20 and 17, little did they know they would soon experience the battles of Fort Henry, Fort Donelson, Shiloh, and Vicksburg under the leadership of Gen. Ulysses S. Grant. Their names are displayed in the Illinois Memorial at Vicksburg with other soldiers of Company K who served as a detachment on the gunboat petrel during the great siege of Vicksburg which ended on July 3, 1863

After fulfilling their three-year enlistment, they were mustered out of the service at Natchez, Mississippi, on August 27, 1864, and returned home to Rose Bud, Illinois, where they both married. William and wife, Matilda Overton, were childless whereas Henry and Martha Ann Davis were blessed with five boys.

Unfortunately, both young men bore the scars of the war and lived relatively short lives. According to his 1880 government pension application, Henry's cartridge box shoulder strap aggravated a mole on his shoulder, causing a cancerous tumor which by 1880 rendered him unable to even dress himself, let alone care for the farm. He died on March 10, 1883, and is buried in the Independence Cemetery near Rosebud.

William's pension record details continual sickness pointing back to the historic cold march many soldiers made through waist-deep water from Fort Henry to Fort

Donelson in early February 1862. William left this life on May 23, 1890, at the Veteran's Hospital in Buffalo, New York.

A Daily of a Union Soldier Record

The following diary was copied from Henry's notes of his first year in the service.

Henry Shappard
Entry Book
Belonging to Heinrich Schaphard of Metropolis City
Massac County, Illinois

Copied by Wilhelm Nopper from Pencil book.
Office, Forest Church, Great Heart

Translated from German by Paul Shearouse, West Frankfort, Illinois, May 22, 1977

{page 1}
I enlisted under Captain Carmichel's Company on 1 August, 1861, and was in Camp Baker until 11 August, 1861. We traveled to Cairo with Charles Bonn, and we were in Cairo until 13 August, 1861. At 4 O'clock in the morning we traveled to Camp Butler. August 13, 1861, 5 O'clock in the evening, we arrived in Elgaden, and we spent the night in separate houses and from where we traveled on 14 August, 1861 at 10 O'clock to Camp Butler where we arrived in Camp

{page 2}
Butler at 4 O'clock in the evening. August 16, 1861, we were sworn into the United States Army. We were in Camp Butler until 29 August, 1861 where we got on the train at 10ten O'clock in the morning and came on 30 August, 1861 into Cairo at 9 O'clock in the morning 1861. We laid over in Camp McClarnend and stayed there until 18 October. We were received in Camp Cairo and stayed until 3 November.

{page 3}
We roused and marched out the same day at 4 O'clock in the evening and stayed that night on the steamboat Memphis in a very thick fog. On 4 November, 1861, at 7 O'clock A.M. we traveled out on our steamboat Memphis and came at 10 O'clock A.M. in Commarc, where we laid over that day. 5 November 1861 we traveled from Commarc at 6 O'clock in the morning past the confederates and came at 5 O'clock in the evening to the place owned by Colonel Hunter, who was serving with the confederates

{page 4}
and was likewise home at the same time on a visit. Our cavalry attacked unexpectedly and he ran off without a saddle. Thus we took over his farm greedily for our rest. We had much freedom and did whatever we pleased. We slew the pigs and sheep both and enjoyed a very good supper and breakfast. But Hunter's wife was very displeased and told her husband would come with 10,000 confederates and would run us off.

{page 5}
We did not get out, but only laughed and said we only wished he would come where we had been several times and found no good water. On 6 November, 1861 we traveled away from there and came at 4:30 in the evening to Wait (White?) River, our cavalry making 20 miles and came on a place in the river where the Confederate Cavalry had captured but in their retreat had broken down the bridge. Unexpectedly, 6 miles from here they would have broken (or burned) down another bridge, but

{page 6}
our cavalry chased them. They shot many times at our cavalry but luckily nobody was hit but among the Confederate Cavalry several were wounded. Surprisingly, our cavalry held by this bridge the whole night. On 7 November, 1861 we traveled out at 9 O'clock in the morning and had to go through underbrush (?) with the wagon we had with us and therefore our march was not orderly and we made 12 miles.

{page 7}
We made camp 5 miles this side of Bloomfield on the river. Here news came to us from Colonel Ross that our army had entered Bloomfield, meeting Jeff Thomson with his army, halted from the pursuit. On 8 November, 1861 we traveled at 8 O'clock in the morning and came at 11 O'clock to Bloomfield. Thus we arrived with great rejoicing from our travels, to meet the 8th and 21st Iowa regiments there were here.

{page 8}
We carried our flag up to the courthouse, where we found a few Union supporters. So were we again in free territory as we wished to trade and badly to swim again. The dogs had been let loose; a few days earlier a store had been broken into and what was not taken was devastated. 3 Union men had been hanged in this place––hanging on the very trees where we had eaten.

{page 9}
November 9, 1861, early in the morning, at 6 O'clock, we roused up and journeyed back toward Camp Caireto. That day we had a few hard paths in which we marched 30 miles, having to stop at a few ponds. November 10, 1861, 6 O'clock in the morning early we began on the march, it was 25 miles toward Camp Caireto, and we arrived Camp Caireto at 5 O'clock in the evening and laid over there until 12 November, 1861. That day at

{page 10}
9 O'clock we took the steamboat Memphis toward Cairo and arrived again in Camp Cairo at 5 O'clock in the evening. On 19 November, 1861 in the morning we held a march while Jeff Thomson was in Commarc and we took a steamboat from Union territory and captured all four that were on it, burned the steamboat up and in the same manner took flight. We came to Commarc at 4 O'clock in the evening but Jeff Thomson had already sent our cavalry out.

{page 11}

On 20 November, 1861, at 10 O'clock in the morning we arrived again in Camp Cairo. We traveled the 30ᵗʰ of November, 1861 away from Cairo and came 1 December in Cave-in-Rock, Illinois. December 10, 1861 we traveled away from Camp Cave-in-Rock and stopped for the night 3 miles from Elizabethtown. We arose in the morning at 4 O'clock on 11 December, 1861 and arrived in Cairo. January 9, 1862 we have an order to march but we could not

{page 12}
march out on account of the thick fog. On 10 January 1862 we left on a steamboat and landed 5 miles below Fort Holt, also called Fort Jefferson. January 14, 1862 we marched, making it the same day to Blentville, which is 10 miles, where we Campton (camped) January 18, 1862 we made our journey away, whereby the same day we made 6 miles

{page 13}
to a large farm Campton (camped?) January 16, 1862 early in the morning we made our journey away and came the same day to Milburn at 1 O'clock P.M. and we were 3 miles beyond Milburn where we heard the news that our army had entered Mayfield. So we likewise again took the return journey and by the Paducah road Campton (camped) 10 miles toward Lovelaceville, so we made 12 miles the same day.

{page 14}
January 17, 1862 we marched out at 8 O'clock in the morning and came the same day near Lovelaceville. Thus we made 10 miles the same day and made camp. January 18, 1862 we marched again at 9 O'clock in the morning, but a very inconvenient matter––a lot of rain all day and we made that day 3 miles. January 19, 1862 we made 7 miles, campton (camped?) 3 miles on the other side of Blentville (Blandville?). January 20, 1862 we made 7 miles, campton (camped) in Fort Jefferson. January 21, 1862 we made our journey

{page 15}
back toward Cairo and arrived at 2 O'clock P.M. in Camp McClarnand, where we were until February 2, 1862. We marched out again February 2, 1862 at 4 O'clock P.M. and at 6 O'clock in the evening we made it aboard the steamboat Emerald. On February 3, 1862 at 8 O'clock in the evening we departed from Cairo and on February 4, 1862, landed in Paducah at 6 O'clock in the morning. We traveled out at 8 O'clock in the morning and made it to the Tennessee River and landed

{page 16}
4 miles short of Fort Henry. We left the steamboat at 5 O'clock in the evening and remained here until February 6, 1862, when we marched out at 9 O'clock in the morning. At 1 O'clock P.M. the gunboat attacked Fort Henry with 10 minutes of increasing destruction. The general of Confederate forces unceremoniously ran up the White flag

{page 17}
and pulled down the Confederate flag. The the Confederate soldiers left the fort and

jumped on us in all directions, brainlessly springing on our artillery to try to capture it. At 4 O'clock P.M. we entered Fort Henry with triumph. We ran toward the tents and found many weapons and other things

{page 18}
which we turned to our own needs. February 10 we had an order to march and we marched out 4 miles from Fort Henry, where we camped. February 11, 1862 we marched out at 8 O'clock in the morning and marched toward enemy Fort Donelson. At 4 O'clock our advance guard got into a small skirmish from which we had 4 wounded.

{page 19}
7 O'clock in the morning––the Confederates had fired on our regiment, resulting in 3 dead and 7 wounded on our side. February 12, 1862, at 7 O'clock in the morning our artillery began to open up and our regiment was in support of the artillery. February 13, 1862 we had the fort surrounded and our forward troops were under fire all day long. February 14, 1862, our gunboat began again to pump rounds of shot

{page 20}
from 1 O'clock P.M. to 4 O'clock P.M. February 15, 1862 at 6 O'clock in the morning we attacked on the right wing, consisting of the 18th Illinois, the 8th Illinois, and the 30th Illinois regiments. After a half hour more we began to link up, bringing our regiment under attack, namely: 29th Illinois Regiment, 31st Illinois Regiment, and the 11th Illinois Regiment. After a half hour we were hit hard and had lost 2 field guns, so some Ohio and Indiana regiments came

{page 21}
upon the Confederates. Thus the Confederates withdrew into the fort again so that our forces surrounded the fort on all sides. February 16, 1862 very early in the morning our General Grant held a parley with the Confederate general and gave him the following message, "I will capture the fort today and I will give you 15 minutes to decide whether you will surrender or not".

{page 22}
The Fort was surrounded and the same morning we filed into the fort with great rejoicing, and we took 18,000 prisoners, including 3 generals. On March 4, 1862 we marched away from Fort Donelson and made 6 miles the same day. On March 5, 1862 we marched out at 7 O'clock in the morning and at 3 O'clock P.M. we were at the Tennessee River and campton (camped) here the same––(night?)

Pages 23 to 26 of the notes are missing which covered the battle of Shiloh.

{page 27}
and the day in which the Confederates fought a skirmish with the 45th Illinois Regiment. The Confederates captured Company C from the 43rd Illinois Regiment. Then the 30th Illinois, 20th Illinois Regiments came into battle at 9 O'clock A.M., 8 miles from Medon Station and lost 2 cannons that the Confederates destroyed. On September 3,

1862 at 9 O'clock A.M. we again journeyed by train to Jackson. On September 9, 1862 our company marched

{page 28}
out of Jackson and came at 11 A.M. to Corolls (Carrolls?) Station. On the 10th day of September 1862 our picket came under fire. We attempted to form a battle line, whereupon the Confederates took flight. On September 11, 1862 we began to work on the entrenchment, being helped by the blacks in the neighborhood. On September 20, 1862 we arrived again in Jackson. On September 22, 1862 we came on the train toward Bolomer (Bolivar) and we

{page 29}
arrived in Bolomer (Bolivar?) at 6 O'clock in the evening, 1862 and remained there until September 24, 1862. That same day we again took the train toward Jackson and arrived in Jackson at 11 O'clock A.M.

Union Flag
36 Stars

Confederate Flag
13 Stars

The Meng and Shamhart family history in the German
news, with mention of a movie?

English translation of the news paper article

Foto inside the large famihouse: from left is farmer Adolf Steinhage, his grandmother was a Oberschabbehard and Werner Schabbehard.

Under the large farm foto: **Farm Steinhagen No.3**: Amateur genealogist Werner Schabbehard (small picture, on the right) andfarm owner Adolf Steinhage present the genealogy book which an American descendant has published the USA right now.

Under the crossbeam: **Contemporary witness**: The inscription in the beam above the big door reminds of the reconstruction of the house 1842, after it had fallen victim to a frre.

Below the smal house: **Historical building**: In 1837 was built the sheepshedl which was used during later years as a cowshed.

Family connections to America

Hobby genealogist Werner Schabbehard presents publication from the feather of one of his descendants from the USA

Steinhagen. The amateur genealogist Werner Schabbehard and owner Adolf Steinhage stand before a piece of stone history. The fotmer farm Oberschabbehard today farm Steinhage-.being not only for the century old history of the municipality of Steinhagen of interest. Besides, numerous Schabbehards have emigrated to America. Now one of these descendants has lighted up his Steinhagener roots and has summarised his results of the research into this book. In this appearance Werner Schabbehard had a determ.illing portion.

"Then Meng and the Shamhart Family History and Genealogy in Deutschland ans America" has James L. Meng titled his book. Shamhart, because the German name Schabbehard has been americanised at the immigration. "His mother is a Shamhart and her forefathers came from thisfarm Oberschabbehard", explained Werner Schabbehard thefamily connections. The farm Steinhagen No. 3, as the former farm Oberschabbehard is also called (No. 1 is the Austmannfarm, No.2 the today's Westphalian's farm, early Niederschabbehard) is mentioned already in 1556 in the Ravensberger "Urbar". By his searches in church registers and the states archive Detmold the Bielefelder Werner Schabbehard bas found out that the American Shamharts are descended from a Schabbehard from Varenholz.

"There one of the supernumerary heirs of the farm Oberschabbehard has moved to step in to work with the noble family of Wendt" to which towards the Oberschabbehardts had to pay taxes reports

Werner Schabbehard. One of these Varenholzer descendants emigrated in 1802 to America and disposed before of his whole possession to which also various distillery utensils belonged.

"This Simon Henrich is the founder of the American Shamhart clan", is Werner Schabbehard sure who helped James L. Meng, as he found many boxes of old photos and family documents. Together with ancestor researcher Ulrich Siebrasse did the two helped him with pleasure with the searchfor his ancestors.

"The book has provided in America, where genealogy is at the moment very much in fashion for a sensation", says Werner Schab be hard. "There are even efforts to make a film at the original scenes here in Steinhagen".

CHAPTER 28
THE FOSTERS

William Foster
Jessie nee Shamhart Meng's grandfather
(b. 25 Aug. 1838, Franklin Township, Jackson, Ohio; d. 10 Feb. 1884, Tillamook County, Oregon)

Parents and Siblings
Thomas (no middle name) Foster (1816–1860)
Mary "Polly" D Trexler (1819–1905)
Jonathan Foster (1840–1863)
Evelline Foster (1844–1863)
Elizabeth Jane Foster (1844–1926)
Rachel E Foster (1846–1868)
Job Craycraft Foster (1847–1927)
Sarah Ann Foster (1847–1926)
John Vinton Foster (1851–1915)
Catherine E "Kate" Foster (1853–1926)
Nancy Jane Foster (1854–1881)
Thomas Hartley Foster (1855–1926)
Francis Samuel "Frank" Foster (1857–1930)

Spouse and Children
Henrietta Crail (1843–1933)
William Sherman Foster (1865–1942)
Harry Franklin Foster (1868–1869)
Winnifred Dean Foster (1869–1949)
Evaline "Eva" Foster (1871–1917)
Charles Lawrence Foster (1872–1945)
Augusta Foster (1874–1918)
Olive "Ollie" Foster (1876–1962)
    (Jessie F Shamhart's mother)
Frances "Fannie" Foster (1878–1934)
Arthur Garfield Foster (1881–1933)

The Foster Family Linage

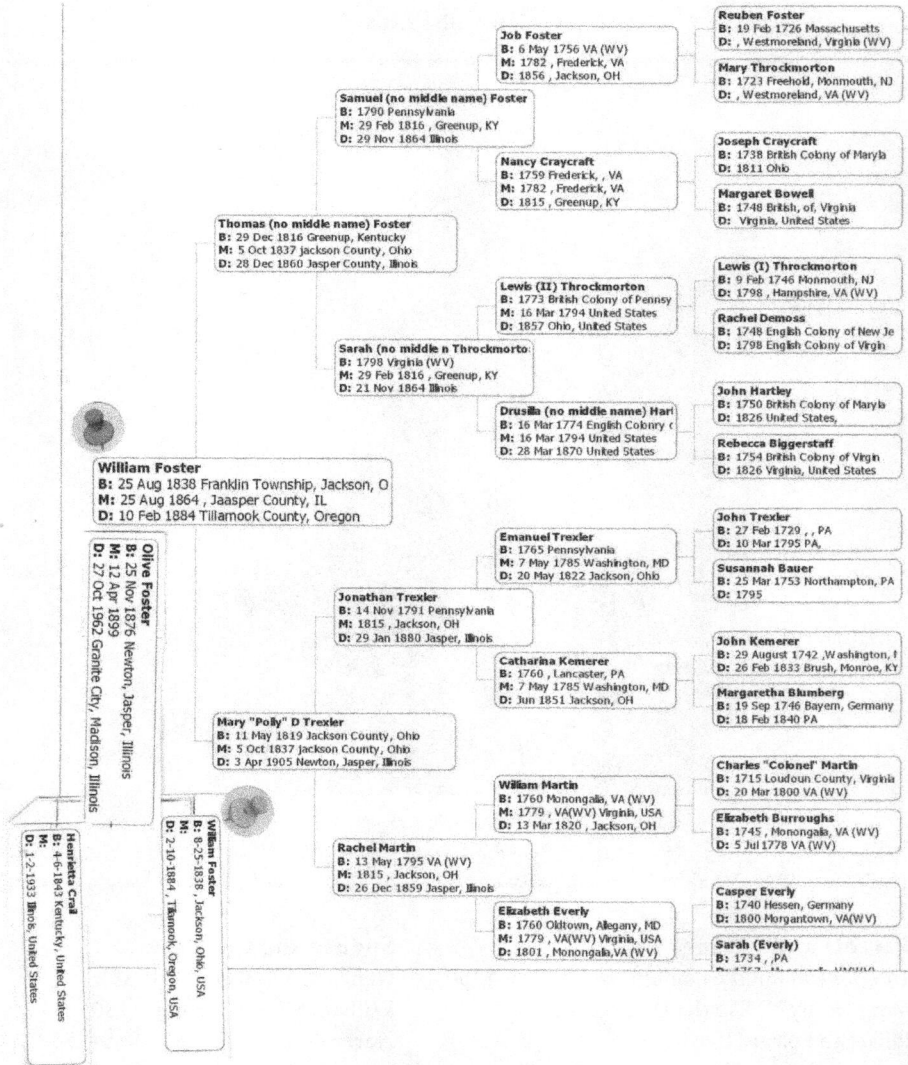

William Foster
B: 25 Aug 1838 Franklin Township, Jackson, O
M: 25 Aug 1864 , Jaasper County, IL
D: 10 Feb 1884 Tillamook County, Oregon

Thomas (no middle name) Foster
B: 29 Dec 1816 Greenup, Kentucky
M: 5 Oct 1837 Jackson County, Ohio
D: 28 Dec 1860 Jasper County, Illinois

Samuel (no middle name) Foster
B: 1790 Pennsylvania
M: 29 Feb 1816 , Greenup, KY
D: 29 Nov 1864 Illinois

Job Foster
B: 6 May 1756 VA (WV)
M: 1782 , Frederick, VA
D: 1856 , Jackson, OH

Reuben Foster
B: 19 Feb 1726 Massachusetts
D: , Westmoreland, Virginia (WV)

Mary Throckmorton
B: 1723 Freehold, Monmouth, NJ
D: , Westmoreland, VA (WV)

Nancy Craycraft
B: 1759 Frederick, , VA
M: 1782 , Frederick, VA
D: 1815 , Greenup, KY

Joseph Craycraft
B: 1738 British Colony of Maryla
D: 1811 Ohio

Margaret Bowell
B: 1748 British, of, Virginia
D: Virginia, United States

Sarah (no middle n Throckmorto
B: 1798 Virginia (WV)
M: 29 Feb 1816 , Greenup, KY
D: 21 Nov 1864 Illinois

Lewis (II) Throckmorton
B: 1773 British Colony of Pennsy
M: 16 Mar 1794 United States
D: 1857 Ohio, United States

Lewis (I) Throckmorton
B: 9 Feb 1746 Monmouth, NJ
D: 1798 , Hampshire, VA (WV)

Rachel Demoss
B: 1748 English Colony of New Je
D: 1798 English Colony of Virgin

Drusilla (no middle name) Hari
B: 16 Mar 1774 English Colony c
M: 16 Mar 1794 United States
D: 28 Mar 1870 United States

John Hartley
B: 1750 British Colony of Maryla
D: 1826 United States,

Rebecca Biggerstaff
B: 1754 British Colony of Virgin
D: 1826 Virginia, United States

Olive Foster
B: 25 Nov 1876 Newton, Jasper, Illinois
M: 12 Apr 1899
D: 27 Oct 1962 Granite City, Madson, Illinois

Mary "Polly" D Trexler
B: 11 May 1819 Jackson County, Ohio
M: 5 Oct 1837 Jackson County, Ohio
D: 3 Apr 1905 Newton, Jasper, Illinois

Jonathan Trexler
B: 14 Nov 1791 Pennsylvania
M: 1815 , Jackson, OH
D: 29 Jan 1880 Jasper, Illinois

Emanuel Trexler
B: 1765 Pennsylvania
M: 7 May 1785 Washington, MD
D: 20 May 1822 Jackson, Ohio

John Trexler
B: 27 Feb 1729 , , PA
D: 10 Mar 1795 PA,

Susannah Bauer
B: 25 Mar 1753 Northampton, PA
D: 1795

Catharina Kemerer
B: 1760 , Lancaster, PA
M: 7 May 1785 Washington, MD
D: Jun 1851 Jackson, OH

John Kemerer
B: 29 August 1742 ,Washington, I
D: 26 Feb 1833 Brush, Monroe, KY

Margaretha Blumberg
B: 19 Sep 1746 Bayern, Germany
D: 18 Feb 1840 PA

Rachel Martin
B: 13 May 1795 VA (WV)
M: 1815 , Jackson, OH
D: 26 Dec 1859 Jasper, Illinois

William Martin
B: 1760 Monongalia, VA (WV)
M: 1779 , VA(WV) Virginia, USA
D: 13 Mar 1820 , Jackson, OH

Charles "Colonel" Martin
B: 1715 Loudoun County, Virginia
D: 20 Mar 1800 VA (WV)

Elizabeth Burroughs
B: 1745 , Monongalia, VA (WV)
D: 5 Jul 1778 VA (WV)

Elizabeth Everly
B: 1760 Oldtown, Allegany, MD
M: 1779 , VA(WV) Virginia, USA
D: 1801 , Monongalia,VA (WV)

Casper Everly
B: 1740 Hessen, Germany
D: 1800 Morgantown, VA(WV)

Sarah (Everly)
B: 1734 , ,PA

Henrietta Crail
B: 4-6-1843 Kentucky, United States
M:
D: 1-2-1933 Illinois, United States

William Foster
B: 8-25-1838, Jackson, Ohio, USA
M: 2-10-1864
D: 2-10-1884 , Tilamook, Oregon, USA

Henrietta Foster and her children in front of her home in Newton, Illinois

Henrietta Crail Foster (1843–1933)

647

The Civil War

Honorable discharge of Sgt. William Foster of Company "I"
Ninety-Eight Regiment of Illinois Volunteers due to Disability

ARMY OF THE UNITED STATES.

CERTIFICATE

OF DISABILITY FOR DISCHARGE.

Sergeant William Foster, of Captain N. H. Wade's Company, (I,) of the ninety-eighth Regiment of United States _____ was enlisted by N. H. Wade _____ of the 14th day of August, 1862, to serve twenty years; he was born in Lockpart, in the State of Ohio, is twenty-three years of age, 5 feet 4 inches high, light complexion, blue eyes, light hair, and by occupation when enlisted a farmer. During the last two months said soldier has been unfit for duty _____ days.

Station Gallatin, Tennessee
Date March 19th 1863

E. A. Paine
Brig. Genl.
Commanding Company Post

I certify, that I have carefully examined the said William Foster of Captain Wade's Company, and find him incapable of performing the duties of a soldier because of Hypertrophy of the Heart

(Not entitled to a pension.)

Discharged, this Nineteenth day of March, 1863, at Gallatin, Tennessee.

E. A. Paine
Brig. Genl.
Commanding the Regt. Post

The soldier desires to be addressed at
Town Newton, County Jasper, State Illinois

[A. G. O. No. 106 & 10—Prov.]   (DUPLICATE.)

War Department,
ADJUTANT GENERAL'S OFFICE,
Washington, Aug. 5th, 1882.

375: 845

Respectfully returned to the Commissioner of Pensions.

William Foster, a Sergt. of Company I, 98th Regiment Illinois Volunteers, was enrolled on the 14th day of Aug., 1862, at in Jasper Co., Ills. and is reported: On Roll to Oct. 31, 1862 Present. (Nov.) & Bell. Co. Absent Sick. Nov. & Dec. 1863 Absent in Hospital at Gallatin. Nov. & Dec. 1863 discht. Mch. 19, 1863 on Surg. Cert. of disability. Return for Nov. 1862 ... no trace of file.

... The records of this office furnish no evidence of alleged disability. Company muster rolls report, as above stated, sent to Hospital at New Albany Ind. No. 1863 shows him sent to Hospital at New Albany Ind. Regimental Hospital. ... Nature of sickness not stated.

... records not on file. Certificate of disability above described dated at Gallatin, Tennessee Nov. 19, 1863.

E. D. Townsend
Assistant Adjutant General.

State of Illinois }
Jasper County } ss. The People of the State of Illinois
To all who shall see these
presents—Greeting;

Know ye, That licensed
permission has been given to any minister of the
Gospel authorized to marry by the Church or
society, to which he belongs; any Justice of the
Supreme Court, Justice of any Inferior Court,
or Justice of the Peace, to celebrate & certify
the marriage of Mr William Foster, & miss
Henrietta Crail, now both of this County,
according to the usual Custom and laws
of the State of Illinois.

Witness E. W. Curtis Clerk of the County
Court in and for the County of Jasper
and the seal of said Court thereunto
affixed at Newton this 20th day of
August A.D. 1864,
E. W. Curtis Clerk

State of Illinois }
Jasper County } ss. I hereby Certify, That
on the 25th day of August
A.D. 1864, I joined in the Holy State of
matrimony Mr William Foster, and miss
Henrietta Crail, according to the usual
Custom and laws of Illinois
Given Under my hand and seal
this 25th day of August A.D. 1864
Rev Jeremiah Worthey

Page 17.

Sgt. Willliam Foster's application for military disability pension

State of Illinois
Jasper County } ss. I, H. K. Powell
Clerk of the County
Court in and for said county in the
State aforesaid do hereby Certify, that
the foregoing and within is a true
and Correct Copy of the record of the
marriage of Mr. William Foster with
Miss Henrietta Crul as appears from
the record now on file in my office
Witness my hand and the
seal of said Court at Newton
this Eighth day of September
A.D. 1884.

H. K. Powell
Clerk County Court

D   D

WIDOW.

CLAIM FOR PENSION.

WITH CHILDREN.

ORIGINAL.

Ipser 6ir # # 379 40 2

Applicant.

Henritta Foster

Widow of William Foster

Sargent Co. 9ª 8 ª Regt.

Illinois .... Vols.

FILED BY

David Tyler his
Attorney at
Newton Jasper's

News Steam Printing Co., Olney, Ill.

All the blanks in this form should be carefully filled and the requirements of the notes strictly observed.
An honorable discharge from the service in all cases is necessary.
Declarations of claimants, either for original pension or for increase of pension already granted, must be made before a court of record or before some officer thereof having custody of its seal; said officer being fully authorized and empowered to administer and certify any oath or affirmation relating to any pension or application therefor.
The claimant's identity and loyalty must be proven by two witnesses, certified by the judicial officer to be respectable and credible, who are present and witness the signature of the declarant, and certify to his identity and loyalty under oath or affirmation.
Declarations and other papers should be as legible and as clear in statement as possible.
Where any evidence is already on file in any department of the Government, a definite description of and specific reference to it will render it available in any subsequent claim.
The post-office address (naming street and number in all large cities) of the applicant, attorney, and witnesses, should be embodied in or accompany every application, and all evidence in each claim; and each change of residence of said parties, while communicating with the Pension Office or the pension agents, should be stated. The statement of claimants, unless duly corroborated, are not accepted as evidence.
Pensions are, by law, exempt from any liability on account of the obligations of the pensioners, and no lien upon them can be recognized.
All facts, testimony of which is required to establish a claim, must be proven by the affidavits of two or more credible witnesses, unless other evidence is specified. Testimony in support of allegations made in a declaration may be taken before any officer whose authority and signature are duly certified, and who shall disclaim any interest, direct or indirect, in the prosecution of the claim.
With all claims for arrears, increase, or restoration to the rolls, the original pension certificate must be returned, or explanation of its absence must be given under oath. To facilitate the adjudication of claims, all the requisite evidence that is available should be forwarded with the application.

To fold this blank correctly— First fold about three inches at bottom, then in half folds as if there was no 3-inch fold at bottom.

Henritta Foster's pension from Sgt. William Foster

652

State of Illinois }
Jasper County } ss. I, H. K. Powell,
County Clerk of
Jasper County Illinois, do hereby
certify that Henrietta Foster widow
of William Foster, deceased, late of Company
I 98th Illinois, exhibited to me the
family Bible purporting to be the family
record of the above claimant and soldier
and from all appearances is genuine,
which shows as follows:
Bible date 1855, William Foster and
Henrietta Crail was married August,
25th 1864, And the following births:
William Sherman Foster born June 8th 1865,
Harry Franklin Foster born January, 7th 1868,
Wennifred Dean Foster born July 29th, 1869,
Eveline Foster born January 28th 1871,
Charlie Lawrence Foster born August 30, 1872,
Augusta Foster born August 12th 1874,
Oива Foster born November 26th 1876,
Frances Foster born November 19, 1878,
Archie J. Foster born May 3rd, 1881,
Witness my hand and seal, of
said Court this 19th day of August,
1889,

H. K. Powell,
County Clerk.

653

D Declaration for Original Pension of a Widow,—Child or Children under Sixteen Years of Age Surviving. **D**

STATE OF _Illinois_, COUNTY OF _Jasper_, ss.

On this _2nd_ day of _January_, A.D. one thousand eight hundred and _Eighty eight_ personally appeared before me _H. K. Powell County Clerk_ the same being a court of record within and for the County and State aforesaid _Henrietta Foster_ aged _44_ years, who, being duly sworn according to law, makes the following declaration in order to obtain the pension provided by Acts of Congress granting pensions to widows: That she is the widow of _William Foster_ who _Enlisted_ under the name of _William Foster_ at _____, on the _14th_ day of _August_ A.D. 186_2_ in _Company I of 98th Illinois Regiment_ in the war of _the Rebellion_, whose _In said Service contracted Rheumatism and Disease of the Heart for which he was discharged on the 19th day of March 1863 and of which disease he died_ on the _11th_ day of _February_ A.D. 188_7_ who bore at the time of his death the rank of _____, in _Service aforesaid_; that she married under the name of _Henrietta Craul_ to said _William Foster_ on the _25th_ day of _August_, A.D. 1864 by _Rev. Jeremiah Walker M.G._ at _Jasper Co. Illinois_, there being no legal barrier to such marriage; that neither she nor her husband had been previously married.

that she has to the present date remained his widow; that the following are the names and dates of birth of all his legitimate children yet surviving who were under sixteen years of age at the father's death, to wit:

HIS BY HERSELF.

Name	Born		HIS BY A FORMER MARRIAGE	Born
Winniford D.	born July 29, 1869		Arthur G.	born May 8, 1861
Eveline	born Jun 28, 1871			born 18
Charlie L.	born Aug 30, 1872			born 18
Augusta	born Aug 1, 1874			born 18
Olive	born Nov 25, 1876			born 18
Frances	born Nov 1, 1878			born 18

That she has not abandoned the support of any one of his children, but that they are still under her care or maintenance

that she has not in any manner been engaged in, or aided or abetted, the rebellion in the United States; that a prior application has been filed by _William Foster her Husband and allowed in her name to date of his death on certificate # 378.402.2 ask all evidence on file be considered in my claim_; that she hereby appoints _David Mexter_ of _Newton Ills._ her attorney to prosecute her claim; that her residence is No _____ street, and that her post-office address is _Latour Jasper County Illinois_

(Attest)

William Shup   _Henrietta Foster_
William Trainor   (Claimant's signature)

Also personally appeared _William Shup_, residing at No _____ in _____ street, in _Newton Ill._, and _William Trainor_ residing at No _____ in _Newton Ill._ street, in _____, persons whom I certify to be respectable and entitled to credit, and who, being by me duly sworn, say that they were present and saw the claimant, _Henrietta Foster_, sign her name (make her mark) to the foregoing declaration; that they have every reason to believe, from the appearance of said claimant and their acquaintance with her, that she is the identical person she represents herself to be; and that they have no interest in the prosecution of this claim.

William Shup
William Trainor
(Signatures of witnesses)

SWORN to and subscribed before me this _2nd_ day of _January_ A.D. 1898,

Rheumatism and Disease of the Heart for which .... *he was discharged on the 19th day of March 1863 and of which services he died*

on the ....11.... day of ....February...., A.D. 18.., who bore at the time of his death the rank of

................................., in .....Service aforesaid..... ; that she married under the name of

.....Henrietta Crail............... to said .....William Foster.......

on the ....25.... day of ....August...., A.D. 186.., by .....Rev. Jeremiah Winther M.G..

at. .....Jasper Co. Illinois., there being no legal barrier to such marriage; that neither she nor her husband had

been previously married.

that she has to the present date remained his widow; that the following are the names and dates of birth of all his legitimate children yet surviving who were under sixteen years of age at the father's death, to wit:

HIS BY HERSELF.		HIS BY A FORMER MARRIAGE.	
✓Winnifred D.	born Feby. 29, 1869	Arthur G.	born May 8th, 18 81
✓Earline	born June 28, 1871		born, 18
✓Charlie L.	born Aug. 30, 1872		born, 18
Augusta	born Aug. 1, 1874		born, 18
✓Olive	born Nov. 25, 1876		born, 18
✓Frances	born Nov. 1, 1878		born, 18

That she has not abandoned the support of any one of his children, but that they are still under her care or maintenance

that she has not in any manner been engaged in, or aided or abetted, the rebellion in the United States; that ..it.. prior

application has been filed .by William Foster her Husband and allowed as

her name to date of his death on certificate # 379.402. I ask all evidence

on file be considered for my claim that she hereby appoints .David Wheeler of Newton. Ills... her attorney to prosecute her claim;

that her residence is No ...., street,

and that her post-office address is .....Laloma Jasper County Illinois.

(Attest) ....Henrietta Foster......

.....William Shup...... ....(Claimant's signature)

.....William Trainor...... Also personally appeared ..William Shup., residing at No.

in................ street, in .Newton Ill., and .William Trainor

residing at No ...., in .Newton Ill.street, in ...., persons whom I certify to

be respectable and entitled to credit, and who, being by me duly sworn, say that they were present and saw the claimant,

.....Henrietta Foster......................, sign her name (make her mark) to the foregoing declaration; that

they have every reason to believe, from the appearance of said claimant and their acquaintance with her, that she is the

identical person she represents herself to be; and that they have no interest in the prosecution of this claim.

.....William Shup......

.....William Trainor......

(Signatures of witnesses)

SWORN to and subscribed before me

this ..2nd.. day of ....January.... A.D. 18.,

and I hereby certify that the contents of the above declaration, &c., were fully made known and explained to the applicant

and witnesses before swearing, including the words ....

..........................erased, and the words ....

..........................added;

and that I have no interest, direct or indirect, in the prosecution of this claim.

.....A. K. Powell......

(Signature)

.....County Clerk......

(Official character)

1 State company and regiment, if in army; or vessel and rank, if in navy.
2 State nature of wounds and all circumstances attending them, or the disease and manner in which it was incurred, in either case showing soldier's death to have been the consequence.
3 "In the service aforesaid," or otherwise.
4 If either have been previously married, so state, and give date of death or divorce of former spouse.
5 For such claims as are not under her care claimant should account.
6 If prior application has been filed, either by soldier or widow, so state, giving number assigned to it.
Printed and for sale by NEWS STEAM PRINTING CO., OLNEY, ILL.

655

The Foster Family

Standing, L to R: Olive Foster, Evaline Foster, Arthur Garfield Foster, and Frances Foster. Seated, L to R: William Sherman Foster, Winnifred Dean Foster, Henrietta Crail Foster, Augusta Foster, and Charles Lawrence Foster.

William Sherman Foster, 1889, Illinois

Augusta Foster

Evaline Foster

*Henrietta Crail Foster, Frances ("Fannie") Foster, and
Arthur G. Foster spending a quiet evening at home. The marbled topped
dresser in the background is now owned by Heather Meng.*

What do you do on a cold winter night in 1912?

Much of the evening's entertainment during this time period was reading. In Olive Shamhart's possession was a *Peoples' Home Journal*, dated February 1912, which sold for five cents. This issue contained articles on the use of ivory soap in the nursery, Uncle Ben's Talk to Boys, discussing the value of the American home, and the best on earth today providing security and well-being. There were several short stories: "A Bitter Experience" by Etta W. Pierce; "Seven Other Spirits" by Wilson Clay Messemer; "A Tragedy of the White House" by Harry Thurston Peck (about Lincoln); "The Mystery of Mrs. Von Ransaler" by Mary R.P. Hatch; "The Last of the Puritans" by Federic P. Ladd; "The Slender Threads of Destiny" by Agnes Louise Provost, etc.

Of course, no magazine would be complete without recipes for apple salad, date pudding, Neapolitan blancmange, and the all-time favorite stuffed hearts by Marion Harris Neil. Articles on embroidered table linens and the women's winter styles of 1912; how to raise chickens, a sale on corset covers for only twenty-five cents; pork and beans for seven and one-half cents per can, rice for twelve cents, a pound of corn flakes for seven cents, etc.

Evenings were spent around a wood fire, reading short stories, women's dress styles, recipes, etc., before retiring to a warm feather bed (complete with thunder mug) was about as good as it gets. As a time frame, 1912 was five years before America entered World War I.

*Mollie Shamhart, Winnie Kirkam (whose mother
was Etta Foster), and Olive Foster Shamhart*

Arthur Garfield Foster

Some of the Fosters in 1898[7]

This picture of the Buckeye school was taken on December 9, 1898, and is owned by Winnie Reed of Martin Street, Newton.

Front row, left to right: Charley Price, Harry Lambird, Everet Bickers, Harry Sparks, *Perry Foster* (with slate), Oran Worthey, Maud McWorter, Effie Worthey, Clifford Lambird, Ada (Lambird) Riley, and Chris Sparks.
Second row: *Everet Foster,* Everet Price, Winnie (Mahaney) Reed, Myrtie (Lambird) Klier, Lillie (Lambird) Klier, Myrtie (Burnside) Mascher, Dessie Worthey, Minnie Worthey, and Grace (Mahaney) Tate.
Third row: Ira Burnside, George Burnside, Elzie Wooden, Johnie Mahaney, Jasper Worthey (teacher), Alta (Wooden) Varvil, Nelia (Lambird) Klier, and Eli Sparks.
Top row: Floyd Price, Watson Sparks, Arthur Reed, Dell (Johnson) Shoemaker, Ola Burnside, Dell (Wooden) Dyson, and Dora (Burnside) Dillman.

The school was located two miles south of Kedron.

C. L. Foster,   Ingraham, Ill.

POST CARD

THIS SIDE FOR CORRESPONDENCE   THE ADDRESS TO BE WRITTEN ON THIS SIDE

April 5 - 1932

Dear Grandmother :-
    Just a card to let you
know we remember your birthday.
It is tomorrow, Apr. 6th. We wish
you a happy birthday, and trust
you are in good health to enjoy it.
    All are well here. I surely do
wish we could be with you
and help celebrate with you.
    Must close now with very
best wishes to you, from
719   Theodore, Grace and Family.

Mrs. Henrietta Foster,
   W. Washington Street,
     Newton,
       Ill.

663

Theodore Calvert

Grim Reaper

Mrs. Eva Calvert

Mrs. Eva Calvert (nee Foster), 46 years old of 2249 G street expired, Wednesday night at 9:40 o'clock, after several months of suffering with general nervous breakdown. Funeral services were held this morning from the Central Christian church of which the deceased was a member, Rev Underwood conducting the services. Interment was in St. John's cemetery.

Mrs. Calvert leaves to mourn her death, her husband Theodore Calvert, and one grown daughter, Grace and a large circle of friends.

Mrs. Calvert was the first one of a family of eight children to pass away. Her mother, Mrs. Etta Foster of Newton, Ill., is a widow. The other surviving members of the family are Sherman Foster, who resides in this city; Laurence and Arthur Foster, who live at Bridgeport, Ill.; Mrs. Winnie Kirkham of Wheeler, Ill.; Mrs. Ollie Shamhart of Newton, Ill.; Mrs. Fanny Clagg of Latona, Ill., and Mrs. Gussie Kirkham of this city.

The deceased was an active member and worker of the Central Christian church and her presence there was greatly missed.--Granite City Press Record, March 30, 1917.

665

January 20, 1976

Dear Jessie and Ed Meng,

I am the daughter of Vera and Ross Kirkham, and their mail is being forwarded to me now.

On December third mother was making her daily trip to the nursing home. This time she was on foot because her car was being repaired. She was crossing the intersection by the nursing home, with the light in her favor, when a large dump truck made a left turn and knocked her down. She ended up under the rear wheels, badly crushed, and died two hours later.

Dad has been told but he doesn't seem to understand that she is gone. You probably haven't heard that he is totally blind now.

Since none of us children live in Kansas, my daughter who lives in Wichita (and was married just four days before the accident) has been appointed Dad's guardian and administrator of the estate.

Criminal charges have been brought against the man who killed Mother. We also have filed a wrongful death suit against him.

I am sending your Christmas letter to my daughter who will read it to Dad. He still appreciates letters from friends and relatives even though his memory of recent events is often confused. If you want to send him any cards or letters in the future, his address is

Yours truly,

Norma Ireland

Frank Kirkham's birthday party

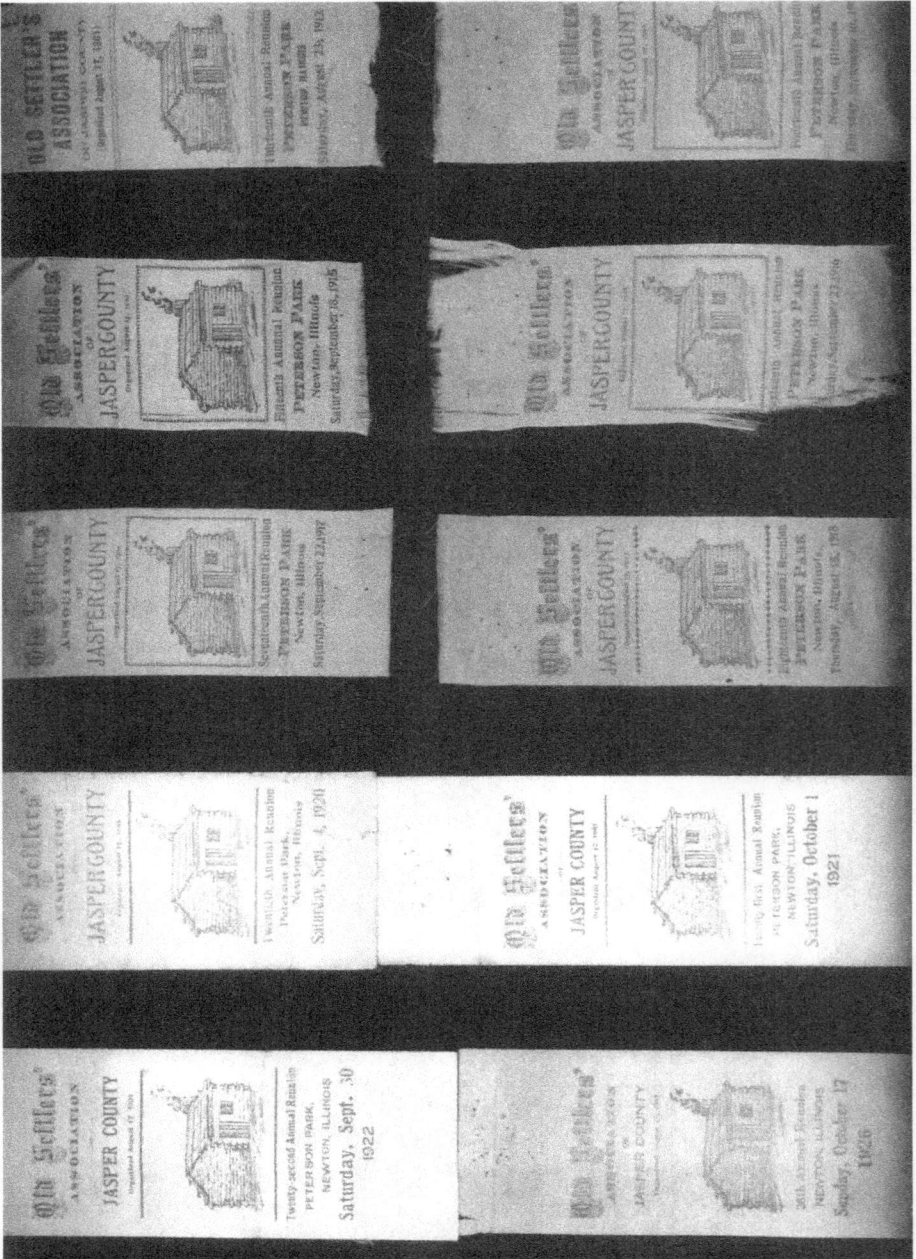

CHAPTER 29
THE TREXLERS

Patriot Emanuel Trexler

The Trexlers

Mary Trexler was the great-great-grandmother of Edward S. and James L. Meng, sons of Edward J. and Jessie F. (née Shamhart) Meng. An excellent book titled *Trexler Family and Related Kin* by John Warren Trexler provides outstanding history and the genealogy of this connection. The excerpts used are from the Trexler Family History and Genealogy book, library of congress catalog card number 72-75594, which includes data on the Meng family stemming from Jessie Shamhart Meng. It traces the Shamhart, Foster, and Trexler family connection back to February 11, 1721. This book was utilized to acquire membership in the *Children of the American Revolution* for both Heather Andrea Meng (national number 126127) and Erik James Meng (national number 126128). Heather and Erik's membership connection was traced back to Emanuel Trexler, a Revolutionary soldier.

John Peter Trexler, who was born in Dettingen on the Mainz River, in Hessen-Darmstadt, Germany, started the Trexler American line. He married Catherine Breinig. They left Germany for England on May 3, 1709. On May 6, 1709, they sailed on the St. Catherine for America arriving in New York, NY.

Just north of Allentown, Pennsylvania, is a town named Trexlertown. This town of approximately 1,000 was named after the settler John Trexler. John Trexler was granted a license to conduct a tavern or house of entertainment by King George II of England. This building known today as *The 1760 House* is used as a Supper Club. James, Beverly, Heather, and Erik Meng had lunch in this establishment in 1981.

Many of the Shamhart, Foster, Crail, and Trexlers are buried in the Trexler Cemetery in Jasper County, Illinois.

An interesting side note to this book occurred when my mom was sent a family questionnaire from the author, John Trexler. We discussed the questionnaire within our family, and my mom replied buying a future book. A year later, I asked my mom if she had heard anything on the Trexler book. Her reply was noncommittal. Another 6–12 months pass, again the same scenario. This is repeated again, but no definitive response. When my mom passed away in 1978, we were going through her room and found the Trexler book! Apparently, when she submitted the family information, she had left my name and dates out and was too embarrassed to tell me.

THE MENG VIA SHAMHART-CONNECTION TO EMANUEL TREXLER
A REVOLUTIONARY SOLDIER IN THE WAR FOR AMERICAN INDEPENDENCE

The following was used in 1982 by Heather and Erik Meng to join the Children of the American Revolution.

JESSIE SHAMHART (11), b. 7-2-1903, m. Ed Meng.
2 children, (12th generation)
1. EDWARD SHAMHART MENG, b. 6-19-1933
2. JAMES MENG, b in the USA

OLIVE FOSTER (10), b. 11-25-1876, d. 10-27-1962, m. 4-12-1899. Wilmer Shamhart. Both are buried on Trexler Cemetery, Wheeler, Ill.
4 children, (11th generation)
1. SYBIL SHAMHART m. Milton Fisher
2. JESSIE SHAMHART m. Ed Meng
3. WAYNE SHAMHART, b. 7-4-1912. He is buried on Trexler Cemetery, Wheeler, Ill.
4. LOIS SHAMHART, b. 11-21-1914, m. Robert Cox

WILLIAM FOSTER (9), b. 8-25-1838, d. 2-10-1884, m. 8-25-1864, Henrietta Crail, b. 4-6-1843, d. 1-2-1933. He is buried at Oretown, Oregon.
8 children, (10th generation)
1. WILLIAM SHERMAN FOSTER m. Effie Mott
2. WINIFRED DEAN FOSTER m. Daniel Vorhees Kirkham
3. EVELINE FOSTER m. Theodore Calvert
4. CHARLES LAWRENCE FOSTER m. Sophronia Reed
5. AUGUSTA FOSTER m. Charles Edgar Kirkham
6. OLIVE FOSTER m. Wilmer Shamhart
7. FRANCES FOSTER m. Alva Clagg
8. ARTHUR GARFIELD FOSTER m. Lola Kirkham

MARY TREXLER (8), b. 5-11-1819, d. 4-3-1905, m. 10-5-1837, Thomas Foster, b. 12-29-1816, d. 12-28-1860.
2 children, (9th generation)
1. JONATHAN FOSTER
2. WILLIAM FOSTER m. Henrietta Crail

JONATHAN TREXLER (7), b. 11-4-1791, d. 1-29-1880, m. 1815, Rachel Martin, b. 5-13-1795, d. 12-26-1859. Both are buried on the Trexler Cemetery, Wheeler, Ill.
10 children, (8th generation)
1. JOHN m. Mary Nancy Jane Dixon and Polly A. Dobbins
2. MARY m. Thomas Foster
3. JOHNSON m. Sarah Jane Ward and Mary A. ....
4. JACKSON m. Louiza Mercer and Deborah ....
5. JOHNATHAN m. Drusilla Forster

6. DAVID m. Sarah Jane Brown
7. RACHEL m. .... Toland
8. WILLIAM W., m. Sarah M. ...., b. 4-28-1841, d. 8-9-1862. She is buried on the Trexler Cemetery, Wheeler, Ill.
9. CATHERINE E., m. 12-22-1847, James B. Johnson.
10. VINTON, b. 7-31-1833, d. 6-6-1862, m. Nancy Ann .. .., b. 8-24-1839, d. 4-4-1902.

EMANUEL TREXLER (6), b. .... 1765, d. .... 1830, m. Catherine Cameron, b. .... 1760.
10 children, (7th generation)
1. SUSANNA m. 4-25-1809, John Jacobs
2. MARY m. William Spriggs
3. HANNAH m. 12-1-1814, Nottingham Mercer
4. RACHEL m. 3-5-1815, Nathan Stewart
5. CATHERINE, b. .... 1803, m. Moses Faught
6. ELIZABETH, m. Collins Bennett
7. SAMUEL, b. 6-1-1787, d. 10-24-1850, m. 5-4-1828, Harriet Mercer
8. JONATHAN m. Rachel Martin
9. JOHN, m. 5-4-1825, Nancy Price
10. DAVID m. 4-23-1826 Sarah Crabtree

Emanuel Trexler (17) was born in Pennsylvania and received a good education. A Revolutionary soldier, on March 10, 1781, he took the oath of allegiance before Peter Trexler in Northampton County, Pennsylvania. On April 22, 1782, he is found on a muster roll call of Capt. John Jacoby, Militia Company in second class of the First Battalion, Northampton County, under command of T. T. Nicholas Karn, in the service of the United States on the frontier of said county for two months' service, said called to turn out and meet together at the house of Col. Stephen Balliet. He married in 1787 in Lancaster, Pennsylvania. He moved to Ohio and brought with him considerable means and was the first permanent settler in Portsmouth, Ohio, in 1796. He planned to lay out a town where Portsmouth is now located, but Henry Massie, a surveyor from Chillicothe, entered the land the moment the land office opened and left *Emanuel Trexler* (17) with no choice but to abandon his plans. In 1798, he was appointed the first Justice of the Peace. In 1804, he built the first grist mill in Jackson County, Ohio, on Four Mile Creek, Franklin Township. In 1811, he built the first bridge of any consequence in the area over Little Scioto River. On September 27, 1814, President Madison deeded *Emanuel Trexler* (17) NW. ¼, Section 20, Township of Range 18, one of the earliest deeds recorded here. He is buried on a private cemetery on his farm.

Jonathan Trexler (54) was born in Pennsylvania and moved with his parents to Ohio in 1796. He served in the War of 1812 with Capt. John Lindsay's company of Ohio militia's Second Regiment. He enlisted at Jackson, Ohio, and was discharged at Chillicothe, Ohio. He moved to Illinois in 1853, to Jasper County, and raised fine saddle horses.

See American patriots involved with the Meng family in chapter 3

Trexler Family and Related Kin

Jonathan Trexler

Mary (Polly) Trexler Foster

L to R: Johnson Trexler, Jackson Trexler, Mary (Polly) Trexler Foster, and Rachael Trexler Toland

Rachel Trexler Toland and Jackson Trexler

The Historic 1760 House

During the year 1731, a log house was built which constitutes the southern half of the present building, and in 1760, the northern half was built. In 1746, John Trexler applied to the court for a license to conduct a tavern upon the site.

The following is a copy of the original petition, now on file in the courthouse at Doylestown, Pennsylvania, which was then the county seat for this locality.

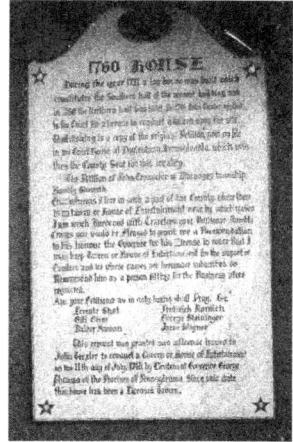

Plaque at 1760 house

"The petition of John Traxseler of Macongy Township humbly sheweth:

That whereas I live in such a part of the County where there is no tavern or house of entertainment near, which reason I am burdened with Travelers, your petition humbly craves you would be pleased to grant me a Recommendation to his honour the Governor for his license in order that I may keep Tavern or House of entertainment for the support of Travelers and we whose names are hereunder subscribed to Recommend him as a person fitting for the business afore requested and your Petitioner as in duty bound shall pray Ec."

Lorentz Shot	*Frederich Romich*
Giti Grim	*George Steminger*
Balzer Haman	*Jacob Wagner*

The request was granted and a license issued to John Trexler to conduct a Tavern or House of Entertainment on the 11th day of July 1746, by King George II of England. Since said date this house has been a licensed Tavern.

1760 House--Trexlertown, PA.

MR. & MRS. TOM HAINES
Present Keepers of the INN

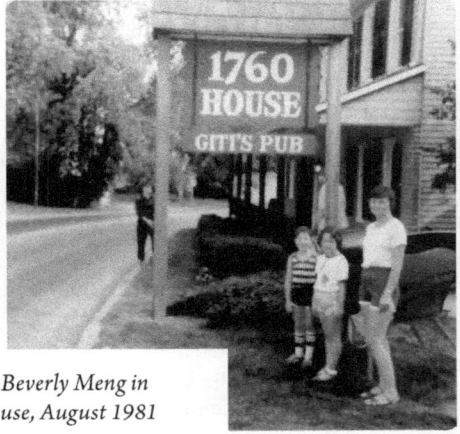

Erik, Heather, and Beverly Meng in front of the 1760 House, August 1981

8-27-24

The Second Annual Reunion of the Trexlers and relatives will be held at Toland's Grove in Jasper County, Illinois, September 21, 1924. Please help make this a success. Notify Others.

COMMITTEE.

Jackson Trexler, one of the enterprising and representative farmers of Jasper County, who resides on section 33, North Muddy Township, is one of the worthy citizens that Ohio has furnished to Illinois. He was born in Jackson County, of the Buckeye State, June 2C, 1828. His grandfather, Emanuel Trexler, was born in Germany, but for many years resided in Pennsylvania, and his later days were spent in Ohio. By occupation he was a farmer, but he also dealt in salt in Portsmouth, Ohio, and probably built the first house in that place. He reared a large family and died at an advanced age.

His son, Jonathan Trexler, was born in the Keystone State, and, during his childhood, went with his parents to Jackson County, Ohio. He was reared as a farmer's son, and there followed agricultural pursuits until 1853. In the meantime, he married Rachel Martin, a native of Kentucky. They became the parents of 10 children, seven sons and three daughters, of whom seven are now living: Jonathan, now a resident of Effingham County, Illinois; Mary, widow of Thomas Foster, of North Muddy Township; Johnson, a farmer of North Muddy Township; Jackson; William, who is farming in Marion County, Oregon; Catherine, wife of Dr. James B. Johnson, of Jackson, Ohio; and Rachel, wife of John Toland, of North Muddy Township. In 1853, Jonathan Trexler emigrated with his family to Jasper County, Illinois, and located in North Muddy Township. He entered between 200 and 300 acres of land and purchased 200 acres on section 2, range 8 east, in town 6, developing the same into a fine farm. He was one of the prominent and thrifty farmers of this locality. In the War of 1812, he had served as a soldier. He died in 1878 at the age of 88 years. His wife, who was a member of the Christian Church, passed away about 14 years previous.

Jackson Trexler, whose name heads this record, lived quietly upon his father's farm during the days of his childhood and gained a good English education in the common schools of his native State. After attaining to man's estate, he was united in marriage, December 12, 1852, with Ms. Louisa Mercer, daughter of Joseph and Anna (Day) Mercer. Her parents were natives of the Keystone State, but in an early day removed to Jackson County, Ohio. After his marriage, Mr. Trexler, in company with his brother Vinton, purchased a farm in Ohio, and his father also gave him a tract of land, but in the fall of 1853, he sold his property in the Buckeye State and came to Illinois to try his fortune.

In Jasper County, he entered 200 acres of land from the government and afterward purchased an additional 60 acres. He has since bought and sold a considerable amount and has given not a little to his children. His landed possessions now aggregate 270 acres.

The greater part of this is under a high state of cultivation and well improved with all the accessories of a model farm.

In 1867, Mr. Trexler was called upon to mourn the death of his wife, who died on the December 22, in the faith of the Christian Church, of which she was a consistent member. They had five children, three sons and two daughters, but Nottingham and Ida Catherine are now deceased, the former having passed away at two years of age, and the latter when a year old. Elizabeth Ann, the eldest child, is the wife of Benjamin Toland, a farmer of North Muddy Township, by whom she has five children: Florence Olive, Gilbert, Arthur, Claude, and May. Rachel is the wife of Arthur C. Pickens, who is engaged in farming in North Muddy Township. They have three sons, Darwin, Cecil, and Ernest. Stanton is yet at home. On January 26, 1869, Mr. Trexler was again married, his second union being with Mrs. Deborah Lake, widow of James Lake, and a daughter of John and Annie (Chezem) Bonce, who were natives of Indiana. Mrs. Trexler had one child by her former marriage, James A. Lake, who married Ms. Viola Gurrell, and is living three and a half miles from Wheeler. They have one child, a daughter, Verda Edith, born February 17, 1893. Five children graced the second union: Elmer C., who on April 2, 1893, married Miss Naomi D. Gillson, daughter of William C. Gillson, of North Muddy Township; Jane; Nora, deceased; Vinton, also deceased; and Clinton J.

Mr. Trexler has resided upon the farm which is still his home for 40 years. When he first came to the county, it was in a wild and primitive condition. Deer and all kinds of wild game could be had in abundance and wolves were numerous. The first barrel of flour which he bought after coming here had to haul by wagon from Terre Haute, Indiana, a distance of 65 miles. He has seen the entire development of the county and as a good citizen has aided in its development and upbuilding. Success has attended his business efforts, and he now has one of the finest farms in North Muddy Township. In politics, he is a supporter of the Republican party. Himself and wife are members of the Christian Church and are people whose many excellencies of character have won them an enviable position in social circles and gained them the respect of all with whom they have been brought in contact.

The Shamhart- Meng book is in the Trexler City, Muhlenburg College, and Allentown Libraries. Plus the Lehigh Valley Heritage Museum

CHAPTER 30
THE CRAILS

US Congressman Joe Crail's Connection to Lady Campbell, Daughter of the Duke of Argyll and Descendant of Duke of Marlborough

The Crails

Henrietta Crail was the great-grandmother of Jessie Shamhart Meng. Henrietta was born on April 6, 1843, in Gardnerville, Pendleton, Kentucky. She was married to William Foster. Henrietta died on February 1, 1933, in Newton, Jasper County, Illinois. The Crails originated in Crail, Scotland.

An interesting letter dated January 31, 1938, from California congressman Joe Crail will follow. This letter outlines the Crail lineage going back to 1765 Scotland. Included in the Foster section of this book are the Civil War Pension papers for Henrietta Crail Foster, stemming from the death of Union Sgt. William Foster.

According to the congressman, his grandfather, John Boggs Crail, was the son of Lady Campbell, a descendant of the Duke of Argyll. On his father's side, he was a direct lineal descendent of the Duke of Marlborough. John B. Crail also served two years as an officer in Twelfth Virginia during our Revolutionary War. Henrietta Crail's father, Lilburn Crail, is a direct descendent of John Boggs Crail.

In 1996, James and Beverly Meng had the good fortune to travel to England and Scotland. Driving on the other side of the road for two weeks to the Isle of Skye with no dents or scratches is another story. However, while in Scotland, we stopped in the beautiful medieval city of Crail. Crail which has a family connection was originally settled in 800 and has a Dutch influence.

Crail Scotland is where the Crail side of the Shamhart family came from. Crail is a quaint city on the Firth of Forth with a beautiful harbor on the east coast not too far from Edinburg. It has the seventh oldest golfing society, established in 1786 and is just 10 miles south of St. Andrews, Scotland, with its famous golf course. Crail was granted its royal charter in 1310 by Robert the Bruce. John Knox gave his fiery sermons 200 years later in the church that Bev and Jim attended.

A lot of history is recorded in the congressman's letter. We gave a copy of the congressman's letter and other information that we had to the church in Crail which also housed its genealogy society. However, at this point, further investigation into the Crail genealogy and its connection to the Shamharts is being left to others.

The Shamhart- Meng book is in the Fife City Library in Crail

The beautiful and quaint town of Crail Scotland which dates back as far as the Pictish period. A must see on everyones schedule. Robert the Bruce granted permission to hold markets on a Sunday in Crails marketgait and John Knox delivered sermons at the Crail Church.

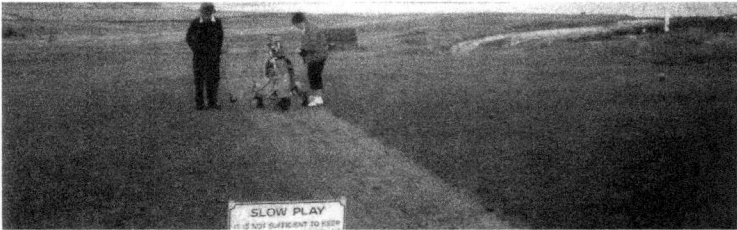

The Crail Golfing Society is the seventh oldest in the world. They have been playing golf here since the 1850's.

Lilburn Crail and Sara Jane Dean Crail, Jessie (Shamhart) Meng's great-grandparents.

Family Group Sheet
From Source unknown

Parents		Parents
Unknown	Unknown	Samuel Purdy

Husband	Wife
Wilson S Crail	Mary "Polly" Purdy
B:	B: 1780
D:	Pennsylvania
	D:1849
	Pendleton County, Kentucky

Relationship Events

Marriage	1800
	Pendleton County, Kentucky

Children

Name	Birth	Death
Henry Crail Son		
Lilburn Crail Son	28 Dec 1801 Pendleton County, KY	12 Mar 1883 Effingham, Effingham, IL
Greenberry Crail Son	2 Nov 1804 Falmouth, Pendleton, Kentucky	25 Dec 1894 Lancha Plana, Amador, California
Nicholas Crail Son	1810 , Pendleton, KY	Cincinnati, Hamilton, OH
Sarah Crail Daughter	1810 Pendleton County, Kentucky	Adam County, Illinois
William Calhoun Crail Son	1814 Pendleton County, Kentucky	1867 Christian County, Illinois
Milton Crail Son	1819 Pendleton County, Kentucky	1859 Cincinnati Ward 5, Hamilton, OH
Samuel Purdy Crail Son	3 Apr 1828 Pendleton County, Kentucky	8 Sep 1855

Husband	Alternate Spouses (1)	Wife
Lilburn Crail		**Sarah Elizabeth D???**

Lilburn Crail	Sarah Elizabeth D???
B: 28 Dec 1801	B: 27 Aug 1814
Pendleton County, KY	Long island, NY
D:12 Mar 1883	D:12 Jan 1883
Effingham, Effingham, IL	Effingham, Effingham, IL

Relationship Events

Marriage	1830
	Ohio

Children

Name	Birth	Death
Sarah Elizabeth Crail Daughter	Mar 1834 Pendleton County, Kentucky	Effingham, Effingham, Illinois
Mary Jane "Molly" Crail Daughter	1836 , Pendleton, KY	1916 Newton, Jasper, IL
Lilbourn Milton Crail Son	1839 , Pendleton, KY	abt 1879 Newton, Jasper, IL
Pendleton Greenberry Crail Son	1841 , Pendleton, KY	1863
Henrietta Crail Daughter	6 Apr 1843 Gardnerville, Pendleton, KY	2 Oct 1933 Newton, Jasper, IL
Hammiel Ann "Hammy A Crail Daughter	abt 1845 , Pendleton, KY	, Pendleton, KY
Mahala Crail Daughter	1847 , Pendleton, KY	
Frances Beatrice "Bea" Crail Daughter	1849 Pendleton County, Kentucky	Illinois
Milton J Crail Son	Sep 1850 , Pendleton, KY	Pike's Peak area, CO
America Dean Crail Daughter	18 Dec 1851 , Pendleton, KY	26 Jan 1854 , Pendleton, KY
Virginia M "Jennie" Crail Daughter	18 Dec 1852 Pendleton, KY	July 4 1949 Lawrenceville, Lawrence, IL

Joe Crail (1877–1938)

Crail, Joe, a United States Representative from California; born in Fairfield, Jefferson County, Iowa, December 25, 1877, attended the public schools and was graduated from Drake University, Des Moines, Iowa, in 1898; during the Spanish-American War enlisted as a private in the Twelfth Company, United States Volunteer Signal Corps; promoted to corporal and served in the American Army of Occupation in Cuba until its withdrawal; studied law at Iowa College of Law, Des Moines, Iowa; was admitted to the bar in 1903 and commenced practice in Fairfield, Iowa; moved to California in 1913, settled in Los Angeles, and practiced law until elected to Congress; served as chairman of the Republican State central committee for Southern California 1918–1920; elected as a Republican to the Seventieth, Seventy-First, and Seventy-Second Congresses (March 4, 1927–March 3, 1933); was not a candidate for re nomination in 1932, but was an unsuccessful candidate for nomination as US Senator; resumed the practice of law; also engaged in banking; died in Los Angeles, California, March 2, 1938; interment in Inglewood Park Mausoleum, Inglewood, California.

Source: Biographical Directory of the United States Congress, 1771–Present

January 31, 1938

Mrs. Virginia Crail Calvert
M. E. Home
Lawrenceville, Illinois

Dear Mrs. Calvert:

Your letter of January 24th came this morning. Enclosed herewith is some information which my brother and I have collected with considerable effort. My father, who was born in Virginia in 1828, had a brother named Milton Crail. He also had seven other brothers and sisters, all of whose names are listed on the enclosure. My uncle, Milton Crail, has a granddaughter living at Santa Barbara and a great grandson practicing law at Santa Barbara, whose name is James Ficklin. My uncle, John Irving Crail, lived at Cincinnatti during his active life and at one time was President of the Chamber of Commerce there, and a very active merchant. His daughter, two granddaughters and two great granddaughters live in Beverly Hills, which is near this city.

Like yourself, I have never known any person by the name of Crail who was not related to me.

Thank you very much for writing me such a nice letter.

Yours sincerely,

JC:GA   Joe Crail

From Congressman Joe Crail

Name:	Joe Crail
Addresses:	Business: 2nd floor, Merritt Bldg., Los Angeles Calif.
	Residence: 247 S. Muirfield Rd., Los Angeles, Calif.
Clubs:	Los Angeles Country Club; Del Mar Beach Club.
Date of Birth:	December 25, 1877.
Name of the Founder of your family:	John Boggs Crail, my great grandfather.
When did he leave Gt. Britain to settle in America:	About 1766.
In what County or Town in Gt. Britain did his Family then reside:	John Boggs Crail was a descendant of the Duke of Argyll and the Duke of Marlborough as appears more fully below. Town of Crail near Edinborough on east coast of Scotland.
Please show, to the best of your knowledge, your line of descent from the Founder:	The said John Boggs Crail had eleven children as follows Benjamin Crail, who was my grandfather, born July 8, 1795; also Edward Crail, Jane Crail, James Crail, Mary Anne Crail, Peter Crail, Althen Crail, Joseph Crail, John Irvin Crail, S. Middleton Crail, and Elizabeth Crail.
	Benjamin Crail, my grandfather in a med above, had nine children as follows: John Crail, Milton Crail, Benjamin F. Crail, Irvin Crail, James Crail, Mary Crail Williams, Ellen Crail Snodgrass, Cynthia Crail Craften, Matilda Crail Hunter.
	Benjamin F. Crail, my father, was born March 19, 1828, and died March 11, 1924.
	The said John Boggs Crail, my great grandfather, enlisted as a private in the 12th Virginia Regiment of Revolutionary soldiers and served two years in the war for American Independence, being promoted to the rank of First Lieutenant.

John Boggs Crail, the founder of our family in America was a son of Lady Campbell, a daughter of the then Duke of Argyll, and on his father's side he was a direct lineal descendant of a Duke of Marlborough. His father was a Landowner of some importance and was the owner of Castle Crail at the town of Crail on the east coast of Scotland near Edinborough.

Brief biography of your career:- Place of Education and Degrees, Details of Vocation, Positions, Official appointments, and special Interests, etc.

Educated in the public schools, graduated from Drake University, Des Moines, Iowa, with the degree of Ph.B, 1898, honored by that institution with the Phi Beta Kappa key. Enlisted in the 12th Company United States Volunteer Signal Corps in 1898, served during the duration of the war with Spain. Admitted to practice law in 1908, practiced law as a partner with my twin brother, Charles Crail, until the latter went on the bench of the Superior Court of Los Angeles, Calif. Charles Crail is now the Presiding Justice of the Court of Appeals of the State of California.

I was elected as a representative in the Congress of the United States in 1926 and was the sole representative in Congress form the cities of Los Angeles and Hollywood until 1933, at which time I ran for the United States Senate and was defeated.

Name and Parentage of wife, and date of your marriage:

Gladys Adelaide Schmidt, born in Berkely, Calif. Father-George Schmidt; mother-Nellie M. Phillips. Married-February 10, 1920.

Names of sons and daughters, with Dates of birth, marriages, and Issue, and present Residences:

Gladys Crail, daughter, born March 30, 1923. Jo Crail, daughter, born Sept. 10, 1930. They are both living with myself and my wife.

Names of your Brothers and sisters, and present addresses.

1. Hon. Charles Crail, my twin brother, Presiding Justice of the District Court of Appeals of the X State of Cal., State Bldg., Los Angeles, Cal.
2. James B. Crail, Washington, Iowa.
3. D. E. Crail, 449 S. Citrus St., Los Angeles, Calif.
4. Mrs. Elizabeth Crail, 1349 W. 11th St., Los Angeles, California.
5. Mrs Susan Steele, 1312 W. 11th St., Los Angeles Calif.
6. W. N. Crail, now deceased, survived by his daughter Mrs. Nancy E. Sames, wife of Federal Judge Albert Sames, Tuscon, Arizona.
7. Robert Crail, now deceased, survived by Scott M. Crail, 307 West 8th St., Los Angeles, Calif.
8. Jane Steele, 1312 West 11th St., Los Angeles, Calif.

THE GRIM REAPER

Mrs. Henrietta Foster

Written for the Press.

Henrietta Crail, was born in Pendleton county, Kentucky, April 6, 1843, and departed this life, January 2, 1933, following an illness from pneumonia, aged 89 years, 8 months, and 27 days. She moved with her parents, Lilbourn and Sarah Elizabeth Crail, to Jasper county in 1861, settling near Bunker-Grove five miles southwest of Newton.

She was married to William Foster August 25, 1864, who preceded her in death, February 10, 1884. To this union were born nine children, namely: W. S. Foster of Winterrowd; Harry Franklin, died in infancy; Mrs. Winifred Dean Kirkham of Wheeler; Eveline Calvert, deceased; C. L. Foster of Hillsboro; Augusta Kirkham, deceased; Mrs. Olive Shamhart of Granite City; Mrs. Frances Clagg of Wheeler; and A. G. Foster of Cloverdale, Oregon. She also leaves one sister, Mrs. Greenlee Calvert of Lawrenceville.

She united with the Church of Christ at Latona in 1870. She resided near there until 1900, when he moved to Newton, where she lived the remainder of her life. She moved her church membership to the Central Church of Christ at Newton, and remained a faithful member until the Master called her to her reward.

Funeral services will be held at the Central Church of Christ this afternoon at 2:00 o'clock, Rev. A. Calvin Stewart officiating. Interment will be in Riverside cemetery.

Henrietta Crail Foster (1843–1933) married William Foster (1838-1884)

Henrietta Crail Foster

Mary Trexler Foster, wife of Thomas Foster. They were parents of William Foster, who married Henrietta Crail. They were grandparents of Winnifred Dean Foster, wife of Daniel Vorhees Kirkham. No known photograph of Thomas Foster exists. She was born in Ohio, as was her husband. She was born in 1819 and died in 1905 and is buried at Kedron (or Tolond) Cemetery about four miles southwest of Wheeler, Illinois. Her husband is buried in a field plot called the Foster Cemetery near there. He was born on December 29, 1816, and died on December 28, 1860. He had brothers, Job, Joe, Daniel, and Samuel Foster. She and husband moved from Jackson County, Ohio, to Illinois.

CONCLUSION

This book is a product of 15 years plus of collecting, identifying, and developing information into a chronological and historical record of the Meng and Shamhart families.

What I have learned with this exercise is a renewed appreciation of these immigrants who left the world that they knew to go to a new country with only what they could carry. However, all the Mengs and Shamharts that I knew both as a child and as an adult brought to their new country a strong love of family, a strong work ethic, and desire to do their very best with their God-given abilities. These traits were not only preached, but expected of all. I attribute this characteristic to their German heritage where hard work is the norm, as is part of their DNA. They were all proud Americans, but believe me, there were times when they were also the preverbal, "hardheaded Germans."

Discovering the Meng contributions to the American War for Independence was personally very interesting, especially learning that several colonial patriots had my name. While another patriot, John Hanson, had my DNA. Think of this, Meng relatives were also working with and talking to our country's founding fathers like George Washington, Benjamin Franklin and Patrick Henry. I would also bet they were also all involved in the Boston Tea Party of 1773. Learning of dead Romans, third and fourth century vases in a Meng backyard is, at least, very unique, while the Meng connection to New Zealand is all new. Then there are the Shamharts being traced back to the start of the Second Crusade in 1147. Additionally, a connection to Lady Campbell, daughter of the then Duke of Argyll, a descendent of the Duke of Marlborough was also unknown by this author until this exercise. To think that some of the original Meng and Shamhart homes in Germany are still in existence and currently occupied in 2015 speaks volumes about German frugality.

This project also put me in contact with some great contributors like Werner Schabbehard and Ulrich Siebrasse in Germany, Belinda Lansley in New Zealand, Barbara Johnson in Oregon, Phil Shappard in Illinois and Hoyt and Scottie Ming in Alabama. We are also indebted to those who are no longer with us, my mother, Jessie Frances Shamhart Meng and Olive Foster Shamhart and other relatives who saved all the family pictures and documents awaiting for some poor soul with a low I.Q. to come along and organize it all into a book.

However, it also should be remembered that the acquisition of official family documents from Germany was not an easy task. Many of the original documents were written in French (who also used a different numbering system) or old German script which all had to be translated into modern German and then into English.

To complicate this process, some of the priest thoroughly enjoyed their beer or wine. Consequently, many spelling mistakes were made requiring double verifications. In addition, many records were destroyed in World Wars I and II or were removed to other European capitals when the territory was once ruled by others.

There were also many times during the past 15 years that I just had to ask myself, why am I doing this? An example of some of the difficulties that I had with this project was attempting to fully understand and implement e-mails like the following from my good friend Werner:

Hi Jim, have a look.

The first document from 1830 is the marriage Johannes Meng, 35 years old, with Katharina, 25 years old, born Barth. Father from Johannes Christian, 67 years old, mother if Barbara, 51 years old, born Stahl.

The second document from 1829 is from the wedding Richard Meng, 29 years old, marries Maria Eva, 18 years old, born Dörrschuck. Reichard has the parents Karl Phillip and Maria Dorothea, born Schneider. Her father Johann Dörrschuck is already dead; her "living" mother is Anna Barbara, born Diehl.

The third document from 1822 is from the city of Worms, for the death of Georg Wilhelm at the age of 67 years. The fourth is the same, when he died in Monsheim. I do not know yet, why there is a second document for the city of Worms, this is unusual! Both documents contain the name of his parents from Hohensülzen: Wilhelm Meng and (no first name known) Schiffmann. That means Georg Wilhelm was not a son of Johann Stephan born about 1725, he could have been a nephew.

The fifth document from 1811 is written in French, because we belonged to France until 1814. Appolonia Meng (née) born Hoffmann was the wife from Georg Wilhelm and died 1811, age 56 years old. Georg Wilhelm was born in Hohensülzen in the year or around 1755. His mother . . . Schiffmann was surely from our village, the name appears already in the seventeenth century.

The next step must be, to find in the church books, when Georg Wilhelm was born. Then we can try to find the former relatives of the Meng family: his father Wilhelm and then, I suppose now, that is, the brother of Wilhelm, Johann Stephan, born about 1725.

I am still sure, that we had only one Meng family 250 years ago, but we know not everything before 1800, because the French burned out documents in our town hall. Only the church books can help to find out.

Since a couple of weeks some student will look in the books of the archive of Wien (Vienna/Austria) for names and happenings in our village before 1800. We belonged in this time to the emperor of Austria (Vorderösterreich). When the French took us, at the end of the eighteenth century, Austria did not take care. We were far away and not important. In documents before 1700 (I have some), there are no Mengs. They came past 1700 to Hohensülzen.

Best regards,
Werner Schabbehard

Many of the documents in this book were retained in the original language. This was done because the information contained within is easily translated and continues the distinctiveness of the German connection. A heritage for which I am very proud.

This project which started with the menial task of identifing old pictures and documents in a box in my basement, proved to be more time consuming and expensive than originally thought. Thus, e-mails like the one cited above and many, many others were a definite challenge to comprehend. However, with gracious help of Werner Schabbehard's phone calls which walked me through all the complexities, plus an occasional adult beverage, the last chapter finally arrived. Consequently, as all my ancestors would say after a long audacious task, *Ich bin fertig!*

Again, I am not a genealogist but all the information contained within is being offered to others for their continued research. More will be discovered in the future which may or may not change some of the aforementioned data. With this recognition in mind, I wish all the highest success in your future genealogical endeavors. Please note I have intentionally entered typos and sprinkled a few wrong dates and misidentifications throughout this book just for others to find. So, when you find them, great! As my father, Edward J. Meng would say, a smile and a kind thought would be appreciated.

James L. Meng

691

Again, from where did our ancestors originate?

The Shamhart's from the town of Varenholz and Meng's from the towns of Ladenburg, Monsheim, Speyer and Hohen-Sülzen.

Deutschland

INDEX

NEWS PAPER AND FOREIGN ACKNOWLEDGMENTS

A special thanks to the following sources for granting permission to use their information and pictures in the formation of this book. Their contributions to the Meng and Shamhart history are appreciated by many.

[1] The Jackson Daily News, Jackson, Mississippi

[2] Werner Schabbehard and Ulrich Siebrasse, Germany

[3] Belinda Lansley and Werner Schabbehard, New Zealand

[4] The Belleville News Democrat, Belleville, Illinois

[5] The Granite City Press Record, Granite City, Illinois

[6] The Telegraph, Alton, Illinois

[7] The Newton Press-Mentor, Newton, Illinois

[8] The Suburban Journals, St Louis, Missouri

[9] The Ashland Daily Independent, Ashland Kentucky

[10] The Orange County Register, Fullerton, California

The historical locations throughout this book, both as quoted and modified, are the contributions of Wikipedia, The Free Encyclopedia. Their assistance in developing the environment in which our ancestors had lived, provide a valuable asset to our understandings of these brave people.

In Memory of Hoyt B. Ming 1934-2009

A very special acknowledgment is due Hoyt Bertram Ming for his many years of difficult work researching and documenting the Ming-Meng family history. Much of the early Meng family history was totally unknown until revealed and connected by Hoyt.

ADDITIONAL BOOKS ON THE FASCINATING AND HISTORIC MENG AND SHAMHART FAMILIES.

The Trexler Family and related kin. 1972. by John Trexler Warren. Schlechter's Printers-Publishers, Allentown, Pennsylvania.

Sebastopol. 2012. by Belinda Lansley. Dornie Publishing Company, Grasmere Invercargill, New Zealand.

The Meng and Shamhart family History and Genealogy in Deutschland and America. 2012. by James L. Meng, Xlibris, Corporation, USA. Revised 2015.

Steinhagen, Bemerkungen und Notizen über, 82 Wohnstätten und Bauernhofe, 2015. By Werner Schabbehard, Rosenheide 21, 33611, Bielefeld, Germany.

Geschichte eines Namens aus Steinhagen in Westfalen. 2014. By Werner Schabbehard, Rosenheide 21, 33611 Bielefeld, Germany.

Northern Roots and Southern Trails by Hoyt B. Ming. Date and publisher unknown.

For more information on the Shamhart families on the Internet: **home.schabbehard.de**

GEORGE W. BUSH
PRESIDENTIAL CENTER
★ ★ ★
RECOGNIZES

Mr. James L. Meng

AS A CHARTER MEMBER
WITH ALL OF THE RIGHTS AND RESPONSIBILITIES
PERTAINING THERETO.
GIVEN AT
DALLAS, TEXAS,
THIS TWENTY-FOURTH DAY OF JUNE, TWO THOUSAND ELEVEN.

PRESIDENT GEORGE W. BUSH

THE HONORABLE MARK LANGDALE
PRESIDENT

FREEDOM ★ OPPORTUNITY ★ RESPONSIBILITY ★ COMPASSION

Mr. Meng, thank you for your support and friendship as a Charter Member from Missouri. With your help we can make America stronger, safer and more prosperous.

Best Wishes,
Laura Bush

www.ingramcontent.com/pod-product-compliance
Lightning Source LLC
Chambersburg PA
CBHW030347050426
42336CB00048B/73